Praise for
You Must Set Forth at Dawn

"[A] sprawling, delightful memoir...As a chronicle of modern Africa and its troubles from the continent's foremost literary giant, *You Must Set Forth at Dawn* triumphs."
—*The Washington Post*

"*You Must Set Forth at Dawn* is more than just the journey of a remarkable and controversial man through the backdrop of the controversial country he loves so much. It is not merely an important book. This is a book that must exist."
—*San Francisco Chronicle*

"The fine detail of [Soyinka's] oppositional activity, involving clandestine border crossings, strange bedfellows and secret diplomatic missions, is presented here for the first time. Adding it up, one wants to set him in the right company. Victor Hugo, Yeats, Byron and Alessandro Manzoni all come to mind."
—*The New York Times Book Review*

"Wole Soyinka is a titan.... Playwright and poet, novelist and pamphleteer, editor and auto-biographer, cultural impresario and unofficial diplomat, democratic conspirator and ferocious, unappeasable warrior for justice, he has earned his Nobel Prize many times over."
—*The New York Review of Books*

"Captivating ... *You Must Set Forth at Dawn* is much more than a memoir.... Soyinka's most powerful weapon has always been the eloquence of his voice as a writer.... [Soyinka's art] will outlive both him and the regimes he opposed."
—*The Nation*

"Profoundly rewarding...the synthesis of a wealth of ancient myths and traditions with the best of humanism and modernity, addressing the drama that is not only the author's life but Africa's contemporary reality."
—*WQ: The Wilson Quarterly*

"Humane, sensible and impeccably written; a fitting summation of a life interestingly lived."
—*Kirkus Reviews* (starred review)

"Engrossing...His lyrical evocations of African landscapes, the urban nightmare of Lagos, the horrors of British cuisine and the longing a dusty fugitive feels for a cold beer will entertain and educate readers."
—*Publishers Weekly* (starred review)

"A must for anyone concerned with human rights and the global web of oil, poverty, and corruption."
—*Booklist*

ALSO BY *Wole Soyinka*

You Must

Set Forth

at Dawn

RANDOM HOUSE
TRADE PAPERBACKS

NEW YORK

WOLE SOYINKA

You Must
.....
Set Forth
.....
at Dawn

A MEMOIR

2007 Random House Trade Paperback Edition

Copyright © 2006 by Wole Soyinka

Published in the United States by Random House Trade Paperbacks,
an imprint of The Random House Publishing Group,
a division of Random House, Inc., New York.

RANDOM HOUSE TRADE PAPERBACKS and colophon
are trademarks of Random House, Inc.

Originally published in hardcover in the United States by Random House,
an imprint of The Random House Publishing Group,
a division of Random House, Inc., in 2006.

ISBN 978-0-375-75514-9

Printed in the United States of America

www.atrandom.com

2 3 4 5 6 7 8 9

Maps created by David Garner

Book design by Barbara M. Bachman

To all the fallen in our common cause,
and to the surviving, scars and all, clamorous or hidden.

. . . . .

To all my stoically resigned children.

. . . . .

And to my wife, Adefolake, who, during the
season of a deadly dictatorship, demoted me
from the designation of Visiting Professor to that
of Visiting Spouse, but was still left with only an
Invisible Spouse as I was swallowed by
my study even during visiting hours.

Contents

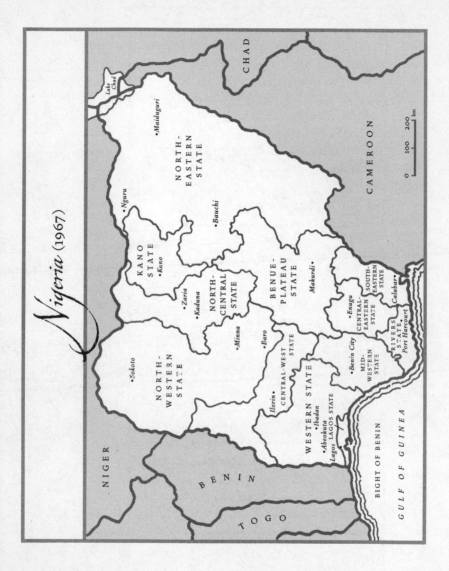

Nigeria (1967)

The States of Nigeria, 1955–1991

NORTHERN
REGION

WESTERN
REGION

EASTERN
REGION

1955

NORTHERN
REGION

WESTERN
REGION

MID-
WESTERN
REGION

EASTERN
REGION

1963

NORTH
WESTERN

KANO

NORTH
CENTRAL

NORTH
EASTERN

KWARA

BENUE
PLATEAU

WESTERN

LAGOS

MID-
WESTERN

EAST
CENTRAL

SOUTH
EASTERN

RIVERS

1967

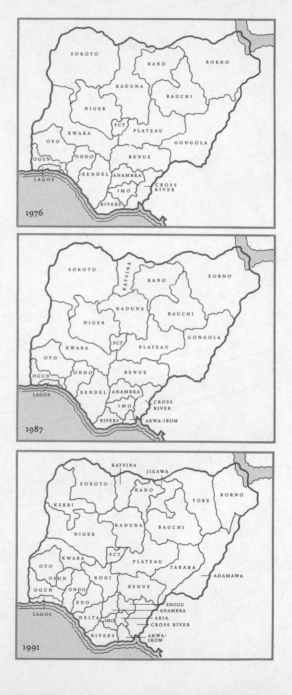

Chronology

1960

October 1   Independence from Britain

1962

May   State of emergency declared in Western Region; abortive census exercise

1963

August   Midwest Region created

October 1   Nigeria becomes a republic

November   Census shows a population of 55.67 million

1964

December   Election crisis

1965

October–December   Political crisis deepens after Western Region elections

1966

January 15   First military coup: overthrow of First Republic and establishment of Ironsi regime

July 29   Second military coup: establishment of Gowon regime

September–October   Ad hoc constitutional conference

1967

January   Aburi meeting to forestall imminent civil war

May 27   Creation of twelve states to replace four regions

May 30   Military governor Odumegwu Ojukwu announces secession of Eastern Region and declares Republic of Biafra

July 6   Start of Civil War

1970

January 12   End of Civil War

1973

November   Provisional census finds population of 79.76 million; later annulled

1975

July 29   Third military coup: establishment of Murtala Mohammed regime

1976

February 3   Twelve states replaced by nineteen states

February 13   Fourth military coup (abortive): Mohammed assassinated. General Olusegun Obasanjo becomes head of state.

1978

September 21   1979 Constitution promulgated; ban on politics lifted

1979

October 1   Inauguration of Alhaji Shehu Shagari as civilian president and establishment of Second Republic

1980

December   Fundamentalist Muslim uprising in Kano (Maitatsine riots)

1981

June 22   Governor Balarabe Musa of Kaduna impeached

1983

August 13–   Federal and state elections
September 3

December 31   Fifth military coup: establishment of Buhari regime

1985

August 27   Sixth military coup: establishment of Babangida regime

December 20   Seventh military coup (abortive) announced; coup plotters, including General Mamman Vatsa, executed

1986

January   Return to civilian rule by October 1 announced; Political Bureau appointed

February   Nigeria joins the Organization of the Islamic Conference (OIC)

1987

March   Christian-Muslim clashes in Kafanchan, Kaduna, Zaria, Katsina

July 11   White paper on Political Bureau Report; timetable for return to civilian rule on October 1, 1992, announced

September   Two more states (Akwa Ibom and Katsina) created

1989

May   Constitution promulgated; two-party system adopted

October 5   National Electoral Commission (NEC) recommends six out of thirteen political associations

October 7   Armed Forces Ruling Council (AFRC) dissolves all thirteen political associations and "manufactures" two parties: National Republican Convention (NRC) and Social Democratic Party (SDP). Opposition calls for a national conference.

1990

April 22   Eighth military coup, led by Major Gideon Orkar (abortive)

August   ECOMOG moved to Liberia

1991

April   Muslim-Christian conflicts in Bauchi

August 27   States increased to thirty

December 12   Federal capital moved from Lagos to Abuja

December 14   Federal, state assembly, and gubernatorial elections

1992

January 2   Presidential election shifted to December 5, 1992

March 19   Census returns announced: 88.5 million

August–September	Party presidential primaries
October	AFRC annuls presidential primaries, dissolves NRC and SDP executive committees
November	Presidential election postponed to June 12, 1993, and date of handover to civilians to August 27
December 5	National Assembly inaugurated

1993

January 2	Transitional Council headed by Ernest Shonekan appointed; National Defense and Security Council (NDSC) replaces AFRC. Calls resume for a Sovereign National Conference.
March 29	Presidential candidates nominated: Bashir Tofa for NRC, M.K.O. Abiola for SDP
June 10	Abuja High Court grants Association for a Better Nigeria (ABN) an injunction to stop presidential election
June 12	Presidential election still held
June 16	ABN secures another injunction to stop further release of election results by NEC
June 23	Presidential election annulled; NEC and transition program suspended
August 27	Dictator Ibrahim Badamasi Babangida "steps aside"; Interim National Government (ING) named, with Ernest Shonekan as head of state
September 10	February 19, 1994, announced as date for new presidential election
September 24	Abiola returns from self-exile
November 10	Lagos High Court declares ING illegal
November 17	Ninth military coup: establishment of Abacha regime. All democratic and transition structures dissolved.

1994

January 14	Commission for Constitutional Conference appointed
May	National Democratic Coalition issues ultimatum to Abacha regime to relinquish power by May 31
June–July	Abiola proclaims himself president, paralyzing antigovernment restoration of June 12 presidential election. Strikes and demonstrations by oil workers and other civil society constituents.

July	Constitutional Conference begins
December	"First Phase" of Transition to Civil Rule program, which stipulated January 17, 1995, as date of lifting of ban on politics, announced

1995

March	Coup plot involving former head of state General Olusegun Obasanjo and forty-four others "uncovered." Obasanjo goes on trial with others. Death sentence later commuted to life imprisonment.
July 27	Report of Constitutional Conference submitted
October 1	"Comprehensive" timetable for return to civil rule on October 1, 1998, announced
November 10	Kenule Saro-wiwa and eight other Ogoni minority rights activists executed; worldwide condemnation
November 11	Nigeria expelled from Commonwealth

1996

September 30	Five new political parties announced
October 1	Six more states and 138 local government areas created

1998

June	Sani Abacha dies. Abubakar Abdulsalami takes over and immediately begins to release political detainees, including former head of state Olusegun Obasanjo.
July	M.K.O. Abiola dies suddenly. Renewed calls for a Sovereign National Conference.

1999

May	Olusegun Obasanjo is sworn in as civilian president after disputed election. Calls for a Sovereign National Conference continue.

2000

December	Oputa Panel for Human Rights inaugurated

2001

December 23	The nation's attorney general, Bola Ige, is assassinated in his house

2003

May   Obasanjo reelected amid accusations of massive rigging. Calls
       for a Sovereign National Conference continue unabated;
       Obasanjo refuses.

2004

       Acquittal of Bola Ige's accused murderers, including prime
       suspect, former Osun state deputy governor Iyiola Omisore

2005

February   To stifle calls for a Sovereign National Conference, Obasanjo sets
           up National Political Reform Conference. Its composition and
           terms of reference are rejected by civil movements and some
           states, which insist on a genuinely representative Sovereign
           National Conference.

June   South-South delegates to the conference walk out over dispute
           on how much oil revenue should go to oil-producing areas

July   Obasanjo receives report of the conference and declares it a
           success. Opposition leaders pronounce it a fraud and proceed
           with plans for their own National Conference.

October 1 People's National Conference inaugurated in Lagos

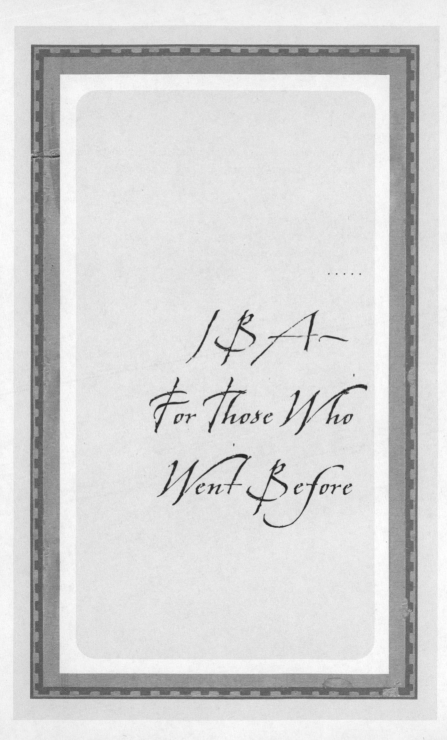

.....

I ♭ A—
For Those Who
Went Before

IBA — For Those Who Went Before

. . . . .

OUTSIDE MYSELF AT MOMENTS LIKE THIS, HEADING HOME, I HESITATE A moment to check if it is truly a living me. Perhaps I am just a disembodied self usurping my body, strapped into a business-class seat in the plane, being borne to my designated burial ground—the cactus patch on the grounds of my home in Abeokuta, a mere hour's escape by road from the raucous heart of Lagos. Perhaps I am not really within the cabin of the plane at all but lying in a coffin with the luggage, disguised as an innocent box to fool the superstitious, while my ghost persists in occupying a seat whose contours have grown familiar through five years of a restless exile that began in 1994. For my mind chooses this moment to travel twelve years backward when, drained of all emotion, I accompanied the body of my friend Femi Johnson from Wiesbaden in Germany, bringing him home in defiance of the unfathomable conspiracy to leave him in that foreign land like a stray without ties of family and friends. And the pangs that assail me briefly stem from the renewed consciousness of the absence of this friend, whose thunder-roll laughter and infectious joy of life would have overwhelmed those welcoming voices that I know await me at my destination. Despite the eternal moment of farewell by his open coffin in the funeral parlor in Wiesbaden, it was difficult then, and remained continuously so, to reconcile that self with the absence of a vitality that we had all taken so long for granted, his big but compact frame in a box, immaculately dressed as though simply from habit—be it in a double-breasted suit with a carnation freshly cut by his chauffeur from the frontage garden, then laid ritualistically beside his breakfast set, or else in his casual outfit, its components no less carefully matched for all its seeming casualness, or his hunting attire, which appeared selected for a genteel English countryside ramble instead of a "rumble in the jungle." Difficult to accept the closed eyes that would bulge at some inspired business idea, at the prospect of a gastronomic spread, at the sight of a passing generously endowed female, or simply when charged with a newly thought-up mischief—but always lighting up the space around him. Still, I could not rest until I had brought him home, exhuming him from the graveyard in Wiesbaden, and the clinicality of my motions at the time made me wonder if I had left my soul in that alien graveyard in his stead.

It must be, of course, the coincidence of the airline that triggers such a somber recollection, in the main—that final homecoming for Femi was also on a Lufthansa flight. And it was a coming home for me also, since my moment-to-moment existence from the time of his death until his reburial was in some ethereal zone, peopled by eyes of the restless dead from distances of silent rebuke. I came back down to earth only when he was himself within the earth of his choice, earth that he had made his own: Ibadan. And it is this that now reinforces the unthinkable and irrational, that this same Femi—"OBJ" to numerous friends, business partners, and acquaintances—is not in Ibadan at this moment awaiting my return, his sweaty face, black as the cooking pots, supervising the kitchen in a frenzy of anticipation, with an array of wines lined up to celebrate a long-anticipated reunion! Femi should be alive for this moment. If any single being deserved and could contain in himself the entirety of the emotions that belong to this return, it is none other than OBJ, and he is gone.

It is a long-craved homecoming, my personalized seal on the end of the nightmare that was signaled by the death of a tyrant, Sani Abacha, yet here I am, trying to find reasons for my lack of feeling, trying to ensure that it is not just a mask, a perverse exercise in control, this absence of the quickening of the pulse. It is that other homeward journey of twelve years past that stubbornly sticks to the mind, that of a friend forever still in a casket in the belly of the plane, I seated among the living but stone cold to the world, conscious of this fact but only in a detached way and wondering why I was still so devoid of the sensation of loss. It could be, I acknowledge, the aftermath of the battle to bring home his remains—plainly, it had left me drained of all feeling. This return has not, so it must be that I have carried that home so obsessively in my head these past five years that I am unable to experience the journey as one toward the recovery of a zone of deprivation. The absence of Femi, who persists in looming large, a territory of dulled bereavement, is only a part of it. The adrenaline had been secreted over time, stored up, and then—*pfft*—evaporated in an instant, there being no further use for it.

One seeks these explanations somewhat desultorily, since I already acknowledge that this is not quite the homecoming I had anticipated, not quite the way my return had been planned, not this legitimate arrival, swooping toward Lagos on a normal flight as if Lagos were Frankfurt, New York, or Dakar. Surely it is not the same white-haired monster, that same "wanted" man with a price on his head, hunted the world over, who is headed home, steadily lubricated by the aircraft's generous bar. I continue to interrogate the featureless flatness of my mind—compared to it, the pastel evenness of the Sahara Desert, over which we appear to be eternally suspended, seems a craggy, wild, untamable, and exotic piece of landscape.

I acknowledge that I am not much given to sentiment, but after all, I am not normally averse to being welcomed home! Indeed, I often wonder if, for others similarly embattled, homecoming does not gradually become a central motif of their active existence. For instance, I find I dislike airport farewells—the exceptions have usually been preceded by some kind of tug-of-war to which I eventually yielded, often through emotional blackmail. By contrast, I am somewhat more accommodating with the motions of being welcomed back, though, even here, I am just as likely to be found sneaking in through the back door. Generally, my inclination is simply—*to have returned. To find myself back in the place I never should have left.* Or where returning is no different from never having left, a routine recovery of a space of normal being, temporarily fractured, restoration of which has no significance whatsoever and requires no special recognition. In any case, each homecoming differs wildly from the last, and this goes back to my very earliest awareness of such an event, the end of a physical separation, when I first returned home from studying overseas—on New Year's Day 1960, the year of Nigeria's independence. Then, feeling already long in the tooth at twenty-five, I had contrived to sneak home, to the discomfiture of parents, family, and relations. Normally, such a return should have been an occasion for celebration, varying from modest and restricted to festive and all-embracing, the latter gathering in distant clans and even total strangers with that ringing invocation that must have been adopted by the first-line beneficiaries of European education—*Our Argonaut has returned from over the seas after a long, perilous voyage in his quest for the Golden Fleece!*—or any of its hundred variations.

It is perhaps the sedateness of this return that continues to sit awkwardly on me, an abrupt usurpation of the other furtive homecoming that nearly was! Not that I regret the change, oh no, not for a moment! *T'agba ba nde, a a ye ogun ja*—thus goes the Yoruba wisdom—"As one approaches an elder's status, one ceases to indulge in battles." Some hope! When that piece of wisdom was first voiced, a certain entity called Nigeria had not yet been thought of. In any case, I appear to have failed in my ambition to "grow old gracefully"—no more strife, no more susceptibilities to beauty's provocation, and so on—a process I had once confidently set to begin at the magic figure of forty-nine, seven times seven, the magic number of my companion deity, Ogun. But at least I accept that there comes a moment when age dictates the avoidance of certain forms of engagement. That makes sense and is also just. There comes a point in one's life when one should no longer be obliged to sneak into one's homeland through mangrove creeks and smugglers' haunts, and in ludicrous disguises!

I worry therefore about the absence of feeling, the absence of even a grateful nod to Providence, and seek some reassurance that my senses are not fully dead, that the emotional province of the mind is still functioning. I obtain a measure of relief, however—indeed, I begin to worry now that the senses may be roaming out of control—when, even within the recycled air of the plane's interior, overflying nothing but Sahara dunes and dust, I could swear, suddenly, that I already smell the humid air of Lagos, the fetid dung heaps, the raucous marketplaces and overcrowded streets. I am certain that I can hear, dominating even the steady purr of the jet engines, the noisy street vendors with their dubious bargains, see the sly conspiratorial grins of some as they offer contraband of the most dangerous kind—and this had become routine even before I fled into exile in November 1994—banned publications that they slide out from under the pile of other journals, like pornography in other places. *Psst!* They sidle up to motorists at traffic junctions and delays, with the mainstream journals on conspicuous display. Then, indifferent to the risk that the prospective customer might turn out to be a secret service agent or one of Abacha's ubiquitous informers, they flash the sensational cover of *Tempo, The News, The Concord, Tell,* or some other hit-and-run samizdat: SANI ABACHA BARES HIS FANGS! WHOM THE GODS WILL DESTROY! ABACHA'S AGENTS ON RAMPAGE: MOTHER KILLED, ELEVEN-YEAR-OLD HELD HOSTAGE IN POLICE CELL! SCANDAL ROCKS ASO ROCK! WHO KILLED BAGAUDA KALTHO? Then the cat-and-mouse games, the mandatory raids—some days, weeks, even months in police cells for these stubborn vendors, some of them no older than ten or eleven. And no sooner are they released than they are back on the streets. Even the police grew weary of the charade. Such sights filled one's bloodstream with a political rush; the truth was, however, that I would rather be miles distant from the obligations they imposed, "taking my gun for a walk" in the bush, far from the stressful streets.

. . .

I CANNOT WAIT to repossess the bush, or maybe it is the other way around, let the bush repossess me. The bush and its furtive breath. Refuge and solace. The mere thought brings in its train the *smells*, and soon my seat is isolated and wreathed in nothing but the very smells of the bush! The thought of resuming my forays into those silent growths finally quickens my pulse, hesitantly, just perceptibly, sobered by the thought that Femi, whom I also taught to hunt, will no longer be a part of it. Yet there, perhaps, is where I would most painlessly recover his presence—in those swathes of isolation, that terrain of so many sensory ambiguities. Enfolded within the tropical bush, the effect is tranquilizing—until of course the moment of the approach of a quarry—not that the pulse quickens all that noticeably even then. It does not matter whether it is the Harmattan season of dry air with its parched or burnt vegetation—except in the early morning when the foliage is misted over and even the earth is deceptively damp—or the rainy season, which leaves you tangling with moist thickets, fording swollen gorges, sliding on treacherous rocks, and being sucked into mud gullies, day or night, at night with nothing but a few stars seen through branches or fireflies to test your patience and judgment as you wonder whether they are the eyes of a wildcat, a tree cyrax, or twin raindrops caught in the light of your night lamp.

All that matters is the escape into timelessness, interrupted by furtive pads of a four-footed quarry or the sudden burst of the brown bush fowl or gray-streaked guinea fowl soaring and screaming over trees. An instant only to decide whether or not the latter is worth the try—even if you downed it, how much time would it demand to plunge into the hostile fastness to retrieve your booty? In the process you become insensitive to the rank presence of a far larger quarry, the prized *egbin**** or *igala,*† or a patriarch or matriarch of the *etu*† family, the archsurvivor of the species—*adimu*—whose heavy meat could feed a fair-sized company of guerrillas long lost in the bush.... Definitely it is the bush, the bush alone—its smells, muted sounds, textures, and often impenetrable silence that finally bathe me in a glow of warm anticipation. It is that, that alone, not any other resumption of relationships or recovery of suspended voices. Is this some form of misanthropy?

Or perhaps it is the suppressed fear that my house is gone anyway, that I

---

* A quadruped of the deer/antelope family.
† Same as above.
† A large specimen of the rodent family.

am returning to a conspicuous gap in the landscape at which I had hacked and quarried, years before my departure, to give expression to my appetite for space. News of the invasion had reached me, but the dimension of destruction had been vague and guarded, as if the kind couriers had agreed to hold back the worst. In truth, regarding the building itself, I had not planned to encase so much space within walls, just a small cottage, after my retirement from university service, but with as much ground as I could afford. Still, hovel or mansion, the soldiers' violation hung over it, as it hung over many other homes that were owned by perceived enemies of the dictator, Sani Abacha. The house had been built almost entirely from the windfall of the Nobel Prize. I had expanded it from its original design only because I wanted to create a space for periodic retreat for writers and artists—typical of the fantasies of those who are suddenly bombarded with more money than generations before them ever laid eyes on! Thus was born the notion of the Essay Foundation for the Humanities, named after my father, whose initials, S.A., had coalesced in my childhood mind as one word: Essay.*

THE HUMAN LANDSCAPE that I left behind has been altered irreversibly, deeply pockmarked with craters of loss. It was already nearly unbearably depleted with the loss of OBJ, the irrepressible Femi Johnson, but that a feature familiar on both the personal and national terrain, Ojetunji Aboyade, should vanish within a mere three or four weeks of my departure seemed a perverse act of some vengeful deities—but to what end? To impart an already conceded lesson on mortality? And the timing, so soon after my escape, seemed cruel.

My escape had become known only when I resurfaced at a press conference at UNESCO toward the end of November. Two weeks later, I was back next door to Nigeria, in Cotonou in Benin, a place populated largely by Nigerian nationals, especially the Yoruba. My family had been smuggled out to join me for a Christmas/New Year reunion that might be the last for—who could tell how long? Our mainstay in Cotonou, Akin Fatoyinbo, himself once a prison actor in a Kafkaesque scenario under the regime of an earlier dictatorship—that of Generals Muhammadu Buhari and Tunde Idiagbon—chose to break the news to me without any preliminaries. I was working at my improvised desk in our bungalow, rented for the season, when he drove in from Lagos. His face was stone as he placed the newspapers before me, wordlessly. A thick black banner across the front page seared my sight as my eyes encountered the definitive

* See *Aké: The Years of Childhood.*

pronouncement: PROFESSOR OJETUNJI ABOYADE DEAD! I swept the bunch of papers off the table, leaped up, and walked away into the bedroom.

It was an indelible warning. By the end of this exile, the human landmarks to which I had grown accustomed would vanish, just like this, irremediably. Oje—hardly anyone ever called him by his full name—had been my vice chancellor at the University of Ife, later renamed Obafemi Awolowo University after the death of the politician and sage Awolowo, a first-generation nationalist of Yoruba stock who never lost his political fire until his death in 1984. I never really knew how my attachment with Oje had developed and deepened, but it was perhaps inevitable. He was one of that breed of tireless intellectual sparring partners, cunning at fashioning theoretical propositions that were guaranteed to provoke you and keep you in animated debate until lunch dissolved into dinner and then into late supper.

The news of his death left me with an irrational suspicion of a conspiracy of progressive abandonment by friends and colleagues, a sinister plan of deprivation of a valued landscape. Oje's cerebration was first nature, as if the gray matter in his massive head churned compulsively and could find relief only in controversy. As a hunting pupil, however, he was a total disaster. All he did was provide light relief at any outing: "Oje, that was yours! Why didn't you shoot?" And Oje would shrug: "I didn't want to waste a cartridge." So we nicknamed him "Silent Gun," in contrast to Femi, who became "O. B. *Lau-lau!*" Femi needed no prompting to blast away at anything that stirred the foliage. The Silent Gun was anything but silent, however, as we filed through the bush paths toward the killing fields; indeed, his voice was raised the lustiest as we startled farmers, villagers, and sometimes cattle drovers, all marveling at three—occasionally more—obviously mad, conspicuously *akowe** types, belting out their "Aparo† Hunting Song," which I had set to the tune of the spiritual "There's a Man Going Round Taking Names." I replenished it with new verses during outings, each addition a giveaway for the result of the day's hunt. Such a day might begin buoyant and demolition-primed, end with the equivalent of Napoleon's retreat from Moscow. Sauntering out with

> An aparo's waiting yonder with my name
> It goes, quaw-awk, quaw-awk, quaw-awk— it's my game
> It just won't go to bed

* Indicating the educated type—from an office clerk to a doctor, lawyer, professor, etc.
† A fast-flying wildfowl of the quail/partridge family.

Till I fill it full of lead
I can hear it simmering gently on the flame

it was not uncommon for the day to end in a chastened recessional:

So, don't invite yourself to dinner chez moi
In this hunting clan, the merrier means fewer
As our forebears' saying goes
If a hunter counted his woes,
He would never invite a friend to dinner—which you are!

THE YEAR 1994 was closing on the brutal reign of Sani Abacha, and the stream of dissidents into exile had begun to increase. As if he had timed it with his annoying, statistical mind, Oje chose the final hours of that year to subsume all other flights into exile under his own irreversible departure, also filling mine with a warning of many frustrations to come. Close by, a mere four- or five-hour drive to his Ibadan home, where he had passed away, and an hour farther north toward Awe, his burial place, I was left to fume that I could not be present at his funeral, could not bid good-bye to an organism that had grown on me over the years. All that was left was to mourn his departure from exile through a surrogate. I was given no time to sink into this new loss and absorb the blow in my own way—no! My farewell words were awaited, and a contact had agreed to pick up the message the following day.

I looked for solace of sorts in recalling how I would sometimes remind him—whenever he proved difficult—that I should, after all, be credited with having prolonged his life, or, more accurately, with having thwarted an earlier claim on his life. In turn, he rejected my claims, insisting instead that all that the "lifesaving" episode revealed was what a soft underbelly was hidden beneath my public carapace. No sooner had he survived the illness that nearly took him away than he took to regaling any willing listener with details of my "unmanly" conduct at his bedside at the Lagoon Hospital in Apapa, Lagos. For Oje, it was the ultimate demystification, the explosion of the Kongi* myth, a reading that he relished and refused to abandon.

He was being prepared for his departure to Germany in an ambulance plane, a necessary recourse, alas, that was itself a damning commentary on the state of hospitals within the nation and the faith of the rulers in a national

---

* The name of a character from the author's play *Kongi's Harvest* that was in turn adopted by others as his nickname.

health service. That consideration presented no problems for the then dictator, Ibrahim Babangida—nor indeed for any of the heads of state before him. Babangida was not about to lose his top policy adviser; he ordered Oje Aboyade's immediate evacuation.

When the moment came to wheel him into the vehicle, however, I balked.

"Well, fly safely. And get yourself back here soon."

His eyes opened wide in disbelief. "You're not coming to the airport with me?"

"No, thank you. I already feel superfluous."

"But that budgetary provision you're so concerned about—the IMF relief package—we could discuss it some more on the way to the airport."

At that point, I came clean. "No way," I said. "I saw Femi off at the airport, and he never made it back. I am not accompanying you."

"I don't believe this!" he shouted. "Look at you! All your *sakara**—beneath it all, soft. You're scared stiff. No, worse, you're superstitious."

I shrugged, unmoved. My mind was already made up. Into the earth-hugging ambulance, yes, but to follow and watch him being loaded into the winged counterpart, taking off into the same ozone that had swallowed Femi forever—out of the question! "Call me what you like. I am not coming with you. I accompanied Femi virtually into the plane, and he vanished forever. This time, no. This way, I know you'll be back in no time."

"Coward! I will never let you live this down."

"I'll survive that. Femi is not around to help you make a perpetual feast of it, so once again—journey safely. I may visit you there, I may not. The beer is very good in Germany, by the way. Tell the doctors to pin the placard 'One Man, One Beer' by your bedside, where you can see it. It will get you up and about in no time."

MY FINGERS FELT considerably lightened, and I began to tap out his graveside tribute, invoking the earlier match that ended in his favor....

Oje Aboyade had had a close brush with death about four years before. Even the specialists at the German hospital who performed the lifesaving operation on him marveled at his survival. He became, in effect, a sideshow for the students at the teaching hospital; they all came to examine his case notes and gawk at the miracle man. His recovery was total, and it most certainly was not that ailment which finally took him away. After that "refurbishment," and coming as he did from a

---

* Bravado.

*long-lived family, I most confidently expected him to outlive the rest of us and
would often say so. That was careless; I should have remembered the Nigerian
killer factor. Simply defined, it is the stressful bane of the mere act of critical
thought within a society where power and control remain the playthings of imbe-
ciles, psychopaths, and predators.*

Oje's close-cropped head, grudgingly pocked with a few white tufts, rose
before me, the deceptively mild roundness of his face lightly lined with cicatrices of his Awe origin. His name was an instant giveaway, to the knowledgeable,
as scion and heir of the family ancestral masquerade, the *oje*. So proud was he
of this legacy—deemed "heathen" by the disciples of Christianity and Islam—
that he ensured that the names of his two male children bore the prefix *Oje*, yet
he was an unfailing Sunday worshiper at his church in Bodija Housing Estate
and even some kind of deacon.

Aboyade had been deeply immersed in a project in Ibadan, the Development Policy Centre, long before I fled into exile. The seed of the idea had been
sown as far back as 1978, under the military regime headed by General Olusegun Obasanjo—who would later resurface as a civilian head of state in 1999.
That original idea for a civilian think tank had ended up as yet another military
appropriation, becoming the Centre for Strategic Studies located in the far
north, in Kuru. General Obasanjo blithely assumed that Oje would still agree
to direct the new institution, but no. It was not what he had envisioned. Not
only had his idea been purloined, it had become militarized. Stubbornly but
patiently, he persisted with his original vision and finally began to see it take
material form twenty years later. During that earlier inception, I frequently accompanied Oje in the search for a suitable location, and we settled on an estate
being developed near the Asejire Dam, just outside Ibadan. I sat with him
through several brainstorming sessions with Obasanjo in Dodan Barracks,
Lagos, then the seat of government, poring over blueprints. A year before Oje's
death, the original idea was back within Ibadan, on a somewhat more modest
scale but as a fully civilian institution, independent of any government dicta-
tion.

Encumbered by other preoccupations, I drifted into and out of the resurrected project, though we would discuss its progress in the usual speculative
manner. About four years before his death, Oje took me to the site, where the
offices were in quite an advanced state of construction. He had already recruited his team and earmarked my own office space—typically informing me
of this with the utmost casualness and no prior consultation.

I wandered around—it seemed a logical retirement home for an aging author and itinerant lecturer who, I had long acknowledged about myself, would remain creatively restless right across the border of senility. The environment was finely balanced within but fully shielded from the sprawling city of Ibadan. Already, the site seemed charged and vibrant, pulsating with intellectual energy—but then, I admit I am biased. Construction sites are often inspiring spaces for me, potent with inchoate forms, and knowing that this one had materialized out of sheer persistence and aspired to become a warehouse of cross-fertilizing minds, it was inevitable that I would imbue even the slurry-caked cement mixer, temporarily silenced, with intellectual fecundity. Sometimes it seemed a pity that a polished, elegant edifice should ever replace the chaotic terrain of the architectural muse in labor, but of course one is ultimately consoled by beauty of a different kind—hopefully! An addict, I wandered over mounds of sand and gravel, stepping over uprooted stumps and negotiating reinforced concrete pillars. Pools of water from recent rains stagnated on the concrete flooring.

There were some smashed rocks, mostly flat slabs, scattered over the grounds, dug up during the laying of the foundation. Oje's collaborator and architect, Alhaji Adetunji, voiced a plaint about how or where to dispose of them—they did not fit into his landscaping scheme. Oje only pretended to mull over the problem; he was already nodding his head mischievously in my direction. The look on his face said clearly "There's your godsend; you couldn't ask for a more accommodating scavenger." My house in Abeokuta—which to him was the structural expression of all unregistered idiosyncrasies —was then approaching completion. I also pretended to think it over. A few days later a truckload of shale slabs and stones was dumped on my grounds, with a message that if I wanted any more, I would have to organize their transportation myself. That was typical of the Alhaji, a self-effacing person who would say very little but act spontaneously and generously. The slabs and rocks went into the paving of the frontage of my Abeokuta home—and the far more restricted Essay Foundation for the Humanities.

The circumstances of Oje's departure resurrected twinges of that far more ancient, far closer bereavement, the leave-taking by my father, Essay, one that also took place in absentia, owing yet again to the exigencies of my political choices. My prison memoir, *The Man Died,* recently published, had not endeared me any more to the regime in power and was unofficially banned from circulation. The dictatorship under which I underwent that prison spell—that of General Yakubu Gowon—still ruled our lives in 1972. It was nowhere near as vicious as Abacha's but not so benign that I dared fail to concede to my

mother—the "Wild Christian" of my childhood memoir, *Aké*—the reasonableness of her warning when she learned of my plans to risk a return home.
Her message to me was in character: "By all means, come home. I'll even send
you a first-class ticket. Understand, however, that you'll be coming for two funerals, the other one guaranteed by such folly." I remained in London. Wild
Christian survived her life companion by several more years and then was kind
enough to transmit to me, in her own way, the moment of her passing away.
Booked to fly to Ghana for a meeting on the fated day, indeed, already standing
at the check-in counter, my feet turned leaden. I refused to take the final, routine step for my boarding pass. Instead, I turned around and drove back to Ife
to await—I did not know what. Doors and windows were locked to give the il-
lusion of absence while I awaited whatever it was that had made me turn back.

Just as they had both done at my father's death, ignoring the fact that I was
now home and, with my siblings, had begun to immerse myself in the tasks
that fall on the children, Oje and Femi took charge of much of my own portion
of the arrangements, aided by Yemi Ogunbiyi, a former student who had become a colleague at Ife. Wild Christian's funeral also took place in our second
hometown, Isara, and she was buried next to her husband. I was able to perform my ritual functions as *omo oloku,* one of the "children of bereavement,"
unlike at my father's funeral, when Oje and OBJ had stood surrogate. Their
functions at his funeral were anything but ritual. They smuggled in a tape on
which I had recorded my farewell, including lines from Dylan Thomas's poem
to his dying father, and ensured that it was played at the funeral service. With
both friends and accomplices gone, it was just as well that I had no more parents to lose!

My mother's warning over Essay's funeral had not been misplaced. Secret
service agents—my eternal chaperones!—swarmed the routes leading to the
town, convinced that I would attempt to sneak into the country. They con-
verged on the church and, on hearing my voice over the loudspeakers, concluded that I had eluded their net and was delivering the funeral tribute in
person. Soon enough, they discovered the mechanical source of the voice and,
once the service was over, swooped down on the church in an effort to seize the
tape—but why? To reassure their bosses that I had not shown my face after all,
that it was only my disembodied voice that had evaded their roadblocks? Or to
interrogate the tape and find out by what agency it had landed in the church?
No matter, my two collaborators took charge, even succeeded in hiding the
recording machine itself, a bulky Grundig, from the police agents and ensuring
that the tape remained where it belonged—with the family. Under Abacha,

those agents would not have waited until the funeral service was over. They would have stormed the place of worship, arrested the tape recorder, and carted off the officiating prelates for interrogation!

ON MY POLITICAL LANDSCAPE, easily the most accusing void, created by one who had been central to my mission in exile these past five years, was that of the industrialist Bashorun Moshood Kashimawo Abiola. Abiola was the elected president of a nation who never did preside over more than his home, his vast network of businesses, and finally his place of detention. It is a pointless habit, one knows, to label what is clearly the crime of others as a failure in oneself, but that irrational speculation sometimes lays claim to such a place in our reverses. Abiola's death was one of unmatchable, lingering cruelty. Robbed of victory, imprisoned and isolated from human contact for nearly four years, and then, on the eve of his second victory, a victory that was signaled by the death of his jailer and usurper of his mandate, Sani Abacha, to end up—wasted!

What the democratic aspirations of the nation had anticipated, following the sudden death of Abacha in June 1998, was a search for a negotiated future in which, logically, Abiola, the imprisoned president-elect, would play a central role, in all likelihood as the head of an interim government of national unity. No one of any note still denied that he had won the 1993 elections for president. Then, one month after the death of Sani Abacha, in the presence of a delegation of U.S. officials—Thomas Pickering, a former ambassador to Nigeria; Susan Rice, President Bill Clinton's assistant secretary of state for African affairs; and others—Abiola was served the cup of tea that has now attained legendary status in the nation, for he suffered a seizure minutes after that cup, collapsed, and died. I try to recall if ever there was a Tantalus in Nigerian history or mythology, but no one seems adequate. Only D. O. Fagunwa's Ogboju Ode, the hero of *Ogboju Ode Ninu Igbo Irunmale*,* buried up to his neck in captivity, victim of a vicious palace conspiracy, comes close, but that was a tale that at least offered its readers the moral reward of a rescue and a happy ending.

The truth, I know, will come out someday. Four years to effect his murder, but murder him they did in the end, and I cannot but feel that it was due to some insufficiency on our part, on mine, though I do not really know what I, or anyone in the democratic struggle, could have done to prevent it. It continues to strike me as grossly unfair that, a few days before his death, I should have

---

* *The Fearless Hunter in the Forest of a Thousand Demons*

been caught up in Vienna by a faxed message warning of his imminent murder. Because of that warning, and despite its futility with regard to both time and means, I tend to drag with me a nagging element of blame. It was small comfort that I would discover later that I was not the only recipient of the message whose text so clearly verged on the hysterical. Even at its most level, matter-of-fact register, this was a source we had learned not to take lightly. In this instance, the frame of mind of this specific writer—we named our key information sources collectively "Longa Throat," after Richard Nixon's nemesis, "Deep Throat"—appeared to have affected his use of upper- and lowercase:

> *The only addendum the new regime and its collaborators has is to: ENSURE THAT CHIEF M.K.O. ABIOLA DOES NOT BECOME THE PRESIDENT OF NIGERIA IN WHATEVER FORM.... Let me state here categorically that this is not a prediction at all. It is a preconceived plan of the new regime, exposed by an insider....*
>
> *THE IMPORTANT REPORT SENT TO ME TODAY: A NOTORIOUS GANG IN THE NIGERIAN ARMY has completed their plan to assassinate Chief Moshood Abiola as a "final settlement of the ABACHA/ABIOLA war" in a "no victor, no vanquished way." Believe it or not, if the report given to me is anything to go by, Chief Abiola's death could come within a few days or before the end of September. This may look ridiculous, unthinkable or like an outright fabrication, but believe it or not, it is true. Tell Prof and other pro-democracy groups both abroad and at home to mount a very intensive pressure on Abdulsalami to release Chief M.K.O. Abiola now!*
>
> *The new regime would fail to protect Chief Abiola from his assassins because it has not been able to persuade them to rethink the Nigerian national question.*
>
> *They might even seize power from Abubakar in order to achieve their destructive plan. These people are hell-bent on destroying the corporate existence of Nigeria rather than see Abiola become the president.*

The last leg in the relay through which the message had traveled was none other than my son Ilemakin, who had long since thrown himself into the struggle on his own, slipped out of the country and begun to carry out some missions for the democracy movement. The desperate appeal finally reached its destination on my last day in Vienna, but only after the departure of Kofi Annan, secretary-general of the United Nations. A day earlier, I had been locked in a tête-à-tête with him for nearly an hour and a half. He seemed quite relaxed; the human rights conference that had brought us both to Austria appeared to have fulfilled all the aims of the United Nations, and Kofi Annan was now looking forward to his next mission: to travel the next morning to Nigeria, where he would visit the new—decidedly interim—head of state, Abdulsalami Abubakar, and of course see Moshood Abiola in prison. Neither of us required any urging to accept that we had to meet and talk before his departure.

My patience was severely tested by his "reasonableness" ... *Yes, yes, Wole, an opportunity has opened up now with Abacha's death, and we musn't waste it. A lot can be achieved, the crisis can now be resolved, but, you know, you must tell your people also to be reasonable. The opposition simply has to be reasonable.*

Reasonable? Were we being unreasonable? After nearly thirty years of military rule, the last five under the most repellent of the species, we were asking for the immediate release of the elected president and all remaining political prisoners and the setting up of an interim government headed by Abiola, the legitimate president—an interim government that would last a year, maybe two. In tandem, the nation's representatives would meet at a sovereign national conference to ascertain the real will of the people and lay the ground for the next elections while reviewing the terms of association of the constituent parts of the nation. Then general elections. What was unreasonable about such proposals? Indeed, what alternative was there? I had the sinking feeling that Kofi was traveling with a prepared script, a script already agreed between the United Nations and a caucus of Western governments. The program of our democratic coalition was not to be part of that script.

Warning of the death threat to Abiola was delivered into my hands only after Kofi Annan had left for Nigeria and had even held his meeting with the prisoner! If I had received it earlier, I would have submerged all political discussion under the urgency of bringing Abiola out of prison immediately! Certainly I would have served formal notice on the United Nations, insisted—for whatever it was worth—that its secretary-general refuse to meet Abiola except at liberty, in his own home, surrounded by his family and political associates. We had learned from experience to trust any warning from "Longa Throat." It was too late, however; Abiola was already dying, his organs weakened by a devilish regimen of slow poisoning. It will all come out in its full byzantine details—of that, I live in total confidence.

So our discussion—and my principal concerns—were taken up mostly with Nigeria's future, not with any thoughts of danger to the man at the center of it all. By the end of that meeting, so convinced was I that that future had already been decided by others that I sent messages home immediately, urging that all pressure should be mounted on the visitor to make him *listen* to our program and press it on the new landlord of Aso Rock, General Abdulsalami. And yet I warned in the same breath that it would be futile anyway. Such were the frequent contradictions that defined many moments of that democratic undertaking. Futility stared one in the face, but inaction was far more intolerable.

Wryly and incongruously, at such moments would float to the surface of my mind one of my mother's favorite aphorisms, with her comic Yorubization of the key English word "trying": *"Itirayi ni gbogbo nkan"*—"The trying is all." Wild Christian applied it to a full gamut of incompatible situations—from the shrug of resignation that followed a failed attempt to charge exorbitantly for her goods to falling with full relish on the dubious results of an exotic recipe that she was attempting for the first time. Abiola was—like the French Socialist president François Mitterrand, which is where the similarity ends—a dogged disciple of the doctrine of *itirayi*. It was not his first attempt to become the president of Nigeria. A Yoruba from the South, his first, overconfident foray was ridiculed and scuttled by a feudal cabal of the North who found it laughable that anyone outside their privileged caucus should even dream of ruling the nation. They took his money—lots of it—but openly derided his ambitions. Abiola made a strategic withdrawal, bided his time, launched himself on a philanthropic crusade, broadened and reinforced his political base. At the second outing, he succeeded. And for that, Abiola was killed.

I AM TEMPTED to hold this last loss responsible, above other candidates, for a homecoming that appears almost completely devoid of emotion, the focus of one's struggle having been violently sucked into a void. But it goes beyond the depressing weight of such absences. I am not returning to any abandoned territory, since this is where I have remained by compulsion, almost with debilitating intensity, these past five years.

Instinctively, I turn toward the window when the captain announces that we have entered the Nigerian airspace. The plane's shadow dances over a few minarets and walled cities of the North. We are still some distance from our destination; the full length of the Nigerian landmass has yet to be crossed. For a moment I think I have caught a glimpse of an oasis, but it is only the sun's glint on a flat, corrugated iron roofing, undoubtedly a factory. My mind moves to the fate of my own house, the modest foundation dream. Now, *that* I had effectively abandoned, perhaps in self-defense, brick by red brick and beam by beam, including its wild, ample grounds, where I had experimented and succeeded—against all odds, I was told—in cultivating the wild, now rarely seen *agbayun*, that stubborn berry that coats every morsel of food for hours afterward with a natural sweetness. The lore, backed by generations of frustrated farmers, was that it never fructified in captivity. Through trial and error, by varying the combination of sunshine and soil, moisture, shade, and whatever else I could recall from my amateur flirtation with viniculture, I produced a freak success, a feat of which I was inordinately proud, since I am no farmer. The oldest and the youngest in the family, Tinuola and Folabo, are the family's green thumbs. Femi, next to me in age—"Jamani," to distinguish him by his childhood nickname from his namesake, OBJ—is the fisherman. I took to hunting. Cultivating the *agbayun* was also an irony, as I do not like sweets and only gave the berries away.

There was also my minifield of wild mints. When I retired from the Nigerian university system in 1985, thinking of various occupations for survival, I considered a project for freezing or drying my wild mint for sale, especially to bars and teahouses around the world. Fantasizing myself as a small-scale trading maverick, one who identified, produced, and marketed a select item or two in demand, virtually from my doorstep, making a living out of it to sustain a retirement into purely creative pursuits—this has long been a favorite pastime of mine. I suppose it was my fascination with the world of Wild Christian, that modest trader in a medley of commodities, that promoted such fantasies. I knew it would come to nothing, but it provided moments of unmatched bliss to sit in those ample verandas, survey my lordly domain, and weave my magic carpet of a life of interdependency between the arts and the farm. The minigrove of wild mints and the *agbayun* were doomed to remain contemplative vistas, nothing more. I enjoyed watching them grow, sniffing the air around them and accompanying their flights to myriad cities in air-sealed bags. But all I did was lace the occasional drink with the mint leaves and distribute the *agbayun* berries to friends. A few hundred were forgotten in my freezer, where they duly rotted when the infamous electrical supply took even its feeble charge away for prolonged periods that coincided with my absences from home.

Perhaps the memory of its one dedication still hovers around the estate. At the first anniversary of Femi Johnson's death—or, more accurately, of his reinternment—the foundation received its first guest, an absentee guest and permanent resident. Then the estate came alive, peopled, that one time, by the very creative tribe it was meant to serve. I try to recollect the animated faces and voices . . . the poet and journalist Odia Ofeimun; the critic Biodun Jeyifo; the poet and playwright Femi Osofisan; Tunji Oyelana and Jimi Solanke, musicians and actors; the singer and lifelong collaborator Francesca Emmanuel; Bola Ige, a lawyer and politician but friend of the arts and occasional poet . . .

then we formally named a wing for our late friend, slaughtered a goat, and consumed gourdfuls of palm wine and cases of its bottled and labeled expatriate siblings. Celebrating Femi Johnson's life? Or assuaging our loss yet again? No matter, he was one of us, actor and singer even though a businessman, and we were sealing his present memory into those walls.

The memories, yes, but the physical casing of the idea? Mentally abandoned—at least, so I continue to hope—flushed into the thin stream that I had widened into an artificial pond, past the catchment groves of repose along the watercourse, now certainly silted up or covered in an oily slick that oozed lazily from that strange soil. I remind myself that I once abandoned even the cactus patch, a bristling phalanx of thorned markers to which I had assigned the role of covering my remains—yes, that was the ultimate proof of my detachment. It was due especially to the dismissal of that last attachment that, faced with the real possibility that I might be killed in exile, I seized greedily on a chance encounter, a revelation, on the island of Jamaica. I imbued the event with a fated dimension, read it as a solemn pronouncement and offering from predecessors to the ancestral realms. Alas, even that substitute would prove treacherous, impressing on me all over again the lesson I thought I had mastered—never to call deeply to anything as mine, never to become attached, not even to a prospective burial ground.

IN 1990—IN MY NOTATION, the Year of Mandela's Release—when he made Jamaica one of his earliest stopping points for his reunion with the living world, I made a startling discovery on that same island. If Nelson Mandela was discovering the space of freedom on a global scale, I was also discovering a microworld that was founded in freedom. Thus did I embark on a pilgrimage that would begin as a sentimental, and evolve into a morbid, attachment.

The timing of my presence in Kingston, Jamaica, with Mandela's—even though we never did meet on that soil—imbued my discovery with an indefinable sense of augury, but then, let it be recalled that, like a large portion of the world, I had carried the calvary of Mandela and the struggle against apartheid South Africa in my head for longer than its continental replacement, the horror of an Abacharized Nigerian nation. Apart from participating in the mandatory "Free Mandela" marches, disinvestment campaigns, lecture sessions, anti-sanction-busting commissions, and so on, I had presented an early student play at London's Royal Court Theatre, *The Invention*, on the insanities of the apartheid system. Decades after that production, I titled a collection of my poems *Mandela's Earth and Other Poems*, and it seemed the most appropriate gesture, as I prepared for Stockholm in 1986, to dedicate my Nobel acceptance speech to him. (That was the speech in which, to my eternal chagrin, I listed Montesquieu among the contributors to European racist thinking—may the shade of Montesquieu find it in his ancestral heart to forgive that libel!)

To find myself again in Kingston for a lecture engagement in 1990, for the first time in nearly fifteen years, just as the entire city was emptying itself out for Mandela, was already more than sufficient. It was a symbolic gift that I regarded as personal, not shared with the millions of ecstatic hordes that had labored for and now celebrated his freedom. To discover a portion of my own homeland in that far-off place at the same time—now, that was a miracle that could be wrought only by a Mandelan avatar!

For it was only on this visit, my second ever to that island, that I was made aware of a slave settlement called Bekuta, a name that immediately resonated in my head as none other than the name of my hometown, Abeokuta. This centuries-wide reunion with my own history sent a tingle down my vertebrae— an encounter with descendants from my own hometown on a far-flung Caribbean island, in the hills of a onetime slave settlement called Jamaica?

The group of slave descendants who founded the settlement, in flight from the lowland plantations, had sought out a hilly terrain that would prove nearly impenetrable for their pursuing owners but would also remind them of home. They found it in the county of Westmoreland and settled among its rockhills, naming it Abeokuta. Yemi Adefuye, the Nigerian high commissioner in the West Indies, had already become acquainted with this history and could not wait to arrange a visit. What was only an academic though exciting discovery for him and others was, in my case, a most affecting experience. I found it strange indeed that during my first visit to Jamaica, in 1976 for Carifesta—the Caribbean Festival of the Arts—no one had thought to mention the existence of this settlement or propose that we pay it a visit!

A famous Nigerian, now also deceased, had preceded me on this voyage of private discovery, I was informed. This was Fela Sowande, a composer, but a totally different spirit from his younger and more famous namesake, the "Afro-beat king" and iconoclast Fela Anikulapo Kuti. Sowande had been completely overwhelmed—he had broken down in tears. This older cousin would exact his emotional revenge on me some years later, unintentionally, for it was his symphony *Obangiji*, based on melodies from our common birthplace, that, unexpectedly swarming out of the violin and cello strings of the Swedish orchestra as I moved forward on the Stockholm stage to receive the Nobel Prize, nearly succeeded in making me a victim of the shamelessness of tear ducts. It was a brief but tense struggle! The rockhills of origin stood me in good stead, but it could have gone either way. (The horror of it—the immaculately pressed, ribboned, and sashed master of ceremonies, the Swedish prince consort himself, compelled to lend me his handkerchief!) Really, the Stockholm ceremonials should not spring such surprises on middle-aged susceptibilities!

As the island slowly recovered from the hangover of Mandela's visit, I could not wait to answer the call of Bekuta. There I encountered one of my yet living ancestors, the oldest inhabitant of the settlement, frail, as one would expect a being of more than a hundred years to be. Now, let no one dare tell me I do not know an Egba face when I see one! The parchment tautness of her face, the unmistakable features of the Egba death mask, captured so immutably in Demas Nwoko's* painting *Ogboni,* attested her origins distinctly against any skeptical voices. Not much motion was left in her body, or else her body rhythm, I was certain, would have reinforced what her face pronounced. As she became bedridden, she ordered her bed moved to the window that overlooked the rockhills. Now all she sought was that her eyes would open and close on those rocks, dawn and dusk, until her final moment.

She was the sole survivor of the original settlers. Her voice was still remarkably strong. Did I imagine the unmistakable Egba twang in her Jamaican patois? Of course I did, but what a conceit to let it linger in the resounding chambers of one's head! *Oh yes, the real name is A-be-o-ku-ta*—never did music sound so tanned, so ancestral in authority—*but it gradually became corrupted to Bekuta. I tell them all the time—the name is A-be-o-ku-ta, but how many of them can remember that? They don't even remember what it means, unless I remind them. I was a child when we came here. When our people dance for you and cook you* fufu, ewedu, jogi, *and other foods from home, no one come tell you that we descendants of slaves from A-be-o-ku-ta. But yes, much has been lost. The government help a little, they come here sometimes, bring visitors, and the local council preserve our history by staging shows every year. We observe the seasons of the gods . . . Sango, Obatala, Ogun[†] . . . we used to have a* babalawo,[‡] *but I don't think anyone remember how to read Ifa[§] anymore . . . some of the children go away and never return . . . in fact, the best dancers are the older ones, they the ones who keep our traditions alive. They teach their children, but the children not very inter-*

---

* Nigerian painter and sculptor.
† Yoruba deities.
‡ Diviner, priest of divination.
§ The Divination Corpus.

ested. They only do these things when there are important visitors, so I don't know
what going happen when the older ones die off....

Shadowed by soaring rockhills—if the god Ogun sought congenial habitation, it would be nowhere else—they danced for us the sedate, ceremonial steps of the Egba, and fed us dishes whose recipes had been carefully preserved from the vanished home. These were the life exiles, generation exiles, those who had died to a faraway homeland and awakened to a new earth, exiles to whom the call of origin had thinned over time and dissipated into the winds of passage, drifting with mists from the cascading waters of Bekuta rockhills and evaporating the same way. It vanished wistfully into the territory of legends, of the deities of mountains and valleys, was fleshed out in purely performance modes that increasingly underscored its now vestigial status. Recollection stepped gingerly into temporary recovery spaces of town halls or school fields, ever submissive to the present. The exigencies of that present—careers, economic survival, politics, and the rest—reinforced their supremacy over memory or sentiment. After each emergence, the adaptive masks and costumes of origin reentered their normal abode of camphor-saturated boxes and shelves—until the next festive or commemorative occasion.

Not the sheerest thought of that vivid state of suspended animation, exile, had I entertained on my encounter with that settlement in the Year of Mandela's Release. I was paying a call on family and preferred not to see the sparse population of Bekuta as exiles but simply as one of the many branches of the Egba—a clan of wanderers who had vanished into the forests one day and could not readily find their way back. Regarding my own future, exile was simply not on the divination board.

Three years later, all had changed. A new dictator, Sani Abacha, an identical agenda—the perpetuation of military rule—but a different cast of mind, and with an increasingly ruthless, ever-widening network to act it out. The thought of real death—not the remediable conceit now of exile as a mimic death—became an insistent, strident companion. As I set out on one mission after another, in pursuit of what surely, simply had to be the vital key to repossession of one's real space, my mind took refuge in Bekuta. It was not a morbid condition, just a matter-of-fact possibility that stared me in the face. Agitated by the thought that some misguided friends or family would take my remains to Nigeria, I announced openly that, if the worst happened, I did not want Abacha's triumphant feet galumphing over my body and would settle for the surrogate earth of Jamaica. And I began to make preparations to buy a patch of land in Bekuta.

· · ·

FATE, I CONCLUDED, lured me back to Jamaica for the next, determining visit in 1995, barely two years into the exile that followed the ascent of Sani Abacha. The vehicle was *The Beatification of Area Boy,* a play that was originally intended for Lagos but was now headed for production in the land of the Rastas. Bekuta beckoned. My first free weekend in Kingston found me motoring through the hairpin bends of the mountain road toward Westmoreland. I could not wait to transfer the deed to my cactus patch to Bekuta.

Motoring with me was Gerry Feil, my American friend and filmmaker, whose bulk belied his restless energy, with permanently irritated features that grumpily matured with age into a passable double for the patriarch of the Flintstone family. He arrived in Kingston with his daughter, Anna, titled my wine-daughter, a special relationship that came from her ceremonial induction into wine from childhood, a rite of passage that is de rigueur in my own household, where the mother has a choice of being a voluntary accomplice, is herself immobilized by a generous dosage, or else is locked in the toilet until it's all over. Such sustained devotion to the cause of wine must have been mystically transmitted to the oenophile nobility of France and resulted in my most treasured recognition, to which even the Nobel takes second place. During a lecture visit to the University of Tours, the vice chancellor and I were dragged off to a deep underground *cave,* a multichambered grotto. There, over feeble protests at my unworthiness, I was inducted into the Commanderie de la Dive Bouteille de Bourgeuil et de St. Nicolas de Bourgeuil, a centuries-old order that boasts as members Rabelais and Voltaire, among other illustrious humanists. It was definitely the highlight of my career.

Gerry had visited me in Nigeria several times—in Ibadan, Ife, and Abeokuta—the first time as a member of the exploratory team of the British director Joan Littlewood, who was seeking to film my play *The Lion and the Jewel.* Each visit was marked by one memorable event or another, but perhaps none more unsettling than his stay in Abeokuta while I was still living in a rented house, supervising the building of the first-ever home—modestly conceived at the time—that I could call my own. Gerry, to whom the combination of heat and humidity remained a potentially fatal threat, spent all night in my motorcar with the engine running to guarantee an air-conditioned environment. My home, alas, lacked such a basic amenity. This meant, quite simply, that I got no sleep that night, since a stubborn specter stuck to the inner membrane of my eyelids: Gerry's corpse in the morning, gas fumes having seeped into the interior of the car. Earlier efforts to make him seek remedy in a bathtub filled with cold water—where drowning in his sleep was less likely than carbon monoxide poisoning—had proved futile. My guest insisted that he entertained no fear of death by water but argued that submersion in water all night would only aggravate his condition. I went downstairs every half hour to seek a clear patch in the misted-over windows through which I could check if he was still breathing. The following night, after intense persuasion, I induced him to transfer to a commandeered air-conditioned room not far from me, just for the nights, while he returned to spend waking time with a host who otherwise would have turned into a nervous wreck.

The invitation to Westmoreland was mainly for Anna. She was then looking for a subject for her thesis in social anthropology, and it occurred to me that the story of Bekuta was a ready-made subject: a violent dispersal, exile, enslavement, liberation, the search for a substitute homeland and—resettlement. It was a research subject for which I made no attempt to disguise my own vested interests. What was left of the cultures of the original homeland? How had the descendants adjusted? Had polygamy survived? That last was inspired by more than a cursory interest in a return to roots. It could produce, maybe, objective criteria for evaluating a social philosophy that contrasted so profoundly with serial polygamy, as practiced in the "progressive" Western world. Was there any syncretism in the new microculture of the *araa Bekuta** with the cultures of other Jamaican settlers or indigenes? And so on. Anna came armed with a tape recorder and video camera, seeking preliminary material with which to persuade her supervisors that this was a worthwhile subject for a thesis. I was prepared to accompany her project statement with a recommendation of such enticing prospects—even in blank verse, if that would help—that it would make her supervisors salivate and even attempt to take over the project to boost their résumés.

It took a while to find the village on this decisive encounter, far longer even than the journey from Kingston, where the driver had done his best on those treacherous, sometimes vertiginous roads, to ensure that we prematurely gained my dream patch of the afterlife. On the way back to Kingston, however, I had cause to regret that he had not succeeded, had not ended the dream in the most brutal way that he appeared mindlessly capable of doing, so complete was the collapse of my anticipations. Only five years had passed since my "Mandela" visit, and yet not many people in neighboring, virtually next-door villages ap-

---

* People of Bekuta.

peared to have heard that exotic word—*Bekuta*! Those whose eyes lit up at the sound were no longer sure if it still existed. *Bekuta? Sure, me once know the place. But is it you going find anyone still living there?*

We had embarked on the search on our own, seeking, unlike black Americans, tributaries, not roots. It was an extended holiday in Jamaica, one of those infinite weekends, so there were no officials to act as guides—not that I needed them, I boasted, Egba blood would call to Egba, never mind that I routinely refer to myself not as Egba but as Ijegba—a marriage of Ijebu and Egba, the two Yoruba branches of my parentage. As for any local descendants of the Egba clans we might chance upon, they had long substituted rum and ganja for palm wine and kola nut, the calypso and reggae for juju and *agidigbo*.* Fortunately, such was my impatience that, the very afternoon of our arrival, late as it was, I decided that we would do some reconnoitering before dark. Thus we would eliminate several false leads, leaving only a handful of blind alleys and mountain cul-de-sacs for the following day.

And we did find Bekuta with only a little extra agony the following morning. The old lady was dead, but that was to be expected, she had long been ready to be called home. Something far larger had died, however, and that was Bekuta itself. It was the old lady who had kept up the settlement and its traditions through sheer willpower—we knew that already, but had not guessed how solitary a task it had been, how her spirit had been the existential force of the village. Now the homestead had died with her. The younger generation had pulled up stakes and departed. Her granddaughter, who was settled a modest walking distance away from Bekuta, found my pilgrimage amusing . . . *but no one pay much time for that Africa foolishness. She only one keep all that in she head, so when she gone, no one pay any mind to such things.* If only she knew what rusty daggers she was using to slash at my entrails!

Yet some stubborn retention was in evidence, as we found when we visited the original site with its few surviving relics. We put questions to them one after the other, Anna ran her miniaturized camera on the miniaturized village and took notes, but it was clear that this was no treasure trove for the would-be researcher, and there seemed to be even less substance to my quest. It was some consolation—as if the spirit of the dead matriarch still ruled in odd corners of a few hearts—that the daughter, that same dismissive daughter, was still unable to tear herself away from the terrain completely. She had stayed behind, and her mother's grave was in her small orchard, neat, carefully tended,

---

* Yoruba traditional social music.

and overlooked by the rockhills, upon which, I could only hope, the matriarch's eyes had closed at the end.

But the times had been unkind to Bekuta. Piece by piece, the story of the death of a village was elicited through indifferent voices. Some years earlier, a flash flood had sent torrents cascading down from the mountains and swept away much of the hillside settlement, washed away the crops, and even taken a toll in lives. The survivors had relocated in a few terraced plots scooped into the hills, protected by overhanging rocks, but mostly in the plains below. A year later, Nature had struck yet another blow—a renewed flooding—and the spirit of Bekuta had been broken. The village was now in the throes of death, and the old lady's passing simply had sealed its fate. Three, four years after her death, the last of the small community—with any shred of vitality—had vanished. The jungle had reclaimed its space.

DISPIRITED, WE RETURNED to our hotel. And then, while I lay in bed licking my wounds, from across the ocean, thousands of miles away, another Egba spirit flew away. The news came on my portable radio, and it sounded so strange, a floating contradiction that was at once detached from yet infused with the world from which I had myself just earned a lover's rebuff. My young cousin, the *abami eda** whom the world knew as Fela Anikulapo Kuti, was dead. He had not yet attained his sixtieth year.

A naked torso over spangled pants, over which a saxophone or microphone would oscillate onstage, receiving guests or journalists in his underpants while running down a tune from his head, in the open courtyard, at rehearsals, or in any space where he held court—all constituted the trademark of his unyielding nonconformism. Far more revealing than such skimpy attire, however, were his skin-taut skull and bulging eyes, permanently bloodshot from an indifferent sleeping routine and a dense marijuana infusion. His singing voice was raspy, intended not to entice but to arrest with trenchant messages. Sparse and lithe, Fela leaped about the stage like a brown, scalded cat, whose *miaow* was a rustle of riffs eased from a saxophone that often seemed better maintained than his own body. Fela loved to buck the system. His music, to many, was both salvation from and an echo of their anguish, frustrations, and suppressed aggression. The black race was the beginning and end of knowledge and wisdom, his life mission to effect a mental and physical liberation of the race. It struck me as a kind of portent, that it was while visiting this distant outpost of my home,

* A weird, unique being.

Abeokuta, in Westmoreland, propelled—but quite soberly, objectively—by thoughts of death, that I would receive news of the death of that other musician member of my family: the irrepressible maverick Fela Anikulapo Kuti.

How would one summarize Fela? Merely as a populist would be inadequate. Radical he certainly was, and often simplistically so. Lean as a runner bean, a head that sometimes struck me as a death mask that came to life only onstage or in an argument—more accurately described as a serial peroration, since he was incapable of a sustained exchange of viewpoints, especially in politics. Only Fela would wax a record according heroic virtues to such an incompatible trio as Kwame Nkrumah of Ghana, Sekou Toure of Guinea, and—oh yes, indeed—Idi Amin Dada, the terror of Uganda. It was, however, sufficient for my cousin that, at one time or the other, they had all challenged, defied, or ridiculed an imperial power—any voice raised in denunciation of the murders by Idi Amin or the torture cages of Sekou Toure was the voice of a Western stooge, CIA agent, or imperialist lackey. There were no grays in Fela's politics of black and white.

Memories flitted across the night—such as one of my least treasured experiences, the feeling of being designated as dog food! It was 1984, and I had traveled to Paris in order to campaign for Fela's freedom at a mammoth music concert under yet another dictatorship, that of General Buhari. Buhari's government had flung him into prison on spurious charges of a currency offense. Under the general antiracism and human rights slogan *"Touche pas mon pot!"*— "Don't touch my friend!"—the organizers of the concert planned to devote a special spot to publicize Fela's unjust imprisonment and mobilize world opinion on his behalf. I had accepted their invitation at extremely short notice, and had never before attended a pop music concert, having no inclination toward high-decibel events and mass excitation.

The trouble came from my efforts to approach the sacred arena where the artists, handlers, and other participants were tented. I shot to the venue straight from dumping my bags at the hotel and without the dozen or more passes required to open up the succession of barriers—someone had omitted to provide them. My lasting image from that concert was that of me about to be eaten at each barrier by teams of obviously starved Alsatian dogs, launched—it appeared—by their handlers, even while they pretended to restrain them. Nobody will ever persuade me that those dogs are ever fed or that they are not trained to identify innocent humanity as their next meal! I had seen footage of white police officers unleashing kindred monsters on black protesters in apartheid South Africa. At no time did the thought ever cross my mind that I would someday come close to taking over those victims' role in Paris, especially as an honored guest. My mission, I assumed, was to deliver a message to the world, thereafter escaping into the sanity of the farthest café from the raucous, stoned environment within which millions of presumably sane people would actually find a night of ecstasy. Still, once within the protective barriers, I carried off my mission with all due dignity, as became an ambassador of the "Black President," one of Fela's many unofficial titles, and delivered my message against the background of his blown-up image even as his music was blared out to the Paris night.

For nearly the last five years of his life, Fela was fully convinced not only that he was a reincarnated Egyptian god but that he had actually begun to reverse the aging process and would again revert to childhood and infancy. By that token, my *aburo* would have watched his own funeral, unobserved by mere mortals. Wreathed in a marijuana-induced serenity—for I have no doubt that there would be gardens of vintage ganja in Fela's Heaven—he would have enjoyed the irony of his funeral, the magnitude of which was an unintended gift to us on the outside. He was laid in state at the huge Onikan racecourse in the heart of Lagos, a now-degraded monument to vainglory that an earlier dictator, Yakubu Gowon, had built for himself. It had been designed as a parade ground that would show off the might and splendor of the military regime, and the first visiting dignitary to grace those grounds would have been Queen Elizabeth II of England. Alas, while attending a meeting with other African heads of state in East Africa, Yakubu Gowon learned that he had been overthrown in a coup mounted by his own palace guard, and the royal visit was canceled. I found it altogether fitting that Fela should lie in state on those grounds as nearly a million of his countrymen and -women came to pay him tribute.

On the day of Fela's funeral, the whole of Lagos stood still, all businesses were suspended, and all governmental presence was banished. The mammoth crowd at the funeral of this most vocal and unrelenting dissident being was, first, a tribute to his person. Following this, however, it was also a statement of defiance to the regime of Sani Abacha. Despite his quixotic outbursts, nearly blasphemous since they appeared to support the rule of Sani Abacha, the fundamental message of Fela's art and lifestyle was anathema to any military or dictatorial regime, and thus he remained persona non grata even to Sani Abacha, whose persecution of Beko, Fela's brother, was a reminder to the maverick tunesmith that not even he was untouchable. Fela's funeral was thus an occasion that the people exploited to the full, pouring out in a way that defied the regime's ban on public gatherings, making the Black President the mouthpiece of their repressed feelings, even in his lifeless form. Neither the police nor the military dared show their face on that day, and the few uniformed exceptions came only to pay tribute. Quite openly, with no attempt whatsoever at disguising their identities, they stopped by his bier and saluted the stilled scourge of corrupt power, mimic culture, and militarism. It was a much-needed act of solidarity for us.

Outside of public adulation, however, my mind remained retentive of a decades-old image of Fela, a private one, not the familiar stage torso swiveling above sequined trousers, leaping about onstage with inimitable verve, a leaner version of James Brown. It was a fleeting moment of revelation, glimpsed during one of my infrequent visits with him, a trapped moment of repose when his inner thoughts appeared to overcome his darting eyes and they remained in place, deep windows into a wistful, deeply dissatisfied being. There was no audience, no need for role-playing. His familiar, loosely wrapped marijuana stick of almost midsize-cigar proportions smoldered over his lower lip, diffusing sufficient smoke to intoxicate an audience of a hundred or more. He had a faraway look, filled with discontent, and I thought I read in those eyes a longing that they could will the pungent fumigation that emerged from between his lips into a transforming agent for a nation's putrefactions, yet acknowledging that he was powerless to effect this dream, that the mocking immensity of the task would forever render him tormented, inconsolable.

I found a private symmetry about his passing, mostly in the way it chose to touch me in a remote space of separated yet close kinship, as if this public death had been sent across radio waves to reattach me to that distant but progressively depleted landscape. Despite the weight of a double bereavement, I accepted, quite factually, that I was not destined to be buried in Bekuta but remained cautious about whether or not I should read the loss of Fela-Bekuta as an omen that I was not meant to perish in exile.

Bekuta is dead; long live Abeokuta? Or whatever else tugs at one, inexplicably, like the power of Ogun's magnet directed at one of his metallic vessels. That hope/prayer/doubt, addressed to the rockhills and their presiding deity, Ogun, or whatever emanations remained within those granite veins, had the effect of simplifying—and intensifying—my mission in exile. Back in Kingston, I seized the first occasion to make it known that I had changed my last will and testament! Burying me in Bekuta, I announced, would be the same as burying me in some pristine jungle that had bartered away its soul. Since hoping to find another Bekuta outside Nigeria was stretching the laws of probability beyond limits, my mission in exile became even more personalized—to exploit every second of my living hours toward the retrieval of my cactus patch, but purged definitively of the possibility of a tyrant's triumphalist tread.

PART I

. . . . .

Ogun and I

Early Intimations

THE SUGGESTION THAT I WAS POSSESSED QUITE EARLY IN LIFE BY THE creative-combative deity Ogun is a familiar commentary of some literary critics who stretch my creative fascination with that deity, undeniable in my works, beyond its literary purlieu. If I were persuaded of that, I would have headed long ago for the nearest *babalawo* for the rites of exorcism! I am, contrary to all legitimately cited evidence—and none more damning than the accused's own history—actually a closet glutton for tranquillity. An oft-quoted remark of mine—"Justice is the first condition of humanity"—does, however, act constantly against the fulfillment of that craving for peace, an insertion into my mental template that can be regarded as a "categorical imperative." There is nothing mystical about it, nothing beyond an overacute, remedial sense of right and wrong, of what is just and unjust.

A casual involvement, at a most impressionable age, with the Abeokuta women's movement, narrated in *Aké*, may have prepared the soil. That began in the late 1930s, when the women, led by my aunt, the formidable Funmilayo Ransome-Kuti, rose against unjust taxes and chased the feudal lord, the Alake of Abeokuta, from his throne. So might also the induction, in my school days, into the propensities of the class bully, merging onto a broader canvas of the arrogant ways of colonial domination. That last in turn formed a continuum of visceral identification with the apartheid victims of South Africa, a condition that ironically honed itself to an insurgent pitch only when I arrived in the United Kingdom in 1954, into the homeland of a colonial power that ruled with violence in parts of Asia and Africa, Kenya most notoriously on the latter continent.

When I was studying in England in the mid-1950s, vacations found most of us African students headed for London from all over the British Isles to earn some extra money—mostly as porters in railway stations and post offices. We would then gather at the Overseas Students Club in Earl's Court, the University of London Student Union, or the West African Students Union in Porchester Terrace, Bayswater. There, virtually only one topic dominated all conversation: colonization and how/when to end it! The West African colonies appeared to be on their way to negotiated independence, so our agitated sights were set in other directions. Kenya was embroiled in the Mau Mau revolt, a truly indigenous, internally generated struggle, in which the forests favored the liberation fighters. South Africa, however, occupied a special place of bafflement, rage, and despair. Awareness of that degraded zone of existence on the soil of our own continent, the apprehension of a world that assigned to one's race a condition of subhumanity, was all-consuming. We began to prepare ourselves for the day when we would reclaim that humanity—by force of arms if needed.

This obsession with the humiliation of racist entrenchment in southern Africa was not one of bloodless empathy—we did, after all, savor mild doses of that condition in our encounters with the white natives on their own territory. Even as a student, occupying a mostly sheltered environment, I did not escape pointed acts of contempt or rejection. My overanthologized poem "Telephone Conversation," the record of an exchange with a landlady, was only one of my many trite encounters with British racism. On public transport, for instance— although admittedly I *enjoyed* having a seat to myself in a filled-up double-decker bus, which made turning over the abnormally broad pages of *The Yorkshire Post* much easier—could I really pretend not to notice, or fail to be stung by, the fact that a boarding passenger had traversed the length of the bus, seen the one empty seat next to me, but had chosen to retrace his or her steps and climb upstairs to search for a vacant seat? That the same passenger had come down again—no standing allowed upstairs—and chosen to attach his or her arm to a strap sooner than take that empty seat? Or, even more blatantly, when I was about to take the nearest vacant seat on a two-seat bench, that the occupant next to the window would shoot up, quickly extricate his or her body, and move to another seat or remain standing? Incidents like these, even in the mid-1950s, were mind-numbingly commonplace.

In shops, you turned invisible. The shopkeeper ostentatiously pretended not to see you and turned to attend to someone who had entered the shop long after you. He was quick with the apology and excuses, of course, the moment you shouted a belligerent "Excuse me!" Then followed the predictable "Oh, so sorry, were you next?" with an oiled, hypocritical voice the worse for being in a thick regional accent, when—irrationally—you somehow expected the country yokels to be more human than their cosmopolitan sophisticates.

How did one cope? Sometimes by invoking the inner confidence of one's mental superiority—that was easy enough; many of the natives were ignorant of much that was routine knowledge to any student. For a start, they did not even know where on the globe Africa is located. More to the point, in our own colonized territories, a white man was always associated with lordly positions of authority, yet here they were, finally exposed in all their grime and sweat, workers and peasants like our own mortal beings, often more wretched and impoverished than the poorest menial at home! Corporeally, all our student nostrils were in complete agreement that white people—almost uniformly—stank! They gave off a most upsetting odor, only slightly less upsetting than the belated discovery that they actually thought that we also stank! On balance, it was impossible to make an issue of racial slights all the time, and the more politicized of us, faced with a racial affront, simply switched our minds to that distant bastion of racism itself, apartheid South Africa: *You wait!*—an inward, vengeful mutter—*You are not remotely close to the league of your apartheid kin. When we have wiped out that main reservoir of racial disdain, these poisoned outposts of the same affliction will simply wither away, atrophied from lack of further nourishment from the ultimate exemplar.*

Writing poems such as "Telephone Conversation"—together with the satisfaction of reading it over *their own* radio station, the BBC—also helped. So did attempts to write for theater. A full-length play over which I labored for months had a Boer family trapped in their farmstead, where they were slowly eaten by black soldier ants—I rode the horses of vengeful symbolism to their knees! A lecturer commented that the play was long on purple passages. I was encountering that phrase for the first time but instantly understood what he meant and promptly added it to my vocabulary of self-censorship. The play also owed far too much to Eugene O'Neill, whose works I was studying at the time, so after reams of sheets trying and failing to expunge all further borrowings, I committed the first auto-da-fé of my career and set the play on fire.

A shorter play, *The Invention,* was produced as one of the Royal Court Theatre's Sunday-night experiments in December 1959. It climaxed in an explosion that wiped out a group of white scientists who had been researching the accurate determination of racial types in South Africa—so much for wish fulfillment by the theatrical route! To make matters worse—a cautionary portent for our future plans, perhaps?—the explosion refused to occur on cue!

Offstage, we followed the descent of South Africa into a solidifying black negation. By 1955, the nation's apartheid stucture was cemented by the Nationalist government, uprooting the black population from proximity to white estates—except under license as daytime servants and menials—and resettling them in the so-called townships, more accurately described by another name: shantytowns. In our projections, this pointed to only one conclusion: at the first sign of uprising by the black population, those shantytowns would be surgically taken out, bombed out of existence with no danger whatever to the white population! It was that stark, that logical. An internal war of liberation, in the manner of Kenya's Mau Mau, appeared to have been rendered impracticable, literally overnight. As a counterinsurgency action in the preventive mode, the Boers' move was a masterstroke.

We knew our history, however. The Spanish Civil War had given birth to a volunteer international force, of which the writers and artists units, such as the Abraham Lincoln Brigade, played courageous but mostly tragic roles. As we argued and constructed possible scenarios at the student clubs, buoyed by tea and biscuits, lager-and-lime and cider, sandwiches and sausage rolls, warmed by the glow of the fireplace after a hard day's work delivering Christmas parcels or lugging railway baggage, our conclusions pointed us in a similar direction—to prepare ourselves for the liberation war in South Africa. We saw that ill-used tip of the continent being restored to the black race by a Continental Brigade of volunteers converging on the South from every corner of the black landmass. It was the most obvious solution. That future was so clear to us—our generation could not escape the destiny of marching down to terminate the racial insult that rebuked our very being as black peoples. Whenever I had cause to think of that prospect, I confess that I felt nothing but a warm glow of anticipation. It made personal encounters with racial prejudice easy to ignore—I *knew* something that my local tormentors did not!

We knew, beyond all doubt, our place within the evolving organism of new nations. We, the young generation of that independence phase, were a renaissance people who would transform the strange bequest into a world marvel. The only way to grasp this confidence, this self-assurance, was to treat it as *pure knowledge.* Not intuition, not revelation, not blind faith, not ambition, not deductive reasoning or a conscious sense of mission—no, simply as *knowledge* in its purest, unassailable form! We *were* the renaissance people! And we were working in our various fields—quite indifferent to any special designation—to bring about this renaissance.

If there was a "plan of action," it took place within continental leadership, and took its substance and bearing from the merging of nationalist forces at the leadership apex. Beginning with two mutually antagonistic blocs, the "Casablanca" and the "Monrovia" groups, a collective effort was progressing toward the formation of an Organization of African Unity. But even more significant for us was the struggle at the grass roots, the wars of liberation from settler colonialism in Kenya and from the Portuguese "assimilationist" deception in Angola and Cape Verde. Defined by these efforts, we would be the transforming auxiliaries of an inchoate entity, of spaces that just happened to be called Nigeria, Gold Coast, the Rhodesias, Ivory Coast, Senegal, Cameroon, and so on. The future spread itself before us: the reassemblage of a much-abused, much-violated people on whose heads the ultimate insult had been heaped—broken into pieces and then glued back together like the shell of the tortoise in folk mythology. We were unstoppable.

But first, we had to liberate our kinsfolk to the south!

I ENROLLED IN the Officer Training Corps of my university in 1955, opting for infantry. Alas, my membership in that unit was brief. In 1956 the Suez War broke out and I received my call-up letter. I learned that, as a colonial, I was liable to be called up anytime to serve Her Royal Majesty. I had imagined that I was conveniently exploiting Her Majesty's training facilities to prepare myself for a liberation war, but it appeared that Her Majesty's government had other plans for me. Although I was required only to present myself for training with other reserves, all I saw was my overclever self being loaded onto a landing craft, heading away from South Africa, fighting on the side of the French and British against Gamal Abdel Nasser over a canal situated on his own soil! This ill-disguised attempt to recolonize Egypt and compromise her sovereignty did not appear to be a logical progression from the Continental Brigade that we had conjured up by the fireplace at Porchester Terrace. I sent in a letter declining my call-up. I was summoned to the recruitment office and reminded that I had taken an oath of loyalty to the queen and that my enrollment in the Officer Training Corps meant, in effect, that I had enlisted. The refusal of an order, I was quietly informed, could earn me a court-martial.

It was quite true about the oath of loyalty. There was an anteroom in which we all, new volunteers, were assembled, and from which we were summoned one by one. One officer sat behind the desk while beside him stood another, a card in his hand. That card contained the oath. The words were unambiguous... *to be ready to serve and protect Her Majesty at all times*... or something to that effect. I was unprepared and, frankly, shocked. I was a citizen of an upcoming nation called Nigeria—not yet fully independent, admittedly, but my passport declared me a citizen of Nigeria, which, in turn, was defined as a British protectorate. Nigeria was a hotbed of nationalism. Herbert Macauley, Nnamdi Azikiwe, Mbonu Ojike, Bode Thomas, Obafemi Awolowo, Nwafor Orizu of "Boycott the Boycottables" fame—meaning boycott all foreign products— these were men whose joint endeavor was the separation of Nigeria from the control of that same Majesty the Queen. How, then, was I supposed to swear an oath of loyalty to her and her dominion?

But I never thought of backing out at that point. I had come this far, I had decided on the training, and in any case, the juggernaut was rolling and I was strapped within it. To the two officers conducting the proceedings, this was purely routine. There were several more of us to put through the same ritual, and I guessed that neither was really listening to the responses we recruits were uttering. So I put on my thickest Yoruba accent, ensuring that nothing intelligible emerged from my throat. The administrator of the royal oath naturally assumed that this African could not really cope with the Queen's English—that is, if he was listening at all. As if it mattered in the slightest! My signature in the register was an affirmation of the oath I had taken—legal and binding! Still, I clung to the crumb of consolation that the oath had not truly passed over my tongue, which, as soon as I left the induction room, I proceeded to rinse, with others, in the bar with a glass of celebratory sherry—cost threepence, subsidized mess price.

Now came payment time, premature and politically unthinkable! I packed up my supply kit, tucked it into the farthest corner of the neglected attic of my lodging in Ash Grove—where, for all I know, it may still be gathering dust today—and vanished. One thing I was sure of: there was bound to be further correspondence before I was press-ganged and sent to camp, formally arrested and court-martialed, and/or deported. I sent off a letter saying that a mistake had been made. I am a citizen of Nigeria, I explained, not of Great Britain. There was silence from wherever the menace had emerged. Later on, I discovered that the deployment office may have had a legal question on its hands. If I had been a native of Lagos, it would have been a different matter. Lagos was a colony, and its citizens carried a kind of quasi–British citizen passport which made them colonial subjects of Britain. I, on the other hand, being from the interior, belonged to the second-class citizenship of the extended British Empire. As such I was a "protected" being, not a colonial subject. It was the only time I felt grateful to be classified as a second-class citizen.

The war soon ended, mercifully, and Her Majesty's army lost all interest in me. I would not smell any form of training until some months later, when the

Soviet Union, taking advantage of the West's misadventure in Suez, invaded Hungary, and a volunteer student training camp opened in Nottingham in the North of England. I signed up immediately. This was closer to the kind of training I needed. I must state this clearly: I did not intend to go into Hungary to fight, but there were support functions that I felt I could perform for the cause of those nationalists in return for my training. A black face would be far too conspicuous in the midst of such a war, and sympathetic though I was to the Hungarian national cause and the right to take up arms to repel a bully— even an ideologically progressive one—I had my priorities and could not really see how a black face would be justified in slinging Molotov cocktails in the streets of Budapest. The prospect of getting killed in a strange land that I knew only from history books and for its robust red wine Egri Bikaver struck me as grotesque—a black festering corpse alone in a snow-clad street, all other casualties vanishing into the protective coloring of their natural environment? On the other hand, that prospect was balanced by the lure of acquiring the experience of urban warfare, which, according to the news bulletins, was largely what the Hungarian nationalists were waging against superior forces—Molotov cocktails against tanks, street-to-street fighting. It looked like a perfect rehearsal opportunity for what we had conjured up—*Destination, Johannesburg!*

Given the unpredictable situation in Hungary, the uncertainty of my position resulted in my writing a rare letter to Essay—my father—taking him into my confidence. It seemed only fair, in case I was wounded, taken prisoner, or worse. Only years later did I find it curious that I ever imagined that his response would be at least sympathetic, albeit disapproving. Instead, it was scathingly dismissive. I could picture him seated at his desk, his pen moving swiftly and noisily over the lined sheets: "You were sent over there to study. In any case, charity begins at home, so if you feel inclined to jeopardise your studies by succumbing to some warlike urge, kindly return home and make this your battlefield." It was such an infuriatingly rational response that I refused to write him another letter for even longer than usual. And the abrupt end of the conflict appeared to have taken his side. The Hungarian resistance collapsed and any further discussion became academic, with him having won the argument by default. I felt intensely annoyed and held him personally responsible for the defeat of the Hungarian nationalists.

ESSAY WAS RIGHT, though he did not know it at the time, although "prescient" would be a more accurate expression for his proposed amendment to my battle plans. Indeed, I often wondered if, once I had become embroiled within my own borders, he did not wish from time to time that he had encouraged me to go and take my chances on the Hungarian front! By then, of course, he no longer had a say in the matter, because in the meantime, in company with my University of London/Porchester Terrace master planners, I had made a startling discovery!

The nationalists, the first-generation elected leaders and legislators of our semi-independent nation, had begun to visit Great Britain in droves. We watched their preening, their ostentatious spending, and their cultivated condescension, even disdain, toward the people they were supposed to represent. There were exceptions, but, in the main, they did not appear to have emerged from the land and people we had left behind when we journeyed out to acquire some skills and learning. While we dreamed of marching south to liberate southern Africa, they saw the nation as a prostrate victim to be ravished. We accepted invitations to their public talks and informal meetings, even partook of their lavish receptions. Some were stark illiterates, though full of bombast. This strange breed was a complete contrast to the nationalist stalwarts into whose hands we had imagined that the country could be safely consigned while we went on our romantic liberation march to southern Africa. The exceptions engaged us in serious discussions, outlined their vision not only for the nation but for the continent, and pleaded earnestly that we hurry home and join hands in building the future. Most of the time, however, as we ran eagerly to welcome the protagonists of the African Renaissance, we were bombarded by utterances that identified them as flamboyant replacements of the old colonial order, not transforming agents, not even empathizing participants in a process of liberation.

Some turned students into pimps, in return for either immediate rewards or influence in obtaining or extending scholarships. Visiting politicians financed lavish parties for one sole purpose—to bring on the girls! They appeared to have only one ambition on the brain: to sleep with a white woman. For that privilege, in addition to discarding the dignity of their position, they would pay more than the equivalent of our monthly student allowances. We watched them heap unbelievable gifts on virtual prostitutes, among them both British and continental students. It was a lucrative time for willing "escorts." We were not prudish; we drank and danced with them till cockcrow and took women off them between their first drink and last boast. But, we asked ourselves, were these men, who routinely conducted themselves with such gracelessness, the true representatives of a national mandate? And their version of the message of the committed minority that also urged our early return home was "Come back quickly and stake your claims. The earlier you position yourselves, the bigger your slice of the national cake!"

I recall one publicly humiliating instance: a revered national figure in a highly sensitive political position got so carried away with his date that he paid for a one-night stand with a check, at the bottom of which, just in case his scrawl was indecipherable, he had written his name, complete with his official position. The girl, a brilliant student from an upper-class British family but a notorious nymphomaniac, flounced to our table at the students' cafeteria and flaunted the check in our faces, asking loudly what kind of a would-be independent nation would produce a political leader who could act so stupidly. I could so easily blackmail him with this, she boasted. We succeeded in coaxing the check away from her—a medical student promised to introduce her to a new, "virile" boyfriend if she surrendered it. She agreed, and we destroyed it. She was completely indifferent to the money—it was sufficient that she had our "national figure" in her power.

One scandal after another was hushed up by the British Home Office, which was the main sponsor of many of these "study" or "familiarization" tours—familiarization, that is, with British-style democracy, its institutions and bureaucracy. The Crown agents, the main purchasing and forwarding agents for the colonial governments and visitors, continued to ship home luxury items for our overnight Croesuses; reams of indents—the order forms—and payment demands flowed between Nigeria and the United Kingdom as the august visitors blithely took possession of goods and ignored the payment half of the transaction. Often, the Home Office stood indemnity.

Their conduct on home territory, from the news that reached us, appeared to be of the same nature. The pan-African project was becoming farcical. The alienation of many of the first-generation leaders was total, and, for the first time, we began to wonder if the power relationship between the political elite and their people was not paralleled by that between the Boers and the black South African majority—a master-servant relationship, the monopoly of privilege by a minority, with its complement, the denial of rights or human respect to the people. We read in this a double betrayal, an act of treachery from within. We came to only one conclusion: the writers and artists brigade could wait—first, it was essential to secure our rear. The weapons of confrontation need not be the lethal kind; we could join forces with the progressives, make trenchant use of the pen and the stage, propagate progressive ideas, mobilize the people, and expose their betrayers. The contested arena would be strewn with words and polemics, not soaked in gore. My adopted muse would remain Ogun, but only he of the biting lyric.

Alas, that willful deity would refuse to bow to mortal preferences within his dual nature!

Reunion with Ogun

. . . . .

A SPECIAL BOND, A VERY PERSONAL COMMUNION, WITH THE ROAD HAS remained an essential part of my relation with the physical world from so early in childhood that I can no longer recall how I came to embrace, almost osmotically, the road as the fusing agency. This went beyond the merely physical—the road's linkage of Isara, my father's birthplace, and Abeokuta, my maternal origin, where I was also born and mainly raised. The forest paths and lanes that laced the rust-roof farmsteads and lush farms fed the rudimentary roads between villages and towns, providing a seamless weave of mystery and discovery. The women traders from Isara, heads pressed down with bales and baskets, who trod those roads and pathways every market day laden with merchandise, perfumed the household in Aké, the rockbound parsonage of childhood. They were caravans from distant lands, their indigo-dyed feet covered in red laterite as they filed into our backyard, bringing the exotic, animistic world of Isara into the Christian aura of Aké. Then, right from my first journey between those two axes of my then total existence, in a wood-paneled lorry, jammed against basketfuls of vegetables, yams, dried fish, beads and trinkets, bales of *adire, kijipa,* and *aso oke,** the still vegetal passages opened up into a succession of way stations before the final destination. The road was a magic lantern whose projections, by some potent hand hidden in those dense forests, unwound like a sash of multiple designs on which we rode from marvel to marvel.

This revelation of the road's infinite resources endured for a while, competing with the railway, which had an ambiance all its own, its rhythmic raucousness subdued, turned even mesmerizing between stations by the pristine

---

* Tie-dyed and woven textiles.

awesomeness of the nature through which it snaked, leaving the viscera suspended between a pastoral innocence and the chants of commerce that began with an echo and invocation of the names of the market outposts—Olokemeji, Otta, Wasimi, Lafenwa. . . . The women were my first mystics of the road, but they were no less palpable, powerful, and political. It was the same women, or their market companions, who formed the vanguard of the assault on the feudal bastion of a repressive monarch, the Alake of Abeokuta. Despite the support of the colonial district officer, they routed him and sent him into a prolonged exile.

With the years, the magic of the road would begin to dissipate, but not so completely that, by the year of my first homecoming at the end of my study stint in England in 1960, I could not recover, or maybe simply stubbornly imbue, this ageless sibling with something of its childhood retentions whenever I motored along the highways. The five-year interruption in England and Europe did, through the road's pure functionality, its place on the landscape as an efficient conveyor belt, sober me down somewhat, but not entirely. A special responsiveness remained, even patches of its mystic rapport.

Is it necessary to admit that I felt little of that mystic rapport with the highways of Europe? Maybe there were once gods in Europe, but they are all dead or have migrated elsewhere—except perhaps those in the isolated crags and music of Wales, the poetry and drama of the Irish, the extant rituals of the Celts, and the fjords of Scandinavia. Greece has kept her gods—the peaks and gorges of Delphi remain eternally god-suffused. Also, grudgingly perhaps, the Carpathian Mountains of Yugoslavia. The new gods and goddesses of Europe, alas, were mainly to be found on the cinema screen and on the pop stage; confronted with their iconic eruptions, I was able to understand, at last, the true meaning of pagan adulation.

It was good fortune that I could return home—where the gods were still only in a state of hibernation—under conditions of personal independence. I arrived on the wheels of a Rockefeller fellowship on New Year's Day of 1960 to research traditional dramatic forms. My most essential piece of equipment was a Land Rover, and that vehicle became an extension of myself through which I negotiated relationships with the overall society. I penetrated east, north, south at will and toured the entire West African coast on the trail of festivals and performing companies, keeping touch with gods and goddesses everywhere and celebrating their seasons, encountering and savoring exotic names such as Dorma Ahenkro, Koton Karfi, Maiduguri, and Ouagadougou, constantly at war with self-installed lords of remote inland borders who held the keys to the gates of some invisible, paradisial independencies that presumably floated above the artificially divided peoples of West Africa.

My forays outside Nigeria were infrequent, but they triggered a habit of marveling at a meaningless separation. Ghanaian, Togolese, and so on—just what did these terms mean to those who were so described? Culture and language differed within each nation as frequently and as profoundly as they found identities across the borders of such nation spaces; the arbitrariness and illogicality of their groupings hit any traveler in the face—and remained meaningless to a huge majority of those whom the borders enclose or separate. It was true of the preindependence entities, and it is still mostly true today.

The road and I thus became partners in the quest for an extended self-discovery. Early morning was my favorite hour; you caught the road's exhalation as it rose from the tarmac with the sun's heated awakening, piercing the early mists in a proprietorial mood—you owned the road and all that lay revealed along its rises and plunges, its contortions, and its arrow directness on both flatland and crests that sometimes appeared aimed at a horizon shimmering at the very edge of the world. Even the rarest encounter with another vehicle in that sublime hour was an act of generous concession on your part; it was only your early-morning kindness that permitted it to trundle past, another wraith from the bowels of the earth.

I would throw a few clothes into what I called the "Mungo Park" trunk that remained permanently screwed down into the back of the jeep. Nothing, absolutely nothing, could substitute for setting out at that hour of the gods' retreat. Then, over the next days and weeks—Akure; Idanre, the mountain retreat of Ogun; Kaura Namoda, a landscape of baobab sentinels ushering the traveler into Sokoto and the sonorities of the muezzin; the return track, hugging the Dahomean border; Kishi, cornfields into the horizon; Iseyin, weavers' looms under lean-tos; Abeokuta, balanced on boulders; and—Lagos. I camped in villages or in the truck, or sometimes gratefully enjoyed the courtesy of rest houses built for the colonial district officers, where the uniformed waiter, immaculate in standard attire, service-conditioned from colonial days, would pad in gently in the morning with a tea tray....

But I did not ask for tea! *Yes, master,* he (old enough to be my father or even grandfather) replies, setting down the tray and pulling back the curtains.... No! Leave that alone, I'm not awake. . . . *Yes, master,* he replies, pulling the curtain open all the way.... *Will master like me to make fried or scrambled eggs with the toast?* Oh, you house-trained antiquated robot, master would like to scramble Papa's head for breakfast! It was surreal! But for those stubborn early-morning rituals, such interludes of luxury were only too welcome.

I suppose the "University of Ibadan" logo had much to do with such undeserved courtesies—the university counted for something in the early 1960s, and nowhere was reverence for any symbol of learning more solemnly manifested than in the hinterland. I sometimes arrived in the midst of a festival, the turbaning of a village head or a wedding, where I became an instant honored guest. I was confronted with deep dishes of pounded yam, steaming stews and venison, gallons of fresh-tapped palm wine or the most exotic bottled brands, which had no business being in such rural, isolated corners of the world.

Another trajectory took me through Oyo, city of the fiery god Sango, leathercraft, and decorated gourds; Oshogbo, watched by her river goddess, Osun; Ilorin; Bida of glass beads and hennaed women!—then Minna, scattering hordes of monkeys and apes; plump, mouth-watering guinea fowl all the way to Kaduna, Kano, and Maiduguri of dry dust, turbaned horsemen, and minarets, from which the obvious route back was to hug the Cameroon border to the east—Yola, Markurdi, and the confluence of the great rivers Gboko and Abakaliki—pounded yam and roadside venison—Awka of furnaces and open smithies—then a plunge southward into the riverine areas, Ikot-Ekpene of outsize *ekpe* masks; Calabar of fiery *ogogoro** and light-toned pulchritude; the sweep of the Niger through Port Harcourt, gathering toward its assignation with the sea; sleepy Sapele, pontoons and potfuls of *pito*†; then historic Benin and her outsize coral bangles, bronzes, and women's landscaped coiffures....

In some mountainous areas—Obudu, Idanre, Enugu, the Jos Plateau—in moments of utter sublimity, the road winds like a cummerbund around the sagging waists of clouds, slicing off the peaks and dipping vertiginously into bottomless basins, a trampoline strung across treetops on which you know the gods take their night's repose. Reluctantly I take my leave of them, head back into Ibadan or Lagos, where the muck, dust, and grit of weeks were dissolved in beer and highlife bands in the nightclubs—Victor Olaiya, Roy Chicago, Eddie Okonta, Bobby Benson—and the more intimate air of the juju bands—Orlando Owoh, Dele Abiodun, Denge, or the appropriately named one with the high-pitched voice, Tunde Nightingale.

The road was dust, laterite dust for the most part, or narrow ribbons of

---

* A gin distilled from wine of the palm tree.
† A beer made from millet.

macadam, but reasonably well maintained, some no smoother than quiltwork. Pontoons, not bridges—there was no Lokoja bridge, no Asaba–Onitsha bridge, none between Warri and Sapele, only pontoons. The few bridges that interrupted the stretches of highway were single-lane bridges that could take only one vehicle at a time, and some were even shared by the railway line.

Indeed, it was while waiting for a pontoon at Lokoja that the doyen of the indigenous-language novel, D. O. Fagunwa, would vanish in the most mysterious manner, as mysterious as his novels, which formed our fictional sensibilities from childhood and peopled that accommodating world with its strange characters—*Ogboju Ode Ninu Igbo Irunmale, Irinkerindo Ninu Igbo Elegbeje*, and so on. I translated the first into English as *The Fearless Hunter in the Forest of a Thousand Demons* and thereafter wisely gave up my ambitious project to translate *all* his works, so taxing did I find the density of his Yoruba usage!

There are so many versions of Fagunwa's death—or disappearance—but all agree that he was standing by the Niger River in broad daylight, waiting for the pontoon to take his motorcar across the river. Perhaps he strolled along the embankment and slipped—here the versions diverge—but he was never seen again, nor was his body ever recovered. It was as if he had been claimed by one of those very creatures that crowded his imagination and were vividly brought to life in his works, as if one of them had emerged from that naked sunlight, visible to him alone, taken his arm, and led him off into the unfathomable habitations of the mind.

IT WAS NOT all idyllic, nor was death always mysterious, even awe-inspiring, in the manner of Fagunwa's disappearance. Like the many faces of Ogun, god of the road, the road was also a violent host. I stared into the many faces of death, but most often death just taking its leave, its back indifferently turned on heartbreak and destruction. In the early sixties, just after independence, the bridges that had been inherited from the departing British not only were narrow and rickety but some were suspended, it seemed, between earth and sky, between the worlds of the living and the ancestor, attached to some mysterious anchor that was invisible to all but their original engineers. They appeared to lie in wait for unconscious participants in some infernal lottery. These—in addition to the still, neatly broken forests—mostly formed the backdrops to the scenes of death that were enacted before me so often in the West African interior, as if the ritual audience they awaited had to be a stranger.

By the side of the road, a small cluster of men and women, mute, isolated still forms, their faces partly hooded. Strewn around them, the shattered contents of what were once tall jute bags. Now the kola nuts are strung around their feet, outsize chromatic beads under the early sun. Only when one sees a row of corpses, neatly laid side by side, does one grasp the inexorable loneliness of mortality. The stillness confers on the senses a replete, understated solitude that the frenetic realms of community, service, friendship, love, and other relationships routinely obscure. A vehicle or two upended, torn, mangled, wrapped around a tree, or simply neatly chipped, a fatal slice taken off its corner, or else nothing but a telltale swathe through the forest and the camouflage of shrubs and trees that the errant vehicle had pulled around itself like a resentful shroud. A jagged opening through the railings on one side of the bridge might narrate the beginning of a trajectory that ended on the distant rocks below, waters swirling around a few scattered pieces of metal and wooden body frame, all unearthly still. Such tableaux instigate the reconstructing functions of the mind, instantly at work to figure out the progression of events, stringing the vanished sequences together. Without that, the laid-out forms could well be outer-space forms in suspended animation, awaiting revival on arrival at their destination, or else wrapped-up exotic tubers, levitated from within the deepest recesses of the earth.

Those early scenes of death had a solemnity about them, a graceful pronouncement of leave-taking where the precedent violence is gently absorbed by, indeed sublimated beneath, that shawl of multiple existences that the Yoruba wrap around their consciousness as a testament of continuity: the world of the living, the ancestor, and the unborn. Then and only then—in those early 1960s, when death on the road was an isolated, discrete event—was it possible to sustain one's early mystic rapport, however tenuously, with the road. The road was old and it was young, ageless as the peoples through whose lives it threaded and young as the same peoples, who were being collectively transformed. Perhaps I assumed the function of the wanderer whose occupation was to bear witness to the road's many phases that mirrored not merely human fate but, more directly and effectively, an immediate entity in formation.

The newly demarcated space had been christened "Nigeria" by the spouse of a colonial officer, but it was one whose ancestral exhalations stubbornly overwhelmed its merely convenient administrative identity. I wandered through those arteries with mixed feelings, bounced not only up and down on the seat of the Land Rover but—as the sun came up—between the delineation of the physical world and the misty trails of unseen presences. Undoubtedly something of this consciousness went into my encounters with those scenes of death in the early days, robbing them of the reality of violent rupture and leaving in its place the mere rites of passage, insinuating a pervasive aura of the invisible world of ancestors. The simplest way to put this, therefore, is perhaps that death, in those early days, had a sense of proportion—death knew its place.

My soul has grown deep like the rivers...

If Langston Hughes, the black American poet, had driven through Nigeria in a Land Rover at the beginning of the sixties, he would have written, I am certain—*My soul has grown deep like the road.* He did visit eventually, but I doubt he ever took up that general invitation that I issued soon after my reunion with Ogun:

> *Traveller, you must set forth*
> *At dawn*
> *I promise marvels of the holy hour....*

In the road's later decay, rather like the sustained conceit of *The Picture of Dorian Gray*, is recorded a nation's retreat from a humanism that I had imbibed, quite unconsciously, from childhood. I was fated to watch the nation turn both carrion and scavenger as it killed and consumed its kind, the road remaining an obliging stream in which a nation's fall from grace was duly reflected. To the scenes of violence and contempt for kind that would later become commonplace, a strange encounter from those idyllic days underscores the flight of marvels and the end of the holy hour. It was recorded by a journalist, and I had myself witnessed variants of such enlightenment from "dumb beasts" on the road. I have a distinct recollection of this solemn choreography, once not far from Akure, and then further north, between Jebba and Kaura Namoda.

> *A crow had been killed by a motor vehicle and then, in what seemed like a practised ritual, the corpse was surrounded by other crows. One after the other, they landed, then began to circle the stricken bird in deliberate formation. After a while, they stopped, moved nearer the lifeless form in what appeared to be a tightening of the circle, closing the gap between them and the corpse. Then they began a chorus of cawing, moving their beaks up and down in unison—it was a kind of ordered ululating, and the eerie scene looked strangely like some kind of service being held*

over their slain companion. Shortly after, they lifted the corpse with their beaks, taking little hops, until the entire gathering had disappeared with the corpse over the verge.

The journalist had narrated that encounter in the newspapers at the time, awed by the scene. My instant reaction to the story was gratitude that I had not narrated my own experience of that nature. As a known writer, tarred with the brush of a profession known for poetic liberties, no one would have believed me. Still, there it was; even the crows appeared to accord some dignity to their dead. And the humans did no less at that stage when I still boasted a visceral companionship with the road. Death was a constant companion, but its victims were not mere carrion on the road. Each scene of death was—after the initial disorientation—almost a haven of tranquillity. The survivors, even the injured awaiting help, formed a serene community—transfigured, it seemed, by a surreal wind that had blown across them briefly and altered their lives forever. Enfolding such scenes in an immense, invisible cloak was a palpable presence of time in its absolute stillness.

There was a practical reward to my preoccupation with the road—it was a talisman against alienation, that altering phenomenon that separates the individual from community. This condition had begun to disfigure the social landscape of the nation not long after independence, especially in the cities. Out in the hinterland, one could still wallow in a mystic bond with the land and thus with a people's eternal, collective being. If I was an initiate in this process of the coming-into-being of a nation, the road was my personal mentor, conspirator, and—in the growing face of alienation—an unassuming safeguard. Alas, its revelations also plunged me into the parallel politics of its violent being.

ʄ*irst Skirmishes*

. . . . .

Wʜᴇɴ ɪ ʀᴇᴛᴜʀɴᴇᴅ ᴛᴏ ɴɪɢᴇʀɪᴀ ᴏɴ ɴᴇᴡ ʏᴇᴀʀ's ᴅᴀʏ 1960, ɪᴛ ᴡᴀs ᴀ ɴᴀ-
tion wound up to a fever pitch of social expectations—and self-confidence—
as its date for independence from British rule drew close. Its future was already
mapped out, however, for the eve-of-independence elections had taken place
the previous year, and all that was left was for the British government to hand
over power to the victorious party and take its leave.

I was not pessimistic about the future but extremely cautious, having come
into contact with the first-generation leaders in my student days in England.
The enemy, as I had identified it, was power and its pitfalls, a cautionary motif
that dominated my would-be independence play, *A Dance of the Forests*. The
view was not shared by the cultural bureaucrats, quick to smell out subversion.
They cautioned that the play contained a subversive message. It had won the
contest for the official theater presentation for the occasion but was now
deemed a damper, unsuitable for a festive occasion. I staged it anyway, in an alternative venue, using the prize money and forming a theater company, the
1960 Masks, in the process.

On the much-anticipated day, October 1, 1960, the "subversives" presented their shoestring worldview on the stage of the University Theatre,
Ibadan, while the nation celebrated its formal liberation from colonial bondage
with a series of sumptuous events and ceremonials in the capital, Lagos. The
nation space known as Nigeria had come of age, a federation made up of three
semiautonomous regions—the Eastern Region, the Western Region, and the
Northern Region—the last occupying a landmass larger in size than the other
two combined. Each had its own legislature in its regional capital, while a federal house sat in Lagos, the nation's capital. Those regional legislatures—or

Houses of Assembly—had been in place since 1954. However, the results from the preparatory federal elections of 1959, conducted by the departing British officials, that decided who would hold power at the center had been most bitterly disputed, and it was already a divided nation that ritually lowered the British Union Jack that October, folded it away, and hoisted the green-white-green of Nigeria—surely the most uninspiring national flag on the surface of the earth! The white was said to symbolize peace, green stood for agriculture; combined they misrepresented the sum of a nation's imagination.

Recent memoirs* by former colonial officers have revealed how crooked that beginning was. The elections that placed a government in power at the center were rigged—by the British! John Bull was not about to leave an independent Nigeria under the control of any uppity radicals, as the southern nationalists—the East and the West—were perceived. Thus, on instructions from the British Home Office, even the Nigerian census was falsified, giving an artificial majority to the North, which was largely feudalist by tradition and conservative in political outlook. The census was actually based on sample head counts—random or selective, no one knew—which were then roughly multiplied by the acreage of the landmass, irrespective of actual population densities!

In its resolve to ensure that the nation was handed over to a conservative power, the British did not rely on numerical strength alone: after all, the North did harbor radical or rebellious elements—such as the Tivs, in what was known as the Middle Belt, or the Northern Elements Progressive Union—in quite sizable numbers. And so, to make absolutely certain that power did not fall into the wrong hands, specific instructions were issued by the British Home Office to its civil servants: the final results of elections to the federal legislature must be manipulated, where necessary, in favor of the political conservatives. Archival material, now free of the time constraints of the Official Secrets Act, testify to this. An admission, and even a statement of regret, was wrung out of a serving British minister during the Abacha years. The precedent had, however, been set, and rigging now answered the name of democracy.

Not surprisingly, the national flag began to unravel rather quickly after independence. To begin with, each of the three regions, West, East, and North, had its own restless minorities. Low-intensity armed warfare, largely unpubli-

---

* In 1992, the memoirs of a former colonial officer, Harold Smith, were ready for publication but suppressed by the British government. The author sent me the manuscript, in which he revealed that he had been ordered by the Home Office to take part in the rigging of the 1959 elections. In his own words, "It was the British who taught Nigerians the art of rigging."

cized, accompanied the nation into independence in the Tiv region of the North. Elections merely modified the geography of hostilities.

At independence, my own West was ruled by the Action Group, led by a dour, ascetic Yoruba, Obafemi Awolowo, affectionately known as "Awo." However, his party lost the fight for federal control at the center to the Northern Peoples Congress (NPC), the North-based party, which was headed by Sir Ahmadu Bello, a feudal Fulani scion. Ahmadu Bello claimed descent from the legendary Othman dan Fodio, the jihadist who had once sworn that he would dip the Koran in the Atlantic.

The Northern Peoples Congress also controlled the Northern Region. In the East, the party that held power was the National Council of Nigeria and the Cameroons (NCNC), led by the charismatic, U.S.-educated Nnamdi Azikiwe, an Igbo and self-described Fabian whose oratory at public rallies drew shouts of "Ze-ee-eek" from ecstatic crowds. That party also lost to the NPC at the federal level but teamed up with the winner to form a ruling coalition at the center. The position of the nation's prime minister fell, naturally, to the senior partner, the NPC.

Nnamdi Azikiwe, having failed to capture power at the center, announced his retirement from politics, waxing biblical in a valedictory speech that declared that, with national independence, his "task was done." He was compensated with the ceremonial position of governor-general of Nigeria, representing the queen of England (Nigeria had chosen to remain within the British Commonwealth, headed by the queen). Sir Ahmadu Bello, the leader of the victorious party, chose to remain at the head of the regional government, nominating his lieutenant Abubakar Tafawa Balewa, a former schoolteacher, as the first prime minister of the newly independent nation; regional heads of government were designated "premiers." The Action Group of the West thus remained the minority opposition party in the federal legislature. Unlike his Northern counterpart, however, the leader of the Action Group, Awolowo, chose to lead the opposition at the federal level, leaving his second in command—Ladoke Akintola, a nationally acknowledged master of Yoruba oratory and a shrewd political strategist—as premier of the West.

THE DEVELOPING FISSURES, nationwide, were perhaps inevitable, given the artificial grafting of the British parliamentary system onto a patchwork nation with different precolonial histories and systems of self-governance. The West was the first to manifest the contradictions. An open rift developed between the party leader, Awolowo, and Akintola, his lieutenant in the West, a region whose politics had always been as volatile as its people were politically advanced. The rift intensified, and the party broke in two, with a little help from the recruiting ambitions of the ruling party, the NPC. The breakaway group, transformed into the Nigerian National Democratic Party, the NNDP, was led by Akintola. It became increasingly perceived as an ally of the ruling party, the NPC; certainly its political ideology became more conservative, more openly impatient with the "radical" tendencies of Akintola's parent party. Defections, intrigues, ideological polarization, political blackmail, greed for a "slice of the national cake"—finally all the ingredients were in place for a new political experience, an arbitrary order of governance. In 1962, the elected government of the West—and with it, democracy—was suspended, and the region was placed under emergency rule.

The immediate justifying episode for taking over the West, one that fulfilled the condition of "a breakdown of law and order," was provided when the Western House of Assembly converted its chambers into a boxing-cum-wrestling arena. This well-laid plan to destabilize that region was activated by a preset signal in the shout *"Ina l'ori oke!"*—"Fire on the mountain!" A legislator vaulted benches and desks, seized the speaker's mace, and attempted to make off with it. It ended up in two pieces, but only after first drawing blood from the head of a fellow lawgiver. A famous image, captured by an alert photographer in the press gallery, showed my favorite political maverick, Tony Enahoro, escaping the melee through a window.

Tony Enahoro would once again take to flight, this time clandestinely through the borders, but that was yet some months away. For now, the organizers of this legislative rout had achieved their purpose, and the nation—the Western Region, at least—embarked on a novel adventure. The region was placed under an administrator, a medical doctor then in government service and, we would learn later, the personal physician to the prime minister, Tafawa Balewa. He had the power to rule by decree, detain citizens without trial. The nation had heard of such things in other places but never imagined that we would actually taste of it in Nigeria—little did most imagine that this was merely a rehearsal for worse. The administrator wasted no time in placing political leaders under his sanction, including my friend from student days Bola Ige, a lawyer and rising leader within the Action Group party.

Bola Ige's final and most prolonged place of detention was known as Lekki Island, a then-desolate place famous for its attack-helicopter mosquitoes. His party, the Action Group, was undisguisedly the real target of federal intervention. A few token politicians from the breakaway branch of the Action Group, the NNDP, were also detained, but mostly in cozy circumstances. Government-catered rest houses were their favored choice, where they continued to conduct party affairs and even receive connubial visits. A quite substantial proportion of Nigerians, including myself, read in the move of the federal government the beginning of an attempt to stifle the democratic infant in its crib and turn the nation gradually into a one-party state. So soon—I could be forgiven for thinking—the actualization of warnings from *A Dance of the Forests*?

A more adaptable, more pugnacious theater company than the profession-ally competent but top-heavy 1960 Masks was clearly required. Enter Orisun Theatre, primed for instant, improvised sketches on the political situation. The administrator's dictatorial conduct in the West, his uneven apportionment of sanctions, and suspicions of a "secret agenda" provoked my lampoon on his office and governance style. It took the form of a song adapted from *The Vicar of Bray* and was published in the media. Nothing untoward resulted from this foray beyond a friendly warning passed through the "official channels" of Ibadan University, where I was serving my stint as a Rockefeller fellow in drama. The vicar was not pleased. He was prepared to tolerate the exercise of my freedom of expression but wanted me to know that he was in the West, after all, to carry out a repair job, to stop the West from descending into chaos. This, he urged us to appreciate, was a delicate task of healing—for which, pre-sumably, his medical training especially fitted him. He expected the academic community to cooperate with him in the achievement of his mission. I assured my interlocutors that I was indeed engaged on an important contribution to his objectives as I proceeded to prepare a series of political satires, the first of which would appear on stage as *Before the Blackout*. It included a dramatized version of the adaptation from *The Vicar of Bray*.

AND THEN, AS IF the political scene were not sufficiently heated or complicated for such a young democracy, the nation was riveted by news of a far grimmer dimension than a mere rough-and-tumble among lawmakers—a conspiracy had been unearthed that sought to execute what would have amounted to a civilian coup d'état. The nest of conspirators was located in the Action Group. There was talk of proscribing the party altogether. Its leading figures were rounded up; some were placed under house arrest, others taken straight to prison. It all left the nation, especially the Western Region, in shock. Gradually the net contracted, closing in on the real target. No one was especially sur-prised when the party leader himself, Chief Obafemi Awolowo, was arrested.

The trials followed lengthy, drawn-out investigations, during which the

name of a white South African police officer, Ceulman, pioneered the confla-
tion, in Nigerian modern history, of an individual name with torture. When the
trials began, a number of the accused protested that their statements had
been made under duress, their confessions extracted under torture. The statements were nonetheless admitted as evidence. Not surprisingly, virtually all
the accused, including Obafemi Awolowo, were found "guilty as charged" and
sentenced to long terms of imprisonment. The judge then committed the astonishing indiscretion of proceeding to recuperate from his marathon hearing
as a vacation guest of the head of the ruling (and "persecuting") party, directly
after convicting and sentencing the accused. Never was a well-known Yoruba
saying more eagerly seized upon: "The witch cried one night, and the child died
the morning after; who still disputes that it was the witch that consumed the
child?" It contributed in no small measure to the interpretative twist given to
the judge's words when, before delivering judgment, he declared, "My hands
are tied." Even while considering his verdict deeply flawed, I still believe that
his words were completely innocuous, being no more than the standard observation by any judge that, no matter his personal inclinations or public expectations, he was duty bound by the law. To the majority of government adversaries,
however, the judge had admitted that he was carrying out orders!

With those trials, the Nigerian political atmosphere was drastically transformed. The hunt continued for the fugitives, including Tony Enahoro. Nearly
all of them had taken refuge in Ghana, then enjoying the reputation of a radical nation under the leadership of Kwame Nkrumah.

I remained one of the skeptics. I believed there was never any weighty matter to the treason attempt, and hold till today that Awolowo, in particular, was
a victim of political intrigue, largely fomented by the NPC but with the full collaboration of elements from within the breakaway party, the NNDP. This, perhaps, was because I was aware that, in pursuit of its increasingly socialist
objectives, the Action Group leadership had decided to send some cadres to be
trained at the Winneba Ideological Institute in Ghana. A number of young
African revolutionaries in the anticolonial struggle also attended the course;
some of them returned home to take up armed struggle against colonial domination in Angola, Guinea-Bissau, Mozambique. Additionally, however, clobbered
by the strong-arm tactics employed by the governing parties as well as the
extralegal deployment of the local constabularies under the control of the governing parties—thugs and local police were becoming indistinguishable—the
Action Group engaged in some soul-searching and concluded that it had been
negligent in its physical department. The party thereupon assigned a number of

its youths to specialized training—self-defense and general toughening-up sessions—in a camp said to have been set up in northern Ghana. I had a good rapport with some of the inner circle of the Action Group and its allied opposition groups. In addition to Bola Ige, who was never arrested or charged, I had become quite close to Dr. Chike Obi, a wiry, eccentric mathematician who was reputed to have come close to uncovering the proof of the elusive Fermat's theorem—nobody knew exactly what Fermat's theorem was about or who Fermat was, but academic folklore had placed this theorem at the pinnacle of mathematical genius, and the media had enshrined the name in public consciousness. It was a surprise to me to learn that Chike Obi had launched a political party in the Eastern Region, the Dynamic Party, but no surprise that it was a radical-leaning party that preached revolution—and even dictatorship!— as the only recipe for the nation's ills. The latter remained our main point of disagreement. It was typical of the mathematician to have driven one of the suspects—Tony Enahoro himself?—to safety across the border, for which he was arrested but later released. Between Bola Ige and Chike Obi, I obtained quite reliable information on the thinking within the party.

That some elements within the Winneba trainees may have been converted by the actual revolutionaries in waiting at that school and organized themselves into an insurgent unit bent on overthrowing a government that was considered reactionary, a stooge of the British government, and so on, was a distinct possibility and probably closer to the truth. That Obafemi Awolowo was involved in such an attempt was a charge that I found incompatible with the man's nature—he was legalist-constitutionalist to a fault. Chike Obi was an astute reader of politics, quite close to Awolowo, and he was contemptuous of those charges. I visited him at Kirikiri prison a few times, taking, naively, a bottle of cognac to keep him company. The bottle was taken into charge by the prison officer, who promised that it would be kept among his other possessions until his release. That was my first intimation that such indulgences were not permitted on the prison menu.

Tony Enahoro became Nigeria's "most wanted," accused of being one of the masterminds of the plot—now, that, I felt, was likely to contain more than a grain of truth. In the anticolonial struggle, Enahoro's record was one of direct, confrontational activism, while Awolowo was a convinced, indeed punctilious, legalist. Alerted in good time of his impending arrest, Enahoro fled to Ghana, then to the United Kingdom, convinced of his safety in a thriving democracy. At the request of the Nigerian government, he was arrested and detained in London. A determined attempt to extradite him back to Nigeria to stand trial with others turned into a cause célèbre. It wound its way through the British courts, the Houses of Parliament, and the Privy Council, then the final court of appeal. Whether Enahoro was guilty or not, I found it intolerable that all the progressives were being netted and incapacitated. In any case, there was the issue of equity: any means to recover what has been unfairly or illegally acquired cannot be unfair or illegal. Electoral robbery, rather than equitable contest, was already the rule in the nation.

Enahoro's case now took center stage in the British Houses of Parliament—to sustain the time-honored claims of political asylum or to butter up the egos of democratic neophytes in apprentice nation-states? I became restless with the knowledge that I was fortuitously placed to lend a hand, thanks to relationships I had developed with one or two figures in the British establishment while undergoing my apprenticeship at the Royal Court Theatre in London. An interventionist tendency had begun to manifest itself in my temperament, though I was yet to become fully conscious of it. I scraped together what money I could find, borrowed the rest, bought a ticket, and flew to London to add my own quota to the lobby against his extradition, profiting from my friendship with Tom Driberg, an enfant terrible of the British Labour Party, and Lord Kenneth of the House of Lords, whom I had known in his plebeian days as Wayland Young.

To my astonishment, the battle was lost. The space of political sanctuary had always seemed a universal given; now it appeared that there had been huge gaps in my history education. Tony Enahoro was flown home to stand trial, like the others, on the charge of treasonable felony. He was found guilty and joined his leader, Awolowo, and other party leaders for a long sojourn in prison.

THE RULING PARTY and its allies could now afford to throw all democratic restraint to the wind, the opposition having been demonized and discredited. The government was now well placed to lay claim to the mantle of democratic defenders even as it engaged in undemocratic conduct. Alas, it had completely misread the mood of the West!

Long before the convictions, the emergency had ended, the worthy doctor had retired to his clinic, but not without first restoring order—that is, overseeing the emergence of the breakaway party, the NNDP, as master of the West, with its leader, Ladoke Akintola, as premier. In the federal chamber, the NCNC, having served its purpose, found itself increasingly marginalized, fed only crumbs from the "national cake." The honeymoon was over, and the NCNC filed its divorce papers, citing spousal abuse and public humiliation. It was promptly replaced by the bride in waiting, the NNDP.

The power of incumbency now decided electoral results. The Action Group, leaderless, lost direction. It would boycott elections, reverse itself, box itself into strategic corners, retreat, lick its wounds, reorganize, and await the next elections. From his prison cell, Obafemi Awolowo gradually acquired the image of a victim of political intrigue and injustice, a martyred visionary and leader, thanks to NNDP misgovernment and repressive measures. There was no ambiguity about it—the NNDP was unpopular. The West seethed with resentment.

The regional elections of 1965 approached. Virtually every woman and child, the aged and ailing, donned their battle gear in readiness for a desperate fight. For that contest, the Action Group teamed up with the former partner of the ruling party—the NCNC—to form a new coalition, the United Progressive Grand Alliance (UPGA). The alliance boosted the morale of both the Action Group and the Western electorate. Tacticians were exchanged. Badly needed resources flowed into the strangulated coffers of the Action Group. The region simmered as even the normally apolitical prepared for what they embraced as a revenge match, where scores would be settled definitively and the world would know just who enjoyed the people's support. It would prove to be a contest between terror and resistance into which I would be drawn for my first taste of political blood.

MY LIFE OF SPONSORED and footloose research—and private theatrical activities—ended at the University of Ibadan in 1962. After a few months' unemployment, I transferred to the University of Ife to earn an honest living as a lecturer in the English Department; Ife's temporary campus was then still located in Ibadan, the seat of government of the Western Region. The NNDP government, which now ruled the West, was proprietor of the university—and this was where the problem began.

In preparation for an electoral blitzkrieg throughout the region for the 1965 fight, the NNDP designated the university a den of opposition that had to be either bought or crushed. Thus, one unexpected day, the deputy vice chancellor, standing in for his boss, summoned a special congregation. Its sole purpose, conducted with all pomp and due solemnity, was to announce a new university credo. The word was actually used in the address: *The credo of the university is that it must support the government of the day!* It was that crude, an inglorious performance whose shame, or thought of potential consequences, must have overwhelmed the messenger himself, since he did not even wait for the usual comments or debate but fled the hall—and the campus—immediately after. He did not return until a week later, after the government had virtually taken over the campus. He could hardly be blamed—the vice chancellor had himself earlier transferred to Lagos, leaving the unsavory work to his deputy.

Five or six resignations followed immediately, among them those of the taciturn—except in political matters—Professor Victor Oyenuga, a biologist and die-hard card-carrying member of the Action Group; Sam Aluko, an economist and another Action Group strategist; myself; and two or three expatriate lecturers, notably Robin Horton the anthropologist, who would move East and settle down with a Nigerian wife. We gave the university the required three months' notice. Obedient to instructions from the Ministry of Education, however, the university responded by accepting the resignations—but with immediate effect. All resigning lecturers would be paid three months' salary in lieu of notice, and we were ordered to vacate our university residences within forty-eight hours!

The arena of polemics outside campus had already degenerated into the physical. Even theater—especially political satire of our kind—had become fraught with such violence that the actors had to be trained in basic self-defense, my favorite innovation being an unorthodox use of fire extinguishers in enclosed spaces. We learned quickly to adjust, since those performances, to reach their audiences, required spaces where the actors could be exposed to instant reprisals. Now the ivory tower itself was about to be physically assailed by the crudity of political intolerance.

Sam Aluko was a smallish lecturer with slightly bulging eyes that blinked furiously above a permanently truculent posture while he launched his rapid-delivery tirades in a heavy accent that was easily recognizable as that of the Ondo people. An Action Group economic adviser, he was away in Lagos attending a political meeting when the strong arm of the NNDP government descended. To leave no doubt whatever in the minds of the anticredo group that the government's intent was understood, the permanent secretary of the Ministry of Education filled his white Mercedes-Benz with thugs, invaded Sam Aluko's house, terrorized his wife and children, flung their furniture and luggage all over and out of windows, and smashed a few household items. They left, warning that they would return after twenty-four hours. They tried also to find the residences of the other lecturers but failed—in any case, they were not eager to remain too long on campus, and two of us actually lived off campus.

We heard the news, mobilized what forces we could, and rushed to protect Aluko's family. Legally, the resigning lecturers were entitled to remain in their residences until the end of the three-month notice, so we prepared to keep guard over Aluko's home until the time had expired. Sam's wife, Joyce, and the children were, however, much too traumatized; all they wanted to do was quit campus as fast as possible. I could hardly insist, since I lived off campus and my quarters were well secured. We had to content ourselves with guarding the premises until she and her family could leave in an orderly and dignified manner, then occupying the house for a week or so afterward in the hope that the permanent secretary's goons would return, expecting to find a defenseless family.

The "refuseniks" had learned their lesson, however. What was a hastily improvised group of "vigilante" volunteers—actors, academics, the odd poet and writer, a few civil servants, a handful of fiercely politicized patrons, the Mbari Club, which badly "wanted to do something!"—was whittled down, streamlined into a close-knit group to develop tactics for confronting the incipient fascism. At the time, it did not even bother to give itself a name.

THE MOBILIZATION WAS TIMELY. It meant that we were not too ill prepared when the elections began and the people's will was openly ridiculed by the incumbent government. Before all-out violence finally replaced all pretensions to legality, the opposition had circumvented the government-controlled public radio with its steady announcements of falsified results. The true results from both urban centers and far-flung villages, straight from the desks and trestles of the counting rooms, certified by the contending candidates and returning officers, were telephoned to the broadcasting studios of the Eastern Region, from which they were broadcast to the nation and to the outside world. A team of radio journalists from the alliance partner, the NCNC-controlled East, also arrived in the West to cover the elections. Led by a seasoned broadcaster, Mazi Ukonu, who was also a comic performer on radio, the team arrived with a transmitter that was installed—I discovered to my horror—in the home of the imprisoned leader of the Action Group, Awolowo!

It was too late for relocation; we could only monitor what knowledge or plans the government had for the transmitter and make contingency plans for its evacuation, if necessary. The field team from Enugu, pointed in the direction of key areas by our group and sometimes escorted for their safety, recorded and transmitted comments on the ongoing electoral charade and reported graphic incidents of violence. Hunted by NNDP police and "stalwarts" and denounced by the government as foreign infiltrators sent to rig the elections, they had intended their operation to last only two or three days, but we managed to persuade them to remain until the very last result from the remotest hamlet had been recorded and broadcast. Ukonu and his team were "held prisoner" till their task was completed, but never were prisoners more willing and obliging, even though somewhat apprehensive for their safety.

On the penultimate night of the presence of the Eastern Region broadcasters, we were finally alerted that the location of the transmitter had been discovered by the police, who would raid Awolowo's house the following day. The information came too late to dismantle and transfer the equipment, so we slept in strategic positions and quickly improvised a defense of the transmitter, awaiting the police assault. Some set up a diversionary ambush around a school across the road from Awolowo's home. My favored couch was the carpeted floor beneath a massive oak desk of the imprisoned leader. The assault did take place, but only after the final broadcast by Ukonu's team. When the police forces arrived for the planned dawn raid, Awolowo's house had been emptied, and Ukonu and gang were well on their way back to safety. The band of volunteers had had their baptism of fire; they slipped out before dawn, returned to their homes with relief, and awaited the next developments. The region hung on edge. An election had been stolen—would the robbers insist on clinging to stolen goods?

THE ANSWER WAS PROVIDED in time-tested ways. More opposition leaders were arrested, their homes and businesses vandalized, and, in some cases, thugs were sent to rape their women, at times with the husband forcibly held down as witness. The people, at first on the retreat, began to respond in kind. The homes and offices of government loyalists were torched, agents killed— sometimes in broad daylight, openly, and in urban centers—and ambushes laid for the marauding police squads. A new expression entered the vocabulary of politics: *Weti e!*—literally, "Douse it" (with petrol, then set it on fire). The police had their tear-gas canisters, Mark IV rifles, pistols, and even the occasional submachine gun; the resisters had in the main just the locally fabricated Dane guns, some shotguns, machetes, and—improvisation. The recipe for a concoction invented by the farmers and used to deadly effect remains elusive still. When the police arrived for their raids in rural areas, the seats and backrests of their unguarded trucks were smeared or sprayed with this substance. Minutes after the raiders returned and regained their seats, the effect began— presumably by then the mystery unguent had percolated through their clothing, the process being accelerated, we learned, by the amount of sweat on their shirts. They would leap up and tear off their clothing, convulsed in pain. It was nothing I ever witnessed personally, and nobody seemed to have died from its effect, but it was narrated by the victims themselves, who described the effect as one of intense, sticky burning. An African prototype of napalm, perhaps? I called it the Medea effect.

Finally, seeing that the campaign of intimidation had failed at voting time, the final "voter returns" were simply plucked out of thin air and announced on radio and television, fulfilling the blasphemous boast of the then deputy premier of the region on state television that had launched the doomed elections: *Whether you vote for us or not, we don't give a damn, since we're going to win anyway. The angels will descend from the heavens to cast their votes on our side.*

Spells of Sanity

The "roaring sixties" were not, however, an unbroken period of political outrage and response, of impositions, of a bleak intensity that sometimes appeared to have dominated, even defined, the life of a young man of thirty. It was not without periods of enlivening relief, both within and outside the nation. Teaching remained a constant respite, a mental undercurrent that restored a sense of proportion and highlighted the absurdity of much of the political reality. It was, however, a rather difficult time for my head of department, a pleasant Scottish lady whose real specialization was bibliography. She could not understand why the departmental timetable was never good enough for me, so that I had to make independent arrangements with my students and my classes took place at any time of the day, night, or weekend, and sometimes simply occupied a continuous weekend, before another vanishing act! Once she happened to read an essay submitted by a student, who had taken to heart my proposition that for Emily Brontë's Heathcliff—yes, Emily Brontë did fall into my lap!—an arguable metaphor would be the vampire. With the same intensity with which the student had pursued the theme, she tried to contest the notion, without the slightest trace of humor, thereby provoking me to improvise a sturdy correlative of clues from which I refused to budge. Finally she sighed, shook her head, and looked out of the window at a huge tree on whose branches bats clustered in their thousands. Instantly, her face lit up and she pointed to the leathery blobs: "When you teach *Wuthering Heights* at night to the background of those squeaky little things, I suppose you're bound to see vampires."

The Mbari Club remained a place for shedding political tensions, even

while introducing some of its own—workshops, exhibitions, plays, music re-
citals, a well-stocked bar where both the locals and the expatriate community
would stay up till the early hours ... eccentric individuals whose interests and
activities provided periods of escape, like the artistic projects of a truly talented
artist who was nicknamed "Mr. G." for his unfailing regularity in picking up the
common social disease in brothels, to the exasperation of his doctor, a Nigerian, who did not believe in patient confidentiality. A totally different kettle of
fish, who also drank like one, was Mitholfer, of an impressive but well-packaged
girth. An officer of indeterminate functions in the U.S. Information Agency,
Mitholfer lived near Femi Johnson in his first home at Onireke, so we often
met there. Mitholfer showed such fervid interest in my take on the political
goings-on that Femi and I challenged him to deny that he was a CIA agent,
specially assigned to me. He would only respond with his Buddha smile, then
go to sleep in his chair. Always good for the latest rumors, for "complots and
stratagems" behind enemy lines—the corridors of power—Mitholfer, who always thoughtfully visited with a bag holding ten or twelve cold bottles, was the
only being I knew who, after downing six .75-liter bottles of Star Beer, could
still hold an impeccable conversation. Even more impressive was the fact that
he could balance a frothing mugful of the seventh in one hand, holding the
mug against his chest or with his arm extended across the armrest, fall asleep,
stertorous snores issuing from ample caverns, then wake up with a jerk as his
head threatened to snap off the edge of the backrest but—not a drop spilling
from the mug! He would seamlessly continue the upward journey of the mug,
take a swig, resume the conversation exactly at the point where he fell asleep,
then go into the same routine, over and over again. At first we thought it was
an act, faking sleep so that he could pick up unguarded tidbits, but we tested
his condition in several ways and there was no doubt about it—after the fourth
bottle, Mitholfer was on his way to star-spangled dreamland. So we nicknamed him "Lanke Omu," after the adventurer of Amos Tutuola's *The Palm-
Wine Drinkard.*

"Carlo Mancini," a chubby, unflappable Italian, also a neighbor of Femi
Johnson, came to Nigeria through Ghana, where he worked for a construction
firm, going through his monthly salary with a steadfastness that sustained
Ghanaian nightclubs and their habituées. After nearly two decades in anglophone West Africa, Mancini yet retained his own stimulating vocabulary and
syntax of the English language. Certain words, sometimes of the simplest and
most common usage, stubbornly eluded him. For instance, he could never recall the word "eraser" or "rubber." Instead, after scratching his head for a long

time, he would hit on a substitute that exploded with relief and clarity: "Give me a *write and cancel!*"

In Accra—so went his own life account—a favorite habituée had taken him in hand and pleaded, "Carlo, you strike me as a very bright person. I know you're good with your hands. So why do you dissipate your money and life this way? I want you to try handing me your salary every month. You can drink all you want in the house, far more cheaply, and we'll put something aside every month so you can start your own business. I want you to be your own boss!" Carlo had found the idea outlandish but not too unwelcome, so he decided to give it a try. Before long, they had moved in together and entered into a "write, no cancel" marital bond that netted three children and a thriving business. They then transferred to Nigeria—not that it stopped Carlo from making the occasional foray into Nigerian fleshpots, but then, the sixties nightclubs were the true melting pots of all classes and nationalities, genial, music-saturated joints with exotic names or simply intriguing ones—Risikat, Agoji Mayor, Seven Sisters, Black Morocco, and Caban Bamboo—the last being a Lagos favorite where the erratic bandleader and proprietor, Bobby Benson, presided over a motley crew of barmen and stewards and his own band, among whom he rotated his bouts of fisticuffs as if on principle or from boredom.

Benson's complaints covered the full range from his musicians selling his musical instruments or their services to others and thus missing engagements to stewards making off with the takings, drinking his beer, watering his whisky, being drunk and asleep on the job, rifling the till, or shortchanging customers. He punched them out of doors, but a week later, they were back on duty. Bobby Benson arranged my adaptation of the traditional song "Ma a fee" and never missed his mischievous ritual of attribution, always introducing the number as "Wole's song—don't blame me" before its rendition.

On the night waves rode also the other class of musicians, deeply indigenous juju, *sakara, apala,* and *agidigbo* bands that played till the early hours of the morning, when rival political thugs exercised a choice of declaring a truce or busting up the joint the moment they set eyes on one another. My play *Kongi's Harvest* took its life from the night clientele and from variations on the theme of power, its obsessions, pretensions, and sensualities. Fittingly, we used Bobby Benson's place as a daytime rehearsal venue during preparations for the staging of that play at the Black Arts Festival in Dakar in 1966.

Erratic even in friendship, Bobby would lock us out in a sudden fit of pique, provoked perhaps by abandonment by his latest paramour or by frustration at a debtor who had again given him the slip. He would lock himself in his permanently pitch-black living quarters, which seemed to have been quarried out of Caban Bamboo's underground warrens. I knew the back door into the interior, so he had to open up when I beat on that door. He would appear in his velvet, ankle-length dressing gown with a boyish, apologetic grin, baldly lie that he had not known that we were coming, and, in any case, when were we going to pay for the hire of the rehearsal space? Moments later, freshly bathed and wreathed in perfume, he would stroll out, his neat goatee leading, in a three-piece immaculately pressed striped suit with a gold waistcoat chain across a mere suspicion of a paunch, a silver-topped black walking stick, and a fedora set at his "rascal" angle. Followed by a steward with plates of fried rice and chunks of peppered chicken, he would regally gesture to him to set it down, tip his hat toward us, and saunter out for the day. We had not ordered it, yet there would be a bill attached—Bobby never joked with his accounts.

Head for Osun, northeast of Ibadan, home of Susanne Wenger, the Austrian artist, and a greater contrast could not be imagined. An assignment roulette in Europe had brought Susanne and her husband, Ulli Beier, into Nigeria, and both had promptly "gone native," Susanne not just culturally but viscerally and spiritually, holding nothing back in herself. She had, in effect, found that self. She was inducted into the priesthood of the goddess of Osun River, whose mystic grove she proceeded to adorn with startling, sometimes controversial, sculptures, aided by a circle of local artistic initiates that she progressively gathered around her. Together they turned the grove into one of the weirdest yet most meditative spots in the nation. Wiry and sprightly, with large green eyes and a remarkable sense of self-deprecation, Susanne always declared herself insulated from politics, yet remained intensely political. One hand fought off the indiscriminate loggers who had no regard for the pristine serenity of the grove, a tranquillity that she had absorbed and carried around with her everywhere, yet uncoiling its serpentine energy at will. These were desperate men who even once sent assassins to deal with the "interfering white witch"—if only they had known that this was a woman who had risked the Nazi concentration camps for her role in hiding potential victims of the gas chambers! Her other hand she kept for fending off the overenthusiastic tourist entrepreneurs—both private and governmental—who also saw the grove as a moneymaking enterprise, to be enhanced by tinselly, exotic events. That left just her body and spirit to paint and sculpt with!

Osun grove, paradoxically, must have been created by the gods specifically for the "wild, wild West," a region that needed a spring of healing—or at least escape—a periodic immersion in the quiescent depths of the pacific deities. To

escape into Osun grove was always a journey into timelessness, a most dangerous indulgence, since the question on leaving was always—Do I really have to
leave? Why need I leave? To achieve what, exactly? This temptation to take
Osun with one, inside one, was the strongest internal battle that had to be
fought—Osun tugging at one end of a long, frayed rope, Ogun at the other...

And sometimes it was outward-bound—there, I was more fortunate than
most. I was unemployed twice in the first five years of my return home, and for
stress-inducing lengths of time—not for a total lack of opportunity but for a
lack of the ideal mold that would cater to both body and spirit, flexible and
stimulating. During such slack phases, I would take out my slim conferences/
lectures file and with a new regard—of longing and of necessity!—reconsider
those overseas invitations that I had shunted aside for some time, being too
preoccupied with unequal dialogues with sole administrators, political (and
academic) vampires, and allied modes of ungainful employment. It was not
that I had never busied myself evolving lucrative schemes for keeping Orisun
Theatre—my most immediate responsibility and political vehicle—afloat and
active, envisioning it as a formidable enterprise that would be quoted on the
stock market. No, there was no failure of ideas in that direction. Art could be
made to pay its way, I contended, and I was the mogul especially destined to
prove it. All schemes, alas, collapsed on the drawing board. Then my economic
health prescribed, without further consultation, a spell on the lecture and conference circuit of the United States and Europe. Even the batteries of conflict
require periodic charging.

The Transcription Centre for African Arts and Culture in London, managed
by Dennis Duerden, the art historian with the Albert Einstein head of hair, was
the central magnet, a dependable refuge for many impoverished or simply displaced writers and artists, especially from South Africa—Ezekiel Mpahlele,
Lewis Nkosi, Mazisi Kunene, and others—reminding one that there was still a
world out there with even more intractable problems, both political and artistic.
Even the campaigns against the atom bomb, the Aldermaston marches, provided spaces of political recuperation, since the problem of nuclear destruction
did not reach down into a personal core of identification but was widespread
as a diffuse, generalized concern with millions of unknown others—*Orun ma
a wo, orun ma a wo, ki nse oro enikan.** By contrast, the affairs of the Western
Region of Nigeria seemed to have possessed me in a very personal, obsessive
way.

---

* "The heaven is falling, the heaven is falling," is hardly a one-man preoccupation.

After my 1960 return to Nigeria, fortuitous timing enabled me to participate in the Aldermaston marches twice. It was both an act of solidarity with
former colleagues on the march and a chance to renew a rather specialized
sphere of acquaintances, among them the pipe-smoking British philosopher
with the willful shock of white hair, Bertrand Russell. My encounters with him
remained largely tantalizing, but I was impressed by his contempt for American racism and British colonial policies in Kenya. Outside the marches, we met
in a soggy British café or two with other admirers and disputants, but also in
his own home, thanks to my friendship with his secretary, Ralph Schoenman.
Ralph was a white American fugitive from Mississippi who had once spirited a
black youth away from near lynching and barely escaped evisceration as a "nig-
ger lover." The youth was a budding blues writer and singer who had watched
as his father was lynched, and it was thanks to a fragment of one of his compo-
sitions, retained by Ralph, that I came to experience, vicariously, the fatalism
and despair in victims of Jim Crow culture:

> Sometimes, I feel I could kill a man
> Just for being good lordy, just for being good....
> Little black mother with my heavy child
> Take that child out of here.
> Take him out and leave him there
> Before he find he's black

Ralph appeared to devote every free weekend to perorating in Speaker's
Corner in London's Hyde Park. His interest lay in two topics only: the atom
bomb and American racism. I wandered to his spot from time to time, fascinated by his ability to repeat the same two speeches over and over again without the slightest variation, not even in tempo or inflection.

In Joan Littlewood's theater of sheer lunatic genius at Stratford, England,
sometimes an entire day or more would be passed moving from rehearsals to
bar, then to a restaurant and back again. Even though she knew you would be
long gone before performance, if the spirit moved Joan, she assigned you a
character onstage—or urged you to create your own. The problem began when,
struck with the possibilities of that moment's intervention, it became an obsession, and she turned on the spigot to hose you down with her most elegant
spiel: *Damn you, fuck face, you can take off for your fuckin' country, be back in
time for performance, can't you? What's keeping you in that fuckin' place anyway?
They're all fucked up, I hope you know that, they don't have room for fuckin' poets*

there, anyone can tell that. Gerry, you tell him the fuckin' truth. Tom Driberg knows the fuckin' lot, he's a friend of Nkrumah, you know, and he says he's the only one worth a shit!

But it's off to a literary conference in Italy hosted by a San Giorgio Foundation in Venice. I had never been to Venice, and so not even Joan's persuasive skills would keep me from going there. Just as well; it turned out to be one of those bashes tailored for an unemployed dramatist on the run from polite creditors! The organizers at San Giorgio thought nothing of making available six different brands of wine during coffee breaks. And where else would I have run into W. H. Auden? Stephen Spender I had already met. Feeling always unsure—not exactly insecure but lacking absolute self-assurance—in my relationships with older, established writers (some of whom had provided the subjects of my student essays!), it was a relief to find myself adopted—indeed appropriated, fusslessly monopolized—by the two icons of British poetry. W. H. Auden's face—I have read at least a dozen descriptions of that phenomenon, so I'll add mine—struck me instantly as a compressed lump of volcanic lava in controlled convulsion.

They took me in tow, unveiling the surprises of the local culture, including the glass factory where I bought a delicate, spiral-lined decorative flask that has miraculously survived all displacements to this day. For an operatic performance, the duo proceeded to commandeer the subscribers' box of the Venice-domiciled Guggenheim heiress, where the audience, instead of keeping their eyes on the stage, swiveled around at every opportunity toward *the* box. I assumed that the two doyens of poetry were the objects of attention. I was wrong! Stephen Spender had planted a rumor that I was an African prince on a world tour and a special guest of Peggy Guggenheim. My habitual plain Yoruba smock, nothing flowing or trailing, nothing at all exotic, was sufficient to lend minimal credence, and the opera habitués could not have their fill of gawking. The Guggenheim heiress owned her own palazzo—palazzi came in different sizes, and hers was certainly above medium range—and it was befittingly stocked with artworks from classical antiquity to the modernists. Sculptures—open-air and gallery-cloistered—jostled for attention with priceless paintings; she threw her collection open to public viewing at set hours.

Stephen Spender's concoction, it turned out, was only half the story. For the heiress, he and W. H. Auden had planted a slight variation: an African prince with a large entourage, a collector and patron of the arts, was on a world tour. Happily, she surrendered her opera box to the prince and his entourage—which of course ended up as just the two English poets. Later, they explained the thinness of bodies in the box to her by claiming that they had learned only at the last moment that the "entourage" was not allowed to sit with His Highness, so they had been allocated seats elsewhere in the circle. I was somewhat puzzled—they were her friends anyway and could borrow or share her box any time they were in Venice—so I asked them, Why the fib? Spender nodded gravely as he explained in his gentle, reasonable voice that the poor girl had more money than she knew what to do with, so she should have something money can't buy—royalty.

They of course owned up to the convoluted deceptions afterward. The heiress was sending her private gondola to bring us to lunch, and the continuing absence of an entourage had became impossible to explain. W. H. Auden persisted in distracting me from feasting my eyes on her collection—"Don't miss it when she turns her arse, dear boy. She had it sliced off, surgically, you know, flattened it, so she could wear those Charleston dresses of the Swinging Twenties." Poetry, literature, and cultural issues were not neglected—the foundation's agenda occupied the conference hours—but neither was mischief by that deadpan duo, a wildly differing image from what I had built up from reading and studying their poetry.

Not a note of mischief, by contrast, did I ever detect in their Paris counterpart Pierre Emmanuel, but rather an abundance of good humor and a warm urbanity. In addition to writing poetry, Pierre was both historian and social philosopher. He completed the small circle of the expatriate company of which I greedily availed myself as respite from tilting at windmills in my own local landscape. A member of the board of the Congress for Cultural Freedom, he also occupied some kind of position in the French government. Ironically, usually in a fit of frustration, I sometimes experienced intense bouts of resentment against them all, on both sides of the English Channel, but only for my inability to conjure up their presence at will, including their roosting spaces— living room, bar, restaurant, concert, or seminar setting—and vanish into their contrasting, uninvolved environments, if only for an hour or two, a day or more. Quite early in our encounters, perhaps fresh from a contestation with some of my Francophone colleagues—the Mauritian poet Édouard Maunick and the Congolese Tchicaya U Tam'si, some of whose uncritical advocacy of *la civilisation française* triggered off my periodic bouts of mild Francophobia—I would accuse his nation of brainwashing its colonial subjects into becoming mimic French. Pierre's indulgent response was to reward me with that uniquely French moue of the lips, accompanied by a hand gesture of modest negation unknown to any other nationality of my knowledge—and a prolonged postprandial afternoon would be taken up with his defense of French colonial history.

My enduring education by Pierre Emmanuel, however, took a different form; I was inducted into the secret of controlling garlic breath—a few coffee beans, chewed slowly—"so next time, you won't have to turn down the chicken cacciatore on account of the garlic." Pierre had accurately guessed why I had turned down his recommendation, the specialty of the restaurant where he had once hosted me, observed my reaction as the waiter described its recipe! I warned him, however, that not all the coffee beans in Colombia or Kenya could meet the requirements of a friend of mine named Femi Johnson, who ate garlic as if he wanted to drown in its juice. "Well, bring him over if he is ever in Paris, and we'll try a few garlic recipes together," he said. I did, sooner than either thought likely. Femi visited Paris after traveling with a Nigerian drama troupe to the Nancy Festival, while I attended to an engagement at the Sorbonne. I halfheartedly participated in their garlic-saturated lunch in Pierre Emmanuel's apartment, as we continued the former discourse on the comparative merits and demerits of French and British colonial policies, the simmering cauldron of Nigerian politics totally banished or at least relegated to a niche within the larger context of world politics, colonialism, and its consequences. It was one of the unmatchable luxuries of this period, entangling one's mind in any tissue except what was being spun in the political looms of my Western Nigeria.

The Congress for Cultural Freedom (CCF), founded to promote freedom of speech and cultural expression, was always a generous host. It occupied offices in Boulevard Haussmann and operated like a more formalized version of the Transcription Centre in London, that dependable host to passing African writers. It also had a far more efficient machinery and clout for mobilizing international outcry when such writers were endangered. Funds from the CCF went into projects of our own Mbari Club in Adamasingba, that cultural roosting place that doubled as a venue for artistic manifestations and political intrigues. The literary and intellectual European journal *Encounter*, edited by an American expatriate, Melvin Lasky, his neatly bearded face a passable but fleshier copy of Lenin's, was the British window on artistic trends in a post–World War II era, and a voice that did aspire to some objectivity during the Cold War.

Like so many other writers and artists from the African continent, I always looked forward to meeting Melvin, who had a wide-ranging mind, full of cultural schemes. In turn he had toured the continent, spending several days in Nigeria. One evening, as I drove him in my Land Rover back to his hotel, close by Ibadan's pioneer television station—WNTV: First in Africa—I swerved suddenly to ensure that I did not miss a large, shiny snake attempting to cross the road. I appeared to have succeeded. I reversed the car, and there it was, stopped in its tracks but still writhing in the light of the headlamps. I ran over it two more times to make sure it was quite dead; still it continued to writhe. So I reached for the engine crank behind me and descended, ready to apply the coup de grâce, Melvin wisely declining my invitation to join in the fray. It turned out to be no snake at all but a discarded filmstrip—very likely thrown out by the television station! Melvin used the incident to end the narrative of his African excursion, published in *Encounter*—his concluding words continued to ring in my head for some time afterward: "In Africa, you confront a serpent, and it turns out to be a filmstrip!" How I often longed for his mots justes to be uniformly true!

Soon enough, we would discover that we had been dining, and with relish, with the original of that serpentine incarnation, the Devil, romping in our postcolonial Garden of Eden and gorging on the fruits of the Tree of Knowledge! Nothing—virtually no project, no cultural initiative—was left unbrushed by the CIA's reptilian coils. The first All-African Congress of Writers and Intellectuals in Makarere, Uganda, after the wind of independence blew across the continent, had been sponsored by the Congress for Cultural Freedom and *Encounter*. The same source infiltrated *Transition* magazine, the pioneering journal of ideas in postcolonial Africa, under the editorship of an East African Indian of Brahmin extraction, Rajat Neogy. Not one of us had the slightest suspicion that a certain U.S.-based Farfield Foundation, which lavishly expended its resources on the continent's postcolonial intellectual thought and creativity, was a front for the American CIA! When the scandal blew open, Melvin Lasky did not deny having had direct knowledge of the fact. My mind flew immediately to Pierre Emmanuel, who was on the board of the Congress, hoped fervently that he was as ignorant of the origin of these resources as was most certainly Stephen Spender, who attempted to rescue that truly stimulating journal *Encounter* from its tainted origins by taking over the editorship and seeking fresh resources for its continuation.

The struggle for the continent's ideological adhesion was not, however, strictly bipolar, a contest between East and West, between KGB and CIA, whatever names under which their cultural surrogates operated. It raged between one European country and another in varying degrees of subtlety and seduction. What mattered to us was that it provided numerous platforms for the cultural vanguard of the contested continent. With a somewhat less disinterested outward reach than, for instance, Sweden and other Scandinavian countries, there was also Germany, with her own courtship of Africa's immediate postindependence writers and artists, opening up venues in Berlin, Erlangen, Tegel, and Munich to Francophone, Anglophone, and Lusophone writers. Perhaps because the Scandinavian countries had no colonies, they appeared to be less inhibited, and perhaps less calculating, at pursuing a collaboration with the African liberation struggle—they had no excess baggage from the past!—and sought to channel that continent's creative and intellectual surge into a close association with their peninsula. Black American jazz musicians, some fleeing from the draft for the Vietnam War, had found refuge in Sweden, enlivening her nightlife. Perhaps this also triggered off a special interest in the continent of origin itself—it was difficult to tell. All that mattered was the evident and open-minded reach of that region into African arts and literature, leading to encounters between the two cultures in which we were more than ready to participate. As for Germany, she had lost her African colonies, but some cultural links remained, and her cultural front, the Goethe-Institut, was determined to reinforce those links and give the Alliance Française and the British Council a good run for their money. The rivalries guaranteed days of greedily imbibed camaraderie among African products of the colonial adventure on neutral grounds, nurturing—without conscious intent—a renaissance hankering for the generation's creative energies. Kindred spirits, with different levels and contexts of embattlement, engaged in a moving feast of cultural and political narratives of comparative fortunes—Tamsir Niane of the Republic of Guinea, a refugee in Léopold Sédar Senghor's Senegal, safe from the increasing paranoia of Sekou Toure, the revolutionary turned dictator of the Republic of Guinea, quietly assuming proprietorship of infamous torture cages that would not be exposed until years later; Ama Ata Aidoo, her playwright career just beginning, and Kofi Awoonor, poet and novelist, basking in the progressive limelight of their Ghana under Kwame Nkrumah; Okot p'Bitek—*Song of Lawino*—who would later drink himself to death in Idi Amin's Uganda; David Rubadiri, the soft-spoken but steel-willed Malawian poet, cautioning his listeners about the increasing authoritarianism of the Malawian ruler, Hastings Banda; the South Africans, in their own unique category of the displaced, gradually reconciling themselves to an inevitable armed struggle; Taban lo Liyong, a poet solidly entrenched in his Africanity, unlike Tchicaya U Tam'si, the Congolese poet with the game leg who remained incorrigibly French yet passionately black, reading his moving poem to the lynched American boy Emmett Till; Camara Laye, author of the elegiac childhood reminiscence *The Dark*

Child, seated at a café terrace in Erlangen, his eyes turned toward the mercury skies as he sighed, *"Regardez! Ici, ce n'est pas un pays. En Afrique, il y a de soleil, il y a du riz, il y a de piment, mais ici"*—and again a dolorous sigh—*"ce n'est pas un pays."* ("Take a look at that! This is not a country. In Africa, you have the sun, there is rice, and there is hot pepper sauce, but here—no, this is not a country.")

We did not require much urging—few, if any, passed up the opportunity for such encounters. Some were already domiciled, by choice or by circumstances, in the home of their colonial patrons. For others, each invitation was a respite, a banquet to be savored, sometimes greedily devoured. We met, debated, wined and dined, pursued amorous prospects, and felt recharged. . . . All too soon, it was time for each to return to a different clime and terrain and confront his or her own serpents.

In 1983 I fulfilled a long-held craving: to visit postrevolution Cuba for the first time. An invitation arrived from Casa de las Americas and found me more than ready. It was an invigorating respite, not unexpectedly, debating the purpose of art and ideology with the Cuban intellectual vanguard of the revolution. A former Royal Court colleague, the working-class playwright Arnold Wesker, somewhat self-conscious in his custom-tailored Mao suit, was at least well suited for a photo call when news came unexpectedly that he had won a prestigious prize. All ideological tussle was forgotten as we suspended the agenda and moved into the celebration mode in the Casa, continuing late into the night. Edward Albee's *Who's Afraid of Virginia Woolf?* found unexpected popularity among working-class revolutionaries—it seemed a paradox, this rite of exorcism between a middle-class American couple being so totally divorced from the ideological concerns of a world in turmoil. Then a four- to five-hour harangue by Fidel Castro at the Conference of Socialist Architects with a fear building up in me that I was watching a personality cult in the making, one that might breed a nation of revolutionary sycophants. A tour of the island, visiting the high-water landmarks of the revolution. Starved for wine by the rationing policy in Havana, we found the countryside more accommodating. In a modest seaside restaurant where we stopped for lunch, a cask of robust red wine, allegedly "washed up" from a Spanish smuggling vessel, was unstoppered in our honor by the straight-faced restaurateur, who appeared unfazed by the presence of the revolutionary watchdogs. We did not get to Santiago de Cuba until late that night, blissfully drunk.

I fell in love with a dancer in Havana, came close to eloping with a widow in Santiago de Cuba, ate frogs' legs in a restaurant for the first time, and marveled at the Cubans' technical ingenuity in keeping ancient Yankee Cadillacs purring smoothly with improvised spare parts. From time to time, the question of Albee's play would come up, our fellow confreres still amazed that such a play should find a place in a revolutionary environment. Ritual, I offered, ritual. Ritual is largely classless; and a debate erupted, as stridently as when I had offered that proletarian art—like the arts of indigenous peoples—had its secure place but should not be permitted to tyrannize over individual departures that offer insights outside the blinkers of the party line. What was remarkable was that the Cuban revolutionaries, in the main, agreed, but the European socialists—in the main—deplored the notion as bourgeois.

"Bourgeois" was also enemy territory in the United States of the 1960s, and was sometimes interchangeable with "white," "racist," "segregationist"—against all of which the black writers were producing a powerful body of revolutionary work. That visit, in 1964, was a lavish concourse, openly sponsored by the U.S. State Department, its intent being to bring virtually all of Africa to dialogue with the United States. No expense had been spared. All disciplines—from the arts and sciences to economics, philosophy, and possibly even religion—were in attendance, making it look as if Africa had been emptied of all analytic, creating, or governing structures for this grandiose effort to capture minds in the open contest between the ideological blocs, East and West. Africa was a much-sought prize, and one side at least, the West, was prepared to spare no expense to grab it and keep it within its orbit. I said to my colleagues, "Listen, we had better indulge to the fullest"—we did—"because it will never happen again." It never has!

It was a chance not to be missed, seeking out kindred spirits in the combat zones of the black nation within the outer embrace. The Spirit House of Leroi Jones—later Imamu Amiri Baraka—hovered between a monastery and a revolutionary training school, joined in a regimen of rigorous discipline and leader worship that was nearly cultic in character. It was wildly different in style and mood from the more democratic setting of the Lafayette Theater in Manhattan, also a revolutionary den for black liberation and equality, where Ernie McLintock, Ed Bullins, Ben Caldwell, and others held sway through their plays, smoked marijuana, needled the white establishment, and warned, just like Leroi Jones and others of that movement, of the apocalypse to come, unless...

Into others' battle zones or cultural oases—those visits were valued furloughs, interjections of comparative sanity, since even the insanities of others, as long as one remains sufficiently detached, inject a sense of proportion into one's close concerns. Every planned escape was guaranteed to be curtailed, however, and thus, ultimately, I was constantly left feeling shortchanged afterward. Still, they were much-needed interruptions in what was fast becoming an existence dominated by the politics of the immediate, demanding instant response. Sometimes the curtailment of the duration of such external relief was of my own ordering, not of any urgent summons from home that stemmed from an unexpected and menacing development. There would come that moment when the mind revolted. I would look around, listen to the conversation around me—a pretentious note, perhaps, a preposterous proposition, an artificial ardor, a comfortable liberalism or armchair radicalism—and the wine would turn flat on my tongue, my mind would go blank, leaving only the rebuke: *What are you still doing in this place?* The following day would find me at the airport, headed back to that region of the world that would come to be dubbed the "wild, wild West" by a young military officer who, undergoing his Sandhurst training during the Western Regional elections, had no inkling of the political destiny that lay ahead of him.

Wanted!

The most extended break from the gathering firestorm of the West came from the Commonwealth Arts Festival of 1965; then it was back to base to have one's face rubbed in the conduct of the Western regime, aided and abetted by the federal government, increasingly arbitrary, vindictive, and desperate. My series of sociopolitical sketches—*Before the Blackout, The New Republic,* and so on—had served to calm the rioting conscience for a while, and the urge to intervene in a more direct way would have been stilled—perhaps—but for one afternoon of sheer serendipity.

Saturday was the weekly concession to a full-bodied Nigerian menu in the Femi Johnson home. Otherwise, my friend Femi, then married to an English wife, would dine on steak and gravy, lamb chops and mashed potatoes, fish and chips, shepherd's pie, and all the other delicacies that could be found on any English table. My presence in the Femi Johnson household whenever I found myself in Ibadan on a Saturday afternoon had thus become routine. I went there to be overfed! The warm reception of my play *The Road,* most especially through a review by Penelope Gilliatt of *The Observer,* had been gratifying, but that was no solace for nearly two weeks of the barely tolerable to execrable restaurant fare that one could afford in 1965 London. I had accepted a new position in the English Department of the University of Lagos but had yet to settle into my office. A huge craving for some solid Nigerian cooking had thus been stored up, and the first Saturday afternoon after my return I could hardly wait for Ibadan and Femi's gourmandizing company. In truth, I was suffering from double starvation: I needed to catch up with the news and explore the on-going politics of the West that had taken the gloss off my theater debut at the Commonwealth Arts Festival.

In attendance as usual on that day was a mutual friend, Michael Olumide, then controller of the broadcasting station in Ibadan. The election results dominated all discussion, and it was not long before a pall of depression hung over an afternoon that was normally devoted to pure, unabashed gluttony. The West, to which we all three belonged, was being stolen from under our noses.

And then, quite casually and in all innocence, Michael Olumide dropped a bombshell that instantly launched a turmoil in my head. Michael had been summoned by the premier to record his victory speech. There was also the possibility that the premier would come into the studio and do his broadcast live. The recording was intended as a backup in case he could not leave what had become his prime ministerial fortress—and prison. Whatever the final decision, the victory broadcast of the NNDP, and Akintola's reelection as prime minister of the West—our West—would be made that night!

The broadcast had to be stopped! Mazi Ukonu and his radio crew had long departed, so a counterbroadcast, relayed through the Eastern transmitters as the election results had been, was impossible. The premier held all the cards. A fait accompli, consecrated on radio waves, would demoralize the opposition, and that broadcast, from a position of incumbency strength, would commence the process of legitimizing a detested regime, with the consequent danger of resignation and apathy from a cowed populace. Another four years under the NNDP could easily become a life sentence for a struggling democracy; there was the very real danger that the now barely hidden agenda to formalize a one-party dictatorship by the victorious alliance would become irresistible. Opposition would be crushed. There would be money- or contract-induced defections. Some would succumb to blackmail. Others would be squeezed into submission through assaults on their means of livelihood. Some of the NPC and NNDP politicians had already begun to raise a chant for a "one-party democracy." The continent was filled with such models of power consolidation masquerading as democracies. Their would-be imitators in the nation virtually drooled in envy as they cast glances at such bastions of the crudity of power. The formal capture of the West was bound to reinforce the proponents of an iron hand.

I had wrestled intermittently with the problem of violence. To be caught up in a violent situation, compelled to respond to it, presents no agonizing choice; to initiate one is another matter. I had never seen myself as a pacifist, never persuaded myself that the liberation of any tyrannized space can always be achieved by nonviolent means. I tried to caution myself, however, about the dangers of unstructured violence, violence that comes to exist for itself, as a glorified end that loses all focus and control and no longer discriminates between its two principal clients positioned at either end of a living axis: Power and Freedom. The most principled of struggles has its share of psychopaths—and I was fortunate to have received early education through encounters with a few of these almost from the start of my political involvement. I was equally lucky to find myself within a close-knit group whose members believed that violence was a stage to be avoided for as long as and wherever possible, insisting, however, that self-defense constitutes its own justification. This includes defense against violation, such as acts of robbery or extortion. Rape. Any form of dehumanization. Even to be robbed is to be diminished, and to be robbed of the seemingly intangible—such as a civic voice—is to be diminished as a citizen. To resist such a diminution meant, in my view, a simple act of self-defense, of self-preservation.

The elections had thrown up many instances where the most diffident individual found himself compelled to write his own limited rules of engagement in response to real violation. My favorite recollection was that of a young politician, Soji Odunjo, a few years younger than I. He was probably the youngest of the Action Group candidates, a wispy, normally mild-mannered youth, rather retiring in demeanor. I had long known him, before he entered politics, only as the junior brother of a colleague from the old University of Ibadan. Perhaps politics did course secretly through Soji's veins—he was, after all, the son of one of the founding members of Egbe Omo Oduduwa, the Yoruba cultural organization that later metamorphosed into the Action Group. Nevertheless, I was quite surprised to discover that Soji considered entering the wild world of politics of the mid-sixties.

After voting had ended and the votes were tallied, Soji found himself faced with a crooked returning officer who refused to release the results in his electoral ward. He had campaigned hard and fair, against all odds, displaying unsuspected political instincts, and now all he wanted was that the results, already announced to the waiting crowd, should be set down so that he and his opponent could sign the returns as required by electoral law. The officer, however, insisted that the results would be released only at the state capital, Ibadan, and from there be broadcast by the radio station. Since Soji knew by then—as did the entire nation—what happened to returns en route, he dashed home and returned with a loaded shotgun, whose muzzle he then pressed against the head of the returning officer. I remain convinced that Soji would have been incapable of pulling the trigger even if the officer had persisted; still, by the count of three, the man had handed over the card. His mission accomplished, Soji drove to the collating office in Ibadan, where he logged the results. Then he went home to sleep the sleep of the just.

Thinking of the course I was about to embark upon, I found my position no different from Soji's, except that I was not even a candidate but was acting as one of the electorate who felt bound to protect his rights. In consonance with the majority of the populace of the Western Region, I was being robbed of a voice. A series of false results had already been announced, of increasingly cynical attributions. Now this act of robbery was about to be made official by the head of the robbery consortium, the premier, also the principal receiver/ beneficiary of the stolen goods, all rolled into one. Picking somewhat distractedly at my plate in Femi's dining room, I found it only slightly incongruous that I should be considering, and with complete equanimity, whether or not I should arm myself before going to recover—or at least prevent the formal acquisition of—this stolen property. I would have preferred that we take over the broadcasting station entirely and occupy it for some days, stoking up the now-inevitable uprising with the usual messages of resistance and solidarity, but what forces we could muster were hopelessly inadequate for such an undertaking. We had no precedent to follow, not even the time to stock up for a prolonged siege. A well-directed police action would flush us out in no time!

That afternoon, with its lack of alternatives, informed me with a quiet certitude that I was finally tired of dramatic sketches that, however scabrous, drew only symbolic blood from the veins of Power. Suddenly, that language of intervention—despite the occasional physical assaults on the actors and threats of disruption—became inadequate, even self-indulgent. Fast receding was that homecoming projection of my role as being no more than that of a truth crier, with weapons no more lethal than my portable typewriter and paper.

The next few hours flashed before me in that instant—as already defined motions as well as logistical options—but not the likely consequences; that section was blanked out. Looking back, I appeared to have been focused entirely on practical matters, details. I knew at once that I had to obtain a good tape recorder and recollected, in that same instant, just who possessed such high-fidelity equipment: a serving U.S. Peace Corps volunteer doing some field research at the University of Ibadan. Now all I saw, detachedly, was my doppel-gänger walking up the back stairs of the broadcasting station where I had been a frequent contributor, into the corridor where the director's office was located, past his office, past Amos Tutuola's cubicle, then up a short flight of steps to the left before a right turn at the landing. The crucial door was on the right. It led into the control room through which one had to pass in order to enter the studio where I had done dozens of broadcasts. I would not be going into the studio, however. The control room from which the tapes and records were played was the target. I wondered who would be on duty, knowing, however, that I could rely on the commitment of the majority of the staff in that station.

Would the premier come in person? The political situation was unraveling fast, and the premier was a shrewd calculator who instinctively homed in on survivalist tactics; it was therefore quite possible that he would decide to make a live broadcast. Between recording and broadcast, much could happen, and Akintola, a master of improvisation, would want to enter any last-minute development into his speech and manipulate it to his advantage. This complicated my thinking, since the prime minister would then travel in a motorcade and the studio would be swarming with police escorts and perhaps a truckload of his party's "irregulars." Obviously I would have to arrive early, just before nightfall. A curfew was in force, which was good, since we were masters of the curfew. We needed the dark. I chose the record library as the most strategic position in which to place myself; one had to walk past it to reach the studio. If the premier came in person, however, what would we do?

We? No, in my mind's eye, everything was reduced to one person. I am always amused—or irritated, depending on my mood—by much that has been written about my so-called loner mentality. As if the one individual in a mountain climb who plants the flag on the summit and beats a quick retreat before a snowstorm obliterates all landmarks were not backed up or preceded every step of the way by the rest of the team! On any of them could have fallen the task of making that final sprint to the summit. Of course I entered the studio alone. There were armed police swarming all over the outer premises. If I were to take others with me, detection would likely occur before we even breached the perimeter of the building—unless, of course, the intention was that others should expose themselves to detection and so create a distraction for my entry. That option was unnecessary. It was much easier for one person familiar with the building to slip into and out of the storage space, record library, offices, and corridors all the way to the studio. If we had had one more day, we could have found an excuse to bring others into the building in broad daylight, given them the opportunity to memorize the geography of stairwells and landings. There simply was not time.

The recording of my countermessage settled, it was easier to concentrate on peripheral but crucial details, such as who would drive me to Broadcasting House. Next thought: guns. To go armed or unarmed? That did not generate much agonizing; the unpleasant but unavoidable word was *coercion*. I was not going into the studio to preach to the studio engineer and the continuity officer that their moral duty lay in removing the prime minister's tape and substituting my own. I had no idea who would be on duty, and even if I did and their sympathies were with the opposition, they were entitled to their overt neutrality. If they were militantly with us, they would enjoy the charade of submitting—like the broadcaster, Ukonu—to force majeure. If they were not... well, then they could wallow in the indignation of having been made to act under duress. If things went wrong and the police were somehow alerted— there was no time to think of consequences beyond knowing that unless I was shot at or about to be shot at, I would calmly surrender myself for arrest *once the tape was running*. I was of no two minds about that.

Finally, there persisted one critical question: Suppose the man came himself, surrounded by his entourage? The only answer was to prevent him from entering Broadcasting House in the first place, scare off his motorcade en route. Again, the niggardly collaboration of time! There was not enough of that commodity to mobilize the entirety of our small band. Still, I knew the normal haunts of the marginal members, including the faithful Kodak, a former thug and mercenary who had chosen to throw his lot in with us. In turn, he could rouse another four or five from whichever dens they had thought to pass an uneventful or predatory weekend in. Hidden in the dark among the buildings, behind vending kiosks or trees—the trees had not yet been eaten on Ibadan roads, or in other urban centers for that matter, to assuage the hunger for development—they would man the immediate approach to the premier's destination and pepper the motorcade with a few shots. Knowing the high state of alert in which the town was seized, it was certain that the immediate reaction of his security outriders would be to accelerate and tear past Broadcasting House without pausing. Unable to determine how large a force was firing at them from the darkness and the ominous emptiness of streets under curfew, that was only common sense.

At last I could feel inwardly at peace. I rejoined the conversation, putting a few innocent questions to Michael, and abandoned the rest of the Saturday feast.

. . .

IT ALL PROCEEDED according to plan. The duty officers responded as any sensible persons would under the gun: they removed the premier's tape and replaced it with mine. It ran long enough for the message to the government to be clearly transmitted: *Drop your stolen mandate, leave town, and take your reprobates with you,* and so on, and so on. Then a disbelieving senior operator in another control room roused himself from his paralysis and depressed a control button that cut off the transmission. By that time, I had slipped away. My retreat was unhindered.

Before dawn, I was in flight to the Eastern Region, later to confront the weird experience of seeing my face pasted on the pages of newspapers as a "wanted" man. One of the studio staff, A.O., had sworn to the identity of the intruder! Indeed, he recounted in detail a conversation that, he claimed, had taken place as he carried out the intruder's instructions—under a gun pointed directly at him, he repeated ad nauseam—to remove the premier's tape and substitute it with his. The evening of the raid, A.O. had indeed proved an unstoppable conversationalist; perhaps he did need to babble in order to steady hands that quivered so badly that, in the end, it was a junior assistant, Friday Ifode, who completed the task of threading the tape.

Once the police investigations began, A.O. continued to supply details of the one-sided exchange, a virtual monologue: how he had expressed astonishment at seeing me in Ibadan since I was supposed to be in London, and so on. The others swore they had heard nothing of the kind or else had caught only snatches of the exchange not sufficient to identify the gunman. We thought the intruder was his friend, they said with a shrug, since A.O. appeared to know everything about the stranger's movements, even while he was in London.

I WAS ALREADY UNDERGROUND when I was declared "wanted"; that was all part of the decision of the small band of "irregulars" that went under different aliases for the purpose of a public but elusive voice, including, at one stage, the Committee of Writers for Individual Liberty (CWIL)—a most misleading title, since only the poet Christopher Okigbo and I thought of ourselves as writers. There were, however, two or three lecturers from Ife and Ibadan University. Other members, such as Kodak, belonged on the fringes of mainstream society. Members of my itinerant performing group, the Orisun Theatre, had slipped, imperceptibly, into the role of an informal intelligence-gathering unit, a productive network that co-opted friends, families, lovers, and former schoolmates working in junior positions within the establishment. The Pyrates—that campus fraternity that meant so many contrary things to bemused or terrified Nigerians—refused to be left out of any direct action, though their participation was limited to a hard core of three or four at any time. Doig Simmonds, a British medical illustrator, was the sole expatriate member—mostly on the periphery. A designer and printer of most of our leaflets, he was not involved in any of the public activities. Doig did, however, surrender his fowling piece to me, a skeletal gauge that could just about pluck the feathers off a bush fowl at a ten-yard distance but made an impressive amount of noise, especially in an enclosed space. It earned its keep in some of the encounters that took place as we monitored the electoral process in remote areas, where violence had replaced even the semblance of an electoral choice.

By the time the police felt sure of the identity of the intruder, I had left Ibadan town and indeed the borders of the Western Region. I resurfaced in Enugu, Eastern Nigeria, whose premier, Dr. Michael Okpara, was in active alliance—United Progressive Grand Alliance—with the opposition Action Group of the West. I told him of our plans to muster a sustained resistance against the NNDP government, and he gave me the run of his state, requesting only that I keep out of sight of the police force, which was under a central command—that is, mostly took orders from Lagos. Just to be on the safe side, however, he invited in the commissioner of police in Enugu and introduced us to each other. Nothing more was said.

MY HOST IN ENUGU was Dr. Sam Aluko, the economist who had been crudely ejected from the campus of Ife University. Through some strange workings of his mind, he would find himself, a quarter of a century later, quite comfortable in the position of economic adviser to the nation's most notorious despot, General Sani Abacha, who looted the nation's monetary reserves with as much abandon as he tortured, imprisoned, and killed her citizens. It was, however, the familiar face of my activist colleague that welcomed me without a thought while the police pursued my imaginary trail to phantom sightings all over the country.

It did not take long before the police tracked me down to Enugu. My telephone calls to Femi Johnson had been monitored and their originating station easily traced. If the fugitive was in Enugu, thought the NNDP police, it also stood to reason that an obvious point of contact for him would be his erstwhile colleague Sam Aluko. Within two days of my arrival, the Eastern Region police command received a signal from Ibadan that Aluko's house should be searched.

Sure enough, Sam received an advance notice from the Enugu police that they would arrive the following morning on their hunt for the fugitive.

They arrived as promised, armed with copies of the "wanted" notice with my photograph. A charade ensued. Sam accompanied them as they looked through the rooms one after the other, passed through the living room, where I was seated. They looked right through me as through a windowpane. Content with the futility of their mission, they sat down with the Aluko family in the same living room. With straight faces, they inquired of Sam Aluko if he had had any news of me. Sam shook his head in the negative. "Well, be sure you keep us informed if he makes contact—we'll leave this 'wanted' notice with you in case you lay eyes on anyone resembling him"—again looking straight through me as I sat sipping my coffee. Sam took the poster, scrutinized the photograph, nodded, and assured them that he would definitely get in touch, then accompanied them out of the house.

Some days later the same police advised Sam that I should move to a new place. A fresh group of detectives was being sent directly from Ibadan to ferret me out. Sam Aluko, they sensed, held the key to my whereabouts. The new squad would be paying him a visit and would likely remain in Enugu to monitor his movements, convinced that he would eventually lead them to my hiding place. By then, however, the situation in the Western Region—the breakout of insurrection and the disintegration of the NNDP regime—had created the right conditions for my return to Ibadan and the certainty of a trial. Dr. Okpara provided a nondescript Volkswagen that took me straight to Lagos and to the safe house of a colleague, Dapo Fatogun, a journalist and Marxist with ties to Red China.

Dapo was a saturnine intriguer, virtually expressionless, with a complexion that seemed to shroud him in perpetual darkness. I had a hat on, no other disguise, except that I had shaved off my wisp of a goatee. Dapo took over and drove me around the newspaper offices, where the shock on the faces of the editors and staff was worth the sometimes uncomfortable maneuvers Dapo took me through to ensure that we escaped police detection. At each newspaper office, I followed the prepared script, high on indignation, telling how shocking it had been for me to discover, after my return from a habitual creative retreat, that I had been declared wanted by the police! I took the strongest exception to such criminalization tactics. If the police wanted me, I protested, all they had to do was to look for me seriously. The friendly press, as usual, hammed it all up in full accord with a favorite subject and set to work to prepare their sensationalist copy for the following day.

We drove to Ibadan. I had to decide on a place where I would spend my last night of freedom, my own home being out of the question. I had been briefed regularly about the police inquiries, interrogations, and so forth, information supplied even by some of the police who had been sent after me. I knew in detail who had volunteered information, even unasked, and who (especially two expatriate colleagues) had been terrorized into collaborating, revealing some of my movements that could invalidate an alibi. Others, however, Femi Johnson among them, had refused to oblige the police in any particular.

All I knew of Femi's politics was his outrage at the electoral fraud. He was not a member of CWIL; I had never subjected him to any test of solidarity or asked him to participate, even marginally, in our activities. Yet Femi had taken extra pains to frustrate the police every way. Indeed, so eager was he to confuse the investigators that he deliberately distorted the time and content of our telephone conversation, little realizing that the distortions would prove useful to the prosecution! That very gaffe, its touching motivation, contributed to my choice of his home for my last evening at liberty. It was an intuitive feeling; I knew I could feel as safe and secure with him as I did in the professional hideout of my Marxist colleague Dapo Fatogun, with its elaborate network of communication and warning systems.

THE DRAMA NOW SHIFTED to the court. My lawyers—all, with the exception of the senior counsel, volunteers who never asked a penny—joined me in secret later that night. They were Tayo Onalaja, Kayode Somolu, Jide Olatawura, and Dele Ige; the first three would become High Court judges years later, while Dele turned to business. Dele's brother Bola Ige, also a lawyer, stayed on the sidelines, contributing legal advice from his chambers. As he was a noted politician in opposition, it was not considered advisable that he participate openly in my defense. Together we worked out the strategy for my surrender.

By morning, the papers would be filled with the news that I had resurfaced and would submit myself for arrest sometime that same day. My lawyers would contact the police, laying a false trail by inviting them to come to my own house in Felele at ten in the morning to pick me up. I would, however, remain in Femi's house and report directly to the Iyaganku police station at the same hour. That would prevent any act of bad faith on their part, such as storming my house and pretending that they had found me in hiding and had conducted a difficult arrest. Such moments were bread and meat to Femi. His eyes shone with the sheer enjoyment of scheming and counterplotting. That light dimmed only when the terms of my indictment were announced, framed to ensure the maximum penalty possible, short of capital forfeit: robbery with violence, carrying a life sentence. The stolen item: one magnetic tape. Cost: two pounds, seven shillings.

We had indeed underestimated the regime in that one respect: its choice of the charges under which I would be tried. We were more than prepared for a political trial; indeed, I looked forward to it. But not armed robbery! The possibility of such a vindictive interpretation of a purely political act had escaped both my little band and the lawyers altogether; if it had occurred to me, I would most certainly have dug deeper underground, burrowing away from both East and West as far as possible!

It was, when all is fairly considered, a most uncharitable way to respond to what, in essence, amounted to no more than borrowing some airtime on a public facility. True, I had made away with the tape of the premier of the Western Region—and there was the unavoidable introduction of a firearm in the process—but I did leave my own tape in its place. And if it was a question of content, well, the comparative value of both messages was something that could have been settled amicably in a court of arbitration. I would be the first to admit that, in wit, wordplay, and verbal resonance, my humorless message— and in the strident accents of the English language to boot—was no match for Ladoke Akintola's adroit Yoruba. Still, the cost of both tapes was the same, and the labor I had put into ours certainly equaled that of the premier, who had had all the resources of the state at his disposal for recording in his living room. Such basic principles of equity notwithstanding, forgetting our people's own wisdom that is expressed in the sentiment "Exchange is no robbery," Akintola's government still insisted that I be charged with robbery, and of the armed variety.

THAT CONTEXT OF CRIMINALITY was the only sinister element in what would otherwise have proved a period of welcome rest, enforced immobility. I could catch up on neglected reading and calmly observe the world of petty criminals and their hunters, accomplices, and relations as they milled around the police yard and passed by my makeshift cell. Despair, desperation, a world of deceits and opportunism, and the occasional impulsive act of kindness. Interrogations sometimes took place in my presence, or else I would have to sit in the corridor within earshot of threats, cajolery, whining, denials, and the most odious lies, delivered with a stolid, inflexible countenance. Most memorable, perhaps, of the many revelations of this world of crime and detection was an encounter between a known kingpin of the underworld and his interrogator, the latter clearly terrified of a prisoner who openly relished his reputation as a most violent specimen. That underworld figure was short, jet-black in complexion, and had a square-set face but was built like the concrete cylinder that serves as the wheel of a primitive tarmac compressor. He gave off a thick air of menace that percolated through even to me.

The poor "E" branch officer to whom fell the work of interrogating him tried to carry out his preliminary task, which was to physically secure his charge. In the most diffident manner, virtually plaintive, he asked permission to clamp him with leg cuffs. The lord of the underworld gave him such a look of dare and disdain that the officer fell to whining and pleading. The cuffs were left alone, and a dialogue—supposedly an interrogation—ensued between cat and mouse, with the prescribed roles reversed. Another officer happened to walk by—maybe on a casual inspection—and quickly demonstrated that confident authority often achieves what physical force cannot. It was then the turn of the gangster to fall to whining, swearing that he had never at any time objected to being restrained with the cuffs. The officer said nothing further, merely fixed him with a telling look and pointed to the abandoned cuffs. King Kong took the cuffs in his own hands and aided his earlier captive of terror in securing his ankles. It was easily the most abrupt, most dramatic change of attitude that I had ever witnessed in any human being.

The formal security around me grew quite slack as the case wore on. For instance, a famous picture—it appeared also in foreign newspapers—showed me being escorted across the road from my police cell by one policeman only, unarmed. Before then, pictures had shown me apparently with no escort; in reality, I was constantly under the far more efficient guard of three plainclothes officers. Infuriated that the prisoner was photographed walking—to all appearances—without guards, the government ordered that I must never again be seen without the visible company of a uniformed officer. *He's a common criminal, accused of a serious crime, and should be presented as such!* So the plainclothes detail was removed, and only the somewhat tubby uniformed police remained to ensure my security. During any of those walks across the road to the court and back, I could have been rescued by any single member of our group if I so wished and rushed into a car conveniently parked or cruising along the road before that solitary officer could raise an alarm.

The NNDP government, finding unexpected and growing international interest in the prisoner, was unsure how to respond and yet continue to depict itself as a legitimately elected democratic body, deeply wronged by the disruptive act of one individual. Questions were raised in the British House of Commons. Was the writer being unjustly persecuted? Was a fair trial possible in a situation of political chaos? Was the prisoner being kept in humane conditions? Had democracy failed in its largest ex-colony? And so on. In its desperation to respond to these and other hue and cry from outside, the government fell into one self-contradiction after another. Its predicament was not helped by an untoward incident that resulted from a noncooperation campaign I had embarked upon, a quite unscripted event that no one, certainly not I, could have foreseen.

Fed up with delays over bringing me to trial, I went on a hunger strike and demanded to be moved from my makeshift detention place in the police office to a proper cell with other criminals. An interlude of tranquillity had been welcome at the beginning—I had, after all, prepared for it when I agreed to the decision over my return—but after two, now approaching three months of "ongoing investigation," the wait was becoming oppressive. My outward composure and resignation were fast becoming lies, increasingly difficult to sustain. I became convinced that the government was deliberately stalling my trial. The longer I could be shown off to the world as being accorded VIP treatment—detained not in prison, not in a cell, but in a police office—the longer the government could afford to delay my trial and thus place me out of circulation indefinitely. The West was boiling, and, frankly, I felt deprived of my rightful share of action. My demand was granted, and I was taken to the regular police station cells and locked up.

I made one immediate discovery: those cells were far filthier from the inside than the griminess that was evident when one merely looked in from the outside! The smears against the wall established a definition—it could only be human excrement!—that made the body shrink from touching them. Still, I had asked for it, and all that was left was to look forward to a clean bath when this was all over.

That same night I received unexpected visitors, a development that, considering my yet-unpublicized transfer to a new residence, could not have come about as the result of a chance visit, as later claimed in court by my police assailant. A deputy commissioner of police, Loremikan, escorted by a detachment, stormed the station and demanded access to my cell. The duty officer had no choice but to comply. My door creaked open. Before me stood a stranger, staring at me with indescribable venom. He was dripping with tear-gas canisters, grenades, sidearms, and drunken saliva. Before I could begin to assess the nature of the invasion—beyond the clue that his slobbering face offered as it accused me of causing problems for the government—this apparition had baton-charged me repeatedly at the base of my rib cage and I was left gasping for breath.

When I was taken to the hospital the following day, the X-rays revealed contusions but, luckily, no broken ribs. My lawyers took a complaint to the judge a few days later. The judge—Justice Kayode Eso—was infuriated, summoned Loremikan to court, turned him into a mop, and scrubbed the floor with him, leaving him dribbling yet again, this time in sheer terror. The courts, at that time, did command authority! Justice Eso sent for the police inspector in charge of the station, ordered him to take me back to my former place of detention—his office—and charged him personally with responsibility for my body. The inspector was to consider himself answerable to the court for my safety.

The press, both local and international, covered the episode with vengeful glee. From then on, the atmosphere around me changed completely. The police insisted that I return periodically for treatment to the University Teaching Hospital, where, as the gods who oversee these matters had evidently decreed, a nurse with whom I was having an affair also resided. Since orders had been given that I was to have minimal contact with the public outside the police station, I was given appointments at odd hours—again at the insistence of the police— mostly in the evenings, outside the regular outpatient hours. It became routine. After examination and treatment, my obliging police escort—now back to mufti—would take the route to a particular block of apartments in the hospital complex. He would stay downstairs, nursing a cold beer, while I went up to be nursed. A baton charge by a drunken police officer was something that I—and most prisoners, I am certain—would consider a small price to pay for such conditions of restraint.

Such reliefs, to tell the truth, were relished far more for their context of defiance, as a statement of some personal control over my environment, than out of necessity or desperation. Of far greater value to me was an event of touching revelation, one that occurred on the night before the verdict. This was when I first experienced, with sheer wonder, the potential depths of human friendship. First, Femi Johnson had hardly missed one day of visiting during my detention and trial, turning up sometimes even twice or thrice—on his way to the office, returning home from the office, or setting out from home for no other purpose than to keep me company, remaining as late as the police would permit him. Only one other person came close in the consistency of his visits: the poet Christopher Okigbo, then representing Cambridge University Press in Nigeria and an informal member of CWIL. He would bring his latest verses in typescript, scribbled over in his neat, tiny handwriting, and read them aloud to me, sometimes with Femi as his only other audience. Armed with a hamper of food and drinks, we might even have lunch or dinner together in that office turned residence. A young German journalist, Gerd Meuer, then married to an Indonesian, would also drop by occasionally, with an Indonesian spread prepared by his wife. On this night, however, the last before my sentencing, it was Femi who appeared with his now-familiar basket.

I was reading. I looked up suddenly with that feeling that someone was watching me. There he was at the window, just looking in.

"How long have you been standing there?"

"Ages!" he sighed. He shook his head in a gesture of disbelief, his shoulders unusually slouched as he came around to the door. My guards were chuckling—he had signaled them to keep silent, not reveal his presence, while he simply waited until I looked up or he got tired of waiting. His entire manner was uncharacteristically down at the mouth. I waited for him to throw off the mask, to detonate the joke behind it. But there was no hidden mirth lurking in Femi's throat.

"What's the matter?"

"I don't understand," he said. "I've been standing there watching you for at least thirty minutes."

"Don't exaggerate."

"But . . . how can you? Tomorrow is the day, isn't it?"

"You mean, the verdict?"

"What else is there tomorrow? You know, you're not normal. Wole, *eda ni e o. Eda ni e.** You are not normal at all. How can anyone normal just sit there reading as if nothing is happening?"

He put down the hamper. I must have been truly absorbed to have failed to respond much earlier to the aroma, but then I had developed a fussless capacity for obliterating my environment. I lifted a corner of the cloth, drew in a lungful of delights.

"Hm. Last supper."

"It's not a joking matter!" he protested.

I lifted the cloth aside to inspect the dishes. "I am not yet condemned, you know. And if I were, even the condemned man is allowed his last breakfast—and of his own choice."

"You're not normal."

We ate, but it was all I could do to eat as heartily as I felt, since Femi's mood

---

* "You are a weird being. A weird being."

could not be breached. For once, his famous appetite appeared to have deserted him. "You're ruining my dinner," I complained.

"Look, suppose the judge hands you the full life sentence?"

"Femi," I assured him, "there is nothing like life imprisonment in what I see of my future."

"What makes you so sure?"

"Just take it from me—no lifetime in prison. In fact, no prison stay at all."

"So what are you doing here?"

"Resting. In police detention."

"You can afford to be flippant," he complained.

"That's a good one, coming from you."

For the umpteenth time, he cast his eyes around the prison cell, took in my camp bed, which was folded against the corner, as usual, until it was time for me to turn in. Femi shook his head, as if he were seeing it for the first time.

"You may not get that in prison, you know."

Again, I assured him that I had no intention of rotting away in prison. "It does not matter in the least if the verdict goes against me. I promise you, I am not going to prison."

"You think he'll give you a suspended sentence? You think he can?"

"I have no idea what sentence he's going to pass. He can give me the full life sentence. I'm simply assuring you that I am not going anywhere near the prison."

There seemed no other way to handle his dolefulness. It hung over him like wet smoke, blotting out the sheerest vestige of his normal ebullience. In a way, it was quite comic, since it ill fitted an irrepressible prankster and raconteur who could tell the same story a hundred times to the same audience yet drag a laugh out of them. He drank, and that appeared to give him a little appetite. I tried to fill the space with conversation, but his responses were desultory.

Finally, it was time for him to go. A huge sigh came from somewhere in his bowels and he dragged himself up heavily. I watched him walk to the door and step into the corridor as if he were taking in the air. His purpose, however, was to cast a rapid glance right and left, to ensure that no one was within earshot. He then dashed back into the room and spoke rapidly.

"Look, just listen. I am not a brave man. I am not crazy like you are. I couldn't stand even this condition, being cooped up like this. I would simply break. My driver over there, Mufu, he's different. More like you. And you can't imagine what a fanatic of yours he is. He's ready to do anything for you, you have no idea. So he's all yours. I don't know what your plans are, but I know you're planning something. You're so secretive. Just as well, because I don't want to know. If I don't know anything, then I can't give anything away. I can't imagine torture, I tell you. I'll break before a hand is even laid on me, so it's better for me not to know."

I tried to stem the rush of words. I assured him that I had no sinister plans, but he bore down on me with his intensity and sense of urgency. "You can abandon the car anywhere you want or take it with you wherever. When I leave you, I'll send Mufu to pack up the plates and things, then you can give him any instructions you want. If you want him to park at a spot near the court premises or somewhere else, go and wait somewhere, at the border or wherever, just tell him. I have to make some contribution to what is happening. After all, those who are taking on the government's murder squads, they're human beings too. And they are fighting for us all, same as you. Well, that's all there is to it."

I succeeded in interrupting him at last. "All right, all right. I accept your offer. You're being unduly alarmist, I tell you. But if it will make you happy, send in Mufu. When you've said your good night, send him in."

I lay awake for a long time after his departure, marveling at this man who had said of himself "I am not a brave man," wondering what his definition of bravery might be. I recollected the many hours he had spent with me in my police cell, the arguments we'd had, the many points of agreement, his total passion for the cause that had landed me in a predicament whose gravity I resolutely refused to confront but that oppressed him so heavily. Now it was time to begin to wonder when next we would meet. In the more natural condition of liberty? Or in the formal visiting room of a walled prison? For now, only one thing was certain—I knew that I was going to have a sounder sleep on that eve of judgment than this friend was likely to have.

I COULD SCHOOL MYSELF to appear as indifferent as I wished; the truth was, the trial had not been without tension, even for me. Indeed, there were days of testimonies and cross-examinations when the mood swung from euphoria to despair. The prosecution would secure an unexpected piece of evidence or testimony. A surprise witness had seen me somewhere or the other on the crucial day, when I was supposed to have been elsewhere. Evidence was given that I had attended a university senate meeting on the day in question, and the prosecution—to all appearances—had turned this to its advantage. I had indeed attended the meeting, and deliberately, to establish an alibi. From the corner of my eye, I watched the sympathetic security agents share the crowd's anguish when hostile witnesses took the stand, providing evidence that sounded damning, since they seemed to puncture the alibi on which my lawyers had built part of the defense structure. On such days, one would sense the spectators drooping, while the prosecutor's team adjusted their wigs at a cocky angle that signaled vindication and triumph, cast challenging looks in the direction of the defense team, and departed to the congratulatory smirks of the sprinkling of individuals who came to see the government win its case. And thus it proceeded, roller-coaster fashion, day after day, until the day of the verdict.

All we knew of this judge was that he had remained impervious to numerous attempts by the government to pressure him into delivering a "guilty" verdict. Justice Eso advised such extrajudicial lobbyists for the regime—including the deputy premier*—that their time would be more wisely spent assigning a competent prosecutor to their case. All through the resistance to the regime of the NNDP, the telephone operators—then situated at Oniyanrin, Ibadan—voluntarily tapped into all calls to and from highly placed government and party officials; indeed, all telephone conversations from Government House routinely passed through the ears of one member of the opposition or another. In several of those calls, every effort was made to "bend" Justice Eso, but he would only respond with a calm assurance that yes, he fully intended to uphold the law.

I meant it when I said to Femi that I saw no life imprisonment in my future, but this went beyond our confidence in the integrity of the presiding judge. The political charge throughout the West was such that change, in one form or another, was imminent. The issues that cried for resolution were already beyond the jurisdiction of the courts. Femi was quite right: I was indifferent to the verdict, except insofar as it could be used—if it went against us—in intensifying the insurrection. Looked at in any way, I was confident that I would not remain a prisoner for long. The government was being brought down, and the trial of one "armed robber" was only a small part of the process.

Came judgment day and—what a sense of drama this judge had! As he reviewed the evidence with a granite scowl on his face, most people in court, Femi most agonizingly, had broken out in rashes, were perspiring blood, or else were intoning last-minute intercessionary prayers, expecting the worst. Justice Eso assessed the case for the prosecution at length, upholding most of its arguments, then spent just a fraction of the time in outlining the holes the defense had punched in the prosecution's case, and, suddenly, there it was—Eso upheld the submission of our defense: no prima facie case to answer. The

---

* See Kayode Eso, *The Mystery Gunman*.

prosecution had undone itself. We had secured a verdict through a pure technicality that came from a crucial contradiction within the prosecution's elaborately presented case. The defense strategy had worked, and I had not even been placed on the witness stand.

The court exploded, earning the stern, unsmiling rebuke of Justice Eso. "This court is still in session!" he spat. "Any unseemly conduct, and I shall not hesitate to cite the offender for contempt." His pebbled lenses raked the interior of his domain, daring any contradiction. The spectators fell silent, restraining themselves until the figure of doom had retreated into his chambers and the door was closed behind him. Then the explosion resumed, engulfing even the policemen and the judicial staff—registrar, court orderly, recorder, everyone. These took advantage of their proximity to the dock in which the accused stood and were first to dash over and shake hands. Our squad—Kodak and company—postponed any indulgence in jubilation; they positioned themselves in a different mode, allowed a few moments' intermingling with the crowd, then formed a protective sheath and swept me through.

Mufu, Femi's driver, parked at a distance but deprived, of his own volition, of the moment of victory, had heard the roar, and he was elated—and a little disappointed. He was already primed for the role his employer had fantasized in case of a "guilty" verdict, but now all that was left to do was to sense his adrenaline evaporate. Still, he made the most of the situation: drove his car right at us and screeched to a halt. The next moment I was in, alone, and he took off like the wind, headed toward Lagos in a deliberate feint, slowing down only when he had assured himself that he had shaken off any likely pursuit of supporters or press, then doubling back to the Johnson home, the only place where I wanted to release all hidden tension and ease myself gradually into legalized liberty.

We did not deceive ourselves that it was all over. The government had lost face and would begin, we knew, to seek an extrajudicial solution to the predicament in which it had placed itself. For now, there was only one duty to fulfill, and this was to myself: I *luxuriated* in this welcome home by a man who, even while denying it to himself, had tailored the concept of bravery to a unique definition of his own.

PART II

. . . . .

Ogun, Less Benign

Uncivil Wars: The Third Force and the Midwest Incursion

. . . . .

IT WAS TO BE EXPECTED THAT THE MILITARY COUP D'ÉTAT OF JANUARY 15, 1966—the first in the "stable, moderate, democratic exemplar, the giant of Africa"—would divide the Nigerian nation more sharply than any other event in its six years of full independence. Up till 1914, the British had ruled present-day Nigeria as two distinct protectorates, the North and the South. In the march toward independence, however, the South had been split into two: the East and the West. After independence, the Western government had allowed the Midwestern people their own region, thus turning the South into three regions: East, West, and Midwest. The North, a mostly Muslim region, remained intact, and culturally distinct—quite apart from religion—from the South. It was this North, with its largely feudal and conservative outlook, that had held political power since independence in 1960. The coup changed all of that, effectively pitting the North against the South.

The coup had taken a bloody toll on the North, which had lost several of its senior military officers and political leaders. Ahmadu Bello, the Sardauna of Sokoto and premier of the Northern Region, a public enigma behind the facial seclusion of his Arabian turban, was shot dead in his palace. Some of his wives were also casualties. The first prime minister of the independent nation, Tafawa Balewa, also from the North, was abducted and executed. So was the minister of finance, the flamboyant Chief Festus Okotie-Ebo, albeit from the Midwest. Several of the killings, objectively considered, were not remotely essential to the success of the coup.

In the West, however, the "wild, wild West," where the people had inhaled nothing but flames at close quarters for most of the preceding years, the coup was a hand of salvation, and they did not especially care by what means it was extended or how bloodstained it was. Mostly, there was jubilation to the south—in the East, West, and Midwest—while the North was plunged into mourning and into a deep, visceral distrust and resentment of the South. The Eastern Region earned the greatest loathing from the stricken North, since it soon became noticeable that the leadership of the coup was mostly Igbo, the dominant population of the East. In addition, the Eastern political leadership had been left untouched.

There were a few days of standoff between the rebels and the military command structure, headed by General Johnson T. Aguiyi-Ironsi, himself an Igbo. The rebel leaders—mostly middle-ranking officers—eventually surrendered to his authority, and Aguiyi-Ironsi emerged as Nigeria's first military head of state. Once he felt confidently installed, he imprisoned the leaders but dithered over what to do with them: bring them to trial, simply dismiss them from the army, or—set them free? To many Nigerians, mostly in the South, they were heroes. To the Northerners, they were murderous villains.

Eventually, in May 1966, the North rose up in reprisals, killing several Igbo and other Southern residents in their midst and torching their homes and businesses. The Igbo fled to their homeland in the East but, as the wave of killings subsided, were persuaded to return and resume normal life in their adopted homeland. This uprising did not involve a military coup, however, and General Aguiyi-Ironsi remained in power.

The countercoup of July that same year was the bloodiest yet. Aguiyi-Ironsi was abducted from the state house during an official visit to the Western Region and killed, together with his host, the military governor Lieutenant Colonel Adekunle Fajuyi. Many other Igbo officers also lost their lives, often in a gruesome manner, some of them—suspected participants in the January coup—dragged from prison detention and butchered in the streets.

Fajuyi had been appointed the first military governor of the Western Region following the January coup. I had struck up a rapport with him in his first months in office. Our first meeting was at his request—perhaps he was curious to meet the man who was alleged to have held up a radio station. This encounter led to others. He attended my premiere production of *Kongi's Harvest* in the Arts Theatre of the University of Ibadan and was full of schemes for the development of the region so unexpectedly placed under his charge. It was quite in the character of this officer, whom I came to know so well in such a short time, that when the coup makers broke into his residence to arrest his commander in chief and guest, he refused to hand him over and insisted on accompanying him. For his gallantry, he suffered the same fate as his superior.

They were both taken to a forest outside Ibadan, cruelly tortured, and executed. His end would later wring a poetic tribute out of me.

With the killings more or less over, power reverted to the hands of Northern officers, their Igbo colleagues having been thoroughly routed and decimated. This was when the name of an officer named Murtala Mohammed first came into Nigerian lore; he was widely rumored to have masterminded the countercoup and was expected to take power. However, a young officer from a minority Christian group in the North, Yakubu Gowon, ended up as Nigeria's new head of state.

And there, with the shift of power, the nation hoped that the bloodletting would cease—but no. A progressive pogrom of the Igbo erupted in October the same year, a hunt for Easterners of all ages who were unfortunate enough to have heeded the call of the new regime to return to their places of work and residence in the North, reassured that all was well. They were gruesomely mistaken. Not merely from the North but from every corner of the nation, the Igbo fled homeward, wheeled contraptions of every kind bearing their dismal remains and possessions into Igboland. The trainloads of refugees from the North bore pitiable cargoes: some survivors with physical mutilations, some women in such a state of shock that they clung to the severed heads of their spouses or sons, cradling them on their laps. Even within Lagos, the hunt for the Igbo continued unabated, in their homes and at roadblocks. The depletion of my wife's wardrobe during the months of October and November was only one of many private testimonies to the desperation of one's Igbo male acquaintances—not all of them soldiers—who resorted to female disguise to escape detection as they fled eastward. Images of death and mutilation in Eastern journals and the television coverage of a savaged humanity erased the final sense of belonging in a people who saw themselves isolated within the nation and catalyzed their resolve to secede.

The discovery of oil in huge reserves in the East, largely in the Niger estuary, played a role, unquestionably, in the propulsion of the Biafran leaders toward secession, but it would be a distortion of history and an attempt to trivialize the trauma that the Igbo had undergone to suggest—as some commentators have tried to do—that it was the lure of the oil wealth that drove them to seek a separate existence. When a people have been subjected to a degree of inhuman violation for which there is no other word but genocide, they have the right to seek an identity apart from their aggressors'.

I was not alone in writing embittered articles on the massacres, especially denouncing the lackadaisical attitude of Gowon's government toward the killings. We accused the government of condoning genocide and urged our own people in the West to distance themselves from any act that might suggest approval of such insensate slaughter. In addition, however, the suspicion developed of a Northern-dominated agenda, this time through the agency of the military.

It was a period of great tension and mutual suspicion. Violence hung in the air, threatening to break out at any provocation and consume the nation. The various forces in the West that had resisted the NNDP reign of repression regrouped and resumed their meetings, watchful and suspicious of the new military government. When Gowon summoned a meeting of "Leaders of Thought"—selected prominent citizens in various fields—to Lagos to decide the future of the nation, we worked on the sidelines, contributing to the position of the West through my friend Bola Ige, a stalwart of the Action Group and close lieutenant of that party's leader, Obafemi Awolowo. Awolowo was, of course, regarded as a hero and the political voice of the West, and his release from prison, shortly after Yakubu Gowon was installed in power, was easily one of the shrewdest political moves of the new regime.

Most of these meetings took place in Femi's house, then at Onireke, Ibadan. They were fertile exploratory ground for Bola Ige, the only party politician of the brainstorming group and a member of the Western Region's delegation to the Leaders of Thought assemblage. Little did this colleague dream—or perhaps he did already?—that he would one day become an elected governor of the same region, after it became known as Oyo state. For now, he was only a junior member of the Leaders of Thought—whose meetings, we would later find out, were closely monitored by the British High Commission.

I would occasionally accompany him, but only to those preliminary, informal meetings, where the various regional groups tested one another's positions and traded tactical moves. It all took place in an atmosphere of indescribable tension. Delegations stayed in fortified apartments, went about under the protection of armed police and army squads. Lieutenant Colonel Chukwuemeka Odumegwu Ojukwu, the military governor of the Eastern Region, used the alibi of this insecure environment to stay put in Enugu and refuse to participate in any of the meetings, even symbolically, by sending observers. It was a ploy—Ojukwu was already making plans to secede—but I had personal cause to agree with his dismissal of any notion of a secure environment.

ONCE BOLA IGE nearly got us both killed in the sedate residential part of Ikoyi, where we had gone to consult with the leader of the Tiv delegation, J. S. Tarka.

The Tiv are a people who live within what is known as the Middle Belt of Nigeria—hence the name of their political movement, the United Middle Belt Congress. Politically merged with the Northern Region, they chafed under domination by its ruling oligarchy and commenced armed resistance long before the nation's full independence, continuing, albeit underreported, even for some years afterward. In later years, one of the officers who commanded the pacifying forces of the Tiv uprising publicly lamented his contribution to their subjugation.

Tarka, a figure of unquestioned charisma, led the Middle Belt Congress, a traditional ally of the Action Group of the West. Tarka and I were not close, but we seemed to respond to each other through some hidden waves. On the way to my assignation with the radio station in 1965, I had made a brief stop at Bola Ige's house to let Bola know that I might be away for a while, although I did not tell him why. It was there that J. S. Tarka and I met for the first time. I was instantly drawn to this man of very gentle bearing, sensing that behind a face that smiled so readily were a cast-iron will and a radar mind that constantly scanned his environment and its occupants. We spoke briefly in the living room while I waited for Bola to emerge.

Suddenly Tarka's demeanor changed; it was quite sudden and startling. He looked at me very strangely, broke off in midsentence, and did what, to me, was even stranger. He thrust his hand into his pocket and brought out a slim wad of currency notes, which he offered to me. I looked at him, questioning, but he insisted that I take the money. I was naturally taken aback but finally accepted a pound note. It was a spontaneous gesture, lacking any explanation, except that he seemed to obey an inner impulse. We had only spoken briefly of the political situation; nothing in our exchanges had suggested my being in need of money or on the verge of plunging into some dangerous straits. But he had looked at me as if he knew that he was supposed to help me in some way, was not sure what form the help should take, and could think only of the money in his pocket. Now, a year and a half later, I looked forward to seeing him again, smiling to myself at the thought of what his reaction would be when I solemnly handed back his pound note. I had no thought that I would nearly get killed before I settled my unsought indebtedness.

Bola was at the wheel. At the end of a long driveway into the block of Lagos apartments where Tarka was staying, off Glover Road in Ikoyi, soldiers suddenly emerged from behind the shrubbery. One of them barked out some orders, gesticulating in a manner that was open to myriad interpretations. Bola thought that he was being ordered to go back. Ramming the car into reverse, he began to tear off at full speed. His neck twisted around to maneuver through the driveway, he failed to see the rage-distorted face of the foremost soldier, but I saw him. He slipped off the safety catch of his gun and leveled it at the car, screaming and swearing at us to stop or else! I did not understand the words, but the language of all his body parts was most eloquent! The more the soldier screamed, the faster Bola drove, and my transmission of what I understood as the soldier's wishes appeared to confuse Bola even more. All this took place in seconds, but it was sufficient to instruct me in the often-understated measure of eternity. In desperation I hit Bola on the chest, screaming at him to stop, and this finally gained his attention. He stepped on the brakes, perhaps just in time. The soldier caught up with us, his body convulsed with violence, coiled up for a release that could be obtained only by pulling his trigger. Then Bola remembered that he spoke fluent Hausa and plunged into a torrent of explanation in that language. It calmed the man somewhat, and only then was Bola able to state our business. It was a very relieved Tarka who opened the door to us, having watched the scene, horrified, from the balcony of his third-floor apartment.

Such scenes were being enacted all over Lagos—indeed, all over the country—many of them ending tragically. The cheapest recruit held the power of life and death, not merely through accidents or misunderstandings, as in our case, but through cold-blooded executions carried out with the confidence of impunity. The nation teetered on the edge of disintegration. I continued to write in the media, debate in private. At campus encounters, open-air bars, and other informal gatherings, at which the secret service made no pretense of disguising its presence, we railed at the government's lukewarm concern for the plight of the Igbo. The meetings of the Leaders of Thought continued, but it was clear that any national gathering was incomplete without Igbo participation.

Within my own caucus, our suspicions of Gowon's ultimate goal also continued to deepen. The underlying agenda had begun to emerge, the signals had become more overt: the military was digging in and would remain in power indefinitely. It was being encouraged to do so by the North, but also by a handful of Western politicians—the remnants of the NNDP faction who had now lost out in the politics of the West, and even groupings of Western professionals and intellectuals, such as the Committee of Ten, who for reasons of their own began to work for Yakubu Gowon's continued stay in office. The British government, acting through its high commissioner, had long since committed itself to a military-dominated agenda, as long as it was led from the North.

After the first military coup, on January 15, 1966, the North had raised the shout of *araba*—"secession." Indeed, at the first Leaders of Thought meeting in Lagos, the Northern delegation's position paper was based on its right to secede from the nation. However, the North was now beginning to lose its secessionist craving. The halfway house of a loose federation, or confederation, was also nixed—governance was to remain under centralized control. Actively prodded by the British government, the North gradually abandoned its secessionist agenda. "You have the whole cake in your hands," the high commissioner admonished Gowon. "Why do you wish to settle for half?"

It did not take long for me to regain my place on the security list. Our friends within intelligence soon let me know that I had been classified as hostile to the government, someone to be closely monitored. Nothing of this, however, deterred Femi Johnson from remaining openly identified with me. That his brother, a staunch military loyalist, had been retained by the new regime as military administrator of Lagos—Lagos was not yet a full state, so it did not merit a governor—meant little to him. Femi was uninterested in ideologies, but we shared a common political principle: justice as the basis of society. The Igbo, he felt, had been cruelly and unjustly treated.

The prospect of war between the East and the federation loomed larger every day. A last-minute effort to avert it took place in Aburi, Ghana. Since the Igbo leadership remained adamant in its refusal to participate in any meetings outside its Eastern enclave, persisting in its plaint of a lack of security for its people, the avuncular military dictator of Ghana, Lieutenant General Joseph Arthur Ankrah—military dictatorship was now in vogue everywhere!—stepped in and offered the disputants the facilities of his famous retreat at Aburi.

They met over several days in this soothing arena, away from the volatile atmosphere of Nigerian coups, countercoups, and massacres, away from the intrigues and self-serving counsels of still-active colonial powers and other behind-the-scenes interests, especially of the business world. In Aburi, those who were enemies within Nigeria embraced, saluted, and held dialogue in a reportedly constructive and pragmatic manner without. They exchanged notes on resources, boundaries, military rankings, and pecking order; they even yielded up the locations of missing bodies—the hasty burial grounds of assassinated national leaders, military officers, and other casualties of the various coups, including former heads of state. When their reinterments took place some weeks later, many in the nation clung to the belief that the remains were not truly those of the victims, that a symbolic farce, with a laudable goal—reconciliation—had been staged. All parties agreed to a solemn undertaking not to resort to violence in the resolution of yet-outstanding disputes. It was an undertaking as empty of substance as some of the caskets that were solemnly interred after Aburi.

THERE WAS A MARKED difference of approach for the Aburi encounter, one that already signaled the certain repudiation of whatever agreements were made. The federal side, led by Yakubu Gowon, attended the meeting with an open book, a laissez-faire state of mind. By contrast, Odumegwu Ojukwu, still governor of the Eastern Region and de facto leader of the Igbo, had arrived meticulously prepared. Not surprisingly, he largely had his way. The protocols and agreements were signed to fanfare and popping champagne corks, and everyone returned home with the map of the nation superficially intact but visibly shredded.

On his return, Yakubu Gowon was assailed by his people for having given away far too much to the Igbo, who continued to press for the implementation of all agreements to the letter, screaming bad faith at any seeming delay. By now, the victims of both the January and July coups had received their ceremonial burials. That ritual appeared to douse political passions for a while, but it was clear that this was only the lull before the storm. Soon enough, Nigeria experienced its first aerial hijacking as a federally owned plane was seized in flight between Lagos and Benin and piloted to Enugu, capital of the Eastern Region. Gowon retaliated by freezing a number of assets that belonged to the rebellious region. A Nigerian Navy vessel went the way of the purloined plane—a mere sharing of joint assets, the Easterners crowed. The drums of secession were beating loud and clear. A mass exodus of Easterners began from all parts of the nation. Once again the roads were clogged with laden vehicles, but this time in all directions; the regional leader, Odumegwu Ojukwu, had announced that he could no longer guarantee the safety of non-Easterners in the region under his control. Some weeks later, he formally ordered all "foreigners" to leave.

It was obvious: the secession of the East was only weeks away. Yakubu Gowon had terminated the meetings of the civilian "Leaders of Thought" and told the bigwigs to remain in their constituencies until further notice—which would never arrive. All talk of a return to democratic rule, on which the Leaders of Thought had spent so much time in sterile debate, was formally abrogated. The military was now free to act as it pleased, without any pandering to the civilian constituency. With every act and public pronouncement, the breach between the federal government and the East widened. A delegation of public figures—politicians, crowned heads, prelates, and others—made a last-ditch effort to head off what now appeared inevitable: declaration of independence by the Eastern Region. They were courteously received by the leadership but returned empty-handed. The position of Yakubu Gowon's federal government hardened.

Consolidation of military power would be inescapable once war was declared. In the thinking of many of us, a military dictatorship with no foreseeable end appeared to be the worst of all possible evils, including even the "evil" of secession. The West, untainted by any coup initiative and blameless of any genocidal participation, still held the few potential checks on the slide toward the precipice of war, but that potential was fast diminishing.

With the dissolution of the Leaders of Thought, Bola Ige now spent even more time with our ad hoc group. This was an eerie period when nothing seemed to be happening; the heart of the nation appeared to have stopped beating, while its body remained suspended in a void. In grim reality, however, the military leadership was extremely busy, vetting names for a civilian-military cabinet and consulting with the nation's former colonial master, the British High Commission. It was during this seeming suspension of reality and intense speculation that we decided that the state of mind of Obafemi Awolowo had to be ascertained, and urgently. As I was an "outsider"—that is, not a member of any official group—that task was given to me. Bola set up the appointment with the leader of the former Action Group, now bestowed with the superfluous and unenviable title "Leader of the Yoruba" by the governor of the Western Region, Colonel Adeyinka Adebayo.

The question on our minds was straightforward: How would Awolowo respond to the looming offer of a position in Yakubu Gowon's government? It was clear that if Awolowo became a part of that government, the last restraints on its policy toward the East would be removed, with the predictable consequence of a civil war. There was, however, a subsidiary question, one that arose from the first—we were deeply apprehensive for his safety, perhaps no one more deeply than I. Had a swaggering officer, a major and of the same Yoruba stock, not boasted to my face that he would personally take Awolowo to the nearest crossroads, tie him to a stake, and shoot him as an example because "we know what he's up to, he has not yet given up his tribal games"? The officer's definition of Awolowo's "tribal games" was so simplistic it was frightening, being none other than the Old Man's reported reluctance to serve under Gowon's government if it was bent on war and his insistence that the West of the Yoruba should not become a war zone if that prospect did materialize.

That Major B.M. should have spoken to me in such a manner was in itself revealing—he could not conceive, even for a moment, that, as a "social critic," and one with supposedly progressive credentials, I could be anything but the loudest voice in the unreflective chorus of "One Nigeria!" The two concepts—progressive politics and national unity—were so thoroughly conflated in his mind that to be progressive or radical was to reject the possibility of perceiving any flaws in the very basis of national being or question the structural arrangements that held the nation together, however precariously. The same officer, like many others, has since repudiated such mindless adherence to the unqualified mantra "*One* nation, right or wrong." At the time, however, he was totally ensnared in such rhetoric and blissfully indifferent to whatever political ideology such a "unified entity" espoused.

Awolowo received me in his office, which was dominated by a massive desk. It seemed even more substantial than it had two years before, when I had slept under it, keeping vigil with others over the radio transmitter as we anticipated an attack by the police and prepared to repulse it. I could not resist a sneak caress of the desk, like a long-missed comrade, then succumbed to the temptation of regaling the Old Man with an account of the episode.

Awolowo's eyes lit up with childlike mischief, eager for details. At the mention of Mazi Ukonu, the leader of the broadcasting team and a well-known radio comedian, he burst out excitedly, "Ukonu? In this study? You mean, in my study? And you under this desk? This very desk? Both of you in here? The election broadcasts were transmitted from here? And by Ukonu himself? I used to listen to his shows over the radio in Calabar [prison]. He has a great sense of humor!"

I satisfied his curiosity for all the juicy details, then we settled down to business. I restrained myself from telling him that I knew that the letter from General Gowon inviting him to serve was already in his possession, that in fact I knew its contents. It was a secret I felt bound to respect—I had kept it even from Bola Ige, a close lieutenant of Awolowo but not a member of CWIL. On the way to the Old Man's home in Ikenne, the courier, a highly placed police officer, had stopped to see his lawyer friend from Abeokuta whose chambers were in mainland Yaba, Lagos. Together, they had opened the letter—yes, the old-fashioned way, steamed it open—read, and copied it. The lawyer, S.S.—a member of the volunteer Committee of Ten that had been formed to drum up support for Gowon's regime and who had fanatically assigned himself the mission of my own conversion—revealed the contents to me shortly afterward, perhaps in an endeavor to make me believe in Gowon's goodwill toward the

"Leader of the Yoruba." Many years, coups, and revelations would pass before the same lawyer found himself renouncing every act that he had done to win support for the regime, advocating nothing less than a separate, independent existence for his own Yoruba portion of the nation. His mantra, which no one could have believed possible in those nationalist 1960s, had become *"K'oluka-luku ma lo n'ti e."**

As I sat across the famous desk in Awolowo's study, however, my mind was not on my "elder brother" from my hometown but very much on the encounter with the young major who had threatened summary execution for the politician—among several other ominous signs. I asked Awolowo, "Sir, I think you'll agree that Gowon is bound to offer you a cabinet position. Suppose you decide to decline the offer; you realize that your life may be in danger?"

Awolowo looked at me, paused thoughtfully, and nodded. "Yes, I suppose I could find myself in that situation."

My next statement to him was made with great hesitation, since I could not be certain that he would not begin to have doubts about my sanity. "If you decide to refuse," I stammered, "have you thought of going underground? I'm sorry, sir, I know that after such a long spell in prison, it is a hard prospect to even consider, asking you to resign yourself to another kind of prison, but I still have to ask it."

Awolowo sat bolt upright at this, then relaxed, again thoughtfully. "Well, I have never thought of that. But I've always insisted to myself that my first duty is to the Yoruba nation. We are a nation, you know. And I put that nation first, then the one called Nigeria. If the moment comes when I firmly believe that it is in our interest for me to disappear, of course I will not hesitate. But, you young radical people! What could have moved your mind in such an extreme direction?"

I shrugged. As I sat facing him, I became painfully conscious of his personal history, the travails of this Job of a politician who had been deprived of the merited electoral leadership of the nation, spent several years in jail for alleged treason, lost his firstborn, Segun, a promising young mind, in a motor accident even as he measured out his days in prison. I wondered if it was even right of me to have suggested such a possible course of action to a man with such a history, but it was too late to back out.

"We like to look at the so-called worst-case scenarios," I explained. "If you stay out of Gowon's government, you will hold a very strong card. For a start,

* "Let everyone go his own way."

the war—if it comes to that—will lose much of its moral backing and inter-national support. You wear the hat of leader of the Yoruba people—that's nearly one-third of the national population. It's a powerful card. To take that card away from you, there are desperate soldiers who will stop at nothing. Sir, if you are killed, I leave you to imagine the consequences. I merely want you to know that we have the means of making you totally inaccessible for weeks, months, and even of smuggling you out of the country."

I was conscious of exaggerating our underground facilities, but what I claimed was not very far from the truth. Since the abrupt end to the Leaders of Thought conferences that had been designed to establish the basis for continued demo-cratic coexistence, we had begun to prepare for every kind of eventuality.

Out of the blue, Awolowo said to me, "One thing I have made up my mind about—I have not led the Yoruba people so far as to have our land turned into a battleground."

I had no idea where his thoughts had taken him, but he continued to speak in that vein for some moments, as if his mind were elsewhere, pondering some decision. Then he leaned back in his chair, fixed his gaze on me through his wire-rimmed "grandpa" lenses that had become, like his cap, his distinctive public symbol. Speaking almost softly, wistfully, he revealed the little-known story of his nocturnal encounter with Ojukwu, the Eastern leader, just a week before.

The 1967 eve-of-secession delegation of national public figures, autho-rized by Yakubu Gowon to engage in dialogue with the Eastern leadership, had been led by Obafemi Awolowo, and the formal, well-publicized meeting be-tween the two sides had lasted nearly all day. The Easterners had listed their grievances and demands, spoken with all apparent seriousness, and seen their guests off to their chalets. Late that same night, however, Awolowo was dis-turbed by a knock on the door.

It was Ojukwu himself. He admitted that he had waited till late into the night so as to be able to speak to Awolowo in strictest privacy. Sure, said Awolowo, but he also insisted that at least one or two persons join him. That was agreed, and Awolowo called the adjoining chalet and woke up the police commissioner for the Western Region, Olufunwa, and a close political aide.

Accompanying Ojukwu was a small team that included a professor of his-tory from the University of Ibadan who, like other Easterners, had fled to their beleaguered state. Years afterward, in 1996, during the struggle against the Abacha dictatorship, the same don introduced himself to me at a meeting in the United States and revealed his participation in the nocturnal meeting of thirty years earlier. His account was a consistent and detailed confirmation of what Awolowo confided in me that afternoon.

Odumegwu Ojukwu's mission was unambiguous, Awolowo told me. "The young man had come to inform me that the East had decided on secession and that there was no going back. All that was left was the announcement of a date. He said, 'Sir, I have come not to argue but to inform you. It has been decided.'

"It was clear that any discussion was futile," Awolowo continued. "After all, we had done nothing but talk all day. Ojukwu confessed that he had agreed to meet the delegation at all only out of respect for my person. Biafra had already made a decision.

"I was not surprised," the chief admitted. "I did one thing, though. I made one request of him—in fact, I insisted on it. I said to Ojukwu, 'At least let us in the West—me, specifically—have a minimum of two weeks' notice before you announce the decision.' And he promised. Yes, he promised me that much."

I hesitated but could not resist asking. "Why two weeks? You told him you needed two weeks—to do what?"

Awolowo gave one of his enigmatic smiles. "You know Olufunwa, the police commissioner?"

I nodded yes.

"Well, apart from me, he is the only one who knows the answer to that question. And he's not likely to tell you, either."

I did not press him.

Hardly had Awolowo's delegation settled back into federal territory than Ojukwu declared an Independent State of Biafra. The date was May 30, 1967. A short while after, Chief Awolowo agreed to serve as minister of finance under Yakubu Gowon.

The federal government had, however, made a preemptive move. On May 27, Gowon had abolished all four regions and split the nation into twelve new states. This achieved the goal of dangling before the entities that were newly carved out from the East the attraction of their own autonomous governance, with all the resources of the oil-soaked Niger Delta. Between the two strokes, loyalties in the former Eastern Region were split. War appeared inevitable.

AS THE RUMBLE of the drums of war became truly deafening, I found myself in Stockholm. That outing was for the first conference of African and Scandinavian writers in the serene setting of Hasselby Slott, initiated by Swedish PEN. It was bliss to get away from the newly overheated nation space of Nigeria and interact with others of one's professionally acquired tribe. It was on that occasion that we met, most of us for the first time, Per Wästberg, the Swedish novelist who was actively involved with African liberation movements in Mozambique, Angola, South Africa, and so on, though we did not suspect it at the time. Per was a close associate of several of Africa's liberation warriors, especially Eduardo Modliane of Mozambique—even today he remains one of the most consistent rescue stations for beleaguered African writers and dissidents. On a personal note, it was Per who introduced my work to Swedish readers.

Within Nigeria, our writers-and-artists clan had been scattered by the coups and countercoups, massacres and consequent insecurity, and now it was flung to the four winds by the secessionist movement. Chinua Achebe, Christopher Okigbo (the poet of *Heavensgate* and *Labyrinths,* and a volunteer from the Western imbroglio), Cyprian Ekwensi, Gabriel Okara, and others were holed up in the breakaway state. J. P. Clark, Mabel Segun, Amos Tutuola, and others—all founders and animators of the Mbari Creative Arts movement of Ibadan—were stuck on the federal side. It had never been much of a close family; we all tended to do our work independently, meeting occasionally, mostly for planning creative workshops, exhibitions, readings, and other special events. However, the poet and playwright J. P. Clark and I had been quite close to Christopher Okigbo—all three of us having been based in Ibadan in the early 1960s—and now I experienced something close to the sadness of a family breakup. I had hoped that Chinua, Christopher, and others would come to Stockholm. In that tranquil atmosphere, we could attempt to form, across the belligerent regions, a common front against the looming war. I was against the secession, but only for practical considerations: I doubted Biafra's ability to survive the inevitable onslaught from the federal side. Not for one moment did I consider the secessionist movement itself an act of moral or political felony—it was simply politically and militarily unwise.

No one turned up from the Biafran side. If someone had, I never would have needed to embark on my fateful mission to Biafra. Far more likely, I would have taken up the invitation of an attractive young lady whom I met in Stockholm, an air hostess, to go hunting reindeer with her father, then traveled to Greece for that nation's autumn wine festival, a cultural indulgence of many dimensions that I had promised myself ever since I had first recognized in the Greek deity Dionysus a long-lost sibling of my personal demiurge, Ogun.

Ogun had other plans for me, however. War was declared—no, not in such terms; at the beginning it was simply a "police action." Very few people in the nation were fooled.

. . .

AFTER STOCKHOLM, FRUSTRATED BY the absence of our Biafran colleagues, I traveled to London, this time to carry out a series of recorded "conversations" at the Transcription Centre for African Arts and Culture, a center of activity—and respite—for a relay of African writers and artists. It was run by the art historian, critic, and broadcaster Dennis Duerden. The center was funded mainly by an American foundation, the Farfield, that was later proven to be affiliated with the CIA, though none of us knew it then. Dennis, a loose-limbed Englishman with a shock of hair who somehow, even in a new suit, succeeded in looking permanently rumpled, enjoyed the unpredictable assistance of one of my associates at the time, Aminu Abdullahi.

Urbane and seemingly unflappable, Abdullahi, a stocky Hausa with a conspicuous single cicatrix on the side of his head, was easily the most passionate and knowledgeable African lover of modern jazz that I ever knew. He could tell an improvised riff by Dizzy Gillespie from one by Miles Davis after only a few notes, and his collection of LPs—long-playing records, now dinosaurs—overflowed his guest room in Dennis Duerden's home into the passageway. It would be much, much later before I would discover that Aminu was the cousin of M. D. Yusuf, then head of Nigeria's secret service, the "E" branch, and even worked for him—if not at the time, then certainly later. That did not diminish the genuineness of his concern about Nigeria's lurch toward all-out war.

A few sleepless nights spent brainstorming in Dennis Duerden's apartment resulted in a decision: someone would have to go to the East and have a talk with Ojukwu, head of the secessionist state, and meet with Chinua Achebe and other leading writers and intellectuals in Biafra. What was required, we concluded, was a revocation of the declaration of secession and the calling off of all hostilities. Then, using our international connections to invoke the aid of neutral countries such as Sweden, with her sound credentials of assistance to African liberation, we would facilitate a return to the conference table. Aminu declared himself ready to make the journey, but there was an insurmountable obstacle: he was not only a Northerner, he looked it, and his accent was a straightforward giveaway. It was difficult enough for even a Southerner, a non-Biafran, to enter the now-xenophobic entity called Biafra. A Northerner who entered that breakaway enclave was unlikely to survive his first step. I volunteered to go in his place.

. . .

FINALLY I COULD RETURN to Nigeria unburdened by a sense of impotence. The very night of my reentry, I was ensconced at my favorite place for both innocent and dubious undertakings: Femi Johnson's house. I gathered my usual group together and outlined what I had brought back, quite fortuitously, from London. The discussion was not complicated—every voice stressed the need to find language that would convince Ojukwu that the Igbo were not abandoned. That sense of rejection, of isolation, was what stood in the way of any form of rapprochement between the federal government and the breakaway Biafra. It went beyond politics, moved beyond the implacable Biafran hostility toward Yakubu Gowon's government. The orbit of guilt, as assigned by Biafra, had now expanded to include the Yoruba West, whose people, the Biafrans felt, had betrayed them. Such a Biafran position was rationally untenable. One had only to recall the coups and countercoups that had resulted in a West that was thoroughly invested by the military, mostly of Northern and Middle Belt origin, thus leaving the West bereft of any military clout or bargaining power. The perception of the West's indifference, or leaning toward the federal cause, had taken root, however, and it was not subject to reasoning.

There and then, in Femi Johnson's house—and all other accounts of this origination can be authoritatively disregarded*—was coined the expression that would later feature in many commentaries, achieving its maximum notoriety in the military incursion of Biafran-led forces into the Midwest Region: "the Third Force." In the confrontation between the federal side and the Biafran, a third force, opposed to the civil war and prepared to mobilize against it, had become a necessity. If Nigeria was the thesis and Biafra the antithesis, then the Third Force resulted from the synthesis—all impeccable dialectics, lacking only an organized movement and the necessary force to back it up!

When, after Femi returned from his insurance brokerage office and settled down to dinner, I told him I was going to Biafra, he lost his appetite in midmorsel. "Madness, madness, nothing but madness! You'll get shot for nothing." Crossing the firing lines meant, for Femi, crossing the boundaries of sanity. It was not much of an argument, as I had already made my decision. In the end he offered a well-reasoned bit of advice: I should at least speak with someone from the federal side before venturing across.

---

* These include my own in *The Man Died*, where a number of individuals still needed to be protected.

. . .

REVEREND FATHER MARTINS was the chaplain for the federal army, a blunt-speaking soldier, compact in build and rock-solid. He had the reputation of not permitting his priestly duties to interfere with his lover's ardor. Once, a totally reliable source informed me, his fellow prelates had gone to remonstrate with him over an affair that, they warned, was causing embarrassment for the church. They picked an unfortunate moment when Father Martins was ministering to the young parishioner in question, and they entered without knocking—or perhaps Father Martins had simply not heard them. Finally becoming aware of their presence, Martins snatched his priestly garb from the floor, flung it over the heads of the intruders, and, while they were still entangled in the robes, pummeled the muffled mass, kicked it down the stairs, and went back to his interrupted offices.

This was the soldiering prelate whom we decided upon as a logical intermediary with the federal government for my visit to Biafra. We met again thirty-five years after the civil war, at a social reception, when the reverend father was eighty. I thought of asking him what the truth was about the story that we had all enjoyed for upward of thirty years. Fortunately, I first made the mistake of offering him my seat when he came around to say hello. He sat me down with such indignant force, truly unbelievable even in a sixty-year-old, that I decided that it would be wiser to let him take his secrets to the grave.

As expected, Father Martins was delighted to learn that not everyone had given up and gave his blessing to the effort at a last-minute appeal to Ojukwu. He promised to speak to General Gowon, brought out his best noncommunion brandy, poured us both generous shots, and wished me luck.

Even so, it was with great reluctance that Femi reconciled himself to my going. The very thought of guns going off was something to which he was allergic; little did he imagine that, as the war endured, he himself would visit some of the towns liberated by the federal troops, drawn by the demands and opportunities of his insurance profession and sometimes within earshot of bombardments across the firing lines. In 1967, a battlefront still signaled for him the nearest that any mortal could conceive of the promised end of the world—a point over which not many people would disagree.

I set out from his house with the doleful face of a normally ebullient friend staring at me across the table. He was especially troubled by the latest rumors, that attempts by the federal troops to infiltrate Biafra had moved the skirmishing to Auchi, a border town in the Midwest state, next to my destination. The Midwest, separated from the seceded state by the Niger River, served as a buffer state between breakaway Biafra and our Western Region. Nothing would dispel Femi's forebodings until I returned a week later, in one piece, but in far greater danger than I had ever been while close to the firing lines.

THE IGBO ARE the predominant ethnic group in the region that became Biafra, but they also shared the Midwest state with other ethnic groups, such as the Itshekiri, Urhobo, Ijaw, and others. This link across the Niger made it logical that the Midwesterners remain neutral, not be forced to take arms against their kin in Biafra. I spent the night in Asaba, the riverside border town of the Midwest and an Igbo stronghold, as guest of Professor Edozien, once master of Tedder Hall at the University of Ibadan. We spoke late into the night, a discussion that brought in his friends and neighbors, eager to learn the news from Lagos and the West. The atmosphere in that Igbo town was predictably one of apprehension. This anxiety, so evident in my host and his companions, did make me feel that perhaps, after all, I had not embarked on a pointless journey. That sense of futility had begun to gnaw into my setting-out confidence as I drove farther and farther from the comparative stability of Ibadan and deeper into that territory of tensions.

Although Biafra was supposed to be under a blockade and the Asaba bridge—the link across the southward-flowing Niger River—was blocked on both the Midwest and secessionist sides, traffic, both human and of goods, flowed both ways through bush tracks to the riverbanks, both north and south of the Asaba bridge. From Asaba, paddle canoes ferried virtually every commodity to the town of Onitsha on the Biafran side and returned just as heavily laden. These tracks were patrolled by federal soldiers based in Asaba, ostensibly to enforce the blockade. I ran into the patrols from time to time and was stopped only once, and that when a soldier wished to be absolutely certain that his eyes did not deceive him, marveling at what W.S. could be doing in the bush so far from Ibadan or Lagos.

Onitsha, a market town on Biafran soil, can be described as the twin city to Asaba, situated directly across the Niger River from the latter. From the moment of my disembarkation from the canoe, it was clear that secession was not just a word to the Igbo but a total alteration of existence, even down to a collective psychology. Any stranger was spotted immediately and either followed, reported, or accosted. In the end he would be arrested and interrogated. Crossing the effervescent market in Onitsha to find a taxi park, I was often recognized and stopped for news. However, the inevitable confrontation was only a matter of time. It included some mild roughing up by young Biafran vigilantes who were on constant and often manic prowl for "sabos"—saboteurs, but a word interpreted to mean "all strangers." I was arrested—at the point of wooden guns, aimed at me in all earnestness!—but generally well treated, especially once I was handed over to the local uniformed officer, who found me a seat in his office. I had taken the precaution of bringing my passport with me, to make everyone understand that I accepted that I was visiting a sovereign territory. Transferred for interrogation to Enugu, now elevated from a regional to a national capital, I was routinely locked up in a police cell and treated as a regular suspect—all possessions confiscated, belt, shoes, and underpants taken away. Then the senior police officer in charge returned and ordered that the latest batch of sabos be brought before him. The moment I appeared, he underwent a moment of utter disbelief, then leaped out of his chair and released me, with a torrent of abuse for his subordinates.

It was while I was waiting for my transfer to a hotel that Christopher Okigbo drove in, kitted for war—in casual civilian clothing, but complete with rifle and ammunition belt. He screeched to a halt in front of the station. He was coming from the front, the excitation of battle still fresh in his eyes. For one brief, nostalgic moment, I believe I envied this friend and colleague who would rather be a poet but had thrown himself fully into a self-defining cause. But he was alone, not within a column of the writers and artists brigade of our student dreams, heading south to demolish the apartheid kingdom. Was there really much difference? How is one craving for liberation to be faulted but not the other?

Christopher had come for promised reinforcements, of both men and weapons. The police commissioner let him into the office, having first made me hide behind the door. When the door was shut and I stood revealed, Christopher let out a screech that brought everyone out of their offices. He broke into a mad jig in front of the astonished officers and wanted to drag me off to wherever. Finally, he had to content himself with accepting that the head of his new state exercised priority over my presence in Biafra. We promised to meet later in the evening, when I would have fulfilled my immediate mission. I watched him load some guns and ammunition into his car, waved to him as he drove off in a small cloud of dust. That was the last time I would see my excitable friend and poet Christopher Okigbo alive. He perished on the Okigwi front, we later learned, with that chant from the Spanish Civil War issuing from his throat: *"¡No pasarán!"** One person, at least, had given his life to the dreams of youth, but how sad that it should have been on a fratricidal field.

THE HOTEL PRESIDENTIAL, where I was lodged as a guest of the government, said it all. Sanctions and a blockade to enforce them had taken their toll, and this once-splendid lodging with a commanding view of the city had nothing left that was remotely presidential—except perhaps the size of its rats! Since I was the sole occupant of that vast, derelict space, perhaps they looked to me for company and even sustenance. They accompanied me everywhere—from the dining room to my bedroom suite, with its discolored ceiling—and formed guards of honor along the corridors of moldy carpets and peeling paint. If I sought a pessimistic portent for the future of Biafra, the Presidential offered itself most assertively. I tried my best to dismiss this pessimistic image, however, eyeballing the rats while I awaited my summons to the leader of the secessionist state.

We met the following morning in an ornate office, a kind of converted hall, its spaciousness a marked contrast to the cluttered office of his predecessor in office, Dr. Michael Okpara, who had shielded me in that city after the radio holdup. The irony was striking: on that visit, I had discussed the logistics of popular insurrection with the civil leader; now I was cast in the role of a mediator between professionals at war making, a role to which I felt distinctly ill fitted. Preaching pacifism, even of a limited, tactical kind, in the midst of evident wrongs has always struck me as a task specially designed to separate saints from mere mortals, and I have never succeeded in finding my proper size in haloes. It became possible to actually exercise conviction in the mission only when I reminded myself that I had really come to call for restraint, even temporary, while accompanying moves were made to reassure the Biafrans of the recognition of their just cause.

Meeting Ojukwu face-to-face, I tried unsuccessfully to remind myself that I was now facing His Excellency Lieutenant Colonel Odumegwu Ojukwu, head of an independent state, not the young "Emeka" whom I had known in Yaba, Lagos, in the early fifties. Then I had been laying siege to the heart of the younger sister of his own object of attention, envying the jazzy sports car that brought him to his trysts while I pedaled to battle on my bicycle. He was heavily bearded and already balding from the forehead, self-conscious of his new sta-

* "They shall not pass!"

tus to the point of unintended self-parody, especially when taken with his exaggerated upper-class British accent, but his delight at my visit was genuine
enough.

I outlined my mission: I was there to persuade him to call a halt to the firing from his side while one more effort was made to resolve the conflict between the federal government and his now-seceded state. The sticky point,
however, was that this would require placing a hold on the secession.

Ojukwu reiterated his charges against the federal side and painted for me
the mood of his people: it was the people themselves, not he, who had pressed
for secession. No one, he insisted, could have withstood the tide of that resentful outpouring. It was a plausible case, but one that I found difficult to
swallow entire. Ojukwu himself had played a role in manipulating emotions.

I joined in his midmorning snack, watched him daintily pick *akara** balls
from a silver salver served by a waiter in immaculate white uniform complete
with white gloves. It all seemed rather incongruous, impossible not to feel that
one was watching an act. The exchange was anything but staged, however; we
were, after all, engaged in an exchange of life and death not merely of human
beings but of his dream of Biafra.

He would not commit himself. Instead, he insisted that I speak first to a
few civilian leaders, some of whom I did meet later on. In turn, I requested to
speak with Major Wole Ademoyega, an officer from the West who had been
imprisoned for his role in the January 15 coup and transferred to Enugu prisons. That transfer had saved his life. When the countercoup had taken place in
July that year, the plotters had invaded prisons under federal control, abducted
the officers, and subjected them to cruel forms of death. Ademoyega, however,
lived to write of his role in the January 15 coup in *Why We Struck*.

MOST FATEFUL OF ALL my meetings in the seceded enclave was that with Victor
Banjo, a Yoruba officer. Following some convoluted chain of incidents, Victor
Banjo had been accused of menacing the former head of state, General Aguiyi-
Ironsi—and had ended up in Enugu prisons. After the declaration of Biafran
independence, he was released by Ojukwu, as were other Yoruba officers and
soldiers from the Western Region, some of whom had certainly been involved
in the original January 1966 coup.

Loose-limbed and slightly bandy-legged, Victor Banjo reminded me very
strongly of a browsing *igala*, that rangy, powerful deer, when it is totally un-

---

* Fried bean-cake.

conscious of any intruder. He exuded a quiet, commanding presence, as one who would be at ease in any environment, looking as if he were in studious contemplation of a world devoid of strife. A total contrast to Ojukwu, his bearing still struck me as a contradiction to the frenzy of war, as if the outer reality had nothing to do with him personally. Yet the war map on the wall, the guns, even the Spartan nature of his office and the stiff, attentive poise of his batman told a different story. I noticed the lenses of his glasses at once—very thick—and from the way his eyes appeared to adjust to distance, I guessed that he was shortsighted. Impeccably groomed even in his khaki uniform, this stranger soon revealed himself as an idealist whose politics were quite close to ours in the Third Force. He made no attempt to disguise the fact that he was subjecting me to some deep scrutiny—or perhaps that was simply the effect of his thick lenses—then abruptly appeared to have made up his mind.

A stream of indignation followed as he castigated the failure of Western leaders to condemn the massacres of the Igbo and ridiculed the visits of traditional rulers who had come to the East to commiserate with widows and orphans—too little, too late, and short on sincerity, was his verdict. For the leader of the Biafran secession, he had even harsher words. If Odumegwu Ojukwu had displayed true leadership, the secession, he insisted, would never have taken place.

Then, again abruptly, he shrugged it all off, dismissed the past with a wave of his hand. He had relieved himself of a long-pent-up resentment, and now he had no further use for it. A slim, light-complexioned, quite good-looking man in uniform joined us and was introduced as Phillip Alale. He was a complete contrast, restless and excitable. Alale spoke agitatedly and volubly of the lack of ideological grounding in the conflict, slashing the air right and left as he outlined the cleansing that was needed for the diseased polity called Nigeria. For him also, Ojukwu was not the answer to the threat of Northern domination in Nigerian politics. What was desperately needed was a third force, though he did not actually use the expression; still, his prescription was for a new entrant that would neutralize the two combatants. It was Phillip Alale, however, who was fated to be neutralized at the firing stake in Biafra, convicted of treason against Ojukwu's government, together with Victor Banjo and two others.

Banjo let him run on for some time, then interrupted with a gesture that was nearly imperceptible—he appeared to be used to commanding effortlessly and economically, like one who needed to conserve his energy. My appearance in Enugu, he pronounced, could not have been more fortuitous. The face of the war was about to change, dramatically, and I was the only one who could transmit certain crucial messages to the other side, that is, to the leaders of the West, both military and civilian, but especially to a certain Lieutenant Colonel Olusegun Obasanjo. It was there, right in Victor Banjo's command room, that I heard that name for the first time and was informed that Obasanjo had only recently been appointed commanding officer in charge of the Western Area Command, with his headquarters in Ibadan. Obasanjo had once served in a subordinate capacity to him. His response to the message I would take, Banjo stressed, would be crucial to the changes that were being contemplated on the Biafran side.

I BECAME A MARKED man on account of my visit to Biafra. Delivering the messages that I brought back with me, however, turned me once again into a wanted man, but this time that designation had turned sinister and all the more deadly for being unannounced.

On the third night after my departure from Enugu, Victor Banjo broke the federal stranglehold on Biafra and led the breakout military unit that had been in secret training. The obstacles that blocked both the Biafran and Midwest ends of the Asaba bridge were flung aside, and Banjo's army crossed the bridge in a rapid move and took over the Midwest state on the other side of the Niger River. It could be rightly considered a politically fatal move for the Biafrans, even militarily self-defeating—unless of course such a move was proceeding strictly according to plan, which was to plunge straight through to Lagos in an all-night advance and swarm over the seat of government without a loss of momentum. That invading force did not, and the result was that the rebel forces were soon spread too thin to be effective. The move also played straight into the hands of the federal government both militarily and politically. What had formerly been a limited war, in which one of the states still retained sufficient autonomy to insist on its neutrality—"No shooting on Midwest soil," declared the governor, David Ejoor—that war now expanded to involve the entire nation. It changed the terms of conflict, enabling the federal government to mobilize the nation against the allegedly expansionist agenda of the Biafrans. It altered the scale and tempo of the war from a desultory "police action" to one of "total war," leaving no room for further neutrality.

If I had earlier had any hesitation about delivering the messages from the architect and leader of that Midwest incursion, they vanished completely and even took on an urgency once Victor Banjo's troops made their move, although not fully according to script. The crux of his message was this: *Let them under-*

stand in the West that I am leading not a Biafran army but an army of liberation, made up not only of Biafrans but of other ethnic groups. Make the governor of the West and other Western leaders understand this. Urge them not to be taken in by any propaganda by the federal government about a Biafran plan to subjugate the rest of the nation, especially the West.

Moving as rapidly as I dared, since it was clear that I had come under heavy surveillance, I carried out my mission to the civilian leaders, with one exception: Chief Obafemi Awolowo. Even before I left Enugu, I refused to accede to Banjo's insistence that I speak to "Awo." After my meeting with that politician, I simply felt, intuitively, that the approaching conflict was not one in which he should be involved.

A Moment of Truth—and the Lies of History

. . . . .

I WAS LEFT ONLY ONE INDIVIDUAL ON VICTOR BANJO'S CALL LIST, THE MOST critical: Olusegun Obasanjo, Officer Commanding, Western Zone. It was the moment of truth, the hardest, most risk-laden decision of all. Obasanjo's junior officers, with whom I had maintained steady contact since my return, warned me to beware. In the same breath, they clearly wished—well—maybe if . . . I weighed the risks. They were difficult days for objective, rational choices. While I hesitated, Victor Banjo broke through to the Midwest, but now he paused to secure the Midwest militarily and politically, making inflammatory broadcasts. The West became confused and awaited direction from its leaders. I chose.

I called Obasanjo over a secret telephone in his bedroom, of whose existence he had not known. In his memoirs,* Obasanjo tells the story of how he had to search for the source of the mysterious ringing that he eventually traced to a wardrobe in his bedroom, one of the few details in that narrative that can stand the test of veracity in the midst of so many half-truths, outright lies, and coy adumbrations. A few more calls and we agreed to meet "unaccompanied and unarmed"—another truthful detail from his memoirs—at a petrol station on the road between the noncommercial Jericho and Mokola sections of Ibadan. Now I had truly burned my bridges, I told myself. There was no turning back.

Even before the fateful meeting, Femi's brother, Brigadier "Bolus," had cautioned Femi about his association with me. I still recall the exact words that Femi said his brother had used: "*So'ra l'odo e o, enu nfe si la'ra. Mi o tii mo kini*

---

* *My Command* (Ibadan: Heinemann, 1980).

n'lon gan, sugbon, so'ra l'odo e"—"Watch yourself with him, tongues are fanning the wind in his direction. I don't know exactly what is going on, but watch yourself." His brother was right. What he did not know was how far committed Femi was—not to the Biafran side as such but to the liberation of the Western Region from the domination of the North.

With the incursion of Victor Banjo's troops into the Midwest, all subterfuge, all fence-sitting, came to an end, affecting soldiers and civilian leaders alike. Obafemi Awolowo surrendered his bargaining powers. The Midwest, formerly a part of the West, a self-declared neutral until now, had been invaded and occupied. That region now threw its weight formally behind the federal government, where Awolowo was now minister of finance under Gowon, and it put an end to all his options. Nnamdi Azikiwe, "Zik of Africa," an Igbo and former president of the Nigerian Federation, had already taken his place on the side of his fellow Biafrans. Not that he'd had much choice. At the time of the January 1966 coup, which had been led by a preponderance of Igbo officers, Azikiwe had been on a seemingly endless "health cruise" in the Caribbean, and news of the coup had caught him, incongruously, on the isle of Haiti, then groaning under the misrule of "Papa Doc" Duvalier. The timing of the cruise had been too pat, and the Northern proponents of the countercoup that brought Yakubu Gowon to power in July did not believe for one moment that Azikiwe had not been taken into confidence over a coup that oversaw the decimation of Northern leadership. Azikiwe wisely kept beyond reach of the new regime, becoming a roving ambassador for the breakaway region, a powerful voice internationally in the Biafran cause.

Azikiwe's counterweight on the Nigerian side was Anthony Enahoro. Tony Enahoro was a most effective minister in Yakubu Gowon's government. Indeed, his advocacy contributed much to the international acceptance of the federal cause. Enahoro exuded an easy charm and was gifted with intelligent eloquence, a persuasive Edo nobility in the midst of so many fakes. He was one of the early youthful nationalists, a political model from our school days. Enahoro had learned at the feet of Azikiwe, who would, however, denounce him during that anticolonial struggle as an intemperate agitator when the younger man stood trial for sedition against the colonial government. Enahoro never forgave Azikiwe for that act of repudiation and later switched his allegiance to Obafemi Awolowo and his party, the Action Group, joining his leader in prison as one of the casualties of the treasonable felony trials. He was among those who were freed by Yakubu Gowon in the shrewd political move to gain support among Southerners in the conflict with the breakaway Biafrans. Enahoro was a die-hard federalist—at least then. Together with Obafemi Awolowo, he outweighed the influence of Nnamdi Azikiwe in mobilizing international support.

In his position as commissioner for information, Tony Enahoro was the government spokesman who would read to the international press, after my arrest and detention, an infamous confessional statement that had me admitting that I had been negotiating the purchase of warplanes for Biafra! It was, of course, intended to silence any further hue and cry over my continuing detention without trial. I found it rather ironic—and a little depressing at the time, I must confess—that the "fugitive offender," not many months out of jail, would be the one to read such a damnable fabrication and wave the "confessional statement" in the face of the international press. Perhaps the most easily disproved of the charges—next to the ridiculous claim that I was purchasing arms, including planes for Biafra—was my alleged admission that I had held a meeting *in Benin* with Victor Banjo, the leader of the invasion, on the very night when his troops had taken over the Midwest state. A few weeks after Tony Enahoro's press conference, an indignant Femi Johnson encountered the commissioner on the Ibadan golf course and refused to let that chance meeting go to waste.

"That can't be true!" he challenged the minister. "I was with Wole in Ibadan throughout that day; you can check with my wife and a number of other people whose names I will provide you. All day, including dinner. He could not have been at that meeting as alleged. That confession must be a forgery. It's a frame-up."

Enahoro was taken aback. He asked Femi how sure he was of his facts. Femi swore that he was ready to back up his statement anywhere. The minister asked him to write a formal letter to that effect, which Femi did the following day, making sure that Enahoro had it in his hands before he returned to Lagos. To further engage his interest, Femi reminded Enahoro of his own past predicament as a "fugitive offender"—the title of Enahoro's account of that experience—and of the voluntary role I had played in the efforts to prevent his extradition.

Tony Enahoro replied, "Oh, that was then. This is war, you know. The rules are different."

Curiously, I found myself in agreement with Tony Enahoro—it *was* war—and I never held his indifference against him, which was just as well, since we were destined to join forces two decades later against a far more detestable foe, the dictator Sani Abacha. Even so, I must confess that I was rather nettled at the baldness of the dismissal. I suppose one always nurses a secret expectation of some kind of reciprocity, even if it exists on a purely rhetorical level. As for the statement that Femi handed to him the following day, that was the last he ever heard from Tony.

FEMI HAD CAUSE to be a hundred percent certain of my alibi. Not only had I been with him most of that crucial day, I had again involved him in my course of action, imposed a chore on him—which was to find me a new hiding place. It had become necessary to "go under," even while remaining active. His house was now "hot," and I had no wish to implicate him any futher in this latest entanglement. Tongues from the police and military intelligence were indeed fanning the wind toward my person, and I still had some urgent tasks ahead, tasks that required total seclusion. I also needed a secure place for the two or three final meetings that were left—with members of my group, for instance, even with Bola Ige, and indeed one or two military contacts. I could no longer go to people but could get them to come to me if I succeeded in finding a secure venue. Obasanjo was the sole exception—we had agreed to meet at Jericho.

Femi went away to make inquiries, returned with information about an expatriate civil servant who had gone on leave. His house was unoccupied; not even the servants' quarters were tenanted. Femi obtained the number and address of the bungalow—in the Iyaganku government quarters, virtually under the nose of the police—and drove me casually past the house in daytime while I looked it over. Close to the police though it was, it was most obligingly secluded; the expatriate owner was a kindred spirit, he believed in a surround of lush vegetation. Best of all, it had a functioning telephone.

Later that night, he dropped me by the fence, armed with a torch and the now regulation hamper of food and drinks. Gaining entrance through a window was easy. Once assured of entry, I told him to get lost. "Don't come near me again. From now on, you don't know me, never saw me in your life. If I am absolutely desperate for some item, I'll telephone or get a message to you somehow. You can bring it at nighttime, drop it at the point where you've just let me off, and keep going. You've done enough, you've done more than you should have done. Now get out and look after yourself." The shocked look on his face was a marvel to see, but he saw at once that I was in deadly earnest, sensed at once that this bout of conflict with a military government, and in wartime, was far more serious than my earlier political skirmishes.

I underestimated Femi yet again, forgot that he did not willingly let go of some space of collaboration. The many times when I denied him participation, he succeeded in inflicting on me a sense of betrayal, as if I had deprived him of a natural entitlement that was well within his conspiratorial competence. He insisted on driving me to the rendezvous. In vain I impressed on him the fact that I had my arrangements well in hand, that one of my own group was far better equipped to handle any untoward situation, but, most important of all, he would be exposing himself to unnecessary risks. He flared up—"Why shouldn't I? If I get arrested, well, what exactly would they charge me with? That you had dinner in my house, told me to drop you at the petrol station and return for you after an hour—since when did that add up to a crime? You're going to meet the man in charge of zonal security on some crucial national matter, leaving from my house—everybody knows you stay here, after all. So I drop you and pick you up again, what's wrong with that?" And then the clinching argument: "In any case, we know each other. I've done insurance for him and his colleagues—we get on quite well. In fact, I'll say hello to him as I drop you."

I drew the line there, surrendered the others. Just drop me at the petrol station and take off, I insisted. As it happened, the rendezvous was close to Femi's home. He would pick me up at my hideout after dark, take me to the encounter, I would satisfy his burning curiosity over a late dinner, and then my man—not he—would return me to my base.

I got busy on the telephone, even as I continued to ask myself, Do I really want to meet this man? More meetings with his junior officers followed where we debated that issue.

I had already delivered the core of Victor Banjo's message over the telephone, but Obasanjo wanted very much to discuss it in some detail. I knew what the truth was: he needed to ask questions. Questions to help him decide which side to support? Or questions that might yield snippets of intelligence for securing his own base in aiding the federal cause? It was all very suspicious, and, to make matters worse, the character references from his own officers were not especially reassuring; the kindest word that summarized their assessment of their commanding officer was—cagey. The situation in the Midwest remained fluid; indeed, there was a lull for several weeks, as if the federal government and Biafra were weighing up each other, or else—which was more likely—waiting to see which way the West would respond to the new situation. Fighting had not yet flared up on the next obvious front: the border between the West and Midwest. The West itself was undergoing its final moments of fence-sitting, never mind the stout declarations of allegiance to the slogan of "One Nigeria"!

The British High Commission intelligence network, for once, had been caught on the hop, though we were to learn later that it had not failed completely—the high commissioner did report the likelihood of the Midwest crossing to Yakubu Gowon's government but could not pinpoint the date. Much, so much, now depended on the decision of the Western command. It was a military situation, and not even the governor of the West could make that decision, as he had no forces under his command. Banjo was holed up in Benin. The bulk of the federal troops, weapons, and logistical resources was bottled up in the Northern sector, since the Midwest had earlier refused to allow any fighting on its soil—a position that was no longer tenable. The federal government desperately depended on the West holding firm to the federal cause. In short, one man now held the key, and that was the officer in charge of the Western Area Command, Olusegun Obasanjo.

Several of Obasanjo's officers had no sympathy whatsoever for the federal cause. It was not that they were against a unified nation; no, they simply felt that the internal arrangements of the existing national entity were lopsided, weighed in favor of Northern privilege. Even within the army, they knew what it was to be second-class citizens—given the chance, they would be Biafrans! Again the question remained suspended: Should I really meet this man or not? It all boiled down to the fact that, in the view of his own officers, Obasanjo could not be trusted. He could set a trap, have me arrested for "consorting with the enemy" or whatever. And so they insisted on leaving such a risky decision to me, even while stressing that a voice like mine might just do the trick. There was not much time. Finally I abandoned all further hesitation and I called him once more. Obasanjo remained more than eager to meet.

The venue remained Jericho, at a petrol station in a quiet part of Ibadan. Again we set out the conditions: *both to come alone, unarmed and unaccompanied.* Even then, I continued to battle with unresolved doubts—going underground and operating from there seemed a far more rational option. In the end, it was probably those frenzied four or five days of intense cloak-and-dagger meetings (of whose existence Femi would be kept completely oblivious) with Western leaders—politicians, labor leaders, even senior police officers—that tilted the scales. Time was running out for Victor Banjo and his version of the Third Force, and the leader of that incursion continued to await a sign from the West. I had no further contribution to make, no more unfulfilled chores. I was drained. It was time for a decisive act. I agreed to deliver yet again—but this time face-to-face—the message I had brought back from Biafra, one that had been given to me in Enugu—*not* Benin!

Femi picked me up as agreed. I had already organized a driver, one of our group, to wait for me by Christopher Okigbo's now abandoned and locked-up domain, Cambridge House, a mere walking distance from Femi's house. I tried a last-minute variation: would it not be simpler, I suggested, for him to drop me by the waiting car and go home, and I would join him for dinner and the eagerly awaited debriefing? OBJ would not hear of it. Well, would he at least drive past the road junction by Cambridge House, where my man was waiting, and pause long enough for me to change his instructions? Was it all right if I told the fellow to tag along, follow us to the rendezvous but continue straight on, just checking that we were safe? My friend, addict of intrigues, ignored my sarcastic tone and generously gave his consent.

Neither Obasanjo nor I, it turned out, kept strictly to the agreed conditions of our meeting. In my own case, however, the failure was unintended. Femi at the wheel, we stopped by the desolate Cambridge House to brief the waiting driver of the slight change of plans. He was to follow us the short distance to the petrol station, drive past, and park his car at a distance from where he could ensure that the other side kept to the bargain, then return to Cambridge House to await my return.

At the petrol station, Femi pulled up in the shadow cast by the street lighting off the low enclosure wall. A few moments later, Olusegun Obasanjo's Volkswagen Beetle drew up, stopped at the other side of the pumps. With a Yoruba cap, an *ikori*, firmly pulled over my forehead, I walked across from where we had parked and jumped into the seat beside him. From the shadow of the wall, Femi turned around to go home immediately—keeping at least to the terms of our agreement. Obasanjo took off just as fast in the direction of nowhere, followed, however, by a car that—he would later admit—was his security detail. That uninvited guest was spotted by my own Third Force driver, who promptly threw out all instructions and followed the intruder. The agreement had been broken, and he considered his original instructions no longer valid.

And my good friend O. B. Johnson? As he recounted it to me later that night, he had indeed been headed home when he observed through his rear mirror that Obasanjo's vehicle had acquired two tails. Trust my friend: he turned around and followed the convoy of three vehicles, sensing foul play! Spotting the anomaly was not difficult. The sight of any vehicle on the streets at night was sufficient to generate attention at such a time—a partial, largely self-imposed curfew was being observed on Ibadan streets, and in any case, Onireke was a very quiet part of Ibadan at that hour. Thus began the only comic relief that would come my way since my return from Biafra.

To adapt one of Fela Anikulapo's antiestablishment songs—"Wetin follow be say Follow-follow *follow* Follow-follow."* I turned in my seat, looked back quite openly, and saw what was going on. Obasanjo drove in a way that might suggest that he was merely taking precautions, attempting to throw off any incidental tail, and I pretended to "swallow-swallow" the deception. I have sometimes wondered how an aerial shot of those minutes of the pursuit would have looked, with cutbacks to vehicle interiors and the bewildered faces—and thoughts—of the various occupants! It continued through the twists and turns of Ibadan roads for several minutes before Obasanjo somehow succeeded in losing everyone, including his own security detail. The soldier wore a loose *agbada*. I took the opportunity of the first lurch to lean into him. Of course he was armed, as he would cheerfully admit years later in the home of Ojetunji Aboyade, our perennial peace broker, when we reviewed the events of that night. "Me? I am supposed to be a soldier, do you think I would agree to meet someone just from Biafra, in the dead of night, on a deserted street, without protection? I would deserve to be court-martialed!"

In the flickering lights of the streetlamps, each of us tried openly to assess the other. Even beneath his *agbada,* I could discern the beginnings of a slight paunch, while his face bore the recognizable tribal marks of Owu stock, one of the branches of the Yoruba. The Owu are reputed to be pugnacious by nature; there was, however, nothing remotely soldierly about his bearing. His expression remained inscrutable, but his voice sounded relaxed, even self-confident, and he asked his questions as if the answers carried no import that extended beyond the two occupants of the car. There was nothing whatsoever to indicate which way he felt about the war, no sense of his awareness of the critical position in which he found himself. He sounded more like a village headmaster who was awaiting the visit of a schools inspector and wanted to know all about the likely areas of interest of the visitor. His face became animated, taking on a queasy slyness, only when he asked how I had come to know about the telephone in his wardrobe.

Again I tried to justify the physical encounter to myself. The core of Banjo's message had been delivered. The man's insistence on our meeting therefore had to be his need for a direct "character reference"—in short, to see the messenger in person, assess his genuineness, and hopefully believe in the truthfulness of his message: that in breaching the neutrality of the Midwest, Banjo was not acting for Biafra but planned instead to bring the war to an end. Again and

---

* That is, what then developed was that the follower found himself followed by another follower, and so on.

again Banjo had urged me—as if I needed any urging!—to emphasize this to
Obasanjo: "This is not a Biafran army, and this is not a Biafran agenda." I was
to detail how he had persuaded Ojukwu to let him train an independent force
ostensibly to promote that leader's ambitions. The training had gone on secretly in the Midwest, right under the nose of David Ejoor, the military governor, who had remained genuinely oblivious to such activities. To obtain both
men and weaponry, Banjo had had to agree to train and move an independent
force through the Midwest, sack the center, and install a regime that would endorse Biafra's secession. However, there Victor Banjo's and Ojukwu's interests
were supposed to part company. Banjo was solidly against the secession.

However, Nigerians are weaned on the caution "Cunny man die, cunny
man bury am."* Victor Banjo understood clearly—as I also did even from my
single encounter with Ojukwu—that the warlord meant to take over the nation. It was a view that has since been confirmed by some of the historians
from the Biafran side. It was equally clear that Victor Banjo meant to ignore
Ojukwu's ambitions once he himself had seized Lagos and was guaranteed the
support of the Western command. Banjo then intended to take over the nation, including Biafra. I do not believe for a moment that he meant to terminate
the secession by force of arms; indeed, that would have been nearly impossible,
considering the fact that his liberation force was made up largely of Biafran
soldiers. Guaranteed the support of the Western Region in overwhelming numbers, however, Banjo could have ensured that any ambitions of Ojukwu in the
larger national context were successfully thwarted. Banjo's immediate constituency was the West, and he needed, at the very least, some form of assurance from the Western leaders. This was why he was desperate that his message
to Obasanjo be couched in unambiguous terms: "Tell Obasanjo that the liberation forces at my command do not wish to fight on Western soil. All we
seek is unimpeded passage to Lagos through the Western Region."

This was the message I reiterated to Obasanjo that night as we drove
through the deserted streets of Ibadan warrens.

But now a necessary digression on the minor but instructive theme of revi-
sionism in purported historical narratives, using as an intimate example the
notorious fictionalizing of my telephone exchanges and eventual meeting with
Olusegun Obasanjo during those crucial nights when the fate of a nation hung
in the balance and one man held the key to its future—at least its immediate
future. That man of fluctuating destinies Olusegun Obasanjo would later

---

* The con man fakes death, but another con man will bury him.

become a military head of state, a prisoner of another military dictator, an occupant of death row, and then a civilian president—albeit elected under extremely dubious circumstances—in 1999 and, under even more discredited circumstances, in 2003 (see *Supreme Court Judgement, Buhari vs Obasanjo, 2004*). Obasanjo has earned himself a reputation as an assiduous chronicler of the immediate past, but one most prone, alas, to the extreme latitudes of creative license.

The mission that I had undertaken just before, during, and immediately after the Midwest invasion was to transmit Victor Banjo's objectives to Obasanjo. I was to tell him in very bald terms that Banjo wanted unimpeded passage to Lagos, that he wished to avoid a battle in Western Nigeria—*finis!* This was the exact message I delivered. What I did or said outside that meeting was a different matter, and this included how my future activities were influenced by Obasanjo's response to the message that I had delivered to him.

The decision to meet him at all had been a most difficult one, fraught with warnings. The most forceful had come from the young officer in military intelligence who had revealed to me the existence of the secret telephone in Obasanjo's bedroom, and its number, to facilitate direct contact. Yet even he could not bring himself to wholeheartedly endorse the final meeting. His distrust of his superior officer was unambiguous. Such warnings were responsible for my writing down, then *memorizing*, the precise words in which I proposed to deliver Victor Banjo's message. If I were arrested and brought to trial, I wanted to ensure that my words would not be distorted or taken out of context.

That simple precaution would generate a not inconsequential footnote years later, in 1980, during an encounter between Obasanjo and myself. Our destinies had long taken off in different directions, and Obasanjo himself had served as a military head of state.

I had crammed my lines so efficiently that I still remembered them years afterward, when Obasanjo published his account of the war in *My Command*. There, among other lies, he claimed that I had asked him to name his price for letting Victor Banjo's troops through the West! Even combatants who have done their best to disembowel each other in wartime do embrace and carry on with life afterward, and so, although Obasanjo's betrayal of the very event of our meeting was certainly the most crucial factor that led to my incarceration, I found—to my pleasant surprise, I think—that I could meet him afterward without rancor. I experienced no obstacle to resuming our brief and untoward relationship on a new footing and was able to collaborate with him on a number of national schemes when he became head of state.

What I found impossible to stomach, however, were his constant attempts to rewrite—and tendentiously, to boot!—a history of which I had been a part, in no matter how minor a role. And so, both privately and publicly, I was drawn into the repetitive, excruciatingly boring and frustrating imposition of setting him right whenever—in order to secure a temporary advantage, often petty but distracting—he resorted to twisting the true narrative of events. Following the publication of his book, and after the ensuing bout of public exchanges, we met in the home of Ojetunji Aboyade, then vice chancellor at the University of Ife, who sometimes complained that he felt that his life mission was to act as referee and conciliator during our frequent wranglings.

It was virtually no contest! I began by reciting from memory my opening statement to him on the occasion of our "Follow-follow" meeting, word for word. Then, not nearly so precisely but as close to exactitude as made no difference, even by his own admission, I repeated his comments, questions, my responses, and his final statement. Even the unscripted exchanges were still fresh in my mind; one passes much time in total recall in the quiet of prison solitary confinement! The recalled exchanges were so logical in their content and sequence that Obasanjo could only stare, dumbfounded. I accused him of coming armed to our meeting, contrary to our agreement. He laughed and admitted it. I repeated yet again that I had offered no opinion, no comment on the message I had brought, had said nothing that could be remotely construed as an attempt to sway him one way or the other. Obasanjo remained mute for several moments, then gave his familiar schoolboy-caught-in-the-act mischievous smile and—*apologized!* Aboyade gave his verdict, exhorting me to accept his apology as gracefully as he had proffered it.

And that should have ended this matter—but Olusegun Aremu Obasanjo, "conqueror of Biafra," would not have acted his true self if he had not seized the next opportunity of a public disagreement in the media to repeat, and in the very language that he had himself repudiated, the falsehood he had tried to implant in the public perception. One such occasion was his failure to obtain election as secretary-general of the United Nations, a failure that he attributed to me, with some justification. In common with a number of civic organizations, we had warned that he was not fit to be placed in charge of such a body on account of proven human rights violations that continued even on his private (militarized) farm after his tenure of office. Nettled, Obasanjo exhumed a discredited account of our encounter during the civil war and commenced a new round of doctored narratives.

Lies should never be allowed to lie. I seized the next anniversary of Victor Banjo's Midwest invasion—September 1980—to organize a public lecture at the International Institute of Public Affairs, Lagos, simply to denounce once again, and authoritatively, the man's compulsive need to consolidate a private invention, demanding to know why it is never sufficient that one accept sole responsibility for one's deeds, for better or worse, without being compelled to deal with the emendations of others, who are mostly impelled by concerns for their career, their image, or psychological needs.

It is necessary to make a distinction: this is not to deny that I would have preferred that Obasanjo accede to Banjo's request. It is simply that I had set out with the resolution *not* to attempt any persuasion or—to use Obasanjo's own favorite word—apply any "pressure" on him. I stuck scrupulously to my brief, delivering a "plain, unvarnished tale" and consciously avoiding any futher expansion of the danger I had already incurred by meeting with an unreliable factor in the developing scenario. I could not rule out recording equipment having been installed in his car; after all, a telephone had preceded him, the commandant of the vast Western domain, into his bedroom, and he had known nothing of it! Far too many details in personal memoirs are not even slips of memory but self-serving fiction. Obasanjo wanted to ingratiate himself with his superiors in Lagos, even to the extent of claiming that I had asked him to name a price for his "treason"—against which temptation he had of course presented an armor of loyalty that could not be dented by filthy lucre! Not once, in my entire involvement in this saga, did I encounter any situation in which "ten pieces of silver" ever featured. Ojukwu neither discussed nor offered any, nor did Victor Banjo propose it. Then who was financially placed to ask our man to name his price? This courier, who hardly ever balanced his monthly salary?

Just as unprincipled was the so-called confessional statement read out by the then minister of information, Anthony Enahoro, on behalf of the government—about my alleged meeting with Banjo in Benin, the attempted purchase of arms, and so on—all baseless, cynical concoctions by the government, concerned that the provable extent of my activities might not provide sufficient grounds for holding me in prison indefinitely or for convicting me of some heinous offense in a court of law. Still, it was wartime, and on balance my activities could easily have resulted in a kangaroo trial and execution or other extrajudicial solutions of a terminal kind. None of these consolations reduces the intensity of one's violent dislike to being lied against. Watch even a notorious Nigerian thief defending himself in a court of law: "Your Worship, why do they keep accusing me of stealing a chicken? As God is my witness, all I stole was a goat!"

It must be admitted that many coup makers on the continent—and Nigerian career officers are no exception—sell their allegiances, indeed, put themselves out for hire by businessmen for instigating a coup. This was a real development that came years later, definitely long after the civil war and even after the coup d'état that ousted the regime of Yakubu Gowon, a coup that no one could possibly accuse of having been prodded by moneyed interests. We simply were not in the buying and selling business, and in any case, we had no funds to throw around. Even if we had, we would not have spent such funds on dubious allegiances. I owe it to the memory of Victor Banjo to contest such dishonorable, even unsoldierly, distortions of his motives and conduct; to testify, above all, that he had *not* acted to promote Biafran secession or aid Ojukwu's takeover of power in Lagos. If anything, Banjo felt that he himself should take over power, and, confronted with the two discredited combatants who were propelling the nation toward a bloodbath, those of us who were self-described as the Third Force had no doubt whatsoever that Banjo represented the most viable corrective.

Obasanjo's response at the end of our nocturnal ride through the sleeping streets of Ibadan, a response that I would later transmit to Victor Banjo from my hideout, nearly word for word, was this: "Well, tell him I have taken an oath of loyalty to Lagos. There are other routes to Lagos—by water through Okitipupa, for instance. If he makes it to Lagos and takes over, well, my oath of loyalty is to Lagos, and I'll stand by that. But to let him pass through my Western command, that would be betraying my oath of loyalty. Whoever is in power in Lagos—that's the person to whom I owe my allegiance." Words to that effect, not nearly as close to the original today, I am sure, as my recollection of them in 1980 in the Aboyade home, with both husband and wife as audience, but close enough.

MY FATEFUL MEETING with Obasanjo concluded, I took up permanent residence in the hidden bungalow, where I dared not switch on the lights at night. It was from this bungalow that I telephoned Obasanjo's reply to Banjo in Benin, verbatim. I kept up communication with him, acting as intermediary between him and his increasingly impatient collaborators in the West—our faithful colleagues at Oniyanrin telephone exchange ensured that no one was tapping the lines. I would phone and exchange notes also with Banjo's sister, Mrs. Ogunseye, then lecturer in librarianship at the University of Ibadan, in an attempt to assess this warrior's likely, real, immediate, and/or long-term intentions, to understand why he remained in Benin playing governor or administrator or kingmaker, why he had taken the irrational step of proclaiming yet another secessionist state—the Midwest—instead of moving straight to Lagos and dislodging Yakubu Gowon's government.

Haba! The people of the Midwest had not requested their own independent state *à la* Biafra, so what was the point? On the contrary, they were seething—at least in the non-Igbo parts of the state—under what they read as a Biafran force of occupation. In any case, why should Banjo, an outsider, attempt to donate independence to a people whose neutrality had been breached and who were now drawn into a widening conflict? Each night I issued the same plaint, with ever-increasing desperation: What was keeping him in Benin? We spoke in coded language: *Grandfather is gravely ill. The doctors say they must operate tomorrow; any further delay and it will be too late—do you understand that? Can you make it to his bedside in time? The theater is fully equipped, but the clinic itself may shut down any day ... there is a problem with the expatriate staff; the nurses are threatening to walk off the job ...* and so on. And Banjo would reply, yes, definitely he would be at the clinic in the morning. Most definitely. And again his supporters in the West would prepare to facilitate his passage.

Then he was recalled to Enugu by Ojukwu, who had become suspicious of his procrastination, only to be sent back again to his Benin command. Time seeped away, the initiative and all its advantages shifting day by day to Lagos. Banjo no longer appeared to be the independent operator who had set out from Biafra at the head of a force that was motivated, at least, by some ideological pretensions. His public pronouncements became more and more erratic and contradictory, while our position underground turned increasingly precarious. The uprising that was planned to accompany his entry and provide a popular base for his incursion began to lose momentum. Whatever public support he enjoyed in the West was gradually eroded as the federal government, thoroughly panicked and poised for flight at the earlier stages, uncertain which officers and commands it could count upon, recovered from its fright, rallied wavering support, mobilized, and moved against the invaders. The role played by the British mission at this critical time in shoring up the confidence of the regime has yet to be fully narrated; it certainly was not a negligible factor. The result was all that mattered; Victor Banjo's dawdling in Benin had closed down one possible chapter in the direction of Nigerian history—with whatever consequences, good or ill.

The moment came when everyone, even the most ardent optimist, knew that Victor Banjo would never make that crossing to Lagos. He had left it till too late, and now the federal government had repositioned its forces and was moving in to recapture the Midwest region. It was time to disband.

I had become worried for the safety of many of those with whom Banjo had also made direct contact, his sister, Mrs. Ogunseye, most especially. Banjo telephoned her constantly, sometimes passing messages to me through her, especially if he had missed a call from me. Otherwise, he appeared to dispense with caution, depending on the state of his mood, brimming with confidence or desperate and frustrated. Then he would speak unguardedly, mentioning by name politicians and even military officers from whom he expected support, complaining of their lack of action.

What he had expected these people to do exactly, I never really understood. Of course plans for a popular uprising in his favor the moment he moved into Lagos had been agreed upon—but that the people should mount such demonstrations *ahead* of his arrival? Or perhaps invite him in to come and declare an independent Western state, as he had in the Midwest? The West was submerged under federal guns! But Banjo's telephone calls to many individuals—politicians, labor leaders, intellectuals, and others—in the West and Lagos merely grew wilder. He telephoned even Obafemi Awolowo, harangued Yakubu Gowon, spoke to Adeyinka Adebayo, the governor of the Western state, rebuked several of his military colleagues, both die-hard federalists and sympathetic ears. Telephone lines were constantly tapped—after all, we did some tapping ourselves—and I feared that Victor's careless conversations with his sister would get her into trouble, and over nothing. It fell to me, finally, to tell her to cut off all communication with her brother and begin to act to protect herself. She agreed to take no more calls from Banjo.

The breeze that tongues were fanning in the direction of my person had turned into a powerful wind! By now we had ample proof that Obasanjo had disclosed our conversation to his bosses in Lagos, passing it over the telephone, with his own deadly slants, to Gowon. The young officer from military intelligence was the first to alert me, offering to spirit me to a safe place. Several others urged flight, insisted that I disappear altogether. I did not require too much persuasion and began to prepare. Bayo Oduneye, a young colleague in the Ibadan University Theatre Arts Department, became one of the many peripheral—but quite innocent—bit players in the escalating drama. He offered me his Volkswagen Beetle, in a kindred spirit to Femi Johnson's: "Take it. If you find some means of sending it back, do so. If not, whenever you're settled, send word where I can go and pick it up." He had friends in the military and had also learned that there was an unannounced dragnet for me—indeed, who did not know it by then?

My arrest, in fact, need not have happened. Halfway to safety, going by habit through a mental checklist, I pulled over with a shock. There was a base—one of a handful—used by the veterans of confrontations with problematic governments. Seasoned over the years from neophyte volunteers in the Western electoral struggle of 1964–65 into organized cadres by the time of the civil war, their commitment had transferred to the cause of what now called itself the Third Force. Now they were standing by, ready to ignite popular demonstrations in support of Victor Banjo once he crossed over into Lagos. More alarming still was the fact that they had links with other groups all over the West and Lagos—even I did not know, by this time, how widespread they had become, since some of these links were run by politicians—but they had turned most restive since the West had begun its protests against federal military presence in the West, decrying it as "an army of occupation" and demanding its removal.

I had suddenly realized that my final instructions to disband were extremely likely to have missed this very special base. It was tucked away in Abadina village, the site of the University of Ibadan, close to the farms of the Agriculture Department. It was a most convenient place, the humble quarters of a junior university employee, situated virtually at the very edge of campus. Additionally, a drivable swathe, the handiwork of an agricultural tractor, bypassed the main entrance to the university and led directly onto the road to Oyo and from there to a number of safe houses in any direction, including back to Ibadan or Lagos or, in extremity, in the direction of Shaki and a choice of smugglers' routes to the border with the Republic of Benin. There were no telephones in that part of Abadina, so it could be reached only by a human courier. Its very security meant, however, that it had received no news from me of the changes in events.

I became worried that the members, still congregating around that post, might embark on some harebrained action of their own. Failing to hear anything, they might act impetuously, endanger themselves, and decimate the remnants of the organized civilian opposition to the regime. Agitated, I turned back and drove undetected for the hundred kilometers to Ibadan. On the way

I stopped at the Mbari Club at Adamasingba to pick up any idle member of my acting company, the Orisun Theatre, to act as courier. Only the tall, statuesque Betty Okotie, an early member of that company, was available.

She too had learned of the manhunt. She entered the car and we arrived on campus—again sticking to the back routes, joining up with the road that led to the College of Technology. My intention was to remain in the car some distance from the Abadina post while she went in and brought out whoever she found in place; there was always the possibility that the police had tracked it down and now had it under surveillance. That final base scuttled, I would wait for dark, then head for one of the unofficial border-crossing points to a safe house, or even, if the situation demanded it, into the neighboring country.

At the barrier that separated the College of Technology from the University of Ibadan, however, a policeman was waiting, armed with a rifle. He looked into the car, blinked, and sighed. That was the first and only sign I would obtain that the manhunt had extended to the peripheries of the university campus. Crestfallen at what he had to do, the policeman pulled me aside and, as if he knew what had brought me back, quickly whispered that he would escort me wherever I wanted to go before turning me in "in case"—his whisper went even lower—"in case there are urgent things you wish to take care of—sensitive documents and things like that. They will come and search your house, you know. It's the least I can do for you, Mr. Soyinka."

Not one shred of misgiving did I entertain. I had learned to read faces and voices—with varying degrees of accuracy, admittedly. In this case, I was more than a hundred percent certain of the man's sincerity; this was not a trap. We dropped off Betty Okotie, whom I sent off to Femi with news of my arrest. I visited our last operational base, closed it down, and dispersed the lingering faithful. Then, with my policeman still in charge, I stopped at my university quarters on Ebrohimie Road, informed my family that I might be away for a while, enjoyed a light but tasty meal, shared by my police captor—I did not know when next such tastes would be afforded me—and set off on the route to prison detention.

A tussle then began for my body. The governor of the Western Region, Colonel Adeyinka Adebayo, anxiously discussed my situation with some of his commissioners, knowing that one of them, Bola Ige, would convey his assessment of my predicament to me. Adebayo stood his ground for some time and stalled my repatriation to Lagos. Any interrogation, he insisted, should take place in Ibadan, where I had been arrested. Indeed, he later sent me assurances in my place of detention that I would not be removed from Ibadan, only to send the same emissary, some days later, to tell me that it had been agreed that I should proceed to Lagos, but that he had received an assurance from Yakubu Gowon that he personally wanted to see me and ask me some direct questions about my visit to Biafra. I would leave in the morning, the governor said, escorted by his own people, and would be back in Ibadan that same day.

I had to smile at that! The truth, of course, was that most of the West, including the governor and his cabinet, was against the federal regime but lacked the means to enforce its will. The time had passed when the Western Region government, backed by its Leaders of Thought, could demand that all non-Western troops, bluntly described as an army of occupation, be removed from the West. With Banjo's military incursion into the Midwest state, Gowon had further consolidated his authority all over the nation. The slogan "To keep Nigeria one / Is a task that must be done" meant that there could be no fence-sitting. Centralization—was anyone surprised?—had made a dramatic comeback. You bowed to the central authority in totality or were considered to have ranged yourself with the rebels—spelled d-e-v-i-l-s! You were an agent of destabilization, fifth columnist, neocolonial agent, never mind that it was the former colonial masters, the British, who were standing solidly behind the regime. Gowon was riding on a high crest of nationalist fervor, and nationalism meant: no Balkanization. The very name "Gowon" was turned into a quite clever acronym: "Go On With GowOn." Civil servants "voluntarily" donated a percentage of their salaries to the war effort, to a special fund called Troops Comfort Fund.

Regarding that "patriotic" exercise, there was one exception, one of a virtual handful, who defied that hysterical phase of patriotism. This was my elder sister, Tinu, then deputy principal of the Nursing School of the University Teaching Hospital, Lagos. She had nothing against keeping Nigeria one, offered no opinion regarding how one should go about it, but as long as her brother was in prison detention without trial, nobody had better touch her take-home pay! She refused to sign the "voluntary donation" form and declared her lack of interest in comforting any troops. Throughout the entire period of national jingoism—indeed, throughout the war with Biafra—no one dared touch Tinu's salary.

MY LAST TELEPHONE CALL, made from my home, where I shared a meal with my police captor, was to Femi. He was still in his office. I told him that there was a message—concerning rehearsal schedules—on its way to him through one of the Orisun company. To this I added tersely: "This is just for information. You are *not,* repeat, *not* required to be at these rehearsals. I have no idea how long they might take. This is a different play altogether, and—I already warned you—there is no longer any role in it for you. So take a sabbatical, will you? Understand?"

His voice was heavy with sadness and foreboding, but it did say that he understood.

*T*he Conquest of Civilian Pride

. . . . .

TWO YEARS AND FOUR MONTHS LATER—A YEAR AND TEN MONTHS OF IT spent in solitary confinement—I emerged from Kaduna prison,* armed with a rehearsed slogan. It was my chosen antidote to the national jingle, which continued to set my teeth on edge: "To keep Nigeria one / Is a task that must be done." I had nothing against the oneness of the nation called Nigeria— indeed, as I once remarked, why should I wish to add yet other consulates to my rounds of visa applications? The travails of my passport, sometimes three stuck together, under the hostile frowns of immigration officers searching not only for their nation's visa but for space on which to place their stamps, were sufficient to warrant a subjective opposition to the infestation of the global map with new national entities! What I did contest was the basis on which a nation calls itself one, a crucial debate that was easily obscured by cheap, meaningless slogans. I had long resolved that this basis could be one thing only: equity among the constituent parts—in short, political parity, also known as political justice for the parts within the whole. And so, as I descended from the plane at Ibadan airport in January 1969 and found myself confronted by the press, I had only one statement for them: "To keep Nigeria one / Justice must be done."

Then came the shock. The then chief justice of the Federation, a scion of Egba royal stock—that is, from my own birthplace—felt compelled to respond to my slogan. Though it had no immediate relevance to the purpose of his next public outing, the worthy judge could not wait to declare that justice not only existed in the nation but was well and thriving! The media were after me im-

---

* See *The Man Died: Prison Notes of Wole Soyinka.*

mediately, eager to offer a platform for me to take the battle to him. I declined
the bait, yet I was deeply troubled. Unknown to him, the judge had set me the
first puzzle in my reintegration into society. I needed time to digest what
struck me as a most unnecessary self-interposition between a government
with which I was undoubtedly at war and myself by the symbol of an institution that I had not assailed in any way. It was such a gratuitous intrusion that
I feared it had a deeper meaning that was yet hidden from me, something my
long absence from society had made me miss. Why—I asked myself—should
a supposedly independent judiciary concern itself with the grouching of a
known dissident? Was that institution now a mouthpiece of the state?

I was thrown into a mental quandary. I had not, after all, addressed or assailed the formal structure of justice, and I assumed that this was obvious.
Alas, my prison existence, in a circumscribed world with its limited but coherent relationships of objects and events, its internal logic that defines the very
nature of routine, had totally unfitted me for such an arbitrary, adversarial in-
terjection. It was my first test on returning to the real world, and I was thrown
off balance. I recovered an emotion that I had long forgotten: *fright*! Was this
what was in store for me after even such a brief confinement—a mere two years
and four months, no matter how endless it had appeared at the time? What had
become of the nation? Its civic institutions? How deeply had the militarized
state eroded their foundations? Suppose the state had chosen to bring me to
trial after all; where was the impartial arbiter into whose hands my fate would
have been thrust? Only at that moment, when indeed there was no longer a
likelihood of being brought to trial for any crime, did I first experience fright!

Was the statement of the chief justice intended as an official affirmation of
the *justice* of the war? The definitive word on the tragedy? What was the view of
his peers on the Supreme Bench, those who were Igbo or sympathizers, or perhaps had lost friends and relatives in the war? He was, after all, only a first
among equals.

I proceeded to review the immediate actuality of our national being, given
the costly, devastating war that was now, thankfully, drawing to a close. War,
after all, must be considered an abnormal event in any nation's life. To start
with, by the very nature of war, all norms of justice are surely set aside. You do
not invoke some code of jurisprudence to decide whether mercenaries should
fight your war or foreign pilots be brought into a conflict to bomb one side or
the other into submission. Once the shooting has begun, attempting to obtain
a court order for the restoration of the status quo ante between the combatants
is an absurdity; the deciding role has been conceded to force majeure, with or

without the restraining hand of national or international realpolitik or the Geneva Conventions. Thus, somewhere within the nation called Nigeria, some feeling of a suspension—at the very least—of the expectation of justice had to exist, some plaint of unmerited affliction, of deep-rooted suffering. Any thinking being must surely concede that elementary probability! There had to be innocent victims, both individual and community. The Biafrans, major actors in this war, assuredly nursed a feeling of injustice. The Midwest Igbo, first compromised by their kin from across the Niger, then "liberated" by federal forces and slaughtered in batches for "collaborating" with the Biafrans, must feel engulfed in blood founts of injustice. The minorities of the delta region, forced into an unwanted entity called Biafra and brutalized, had surely undergone at the hands of Biafrans a monumental injustice. The very process of their liberation must have caused some undeserved suffering, thus breeding a sense of double injustice. Justice denied, injustice unmerited, even as expressions of the barest possibilities, surely existed beyond dispute. What, then, I continued to demand of my captive audiences—close friends and comrades—what problem could the chief justice possibly have with that?

Mentally, I began looking over my shoulder with a burgeoning paranoia. It was not quite how I had envisaged my induction into normal existence. I was made more acutely aware how deeply that commodity called justice, however qualified, was central to my self-apprehension and ordering of the human community, and it was not a healthy feeling. The world, I felt, was out of tune if the pinnacle of the structure of justice considered it necessary to assume the responsibility of responding to a man who had just emerged from a confinement to which he had been consigned without trial, most of it solitary confinement, who had been lied against without a means of defending himself. If only in his own right, for no other cause besides his own, this emerging recluse surely had a right to proclaim a prima facie case of injustice, since he had never been brought to trial for any crime. The legitimacy of a chief justice was nonexistent outside the basis of Nigerian ground rule: *deemed innocent until proven guilty!* But the main shock for me was the fact that anyone at all, apart from a recognized government mouthpiece or a political adversary, should assume the responsibility of attempting to counter what, at most, should be considered no more than the rhetoric of defiance!

I was truly obsessed with the need to find a meaning—so compulsive must have been my need for clarity after my prison sojourn. Everything had to make sense. I had to find a logical process, a credible sequitur to what had gone before, a rational cause in any situation that aspired to produce an effect. I worried about this statement as a dog does an unraveling ball of wool, little realizing that I was taking it so personally! The chief justice had not, after all, sentenced me to prison. I wore out the patience of my handful of listeners: Did the man interpret justice in the titular sense—that is, "justice" as in chief justice of the Federation? Did he imagine that I had cast doubts on his existential definition or indicted his functional reality? What had happened to the national edifice, its pillars, in my absence?

It was an unsettled period of intense speculation. Perhaps it was a continued variation of that phase in prison when I had created totally theoretical problems and sought to solve them mathematically—a subject I had hated in school—just to pass the time. Solitary confinement is a state in which one creates a microcosmic but coherent world, albeit a world of the lowest hierarchy. The prisoner's condition depends, first, on the will of his principal jailers, far removed from his predicament, and next, on their immediate agents, who regulate his day-to-day existence. Below those levels, however, the prisoner is the complete master of his universe, and that universe is regulated—if only for sanity—along strict, objective lines. Mine was certainly a world that was populated by trivia, by the mundane, but its very ordinariness was ordered and predictable. An improvised pen remained exactly where you chose to hide it, day after day and week after week. If by chance it was discovered, that probability had long been built into reality and thus became a logical development. My ink—*soyink*, I called it—was developed experimentally, but, once perfected, it followed the laws of supply—and quality—precisely as anticipated. The trusty left your food tray on the same spot day after day, and you reciprocated in like manner when you were done. Toilet paper was supplied—one roll for so many days. So were cigarettes. If there was a change—a rare occurrence—in the routine, there was a reason for it. When the superintendent paid a surprise visit, that also slid into a niche of normality—a surprise visit was exactly as it should be, a surprise. And so on and so on. Any unpredictable or irrational element was banished from that universe as a phenomenon that belonged to other hierarchies where one was not in control. By contrast, the environment from which I had been forcibly removed two years before, which I was now reentering, I began to discover was a more palpably humanized terrain, yet one that refused to answer to the name of logic and coherence. It did not guarantee the security of the predictable or rational explications of the unexpected.

MY REEDUCATION WAS GRADUAL, and of course it began with recollections of what daily existence had been like before my detention. The chief justice had unknowingly administered a salutary shock. I now learned to recognize that I had been released from prison into a paradox—a nation that wallowed in triumphalism yet was under subjugation. It was a society that fed contentedly from a common trough of humiliation but paraded itself as the People of Victory. Paradox did not exist in my prison environment; hence my disorientation by the quite commonplace response of a chief justice. I did not immediately recognize the nation I had left behind, yet my absence had not really amounted to much in a nation's life. Perhaps if nearly two years of those twenty-eight months had not been spent in solitary confinement—if, for instance, I had had steady contact with visitors, newspapapers, radio—I might have been inducted into the altered psyche of the nation, and would have been better prepared for the norm of citizen sycophancy and self-abasement that had replaced the self-esteem on which we had earlier ridden, as the rightful place for a people who had no history of internal subjugation. A new social culture had, however, emerged in civil society: allegiance to the military and a need to promulgate the righteousness of a war now in its final days. I had done nothing more than provide Justice with its own opportunity; there was, apparently, more than one means of contributing to the Troops Comfort Fund!

With victory go the spoils of war. Civil society lay at the feet of the conquerors, and within that civil society were many who had genuinely cheered, even sacrificed for, the war of oneness. For others, the military had become enthroned as the new elite, and the level of fawning and jockeying to be merely noticed and smiled upon by any pretender in uniform already spoke of a nation that was loudly pleading to be crushed underfoot. The army was only too willing to oblige, the message ground into public consciousness—of young and old, big man and nonentity—that there was a new overlordship sprung to life in full formation, that the ragged boot of the lowest corporal rested permanently on that rung of the ladder where the hands of the civil engineer, the business tycoon, the university professor, the crowned head, and even the cleric competed for a hold that might eventually haul up the rest of the body one more step. And as each military boot scraped itself onto the head of the civic worthy below, that head turned upward with a most ingratiating smile and received the full dollop of the scrapings in its wide-open mouth.

With the entrenchment of the military, the season of unsolicited résumés began: *Please, sir, I am available for a Parastatal Board membership, diplomatic posting, one-man management board, administrator, commission of enquiry, tenders board, et cetera, et cetera.* There were, of course, uplifting exceptions, individuals who turned down lucrative temptations and chose to stick to their professions, as well as hundreds of unknowns who simply refused to accept any act of humiliation by a soldier, even fought them physically at the risk, sometimes the cost, of their lives. Such was the lady radiographer Dupe Oke, who was slapped by a soldier at a roadblock at Idi-ayunre, some miles from Ibadan. Her crime was no more than failing to understand what exactly the soldier demanded of her. She opened the boot of her car for inspection, opened her glove compartment, but the soldier kept jabbering more instructions. "I'm sorry, I don't understand what you want," she finally said, and was rewarded with a slap across the face. "You no understand, you no understand what? You think I come here waste time for grammar people like you?"

He did not get much further. Dupe flew at him and sank her teeth into his face. It took nearly the entire crowd of motorists awaiting their turn to be searched to pry open her teeth and release the soldier. It was one of the lucky cases—she could easily have been shot. The people rallied around, however. One of the travelers raced to the nearest cantonment in Ibadan and returned with a superior officer and some military police in tow. The soldier, raw flesh dangling from his cheek, was arrested and taken away. His pathetic visage did not save him. He was given the "guardroom" treatment for more than three months, we learned, while Dupe received apologies and an escort to her destination.

NOT SO FORTUNATE was Ola Rotimi, playwright and director, the recollection of whose ordeal, which he himself narrated to me on my return from prison, would sometimes jerk me awake covered in sweat in the middle of the night. In vain I admonished myself: Why do you give yourself this vicarious agony? But it was a scene that persisted in my head for a long while, and at all hours. I would recall it right in the middle of my work and stop. A long time would pass before I would realize that I had been staring at the wall, my heart beating rapidly as I put myself irrationally through a bout of anxiety, one that would sometimes trigger a slight trembling in my hands. In Ola Rotimi's position, what would I have done? What was the right decision at such a moment? Why should anyone be subjected to such a dilemma?

Ola was close to Ikorodu town, on the "old Ikorodu road" as it became later known, after the dual carriageway that now links Ibadan to Lagos was built. There was the usual succession of roadblocks, the personnel at each hardly knowing or caring what the dictator of the last—sometimes within sight of each other—had done. Ola Rotimi, a short man with broad shoulders and a boulder of a head, was a lecturer and dramatist at the University of Ife. He had his family with him, his foreign wife and children. Sometimes when the line of vehicles was long—which was often—the soldiers would go up and down the line, scrutinizing the passengers, pounce on a random choice, and wave the others on. This was what happened to Ola. A soldier came alongside and looked into the car—it was a station wagon without a closed luggage section—asked to see his papers, and then waved him on. Ola pulled out of the line, like others who had been similarly cleared, and moved. Suddenly a soldier stepped out from the head of the queue, stopped him, and ordered him to pull over. Ola Rotimi obeyed.

"Come outside!" he ordered.

Again, Ola did not argue.

"Everybody, come out. Yes, all of you, come out!"

Ola opened the door of the car and helped his family out.

"Stand there. Stand over there."

Ola began to protest. "But what's the matter?"

"Shut up! You no know wetin you do?* You jump queue." Ola Rotimi began to explain that he had been cleared to move, but the soldier again shut him up. "You jump queue, you tink say I no see you? You tink you be big man so you no fit wait like everybody?"

Ola pointed in the direction he had just come from. "Your companion over there passed us. You can ask him, he'll tell you."

The man snarled. "Oh, you telling me what to do? You still dey talk grammar? I show you pepper today. Come on, turn your back."

"What?"

"I say turn your back!" The soldier had slung his gun over one shoulder, and Ola now saw that he had replaced it with a horsewhip. "You getting twelve lashes to teach you lesson—turn your back."

For what must have seemed an eternity, said Ola Rotimi, he merely stared at him, unable to believe his ears. Another soldier had moved up, with his gun pointing at the trapped man. The first one screamed at him again, unslinging his gun, "You deaf or what? If I count three and you no yet turn your back, I fire you on the spot!" And Ola both heard and saw him remove the safety catch on his gun.

"One! ..."

In between "One" and "Two," Ola Rotimi told me, he reviewed his life in a flash. His intense eyes must have enveloped his wife, his three children,

---

* "You don't know what you did?"

through his thick-rimmed glasses, aimed another look at the unprepossessing figure towering over Ola's five-foot-three frame and now virtually frothing at the mouth with insane rage. In that brief moment, his entire world was wrapped up in one thought: Am I about to make my wife a widow and these ones fatherless?

"Two! ..."

Again a flash of his lifeless body on the road, his wife and children kneeling and wailing but helpless beside it. He presented his back to the soldier.

"Put your both hands on the car!"

Ola obeyed. As the lash tore into his back again and again, Ola, who was anything but pro-Biafran, swore that his wish at that moment was that a rogue Biafran plane would penetrate through to Lagos and unleash a barrage of bombs on the very spot where he stood, pulverizing everyone, including himself, equalizing torturer and victim with its deadly weaponry of arbitrary terror.

For a long time after Ola had poured out his bitter heart to me, I continued to sweat out that lethal question: *What would I have done?*

SUCH DEHUMANIZATION OF the populace did not take place only at checkpoints that were formally manned, but these were the most public places, and their audiences were guaranteed to cover the entire gamut of civil life. Day by day civil society endured, witnessed, and passed on the message. The uncertainty with which a traveler set out in the morning, deprived of the authority of office and security of the home, was a constant, debilitating companion. It preyed on innocence itself, instilling an irrational fear because of the irrationality of the lords of existence to whom an unintended slur, a gesture adjudged to be lacking in the respect that was due to the wielders of guns and horsewhips, could result in instant, public humiliation or worse. The most favored school of domination by the occupying force was thus the public arena, or the nearest to it, sometimes improvised or converted, as might be a private occasion such as a wedding, a child-naming ceremony, or a funeral. It might be one of those ostentatious parties—the ubiquitous *owambe* parties—that routinely spilled over into streets sealed off to traffic to accommodate the over-affluent of civil society or relatives and cronies of the military. There, any act deemed lèse-majesté would result in the open "drilling" of the offender or his kidnapping on orders from the unofficial chairman of the occasion, bloated already by commandeered authority, doubly bloated by ample food, XO cognac, Veuve Clicquot champagne—nothing less would do for khaki—and triply bloated by the obsequious attention of his hosts. And if the erratic Electricity

Power Authority chose that moment to inflict a routine blackout on the arena of pleasure, what better sport than to send a military jeep for the local station manager, haul him out of bed, and order him to shed power from other sources and restore electricity to the hallowed spot! Then, to impress on the locals the lesson that such acts of gross disrespect would never be tolerated, he would order his underlings to strip him half naked and frog-march him around the dance arena, then send him to the guardroom, where his head would be shaved with a piece of broken bottle, his body lashed with the infamous twisted cable and subjected to further indignities for days, until friends, relations, local and distant dignitaries of the town came to plead for mercy: "Sorry, Suh, the slight was unintended, he didn't know that your Excellency would be attending the party, or he would have suspended the power-shedding schedule until the party was over." And no question about it, civil society constantly collaborated in its own humiliation. A private quarrel was no longer arbitrated by any of the traditional routes of community intervention or even by the local courts. It sufficed that one knew someone in uniform, however low in rank. Come Judgment Day, the man of khaki connection would descend on the offending party with a bunch of his pals. They would smash their way into the household, slapping, kicking, vandalizing, and often making off with the miscreant—or hostage—until the terms of settlement, as dictated by the complainant, were accepted by the accused.

And it spread and spread, and the culture was imbibed by a prostrate society, one governor and petty administrator striving to outdo the next in sadism. From major and petty contractors to teachers and students, to all seekers after essential documents—title deeds, certificates of occupancy, certified true copies of this and that—to unpaid pensioners, to hoteliers, to local government councillors, and more, more, and more, sooner or later members of all strata of society found themselves knocking at the door of some government office, usually located at the secretariat. Thus the secretariats were guaranteed regular captive spectators as these were turned into stadia of blood sports masquerading as "discipline." And of course, to ensure that the lessons there were driven home, literally, state television and other media would be summoned in advance to capture and disseminate the images—the spruced-up, ticktock, no-nonsense administrator, enforcing public discipline in set-up scenarios.

A BRIGADIER, CAPTAIN, OR colonel administrator arrives at his office five minutes before the official opening hour. On the dot of half past seven, he orders the gates to the secretariat closed while his soldiers take up positions by the main gate and seal off all other entry points. Then any worker arriving late, no matter his or her rank, age, or physical condition, is made to do the "frog hop." A frog hop? Literally to hop or jump like a frog! The culprit attaches his fingers to his ears, lowers himself on his haunches, and hops in one spot, circles a tree or parked vehicles, or goes up and down the road. Laggards are assisted to improve their performance with the application of the *koboko,* the infamous rawhide whip, across their backs or knees. The real horror, however, is not this act of public torture but the ingratiating "Uncle Tom" smile on the faces of some of the victims. It is as if, knowing there is no other purpose to this spectacle, no other intent than to destroy their dignity, they try to draw the sting from their abasement and pass it off as a joke. Don't show resentment, pass it off as merely humoring the strange ways of this unwanted breed, and behold, the shame evaporates. It is all a staged performance in which symbolic roles have been assigned—and without prejudice.

Ogun be praised, there were always a few who hissed their contempt at their would-be disciplinarians, turned their backs on the scene, got into their cars or simply walked away, and went home to write their resignation letters. Some got away with it; others were forcefully compelled to comply or else were arrested and taken away, where they received an augmented dose in the military guardroom. A number of deaths occurred—from heart attack—from this unaccustomed exercise, but it made no difference. Dis'pline was dis'pline, and the civil servant was required to submit to its irrationalities. It did not matter in the least—to come down to administrative realities—that the nature of the employee's duty sometimes required that he or she visit some other offices, do some rounds in a relevant professional constituency, resume the routine of inspection of some critical installations before resorting to his or her desk. No—such explanations were dismissed with full military aplomb. Be at your desk on the dot of 7:30 A.M. or else—prepare to be *dis'plined.*

Humiliation filled the streets, the highways, in competition with violence. It entered the homes on camera cables and infested the media with tales of horror. Freedom had begun to compare most unfavorably with prison existence, yet the mood around me appeared to be one of celebration—of victory over a great evil called secession. I now began to feel like a stranger, though surrounded by familiar landmarks. It was rather like going to sleep in a familiar room, yet waking up each morning in the wrong neighborhood, a feeling that was undoubtedly aggravated by recollection of those months in solitary, difficult as they sometimes proved, in which one constituted the entirety of his world, undisturbed. Resumption of my friendship with Femi provided some solace, but nothing really helped to resolve the question that obsessed me: *What would I have done in Ola's place?* That is, what would I have done in place of the many Ola I knew, some of them old enough to be the grandfathers and grandmothers of the agents of their humiliation? The only certitude in my mind was a negative one—I had not thought that the prison regimen could ever lay claim to leaving the inmate with more dignity than victims of the *dis'pline* in which civil society daily acquiesced.

MY SENSE OF ESTRANGEMENT was compounded by the lingering effects of a loss that had taken place in my absence: that of my private den. All animals need a hole into which they can crawl from time to time. With every passing day, I acknowledged that, while in prison, I had looked forward to retreating into mine once I was released. Indeed, solitary confinement appeared to have deepened what had once been mere habit into a visceral need.

The den was gone. Its shell remained—a converted motor garage—but only as another space of estrangement. A visitation—or a series of visitations—had turned the den into just another warehouse. I had not thought that so much empathy could be lodged, over time, within a mere array of man-made objects, creating an aura of near inviolability. Without that den of escape, I turned increasingly irritable, impatient, and restless—even I could sense that, without the aid of surprised stares and protests. A physical distancing from an alienating environment was only a matter of time.

I was discovering much about myself. I had thought that the state of imprisonment, where the environment is not of one's choosing, would inoculate an inmate with resistant germs against any future sense of privation, make one indifferent to possessions. I gradually learned that the state of freedom also breeds desires and expectations, including the craving for an accustomed space, a sanctuary, a physical, palpable, intimate space, not unlike solitary confinement in a prison cell but, of course, of one's own choice and designation. Already alienated from the public environment, I was now deprived of an intimacy that I had once relished, one within which I could take refuge from the outside world and also regain a sense of fluidity in the creative process.

Perhaps if my marriage—briefly resuscitated by shared tribulations and the emotions of reunion—had held out, the throb of alienation would have been muted. However, the differences that had turned that marriage into a mere effort before my imprisonment resurfaced in no time at all, increasing a daily, prolonged craving for a handy escape, a familiar, welcoming lair. I still entered the converted garage from time to time, but it had lost its deep, self-absorbing aura.

I threw myself into the filming of *Kongi's Harvest*, under the direction of Ossie Davis, the black American actor, with the possessed cineaste Francis Oladele as the producer. Day after day, the designated lead, Gaius Anoka, expected from the Biafran territory, failed to turn up—we later found out that he had been denied a clean bill of health by the debriefing team of the victorious federal side and thus was not permitted to leave the subdued enclave. Ossie Davis filmed around and around his absence, but in the end there was not one scene left that could be shot without the figure of the dictator, Kongi.

All eyes turned to me. Till then, I had contented myself with adjusting the script and tackling Ossie's queries but mostly working with the music. Now—enter the star!—I stepped into the role of the dictator for one of my least memorable performances. Still, the frenzied and intense pace of that preoccupation helped. As I was on location most of the time, a shifting environment succeeded in blunting the need of the animal for his lair. In between shoots, however, on returning home, there was no congenial space into which I could withdraw. Not until I had lost this sanctuary did I discover how deeply dyed I was in that "deadly sin" from which I had so blithely excepted myself: attachment! It was a surprise—and something of a discomfiture—to find that I did own something that I deeply valued. It did not help matters that the blow that routed my assumptions had been struck from within my family.

Ironically, the transgressor, my junior brother—who narrowly escaped decapitation or worse at my hands—would provide for me, as for both family and acquaintances, proof of the redemptive potential of any human being. Kayoos—his favorite nickname—became a born-again Christian. Yes, the real thing, I testify to that! As authentic a born-again Christian and evangelist as you would hope to meet on this side of sin. Kayoos was transformed into an actively caring asset to the whole family with all its extensions, and to friends. At the time, however ... !

As I emerged from prison and was reinstalled in my campus home, it was not difficult to observe that among the endless tumult—family, colleagues, friends, and even total strangers—who invaded the house, one face, with its wide, guileless smile and a booming baritone voice, was conspicuous by its absence. This absence was made all the more noticeable by the fact that the face had made a very brief early appearance on my arrival at Ibadan airport, when its owner had held me in a powerful and emotional embrace. And then it had disappeared altogether!

That was strange. Kayoos's natural place was at the heart of celebrations, and this was an occasion especially tailored to his expansive, adventurous, and outgoing nature. Kayoos was very affectionate. I knew that he had remained fond of me even when I had totally given up on him, having fully taken my turn at the rehabilitation roulette in which he engaged the rest of the family and gotten thoroughly burned for my pains. I had indeed begun to remark openly that only a prison spell would make him confront the realities of life; thus the ironic fact that my mother and I did have a meeting point—in prayer. I prayed that his prison experience would not scar him for life but would be very short, sharp, and painful, thus achieving what all our efforts in the family had failed to do. Wild Christian, needless to say, harbored no such thoughts. She simply importuned God to change him—in His own good time of course, she hastened to reassure Him—but really tomorrow, preferably.

Even before my prison detention, I was undoubtedly the most severe on him. I forbade him not only my home and office but my presence. That did not stop him occupying one of the rooms in the tiny annex to the official residence, intended for the house help but often converted into a colorful student pad. I knew that my wife—another of the rehabilitation team—had let him stay there, but I pretended not to know. He kept out of my way and never entered the main house while I was around. Once I was out of the way, however, Kayoos would come in and help himself to whatever he needed, run errands for my wife, and play with his nephews, nieces, and cousins—in short, everyone behaved like a true Yoruba, or indeed the average African: you snarl at the stray sheep but pretend that you never noticed that the side door was left open for it to sneak in at night.

The garage was home to my modest collection of—mostly traditional— artworks. I lavished all my spare resources in acquiring them, and they were indeed a main source of marital friction. It had become my habit to turn the garage in whatever house I occupied into a gallery cum study, and this was where I spent most of my time, working among the ancestral masks, the gods, their caryatids, shrine posts, and vessels, basking in their aura. It provided a working ambiance that suited my temperament, rather like being within a web of emanations from multiple existences. But the gallery also served a less exalted purpose. Along its backyard, separated by a heavy copse that was home— we would discover much later—to a nest of pythons, ran one half of the dual carriageway that led to the university campus. This meant that a car could stop or be parked behind the house, its passenger walking through the copse directly to the garage without disturbing the household. As my marriage disintegrated, this sanctum sanctorum would serve as a venue for desperate assignations, usually in the dead of night. The snakes, fortunately, did not appear to have been unduly disturbed by these nocturnal intrusions.

Nor were the gods under whose watchful eyes they took place. It was my very private world. Within it, I experienced no sense of betrayal; guilt did not obtrude, did not exist. Marriage, now a mere formality, remained equally protected in its own continually expansive world of responsibilities, emotional impositions, and domestic bargaining, but this arena of deities and ancestors remained impervious to its moralities. Heavy wood sculptures, bronzes, caryatids and votive vessels, ceremonial drums and metallic gongs—they provided relief for the mind when inspiration flagged and my fingers fluttered aimlessly over the typewriter. Most times, however, they proved an additional impetus for those stretches when the fingers tapped a productive rhythm on the keys. While I was locked away in prison, family and visitors found it most touching to see Kayoos turning up from time to time to dust my collection, take out the cobwebs, and spruce up the appearance of his big brother's prized sanctum.

Then one day, my wife visited a colleague of hers. A friend from the United States had been staying with that lady, and now he was getting ready to leave. Strewn all over the floor, in various stages of wrapping and packing, were souvenirs he was taking with him. Quite innocently, she sensed a familiarity in some of the artifacts and observed that her friend's visitor appeared to have similar tastes to mine. Then she picked up another piece. Interesting, that also looked familiar ... and then another, even more familiar. Suddenly, she felt dead certain. The coincidence was too much. There could not be such consistency; the pieces were not merely familiar, they looked identical, and there were far too many of them. One piece in particular belonged in the living room, so she had grown accustomed to it. She excused herself and returned home. Yes, it was gone; so were a number of other pieces within the house and a lot more from the garage-museum.

The collector had no misgivings whatsoever. He had bought them, and legitimately. He knew to whom they belonged but had been made to believe that Kayoos had been given the authority to dispose of them. This was easy enough to believe, as Kayoos was well known in expatriate circles as a dealer in traditional items, though not necessarily antiquities. And what was more logical than to assume that the family of an imprisoned man, incommunicado, might need to dispose of some personal items to take care of their immediate financial needs?

What items that could be retrieved from the hapless visitor were taken back, but of course he was not the only buyer from Kayoos's limitless source. A number of coveted objects had disappeared forever.

While I sojourned in prison, oblivious to my bereavement, a series of family meetings and consultations with friends began. Bola Ige, lawyer and combative politician, undertook the task of extricating Kayoos from the criminal consequences of his enterprise, since the effort to recover other items had necessarily involved the police. Femi Johnson was at hand to give advice and exert his influence in other vital directions. As the day approached for my release, the meetings were resumed with one agenda: how to break the news to me and what to do about this near-unhealable breach. The first decision was predictable, being based on what even those outside the immediate family had instinctively grasped, or had been told, about my attachment to these works of art: Kayoos was ordered to keep his distance from me. He could come and join in the welcome on the very first day, but that was all. And so he seized the earliest chance to break out from the crowd and give me that most expressive hug, disappeared into the crowd, and swiftly left town.

The moment I could escape the throng of visitors, my first visit was to this private den. I had been absent twenty-eight months, but I had a total recall of my collection: how they had been stored, how one related to another across the room or jostled for shelf space with a third. I knew in which direction I turned at my desk to rest tired or questing eyes on an Ogun here, an Esu there; I knew which corner Osanyin reposed in with his skeletal birds, cowrie beads, and train of leather thongs, where the divination tray was propped against the bamboo support, and where, I would joke, a field of force was generated between a phallus-burdened monkey and a caryatid with a split vulva. And there were the bronze miniatures whose patina I caressed as I strolled between the bamboo shelves that I had constructed myself, the uprights festooned with ancestral masks or elaborately carved hunter's fly whisks. Now all I saw were gaps, clamorous absences.

I asked questions, obtained vague answers from my wife.... Oh, some of the items had been sent for restoration and then kept for their own safety ... anyway, Professor This or That would speak to me about them later. Something was wrong, I knew, but I chose to be patient. There were, in any case, more pressing concerns that had been created by my absence.

They came like a mournful delegation to break the news of a family bereavement—an uncle, a cousin-in-law, a mother-in-law, an elderly family dependent; and of course, lurking in the background, ready to interject some balm or whisk me away to some place of recovery was—OBJ. They judged that the moment was right, having allowed me a few days to settle back into domesticity, be reabsorbed into a living community, but also to recover from the overpowering waves of well-wishers. Now there was this family matter to be settled, a breach to be healed. I listened to voices of entreaty, numbed ... *You have to remember, whatever it takes, he is still your brother. The important thing is that we are able to give thanks to God for your safe return. Add this to the list of the trials that you underwent; even though you did not know it at the time, this loss is part of those trials nonetheless. Only God knows what he has in store as compensation, but certainly he means to make restitution a hundredfold. You have your family, your children; your standing in the world is a thing of envy in the minds of thousands you've never heard of. . . . Family is family, no matter what . . .* and on and on and on. . . . The case was still with the police. They were waiting for me to return before they could close the files. As the owner of the stolen or missing goods, only I could give them instructions to do so. If I could find my way to doing this as soon as possible, then we could all get over the nightmare and put it behind us.

They had done their duty. I thanked them. I replied that I had listened carefully to what they had to say and assured them that I had taken the disaster stoically. I had no interest whatever in exacting the appropriate penalty from the scoundrel. As far as I was concerned, there was no case, there was to be no criminal pursuit, and the case should simply be allowed to lapse. None of them should, however, expect that I would go to the police station or write a letter asking that the case be discontinued. Just let it lapse. If they wanted me to get over this blow as quickly as possible, it would be the only way—that it be dropped like a stone into a pond. *Finis!*

They remained worried. It seemed to them a kind of closure but one that lacked an impermeable casing. Yes, they were in full agreement. It would be asking too much of me to take the active step of approaching the police. But suppose they brought the officer in charge of the case to me and I gave him instructions? I considered this, then thought up an even better idea for my peace of mind—I wanted so desperately to be alone. Look, I proposed, why don't you write the letter? Make it short and to the point: *I, Wole Soyinka, complainant in the matter of the stolen antiquities, hereby declare that I do not wish to pursue any criminal charges and hereby authorize you to close the case.* Something along those lines. Just write it and I'll sign it. I don't even wish to read it. Write it now, right now. I want the matter closed.

They all turned to my friend Femi Johnson. He had been part of the conspiracy from the beginning, though he had said nothing so far, since this was basically a family matter. Quickly, he wrote the short one-paragraph letter. I signed it. Then there was some hemming and hawing. I looked around at the faces; obviously they were not done.... *Well, there is still the family matter.* Family matter? What family? *Well, your brother... when can he come to see you? He has to know that you've forgiven him.*

I was puzzled. What were they talking about? Had they really failed to fasten on the one conclusion that occupied my mind? Yes, of course, there was the sense of betrayal, but it went further. The collection had been my life, so I felt as if I had been murdered. It was quite simple: anyone who was capable of doing this could only have done it out of one conviction—that I would not emerge from prison alive. I looked at their faces, surprised that this obvious awareness had eluded them—*he had wished me dead, he had assumed me dead, he was stealing from a dead man!* Could they not see this as clearly as I did? I heard one of them say, *We've told him to stay away for now.* No, no, you tell him to stay away for good. For good! It's no longer a family matter, because I no longer consider him family. So tell him to keep away. I don't wish to see him ever. I don't wish to know him. In fact, I do not know him.

That evening, after they had left, I went into the garage and packed my books and papers. I did not bestow so much as a glance of regret at my silent companions, feeling only an expanse of deep violation, of betrayal and deep distrust—not focused on any being, since I had truly wiped out my assailant's existence from my mind. All I had left was a void, the loss of a vital organ. But it also triggered off a process of self-chastisement: *See? That's what comes of becoming attached to material things. Now see how devastated you are. Were these really anything but props? Crutches! Deprived of your crutches, you are crushed! Yes, crushed! So much for those phases of self-dissolution in which you indulged in prison confinement, when even your physical self vanished and you found peace in the abode of nothingness. So much for your claims of companionship with the hermit priest Malarepa: "I need nothing. I seek nothing. I desire nothing." Does it require the barrenness of a prison cell to induce such wisdom in the mind, and is such wisdom so soon dissipated on emerging from confinement?*

Still, no one could deny that it was my right to remain attached to my books and papers, or at least to need them for my living, so I piled them into the car and drove to my office behind the theater. I tumbled them into a corner and, in that deadened state of mind, chloroformed by loss and repudiation, proceeded to set up a new work space. The gods remained in their own abode, abandoned, but this was a condition to which they had been accustomed for the past two years anyway, and even since eternity. They were free to seek their own remedies; all I asked for was my peace of mind. My reinstallation in this neutral space completed, I drove furiously to Femi's house, late as it was. He was expecting me. We drank late into the night.

IT TOOK YEARS before I would again acknowledge the right of this rump collection to a place in my existence or move to replenish it. The healing came gradually; Kayoos underwent a virtual transfiguration, becoming almost one with the playful, even sometimes watchful presences in his own inner sanctuary. At the time, however, the void in my private space only augmented the hollowness that beset me whenever I was thrust into the public arena, from which I had become even more viscerally alienated. It left me craving distance, a tactile and sensory severance. I slipped out fusslessly and, into my first—and only—spell of voluntary exile.

PART III

Interlude to a Friendship

Interlude to a Friendship

. . . . .

LOOKING BACK, IT STRIKES ME WITH SOME ASTONISHMENT THAT, UNTIL his death in 1987, one constant, a large presence in the "extracurricular" undertakings of my adult existence, was Olufemi Babington Johnson. Just who was this being?

I have often wondered what he would have made of Sani Abacha. What role would he have played in our struggle? I know that he would not have hesitated one moment to place resources at my disposal, most especially for Radio Kudirat, the opposition radio that drove Sani Abacha to distraction. Femi once paid me an unusual compliment, an invaluable gift, if only he had known it! He confided it to his second wife, Folake, who passed it to mine, her namesake. This man said of me, "You can leave your heart with Wole and travel to Hong Kong. When you come back, it would still be beating." I must confess that I have never ceased to ponder and be moved by this tribute. The views of women with whom I have had disastrous relationships will probably differ, but—best to stay away from that literal track!

This, of course, was a tribute that was infinitely appropriate for him, and I wondered if he ever thought about himself that way or made it a guiding principle of his existence. I only know that his words hovered around my head like a talisman long after his death, as if in silent exhortation. To a degree, we do aspire to live up to the view of others, no matter how stoutly we deny it. During the fight against Sani Abacha's tyranny, I could hardly deny myself the echo of Femi's words urging me on in that obsessive mission: to keep the heart of a nation, of a people, beating, even after a demented dictator had ripped it out and squeezed its lifeblood down his throat.

Femi's generosity was not limited to tributes to a friend. As one frustrated year succeeded the last, I would imagine scenes of clandestine meetings—in London, Kampala, Paris, Lisbon, Dakar, Vineroz, and other venues—where his first question would most certainly have been: How can I contribute? Then would follow a self-deprecating catechism of his lack of physical courage. The cloak-and-dagger arrangements that would have preceded such a meeting— for his own protection—would have set his eyes dancing with relish. We would meet for lunch or dinner. Straight from the first course, I would spring the surprise, letting him realize for the first time that I knew and had been moved by his tribute. *Femi, you want the heart of that nation of ours to continue beating, not so? Well, help me fund a clandestine opposition radio.* A double take, the inimitable laughter boom, a threat to "hammer that woman's head"—his wife's, for betraying his confidence—and his next question would be: What do you need, and how soon?

Difficult now to imagine that once we did not speak to each other for nearly seven months and I pronounced our friendship at an end. It was absurd, a falling-out that made little sense, but it did happen. I declared it all dead: the years of intense bonding, of arguments, risks, of political and other—far more delectable—exploits, both the casual encounters and others that demanded elaborate organizational skills and complex logistics, covering up for each other as needed. Or the theater and other performance ventures, the hunting expeditions, and of course the hours at his generous table, or at my skimpier one, which gave up, very early, all attempts to rival his sybaritic largeness. A compulsive performer, with artistic sensibilities and a sonorous baritone singing voice, Femi could have shaped his life in a different direction, in a different environment, but he chose to become an insurance broker and entrepreneur, and became an immensely successful one. Perhaps what drew me to him was partly recognition of that road not taken, the repressed artist within the nattily suited businessman, a keen political animal that yet fled politics, one who did not hesitate to take the hearts of others into his hands for safekeeping—or resuscitation.

THE KENYAN WRITER Ngugi wa Thingo never met Femi Johnson, but his wife did. So did Ngugi's comrade in arms Micere Mugo, one of the dissidents of Kenya's intelligentsia, resolutely opposed to the corrupt and repressive government of Daniel arap Moi. At the height of arap Moi's paranoid and draconian rule in the 1970s, I became desperate to make contact with Ngugi, about whose condition in prison we were receiving only disquieting news. I had not yet developed any of the multiple identities that I was later obliged to adopt and owned only one passport. A personal appearance in Nairobi would have been short-lived—a press conference, perhaps, and I would have been back on the next plane under police escort—assuming that I was even allowed into Kenya in the first place. In any case, Ngugi's associates—Micere Mugo and others—had advised against a personal visit by me.

As if by a miracle, the African Association of Insurance Brokers decided to hold its annual conference in Nairobi. I had letters and money to deliver to Ngugi's wife—I was then secretary-general of the Union of Writers of the African Peoples, an organization that I initiated in Ghana in 1972 and that was formally inaugurated in Dakar the following year under Léopold Sédar Senghor's patronage. I had squeezed a little money together from our members' contributions, and this was to go to Ngugi's aid. Even more important than the immediate monetary relief was the need to establish contact, to get a message to Ngugi that we were not simply sitting on our hands, indifferent to his predicament. Never—I am certain—has a meeting of insurance brokers been so conveniently timed in the cause of the arts—but it would happen for Femi and me! My friend readily agreed to carry out the mission.

"If they catch you," I joked, "you're on your own. Only if I learn that you are actually about to be executed will I come for you personally."

"Don't worry. Before anyone lays a hand on me, I'll spill the beans."

"Good. That's exactly what I want you to promise. No heroics. Begin with Micere—either she'll be at the university or someone will know where she is. Micere will take you to Ngugi's wife—it may require a long journey by road."

"I'll find her."

"That's most important. We want to know what she wants us to do, how she wants us to react to what is going on. Who else needs help. Be sure to have a long conversation with her. I want news about Ngugi—when she saw him last, how he is, how he's being treated, et cetera, et cetera."

He gave a mock salute. "Yes, Commandant!"

"And don't forget to insure yourself . . . I volunteer to be your beneficiary."

Femi's trepidation at such assignments was genuine. Equally genuine, however, was his relish of them! He reveled in the business of flattening letters and cash into false compartments of his suitcase, making clandestine phone calls from the public phone in the lobby of his hotel rather than from his room, trying out different verbal codes to disclose his identity and that of the person whose intermediary he was. Our insurance broker carried out his mission to the letter, and then some! He undertook a long, roundabout journey by road to meet Ngugi's wife, delivered the funds—to which, needless to say, he had added his own generous contribution, unasked. Instead of joining the organized safari tours with his colleagues, Femi spent two days in Kenya awaiting the contact that had been sent to penetrate through to Ngugi in prison. He met other contacts, wrapped up his mission, and landed in Lagos still wreathed in the high state of euphoria that only commenced—on his admission—once his plane had left Kenyan airspace. Then he eased himself into his accustomed role as the life and soul of the returning delegation for the rest of the journey, they little suspecting what their extrovert colleague had been up to while they were indulging in the fleshpots of Nairobi. Micere wrote a long, glowing report of his performance. They continued to correspond for a while after his return.

ORLANDO MARTINS, a famous Nigerian film actor who could boast of having had Paul Robeson and Ronald Reagan as his screen companions in the 1950s, had retired home to Nigeria. Now he was old, alone, and incontinent. Femi moved him to his sumptuous home in Iyaganku, the setting of many gourmandizing soirées, set him up permanently in his guest chalet, paid all his medical bills, and ministered to every want, whim, and caprice—and Pa Orlando, as he was fondly known, was more than a trial for Job and all the saints. There Pa Orlando stayed, bullied the cooks if his food was too salty or undersalted or ... *Take it away, I've told you I don't want it swimming in oil ... and this time don't forget the ow-nions!* There he remained, Femi's terminal guest, and Femi paid all the funeral expenses....

... OR THE CHILDREN of the villagers where we sometimes went to hunt, victims of all kinds of diseases that defied treatment. Femi would arrange for them to come into town and be examined by doctors. Sometimes he would assign a car and a driver to ensure that they came regularly for treatment until cured....

"*AJOJE L'ODUN*"—"The joy is in the sharing"—was his favorite refrain. And he lived it! Many experienced this only in those summational occasions that he particularly relished, such as his Christmas parties. Even now, nearly two decades later, at Christmastime, the city of Ibadan still undergoes the pangs of bereavement—and this extends beyond the middle class to which he belonged, since his festive hand extended to stewards, drivers, and his acquired hunting families, who were mostly farmers or working-class. No, he did not invite Ibadan's ten million population to his home, but to listen to complete strangers speak in awe of the famed parties, they must have believed he did.

Both for those who shared his bounty and for thousands of Ibadan's inhabitants who never ate from his table, Femi Johnson was synonymous with the transformation of Christmas/New Year's into one huge feast that could only have been dreamed up in pagan Rome. It became a recognized institution—no one gave a party on the last Saturday before Christmas, that was OBJ's day. You did not give a party because you expected to be invited, and if you were not on his guest list, some of your likely guests might be, and between the two, you did not stand a chance with a rival party. All likely guests were headed for *the* party at Iyaganku, where two or three live bands played till early morning and a film might be screened. At least three roasts, over which the host had personally sweated all day, were now ready for their piecemeal internment.

Literally, the table groaned under the weight and variety. The Lebanese section was standard. He had visited Lebanon quite early in his career—then as an employee in the insurance business—when Lebanon was still Lebanon and the business center of the East. He never tired of narrating the experience, and it was mostly—food! A whole roast sheep—and, as a special mark of honor, he had been served the eyes. Then the creamy dips—hummus, tahini, taramasalata, and labneh—and on to the spiced, scented pine nut rice, grilled eggplant, and—oh yes, what had constituted for him the most hilarious delicacy when he discovered what they were—sweetbreads! He had many Lebanese friends in Ibadan, and there was one Lebanese restaurant that later became his Sunday-dinner haunt. It was owned by the Haddad family, and there Femi would be found religiously with his family, armed with a couple of bottles of wine. It was this restaurant that mostly catered his Christmas parties.

Long before the array of food dazzled his guests, however, Femi would have already entered the festive mode. He supervised every aspect of preparation—except the autonomous Lebanese department, which had become adept at ignoring his constant emendations once his main list had been accepted. And so, apart from his own assignment, which was to turn the pink cadaver of a pig or ram into a work of art, pleasing to the eye and glorious on the palate, Femi busied himself with supervising—that is, choreographing the field of consumption. He was especially delighted with the traditional-food department: the women and their young assistants (usually their children) among huge clay pots and pans, plucking, stoking, kneading, pounding, turning farina, boiled yam, and cassava flour into *eba, iyan, amala,* and *fufu,* Femi among the bubbling vats of seafood, venison, beef, mutton, and vegetable stew, the cracking noises of giant snails being separated from their shells, and the numerous chickens browning on the spit.

"*Awon iya ndi aro*"*—and his eyes would sparkle, surveying the field of the busy women—"just the sight of them all over the compound, bent over the fires and cooking pots, vegetables being washed and sliced, meats being cut up and slapped into the huge *basia*† of oil all day long—yes, that's the best part of it. The festive atmosphere of preparation, even more than the result."

But this was not always part of him, not at the start of the sixties, when we first became really acquainted. It was not part of him, and he wanted no part of it. Later, he would become quite candid—but perhaps only with me—and mock himself over that phase of his choice of a lifestyle, when, in his own words, he must have cut the appearance of a displaced Englishman.

I DID NOT REALLY set out to change him. I accepted him as he was. But then, I was not about to change, either, or accommodate him when my temperament revolted profoundly against his inclinations. Certainly I was not about to join him at lunch or dinner eating boiled carrots, potatoes, tasteless fish fillet or steak, or lamb chops and soggy cabbage—all of which I rejected after my first full year in England, 1954–55, when I dutifully ate anything that was put before me. It was my health strategy for that strange, cold, and dismal land that existed, surely, solely to ensure my death from a thousand cold-related diseases!

My reasoning went thus: British weather was unfit for human habitation, yet the Britishers, including their young, vulnerable children, somehow survived it—the evidence was apparent in the many geriatrics who littered the landscape. The explanation could only be found in the kind of food they ate. Thus, for a stranger to survive, he had better submit to their diet, right down to the last revolting speck of mashed potato and the disgusting lick of brown gravy that covered the tasteless slab of undecipherable meat. I ate it all. Some items were less unbearable than others, certainly the breakfasts—oats or cornflakes, kippers, eggs fried or scrambled, bacon and sausages, slabs of bread with butter and marmalade, mugs of tea or synthetic coffee with milk and sugar—I was yet to lose my sweet tooth! British breakfast was quite enjoyable, but the rest—! Well, I ate it all, dutifully, as one swallows medicine. On the dot of twelve months from my first day in England, however, I deemed my body to have built up sufficient resistance to survive winter, fog, smog, clammy rains,

---

* "Women at the festive hearth."
† A wide-mouthed metal cooking pot.

and darkness at noon. I began to pick and choose, discovering the hideouts of Indian restaurants and the one or two Italian, whose choices were limited to spaghetti bolognese or napoletana.

It was therefore quite a shock to find, in the heart of Ibadan, any human being, and a Nigerian Yoruba to boot, who actually served, of his own volition, British cuisine. I would sit with Femi and his family at the dinner table, nursing a mug of beer, but I reserved my stomach space for dinner at home or in one of Ibadan's "sharp corners."

Saturday afternoon at OBJ's was, however, a different matter. Then the table went totally native. *Eba, amala, iyan,* with half a dozen stews to choose from—this was where I first knew that food was more than simply getting something down into the stomach as fusslessly as possible, that eating actually involved a self-surrender that rendered homage to Opapala, the deity of hunger. The family—and this included his British wife, Barbara—*ate*! They consumed with a gusto that bordered on celebration—yes, the celebration of food. Michael Olumide, the involuntary instigator of the broadcasting holdup, was a regular at the Saturday-afternoon phenomenon. He matched Femi morsel for morsel, but Femi, his napkin always tucked into his shirt collar like a bib, had the edge on him. Lunch began at about one o'clock, but rarely was the table cleared before four or five. It was true that in 1960, when I first witnessed Femi's weekend splurge, I had been away for four years, and perhaps I had forgotten that that was how people ate at home. But no, there was my own father as contrast, his picky style of eating. Even my mother, Wild Christian, who was a far more conscientious trencher lady—neither of them, and certainly none of the grownups around me, had eaten such single-minded quantity. I watched the Johnson family in fascination—nothing in my childhood, adulthood, or foreign sojourn had prepared me for such an elemental performance!

It became a challenge. I could not accept that even mere children—the oldest was then no more than twelve—could consume more than I did. I went without food for a full day before joining them, then two days, after which I refused to push that particular remedy any further. Would stomach exercises help? How did one expand one's stomach capacity? I had no idea. It always ended with my gasping for breath while Femi and others carried on as if the world of food were on the verge of extinction.

Next to the joy of eating, however, was perhaps Femi's love of the city of Ibadan and, conversely, our shared, visceral repugnance for the overgrown city of Lagos.

. . .

LAGOS, OPENING UP TO a motorist from the interior like the fetid tail of a strutting rooster, was a city from which we both instinctively recoiled—quite unlike hundreds of thousands of Lagosians who swear that they cannot bear the provincialism of other towns, even of the large beehive of Ibadan. For them, there is no life outside—or after—Lagos!

The day that Femi formally repudiated Lagos and established himself as a de facto citizen of Ibadan, the modern heartland of the Yoruba commercial world, was not too long after the end of the civil war and my release from prison under Gowon's military rule. That he should take the precaution of entering in his will a wish to be buried in Ibadan was a shock only to his family, not to those who truly knew him. I did not know the contents of his will, nor had he ever thought to mention any of its provisions to me, yet an alternative to Ibadan as his resting place was a possibility that my mind could not remotely contemplate when Femi collapsed in that city but drew his last breath in a hospital in distant Frankfurt.

The end of the Nigerian Civil War in 1969 brought with it a false economic optimism that swelled the population of Lagos, the national and business capital, beyond rational management. What was already a city under stress had become a clear case of swarming, warring, multiple personalities, lacking all coherence and identity. If there was any character left to Lagos by the end of the sixties, it was that of a khaki-and-camouflage ubiquitousness, with the civilian *agbada* and *babanriga,** or a three-piece-suited mendicancy that fawned on the former. Together, they squeezed Lagos until it choked on its own vomit, then stomped on the writhing corpse of a city whose human vitality was rivaled by none other in all of black Africa.

Femi was still an employee of a brokerage firm—Law, Union and Rock—in charge of the branch office at Ibadan. Then one day, he received a letter that would have set many Lagosian—or indeed, provincial—minds aglow: he was not only promoted to a high executive position in the business, he was to take up this new position at the headquarters of the firm in Lagos. Uncertainly, with a visage that belied an elevation in status and spoke more of a prison life sentence, Femi asked me to go house hunting with him. The quietude of Kaduna's prison solitary still dominated my response to crowded places, and I had avoided Lagos since my release. The mere thought of that raucous, overwrought space

---

* The northern version of the *agbada*, usually made of stiffer material.

set off alarms in my nervous system, and I demurred. I found a hundred excuses: lectures, rehearsals, family impositions, unexpected overseas engagements. It soon became clear that my friend would keep putting off his search until I was free to go with him. There could be no more evasion—I got ready for my first visit to Lagos since my release from Kaduna.

IT WAS, AS I FEARED, a descent into imagined hell. All semblance of community had vanished. The noise, the frenzy, the disorder! This was a labyrinth of clogged alleys and overburdened streets, dark mounds of indeterminate sludge, tinsel imports on sales racks or in pedestrian motion, festering carrion, abused and abusive humanity that called itself a city. We looked at four or five houses, and I noticed that Femi's inspection grew more and more perfunctory, more fault-finding and downright dismissive. What went on in his mind, he did not tell, but as for me, I was being driven through a built-up habitation of gaudiness and stench. Gutters were packed with garbage, and rivulets of gelatinous fluids overran the streets. Motorized traffic was a series of hiccups, a fractional circulation of the wheel each quarter hour, no more. The famous Broad Street, then renamed Yakubu Gowon Street, swarmed with a humanity that raced, lemminglike, to some destination of guaranteed perdition. Soldiers were in command everywhere, sheathed in khaki, more often than not a camouflage of ignorance and illiteracy yet with the assumed carriage of a superior race, conquerors from an alien planet, masters of arbitrary humiliation. Ita Faji cemetery, a green area where multitudes had once taken shelter during their work breaks and students had read under the trees in daytime and under streetlighting all night, had vanished, made way for a monstrosity called the Lagos Secretariat.

Of course it had not all happened overnight or begun with the military. The signs were already present at independence time, when the famous Supreme Court, a masterpiece of tropical architecture—solidly constructed, with airy corridors, wide wooden-louvered windows, and a warren of staggered rooms that allowed for the blissful circulation of air and people—was torn down limb by limb, erased from Tinubu Square. In its place was constructed a sterile fountain of cantilevered concrete pancakes—a gift, it was said, of the Lebanese community.

I was close to weeping in the year of independence, 1960, as the metallic ball swung again and again against the stubborn walls, which refused to yield without a fight. We had fought for the preservation of that building, pleaded that it be turned into a museum—if indeed a completely new Supreme Court building was required—but no, some purblind urban planner prevailed on his minister to decree that it make way for the Lebanese fountain, whose brief span of gushing glory, its ascension day on the wings of a thousand doves—or pigeons—would diminish to a trickle, dry up altogether, then turn into just another garbage bin for shopkeepers and food sellers. As for the pigeons let off to celebrate its opening, many vanished in twos and threes, trapped by the locals and turned into pigeon kebabs. Reading their fates at the wheels of motorcars in Lagos rush hour and the makeshift weekend fires around Tinubu fountains, the rest took off to unknown places—probably back to the peace of the cedar groves of Lebanon.

The rot of Lagos had begun long before I vanished behind prison walls, but in the two years of my absence, plus the year after my release when I had studiously avoided entering that city, Lagos had accelerated deep down into that pit of decay that is the complementary face of unplanned, greed-motivated development. Greed for unoccupied real estate produced the violation of virtually every available green space. The lush swathes of land in Ikoyi, the residential retreat of the colonial elite, now enjoyed by the new black colonial aristocrats and lucky civil servants, were being torn up to raise more residences for the equally rapacious military elite who were steadily consolidating their grip on the nation. The famous royal palm tree–lined "Love Gardens" of Onikan had lost nearly four-fifths of their territory. Lagos was choking with mimic high-rise buildings. The city no longer breathed; it coughed, sputtered, and spat phlegm. Even the beachfront, the marina, had been encroached upon all along its length. The oil boom had not been formally inaugurated, but it was clear that some people knew something that others did not, because it was simply illogical that so soon after a costly, inhuman war there could have been such an accelerated pace of costly patchwork development of the capital city.

The canals that threaded Ikoyi and Onikan, bringing fishermen and even passengers to the markets of Sand Grouse at Oke Suna, flowed at a somnolent pace behind the police headquarters at Obalende, opened into the lagoon behind Broadcasting House, and lapped the shores of the University of Lagos—the canals were being sanded in, "reclaimed." Nothing but stubbornly retentive memory and nostalgia came to the rescue to serve as a tenuous backcloth to my radio play *A Scourge of Hyacinths* and its stage version, *From Zia with Love*, set in a prison overlooking a Lagos canal. A network of overpasses was under frantic construction, its necessity justifiable, perhaps, yet nothing but land greed demanded that the canals themselves should be sacrificed. This concrete burden slung across contracting land summarized the condition of the city: Lagos was collapsing on itself, suffocating the expanded road network that had to service a swollen administration, business, and incessant building projects. The traffic, which was guaranteed to crawl at any time of day throughout Lagos and its environs, was the ultimate expression of the general stagnation.

At the time of the radio station escapade, in 1965, I was teaching at the University of Lagos, heading the English Department. Always on the lookout for a residence that would discourage casual access by callers, I waited stubbornly until I could obtain a house on the outskirts even of Yaba, itself a suburb of Lagos. I found one in Igbobi, a university-leased house that was tucked into a hidden green preserve. It was a place of utter tranquillity, yet not very distant from the cacophony of Lagos. There were quiet backstreets from Igbobi to Akoka, the lagoonside village that was home to the university, so I did not have to confront even the comparatively mild traffic of Yaba and would be in my lecture rooms within a mere ten minutes of leaving home. A palm tree grew thoughtfully just outside my office window, serviced by a dutiful tapper. All I had to do was hang a jar outside my window. The palm-wine tapper, on his way down from the crown of the palm, would tip his gourd into my container—undiluted, frothing fresh. I hung an object with a sinister appearance—leather and cowrie shells around a metallic lump—outside my window and warned him that if he dared dilute the palm wine that he dispensed for me with water or spike it with saccharine, he would fall and break his neck—that is, if the *sigidi** of the palm tree did not follow him home and suffocate him at night. He tried to laugh it off, but he believed me.

The university itself was a water-lapped oasis despite the choice of a ponderous boathouse architecture for its main buildings. The design was not at fault; it simply puzzled untutored minds like mine why anyone would wish to build huge sampans from concrete rather than from a wide choice of alternative light material better suited to the tropics and the specific locality. Even if the cement had been donated or dug directly from the shore, such an extravagant dominance of concrete was an oppressive waste, a contradiction also of the maritime environment. It gave the institution the character of an open fortress. Still, it appeared to perch convincingly, almost gracefully, on its watery bed, and one could hardly cavil at the overall houseboat motif of the central

---

* A succubus.

block. The surroundings were still wild enough to attract migrating birds, which made the vast wetlands behind the university a favorite stopover and a private repose, a mere minute's walk from my office, the campus obliterated from sight and mind.

But the lagoon, regularly fished by the scantily clad fishermen with their flashing nets, was the answer to the suffocation of the rest of the two sections that made up Lagos: the mainland and the island. Whenever I found myself obliged to go into Lagos on a weekday, I drove to campus, entered a canoe with an outboard engine, and was at Broadcasting House in Ikoyi some ten minutes later. There, I commandeered a car from any one of my friends, conducted my business, returned the car, and was back in the canoe and into the sanity of Akoka, then Igbobi, all within one, two, or three hours. To make that same journey through the Yaba, then Lagos, traffic, as I was obliged to do a few times, was the ultimate torture—it could last half the day.

Remorselessly, to the rhythm of pile drivers, the lagoon vanished, was "reclaimed," and traffic only succeeded in hiccupping through the streets. Lagos, after all, is essentially an island. Even the mainland part of it, Yaba, is still bordered by water, so it remained a mystery why even the rudimentary water transportation that existed from colonial times should have been gradually choked off. The regular ferry between Apapa and Lagos, which discharged workers and traders by the hundreds at fixed hours of the day, had been allowed to sink into decrepitude, operating in fits and starts, sometimes breaking down in the midst of the lagoon, endangering and even taking the lives of its passengers. Perhaps the military rulers had a phobia of water; certainly it would be years after the first military rule—under the civilian governorship of 1979—before an attempt was made to resuscitate the obvious, generous, and effective form of moving humanity and goods.

FEMI'S CAR INCHED and coughed on our way through virtually motionless traffic as we attempted to view as many properties as possible on a list of available ones obtained from an estate agent. He was like a man being dragged to his execution. As we approached each prospective house, his shoulders sagged. They would lift only when he saw, or persuaded himself that he had seen, some feature or another that made the house unsuitable—then he would become really jaunty. The environment was unfriendly, the ceiling was too low, the elevation of the stairs was for kangaroos, not humans, the interior finish was sloppy, it was too far from the offices, and so forth. I followed him, totally indifferent to these masterpieces of Lagosian fortress architecture. Already, when you looked a house over, you began with its fortifications—armed robbery was yet to attain its full season of rage, but its tentative reaches were being felt by many. The coarsening of human sensibilities that accompanied the civil war, both on the battlefront and behind the lines, was being foisted on the general populace. Violence was palpable in the streets, hung over the bars across the windows, the chains and heavy padlocks from Hong Kong, a predatoriness that embraced the self-advertising rabble and "area boys" who hung around the motor parks and the oily business types who stepped out of the luxurious interiors of the latest car models.

"It's no good turning to me for an opinion," I kept insisting. "I'm not the one who's going to live here. The bush is where I'm at home, so don't bother to ask me."

Finally Femi gave up, refused to tackle the remaining offers on his list. "You know, I think I'll let Barbara come and take a look at these others."

Driving out of Lagos, I felt I had been released from prison a second time.

IT WAS LATE into the night when my telephone rang. Femi, of course. He could not sleep. "I've been talking to Barbara" were the first words I could make out, "and you know, she seems to agree with me."

"Agrees with you over what? And what bloody time of the night is this supposed to be anyway?"

"Since when did time matter to you? I thought you ascetic professors didn't sleep."

"All right, all right, just tell me what you've woken me up for!"

"I don't want to go to Lagos."

"All right. Don't go."

"No, you haven't heard anything I've said. I'm thinking of leaving the company. You know, resign. Set up my own firm."

Now I was wide awake. "Leave Law, Union and Rock?"

"Yes. What do you think? Hey, ascetic professor, have you fallen asleep again?"

"I'm thinking, damn it."

"So. What d'you think?"

"Listen, Femi, if I had a choice at all, I would never work for anybody. So I'm the wrong person to ask for an opinion. I am biased."

"So you agree I should leave Law, Union?"

"I already know you're leaving." And I put down the telephone and went back to sleep.

. . .

THUS WAS THE impulsive beginning of Femi Johnson and Company, the brokerage firm that would, less than ten years later, blaze skyward in panels of
bronze-tinted mirrors to attain consummation in the "Golden Pillar." That day
in 1983, OBJ altered the landscape of Ibadan forever. It was not that it was the
first "skyscraper"—that privilege belonged to Cocoa House, raised as the cooperative headquarters of the Western Nigerian farmers. The Cocoa House and
the new skyscraper were separated by less than four hundred yards and virtually stared each other in the face, as if waiting to see which would blink first.
Cocoa House was of the old architectural style, with concrete blocks and traditional windows. Femi's achievement was a pillar of gold, all thin steel and blind
glass. It reflected the slums through whose intestines it had thrust itself, rising
high above them in its dissociated glory. The Golden Pillar became an instant
controversy: Did such a statement of opulence belong in such a distressed environment? No matter, Broking House, as it was christened by its owner, transformed the face of Ibadan's commercial center.

Rightly suspecting that I would disapprove of both the scale of the project
and the compromises that he had had to make with the Ibadan politicians and
city councillors to obtain approval—not to mention the garish architectural
style—he kept me deliberately in the dark. On his travels he had encountered
this new trend in the urban commercial landscape and had dreamed of bringing the city of Ibadan into the late twentieth century in one single, iconic gesture. He was, however, motivated by much more. Lament at the decay of public
services was a constant refrain in most of our exchanges—the curse of Lagos
had spread inland and affected vital commercial cities such as Ibadan. The oil
boom, now in full rampage, had meant, ironically, a deterioration in, and even
total abandonment of, the most elementary standards in the provision and
maintenance of public amenities. Electricity was at best epileptic. For water,
even government offices relied on delivery by motorized tankers. Often those
tankers had no hoses or pumps to reach the auxiliary tanks mounted on
the tops of buildings, so the staff would come down and collect water in buckets, which they then carried up flights of stairs—the elevators hardly ever
worked—to be left in toilets for flushing. Femi's business required that he visit
government secretariats, commercial centers, hospitals, universities, airports,
harbors, and so on to assess insurance claims, and facilities seeking insurance
coverage. After such visits he would return dispirited, appalled by the decay in
infrastructure. A new building would spring up and be declared open amid

glitz and fanfare by the latest dignitaries and with increasingly extravagant social rituals. For about a month it would remain a shining star in a mottled firmament, and then gradually, inevitably, it would become a slum. The walls
would acquire grime overnight, the pipes would leak and form rust patterns
everywhere, and a familiar smell would begin to percolate through the environment: the smell of humanity dying on its feet.

For my friend, this failure was an affront! Annually, he attended conferences
of insurance brokers—in London, Cairo, Nairobi, Rome, Cannes—somehow
they came to settle in Cannes, year after year. Returning home to an economy
that swam in oil revenue, generating vaster resources than its overseas counterparts, OBJ could not accept that not even a fraction of this resource was being
pumped back into the physical structures to make them as efficient as the businesses they conducted. Privately, he resolved to demonstrate that the run of
this malaise could be interrupted. He would create a model that countered the
stereotype, but he revealed nothing to me.

I watched his ventures grow. The world of business has always been for me
an exotic planet, and I was fascinated by his meticulousness, his capacity for
following up claims. I accompanied him a few times, even while he worked
with Law, Union and Rock, to inspect scenes of disaster that had resulted in
claims. Once it was a school on the remote outskirts of Ibadan, in a village I
had never heard of. It had been demolished in a thunderstorm, but fortunately,
the enlightened headmaster had insured it some ten years before. We asked
our way and lost it again and again. Finally we came to the final stretch, which
had become impassable, thanks to floods. We could see the school at a distance, with perhaps only one wall still standing. The corrugated iron sheets
were stretched crazily over debris that looked more like wooden crates and
mud excavations. Immaculate in his white shirt, tie, and black brogues, the insurance broker cum agent cum inspector rolled up his trousers and waded
through mud and torrent. I followed, wondering why he had to make a jungle
voyage dressed in such inappropriate clothing. Until then, I had never imagined the insurance business as extending beyond sitting behind a desk of papers and negotiating claims.

LIKE A VICARIOUS ACHIEVEMENT of my own, I followed the expansion of
Femi's business from its modest, living-and-dining-room beginnings, watching his credit with the banks and clientele soar through his meticulous han-
dling of their claims and his knack for sniffing out shady propositions. Once
he trapped a Lebanese businessman into admitting that he had driven his car

onto the Lagos–Ibadan road and deliberately set fire to it. Another time, it was a police commissioner, who, forever after, would be referred to as *"Ma a grateful si e"** or *"Ogun re e!"*† During the Western uprising, his houses had been targeted and razed to the ground. He quickly rushed to a crooked insurance broker and obtained a backdated policy. Femi easily detected the forgery and asked the police commissioner to drop by his office. A very civilized encounter followed; in the end the police commissioner was forced—with all cordiality— to admit that the policy had been issued after the event. Even so, the lawkeeper failed to accept that this created any problem. Only Femi stood between his application and approval by headquarters, and of course, if Femi played his part . . . The man removed his pistol from his holster, took the barrel between his teeth—no, not pointing down his throat, simply across his mouth—bit into it, and called on the god of iron and oaths to witness an unbreakable pact if Femi chose to play ball.

"Ogun re e! Ma a grateful si e."

Poor man, he had only supplied the incorrigible raconteur with yet another music box, to be wound up—with exaggerated gestures and mimic variations— in both appropriate and only remotely relevant situations. Those who already knew the story were convulsed in laughter, but strangers to the story sometimes took fright. For, given the slightest excuse—perhaps in order to buttress a promise, in affirmation of some declaration, or simply to illustrate a story— Femi would dive, virtually dive, at a convenient metal object and seize it between his teeth. It could be a letter opener, a piece of piping, a fork, a knife, even a lamp stand—and this in the most staid of gatherings, from Venezuela to Campostela—and suddenly my friend would leap up, sink his teeth into the metallic juror as if he were suffering from a brainstorm, and shout, *"Ogun re e! Ma a grateful si e!"*

MI O RI IKU L'OJU E.† No, I did not. Not until that overcast day on the tarmac in Lagos, in 1987. Only then, as he was laid out on the stretcher awaiting his transfer into the ambulance plane, was I suddenly seized with a premonition that Femi was taking his final leave of a world that often appeared to take its very vitality from his existence.

---

* "I shall show appropriate gratitude."
† "Ogun is my witness!"
† I read no death in his eyes.

PART IV

Dining with the Devil — and an Avatar

Olori-Kunkun *and* Ori Olokun

. . . . .

A Preamble on Menu, Service, and Table Manners
at the Devil's Dinner Table

DINING WITH A CERTAIN BREED OF HYBRID HUMANITY—THE MILITARY, IN
its earthly manifestation—is not without its problems, but not any that is insurmountable for those who are not truly hungry, unless of course one takes
the view that experiencing acutely, albeit vicariously, the hunger of others can
be considered a self-serving rationalization. It is the easiest leap for those who
believe, in any case, that there is a bit of the devil in most of us—*there but for*
the grace of God go I, and so on. Given half the chance, in a nation like Nigeria,
I sometimes feel I would betray, with guaranteed provocation over critical
choices, the dictatorial devil in me! One's social and moral responsibility, however, is to curb such a propensity, especially its abuses, not only in oneself but
in others. Ultimately, there is the question of motivation and goals. I have had
many good reasons to work up a good appetite for that diabolical repast,
though I dare not deny that a number of such meals have left me with acute in-
digestion, symptoms of which persist today!

A public cause, a clamorous need, sometimes imposes choices that appear,
on the surface, to contradict one's democratic convictions and, indeed, lifelong
pursuits. The dilemma of dining with the devil, of cooperation, interaction,
even of the most limited kind, with an unelected regime, will always remain a
cross upon which committed democrats, reformers, radicals, and such, in any
authoritarian corner of the globe and especially the African continent, occasionally find themselves impaled. It is one that I have confronted quite openly
but resolved effortlessly and unapologetically—even arrogantly, as I was once

accused of doing by a television interviewer. What had nettled him was that I insisted that I did not owe him or any other mortal an explanation for my choice, since I considered all justifications superfluous when collaboration is clearly undertaken on behalf of life—and even, occasionally, progressive politics, policies, or creativity.

Or could he also have taken umbrage at my response when, accused of having "sold out" to the military, I retorted, quite truthfully, that not even the entire Nigerian nation, with all its oil wealth, could afford me? That was one of the burdens that came with the Nobel Prize—plain, matter-of-fact, commonplace declarations that had not raised an eyebrow during my pre-Nobel existence suddenly became problematic after that event: "Oh, are you saying that because of . . . are you now bigger than the nation?" At such moments, one longs to tell the nation where to stuff its colonial pride. Mercifully, a rational commentator took time out to explain the obvious: W.S. meant simply that his convictions were not for sale.

That particular confrontation occurred over my role in creating a Road Safety Corps under a military regime, to stem the notorious hemorrhage on Nigerian roads, especially on the Ibadan–Ife road. I named it the Slaughter Slab, since it was mostly on this macadam altar that I habitually scooped up my students' brains after filling them with knowledge. Issues of life and death constantly strike me as deserving more than a genuine or merely rhetorical purism. Certainly I have never undergone any angst in this respect. I concede legitimacy to the uncompromising, no-contact position, whose validity may be equally argued, but it is a position that often strikes me as an unaffordable luxury on a continent like ours, where the culture of militarized government appears to have developed remarkable resilience.

Even in late 2002, the once-democratic constant, Ivory Coast, underwent the once-unthinkable—a military coup! Unthinkable? Ivory Coast's long-sustained policy of exclusionism—*ivoirité*, the elegant word for the disenfranchisement of even fifth-generation "foreigners"—was a purulent boil that finally burst open, providing one military section a righteous cause for self-ingratiation into civic acceptance, albeit of a sectarian nature. Nigeria, with its recent exhilarating experience of exorcising the military incubus in 1999, had already undergone two scares. Still, the same Nigeria went on to play Big Brother, wielding a big cudgel in 2004 to terminate military adventurism in São Tomé. Not to be outdone, Guinea-Bissau followed São Tomé only a month or two later, while Togo, in the same West African region, attempted an original variant in 2005: the military made a crude effort to install a son of the deceased dictator, Gnassingbé Eyadéma, in office, against the provisions of the Constitution, simply to entrench surrogate military rule.

It boils down, ultimately, to one's personal confidence in determining the length of spoon with which one dines with the devil and one's ability to keep a firm hold on it. This involves deriving no advantages, no gains, no recompense in the process—if anything, expending oneself both materially and mentally for the attainment of a fixed and limited goal, retaining one's independence of action. Most delicious of all is the ability to walk away from the dinner table, flinging a coin onto it as a tip for the host.

There is a further consideration: in far too many African nations, the comparative index of brutality, contempt for the rule of law, and abuse of human rights between some so-called democracies and military dictatorships leaves dubious space for absolutes. One has only to consider Kenyan "democracy" under arap Moi or the stale tobacco ash end of the Hitlerite Robert Mugabe of Zimbabwe, masquerading as a passion for land restitution. Within Nigeria, the lesson is served by the contrast between the 1975 military regime of Murtala Mohammed on the one hand, and the 1979–83 fascistic and wastrel "democracy" of Alhaji Shehu Shagari's National Party of Nigeria (NPN; successor to the NPC) and so on throughout the continent. Those who insist on inhabiting the real world find themselves subjected to the clamor of what can and deserves to be extracted from usurped authority on behalf of a nation, on behalf of the nonstatistical, palpable humanity that constitutes one's vital environment. For a temperament such as mine, it has never been possible to shunt aside—not for any prolonged period—a sense of rebuke over how much is lost daily, wasted or degraded, how much proves irretrievable, damaged beyond repair, through maintaining a position that confers the self-righteous comfort of a purist: nonnegotiable distancing.

A line must be drawn, however; across from mine will be found the murdering regimes—of an Idi Amin, an Emperor Bokassa, a Sergeant Doe, a Mobutu Sese Seko . . . and of course, a General Sani Abacha. Behind them are ranged those who forbid all planning for, discussion of, or anticipation of a return to democratic rule, setting the stage for life dictatorship—such as General Buhari. Other categories survive on individual assessment. Notwithstanding such finicky distinctions, however, dining with the devil remains undeniably a mined board—prone to misunderstanding, betrayal, public skepticism, getting the fingers nicely toasted, mud all over one's face, and so on. Sublime intentions are detonated by a diabolical joke—of which one promptly offers it-self in all its madcap, cautionary amplitude; but first, a few paragraphs on the devil in that affair.

SOME CLOSE ASSOCIATES have suggested that I secretly nurture a death wish. They base this claim on the fact that despite what would appear to be the single-minded efforts of one General Olusegun Obasanjo to push me beyond the borders of existence, we remain—albeit qualified—friends. I find it dif-ficult to explain this undeniable paradox, except to shift the responsibility somewhere else and insist that, in some unfathomable way, fate appears un-bending in its resolve to throw us together, through events, mutual acquain-tances, the frequent opposition and less frequent coincidence of interests, and so on, both in and out of office. Of course, one is never bereft of choice, but I also have a tendency—I have come to admit—to thumb my nose at the machi-nations of fate, daring it to do its worst or else know that I am also equally compelled to turn its interventions in a productive direction. Flirting with fate and emerging relatively unscathed tend to go to one's head, however, which might partially explain why one appears to travel down the same mined road again and again.

Observing, and even interacting at close quarters with, someone who is completely without scruples is, frankly, irresistible. One speaks here of a politi-cal leader who—to cite a notorious instance—graces the dedication of the new official residence of his Senate president one night, dines, puts on a perfor-mance as the life and soul of the party, mixing gregariously and clowning with other guests, and dances with the senator's wife, knowing all the while that he has already perfected the plot for the senator's removal from office, which he executes a day or two later. Poor Chuba Okadigbo, he never quite recovered from the blow. Indeed, his death from pulmonary complications from police tear gassing during a rally to protest the rigging of Obasanjo's 2003 "reelec-tion" was due partly to psychological enfeeblement from that earlier shock.

It could be a case of letting one's writer's instinct take one too far, but, per-verse though it may seem, I have remained genuinely fascinated by a complex figure who is convinced that he dominates his environment and thinks he acts the part—but who is, basically, a fortunate recipient of the largesse of fate. After all, how many soldiers, after the bulk of a civil war has been fought and won by others, find themselves positioned to receive the articles of surrender from the enemy, thus appropriating the mantle of the architect of victory? Not one to leave any loopholes in his claims to that laurel, however, the soldier signals his entry into yet another turbulent profession—that of the writer—by producing one of the fastest-written war histories ever—*My Command*—remaining blithely indifferent to furious rebuttals of its details by his comrades in arms.

Through a regional balance in military politics—not from merit, such as participation in the critical coup—our subject becomes the number two in the next military regime. The number one is assassinated after only six months in office, and the war hero becomes head of state by default—and not of just any banana republic, but of the most populous, wealthiest nation on the African continent. He escapes the fate of his predecessor and ends a high-casualty-rate career unscathed, in grateful retirement on his farm, escorted into our shared hometown, Abeokuta, on a white horse with drums and bugles. All agree that the honor is deserved, since, unlike most African leaders, he voluntarily relinquishes power. The gesture catapults him to international notice. Thereafter he settles back into civilian life, but not quite, since he begins diligently to lay the groundwork—establishes an African Leadership Forum, and so on—for becoming a respected statesman, mixing with the powerful in international fora and hosting them in turn on his Ota farm.

The saga has not ended. Fate again intervenes, and the hero finds himself arraigned before a brutal dictator, one General Sani Abacha, on treasonable charges, earning a death sentence that will be commuted to a lengthy prison spell. A little more than two years of prison life, and his persecutor is assisted into eternity in a subtle palace conspiracy—never mind any claims of his succumbing to excess sexual ecstasy. All this takes place without his lifting a finger, except perhaps to attract the trusty's attention. The military, thoroughly discredited as a ruling class and beset by international ultimatums, realizes that its time is up but has no intention of giving up power. And so our hero—now an accredited civilian—is released from prison, formally pardoned, and pressed back into service, but now as an "elected" civilian president.

I suppose I subconsciously acquired the attitude that, as a writer, I had proprietary rights over such a phenomenon, and since he was already indebted to me by an act of treachery on his part, I began to regard him as a private preserve for compensatory study. In any case, Obasanjo is quite personable—much of the time—and it was not difficult to respond to his evident desire for cerebral company; like most rulers, he desperately wanted to be accepted as a political and economic strategist and thinker. Was I evincing a touch of masochism? Or perhaps the death-wish proposed by my colleagues? No matter; our hero represented a model of power of an unusual—and dangerous—kind, most especially as he remained basically insecure and thus pathologically in need of proving himself, preferably at the expense of others. That is one unambiguous assessment that is pronounced by nearly all Obasanjo's acquaintances. Interacting with him at close quarters thus involved—again, at a subconscious level—testing one's confidence in one's own invulnerability, somewhat like those traditional charms that warriors swear by as bullet deflectors: they wore the charms but still ensured that no one was pointing a gun at them.

Also, to my intense chagrin, I have been forced to conclude that even advancing years have failed to eliminate from my system a parental inheritance: a missionary streak. Detecting a productive, even sometimes imaginative, glint in the compost of the soldier turned politician is not difficult—Obasanjo is a man of restless energies—and a waste of human potential is something against which a missionary upbringing revolts. A bullish personality, calculating and devious, yet capable of a disarming spontaneity, affecting a country yokel act to cover up the interior actuality of the same, occasionally self-deprecatory yet intolerant of criticism, this general remains a study in the outer limits of a sense of rivalry, even where the fields of competence and striving are miles apart.

A deprived childhood like Obasanjo's, on his own admission, also makes for some measure of indulgence, at least in explaining his deep-seated sense of insecurity. As his need to prove himself degenerated to obvious sadism, however, one is obliged to compare him with his own townsman Moshood Abiola. Both had similar deprived backgrounds and attended the same school, yet they differed drastically in openness and generosity. It is significant that Olusegun Obasanjo, since he became elected head of state over the corpse of the popularly elected Abiola—who breathed his last under confinement by the same Abacha—finds himself physically unable to utter the name of his thwarted predecessor, even in official speeches. The ex-general routinely dismisses all proposals to raise a memorial to the politician, including the resolution of the Nigerian legislature that the Abuja sports stadium be named after a man who was formally crowned "Africa's Pillar of Sports," by the Organization of African Unity.

Perhaps it is this sense of rivalry, the fear of being surpassed, even by ghosts, that thoroughly defines the personality of the general. While, for instance, the majority of the nation clamored for the designation of, and some states continue to mark, June 12, that day in 1993 when a disciplined people went to the polls, united in the resolve to terminate military rule, as Democracy Day, Olusegun Obasanjo persists in imposing May 31 on the nation, this being the date, in 1989, when he was sworn into office after his emergence from prison. A veteran journalist, Kole Animashawun, writing in *The Vanguard,* summed up the general who came back from the dead in a unique expression: "His ego is bigger than his head."

The size of the general's ego was not uppermost in my mind, however, when I invited myself to dinner in 1978. When a prize such as *Ori Olokun,* the long-lost bronze head of a principal Yoruba deity, shimmers so alluringly within the sight of an *olori-kunkun,** one may be forgiven for forgetting the long spoon, even with full knowledge that a swishing tail may be hidden beneath the khaki uniform.

TEACHING AT YALE UNIVERSITY some years after this misadventure, I found myself neighbor to the *ase*†-driven scholar Robert Farris Thompson. He taught African art history and generally did his best to infect his colleagues and students with whatever Yoruba spirit of possession had presided over his birth—possibly even his conception. If Robert had his way, a pilgrimage to the land of the Yoruba would be a condition for everyone who wished to become an alumnus of Yale or, indeed, any higher institution in the United States. Thompson had the same enthusiasm for certain kinds of music and films, and this was how I came to see what was at the time considered a "cult" film, *Indiana Jones and the Temple of Doom.* Since the attraction of *The Temple of Doom* had temporarily displaced the shrine of Orisa in Thompson's general vocabulary, my curiosity was aroused. Thus, one afternoon, I set out to watch the film in the company of my once student, then colleague, Henry Louis "Skip" Gates, Jr.

I regret to say that I did not enjoy the movie. From the opening sequences, I began to squirm. It was as if, albeit on a drastically reduced scale—no competitive spectacle, cliff-hanger risks, or lethal pyrotechnics—I were watching a souped-up documentary of one of my better-forgotten undertakings. My feeling throughout was that I had been deliberately set up to be lampooned by Steven Spielberg in the storyline, without even the consolation of a love angle. I was grateful for the darkness that covered my blushes.

The beginnings were nearly identical. I was close to the end of a seminar in my office when the departmental secretary entered and announced that some colleagues were waiting to see me, on an urgent matter. I dismissed my class a few minutes early—no, unlike in *The Temple of Doom,* there was no lubricious student bursting at the boobs who sidled up to leave me with a long, caressing

---

* Literally, "a stubborn head."
† The word of mystic potency; the invocatory pronouncement that brings things into being.

look and a lascivious invitation—and ushered in my visitors. There were three of them: Akin Isola, a playwright and professor in Yoruba studies; Wande Abimbola, another professor in Yoruba, an academic as well as a practitioner of the mysteries of Ifa, the Yoruba system of divination; and Olabiyi Yai of Linguistics, a Yoruba whose nationality, of the Republic of Benin, served yet again to remind one of the disservice that the European powers had done to the African continent in their arbitrary division of that continent into so-called national entities. How could I have failed, by the way, after watching *Temple of Doom,* to be struck by the coincidence that it was yet another professor of the Yoruba extended family—Thompson—who had been responsible for my presence in the theater, or that I was watching this sumptuous takeoff on my own escapade in the company of yet another scholar, Skip Gates, who was undergoing his own phase of Yorubaphilia in the persona of Esu, the deity of the random factor and reversals, and quirky messenger of the deities!

Back to 1978 and Ife campus, however: it turned out that my visitors had come to solicit my help in an unusual undertaking. Why me? First of all, they were aware that I did have some kind of access to the then military head of state, Olusegun Obasanjo, and this was a matter that required cooperation at the highest possible level of government. Next, there was the matter of the recently concluded Festival of Black and African Arts, the notorious jamboree that had guzzled millions of dollars and earned the nation the ire of at least half of the visitors for its shoddy preparations. Perhaps the single most significant event of that festival, however, was one that never did take place: this was the repatriation of the original of the symbol—and logo—of that festival, chosen in the confident belief that it would be released by its keepers and put on display.

A famous ivory mask from Benin, exquisitely carved and detailed, remained safely esconced in the vast labyrinths of the British Museum in London. It had been looted in the equally famous sacking of the Benin Kingdom by a British expeditionary force in the late nineteenth century, launched in reprisal for an earlier humiliating encounter between a Captain Phillips and King Overawhen, the paramount ruler of the Benin Kingdom, whose ancestry, one line of legend insists, was none other than Yoruba! The Phillips expedition had insisted on being received by the king during one of his most sacred retreats, when the oba was not permitted to see any strangers. His Majesty's Britannic servants were not to be denied, however, and they forced their way into the city, with gruesome consequences. Such insolence was not to be countenanced! Orders were issued to mount a punitive expedition, and they were carried out with equally gruesome efficiency. Numerous treasures, the spoils of war, were shipped back to England—to offset the cost of the war, the British dispatches stated with admirable candor. Among them was the ivory mask, allegedly the head of a Benin princess.

Now, in 1976, the Nigerian minister of culture, a scion of the Benin Kingdom—none other than Chief Anthony Enahoro—felt that this was an opportunity to bring back at least one of those treasures. The diplomatic bag was scorched to and fro with dispatches from both sides—At least *lend* us the damned thing for the duration of the festival! pleaded Nigeria. Nothing doing, said the British Museum. The British government was, of course, "powerless to intervene"—the autonomy of the British Museum being regretfully but conveniently cited as the insurmountable obstacle. Condescending arguments—such as that the Nigerian nation lacked the means, will, or sense of value required to preserve its precious heritage—require no comment.

I had not stinted words, alas, in expressing my umbrage at both sides—against the British government for its hypocritical double-talk and against our own caretakers, a supposed military regime, for their uncreative approach. From the moment the Nigerian government requested the return of the mask, all was lost! The British government would never part with it, since to do so would only set a precedent for demands for a wholesale repatriation of all art treasures plundered by colonial forces to their rightful homes. Indeed, in a moment of righteous rage at ancient wrongs, I went so far as to offer advice that the government should stop drawing further attention to the mask, since it would only place its illegal guardians on the alert. The mask was stolen property, and the aggrieved had a right to reclaim their property by any means. What I proposed instead was that a task force of specialists in such matters, including foreign mercenaries if necessary, be set up to bring back the treasure—and as many others as possible—in one swift, once-for-all-time, coordinated operation.

Since that unheeded advice, in 1984, a live trophy in the shape of a former minister, the infamous Umaru Dikko, has been kidnapped from London, bundled to Stansted Airport, crated, and loaded into a cargo plane, awaiting repatriation to Nigeria. It was an amateurishly planned, clumsily executed operation under the regime of General Buhari, yet it could have succeeded but for the accident that Dikko's live-in mistress happened to have watched it all from the window. She had the presence of mind to take down both the number and description of the car, even before alerting the police. The ineptness of the kidnappers—who had spent months studying Umaru Dikko's movements—

could be summed up in the fact that they failed to notice that his mistress routinely waved good-bye from an upper window when he left the house in the morning. The police found the drugged minister in his crate, together with an Israeli doctor whose task was to pump him full of sedatives at intervals on the flight back to Nigeria. The majority of the nation was waiting to welcome him, even more enthusiastically than the military.

Spiriting away the Benin mask for FESTAC—the 1977 Festival of Black and African Arts—in good time for the opening of the festival would have been much easier, cost much less, and redressed, albeit symbolically, an ancient wrong. I was quite ready to be part of the team. The potential consequences seemed trivial, considering the prize. If we were caught, we would simply fight the case all the way to the International Court of Justice at The Hague, bringing the issue of ownership of objects of colonial plunder to the fore on a global level. I had no idea what the insides of British jails were like, but I could not imagine them being any worse than the ones in which I had been confined in Kirikiri, Ibadan, and Kaduna. That repatriation proposal had stuck in the minds of some of my colleagues, agitated now by the discovery of a missing art treasure that belonged to Ile-Ife.

INTO MY OFFICE they filed—Olabiyi Yai, small, dark, and wiry behind heavily rimmed glasses; Wande Abimbola, only slightly taller, with soft face and gestures, and a facial immobility that would sometimes waver between bewilderment and a cunning watchfulness; and Akin Isola, bearded, with outstanding cicatrices carved into his light-complexioned skin, a creative writer in his own right and Yoruba philologist. He would later translate my play *Death and the King's Horseman* "back into the Yoruba" in which, Isola insisted, it had originally taken form in my head. Their aspects were so uniformly solemn that I was prompted to ask whose turn it was among our colleagues, such was the regularity with which the infamous Slaughter Slab—the road between Ife and Ibadan—ate us up. But no, it was not the road on this occasion. The subject was *Ori Olokun*, the famous bronze head of Ife whose career had turned rather murky since Leo Frobenius, the German adventurer and archaeologist, had first dug up this ancestral representation nearly half a century earlier.

Olokun—literally the owner, or god, of the seas—was the consort of Oduduwa, the twain thus seen as primogenitors of the Yoruba, the black race, and indeed, of all humanity. If Oduduwa was sent to Earth by Olodumare, the Supreme Deity, to directly create and animate Earth, Olokun, his consort, performed a parallel task for the seas and the oceans. Yet, as is common to the nature of numberless deities, Olokun is often mythologized and represented also as male. Their offspring, Oranmiyan (or Oranyan), roamed far and wide from the ancestral home, Ile-Ife, to found a Yoruba kingdom, whose numerous branches he handed over to his countless offspring.

Other legends differ wildly: it was the Edo Kingdom of Benin that was founded by Oranmiyan, not just any Yoruba kingdom. And Olokun was brother to Oranmiyan, not his mother ... and so it goes in the world of myth and legend. The famous stone plinth *Opa Oranyan* still stands in Ile-Ife and is held to mark the burial place of that warlike brother or be merely a cenotaph indicating the spot from which he vanished. The ancestral link between the Edo and the Yoruba is undisputed, however, and it has remained part of the Benin coronation tradition that any new monarch must first travel to Ile-Ife—or be sent a spiritual emissary from Ife—to secure or transmit blessings from his ancestral fount.

Ogun, my patron deity, is the son of Oranmiyan, through his principal consort, Isedale, and is thus the direct grandson of Olokun. Beyond legend and mythology, therefore, I had a personal stake in the fate of Olokun, whose spiritual descendant—through Ogun—I have long accepted myself to be.

Together with some companion figures, *Ori Olokun*—the head of Olokun—was traditionally buried in the courtyard of Ife palace by the priesthood, brought out only at his annual festival, when it was ritualistically washed, honored, and then returned to its resting place until the next outing.

Leo Frobenius, in *The Voice of Africa*, narrates his moment of rapture when, during an excavation, a pick wielded by one of his assistants struck metal. Work was stopped. Carefully scraping off the soil with his hands, he finally held in his hand a piece that the pick had chipped off the cheek of the bronze. After that, his account is filled with negotiations for the sale of this and other bronze pieces, the news of his find filtering to the British colonial officer in Lagos, a chase by that rival that ended just at the Nigerian side of the border with Dahomey (now the Republic of Benin), and finally his summary dispossession of this invaluable piece by that representative of His Majesty's government. Frobenius claimed that the tiny bronze piece that was chipped from Olokun's cheek was his sole surviving souvenir of his monumental find.

The question that surfaced decades later, however, was this: Just what artifact was it that the British civil servant snatched from Frobenius? The real *Ori Olokun*? Or a substitute by the wily German explorer and collector?

. . .

AN *ORI OLOKUN* WAS on display at the Ife Museum, but any serious art or archaeology student knew it to be a travesty. The whereabouts of the real head had long remained the subject of much speculation, with no real agreement emerging, but its loss continued to rankle in a few knowledgeable minds. As if to place one in a state of permanent annoyance, the image that had been adopted for a national stamp had been taken from the fake head in the Ife Museum. Across the waters from the West African coast, a piece that was either the original or its identical twin had been reproduced on postcards, which are still on sale at the British Museum.

More intimately galling to the university community at Ile-Ife—at least, those whose disciplines touched upon such matters—was that it was the Ife Museum simulacrum, a piece of unparalleled ugliness, that was used—just as on the postage stamp—as the icon of the university crest. To this peeved community also belonged the ancients of Ife, who had known the real *Ori Olokun* and were subjected to the indignity of occasionally seeing the fake piece proudly displayed in its glass case in the museum at Ile-Ife. Compared to the classical proportions of the real head—color plates of which appear in a number of books under speculative, indeed sometimes deliberately obscurantist, notes—the museum piece is squat, amateurish, and misproportioned. Among our circle, it earned only contempt, captured in a nickname bestowed on it in a fit of disgust: *Ipako Elede*, "the Back of a Pig's Head." And now these three dons—one of whom was the author of that apt nickname—were seated in my office, facing me across the desk, quietly informing me that they not only knew where the real *Ori Olokun* was hidden but also who had taken it away!

Brecht, Genet, Cheik N'dao, or whoever it was that had occupied my last hour or two vanished into nothingness or irrelevance. The university itself ceased to exist, or, perhaps more accurately, it shed its ivory-tower pretensions and finally justified its existence. The walls of my office dissolved in mists of ancient legend, turning my three interlocutors briefly into three sons of Oduduwa. From across time, I heard only their plea for the restoration of their being, *my* being, to its original repleteness. I could already see that usurper, *Ogbeni Ipako Elede*, being finally thrown on the dung heap where it belonged and a triumphal procession along the ancient route, accompanied by all the purification rituals, ending with the setting of the authentic representation on the minipodium of the museum. What a feast would fittingly accompany this return! I was outwardly impassive—an instinctive freeze, I have since learned, takes over at such moments—so impassive that my visitors thought that they had failed to arouse my interest. Inwardly, however—if only they had known!—I was dancing to some music, a sublime music of the spheres into which their words were absorbed as lyrics even as they were uttered, for what the threesome were actually suggesting was that *Ori Olokun* could, and should, be brought home!

"...you see? We recalled that you expressed a very strong opinion about the way the problem of the FESTAC mask was handled." The reminder brought me back to the present. "We were wondering—and the dean of faculty agrees, we discussed it with him and he urged us to speak with you—well, considering your closeness to the head of state... maybe some way could be found to bring back *Ori Olokun*."

I found my voice somehow. "And where exactly is it now?"

I could not believe our luck! *Ori Olokun*, these colleagues were telling me, was not locked up in a national museum with fortifications, guards, electronic monitoring devices, crisscrossing laser beams, robotic strangler guards, and all the rest, but was displayed in a private gallery, not even a public one but a kind of studio-gallery, owned by a famous artist cum architect! They had known this for a year, and they claimed to know who had spirited the bust out of the country. There were some pertinent questions to be asked, however, such as: "If you knew this a year ago, why are you coming out with it only now?"

"Well, we were keeping a kind of watch. We didn't quite know what to do after Labiyi brought the news. We thought of confronting Pierre—since he admitted taking it out—but decided that might result in his alerting the possessor, who is a very close friend of his. And the head would disappear once again, maybe this time forever—at least in our lifetime. But now he's leaving the university, and that link will be lost...."

Olabiyi had been teaching in an exchange program at the University of São Paulo. Pierre Verger, a respected ethnologist—indeed, perhaps the pioneer of Yoruba ethnological studies in South America, with *Dieux d'Afrique* and others—had been a visiting scholar in the Congos, France, Brazil, and West Africa while we were still padding toward primary school in bare feet with snotty noses. Yai had met Pierre at a party given by the alleged possessor, the architect Carybe, in Bahia. Let Biyi—Olabiyi—take up the narrative.

"The party was held in the gallery, which is actually at the back of the main house but detached from it. You gain entrance to it by a separate external staircase, quite high up. The gallery contained not merely Carybe's works, finished or in various stages of completion—canvases, designs, as well as sculptures—

but art pieces from all over the world. Seated on one of the shelves was—my eyes were simply tugged there, directly—*Ori Olokun*! The *real* thing! You noticed the difference at once. This was nothing like that abortion sitting in Ife Museum. Beautiful! The proportions were unmistakable. I could only gasp with disbelief—but I said nothing.

"All evening, my mind was in turmoil. How on earth did it get there? We all continued to make small talk, but I had only the one thing on my mind. Who had spirited it out? How long had it been stored away on that shelf? Well, as the evening wore on, I found myself seated on the stair landing, just outside the gallery. I was joined there by Baba—Pierre—and then I simply could not keep it to myself any longer. I asked him if he had noticed the bronze head, and he said he had. I asked, 'Is that not *Ori Olokun*?' and he nodded. So I said, 'What of the head sitting in a glass case in Ife?' Pierre snorted. 'But everyone knows that's a fake. What you see on that shelf is the authentic head.' Well, I decided that, since he was so forthcoming, I might as well ask the next question: 'How did Carybe get hold of it?'

"That was when he put his finger to his lips—exactly like this—and said, 'Shh. Don't tell anyone, but—I brought it here.' "

I was numbed. Pierre? Biyi continued, "At that moment, I decided that I had already betrayed too much curiosity. So I mumbled something like 'Really?' And he reaffirmed it. I tried my best to look as if it was really no concern of mine, looked for some way to change the subject, and we both continued with our drinks on the landing."

My other two visitors nodded to confirm that the story was as they had heard it already. Abimbola added, "He kept it to himself until he returned to the country, and then he confided in us."

"Over the past year we've kept returning to the subject, tossing around one course of action after the other," Isola said.

"But it could have disappeared from there in the meantime," I interjected, pointing out the obvious.

"Ye-es," conceded Labiyi. "But I don't think so. Carybe struck me as one of those collectors who simply enjoy the thrill of having something like that in their possession. You know, just having it there. Think how long we've had that *Ipako Elede* in the museum—that tells you roughly how long he and Pierre have had the real thing in their possession. If they'd wanted to sell it or dispose of it somehow, they'd have done so before now."

That made sense. And in any case, what mattered was that we now had a lead. We had a sighting that was less than two years old, we had a physical location, we had a live witness and a confession, and the transporter of stolen goods was right on campus. The trail, in comparison to past chases, could be held to be unseasonably warm.

"It's a delicate situation," I commented. "Pierre has a formidable reputation all over the world, including right here, within our own academia. We are all friends of his."

"It is tricky," Akin admitted.

"And he's a foreign national," Olabiyi added.

"That's why we think it should be handled from the very top. Somehow we must get the head of state involved."

Here followed a long silence, generated mostly from my side. What was going through my mind was, needless to say, my earlier, hardly edifying encounters with this very head of state. Against the universal wisdom that cautioned "Once bitten, twice shy" stood the summons of the ancient head of a mythical ancestor: *Ori Olokun*!

WE HAD MENDED fences since the civil war, had achieved a large measure of reconciliation, thanks to our mutual friend, Ojetunji Aboyade, and my role in the 1977 Festival of Black and African Arts. First, in response to his plea, I had saved the festival from collapse by a successful appeal to President Léopold Senghor to bring his country, Senegal, back into the festival after a difference of opinion—it all had to do with the ideological ordering of the central event, the Colloquium, and it resulted in Senegal's withdrawal and a threatened boycott by the Francophone countries. Next, I myself withdrew on a different matter of principle: the chairman of the festival, Admiral Fingesi, had insisted on overriding decisions of experts, from his position of military authority and cultural ignorance. Finally, however, with the actual festival having proved a debacle, I was prevailed upon to return and stage a closing event. Fortunately, it proved successful, wiped out some of the sour taste in the mouths of most of the visitors, and sent them to their various homes with a much-tempered memory of their overall experience. Obasanjo had been very moved by the farewell event and grateful for the unexpected reprieve of the national image—indeed, his childlike appreciation had been quite touching, revealing an unexpected aspect of the soldier.

All that did not mean, however, that I was prepared to put my life in the hands of this erratic being, and thinking of what—I knew immediately—we had to do, there could be no room for a dubious ally to the rear. The four of us in that room shared the same thought: this was not a situation that could go the diplomatic route; the lesson from FESTAC had made that clear. Someone would have to go over to Brazil and take back what was ours. If anything went wrong, we would need the full weight of a government behind us.

I saw my colleagues to the door, promising to let them know within a day or two what course I had decided upon. The first step did not require much thinking. I called up our intermediary, Aboyade—who was always equipped with Obasanjo's latest secret number—and asked him to arrange an urgent meeting with our awkward friend, adding that it was nothing I could discuss over the telephone. He arranged a meeting for that weekend. For me, work was over for the day, possibly for the rest of the week. My mind had begun to oversee details of an unorthodox mission, and I knew it would not admit any other thought until every step—with all likely variations—was clearly laid out.

We met in his Dodan Barracks residence. For once, this was a brainstorming dinner that could accommodate only one topic. Obasanjo's Owu eyes twinkled with mischief and glowed with the ardor of a race warrior. By the following morning, a task force had emerged: his foreign minister, Henry Adefowope, and an Ambassador Fagbenle, nicknamed "Docky." We agreed that Olabiyi Yai and I should travel to Brazil, locate the quarry if it was still in Bahia, and, if possible, bring it back. *If* possible? I had already resolved that if *Ori Olokun* would simply do its own part and manifest itself before me, it would end its exile almost immediately, journeying back in the diplomatic bag to its home on that usurped podium in Ife Museum!

I did not allow the feast of love with this uncertain ally to smother my instincts. Matters could go awry, and we would find the ruler of a hundred million people losing no sleep over the loss of two citizens. Obasanjo, I knew, was capable of ordering his foreign minister to negotiate with Brazil to keep us in one of its jails for a few years until the scandal blew over, maybe as a condition for continuing trading relations between the two nations. That knowledge was sufficient safety; it was left to me to negotiate our own insurance policy in advance. I insisted not only that we would travel only on diplomatic passports but that the Ministry of Foreign Affairs must issue a letter to our embassy in Brasilia, instructing its diplomats to lend all necessary assistance to bearers who would be arriving there on a confidential mission. I would copy and store those letters before departure. In the meantime, the university should take on the responsibility of "administratively" delaying Pierre Verger's departure, ensuring that he did not arrive in Brazil while we were present. How that was done, Docky shrugged, was up to us.

BACK ON CAMPUS, I plunged into the surrounding bush for the routine of sorting out my thoughts. It was clear that for the recovery of *Ori Olokun,* I was prepared to dine with the lord of the satanic kingdom himself, even without the aid of the long spoon. I was more than ready to make a Faustian pact—to sell my soul in return for that hollow but weighty mass, hallowed by my history!

I would have preferred to spend a full weekend in one of my deepest hunting grounds, day and night, but that indulgence had to make way for the urgency of further preparations. An afternoon around the campus had to suffice. Calmly, sheltered from all human disturbance, I considered what we were about to do. Why was I plunging—at forty-four—into these melodramatic waters with both feet, and fully clothed? I had never been to Brazil and knew that country only for its large population of Yoruba descendants, mostly mestizized from the slave era, and their preservation of the world of the *orisha,* whose faithful looked toward Ile-Ife as their origin. It was in Brazil that the Yoruba world had most penetratingly captured the soul of the Americas to the south and the Caribbean islands: Cuba, Haiti, Dominica, Jamaica. The *orisha* are still alive in Brazil—their rites, their liturgy, their sacral calendar, their suffusion of popular consciousness—how much more in the pristine forests of the continent that spawned these deities!

It is not everywhere that one feels the pulse of the *orisha,* nor are all their pulsations the same. Away from human habitation, for instance, in the moist forests, one experiences their emanations largely in a serene mode, osmotic and intimate; in other places, they are far more abrasive, intrusive, even querulous. The microclimates of the western part of Nigeria often astonish with their quiltwork variety of growth. Tropical vegetation, home to pristine groves, sheers abruptly away into savannah and next into brushland that is brittle with movement, albeit restrained. There, the slightest wind is a prelude to raspy motions, and one can almost hear the scurrying of ants, inviting dialogue with the intruder or launching questions—in such terrain, one is almost prepared to see the contumacious deity Esu metamorphose from an anthill and perch atop its mud spire, full of impish designs against the world. Within tropical lushness, my preferred haven for meandering, time stands still, consciousness is muted. One is enfolded in the amplitude of Nature, where the incongruities of existence are dissolved or absorbed into numinous forces of which each deity stands as a wordless medium. In these close forests, intuition reigns supreme.

No worshiper at any shrine, I do not hesitate to extract from those moments in the forest—after an internal review of events—either an admonishment and urge to desist from a course of action or an end to all vacillation, buttressed with a pledge of absolution. I feel welcomed by and integrated with forces that sit in silent contemplation over the acts of men, judging or merely marveling. In the lair of deities I reminded myself that we were about to embark on a mission of restitution. In the compressed time at my disposal, there was no indulgence in prolonged contemplation, much less meditation— whatever measures we would take in good faith would have the blessing of all the *orisha* and would readily answer the laws of humanity. I had taken the precaution of leaving my night lamp behind, so there was no temptation to spend the night roaming the woods. There was time left only for practical tasks, and these included hours of collective research in the university library, looking into whatever else had been written since Frobenius's encounter with the *Ori Olokun.*

FOUR DAYS LATER, Olabiyi Yai and I left for Rio de Janeiro, then traveled straight on to Brasilia. A message had gone ahead of us, and we were met by a representative from the embassy. Between Yai and myself, I do not recall that we had any cash that amounted to much. I had taken all the foreign currency in Femi's possession—it was not much, unfortunately. There was my credit card, which, thank goodness, was not too severely depleted. Nevertheless, we would have to conserve its credit as tightly as possible, leaving as much as we could for emergencies. The embassy in Brasilia would pay our hotel bill, but that was all. From then on, we were on our own.

I had barely time to observe what an artificial city Brasilia was and stroll through the authentic "people's quarters"—the humanized space—for about an hour before our flight was due to leave for Bahia. I was not interested in sightseeing anyway, my mind being focused on the distant gallery of an unsuspecting architect and the squatters on its shelves, as described by Labiyi. From one of those shelves, *Ori Olokun* beckoned, awaiting rescue and a rapturous welcome home. Nothing else had much reality.

We needed as much independence of movement as possible, and so, in Bahia, I rented a Volkswagen Beetle, mentally adding up the debit on that card with unaccustomed meticulousness. The story we had decided upon was that we were on an official mission to find a local architect who would collaborate in the redesigning of the Nigerian Embassy. I bought a camera, insisting on a bag that was designed more for a large film camera than a still version. We would take photos of the buildings that had been designed by Carybe—it all lent seriousness and genuineness to the cover of the mission.

With Yai reading the map, I drove into town, marveling at the interminable stretch of beaches, packed with humanity. It was the first time I had seen such a continuous stretch of sand, every square inch of it populated by a throng of sun worshipers, a chocolate gradation of skin tones that virtually ate up the white sands. Gradually we discovered that we had arrived on a holiday. It would appear that, at every drop of a work-free hour, the Brazilians repair to the beaches like lemmings. We drove into Bahia—it was virtually empty.

Rooms had been booked ahead of our arrival by the embassy. The moment we deposited our bags, we headed for Carybe's home to do some reconnoitering. There was no one at home—he had joined the rest of Brazil in their weekend homes, certainly somewhere along the beaches. The residential area where the house was situated was almost uniformly deserted. We drove up and down, I with my camera taking pictures of the neighborhood, for all the world like students of architecture or selective tourists. The residential part of Carybe's home was a low bungalow next to the road. Set far back was the gallery, its top floor visible over the wall of the compound. I could see the stairs leading up to it, the upper flight, and its landing, starkly exposed.

"You're sure that sculpture is up there, beyond that door we're looking at?"

"Oh, yes."

I sighed. It had to be! I thought, if the gallery had been on terra firma, not suspended above the walls between earth and sky, tantalizing two criminals from the African continent, we would have returned at night, scaled the wall, broken in, and retrieved our property. Labiyi had assured me that there were no burglar alarm systems. It was a quiet, middle-class area, crime-free—well, that was about to change. Nevertheless, we returned at night, hoping that maybe, just maybe...

No, there was no maybe. The stairs and landing were floodlit, so brightly that I felt certain that they could be seen all the way from Brasilia. We consoled ourselves with a Brazilian dinner, my first. It was a Saturday. We were obliged to cool our heels all through Sunday, waiting for Carybe to return and open his house to hostile guests.

It was the longest Sunday I had ever known, but that made me absorb what Bahia had to offer even more intensely, especially the visit to the *candomble,* where the *iyalorixa*—priestess of the *candomble*—took one look at us and concluded right away that we were from the original land of the *orisha*. Clusters of phrases in the liturgy were familiar, despite some changes here and there in articulation and tonality, and of course there were elisions that had taken place over time. Even so, much of the Yoruba in that worship was still recognizable. Despite time and distance, the lyrics of the chants were especially faithful to the original. Indeed, some scholars go so far as to suggest that the purest forms of these liturgies may be found among the slave descendants of Bahia, not in Yorubaland itself, but that is typical of scholastic conceit. What mattered to us was that these worshipers had no doubts about the authenticity of their beliefs, their dances, their invocations, the jealously guarded usages and values that defined their unique identity as the *anago*, proud descendants of the Yoruba in Brazil, generations that had never abandoned their roots or let them wither. They danced. There was a possession. The *iyalorixa* prayed for us. I felt uplifted.

Out in the streets, it felt strange, most unreal, eating *akaraje*, the Brazilian identical twin of our very own *akara*, thousands of miles away from its original home, a delicacy—sometimes heavy, doughy cake—made from the paste of black-eyed peas, fried in huge pans, just as one might encounter on a street corner of Abeokuta or Ilesa, where making *akara* remains the domain of women. We cruised the streets, Labiyi showing me landmarks of interest, especially places that narrated the history of the slaves and their struggle for emancipation. There was a poignancy about that day, made all the more troubling by underlying thoughts of what had brought us to this vibrant outpost of the Yoruba people—a marked contrast to Bekuta. Frankly, I would have given anything to avoid such a day; it tended to make the mind somewhat mellow, the will flabby from nostalgic thoughts, a tendency to transcend space and history and merge with long-estranged relations. Perhaps it was the Sunday quiet of the streets, but I felt transported to a space of empathy with this living shard of a scattered past, indulging vicariously in the resilience that appeared to be the one consoling extract of a people's displacement. It was all very well for the innocent locals; the nefarious—or soon to be—needed to have both their feet on the ground, focused and honed to a simple, unambiguous goal that went by just one name: burglary! I still preferred to think of it as a kind of unilateral act of restitution, but—burglary by any other name was still burglary.

We left messages for Carybe on his doorstep, and he was not slow to contact us on his return. We met the following morning; he was an affable, relaxed professional who did not attempt to disguise his pleasure at our visit. We spun him the story of our mission. Was this architect the guilty one? Millionaires are notorious for hiring robbery gangs to break into the best-guarded art galleries and snatch a canvas, not just a miniature but the full tapestry-sized object of lust. Rolled up and transported in furniture stuffing or a dustbin, the artwork arrives at the den of the collector and the bemused felons are paid off, leaving the obsessed recluse to contemplate his captive mistress in solitude for the rest of his life. The fact that he dares not exhibit her to anyone—sometimes not even to close family—merely adds piquancy to his salivation! Was Carybe one of these? He did not appear to belong in the millionaire class, but the collector's lust never did discriminate between tycoon and impecunious artist.

Carybe invited us to dinner, just as expected. As we sat in his living room awaiting dinner, I silently swore that before I left Bahia, I would eat more than *akaraje* from his home! I would swallow an entire head, uncooked, yet simmering in his gallery! He served drinks. I sipped but tasted nothing. Though I was outwardly calm, my inner being was quivering. The evening proceeded as expected. While we were waiting, Carybe offered, quite logically, to show us his gallery. I had unslung my camera bag when we arrived; now I picked it up again as we carried our drinks and climbed the suspended stairs into his lair. The door was locked. With difficulty, I tamped down my anxiety as I watched our host fumble with a bunch of keys. What would we find? An empty space where once *Ori Olokun* had reigned? It had been years, after all, since Labiyi had last set eyes on this bronze piece. Suppose Carybe had disposed of it in the meantime?

THE MOMENT WE ENTERED, I received a shock—but what a most delectable shock this was, taunting yet bracing! There, right across the work desk and canvases piled against the wall, seated on the topmost shelf among a number of sculptural odds and ends in a magnificent indifference to the history-laden voyage that had brought it to an alien yet native land, was the long-sought masterpiece: *Ori Olokun.* The difference between this and the *thing* in the museum gallery of Ile-Ife was instantly obvious; in any case, I had seen photo plates of the authentic piece. This face belonged to those photographs—longer, refined, and anatomically well proportioned. It had the seriated lines with which I had become familiar through illustrations in numerous books, nearly all commentaries directing the reader to accept that the original had vanished mysteriously—and forever.

And then—was it a trick of the light? Or was there really a dark patch on its right cheek, just where Frobenius had written it would be, from that careless moment of "Eureka!" when one of the diggers had indeed "struck gold" and a piece had come off the bronze head before the searchers had even caught a glimpse of it? What Frobenius felt as they proceeded to probe the earth more reverently with their bare hands, bringing out their treasure trove to light, I tried my hardest to imagine. More critical, however, was the need to snatch my eyes away before a fire of lust lit up my innermost wish. I exchanged looks with Olabiyi, after which I ensured that the fevered eyes in my head did not again stray toward that spot of attraction. As for emotions, I concentrated on bending all shafts of hate—no, not on its present custodian but on the usurper far away in Ife Museum, whose image lorded over a national stamp, the university crest, and at least a half dozen other public symbols and logos.

Our host gave us a tour of his canvases, opened up his portfolio of designs, and promised to take us around the physical structures to which they had given birth—that would be the following day. My mind was a philistine blank. We descended for dinner. My heart beat more insanely than an erratic water pump. Some disembodied voice, however, did emerge from within me. It announced that I would like to return the following day and browse among his canvases at a more leisurely pace. I also wanted to take photos of some of his sketches—would that be all right with our host? He was agreeable but regretted that he might have to leave us for some time, since he had an appointment. That's all right, I said, just tell your house help to let us in. Biyi and I again exchanged quick glances. Would we really carry this off?

Dinner was tasteless. No doubt the cooking was of the best, but I tasted nothing. On the drive back to the hotel, we were silent, each wrapped in his own thoughts, and never could a wider abyss have separated two preoccupations stemming from the same cause. Olabiyi was in a state of suppressed excitement. He had been vindicated, and all that was left was to fulfill the rest of our mission. On my part, however, I had begun a process of self-chastisement. Since this adventure had begun to take shape, I had lost my accustomed sense of humor, of an earthing sense of proportion. The last hour in Carybe's house had been deservedly traumatizing. I had taken this mission too seriously, I now realized, the perfect prelude to a punitive deflation. Only a tiny fragment of my corrective sense of mischief came to the rescue at this ponderous moment of absolute negation, and I was grateful when Olabiyi broke the silence, unable to control his excitement any longer.

"Did you see it? Did you recognize it?"

I nodded.

"But could you imagine that anyone could be so brazen? I mean, leaving it on the shelf all these years, so conspicuously. As if he didn't care who might see and recognize it."

"Yes, it's a kind of arrogance, I suppose."

"So how do you propose to set about it?"

I glanced at him in feigned surprise. "Set about what?"

"Well, what we came for. How are we going to lay our hands on it?"

"Oh, that," I replied, and the smile that I attempted to summon, if it appeared at all, must have been twisted. Nonetheless, it would be the only moment of self-satisfaction I would enjoy in that harebrained escapade. "That's been taken care of. We've got what we came for."

"We have? What do you mean? Because we've established its presence in the gallery?"

"A little more than that," I replied. "It's in the bag."

Still Biyi thought I was speaking in metaphors. "You mean, tomorrow? You sound confident. You think it's going to be that easy?"

I nodded toward the backseat. "The camera bag. Look inside it." I watched him scramble to lift the bag over his seat. "Be careful," I warned. "It's not bronze. I think it's clay."

"Clay? What do you mean, clay? And anyway…" He stopped dead. Felt the bulge in the bag. "When…? I mean, how…?" His eyes lit up, and he gasped. "But you weren't gone long enough!"

It was a moment I should have savored, but what I tasted in my mouth at a moment that should have trumpeted triumph or at least satisfaction was—depressingly not for the first time—ashes. It was this that had coated my tongue and subverted all taste in the sumptuous meal served by our host. My throat was lined with the stuff. It had all gone too smoothly. I had set down the camera bag as soon as we entered the gallery. When we were summoned down for dinner, I had left the bag behind. Then, moments after we sat down at the table, I had "remembered" the bag and set off, politely brushing aside our host, who offered to send his steward to look for it. I flew up the stairs, placed a stool that I had marked for the purpose on the workbench, snatched up the prize, and—gasped! It nearly flew from my hands! I had expected to lift heavy metal, but whatever I had in my hands chastised my impulsiveness with an incongruous lightness. It was a moment of deflation. It was too late for questions or theories, however. I brought it down, shoved it into the bag, replaced the step, and was downstairs in mere seconds.

"It has to be the real thing!" Biyi persisted. "If it isn't, then what on earth is it?"

"I don't know," I admitted. "We'll find out when we reach the hotel."

"But what do we do now?"

"Research, research. More and more research. Our next stop is Dakar."

THAT MOMENT OF SHOCK, of lifting what should have been a sculpted weight of bronze and was worth more than its weight in gold but proved lighter than tinfoil, was nothing compared to the news from the backup team at home that greeted us the following morning: Pierre Verger had been released from his "administrative detention," and by none other than my good friends, the State Security Service (SSS). Our backup team in the university, headed by the dean, had been assigned the role of ensuring that Pierre's end-of-employment documents were withheld for the few days we would be away, thus keeping him within Nigeria. However, yet another force of intervention had joined in the fray—and from within a state agency. Even more remarkable was the fact that he had been put on a plane and was now on his way to Brazil!

For hours that morning, we speculated on the significance of this move. Was it the result of intense diplomatic pressure? We were in constant touch with our embassy in Brasilia and had a right to expect that we would be instantly briefed on any development at home, especially one that might have a bearing on our very welfare. The embassy had no messages for us—nothing.

The day's program had to be followed, however. We endured lunch with Carybe and some friends in a favorite Brazilian-Yoruba restaurant, discussed the manifestations of Yoruba culture in Brazil, the race issue, and the comparative merits of the firewaters *caxaca* and *capinrinha*, all the time deeply conscious of the double face we wore, wondering what to make of this new complication.

"We must get out of here," I said to Biyi—unnecessarily—as soon as we were alone.

We left unceremoniously, leaving notes for our Brazilian hosts about some problems at home that required our immediate return. The gods must have felt some remorse for their unkind treatment of their faithful servitors, since it was virtually by a miracle that we obtained two seats on the very next flight out of Rio and heading for—no destination could be more earnestly desired—Dakar!

OUR ARRIVAL IN Dakar brought unusual excitement to the staid laboratories of Senegal's ethnological institute, IFAN, headed by Cheik Anta Diop, whose *African Origin of Civilisation* had committed the ultimate sin of faulting the theories of canonized Egyptologists, Jacques Champollion especially. Most of the staff were only too familiar with the ancient controversy over *Ori Olokun*. They cast their eyes on this head with the greenish patina, the telltale hole in the cheek, and the holes strung around the base of the skull, a feature of bronze sculptures cast through the *cire perdue* technique—and they instantly burst into ululations. They pronounced it, unquestionably, the original.

The problem was the material. If it were clay, was our find the original clay mold from which the final head had been cast? But then who on earth had taken the trouble to coat the head in verdigris and replicate the very appearance of an antique bronze piece? Had yet another set of raiders stumbled on the original clay mold, then faked its surface appearance to hide its authenticity? This was a piece that was cast to perfection. Measurements were taken to compare them with those of Frobenius, that assiduous recorder of weights and measures. Cheik Anta Diop, a long-embattled scholar, was beside himself with excitement: "Just think of it, if somehow the original mold from which the bronze was cast had been miraculously preserved—what a find! What a find!"

And what a dismal find it proved when, sitting down with a riot of thoughts while we awaited the return of the archival researchers, my eyes fixated on this troublesome object, I finally noticed a tiny, clearly embossed line at the base of the head, just where it joins the neck. The light from Diop's window had made visible what the artificial light in our hotel room—and our downsized powers of observation in Bahia—had failed to reveal. I looked more carefully and—all was made plain. That impish agent of reversals, Esu, was clearly not done with us!

This fragmentary line was not by itself but was joined to others. They formed the letter—M! And there, just before M, was yet another faded letter: B. The letters "BM" stamped into this piece, standing for no other institution than—the British Museum! Of course! What we had in our hands was nothing other than a British Museum copy, available for the princely sum of—fifteen, twenty pounds? Certainly twenty-five pounds at the most. The deflation could not have been more definitive than that of a hot-air balloon spiraling down to earth after an unfortunate encounter with a migrating stork!

When Cheik Anta returned to his office, I showed him the stamp. He appeared to take it in his stride, looking only a little disappointed but not in the least crestfallen—which would be a generous description of the condition in which he met us. Then I asked the question: "Where is the original today, from which this was made?"

The question must have struck him as fatuous, since the stamp indicated quite clearly where the copy had originated. But my mind had resumed the hunt. I persisted: "If we say that this is a copy of what Frobenius described in his travelogue, the one that he dug up, leaving a hole in its cheek, the same one that was displayed in both the Munich and London expositions before it allegedly disappeared, then from what bronze head was this copied by the museum? And when?" I rattled off details of the facts I had unearthed in the days preparatory to our departure. Its last acknowledged appearance had been at the London Exhibition of 1938 in honor of King George's coronation. After that—the entire ethnographic world insists—*it disappeared altogether.* So from what bronze piece came this plaster replica? I produced my dossier, flashed the museum postcard. "Look at it. Even on this card, produced and sold to its visitors by the museum, it says, 'Present whereabouts unknown.' So what phantom head gave birth to this copy even while its existence is denied?"

Cheik Anta took the piece, rolled it lovingly in his hands, walked to his chair, and sat in it, shaking his head dolefully. "But you know, our white colleagues in this ethnographic business have always been thieves—we know that. But they also put their scholarship at the service of thieves."

I DRAFTED A telegram for the embassy to send to the Ministry of Foreign Affairs in Lagos. It read: "MISSION ACCOMPLISHED, BUT INCONCLUSIVE. STOPOVER IN DAKAR TO PURSUE INQUIRIES." It was the kindest language—to our bruised selves—that I could conceive. I flashed our letter of mission authorization to the embassy and requested that it check us into a hotel and take care of the bills. This was more than conservation of our remaining finances; more than ever, it became important to ensure that the involvement of the government was established at every stage. Once our flight back into Lagos was arranged, the embassy sent another telegram to the Foreign Office providing details of our travel and requesting that we be met on arrival.

We were not. We waited an hour at Ikeja airport, then concluded that our message had not been received or that arrangements had gone awry. On our way out of Nigeria, we had been taken to the airport by ministry officials, accorded full VIP protocol. Our embassy in Dakar had also been more than hospitable, had placed an official car at our disposal while we remained there, driven us to the airport, and assisted in clearing immigration formalities—in short, we had had no cause to think that we were no longer on an official mission. Still, the bare fact stared us in the face: no official was there to meet us, neither from Adefowope's ministry nor from Dodan Barracks.

It turned out that we had arrived on a day when nearly all of Lagos was at a standstill. Nobody who was anybody was to be found in Lagos—all were headed for Benin, homeland of those close cousins of the Yoruba from whom, according to legend, they were descended in the first place. The oba of that famous kingdom, Oba Akenzua Iku Akpolopkolo, had died, and his nearly interminable obsequies were approaching their climax. Successive military regimes had ostentatiously kowtowed to the traditional rulers—unless, of course, they stood in the way of military will, in which case, the oba, obi, or emir soon learned just who wielded the real power. Otherwise, the military paid due obeisance to the monarch, and the oba of Benin was certainly among the most venerated.

Traffic around Benin City moved in two directions. The top brass and cream of Lagosian society and other cities trooped toward Benin to pay homage, while strangers and beggars trooped the other way—they could not escape from Benin and its environs fast enough! For the tradition was that a certain number of human sacrifices must be made when the oba died, and such victims were selected, so persisted rumors, from among strangers. True or false, many preferred not to find out. In addition, all indigenes of the kingdom, the Edo people, were required to shave their heads as a sign of respect and homage. Even my good friend the democratic litigant Gani Fawehinmi, "Senior Advocate of the Masses," though non-Edo, shaved his head clean—a gesture that struck me as dyeing one's attire a deeper indigo than the weeds of the bereaved. I felt irritated that Gani should lend his authority to a feudal imposition, yet harbored a rapport with the traditional institution itself as an essential part of the cultural landscape.

Thus I lamented a failed mystic linkage between the passing of a descendant of Oduduwa and this return of a pale symbol, a plaster cast of his deified sibling, Olokun, just in time to participate in the funeral rites of one of the branches of the great primogenitor. It occurred to me that maybe Yai and I should also shave our heads, not in homage to the passing of this monarch but in remorse for a mission from which we had returned empty-handed—even worse, returned with a mere shell of the historic weight of the scion of Oduduwa. I tried to console myself that we nonetheless held in secret custody an object that could substitute for the royal death mask, but was rewarded only with a decidedly hollow feeling in my stomach, as hollow as the clay head in our possession.

I sensed that something had gone badly wrong. The absence of protocol—the Benin events notwithstanding—was ominous. Still, there was nothing else to do but await the return of the mourners. We headed for Ibadan. Aboyade, our abetting ex–vice chancellor, was also nowhere to be found, and we assumed that he was part of the official delegation to Benin. Yai proceeded to Ife while I stopped off at Femi's, both to unwind and to relieve him of his predictable, ravenous hunger for the narrative of our voyage.

IN IFE, NEWS OF THE safe return of the "Argonauts" had circulated, and jubilations had begun. The History Department, African Studies, Languages, Philosophy, Drama, the Dean's Office, and so on were gearing up to celebrate in grand style. We had the sobering task of stopping them from slaughtering the fatted calf. Not only had the real objective proved elusive; there was now a serious risk that the leakage of our real objective into diplomatic circles would have one guaranteed result: the authentic *Ori Olokun* would now sink deeper and deeper into an impenetrable hiding place. To have propagated its nonexistence for so long, and now to have a bunch of skeptics taking melodramatic risks to puncture that myth of a mystic disappearance, would send a message to the illegal possessor: *Hide it away, dig a hole like its original habitation in Ile-Ife, bring it out to gaze upon from time to time, and perhaps exhibit it to a few intimates!*

So much for the speculative fate of *Ori Olokun*. Of more immediate concern to us was our own fate, the two *olori-kunkun* who had undertaken this thankless mission. Who was responsible for the departure of our suspected colleague whom we had left in the guesthouse of the vice chancellor? The answer was dispiriting.

In its anxiety to ensure that Pierre remained in the country, the Ministry of Foreign Affairs had involved the police. The consequences could not have been more disastrous. The police, on their own, had decided to "carry out investigations." They had visited Ife Museum and found an *Ori Olokun* in its accustomed place, unscathed. They spoke to the curator: Had there been a break-in at the museum? No, the curator assured them. Nothing missing from the collection? Not even a bronze head? No, everything was in its place. And what would be his reaction if he were told that the *Ori Olokun* was missing? Well, if they would kindly follow him, he would show them the *Ori Olokun* on its accustomed podium in the glass case. The harassed man answered their questions in the strictest manner possible. He did not reveal that we had visited the museum at the planning stages and that he was part of the project, though not of the conspiracy. He knew his archaeological history and had indeed admitted to us that each time he passed by the pretender in its glass case, he felt like smashing the case and throwing out the piece. He had unprintable names for Mr. Frobenius.

The police listened, took notes, returned to base, and filed their report. It was succinct and damning: no theft had been reported from Ife. *Ori Olokun* was in its place, large as life. There had been no disturbance of his peace nor of that of his companions on display at Ife Museum.

Piecing the rest of the story together was easy enough. Pierre Verger was questioned. Did he know anything of a missing *Ori Olokun*? He denied it. Had he made enemies while at Ife, colleagues who might be interested in scheming for his downfall? A puzzled Pierre told them that he knew of none such among his colleagues. Was he on good relations with Wole Soyinka? Absolutely, said Pierre. And Olabiyi Yai? What did he know of him? Labiyi and he worked closely, said Pierre, and he had played host to Labiyi in Brazil. Their academic areas of interest threw them together quite often. Akin Isola? Wande Abimbola? Any contest for academic preferment between you and them? Pierre replied in the negative.

Well, declared the SSS to Pierre, you are clearly the victim of some intrigue. And those first two are at the center of it. Right now, they are in Brazil—to do what exactly, we do not know, since it is now clear that they were never after any missing object. Maybe they went over there to further whatever sinister plot your friends at the university had cooked up against you. No matter, we apologize for all the inconvenience and hope you do not hold us responsible for it. University politics are clearly beyond us, and quite frankly, we would rather be kept out of them. There is a flight out to Brazil tonight—would you like to be on it? Pierre was more than willing; he was ready to fly out of Nigeria and never dirty his feet on her soil for the rest of his life! Perhaps only Labiyi and I, of the entire planet, were more eager than Pierre to depart from alien territory during those crucial twenty-four hours.

Our planes did not cross paths over the Atlantic—not quite. Later, as we conducted a detailed postmortem on the sequence of events, followed up on the actions of the police and the departure of Pierre, we discovered that we had actually been in Rio de Janeiro—in the departure section of the airport—at the very moment that Pierre was passing through to Immigration and baggage claim. Fifteen minutes either way, and the two gladiatorial groups would have encountered each other, perhaps in the parking lot or at the frontage of the airport building!

WE WERE ABOUT to discover that the devil sometimes takes a sabbatical! That other descendant of the line of Oduduwa, Obasanjo, the head of state, became suddenly inaccessible, evaporated as the authentic *Ori Olokun* was alleged to have done. I suggested that perhaps he had traveled to Benin incognito, strayed into the path of the ritualists hunting for sacrificial strangers, and was now keeping company with the late oba of Benin. I called the more-than-familiar telephone number, and a strange voice answered. I announced who I was and asked to speak to the head of state. I was rewarded with a barked response: "Do you have an appointment?"

"Do I what-did-you-say?"

"Have an appointment, I said. Do you have an appointment to phone the head of state?"

I still was not sure I had heard right. I repeated my name, and the voice retorted, "Yes, I heard you say who you are. And I asked you if you had an appointment."

"You want me to make an appointment to call your *oga*? Now, how exactly does one do that?"

"That is not my business to tell you. Do you think you can call the head of state just like that? Without an appointment?"

Well, now, I thought, it is not only the Edo Kingdom that is being turned upside down. The nation itself, Nigeria, appeared to have tumbled into some time warp and was spinning out of control. Maybe some aliens had taken over Dodan Barracks. Could this possibly be the same Dodan Barracks that I called up anytime, the same head of state with whom I had brainstormed together with Oje, sometimes over dinner or a weekend lunch, a wine bottle tucked under my arm to guard against wine poisoning by his indifferent stewards? We had commenced this exercise—could only have begun it!—with his active approval and collaboration. Now here was some strange voice that breezily, even insolently, admitted that it recognized the identity of the caller but required that this same caller somehow make an appointment in order to speak to his boss. I put down the telephone, turned to Akin Isola next to me, and sighed.

"We are in trouble. Deep trouble." And I narrated what had been barked at me from the other end of the line.

"What next?" Akin demanded.

In that moment, my mind was made up. "I leave for London. We've wasted far too much time."

"Leave for London? What for?"

"I'm heading for the British Museum. I want to find out which original this copy came from. Certain forces have entered into this, forces on which we hadn't bargained. Pressures. Diplomatic, certainly. Just think—why was Pierre released without our being informed? I think we are about to be sold, bargained away. Before that happens, I need to have pushed this search as far as possible. From now on, we ignore that devil in Dodan Barracks. We ignore the ministry, and we ignore the police. We are on our own and—so be it."

AND SO IT WAS back on the trail, but in a different mode. There would be no more skulduggery. Between the members of the original team and the recruited art historian in the Fine Arts Department, Babatunde Lawal, we had already compiled masses of literature. I pored over this material yet again, returned to the library to scrutinize bibliographies, indexes, and footnotes even more closely, looking for clues that we might have overlooked or considered unimportant. Now it was desperation for more knowledge, for a closer approximation of the truth, that drove me.

It was strange. Only a few days had passed since nothing mattered in the world but that moment when I would hold a physical object in my hands, restore it to its rightful home, and bask in the contentment of a historic closure. Now all I wanted was the truth, the truth of a location, the meaning behind nearly a half century of deception. I felt the pressure of time. Any moment now, I expected to be warned off in some manner that would be difficult to circumvent—probably summoned and read the riot act, such as that any further action on my part regarding *Ori Olokun* would "jeopardize the bilateral relations with this or that government and will not be tolerated." The next casualty would be my passport, then would come all forms of harassment, such as being summoned for interrogation. Arrest or detention was out of the question, that much at least I was quite sure of. The Obasanjo regime badly craved the reputation of following the rule of law.

Femi's wife, Barbara, was away in England; her location could not have been more fortunate. Femi—he had now joined in the chase—proposed her recruitment for the next stage of inquiry. She would visit the British Museum and find out all she could about the "missing" original. Obviously the British Museum held the key. I was now certain that news of our escapade had spread and the doors battened against any Nigerian-looking researcher. Barbara was British, however, and she would not arouse suspicion. We fed her all the accumulated information and suggested a few trails for her to follow, the most promising of which was that the head had once been acquired by a British family, then lent—or sold—to the British Museum. We supplied the name of the family.

Barbara was thorough. She succeeded in tracking down the descendants of that family, located not far from London. She spoke to them on the phone and confirmed that the family had surrendered the head to the British Museum. From the latter, Barbara extracted the information that the main museum had in turn loaned it to one of its branch institutions. A little more probing revealed that this was none other than the Burlington. I asked her to pay a visit to the Museum of Mankind in Burlington Gardens without attracting attention to herself.

In my head, alarm bells continued to jangle, warning me that discretion was now belated. What mattered was to establish the exact whereabouts of the original, now that we knew that the British Museum had made replicas from it. It would be no exaggeration to state that I had now become obsessed. I wanted *Ori Olokun*—badly—even if it was only to set my eyes on it! I wanted it more than I had ever craved any object in my life. In moments of sober reflection, long after it was all over and I analyzed my state of mind during this period, I came to understand what the mystique of the Holy Grail had been about, or the Golden Fleece, how the *epos* of The Quest had come to predominate in the mythologies of nearly every culture. If I could not bring *Ori Olokun* back, at least I wanted to be able to say, "An end to all these lies, the great distraction contained in 'whereabouts unknown.' " Rubbish! There were those still alive who knew damned well where *Ori Olokun* was. There was a bronze head, the authentic article, on display somewhere, yet the scholars were pretending that it was not *Ori Olokun* but its simulacrum, churning out theories to suggest that there was yet another bronze piece, probably an imitation or "sculpture of the head of an Ife king, sometimes mistaken for *Ori Olokun*." Regarding this attribution, however, there was something else we had observed.

This alleged "twin" of *Ori Olokun* was always photographed from the left profile, never from the right, where the pick had taken off a piece of the cheek and left a distinctive gash. Was this a coincidence? I had researched tome after tome, and while the "missing" original—in black and white or in color—was always photographed frontally, from the rear, and in right and left profile, the "twin" appeared only in its left profile. If there was nothing to hide, why was it always photographed from the undamaged side? The task force had also debated this "coincidence"—Adeagbo Akinjogbin of History, Wande Abimbola the Yoruba expert, Babatunde Lawal of Fine Arts, and others. We had examined photos, monograms, ethnographic and art history books, museum catalogues, and the like, and were always struck by this discrimination—the twin only appeared in its undamaged profile. We had all developed a strong suspicion that there was no twin, that is, there was no bronze head in existence of that particular cast that did not have the crucial hole in its cheek. And there could be only one of its kind! Of no other bronze head did any archaeologist ever report that a piece was taken off the cheek—and at that exact spot!

FROBENIUS'S JOURNEYS through Africa have been remarked, with some justification, as an exercise in Teutonic obsession with measurements and detail. He traveled not only with an artist who produced numerous sketches—with finicky dimensions—of art pieces, architecture, landscape, and so on, but with a mobile smelting and casting factory. He made copies of several objects, including bronzes. When the British district officer learned of his excavations in Ile-Ife, he put his paid informers on the alert and thus learned of the success of the dig almost at the same time as Frobenius was covering up the ravished dig. The district officer kept an eye on Frobenius's movements, learned just in time that he was headed for the border with Dahomey, and moved to stop the acquisitive German as he was about to depart with his booty. The story, according to Frobenius, was that he was compelled to part with *Ori Olokun* and succeeded in keeping for himself only the chip that had come off the end of the careless pick.

Our reconstruction, however, was this: the district officer parted with what he *thought* was *Ori Olokun*. It was more likely to have been an imitation—that is, not a direct replica of the original but a totally separate head, a clumsy handiwork by Frobenius's companion. It is that imitation that has continued, to this day, to occupy pride of place in Ile-Ife. Frobenius's companion had mastered the art of *cire perdue* but lacked the skills to make a copy with the finesse of the original. When the district officer demanded that he disburden himself of the precious head, Frobenius had simply given him an *original imitation*, fabricated by his artist.

Well, I wanted badly to see the original—or its mysterious "twin."

IT WAS INDEED on display in a glass case at the Burlington museum, its jagged hole conspicuously in view. I was overcome with an irrational feeling that the normal, viewing world was seeing *Ori Olokun* for the very last time, that this "twin" would vanish as the next logical stage in a half century saga. I threaded my way through the museum visitors, mildly disguised in case my picture had been circulated through Interpol as an art thief to be watched at all costs. I walked past it only twice or thrice, always making sure that the attention I paid to it was less than the amount of time I spent viewing other items on display.

My fears were soon grounded in factual developments. The moment I arrived in London, I called Barbara and asked her to bring me up to date.

Through her deft sleuthing, she had found that the director of the National Museum in Lagos, Ekpo Eyo, was on his way to London. I phoned Burlington, provisioned with a formal but phony title, and asked directly for the director of the Nigerian National Museum—had he arrived? Not yet, but he was expected; the museum had received notice that he was on his way.

Eyo's visit could not be a coincidence. The police had undoubtedly contacted him for an opinion during their clumsy intervention, and he had begun to conduct his own research; which had led him unerringly to Burlington. How many other roads, and taken by whom, I wondered, now led to the Burlington museum?

That conviction of a multiple convergence on that Piccadilly warehouse of treasures bred a renewed urgency and made me throw all caution to the wind. I returned the following day—to do what, precisely, I was not sure, especially as I did not bother any longer with any form of disguise. I was overwhelmed by the certitude of shrinking time, of an accelerated and definitive resolution, albeit unwanted, of this conundrum. I think I wanted to see the head again, knowing that it might be for the last time. If necessary, I would seek out the curator, declare my interest in this object, and speak frankly but not in great detail of the efforts of Ife University to establish the truth of its identity. Burlington, after all, was a public institution; it admitted paying visitors and should not be shy of answering questions. I would ask him how Burlington had acquired it, ask to see records. I think I had become reconciled to the mere satisfaction of holding it in my hands and letting it speak to me through some secret, ancestral vibrations, just so I could know—and share with others—the knowledge of the present existence of *Ori Olokun*.

My craving would be assuaged by no less. With it went a mental restlessness and fitful bouts of sleep, pocked by the strangest dreams. I greeted dawn with great relief, waited impatiently until opening time, and set off for the museum, a creature under possession, and by the most confused of impulses. I raced up the steps, excited at the prospect of seeing the head again, and headed straight for the hall.

ORI OLOKUN HAD VANISHED! On the podium where it had stood in proud display less than twenty-four hours before, there was—nothing. Not even a replacement. Not a label. Just—nothing. The case was empty.

For what was probably no longer than a few seconds but seemed hours, I remained in still confrontation with that glass case, willing its erstwhile occupant to levitate, demonstrate its pristine potency, and astonish all viewers.

What did levitate instead was a member of the staff, a black girl who was simply going about her normal duties. There was no longer need for reticence and I approached her and pointed to the case. "What happened to this one?"

Speaking quite artlessly, she informed me that it had been "taken downstairs." Any particular reason? I asked. None that she knew of, she replied. It was quite normal for the items on display to be changed from time to time. Rotation of themes was common in that section of the gallery—not throughout the museum but in the sections that were dedicated to special exhibitions. Where was she from? I asked, and she replied that she was from Sierra Leone.

I hesitated only a moment. Was it possible that I could see the head, even outside the display? It was obvious to me that if there was any conspiracy at all afoot, this girl was not part of it. Her guilelessness could not have been faked, and when she said, "Sure, follow me," I nearly catapulted her downstairs, fearful that some superior officer "in the know" might interrupt this totally unexpected visitation. We descended into the netherworld where art pieces were cleaned, catalogued, and stored until their next emergence to baffle, frustrate, or enlighten the world.

Yes, finally there did come the belated reward, a long moment of rapture. There on the table with other pieces was the unmistakable head at last—*Ori Olokun!*

I did not wait for it to vanish. Outwardly calm, I simply leaped on it inwardly and lifted this exquisite bronze head in my hands. The weight was just what I had anticipated when I had climbed the makeshift ladder in Carybe's studio and lifted its copy off the shelf. The gash in the missing cheek was exactly where it had been on the copy. Reverently, I turned it around and around in my hands, peered shortsightedly into the cavity beneath the neck, and sought to guess just how old it was. I laughed out aloud.

The girl looked at me, puzzled. Quickly, I improvised, explained that I was simply thinking of how surprised Frobenius must have been when the British district officer ambushed him at the border and deprived him of his catch. It was a lie. I had just experienced one of those flashes—W.S. taking suddenly to his heels, up the stairs, weaving balletically through the display cases, dodging pillars and visitors, out through the door, onto Burlington Arcade, and into a long stretch heading nowhere in particular, alarms jangling, pursued by the white-coated museum staff shouting "Stop, thief!"—a scene straight out of *Oliver Twist,* only in this case augmented by the phlegmatic London bobbies on the beat blowing their whistles, motorcycle police, Scotland Yard, the Fire Brigade, Boy Scouts, and St. John's Ambulance....

However, the race was over—I knew that!—and I remained rooted to the concrete floor of the chilly semibasement of this outpost of the British Museum, in my hands the authentic *Ori Olokun,* no matter what the Western pundits said. I sighed, looked around at the other treasures looted by the imperial forays of European powers. I think it was in that process that I noticed, for the first time, that the museum worker was quite pretty, indeed more than merely pretty; she had a solicitous charm, just the kind that tended to set off vibrations for a different kind of pursuit. For a few brief moments I wondered: Should I make a pass, turn her into an ally, and commence slow, meticulous planning for an inside heist? It seemed worth thinking about. Take her out, cultivate her slowly, gently, wait until the madcap escapade in Bahia was forgotten, the follow-up by the director of Nigerian antiquities, and—certainly— my own visit, which, I did not need to be told, would have raised a few eyebrows. It did not matter if it took an entire year from planning to execution. At the very least, here was a chance to keep an eye on the movements of *Ori Olokun.* No matter where it went, this girl would take note and pass on the news.

I laid down the bronze head gently, returned the girl's smile. Her charm drew me, in its own right, and I was more than certain that there was a reciprocal tug. Yet, unusually, even that consolation was not one of which I was prepared to avail myself—it carried with it the certain risk that I would draw her into a renewed web of conspiracy. If I had felt that a resumption would stand any chance of success, I probably would have persisted, but—I *knew.* The moment I held that bronze weight in my hands, I knew, with every strand of intuition, that we had reached the end of the trail. Too many cooks now had their ladles in this broth. Best to withdraw and abandon the lord of the seas to his overseas retreat.

ON MY RETURN, I called on Oje Aboyade in his Ibadan home. He had traveled, it turned out, not to Benin but in the other direction—outside the country to escape the hullabaloo generated by the death of the Edo monarch. His first question was—had I briefed Obasanjo since my return? Negative; and I recounted the efforts I had already made. Right, let's do it now, he proposed. No way, I said to him. As far as I was concerned, his man no longer existed.

Oje could not believe that "our friend" had blocked his phone against my calls, so I called him again from Oje's house, announced myself, then split the earpiece between us so that he could listen to every word. It was the same voice, and his answer was, if anything, more curt, rudely dismissive. I hung up.

Oje said, All right, let's wait fifteen minutes, and then *I* will call. I did not doubt what the result would be and remained indifferent. Oje put his call through and as soon as he announced himself received the kind of genial response that I had last received before the fateful trip to Bahia. He made an appointment to see Obasanjo.

Then he turned to me, and never had I seen Oje so woebegone. "Someone has been feeding him lies," he announced.

"And what is that to me?" I replied. "There is only one word for this—treachery! Beginning from him and transmitted all the way down the official ladder. Not only had Pierre been released, he was told the entire truth and put on a plane to go there and—confront us. On his own territory! From then on we were dead meat to this Dodan devil! We were not met on our return, and then, for days, there was no contact. Listen, Oje, if you haven't worked this out by now, the truth is—we were not meant to return."

Oje protested vehemently. I shouted him down. "I tell you, we were not meant to return! These people were getting rid of a problem. We've worked out movements on both sides, and we found that Pierre nearly caught us flat-footed in Brazil. One more night! That devilish den did not expect us back."

Oje was nothing if not persistent. He went for his appointment and had a long heart-to-heart talk with Obasanjo. On his return he announced that he had made an appointment for us both to go and see him. I laughed. No, I never wanted to set foot in Dodan Barracks again or see the face of that head of state. Oje piled on the pressure—"At least listen to what he has to say." I remained adamant; I had had enough. I wanted nothing but the solitude of my bush, nothing more.

Eventually, he prevailed. He had recruited Femi Johnson to his side, yet it was not so much the combined pressure that wore me down but my own curiosity. I wanted to confront the man, study the expression on his Owu cicatriced face, follow those eyes as he tried to wriggle out of this one, then give him a piece of my mind and leave. Even so, I nearly backed out at the last moment. I had developed a visceral revulsion toward not only the seat of government but anyone associated with it. Even Oje had not escaped this guilt by association, I realized. It had, after all, been several days after my return from London before I could bring myself to stop at his house, and then it was only because I had been staying in Ibadan that weekend, nursing back my self-esteem in the congenial setting of Femi's home.

Still, I ended up accompanying him to Lagos and into Dodan Barracks, grim of countenance. As we walked through the deserted complex and passed by the sparse allotment of officers on duty, I scowled at each in turn in case he was the miscreant who had given himself the pleasure of telling me to book an appointment for a telephone call. We entered the familiar space of Obasanjo's private lounge. I braced myself for the diatribe that was coiled at the root of my tongue, untended, but capable, I was certain, of atomizing the heads of a dozen heads of state. We had hardly settled down before Obasanjo himself entered the room and plunged into what must have been a well-rehearsed and difficult text.

"The police messed up," he announced. "But they are my men. The ultimate responsibility rests with me, and so—I accept responsibility for their actions and I apologize. I apologize on their behalf." Before I could open my mouth to reply, he added, "Look, Wole, if I wanted to get rid of you, I would put you against a wall and shoot you. But I could never send you to a strange country to be killed or injured. I would never send a fellow Nigerian to another country to be killed. I could never do that. It is against my soldierly training."

I had too much piled up within me and was not about to let him off easily. I plunged into a bitter reprise of the succession of betrayals Labiyi and I, as well as the others at Ife, had undergone. I was particularly galled at the ignorant intervention of the police—if the police had had to be brought into play, was there no police section better qualified for such a role? What had happened to the Antiquities Squad, specially created to stem the illegal flow of national treasures overseas? Oje interrupted, imploring me to accept the man's regrets and draw a curtain over the entire episode. And then, suddenly, the devil himself was chuckling. I was taken aback—was it all a joke to him, and did this include his apology?

"Look, I've already said—heap it all on my head. I have accepted full responsibility—*abi?*" And, his rotund frontage virtually heaving with—in my reckoning—sadistic mirth, he continued, "But you know, it is also your fault. It doesn't matter what you do, the police have a chronic distrust of you. If they see you walking south, they think it must be a trick and that you're really headed north. That's the problem. For them you represent a permanent headache. Anyway, please, let's forget it. I apologize."

From testimonies among his closest circle, this must have been one of the half dozen times that Obasanjo ever apologized for any action in his life. I had been a recipient twice. I wondered, wryly, how soon there would be a third and if I would have to receive it, like Pierre Verger's from me, posthumously.

Epilogue

Now, what was the real story? How had Olabiyi Yai come to believe that the authentic head had somehow landed, after unrecorded vicissitudes, in Carybe's studio?

The explanation lay in his conversation with Pierre. He had believed it because Pierre told him. When it was all over and the misadventure was put to rest, I asked Yai to go through the scene at the party at which this "confession" had been made—to leave nothing out, consider nothing of no importance, see nothing as lacking in significance. I made him go through Pierre's dialogue and his, their gestures, comportments, states of inebriation—in as full detail as he could recollect.

The exchange, Yai reaffirmed, had taken place on the top landing of the suspended stairs. Pierre had gone outside for fresh air with a drink in his hand. He had sat on a step, and Olabiyi, who, all that evening, had had the hidden eyes in his head riveted on no other object but that bronze piece, had finally said to Pierre, "Baba, is that not the famous head of Olokun sitting on that shelf?"

"Of course," said Pierre.

"But—what of the one in the museum at Ife?"

"Oh, that. Everyone knows it's a fake."

"Are you quite sure about that?"

"There isn't any serious scholar who believes in that thing."

"Then how did Carybe get hold of this? When? How did he get it out of Nigeria?"

And then Pierre looked warily right and left, as if to make sure that there was no one within earshot. He leaned forward, put a finger across his lips, and said, "Shh. Don't tell anyone. I brought it here myself."

I believe that narrative of their exchange. What Yai missed was Pierre's boyish sense of mischief, not too different from that of his countryman Abdias do Nascimento. Abdias's contribution at any symposium on identity, culture, race, and the like was always guaranteed to immobilize his audience in a denunciation of Brazilian racist policies, reeling out statistics and calling for world intervention. And then Abdias, ending his diatribe abruptly and resuming his seat, would turn to me and—*wink*!

That evening outside Carybe's studio, Pierre, the scholar, was making a mockery of all efforts—including his, probably—to solve a mystery that had defeated dozens of archaeologists, art historians, and ethnologists. He was amused, it now seems clear, by Yai's naive belief that this long-sought head was actually sitting among the jumble in some architect's studio gallery in

Bahia. Pierre did not consider for a moment that his act was convincing. He forgot that this was a party atmosphere, with plenty of booze, where lurked the possibility of confessions made—*in vino veritas.*

AFTER ALL THE DIPLOMATIC hassle had subsided, tempers had cooled, and even the police were acting somewhat chastened, I commenced the process of inviting Pierre back to Ife, as a special guest. The university was more than willing to create an occasion to make public amends, offer him an open apology and exonerate him before the university community. But the Ministry of Foreign Affairs refused to approve his visa. Indeed, we discovered that he had been placed on a forbidden list!

There could be only one explanation for this. Many more—undoubtedly vicious—lies that would embarrass officialdom were they to be revealed must have been spilled to Pierre by the police. They could not afford to have Pierre back in the country, where the episode could be aired at a public postmortem, even as we, the principals and associated conspirators, winced in chagrin and wiped mud off our own faces. The role of the government and its agencies would have garnered the greatest opprobrium, however; at worst, we would only have to endure some good-natured mockery.

We let another year or more go by, until a civilian regime had taken over the reins of government. I succeeded in cutting through all obstacles—no one, as usual, could recall how they had come to be placed there anyway or who had ordered them—and obtained a visa clearance for Pierre. Using mutual colleagues such as Doig Simmonds, the dancing instructor Peggy Harper—a refugee from South Africa—and Abdias do Nascimento, we invited Pierre to one public event after the other. I swore that I would meet him personally at the airport and escort him to Ife with full grandeur. We arranged that a Yoruba traditional title would be added to the one that he already enjoyed.

We should not have been surprised that Pierre declined. At seventy-plus, his rough treatment at the hands of the police and his conviction of a betrayal by trusted colleagues were simply too much to overcome. The episode was more or less smothered in Brazil at the time but was exhumed by some enterprising journalists when I was awarded the Nobel Prize. Those journalists homed in on both Pierre and myself. Pierre was still bitter but quite generous in saluting my award. For my part, I heaped all the blame on an ignorant and high-handed police, asked the journalists to pass on our invitation to Pierre yet again to return to Nigeria as my personal and university guest, where he would learn firsthand what had transpired and how the misunderstandings had come about. I added, however, that unfortunately, it had been Pierre's impish sense of humor that had triggered off a chain of events among us, his humorless colleagues.

Many of our colleagues believed in turn that I would not step into Brazil ever again, but I have done so, more than once, and even while Pierre was still alive. I looked for him, but he had traveled out of Bahia and we never met. (Had an unforgiving Pierre quit Bahia because he heard I was coming?) The media appeared to have decided to draw a veil of discretion over the episode. Not one mention of the "quest for the Holy Grail" appeared in the press during my entire stay, when I was also received by the president, himself a novelist of note.

Pierre died some years ago. Reconciliation with that misused scholar was one that I truly craved, but appeasement must now be delayed until our reunion under the generous canopy of Orunmila.

The "Evil Genius"

. . . . .

GENERAL IBRAHIM BADAMASI BABANGIDA, WHO FOR MOST OF THE EIGHT-year dictatorship that began in 1985 affected a convincing indifference to public image, eventually revealed his vulnerability. Nettled by a seemingly consensual and persistent view in the media that he was evil at heart and in intent, he finally retorted that if he was indeed evil, he was at least an evil genius. It was inevitable that he would prove to be another devil with whom I would willingly share a dinner table. If anything, he intrigued me far more than Olusegun Obasanjo. Suave, calculating, a persuasive listener and conciliator—but with sheathed claws at the ready—ever ready to cultivate potential allies, he had a reputation for meticulous planning. I was one of many coup watchers who knew Babangida only by reputation, as the mastermind behind a number of earlier coups d'états.

But first, how—apart from his affable exterior—did Babangida succeed in enjoying, at least at the beginning, a quite remarkable level of national acceptability? The answer to that was straightforward: he rode to public favor on the brutal and hypocritical record of his predecessor, Muhammadu Buhari, one devil for whom, in my calculation, no spoon existed that was long enough to justify the risk even of an impromptu snack.

WITH HIS PARTNER, Tunde Idiagbon, General Buhari blew onto the Nigerian stage, raising a whirlwind of corrective energy. His first port of call was the Ministry of Petroleum, which, during the Obasanjo regime, he had headed as minister. During the succeeding rule, that of Shehu Shagari, a hue and cry had begun about a missing $3.4 billion of the nation's petroleum funds, a sum that was later upgraded to $4.1 billion. The scandal was not new. The accusations were public, pursued with vigor by the social critic and schoolmaster Tai So-larin and by an activist with an even more volatile temperament, Dr. Ayodele Awojobi, a professor of engineering at the University of Lagos. Lithe and in-tense in every inch of his six-foot-four frame, Awojobi was, however, more fas-tidious and persuasive than Tai in his acquisition and presentation of facts. The Shagari government was compelled to set up a commission of inquiry. Its findings were negative: Tai Solarin, it decided, was merely whistling in the wind, and no such funds were missing.

Nevertheless, it raised not a few eyebrows that General Buhari, who was at the center of this scandal, should stage a coup d'état against the civilian regime that had inquired into the affair. The eyebrows were raised even higher when, having seized control of the nation, he made a beeline for the Petroleum Com-mission, raided its offices, and carted away its files, swearing publicly that he would get to the bottom of the missing funds and announce his findings in a matter of months. This was the last that the nation heard of those files or the missing billions. Buhari sacked the incumbent head of the Petroleum Commission, reinstated his right-hand man from his previous ministerial stint in that department, and, at the first opportunity, locked up Tai Solarin on an unrelated pretext—for distributing leaflets calling for a return to democ-racy.

It was a harsh confinement. Tai Solarin was subjected to a life-threatening regimen in an inclement far-north prison. He was refused access to his accus-tomed medication for asthma, one that had been prepared for him for years by a traditional herbalist and had proved a hundred percent effective, whereas Western medicine had failed. As for Professor Awojobi, he died soon after Buhari took over. A vigorous personality and brilliant engineer, Awojobi sim-ply passed away conveniently, ostensibly of hypertension.

That beginning established the pattern. The Buhari regime redefined all concepts of moral scourge, incorruptibility, transparency, and even-handedness in the execution of its own codes of justice. It was this regime that presided over the saga of some fifty-three suitcases that passed through Customs at the international airport of Kano. As a measure to stabilize the Nigerian currency and terminate the business of illegal speculation, currency trafficking, and other dodgy financial dealings, the Buhari regime ordered the production of a new national currency. So comprehensive were the measures undertaken to en-sure that not a single forged or obsolete currency note was blown across the borders, either entering or exiting, that all land, air, and sea borders were sealed tight without notice. If migrating birds were not exactly ordered to be shot on sight, it was only because the Nigerian Air Force was too busy ferrying in the new notes. International transactions were suspended. Too bad for those who were trapped outside or inside until the fiscal exercise of several days was over!

Nonetheless, a Northern emir arrived at Kano airport with fifty-three bulging suitcases and—who would be waiting to clear him through Customs? Buhari's own aide-de-camp, Major Mustapha Jokolo! He encountered and tried to brush aside the stolid opposition of the Customs officer in charge of the airport—an unknown civil servant by the name of Alhaji Abubakar Atiku who would later become the vice president of the nation after the return of democracy. The Customs officer held his ground as long as he could but was no match for the aide-de-camp, who had flown to Kano from his duty post in Lagos solely to facilitate the passage of the emir's camels through the needle's eye of Customs. Entry was eventually effected with only one casualty: not long after, the stubborn Customs officer was unceremoniously bundled out of Kano and redeployed to Lagos. Based on the provisions of an allied regulation, however, Fela Anikulapo Kuti, the Afro-beat musician, would be sentenced to a long term of imprisonment for failing to declare some foreign currency that he had legitimately brought into the country. Fela had kept the funds as immediate living expenses for his band, due to begin an overseas tour shortly after.

After Babangida came to power, the trial judge visited Fela in prison, apologized to him for his role in his conviction, and admitted that he had only acted on orders. The poor judge! Did he really think that my uninhibited cousin would keep quiet after such a confession? "The judge done come beg me o!" screamed Fela to the media, leaving Babangida no choice but to set free the victim of Buhari's reformist zeal and dismiss the judge.

So implacable in its dubiety was the moral code of the duo—Buhari and Idiagbon—that most Nigerians involved in routine, legitimate, decades-old monetary arrangements learned to take self-protective measures. On my part, I ensured that I was thoroughly "sanitized" at least a dozen times before boarding an airplane into or out of Nigeria. The decree was uncompromising. Even the possession of a worthless coin or two guaranteed several years in jail. Currency forms had to be filled going in and out, and an inaccurate entry left the voyager at the mercy of the law. My forms always read "zero" going in and out—a crossed line across the page and my signature, nothing more. After Fela's ongoing ordeal, no one in his senses would take his chance with those reformists who had placed themselves on high moral ground, tasking themselves with the laudable goal of stemming the nation's financial hemorrhage! The decrees extended to foreign accounts. They were to be closed down by all

Nigerian citizens and existing funds repatriated to Nigeria. The results were predictable. Anxious not to lose Nigerian business, foreign banks—and without any prompting from their customers—would offer to send their bank statements to proxy addresses, and many Nigerians took up the offer.

Irrationally, perhaps, there I drew the line! I had had an account with Lloyd's since my student days in Leeds, and I was not going to close it down for any sanctimonious terror. Royalties earned outside the country had always remained outside; those from within, within; and that was the way it would remain. Not seeking martyrdom, however, I instructed my bank not to forward any statements to me or even write me a letter—I would call whenever I passed through London if I needed to check the health of my balance or withdraw from it!

While Fela Anikulapo Kuti languished in jail, a blue-blood scion of the Northern aristocracy, Alhaji Alhaji Alhaji, known as "Triple A," then permanent secretary in the Ministry of Finance, was caught—literally—with his pants down in the Austrian capital, Vienna. He was robbed of a large sum in foreign currency--in cash—well over and above his legitimate entitlement, and by a local "female escort." The dalliance over, Triple A fell asleep. When he woke up, his companion was gone, and so was his wallet. Such was his confidence in his personal immunity that the super–civil servant made a report to the Austrian police, and the escapade was bruited about in the international press, from which it was picked up and nearly flogged to death by the Nigerian press, calling for equity in the implementation of justice. The media dug deeper and discovered that this civil servant kept not one but several foreign accounts. Their screams became deafening and perhaps did succeed in deafening the ears of the corrective duo. They heard nothing and so maintained a stolid silence, confident that, sooner or later, the media outcry would subside.

A MILITARY COUP is usually undertaken to terminate the life of a serving government. The Buhari coup set a precedent in Nigerian history by being openly directed against the political opposition. Leaders in opposition were detained without trial or else sent to military tribunals on charges for which record, unprecedented sentences became mandatory. Some were freed, then sent back again for retrial repeatedly on the same charges, as was the case of a septuagenarian, Pa Adekunle Ajasin, an elder statesman of an opposition party and governor of Ondo state. Even the pliant tribunal found itself unable to convict the old man, and so, after several trials, he was simply left in detention to rot. Those found guilty received multiple sentences—some, hundreds of years in jail, to run consecutively. By contrast, members of the ruling party either miraculously escaped capture—like the one with the fifty-three suitcases—were never brought to trial, or else escaped with comparatively light sentences or easeful confinement.

The truth was that General Buhari, with his partner in terror, Tunde Idiagbon, struck against the regime in order to preempt a coup by some "young Turks." Seeing that the corrupt government of Shehu Shagari was doomed anyway, they moved to prevent a radical wing of the military from taking over.

The media was muzzled by the notorious Decree No. 2, which prescribed mandatory prison sentence for any journalist who published anything at all that "embarrassed" a government official, irrespective of whether or not the publication was a hundred percent true. Two journalists, Tunde Thompson and Nduka Irabor, were the first casualties of this decree; they had published facts—and not even wounding facts but facts that the regime did not wish to be published, even though borne out in detail.

Yet another journalist and public commentator, Ebenezer Babatope, was jailed without trial, not for anything he wrote during the incumbency of that despot but for having called attention, a year or so earlier, to the threat of a coup that Buhari had made before actually carrying it out. "Watch yon general," Babatope had warned, "his ambitions run deep." Unsuspecting—after all, he had said nothing against the regime once it took power, had quietly enrolled as a student at Warwick University, England—Babatope returned home to prepare for his new life. For his prophetic pains, Buhari honored him with indefinite residency in a maximum-security prison. Babatope did not regain his liberty until the fall of Buhari.

Detention without trial or imprisonment after a mockery of justice ran rampant. Beko Ransome-Kuti, president of the Nigerian Medical Association, in the company of some of his lieutenants, took his turn in prison for leading an industrial strike of doctors. Their demand? An end to the neglect of medical services and the deterioration of teaching and government hospitals, and a demand for improvement in their serving conditions. His place of incarceration was set not within the state where he lived or close by, but all the way in the far North, quite deliberately, as far as would make family visits and media attention a near impossibility.

The most unconscionable act of General Buhari and his partner, however, was the enactment of an anti–drug trafficking law that was made retroactive, so that even offenses that had been committed before the law was passed came under the same forfeit—in this case, of life. Three young men were publicly executed by firing squad soon after the law was passed, a deliberate effort to strike terror into the heart of the nation. The degree of public disbelief in the possibility of such unjust killings would not be equaled for many years—and then not until the killing of the Ogoni leader Ken Saro-wiwa and his eight companions. Individuals and civic bodies protested the sentence and warned against the executions of the three young men; there was an especially intense campaign by the Quaker Society and by some women's organizations. On the day of the execution itself, it was as if the nation were under a collective paralysis. This was discernible on the faces of people one met on the streets and encountered in offices and hotel lobbies, faces frozen with that one question: Would it happen? Would this event really take place? It did.

Nigerians had been brutalized—deliberately—by the new culture of public executions, dubbed, with gallows humor, "The Bar Beach Show," after a television show then current. After the Biafran war of secession, no one should have been surprised that violent crimes, mostly armed robbery, would rise in frequency, and the military government of Yakubu Gowon introduced public execution by firing squad as its ultimate solution to this terrorization of the nation. Executions took place on the much-patronized Bar Beach in Lagos, and the general public—to my personal chagrin—took to them with gusto, turning them into public fiestas at which refreshments were hawked and the audience danced, jeered at the felons, and cheered the execution squad. Children were conspicuously present. Eighteenth-century England could not have boasted a more macabre occasion for public roistering.

Not at the execution of these three young men, however! The volume of *Nos* and the wailing rose to a hysterical pitch as the priest moved forward to offer the last prayers and an officer began to apply blindfolds. Then the subdued retreat of the priest, the officer's crisp march back to the line of the firing squad, the order, the shots. There were some faintings. A subdued crowd trickled away slowly, numbed with disbelief. Across the nation, a cold cloud appeared to press down on several million roofs, insinuating the unknown. Some years later, I would write *A Scourge of Hyacinths*, for radio, and its stage version, *From Zia with Love*, creative efforts to cauterize the wounds that came from one's impotence.

If the execution of the three young men was the most execrable deed of the Buhari government, designed to cow the nation and condition its people into an acceptance of unguessable extremes of judicial violence, the actual process of establishing a norm of despotism—in all its ramifications—was much simpler. Buhari passed a decree that forbade any discussion of a return to democratic rule. And that was it! Buhari had interrupted a democratic process that had been thoroughly corrupted by Shehu Shagari and his National Party of Nigeria. All this threw into immediate prominence in public discussion the one question: When? When would the military relinquish power? It took only a few months for Buhari to answer that question. A decree was rolled out: the very word "democracy" was criminalized.

NOT ANYMORE, chortled the suave General Ibrahim Babangida as he served Buhari a taste of his own medicine, overthrew him, and confined him in a government residential house not far from the new ruler's home state. Babangida promised democracy but set up structures that ensured that democracy did not proceed "too hastily." *We must learn from the lessons of the past, do it properly and enduringly this time, get rid of the "moneybags," create an environment that will favor the "new-breed politicians," debate the actual democratic will of the Nigerian people, evolve an unriggable system for the ballot box, construct state-sponsored headquarters of the political parties in every state—which must be two and two only, one "a little to the left," the other, "a little to the right," embark on a "learning process," launch one, then two, then three different structures of mass mobilization....* It was clever and succeeded with many. The people were kept busy. The charade took a while to become transparent.

This dictator made a fascinating study. Some time after he came into power, probably a year afterward, I was invited to participate in a media assessment of his time in office thus far. My contribution took the form of a cautionary tale—a factual though whimsical anecdote that drew a parallel from his "fate" at my hands—unknown to him—in the uncertain hours that followed the first announcement of the 1985 coup, when that coup had yet to identify an heir apparent. For someone who prefers to scoff at auguries and other superstitions, it was a revelation—and not the first—of the irrational part of myself, an authentic component, however, that one learns to accept as part of one's makeup.

I WAS TEACHING at Ife at the time and was on my way out of the country for a conference. Stopping, by habit, at my office for a last-minute desk clearance, I observed a group of lecturers clustered around a transistor radio. Some abnormal event had clearly taken place. Surprised by my evident insulation within a shattered normalcy, they waved me over—Hadn't I heard? What did I think? Where would it all end?

It was, of course, another coup d'état. No new head of state had yet emerged, and my colleagues were caught in a fever of guesswork. Various names were tossed about, known players in this game of deadly musical chairs. The first question, of course: Would the coup succeed? Had it already? Where was Buhari? Idiagbon? Was it Joshua Dogonyaro's turn this time?—his name had been prominent on radio as the John the Baptist of the coup d'état, after which he made way for one greater than he. This time, it was a new town crier: name, Sani Abacha. Other names were trotted out one after the other, chewed over, discarded or pushed aside for the moment. The new herald with a high-pitched voice, who identified himself as Sani Abacha, went through the routine incantation—*All soldiers, except those otherwise authorized, are confined to barracks. Military governors to report for redeployment. Offices, airports, and borders closed*—I shrugged with indifference, though also with a sense of relief; I had not especially wanted to make this particular journey.

With a bonus day in hand, I left my colleagues to their anxieties, drove back home, dumped my luggage, substituted my traveling gear for a rough-and-ready shirt and boots, and set off for the agricultural farm, where I hoped some bush fowl would still be found browsing on a late breakfast. My intrusion was swift, deadly, and productive—unusually so for such a brief spell, well above my average.

The first *aparo*—that bird halfway between a quail and a partridge—flew excitedly above my head, flapping untidily. Without any prior intent, on the spur of the moment, I shouted, "Buhari!" and fired. It came down, plumb line. I drew a sight line with my finger and followed its trajectory to the distant crash site.

A crucial part of the hunt is bringing down the quarry. The rest, depending on the terrain, often turns out to be the harder work—finding the bird in what is often tangled thicket. This first offering was most obliging. I nodded with satisfaction: Buhari was definitely gone.

I had hardly secured it to my waist strap when another took off at some distance, offering a very disciplined flight path. It was all an unusually smooth reflex—I pulled the trigger, muttering, "Idiagbon." Buhari's number two man was away on a pilgrimage to Mecca, but that made him even more dangerous to the coup makers; he could rally loyalists from a distance and try to reverse events. I need not have worried. Down came Idiagbon to join his master.

It was a most auspicious beginning, since this one also proved an easy find. Ogun appeared to be taking a hand, compensating me, perhaps, for my aborted journey. Next, "Dogonyaro!" Smack! Find. Next, "Magashi!"—one of the shadowy ones. I could not believe it—they were all so cooperative, either falling in clearings or staying put where they fell in the bush. As for the actual shooting, there was none of the usual calculating effort; arms moved in unison, on smooth pulleys, guided by invisible hands. But the tempo of flights remained the most astonishing. I had hunted that patch before. At that time of the morning, the *aparo* is more difficult to rouse. Having already breakfasted its fill, it tends to dig deep into the bases of thickets, perhaps take a midmorning snooze, yet here they were offering themselves up as eager sacrifices. I had been in the bush for less than thirty minutes. One more, I thought, and I clumped around, hoping for one parting shot. Up it went and I swung after, then ahead, muttering, "Babangida."

No other word for it, this was—*smoking*! Babangida followed the example of his predecessors—a hit! Eyes glued to the landing spot, I plunged into the bush. This time there was a variation. A clump of feathers marked the spot, but, search as I would, there was not a sign of Babangida. Not a trace! Greedy to post a most unaccustomed hundred percent kill, I devoted another fifteen minutes to the search. Not a sign. I gave up. The sun had risen beyond *aparo* tolerance level. It was time to return home.

As I drove into campus, using the back route that took me past the faculty, I noticed the group of lecturers still huddled around the radio, talking animatedly.

"Well, any announcement yet?" I asked them.

"No," they replied. "Just a repeat of the same announcement, plus martial music."

I announced, matter-of-factly, "Babangida is your next head of state."

I received incredulous stares. How could they have missed the announcement? "Which station was it on?" someone wanted to know.

Another: "Oh, have you been on the phone to someone in Lagos?"

"It's his turn," I repeated. "That one who's been masterminding all the coups, he's behind it, and he's taking over this time, that seasoned escapologist!"

At home, even after a sobering shower and a coffee, I found no reason to examine the premises of my conviction. It was just a factual, inconsequential tug of knowledge, and I turned my attention to other chores. Toward late afternoon, the rest of the nation also learned that the new despot was indeed IBB.

BABANGIDA'S FIRST MOVE was to throw open the prisons, a deft, calculating stroke. And he opened up every space of public discourse on every subject under the sun—from democracy to IMF loans—a most masterful distraction, since he could then carry on his own agenda, indifferent, while debates raged all around him.

Quite unlike my encounters with Olusegun Obasanjo when he was head of state, I never once dined—literally, now!—in Babangida's residence and only once in official circumstances, when I attended a banquet for Nelson Mandela. By contrast, he ate at my Abeokuta home on two occasions. The first was a hurriedly improvised affair, organized in response to his own suggestion that he stop by while in my state, Ogun, for some official engagements. I still lived in my rented house at Idi-aba. At the last moment, "IBB" (as Babangida was known) nearly played his *aparo* game with me, pleading the difficulty of extricating himself from an official reception by royal command of the Alake of Abeokuta, the traditional monarch of my immediate domain.

Earlier, his advance team had taken up positions in the cul-de-sac whose *cul* was my house, with a frontage of bamboo trellises covered in creepers. When the wind blew in the right direction, a poultry yard next door stank to the high heavens. I had once threatened to take the owner to court, but he had pleaded that the ex–head of state Olusegun Obasanjo, now a retired farmer, had obtained a monopoly on the importation rights for the chemicals that were required to transform his chicken shit into odoriferous waste. Obasanjo's prices, he said, were prohibitive; that is, when he chose to sell at all. I endured the stench only because I was hopeful of transferring soon to my own house, then under construction.

Babangida's escorts moved back and forth, talking into crackling walkie-talkies and checking on his probable arrival time. Once they came in and announced yet again that he was on his way, next that he might not turn up after all—the Alake was a tenacious host, and it was proving difficult for him to free himself from the palace. I sent word back that he would be forever persona non grata in Abeokuta if he failed to turn up for a dinner that he himself had requested. A newly acquired military acquaintance fast developing into a firm friend, the beanpole Vice Air Marshal Ibrahim Alfa, an ace pilot who had cheated death often, was a member of his official entourage; at the first opportunity he had detached himself from the official train and arrived quite early in the evening. "I don't know about Ibrahim," he announced, "he's head of state, so he can't escape his hosts—that is, even if he wants to. In my case, my official participation in the tour is finished, and I am here to relax and enjoy myself."

Military protocol is a curious affair, however. Ibrahim Alfa and his two army colleagues shied away from digging into the food until their *oga* turned up. Nine o'clock, then approaching ten. Among the hungry guests were my own hastily assembled terrors of political confrontation, who were there to add some mildly astringent spice to the fare. The "mildly" was specially pleaded by me on behalf of a long-term agenda, the possibility that something similar to the periodic brainstorming sessions that Oje Aboyade and I had shared with IBB's predecessor, Obasanjo, would develop from the first encounter. It made sense not to scare him off by a hostile reception at his very first venture.

When Babangida arrived, halfway through the meal, I was treated to quite a display of body language! One could see that the military group, unlike the civilians, were ill at ease, clearly wishing they had waited for the *oga*! As for Babangida, it was equally obvious that he was peeved that the company had not waited, though of course he kept mute. Only half jokingly, he said to Alfa, as conversation became easier, Who asked for this dinner anyway? Ibrahim Alfa, I suspected, had agreed to start only because he was convinced that his boss would not turn up at all—"I know Ibrahim," he kept sighing, as he looked again and again at his watch. Now he looked a little sheepish and quickly pushed his plate aside. I pretended to notice nothing of the discomfiture of the men of arms, even those in mufti. Another of his officers attempted to hide his wineglass. That annoyed me, and I fished it out, filled it, and went around the table with the bottle.

Babangida soon settled down. From his first taste, he declared an instant love affair with Lebanese food. What was more, he demonstrated a largeness of appetite that was quite unexpected—he ate like a battalion on the move. I was so impressed that I immediately announced that I would have to match him against my trencher champion, Femi Johnson. Babangida agreed to take him on any day.

THE SECOND VISIT, at least a year later, was a more elaborate affair, carefully planned but rich in melodrama. It immediately acquired a certain mythical status—at least in the town of Abeokuta, later spreading out via Lagos circuits. The commencing national honeymoon with the smiling dictator had frayed at the edges; awaiting him this time was a clutch of some truly disillusioned critics, led by my pugnacious friend Sesan Dipeolu. Ses—as he was known to close associates—was a retired librarian from the University of Ife school of leftist disputation, but even there a maverick, ready to associate with progressive groups, but strictly on his own, nondoctrinaire terms. A balding sixtyish, Ses appeared to lend his face to a permanently puzzled look, as if trying to recollect the last resting place of a yet-uncatalogued acquisition. He became a different being, a bull terrier, however, when engaged in a bout of contumacy, even at moments when he found himself in basic agreement with the premise of the debate.

We anticipated a lively afternoon of some unsparing examination of the policies and governing style of the unsuspecting guest, but the manner of IBB getting to my house—yet in a state of incompletion—easily overshadowed the intellectual or political quotient of the afternoon. It acquired, predictably, numerous variations, in Abeokuta most especially, taking impetus from the moment when the Alake of Abeokuta, the paramount king of Egba, was heard to exclaim after the event, *"Hare! Wole Soyinka t'iwa ree s'eyi? L'oju gbogbo wa ne e ro gbe head of state sa lo!"*[*]

The Alake had good cause for his umbrage. It boiled down to this: that we had "abducted" the dictator from the state banquet—with his connivance—and whisked him to my uncompleted house in the jungle fastness of Ajebo. His chief of staff, Sani Abacha, holding down the fort in Lagos during his boss's extended tour, later expressed outrage at the foolhardiness of his superior, who had actually trusted his safety to a known dissident, allowing himself to be driven to an unknown destination with only a half dozen or so of his secret service and leaving his mighty armed convoy behind at the venue of the banquet.

What shocked me, however, as we returned our captive to his venue, was that, despite nearly two hours' absence, all the guests had remained in their position! I had not anticipated this. If the guest of honor vanishes and all eating and speechifying is over, the obvious course of action is—go home! Maybe the soldiers and civil servants—military governor, even ministers and commissioners—were obliged to remain, but what reason on earth had the private individuals, independent citizens—including the traditional monarch—for hanging on? Protocol, I was later informed, and that was the day I discovered that protocol was an eight-letter word, brother to the expletive that involuntarily escaped my throat!

MY INTERACTIONS WITH BABANGIDA were, needless to say, of a qualitatively different character from those with his fellow dictator, Olusegun Obasanjo, who, additionally, came from the same part of the country as I—West, Yoruba, and Abeokuta—though I am also part Ijebu. With Obasanjo, I ritually arrived with my own wine bottle or two tucked under the arm, knowing that my

---

[*] "Incredible! Was it our Wole Soyinka that did this to us? You mean he actually snatched the head of state right from under our noses?"

host—and thus his staff—did not know the difference between *burukutu* and Beaujolais. That weighty problem did not arise with Babangida, since this was one devil with whom I dined only at my own table. With Babangida, my interventions were precisely named—issue-specific interventions, though I do recall two exceptions when our discussions ranged broadly, as had been more common with Obasanjo. Sometimes those sessions with the latter also took place in Oje Aboyade's home, over lunch. Obasanjo appeared to find his thinking aggressively stimulated by our unorthodox approaches to many issues, and of course he loved to be thought capable of holding his own intellectually. Fights were routine. He did not take kindly to being caught wrong-footed. He *needed*, sometimes pathetically, to be right! Oje once called him an economic illiterate—he was out of office at the time—and it rankled in his mind for years afterward. I suspect it still does, even with Oje dead. Babangida, by contrast, never seemed to mind being proved wrong; he carried out his own decisions anyway.

My meetings with Babangida invariably took place in his office. There were exceptions, of course. Once I trapped him in the Nigerian High Commission in London to demand the fulfillment of a pledge to Michael Manley, the progressive Jamaican leader, during his electoral contest with the U.S.-backed candidate, Edward Seaga. Babangida had offered help, but the money had never been sent. I had been involved in that initiative and now found myself being battered by messages from Jamaica. The honor of Nigeria was at stake, but that was never under my custody; what I desperately needed was my peace of mind.

George Dove-Edwin, the Nigerian high commissioner and a friend, was hosting a reception for his president and promised to telephone me once the crowd had left. He did, let me into his residence, and pointed to a large reception room, cautioning that he would deny any knowledge of how I had gotten in—Babangida had wished to see no more visitors that day. My entry was muffled by a thick-piled carpet, and the dictator heard nothing. Slumped in a crested chair at the opposite end of the long reception room was a figure of—there was no other world for it—pathos. For minutes I stood watching this symbol of power, lost in thought, bereft of power and panoply, just another human being who had succumbed to common fatigue, sought a few moments' peace, sunk into its tantalizing solace even as he was already lamenting its looming departure. I felt somewhat remorseful that I had broken in on a moment when, it was plain, he truly needed to be alone—even rulers deserve their moment of peace, after all. Then I recalled that his own negligence or tardiness had disrupted mine, and I coughed to rouse him. He looked up, visibly startled, then annoyed, and snapped, "How did you get in?" I replied, "All right, I'll go away," making no such move. Grumpily, he waved me to a chair.

Fifteen minutes later, we had reached agreement on the modalities of the transfer. I monitored its movements over the next week. Only after I was assured that it was in Michael Manley's possession did I consider any lecture invitations that might take me anywhere close to the West Indies.

FAR MORE EXHAUSTIVE was another closed-door session in his private jet, an unscheduled tête-à-tête that took place on the way back from Egypt, where I had once again undergone one of those reunions with Egypt that have set me wondering just what that fascinating nation and I have against each other! That visit, however, provided one of the three occasions in Babangida's eight-year governance when I obtained a one-on-one meeting with him for truly in-depth and wide-ranging discussions— the Nigerian rumor mill that peddled my access to him on a daily basis notwithstanding.

This infrequency of encounters with IBB was not due to indifference on my part. Whenever circumstances urged the possible usefulness of a meeting with this ruler, I picked up the telephone or contacted my collaborator Ojetunji Aboyade—on Obasanjo's recommendation, Babangida had secured the services of my friend as his economic adviser. However, while the rest of the nation called this dictator "Maradona," my name for him was "Artful Dodger" or "the elusive *aparo*." The flight from Egypt was a godsend, a space without distractions. Babangida slid a panel across the middle of the plane, and the rest of his entourage were shut out. Nothing disturbed a continuous session of about one and a half hours—no telephones, no whisper from a briefed aide tapping his pad to indicate a next, fictitious, appointment or waiting dignitary or delegation. There was nowhere to go, except by parachute.

But first—Egypt! Some pristine secret lurks in that nation that makes it a setting for some of my most enduring episodes of pure chagrin! On this occasion, as I was taking my ease in my own environment, along came a frantic message from the Egyptian president through his ambassador and my own government: Would I kindly present myself in Cairo for a very special honor? The occasion was the elaborate opening ceremony of the All Africa Games, 1989. The invitation sounded attractive—sharing a podium with Nadine Gordimer and our Egyptian counterpart Naguib Mahfouz, whom I would meet for the first time ever!

The notice was short and the timing awkward. The Egyptian ambassador and IBB, however, appeared to take turns, independently, applying pressure on me—some seasoned diplomat from our Foreign Office was definitely latched onto Babangida's ear! There were the usual arguments—the symbolic union of three African Nobelists, three African tribes on show, Arab, African, and South African white—promoting a deracialized African, pan-African solidarity. Babangida was himself flying in to join the Egyptian president, Hosni Mubarak, as co-chairman of the Games. I finally thought of one way of easing the strain on my interrupted routine: since it mattered so much to the continent and to him, would he kindly find me a seat on his official plane? He was more than willing.

I planned to join his flight in Abuja, the capital, but a delayed morning flight from Lagos put a stop to that. Babangida's plane waited as long as the protocol arrangements awaiting him at the Cairo end permitted, then took off without Mubarak's one-third continental symbolism. As the regretful phone call informed me of the plane's departure, the Egyptian ambassador, who had dutifully come to see me off, appeared to be seized by an attack of Saint Vitus's dance. I sought to calm him, opening my palms toward the heavens to indicate that we must all bow to the inevitable. It had the opposite effect. He immediately threw himself into a fermentation cauldron of solutions. He would get me into Cairo, he swore, even if he had to accompany me on camelback! Finally—the Egyptian national airline was due in Lagos the following morning on an onward flight to Cairo. He would come personally, ticket in hand, and escort me onto the plane. A happy ending glowed on his face, nearly infecting me.

The following morning, it was not the airline ticket that called on me, however, but the loyal yet desperate representative of the Egyptian government, incoherent with apologies. *Your Excellency, please, you have to be there! An administrative hitch, I am sure. It's the preparations for the Games . . . you know, the officials are all preoccupied with nothing else. And bureaucracy, yes, bureaucracy, that's our problem. The ticket has not been wired, but for the sake of Africa, Your Excellency, you have to travel. Permit me to assure you, Professor Your Excellency—as soon as you land in Cairo, the Egyptian government will refund your travel expenses. The ceremony will more than compensate for this minor inconvenience. Your friend, your colleague, Mahfouz is waiting to receive you, it will be a historic moment. Historic! Believe me, Excellency, this is as much as my job is worth, if I do not bring you to Cairo. The faxes and telexes have been coming fast and furious from the presidency. The ticket is guaranteed. An administrative hitch, nothing else. I've contacted Egyptian airlines, but unfortunately the ticket has not arrived. The embassy—ah, alas, we have no immediate funds. . . .*

With not the sheerest thought that I was headed for yet another contretemps in the land of the pharaohs, a masochistic streak disguised as race solidarity, I headed for the airport on the authority of my credit card. I quashed a deep-down apprehension as it tried to rise to the surface, those earlier visits that had led me to question if I had been an Egyptian in a previous life—as Fela Anikulapo appeared to have believed of himself. Did my prior sojourn involve some negative, unfinished business in that Nile estuary? Certainly the consistency with which any entry into Egypt results in some level of misadventure—from the hilarious to once life-threatening—has begun to alarm me. Perhaps my mummy is lying in one of the catacombs of the pyramids or, more resentfully, a skeleton of one of the slaves slaughtered to accompany the pharaohs into the afterlife.

Egyptian civilization, as persuasively demonstrated by the scholar Cheikh Anta Diop in *The African Origin of Civilisation: Myth or Reality?* and supplemented years later by Martin Bernal in *Black Athena,* had its origins in the black race, so who is to say if Ogun, my demiurge of war and creativity, did not in some distant age leave his mark on that land, some form of antibodies that now distort the intended trajectory of his followers who happen to stray into Egypt? Something is definitely askew somewhere, calling perhaps for rites of exorcism. I fully intend to delve into the mystery on my next visit, which, to succeed, must scrupulously avoid all traces of officialdom!

For I never did meet Mahfouz. Nadine Gordimer did not appear. No mention was made of any national honors. I was not received at the airport. Hotel rooms were nonexistent. A taxi driver, to whom death in a motor accident was obviously no death at all but preparation for his next, elevated reincarnation, maybe as a priest of Isis, all but ended my career on the road between the airport and the hotel, courtesy of the tourist desk at the airport, which eventually located some vacant form of habitation. It turned out to be a kind of athletes' transient lodge.

I got busy on the phone and left a message with the embassy—surely someone must know of my arrival. The message that remained stuck in the desperate larynx of the abandoned VIP was, however, much richer: *W.S. speaking, you know, national treasure, special invitee of President Mubarak, yes, it's I, the Akinlatun of Egba, the Akogun of Isara, one-third African symbolism at the All Africa Games, commander of the Order of the Niger, et cetera, et cetera, who was to have hitched a ride in the presidential jet but was unpatriotically prevented by some domestic airline—yes, it's me, I made it on my own but don't quite know where I am and what to do. This contretemps is happening all over again—*

HELP! For hours afterward, I awaited rescue. None was forthcoming. History, my cyclic bugbear, appeared to be the presiding muse at these All Africa Games.

After a few hours spent pondering this latest round of déjà vu on my Egyptian incursions—not least of which was a painful recollection of my truncated participation at the laying of the foundation stone of the Library of Alexandria—I was ready to depart. It seemed fated. Somewhere in one of those tombs was the unappeased ghost of a wronged ancestor—mine—and my energized physical aura from the land of the Yoruba had once again aroused its millennial resentments, seeking redress or absolution at my hands. I turned for help to the front desk—literally a desk—and asked for a copy of flight schedules heading anywhere out of Cairo. Even that motion reeked of a mimicry of the past.

Moments before I was to leave for the airport, however, a car screeched to a halt in front of the dormitory and a flustered young man, tall and thin in his well-tailored but flapping jacket, leaped out and introduced himself as a diplomat from the embassy. He had just picked up my message. In a few more minutes I was reinstalled in another hotel, less Spartan, where, it turned out, reservations had indeed been made for me. At the desk, the young man inquired if there was any message from the Egyptian government for his guest. There was none. He then took off to track down his Egyptian counterparts to ensure that I had the necessary passes required to enter the stadium, promising to be back in time to accompany me to my seat—security being rigorously enforced. He returned in no time, crestfallen. He had been unable to find anyone who knew anything of my visit, much less of my being a special guest of the Egyptian government or personally of the president, Mubarak! I told him to go back to his duties; I was more than content to wander through the streets of Cairo, return to the hotel in time to watch the opening spectacular on television, then catch the first flight out of Egypt the following day.

He would have none of it. This windswept young diplomat, whose fragile frame totally belied his energy, took me in tow on one of the wildest drives in my nomadic career. He bullied, raged, and forced his way through barriers of security checkpoints with nothing but his diplomatic credentials and inadequate passes—he had not planned to go near the stadium until this challenge arose. At one stage, while his driver whimpered and cowered, he rode shotgun on the car bumper, screaming and cursing, directing the driver to an alternative checkpoint wherever the resistance proved unbreachable, until he deliv-

ered me right into the sanctum sanctorum of the VIP sector, just to one side of
the presidential box.

The show began, and we were treated to a sumptuous display of the glorification of the Egyptian president, Mubarak, in between snatches of a grand
parade of the pharaohs, the sphinxes, and passages of Egyptian history and
heritage. Where, however, were the black Egyptians? Egypt, after all, had boasted
a black pharaoh or two.

Babangida, it turned out, fared no better at the hands of Egyptian protocol.
It had been announced in Nigeria that he would launch the Games jointly with
Mubarak, but the Egyptian organizers appeared to have forgotten that little
detail. Mubarak's broad shoulders, sheathed in an impeccably turned suit, undertook the onerous task, while Babangida sat passively in the presidential
box, for all purposes just another spectator. I do not think that Nigerian-
Egyptian relations were enhanced by the undoubtedly impressive extravaganza
of that very Egyptian occasion. The beginning of a Yoruba-Egyptian rapport
also suffered yet another setback, as the Akinlatun of Egba, Akogun of Isara, et
cetera, et cetera, was left with yet another African solidarity hole in his pocket.

A Pen Coalition

GENERAL MAMMAN VATSA, A HEAVYSET OFFICER WITH A DEEP-CUT RADIAT-
ing cicatrix that identified him instantly as being from one of the minority
ethnic groups in the North, was an unusual soldier, a versifier on social themes
and private thoughts. Vatsa courted Nigerian writers and artists and dearly
wished to be counted as one of them. Shortly after my spell in prison and the
publication of my account of that experience in *The Man Died*, he wrote some
verses in protest of what he considered an unbalanced attitude in my book.
Critical though they were, I was rather touched by this approach from a man of
war, very different from the more usual "What! Is he still talking? He should
thank his stars he got off with his life!"

Later we met, and I was again taken with his apparent thoughtfulness on
the problems that confronted the nation. We never became friends, but I found
him quite amiable and progressively disposed. During the presidency of
Shehu Shagari and his party, the NPN, I made the LP record *Unlimited Liability Company*, dedicated to the ineptness and corruption of that government
and the general decay of society. When it was launched at the Museum Kitchen
garden at Onikan, Lagos, I was surprised to find this military man present. He
sat quietly at his table and bought thirty copies of the record—for distribution
to his military colleagues, he said.

I preferred to keep him at a distance, naturally, though I studied him keenly
from habit. When a high-ranked military officer attends a "subversive" event,
such as the launching of a sarcastic record against the government, and takes
such material back to the army mess for distribution, he warrants some extra
attention. It was just as well, because Vatsa would later defend—indeed, as it

turned out, actually instigate and direct—a raid on the home of Obafemi
Awolowo, the former opposition leader of the Unity Party of Nigeria, when the
inevitable coup took place in 1983 and the civilian dictatorship of Shehu Shagari was overthrown by the reputed man of discipline General Muhammadu
Buhari.

Obafemi Awolowo was not a member of the ousted government but in opposition. He was rumored to have in his possession some sensitive documents
that related to the $3.8 or $4.1 billion scandal that had remained unresolved
during the previous two regimes. Acting under orders, undoubtedly, Mamman
Vatsa undertook a raid of Obafemi Awolowo's home in Ikenne, looking for
"classified documents," but never revealing the subject of classification. The
writer and "factionist" Kole Omotoso interacted closely with Mamman Vatsa,
through his functions as president of the Association of Nigerian Authors.
During their discussions on Nigerian politics, Mamman Vatsa defended the
raid, even threatened that Awolowo would be placed on trial for being in unau-
thorized possession of classified documents. It was an empty boast, but that
was Mamman Vatsa.

Still, Vatsa, who had been placed in charge of Abuja capital territory, did his
duty by the literary tribe to which he wanted so badly to belong. He allocated
some property toward the project for a writers' village in Abuja and even supplied a military transport plane to take the writers to their annual conference,
landing the association's executive in hot water among some of the members
for getting too close to, and accepting favors from, an unelected regime, even
for the benefit of writers. Quite a few writers did take the purist line: no accommodation, in any form, with any military regime. Others believed that a silver
lining—as long as it was not pocket lining!—could be mined from the darkest
clouds. It all made for lively polemics, sometimes pitting the genuine puritans
against the merely rhetorical contenders for the halo of the holier-than-thou.

Now, however, Mamman Vatsa was in deep trouble. Vatsa and Babangida
had been bosom friends right from childhood. Their wives were reported to be
equally close. Vatsa may have been merely tolerated in the regime of Buhari and
Idiagbon—the story was that he had virtually forced himself on those coup
makers and was fobbed off with the then-lightweight post of minister of the
Federal Capital Territory. True or not, with the ascendancy of his friend Babangida, Mamman Vatsa came fully into his own. He was retained in his earlier
position, but the ministry became as powerful as Mamman chose to make it.
Mamman lived the good life. He devised a cape for his attire and referred to

himself as "emperor" of the Federal Capital Territory, which he ran with a free hand, apportioning valuable real estate to individuals and corporations according to his private laws.

What went wrong between the two friends, no one could really tell, but it was put down to rivalry between their wives as much as to Mamman Vatsa's own ambitions. A peer of both men in the military, General A.A., remarked that Vatsa's ambitions were not unlike Macbeth's—dormant until fanned by a wife with a stronger will. I never did meet his wife, so I cannot tell. But it has proved impossible to erase from my mind the presence of that soldier who sat watching quietly at the launching of my record and openly bought copies for his colleagues. His appearance was the furthest imaginable from Caesar's "lean and hungry," but his sly watchfulness made me think more of his co-emperor's nervous perspective on Cassius than of Macbeth as putty in the hands of his worthy lady.

But in 1985, the nation's mildly watchful life under the smooth dictator was suddenly sent awry by the announcement of a coup attempt, and implicated at the highest level was the poet-soldier, General Mamman Vatsa. It was a numbing sight, watching on television the dapper general, emperor of the Federal Capital Territory and friend of Nigerian writers, led in chains into court in the company of other accused. Nigeria had become inured to coups, coup attempts, and rumors of coups, but this was the strangest yet—the dictator's bosom friend, accused of masterminding his friend's overthrow.

Mamman Vatsa was found guilty, with several others, and the sentence was death by firing squad. Nigeria's military regimes were not noted for commuting sentences for treason—always a cynical charge, considering the means by which the complainant government had itself come to power. The public braced itself for the usual announcements of executions and went about its business with a sense of déjà vu: *Let them decimate one another; maybe when they've become sated with their own blood, they'll return to the barracks and leave the nation in peace.*

But one person felt—no! This was John Pepper Clark, now Bekederemo-Clark, poet and dramatist. We had been quite close in the early sixties, in the heyday of the Mbari cultural project, when Nigerian writers and artists had made a creative home in the slums of Adamasingba, in Ibadan. Indeed I had the distinction of taking off a corner of his German-made Karman Ghia—now an obsolete model—against a palm tree. His coupe, unlike the standard Nigerian vehicle, was a left-hand drive at a time when Nigerians drove on the left side of the road, as bequeathed by the British colonizers. J.P.'s car was one of the rare exceptions. He was also prone to accidents at the time, which was why he readily surrendered the car to me whenever we were together. Such was the rate of his encounters with walls, trees, and gutters that I once felt compelled to slaughter a sacrificial goat on his behalf, right on the open stage, during the production of his play *Song of a Goat*. Naturally, I never really considered that it was I who had caused the accident; rather, it was his car, which, under J.P.'s aura, took a yen to the palm tree on the way to my university apartment.

J. P. Clark had become troubled. Mulling over his drink—as I imagined it—the stocky, pugnacious poet had perhaps run through the reel of casualties in the numerous coups and allied killings, was perhaps even haunted by a sense of vicarious responsibility for the initial coup; J.P., I always suspected, had firsthand knowledge, albeit vague, of the first coup d'état of 1966. With Christopher Okigbo, he had accompanied one of the principals, Major Emanuel Ifeajuna, across the border, the latter in female disguise. J.P. had turned back at the border, while Christopher crossed over to the Republic of Benin (then Dahomey), taking charge of Ifeajuna, who was by then virtually an emotional wreck, haunted—Christopher related—by images of blood cascading from his dying victims, his superior officers, none of whom was a stranger to him.

J.P. brought back with him the manuscript of Ifeajuna's account of the coup, hurriedly put together during his period of hiding by that young major and former athlete—he was one of the four who had set a joint six-foot, six-inch record in the high jump at the Commonwealth Games in Vancouver in 1956. Knowledge of the existence of the manuscript set off a wild hunt by Gowon's military intelligence, desperate for an authentic, firsthand account of those who had plotted the 1966 coup, who had done the killings, what civilians, especially politicians, had had prior knowledge or had collaborated in the putsch. For a while J. P. Clark was deemed a security risk. So was his publisher, Longman, whose editors at one time or the other held the explosive manuscript in their possession, debating the wisdom of releasing its contents onto the market.

I could picture J.P. tabulating the waste, the losses, and the uncertain returns: the 1966 coup and the attendant deaths; the revenge killings of May, known as the "minor massacres"—some distinction!—then the countercoup of July, a truly gory affair where even my serene hometown, Abeokuta, was the setting for the flaying of a garrison commander, tied to the back of a Land Rover and dragged around and around till death took pity on him. Hot on the heels of that countercoup followed the "major massacres" of September, a further revenge killing but also a consolidation of the July countercoup. Then the

bloody attempt of 1976, known as the Dimka coup—a failure, but it terminated the life of Murtala Mohammed, the charismatic dictator, a once military
reprobate himself who, on attaining power, most unusually became a reformed
man and a convinced social reformer, earning adulation beyond an objective
balance of his detractions and achievement. At some point, J. P. Clark must
have sighed, "Enough."

I WAS ENJOYING one of my periods of total hibernation in Abeokuta when my
peace was crashed by a least expected face, at the sight of which I could only
blink in disbelief. I was in fact returning from a successful foray into the bush.
Grimy and sweaty I stepped out of my jeep, retrieved my gun and the brace of
birds, when I heard a voice I had not heard for a long time, issuing from my
front door: "Good God, you mean you actually catch these things when you go
in the bush?"

It was indeed John Pepper Bekederemo-Clark, poet and playwright, with
whom my relationship had not lately been the best. He came close, inspected
the birds, and burst into a loud chuckle. "I'd heard about your hunting, but I
never knew it was something you actually did."

I did not know what to make of that but understood that there was awkwardness on both sides. I could not imagine what he wanted.

"J.P., how on earth did you find this place?"

"Oh, it was tough. But I remembered I knew someone in Abeokuta who
was bound to know where you were." He introduced his companion. "In any
case, I was determined not to leave till I found you. If I hadn't found you today,
I would have returned tomorrow."

I thought, What is he up to now? Our last reconciliation effort had been
short-lived, so what had instigated this visitation from my tempestuous colleague?

"Mamman Vatsa," said J.P., and the words tumbled out. "We must save
him. Not just him but all the others. There is far too much bloodletting. We
have to persuade Babangida that he can break the spiral of blood and set the
nation on a new course. We have to do something, Wole. After all the killing
that followed the Dimka coup, we can't allow this to happen. We have to act.
History will not forgive us if we fail."

J.P.'s idea was that three of us—himself, Chinua Achebe, and I, often
dubbed the "elder statesmen" of Nigerian contemporary literature—should
make a publicized personal appeal to Babangida and the Ruling Council for the
lives of the accused, based principally on the plea that the nation had had

enough of killings and all future action should be directed at national healing. Moreover, Vatsa's attempt, as far as we knew, had been only a plot in the making. We should appeal to Babangida's sense of history and stress that this was an opportunity to map out a different course for his administration from the accustomed pattern of vengeance. There were hawks within the final decision-making body, but there were also doves, J.P. declared, including probably Babangida himself, who might be inclined to save the life of his childhood friend. Our position would strengthen his hand. J.P. paced restlessly, consumed by his optimism. He had spoken to the secretary or assistant secretary to the cabinet, who would facilitate the meeting. It would help, of course, if I also telephoned ahead. In any case, J.P. pointed out, bristling with confidence, if we three walked right up to Dodan Barracks, knocked on the gates, and demanded to see the president, who was going to deny us entrance? Our combined stature would open any door in the nation.

His enthusiasm was infectious. We would pool our resources. I would not only make the call but would co-opt Ojetunji Aboyade to follow up the case after our visit. Chinua Achebe, J.P. revealed, was already awaiting us in Lagos.

Our arrival at Dodan Barracks the following day was a much-anticipated event, covered by the media corps that was permanently encamped at the presidency. It was clear that the civil servant who attended us was no hawk. He welcomed the initiative with more than a functionary's disinterest, took pains to impress on us our chances of success, and offered opinions on what arguments would have the greatest effect, how to stand our ground against any counterarguments, and so on. Babangida was in a meeting when we arrived, but as we were ushered into his wing of the sprawling complex, he came to meet us outside, beaming his famous, later notorious, gap-toothed smile. Once we were seated, he thanked us profusely for the visit, assuring us in advance that he understood that our intervention had been motivated by the highest humane principles.

Chinua Achebe spoke, I followed, and J.P. added his plea, each using the precious minutes we had extorted from Babangida's schedule as forcefully as we knew how. It was a somber, intense half hour, and we were all conscious of—no other way to put it—the near sanctity of our mission. I think both Chinua and I were somewhat startled to hear J.P. introduce a rather arcane dimension that he had remarked upon briefly during our earlier exchanges: he had traced the blood pattern of such challenges to power backward and observed that a cycle of violence appeared to emerge every four years. Babangida was uniquely placed, he argued, to break the four-year jinx. Not for one moment did I imagine that such a basically superstitious argument would impress those hardheaded soldiers, but then, one never knew, and soldiers are notorious for their superstitious outlook anyway. Babangida, the consummate listener, gave equal attentiveness to all the arguments, nodding gently.

We were done. Babangida hung his head for a few moments before speaking.

"Gentlemen, I wish to thank you, believe me, with all sincerity. I don't know if you're aware that Vatsa and I were very close, very close indeed. His wife and mine—they are like sisters. So you see, for me, this is not just a military affair, it is a heartrending situation, a family tragedy. And I am sure you can see how sincerely I welcome your intervention. I suspended a meeting the moment I heard you were here. In fact, I was annoyed that I hadn't been informed earlier. Since when has Dodan Barracks been honored by the presence of the three leading writers of this nation?"

He gave one of his broad smiles, then turned solemn once again. "We need more of this kind of exchange, I mean that seriously. And not just when there is a crisis of this nature. You must feel free to call on me anytime. We could do with your advice on affairs of the nation."

The general took a deep breath, then raised his head to give emphasis to his next words. "Regarding what brought you here, I wish to give you my word of honor—I shall go into the crucial meeting determined to do everything in my power to save them. I assure you, I shall not be party to their execution. That I can promise you. You have no idea how much your visit here has helped me. Again, I give you my word, I shall do my utmost to see that the lives of those men are spared."

How we maintained a semblance of dignity, and refrained from letting out a loud "Whoopee," launching into cartwheels, or breaking into an *atilogwu**
dance, I shall never know, but we all admitted that our lungs were dying to burst into a victory song as soon as we heard that pledge: "my word of honor."

The secretary was waiting nervously to debrief us; it was as if he had a personal intererest in the result, and sure enough, he admitted it. A very close relative of his was among the condemned, and, it would appear, he did not believe that there had been as serious an attempt to overthrow the regime as was claimed. When we gave him a quick summary of the meeting, the uplift in his mood could be weighed. He thanked us profusely. We had done a world of good. We had given Babangida all the moral support he needed to deal with the

---

* An energetic dance of the Eastern Igbo people.

hawks and bring the waverers over to his side. The principal hawk, whom he named, would now find himself isolated, and in any case, now that the commander in chief had set his mind against the executions, that was the end of the matter. The press had picked up news of our visit and were waiting outside. We revealed nothing, gave no interviews, but our presence and purpose at Dodan Barracks went out over radio and television within the hour. The nation, equally sick of the incessant bloodletting, had already begun to breathe some air of hope.

The secretary saw us to our car. I drove. We managed to hold down our euphoria until we had driven around the first corner and then burst into yells—J.P.'s being the most manic. I drove off as if on a triumphal lap on a race circuit. Mission accomplished, and with an affirmation that we had hardly dared expect. We badly needed to celebrate, so we repaired to Bintu's restaurant. We ordered the worthy proprietress to "shake up her kitchen double quick" for a special workout and extract whatever wines she kept in reserve for her brother, my friend OBJ, who came there sometimes to lunch or dine. We kept our secret but did not disguise our euphoric condition, raised glasses to one another and to bemused customers, who must have concluded that the "elder statesmen" of Nigerian literature had gone collectively out of their minds. We knew we were celebrating more than the mere reprieve of our fellow writer and his companions, we were celebrating a reunion—the three of us together and bound in a common purpose—after nearly two decades!

For J.P., it was a personal vindication that brought a very special reward. "My circle of friends," he had admitted in Abeokuta when he bemoaned our prolonged estrangement—and he had made a tight circle with his thumb and forefinger—"my circle of friends has contracted to a mere—dot." I had never known any human being to make such a humble confession, nor heard one ever since. We were thus celebrating J.P.'s renewed embrace of a loosely defined community of literary pioneers, and he, the main celebrant, had engineered it himself, and in such style—saving the life of a footloose member of the wider artistic community. It was a moment to savor.

J.P. wanted us to make a night of it, but I needed my retreat, and the thought of Lagos traffic at closing hours finally pried me from the table and into my car, with the thought that the next Sunday night would definitely be spent at Femi's in Ibadan, since no celebration was complete until Femi and I pronounced it so—through a consummatory, summative celebration. He would be waiting anxiously, insisting on a verbatim account—nothing less ever satisfied him: *Wait, wait, wait, stop! Oh, you know, you really are very* *irritating—don't jump, don't jump. You don't know how to* knack gen,* *that's your trouble, it's not the same as writing. Go back. So he came out of his office to meet you. Right. Begin from there. What did he say? All right. Does he go around with bodyguards? What of Chinua Achebe? All right, in what order did you speak? What do you mean—didn't Achebe come to Abeokuta? He didn't? You mean J.P. sought you out alone, all by himself? What! You see, you have to go back. I keep telling you, you gave me the impression that all three of you made the decision in Abeokuta. See? See what I keep telling you? Now you have to start all over again. Don't leave anything out. So J.P. came to Abeokuta, you were coming in from the bush—which reminds me, where is my share of the* aparo?

Driving to Abeokuta, smiling by myself like a lunatic as I anticipated my "debriefing" at Femi's table in Ibadan in another day or two, I knew that I still needed something to bring me down from the clouds before I could do any work that night—or maybe it was best simply to drink some more wine, go to sleep, and then wake up in the middle of the night to work? I was undecided. There was, however, a good half hour of daylight when I arrived, enough time to go into the walled-in overgrown courtyard just behind my house where a few *aparo* families had made their home. I hunted that patch of land with extreme parsimoniousness, just those times when my body needed to be decompressed or I was confronted by the specter of an empty larder and the rare unexpected—and hungry—visitor.

I rushed upstairs, grabbed my gun, rushed out again, and dashed into the bush. I heard Seyi, my landlady's son, hailing me from the window of their half of the house, but this was no occasion for one of his hunting lessons. I needed my own exulting company, not shared with anyone, least of all an eager young pupil. So I shouted back that I would see him later, feeling a little guilty. Twenty minutes later, I outwaited a bird and forced it to fly.

Seyi came running in after the shot to assist me in finding the victim—so I thought. But no, he was merely waiting until he had heard me fire so he would not alert the quarry, and of course also to make sure that he could safely approach. I heard him coming, and soon enough he appeared. I stood still as usual, with my eye affixed to the landing spot, then signaled to him. Normally Seyi would be leaping and thrashing toward the indicated spot, but now he remained in a kind of apologetic stance, watching me, I later surmised, with a kind of pity.

"It's over there!" I shouted. "Go where my arm is pointing."

---

* Nigerian slang: to breathe life into a good story.

All he said was "The TV covered your meeting with Babangida."

"Already? It went quite well. Move." The light was fading fast. "It's over there by the tree."

"They've shot them," he said.

I heard only the word "shot," so I nodded and moved forward, not taking my eye from the spot. "Oh yes, it landed over there. Let's go find it."

"Vatsa and the others. It was on the six o'clock news, just as you were driving in."

The world froze before my eyes. "Shot who? What are you talking about?"

"This afternoon. About an hour ago."

I said, stupidly, "But the Council . . . they were not to meet until late this afternoon. That's when the final appeal would be decided."

"They met earlier. At three-thirty. They confirmed the sentence, and the accused were taken straight from their cells and shot."

My mind unwound itself like a clock, timing our activities. We had left Dodan Barracks around a quarter to twelve. The Council was not even supposed to meet until five o'clock; the secretary had spelled that out in specific terms when he had made the appointment. Their comprehensive agenda would probably take them late into the night, even beyond midnight. Who had moved the meeting forward? Why? My mind was in complete rout, asking questions haphazardly. Where was Chinua? And J.P.? Had they learned of the disastrous end to our intervention? What part had Babangida played in all this? Had it all been a game to him?

And then—horror of horrors!—could our intervention have accelerated the process that led to these executions?

Seyi had been standing in front of me, but I did not know when he left. I next saw him holding out the dead bird. I shook my head, waved him away, and walked back to the house.

My sense of isolation was overwhelming. Too depressed to work or sleep, too depressed even to think, I dragged myself to Ibadan the following day. It was the only spot on earth from which I could search for a sliver of light to relieve the futility that appeared to lie in ambush for any endeavor in a humane cause. I developed an allergy toward the very sight of a military uniform for a long while after, including even photographs in the news media. I began to think that maybe I was on the wrong planet, certainly in the wrong part of it. *This man had given his word!* If it had all been a game, I really did not want to know these people. For another week, I considered leaving the country, going into voluntary exile for a year, maybe longer, maybe going away altogether and making my reasons public, returning only when the country had returned to democracy.

ABOUT TWO MONTHS LATER, I ran into the secretary whose "brother," or close relation, had been among the casualties of that military justice. "Oh, Prof, I had been hoping I would run into you. IBB wanted me to pass on a message."

"I don't wish to hear it." And I turned away brusquely.

"But you should, you should."

"No, thank you, I do not know IBB. I do not wish to know him."

He smiled, somewhat ruefully. "I can understand. But then I also had a message of my own for you. In fact, I already asked J.P. to pass it on to the rest of you."

I stopped, and he continued, "That Council meeting—you should know what transpired at the meeting."

I shook my head. "It doesn't matter. I really am not interested."

"Prof, listen, you know I was affected. I lost a brother, he was virtually a brother to me. But I know you'll be interested in the truth. Babangida put up a fight, a really good fight for the lives of those men."

"Yeah?"

"He did, Prof. You see, these soldiers, they have their way of doing things. There was a point when the chairman of the judicial panel said to IBB, 'Look, *oga*, we are all agreed on what needs to be done. If you cannot put your hand to it, then please step aside.' "

"What do you mean? Were they asking him to resign?"

"Prof, all I can do is give you a report of how that meeting went. I think it's only fair that you know that IBB kept his word. He has been most anxious that you know it. He begged me to find you and let you know. And I swear, that decision really broke him up, it really did."

I emitted a sound that hopefully translated as a rasp of skepticism, indifference, and disgust. Even as the man spoke, I had already decided to use my own sources to check on the various roles played by the members of the death-dealing Council. I wanted to know if these men of iron wore two faces or more. And then I checked myself in midstride—what did it matter in the end whose voice had steamrolled the accused into their graves? Were they not all an indissoluble part of the collective machinery of killing? I recalled who had cast the deciding vote that had sent General Ilya Bisalla to the stake after the panel had deadlocked over verdicts on the Dimka coup mayhem that had overseen the assassination of General Murtala Mohammed in 1976. It had been none other than my erstwhile military collaborator—and adversary, and friend of sorts—General Obasanjo. And there was the purported role of the affable General Ike Nwachukwu, who had also chaired a panel on yet another coup attempt that had sent several soldiers to the execution stake. I had not known him then, but some years later, it would prove to be the same Nwachukwu, as Babangida's foreign minister, who would provide a support base when I came to engage in secret diplomacy—an attempt to bring South Africa's Mangosuthu Buthelezi and Nelson Mandela together in an effort to terminate an even more brutal cycle of revenge killings.

Predictably, the mood passed, even sooner than I had anticipated. First, I believed the young functionary, whose brother had been among the executed. Mostly, however, there were causes to be pursued, a fellow being to be rescued, a screaming injustice to be redressed, lives that could be made more bearable, and even an insufferable limb of the same power structure that had to be restrained, punished, or even amputated—cashiered from the army—using the same agents of destruction while they remained in power and could not immediately be displaced.

EVEN WITHOUT THE rebuff by Vatsa's fate, the trio of literary "elder statesmen" knew that any intervention by them, after the next attempt to topple Babangida, in 1990, was doomed from the start. Even by Nigerian standards, it had been exceptionally bloody. The mood of the military could be gauged in advance, and the reprisals that followed bore it out, evoking an image of the gutters of Lagos clogged with blood. No fewer than eighty officers and soldiers—mostly from the Middle Belt of the nation—had been led in batches to the execution stakes. It became known as the Orkar coup, after one of its leaders, Gideon Orkar, and earned notoriety not merely from the bloodiness of the attempt but from the unusual agenda of the coup makers, outlined to the nation in their very first radio broadcast. No fewer than five states from the far North, identified as bastions of feudal hegemony, were to be excised from the Nigerian national entity. They were to be cast into limbo, to find their fortunes as best as they could or else reform themselves along specified lines and only then apply for reabsorption into the Nigerian state! The conditions for their readmittance would be revealed in further announcements, the broadcast promised. It was a unique agenda in the history of coups d'état.

Funded by a businessman, Great (his real name) Ogboru, an invading force had successfully trained in secret, undetected for months, in the fenced compound of a fish depot in Ikorodu, some thirty kilometers from Lagos. One section seized the national radio station in Ikoyi while the other moved on Dodan Barracks and shot its way right into Babangida's bedroom with the single-minded purpose of eliminating him, together with his family. From all reports, Babangida seized a submachine gun and fought back but was stopped and spirited out by his bodyguards.

The machine gun mounted on the armored car stationed for the protection of the seat of government had earlier been spiked by an insider, and the young aide-de-camp who rushed to man the gun for the defense of his master was easily mown down. The invaders decimated the sparse force that remained for the defense of Dodan Barracks while others sought out the senior officers of Babangida's government. The attempt would have succeeded—even if short-lived—but for an incredible act of neglect by the coup plotters: their failure to disable the telephone lines. Mobile phones were a rarity in 1990, even within the military. Where they existed, they were so temperamental as to be mostly superfluous. This enabled a missed target, the chief of army staff, who happened to have departed earlier from his anticipated location—quite a bag of glitches!—to make probing phone calls, determine the leaning and situation of his respondents, and mobilize loyalists. Suitably reinforced, that officer, Sani Abacha, launched a counterattack while the coup makers were already celebrating their presumed victory. The rest was a rout, and Babangida's government exacted a terrible vengeance on the losers.

The afternoon of that coup attempt, I was present at the scene that would witness the fiercest battle—Dodan Barracks itself. It was symbolic of my relationships with power that this bloody battle would erupt virtually on the heels of the only other tête-à-tête that I could count as a meaningful, extended discourse with that dictator. This time, it was a one-man "coalition" undertaking a rescue mission, and not just for a fellow poet and his fellow accused but for an endangered species—the entire national entity called Nigeria.

The "summit" had proved long in the setting up, and the list I took with me had built up over time, all items rehearsed in advance in meetings with my coconspirator, Ojetunji Aboyade, the chairman of his Presidential Advisory Council. Our meetings invariably began with some frustrating brain beating that would later end in Oje saying, "Look, why don't you talk to him? Maybe if it came from you, from the outside . . . I think he's beginning to find me predictable." Some moments later—not especially enthusiastic but not totally unwilling—we would put through a phone call and attempt to set up an appointment. Usually accepted, and with vocal enthusiasm, it would suffer one postponement, then another, until the issues were perhaps overtaken by events. This time it was different; Babangida had conscientiously reserved an afternoon when he was truly free of distractions.

That afternoon, April 22, 1990, was a holiday; thus it was just as any day could be wished when one is impelled by serious matters that require a long discussion with the principal executive officer of a nation—unaccustomedly quiet, devoid of the routine officials and visitors, not forgetting the army of hangers-on. From my entry into the waiting room and, almost immediately, into his office, I encountered virtually no human beings. Even the few plainclothes security officers appeared to be in a state of suspended animation.

When one has strayed into an arena only hours before a life-and-death drama is already in its final rehearsals, it is not possible to forget, later, what one did or said within such a charged space. A creepy sensation intrudes—afterward—insinuating that one had somehow participated, albeit unwittingly and disconnectedly, in setting the stage for the coming upheaval. It was late afternoon, but far from dusk. For the first time, my encounter with Babangida was unhurried. The dictator had finally, with all serious intent, carved out the time I had insisted upon for an undisturbed, leisurely voyage through a turbulent list. Recalling the intense absorption on both sides and the thoroughgoing nature of our discussion, an invisible observer might have wondered if the fate of a nation was being decided within those walls, if perhaps all the postponements had been orchestrated by some mysterious force simply to ensure that I was present that afternoon, an afternoon without the slightest distraction—just the dictator, myself, and the specter of death.

Learning, a few days later, that the quiet young officer in mufti who had ushered me in and out had perished in the ensuing action only added to my mind's perturbation, imbuing an afternoon of straightforward exchanges, in retrospect, with a fatedness. That gentle, anything but warlike, face of the young officer, Bello, haunted me for some time afterward, as if it had hovered around the discussion, a silent moderator whose final act was to be the sacrificial lamb, an omen of and surrogate for his master's close encounter with death. The invaders, after all, did hold Babangida by a sheer hairsbreadth away from the precipice of extinction. Indeed, the effect was still with him, months later, when we next met in Abuja. That was at a luncheon where Nelson Mandela, the guest of honor, sat between us. Babangida was haunted by memories of that night of close reckoning. He could not shake the topic free of his emotions at the time, as he yet again outlined the course of events to his sympathetic guest.

"There was no indication," he repeated again and again with a sense of wonder, so unlike what I expected from a soldier whose trade is dealing in and warding off death, "nothing at all, not a sign to indicate that anything was amiss. In fact"—and he leaned across Mandela for the sixth or seventh time, as if I were the sole remaining source of reassurance or earthing device to the world of rationality—"the professor was with me that afternoon. We were in my office, a long afternoon when we covered so much ground. Did you notice anything, Wole, any sign at all?"

I shook my head.

"I was mostly alone," he continued, settling back, his eyes still wide with the wonder of death, death that had come calling, very close, barely missed, "just a few security officers and my aide-de-camp, you know, the young officer"—again he leaned across—"you remember him, don't you, Prof? He was the one who was killed, did you know that?"

From deep within Babangida's eyes, as he recounted these events, shot the shafts of fear that must have assailed him when Orkar's men had broken into his bedroom. Mandela appeared awestruck, turned to look at me in amazement: "You were present?"

I laughed. "No, that's not what he meant."

Babangida looked lost. "But, Prof, you were there. We spent over an hour, no, more than that, over an hour and a half in my office...."

"I meant I left some hours before the invasion."

"Oh yes, of course. But I mean, did you notice anything? Anything suspicious at all?"

"Nothing ominous," I affirmed. That there had been no sign of a warning seemed to matter to the seasoned coup maker—not that he worried the issue as a practical security consideration. It was simply that it appeared to have acquired a kind of mystical relevance. Months after the event, Babangida sounded as if he remained entranced by this omission, found it weird, deeply unnatural, that the coup makers had sent no warning sign of their intentions.

"Prof had come to see me on a number of national issues. You do remember what a wide range of topics we covered?" Of course I remembered! And I remembered also thinking afterward how lucky it was that the army traditionally opted for dawn or nighttime to stage its coups. Suppose the invading force had chosen to break with tradition; it was a public holiday, so there was not much movement about. In my view, that quiet, unprotected afternoon seemed perfect for such an adventure—after all, surprise, springing the unexpected, is integral to military strategy.

The difference between Babangida and Obasanjo had struck me most forcibly that afternoon of the Orkar coup—they both were frustrating in different ways. Babangida hardly ever argued in an oppositional manner; he listened and took notes, interjecting a comment from time to time or else giving an explanation about why a policy had been made in the first place, but always with a hint that it need not be so, that if the situation changed tomorrow, the policy would change. Nothing ever appeared cast in stone when you spoke to Babangida, who, either by temperament or practice, nearly always presented a *reasonable* persona. He did not hesitate to agree with you; then, of course, he later proceeded to do the opposite of what you thought he had agreed to.

Only once during the exchanges did I see his face harden in an automatic, bunker rejection, and that was when we came to the sore subject of his intervention in the University of Ife, where he had ordered the dismissal of some of the academic staff—all acknowledged leftists and radicals. It was as if I had bumped against a boil. He launched into a catalogue of the destabilizing activities of which the dons had been accused. I asked him how he had come by such information, and he kept fingering, casually but suggestively, a folder that he extracted smoothly from a drawer in his desk, as if that action fulfilled all the requirements of rebuttal that the subject demanded. Had he personally ordered the dismissal of the dons? No, he assured me, it had been the decision of his minister of education—only to trip himself up some moments later in a flash of anger that conceded that he had either given or approved the order.

And thus it went all afternoon, a relaxed but occasionally charged exchange, with us unconscious of the armored tanks being repositioned around us, others being rendered useless by some undetected readjustments of their working parts, the final touches being put into place for the execution of what would go down as the messiest coup attempt in Nigerian history—a deadly broth of the arcane and the ruthless. While we probed aspects of a national malaise, skirmished over factors and culpability for the blatant culture of corruption that had become synonymous with Babangida's government, an array of serving officers and ex-servicemen had begun to slip out from their training grounds in a fish depot in Ikorodu, twenty-five kilometers away, infiltrate Lagos as passengers in public transport and private vehicles, regroup, and take up positions to await the descent of darkness.

Unusually, there had been no rumors. The nation—and Lagos—went about its business. Obalende, one of the gateways to Dodan Barracks—the usual hive of swarming humanity, of jostling "danfo" buses, touts and passengers hustling and querulous, steamy and grime-clotted, its nightlife gearing up to encroach upon and eventually take over the daytime market life, was only slightly more subdued than usual, on account of the holiday. Quietly, in air-conditioned complacency, we continued our discussions. The nation was close to explosion unless a virtual U-turn in economic policies was effected soon—did he agree, and did he intend to act to provide relief or face the ire of Labor? Babangida appeared to be confident of having taken the measure of organized labor yet was willing to readdress the implications of the Structural Adjustment Programme.

From the sublime to the ridiculous, such as the overweening conduct of his wife, Mariam, who fantasized she was a Nigerian Eva Perón but was blatantly Imelda Marcos. I had already assailed that affliction, most stridently perhaps during a keynote address at the previous annual convention of the Association of Nigerian Authors, where I formally pronounced the era of FirstLadyism and its attendant toadyism. To Babangida's credit, he had responded by curbing some of his wife's public excesses—but not by much. They crept, then galloped, back until the worthy lady was spoken of as running a parallel government. She plucked long-serving permanent secretaries from their duties to serve as ladies-in-waiting and bullied her husband's ministers at whim and insulted them publicly, engineering one resignation here, a dismissal there. She took to ordering all radio and television stations to tune in to her endless stream of money-guzzling, self-promoting projects.

How much tact can one summon to impress on a dictator that his wife is considered a public pain in the neck? I like to flatter myself that I navigated those sensitive shoals as well as any untrained and reluctant diplomat could! The rebuked husband smiled wanly, gamely accepted that I was right, and said that he had begun to take steps, not only in his own household but with governors and senior officers. Outside, Dodan Barracks remained eerily silent.

And the elections in Jamaica? Could Nigeria aid the progressive candidate, Michael Manley, to regain power? Oje and I had met the former prime minister, now opposition leader, during a lunch in his honor at Ota Farm, the retirement place of Olusegun Obasanjo, then courting the role of elder statesman. Manley was visiting at the invitation of the Guardian Newspapers for its annual lecture series. Tentatively but optimistically, he had expressed hopes that Nigeria might match the dollars that the United States was pouring into the campaign of his rival, tagged a creation of the CIA, Edward Seaga. His cause had been embraced not only by Oje and me but also by the former head of state Obasanjo and the Guardian editors spearheaded by Dr. Yemi Ogunbiyi. There were hints that Babangida was already well disposed toward some help.

Outside, Dodan Barracks remained watchful and pensive—it was still so when I took my leave—as if it were only waiting for the departure of the notorious busybody to explode.

The *aparo* survived. If the coup makers had only taken the trouble to consult me, I would have advised them that his fate was already decried in those scattered feathers, which were all that remained when the Artful Dodger fell to a dramatist's gun but remained destined for the greatest escapist performance of his career.

$\mathcal{D}$inner with an Avatar

. . . . .

THE MOST EXPENSIVE DINNER I EVER ATE IN MY LIFE TOOK PLACE DURING A period of great continental—indeed, global—exultation. I did not choose the menu, the wines served were just about average, I have forgotten details of half the company that framed the large round table at the edge of the Parisian skyline, but I have never regretted or begrudged such unintended extravagance for one moment. I could not even write it off as tax-deductible. Even in 1990, I had yet much to learn about the world of taxation.

The individual at the heart of that dinner, the truly honored guest who honors that often dubious accolade, remains, even today, blissfully unaware of how he came to upset my monthly budget. No, he did not belong to the host of devils for whom the long spoon was invented; only those who jailed him for most of his mature life perceived him as such. For that angelic host, a political progressive or liberation fighter (being only another expression for a Communist) was the human clone of Satan, and they had resolutely advertised that dinner guest as being one.

Out of the blue into my Abeokuta redoubt came an urgent message from the French Embassy in Lagos. The chargé d'affaires—the ambassador was away—wondered if I could travel to Paris the following day for a very important dinner being hosted by President Mitterrand. The embassy was standing by to do everything possible, anything at all to ensure that I was present.

I gave my *ha-ha* chuckle reserved for all outlandish proposals, sent the courier back with empty hands, and returned to whatever was then preoccupying me in my backwater township. Back came an even more intense plea from Lagos. The French president was insistent, my presence was considered vital. And now some further elaboration followed: it was not a state/official dinner but a private one. And it was not François Mitterrand who was offering this dinner but the foundation named for his wife, the Danielle Mitterrand Foundation. A private dinner, yes, but naturally the presidency was involved; thus the invitation had been routed through the embassy. The strange proposal began to attract my interest—to fly to Paris for a dinner; this would be no ordinary dinner, since it could not possibly belong to the typical exhibitionist nature of a dinner-on-the-whim in which some of our Nigerian tycoons indulge—*"Abi k'a ti e sere lo si Paree, ka gbagbe awon olosi ti won npe ra won l'oselu?"**

More details came tumbling through. The dinner transcended privacy—it was secrecy itself. It would take place in the roof garden restaurant of the Théâtre National Populaire, in whose long-suffering bowels I had smothered *la langue française* in Joan Littlewood's quixotic production of Conor Cruise O'Brien's *Les Anges Meurtriers* in 1971. Then came the detail that should have preceded all others: Nelson Mandela was visiting Paris—one of his very earliest ports of call after his release—to consult privately with some French businesses and nongovernmental institutions. The Danielle Mitterrand Foundation was "sponsoring" the visit and had invited to this closed dinner in his honor some ten to twelve guests.

Nelson Mandela in Paris? And I was invited to dine with him? If only that morsel of enticement had been served first, I would have been in Paris before the envoy arrived back at his station in Lagos!

The expected flight tickets had not arrived. The chargé d'affaires implored me to buy my own tickets. Once I arrived in Paris, I would be reimbursed, and of course hotel bills and other expenses would be taken care of. The scenario sounded familiar, it would happen again and again, but pity that individual—never mind Bertolt Brecht!—who has no one to call a hero. There was no way I could miss an intimate dinner with Nelson Mandela, a first direct encounter since he had been released from prison! Have passport, will travel. Visa was waiting. Off I flew two nights later, with nothing beyond the proverbial toothbrush. The refund never did materialize, but there was more chagrin to come—even the settlement of my hotel bill took on an embarrassing drama of its own: I had to pick this, of all visits to Paris, as the occasion on which to lose my wallet!

François Mitterrand attended the dinner, stating demurely that it was his

---

* "What do you say we take off for Paris for a quick spree and forget these ragamuffins who call themselves rulers?"

wife's event, not his—"I have been invited only as a husband." Mandela's team consisted of his wife, Winnie; Cyril Ramaphosa, strongly touted at the time as Mandela's successor; and Thabo Mbeki, who, however, ended up snagging that coveted position. Then there were Peter Brook, the British director and an old friend—author of, among others, *The Empty Space*—and some others of the artistic/political world whose names my brain failed to register. I was seated at the round table next to my favorite avatar, Nelson Mandela. All was resplendently well with the world, and especially the African world—well, almost!

It was one of those long-dreamed-of evenings. Shortly after my collection of poems *Mandela's Earth and Other Poems* had been published in the United States, I had run into a woman friend of an African National Congress (ANC) official during a disinvestment rally at Cornell University, where I was then teaching. When she informed me that she would be traveling to South Africa soon and had the channels to ensure that messages would reach Nelson Mandela in prison, I gave her a copy of the poems. I added, however, that this was not the real copy I intended for him. That copy, I swore, would be delivered to him by my own hands, and I would read a verse or two to him as he sat in the full freedom of his living room. The lady shook her head in pessimism, wondering if such a day would ever come about in her lifetime. I, brimming with optimism, pronounced a date beyond which, I swore, apartheid would not last.

It was not the first time I had done that. At a lecture at the Polytechnic School of London in 1972 during the exile that followed my spell in Kaduna prison, attacked perhaps by some kind of mantic rage, I pronounced the year 1985 to be the terminal year of apartheid. No, not "about," "around," "before," "not long after," or anything else but precisely—1985! A few years later, as the magic date approached, I lost my nerve and extended the date by five years! When the cataclysmic event did materialize, it came with such suddenness that even this prophetic medium was caught completely off guard. So now, seated by my very special prisoner at a round table in a restaurant that offered a panoramic view of the mother of the modern revolution, I felt deeply fulfilled—but also troubled.

As postapartheid elections for the governance of South Africa moved from mere speculation and negotiation to the hard realities of campaign rallies, electoral registers, and ballot boxes, violence—especially between former victims, toned alike by decades of humiliation, disdain, and denial—threatened to tear the emerging nation apart. The daily news from South Africa, and the commonest analysis of the array of forces that had brought down the apartheid government, spoke of a brutal aftermath that would ensue from the rival political claims of the African National Congress and the Inkatha movement of Chief Mangosuthu Buthelezi, the traditional head of the Zulu. The extreme Afrikaner Right was well placed to exploit these differences, and it did. It was not sufficient to brand Buthelezi as a dyed-in-the-wool feudalist, reactionary, and stooge of the Boers. If he were, if that last especially were his entire political tendency, then the worse for the victory over apartheid! What mattered was that he should not be thrown by default, fully kilted for war, into the enemy camp—like Jonas Savimbi of Angola in his turn—through the careful tending of his political amour propre by a common enemy. Above all, Buthelezi was not without a fanatical following, even if not all of the KwaZulu nation favored his politics. Perhaps a civil war in South Africa would be short-lived; all the same, its consequences would be devastating for the continent.

Conversation turned, inevitably, to this retrogressive phase, which was already agitating the world, its grisly killings gleefully registered by certain foreign media. Knowing heads were wagging in smug satisfaction. It was still early in the bloodletting rage. The figures had moved from single digits to double and were now approaching triple. The question on the minds of the genuinely alarmed was predictable, and I turned to Mandela and asked, "Would you agree to meet with Buthelezi if he offered to meet with you?"

Mandela did not pause one second. "Of course I would. He was the first person I telephoned when I came out of prison. We have spoken on the phone several times, and I have suggested to our party that we meet him and find out just what he wants. However, within the ANC, we try to do things in a democratic way; otherwise we would commit the same errors as the regime we are trying to replace. Unless the ANC authorizes it, I cannot meet with him."

I saw both Thabo Mbeki and Cyril Ramaphosa prick up their ears. An unsmiling Mbeki said, "They are killing our people. Buthelezi is power-mad, and he stops at nothing. He wants to create his own power enclave within South Africa. The ANC has not struggled for that. It is not possible to hold a dialogue with that kind of person."

Winnie Mandela's lips grew taut, a contrast to her matronly beauty, which appeared to glow from the glossy skin of a newly bathed and oiled African child. She interjected, "The worst of it is that he actually allies with the National Party. They join forces to eliminate ANC cadres."

"We know where he's headed," Mbeki reaffirmed. "What he doesn't know is that we are waiting for him."

Ramaphosa gave me the impression of a businessman at a board meeting, measuring the opposition but very much in control, secure in the confidence of the majority of stakeholders, whose interests are safeguarded by his reassuring presence. I could not help contrasting these battle-scarred activists with the delicate, nearly fragile, soft-spoken Danielle Mitterrand. Equally arresting were the wax features of François Mitterrand, which had earned him the title of "the Sphinx" from his national media—had he undergone a face-lift at some time that had left his facial muscles paralyzed? It was a thought that flitted through my mind as I succumbed to one of my accustomed flashbacks—my first-ever encounter with the Socialist president when, at the urging of Elie Wiesel, the Auschwitz survivor and peace laureate, he had hosted a meeting of Nobel laureates in the early spring of 1987.

THAT DEBUT AT the Elysée Palace was not one of my most entrancing recollections. François Mitterrand received his guests with a nearly wooden, impassive face. Since he had taken the trouble of conferring on me the order of Chevalier de la Legion d'Honneur some years earlier—instigated, I am convinced, by his minister of culture, Jack Lang—I felt it behooved me to rehearse in advance a sentence or two of appreciation in French. As we shook hands, I delivered them in—surely—impeccable French. The man did not bat an eyelid. Did he even look me in the eye? No, he was a mummified presence that appeared to have been installed solely to gaze across my shoulder at some ancient history, visible to none but him! Yet the French ambassador, who had performed the award ceremony in Lagos, had assured me that Mitterrand had taken a personal interest in the conferment and would have preferred that I come to Paris to receive the medal directly from him—oh, those flattering diplomats! I was now convinced that the man could not have distinguished me from Mobutu Sese Seko, the terror of Zaire. It was rather unsettling. Not a tweak of a smile, only some murmur that I could not decipher and a rather limp handshake. If I had not rehearsed those two sentences to perfection, I would have developed a permanent inhibition over any future attempt to communicate in that language—the only explanation that would have made sense being that I had failed to make myself understood. Still, he proceeded to declare the conference open and left us to our devices.

An unscripted occurrence during the conference did, however, serve to compensate for my initial discomfiture—in a rather curious way. In the midst of solving all the world's problems in the elegant chamber, now festooned with cameras and microphones, one of the laureates collapsed and fell from his chair. I leaped up instinctively to go to his aid, only to feel, the next moment, the restraining arm of an inner calm. I began to laugh silently at myself and ordered that eager self to sit down and relax. Our colleague had collapsed among the cream of the world's medical brains and skills—at least they were considered so by the Nobel Foundation—so what sort of aid did I imagine I was going to render?

I sank into an instantly apprehended but all too infrequently experienced state of detachment from the world of purpose, devoid of all anxiety. Something unsettling had taken place, yes, but there was nothing, absolutely nothing, that was required of me. Others in that hall were superlatively equipped, a collective wealth of experience and familiarity with every ailment in the world. I distanced myself even further from my accustomed self in order to relish this generous isolation from all the furor, from the palpable concern that was evident in the others; I wallowed in the unaccustomed condition of absolution that derived from the competence of others. I basked in my unsought enrollment in the world's unskilled and irrelevant population, immersed myself in the sheer luxury of revelation—*Right now, at this very moment, you are useless, nobody needs you! Enjoy it while you can.* It was a paradoxical potency, to be able to sink oneself in inertia yet feel masterful—through others—for doing nothing, for being incapable of doing anything. My confidence was supreme; all would be well. An ambulance had been summoned, but I was not interested in details. "What do you think happened?" my next-seat neighbor whispered, tortured by the thought that the first-ever gathering of this nature—at least, that he was attending—might end in tragedy. With the most limpid of offhand gestures, eased naturally from my overabundant tranquillity, I calmed him, assured him that it was nothing, that our colleague would be up in no time.

Was it a heart attack? An epileptic fit? A stroke? A diabetic crisis? It did not matter to me in my delicious apathy. *He's in excellent hands*—as if I had joined the doctors in diagnosing the cause of the man's collapse. He was assisted out and into the ambulance—perhaps from Mitterrand's official medical fleet—and the meeting continued. I was perhaps the most serene being in the halls and labyrinths of the Elysée Palace all that day. It was a good thing that my faith was not misplaced. The patient recovered fully and rejoined us for the rest of the conference. Nothing, however, could match that moment when, for once, I understood what a gift it was to be at one with the superfluous population of the world.

. . .

IT BECAME OBVIOUS to me, some moments later, why the flashback had oc-curred. It was not the mere recollection of the bloodless face of François Mitterrand—which, in any case, proved quite capable of some animation and even occasional banter, mostly in the form of self-deprecatory remarks, as the evening progressed. More evocative was the contrast between that other gath-ering at the Elysée Palace and the present. At the TNP restaurant, we were drawn into a tense discussion of life and death, the threatened collapse of a barely rising edifice on which millions of eyes were affixed in optimistic expec-tation. One was denied the luxury of indifference, even of detachment. To make matters worse, instead of an abundance of healers, I wondered—was this should-be celebratory dinner, in the tranquil air of a Paris night, a feast of undertakers?

I looked toward Cyril Ramaphosa, who had yet to speak. His message was similar, but his tone was more accommodating. All expressed grievances against Inkatha, and against Buthelezi personally. Thabo Mbeki was obviously the main hard-liner. He could hardly pronounce the name "Buthelezi" without his smallish, nearly triangular face expunging all expression, leaving only the hardness of his eyes. Mandela returned to the theme. He introduced a novel point of consideration by calling attention to Buthelezi's hurt feelings. He of-fered that perhaps Buthelezi had not been given sufficient credit for what he had achieved during the antiapartheid struggle. The problematic chief had, after all, remained steadfast to the cause.

"Why should we fight among ourselves?" Mandela asked, somewhat rhetorically. "If it were possible, I would go and meet Buthelezi tomorrow, even tonight. I know him. He respects me. If he and I were to sit down today and thrash it all out, all these unnecessary killings would stop."

Mbeki again interjected. His tone was stiff; it cut through the mellow am-biance like a party-line diktat. "His atrocities against our members are unfor-givable. We cannot sit down and talk to such a man. There is nothing to be gained by it. For a dialogue to take place, there has to be a talking point. With Buthelezi there is none."

I thought Nelson Mandela looked rather sad and wistful. Obviously he did not share Mbeki's view. His smile was, however, not quite one of resignation. It could have been my hyperactive antennae, but I had the distinct impression that Mandela's statement did not quite correspond to his inner intent, that he was biding his time. Certainly that surmise was contradicted when he said,

"Well, you've heard our comrades. If the Executive Committee were to learn that I accidentally ran into Buthelezi and exchanged a 'good morning' with him, there would be a riot!"

I turned to Mbeki. "I hope you realize what you're saying. You are leaving yourself no choice but to kill him. You'll have to kill him. And you know where that might lead."

Mbeki gave a slight shrug but said nothing further, at least not on that subject.

By the following morning, the glow of an intimate evening with my—and the world's—favorite avatar had dissipated. It took no special political instinct or intelligence to understand the urge for reprisals. My recollection remained focused on the sharp separation between Nelson Mandela's thinking and that of his "young Turks." Even the body languages of those two—Thabo Mbeki and Nelson Mandela—spoke volumes, and the contrast read out a stark warning. I returned to Nigeria far uneasier than when I had set out for dinner—and had begun to consider if it was not time for another dinner with my reigning devil, the real one this time, but a pliable one!

THE TRUTH WAS, I realized, that my student-days obsession with South Africa had merely gone into hibernation. Now it was bludgeoned awake as the figures of fatalities rose sharply by the day. No-go zones between Inkatha- and ANC-controlled areas in various cities—Johannesburg and its suburbs most notoriously—had become battlegrounds, streets turned into open spaces of death. The predicted was taking flesh; the broken white power had regrouped and begun to exploit divisions between the fraternal enemies. It became difficult to understand—how was it possible that no influential African nation had stepped in, brokered peace between the warring duo, and left the Boer diehards stuck to the starting blocks of their devious plots? It was the looming taunt that haunted me: *See, we hand over power to them, negotiated power, that is, and all they do is slaughter one another.* The suspicions, clashes, and killings were not new, nor were the jostling for political advantage and the fear of being overwhelmed by a more powerful partner in any struggle. It was not a situation that was peculiar to South Africa; liberation history has not been niggardly in its instructional scripts.

The continent needed a South African success! South Africa's task of recovery, black majority–ruled but in partnership with the rest of the nation, would be made less arduous—it seemed obvious—if, during its uncertain period of transition, she had a staunch shoulder within the black continent itself to lean upon. The obvious candidate was Nigeria—her size, her resources, her manpower. As so often happened, the motions began in Oje Aboyade's home. Could it... Was it possible that we could play a role in this? Oje became caught up in the idea, activated his direct line to the Artful Dodger.

My first demand, in outlining a plan for a Mandela-Buthelezi encounter to Ibrahim Babangida, was absolute secrecy. Knowing the torrid ideological space that demarcated the ANC from Inkatha, the very idea of creating a bridge left one exposed. If the plans miscarried, we had to assure ourselves, in advance, of the means of a dignified withdrawal and a stout public denial of any attempt to intervene. Despite the substantial support it had received from successive Nigerian governments, the ANC leadership was especially jealous of its independence. The party was obsessed with its self-image of ideological purity, ostentatiously contemptuous of Nigeria as a nation that lacked political direction or a progressive ideology. The mood within that party hierarchy was not so different from that of the Bolsheviks toward their "liberal" and "bourgeois" allies after the success of the revolution—ANC considered its struggle disciplined and "correct" based on the class analysis of history. By contrast, Nigeria was a spoiled, rich brat, a crude succession of hotchpotch dictatorships and feudal conspiracies. That nation had done no more than its duty in offering diplomatic and material assistance to the South African liberation fighters, perhaps more than any other African country except Libya and the "frontline" nations—Tanzania, Zambia, Angola, Namibia, and Mozambique. There was no reason for any expression of gratitude or special recognition. The ANC was morbidly afraid of contamination by the directionless nature of Nigerian society. Once the apartheid regime had fallen, it set out to distance itself from such an embarrassing benefactor.

This attitude would later cause vocal resentment in Nigerian leadership circles—the ANC (Mandela) was accused of pointedly traveling around the world immediately after his release but refusing to step into Nigeria en route to say "Thank you"! Babangida nursed the same feelings of resentment, grumbling that the ANC leadership was made up of arrogant ingrates. No matter, he soon warmed up to the idea of doing this one thing—acting to stop the looming bloodbath. He had nothing to lose by a little investment; if it worked, his image would receive a boost on the international screen.

Babangida agreed to send his foreign minister, General Ike Nwachukwu, to talk to me. Nwachukwu, with his impressive "soldierly" bearing, was one of those Nigerians who could claim to belong to any part of the country. Born of an Igbo father and a Fulani mother, this general had grown up in the North, where he also spent much of his military career. During the civil war, he had remained steadfast to the federal cause. He spoke Yoruba with hardly a trace of an accent, while his English carried a faint upper-class tinge that was probably consciously cultivated from contacts with the British officer class during his military training in England. Hausa tripped effortlessly from his tongue. Nwachukwu was markedly urbane in manners—the result perhaps of his numerous sojourns in Lagos as well as his training spells and attachments in various countries. We met in Yemi Ogunbiyi's house, the rendezvous for many semiofficial encounters that took place, of necessity, in Lagos. The general arrived in an excitable state and announced that Babangida had offered to make a plane from his official fleet available to Mandela and Buthelezi. They could fly secretly into Nigeria for a meeting, or indeed to any part of the world agreed between them. Then came Ike Nwachukwu's own proposal, one that virtually took my breath away.

Bubbling with enthusiasm, Nwachukwu outlined a plan for the Ooni of Ife, the historic ruler of Ile-Ife and acknowledged spiritual head of the Yoruba, to lead a full-fledged delegation of royal heads into South Africa! Chief Buthelezi, the amiable general reasoned, was a traditional chief in his own right. So was Nelson Mandela—the general had done some homework, I had to give him that! In his view, this shared background held the key to netting the two frisky fishes. The Ooni of Ife, accompanied by a galaxy of crowned Nigerian heads from all corners of the nation, would fly into South Africa in Babangida's private jet. The Ooni would summon his two fellow (but junior) royalty to his presence. He would then chide them for their belligerence— undoubtedly in the special language that traditional chiefs all over the continent use when they are among their own kind. He would say to them, presumably, "Look here, fellows, it's time we crowned heads and chiefs sorted out this problem. We understand one another; we cannot afford to dent the prestige of our crowns in public"—not exactly Nwachukwu's words but definitely the spirit of his plan. The Ooni of Ife would load them into the presidential jet and waft them into a Nigerian seclusion, where our local kings would act as arbiters. After which the combatants would embrace, and the continent would live happily ever after. The world would see that we in Africa have time-tested ways of resolving our problems. I listened. Ike Nwachukwu was so carried away by the sheer originality of his plans that he failed to glimpse anything of my reaction, which was one of plain, undisguised horror.

When I narrated the evening's encounter to Oje, we both conceded that the general meant well but that it would be best to leave the Ministry of Foreign

Affairs out of the project, using that department strictly for logistical support. Thus did I come to embark on my initiation into the world of shuttle diplomacy—an activity that I clearly underrated until firsthand experience taught me differently. The one-off Nigeria-Senegal FESTAC experience had proved a most inadequate training ground; the emphasis this time was on the word "shuttle," not on the diplomacy. In any case, diplomacy of any kind requires, above the necessary training or experience, a very special temperament.

Babangida agreed with our proposal to proceed step by step, making private contacts rather than a royal blitz through the debris of apartheid. I would first of all explore the mood within the ANC very tentatively and discreetly, next move toward a tête-à-tête with Mandela, possibly involve Archbishop Desmond Tutu, then track down Buthelezi. After that, we would consider how best to inveigle the two principals into a secret tryst in a place and at a time of their own choosing, a presidential jet always standing by to take off at a moment's notice. Babangida would send funds to the embassy in Washington to take care of my traveling expenses.

Thus came my saga of meetings—more accurately described as ambushes—and of telephone calls from one end of the globe to another, wondering who had hypnotized then brainwashed me into such an undertaking. Compelled to isolate the most defining of these encounters, I would list three. One was a long walk down a Lisbon avenue with an ANC Communist, late into the night. Another was a telephone discussion with the Inkatha leader, Chief Buthelezi. The third was the last of my telephone exchanges with fellow writer and ANC antiapartheid stalwart Nadine Gordimer.

IT HAD BEEN a long day in Lisbon, a series of sessions—and receptions—at one of those encounters between "North" and "South," in 1991. I shared the podium with Mwalimu Julius Nyerere, then beginning to enjoy his honorable retirement from the presidency of Tanzania. We were interacting for the first time since the Pan-African—resurrection—conference in Dar es Salaam in 1973, a year in which General Yakubu Gowon had been consolidating his dictatorial rule of Nigeria. It was at this chaotic gathering that the original credentials of the Pan-African movement as an all-come, nongovernmental forum had been formally buried.

One after the other, suspect voices were censored, in response to pressure from their governments. Nyerere submitted to some diplomatic arm-twisting from Lagos, and I was successfully excluded from one speakers list after another. Walter Rodney, the author of the seminal work *How Europe Under-*

developed Africa, suffered a similar fate, even though he was actually resident in Tanzania. He was "invited" by the Tanzanian government to absent himself from Dar es Salaam during the conference. To pass the time, I did my best to demonstrate solidarity with a liquid product of that socialist nation, this being the most affordable accompaniment to Tanzanian cuisine: some Roman Catholic priests, fooled by the climate and soil of the Dodoma region in northern Tanzania, had engaged in a valiant effort to cultivate grapes and—table wine! Perhaps that product has improved since then, but, like the experience of a gathering that was intended to breathe new life into the pan-African movement, I was rewarded only with a sour taste in the mouth and a prolonged sense of corrosion of the stomach lining.

LISBON WAS, OF COURSE, a different setting and a far more composed affair: a North-South dialogue. It seemed a perfect pointer. If North and South could dialogue, so could South and South or, in my immediate context, ANC and Inkatha. That a senior member of the ANC was also participating in the conference was a further signal that the stars of dialogue were in the ascendant. I had begun with brief but encouraging snatches of discussion with Nyerere as we sat on the podium, the coffee breaks and reception being hotly contested for by far too many claimants. The ex-president was leaving Lisbon that very night, so I had to seize the few minutes in between the speeches of other members of the panel, and over interjections from the floor. I promised that I would get in touch with him through his secretary, call on him in Tanzania if necessary. It would be no exaggeration to claim that I had engaged his interest—or at least that he was intrigued by the idea.

The ANC delegate was, however, the immediate target. As the conference ended, I asked him to take a walk with me toward my hotel, little suspecting that I was about to undergo a renewed induction into a troubling mindset that bears so much responsibility for the deadly strains of revolutionary rhetoric. I had encountered it on numerous occasions, but perhaps it was the setting of the preceding exchanges of the day, an encouraging contact with that man of vision Julius Nyerere, one of the least doctrinaire of progressive leaders on the continent, that left me so ill prepared. For the bespectacled, flaxen-haired, fortyish white militant responded to my plea that a solution be quickly found to the internecine killings with this: "The ANC is still at war. Nelson Mandela is like a general of an army. Generals cannot pause to take note of the loss, or potential loss, of lives—it's all entered into their calculations in advance."

Aghast, I looked at his pale face lit by the safe streetlamps of a safe Lisbon avenue. It was smug and self-righteous, a composure that, paradoxically, approximated a Buddhist state of the resolution of all the seeming contradictions of a world of pain and strife. It required no thinking; I knew at once that this marked the end of that dialogue. I abandoned my plan to stop at a bar and engage him in a productive discussion, preferably over some Portuguese tapas and *vinho verde*. Denial of my right to free speech by Nyerere—whom I deeply admired in any case—was one thing. Collaboration—indeed, rhetorical justification of internecine slaughter in the name of revolutionary theology—was another. I turned abruptly. It was a most inauspicious beginning to the promise of a diplomatic career.

"Well, good night," I said. "Try to remember, however, that it is not people like you who are getting killed. And it is not your community that is being destroyed."

He looked shocked; perhaps the thought had not occurred to him till then. More likely, no one had ever uttered words in his hearing that conveyed this simple, stark truth. The following morning, he called me and promised to see what he could do within the ANC Executive Committee on his return to South Africa.

My hunt continued for a sympathetic and influential mind within the ANC. All that we sought, after all, was that both Mandela and Buthelezi should know that there was an avenue that could be used to meet discreetly—just meet, talk, and hopefully discover that there was no forked tail hidden beneath either pair of trousers.

I encountered several dead ends and near misses. Thanks to my former student Henry Louis Gates, Jr., then a full-fledged professor at Cornell University, I learned that Winnie Mandela was to attend an investiture at Duke University, where she would also deliver a lecture. I headed for that beckoning rendezvous, posting messages ahead. By the time I arrived in North Carolina, Winnie had called off the event, owing to some emergency recall from home, and traveled back to South Africa.

Buthelezi was also a near miss. The chief had been tracked down in Canada and was expected to remain there for some days before traveling on, consumed with his mission of jettisoning the "collaborationist" label that stuck to him stubbornly. I was then in London. Based on his schedule, transmitted by the Nigerian Mission in Ottawa, I flew to Canada and found that our planes—most probably—had passed each other in the ozone layer. This was getting tiresome, but it was too late to complain. In addition, to one blinded by the dazzle of the prize in view, the quarry always seemed no further away than the arm could reach. There was a fast connection to London to be made through New York, and thus to that city I headed on the next available flight. This time, however, I had learned not to place all reliance on the intelligence network of embassies or be at the mercy of the sudden dispositions of these moving targets. Armed with his phone number and hotel address, I took the precaution of first calling Buthelezi from the airport while awaiting the flight to London.

It was just as well. Buthelezi was packing his bags and would shortly head for Gatwick Airport en route to Johannesburg. All the party leaders appeared to be on the move, even the still-ruling National Party of F. W. de Klerk, preparing for the first postapartheid elections, raising funds, and seeking international recognition and/or understanding of their policies. The ANC, for instance, had mounted a campaign to overcome the general perception of its being a Communist-dominated organization. De Klerk was propagating a scheme for opening up the Nationalist Party to non-Boers, nonwhites. Buthelezi was contesting his "collaborationist" label.

And so my dialogue with Buthelezi took place over the phone—I have yet to encounter him physically. He spoke volubly, making an obvious effort to sound reasonable and objective, but came through as a man deeply aggrieved and hurt—Nelson Mandela was right. Buthelezi forcefully reminded me that, despite having acceded to the "homeland" policies of the apartheid government, he had stoutly refused to accept the offer of the status of an "independent" nation—unlike other Bantustans—by which the regime had sought to consolidate the apartheid ideology and weaken liberation thinking. It had created a false sense of national sovereignty; the ruse was so transparent to the world that it remains a mystery even today that any prescient leader could pretend to have been taken in by its touted theology of mutual cultural and political respect: *separate but equal.*

"My big brother," said Buthelezi, "I am only too happy to do anything to bring me closer to my very own senior brother, whom I have always considered my leader. You may inquire of the de Klerk government. Throughout, I insisted that I would not talk to any of them until Brother Mandela came out of prison. Unlike the others, I refused to accept this spurious self-government. What for? Our leader was still in prison. Brother, I am glad it is someone like you calling me, and if there is anything you are able to do to bring us both together—are you sure we cannot meet before my flight? Maybe if you flew into Gatwick, we could have some minutes together before I take off."

I assured Chief Buthelezi that I could not perform the magical feat of getting into London before he took off, not even if I took the Concorde. I heard his sigh of disappointment. Whatever other impression I received of the KwaZulu chief, this much was certain: he was truly eager to seize any chance of mediation.

Buthelezi sounded most embittered. He felt that he had not been duly appreciated, that his strategy for confronting apartheid had been misunderstood, unjustly misrepresented, and vilified. We spoke—or more accurately, he spoke—for nearly an hour, and the burden of it all was that a wedge had been driven between him and Nelson Mandela by "the hothead extremists" of the ANC. "Those people hate me!" he wailed. "They want to destroy me!"

As I admitted to Nadine Gordimer when I succeeded in contacting her in turn, I detected strains of paranoia even across the transatlantic circuit. Chief Buthelezi accused the ANC of committing atrocities against his people; I reminded him, very gently, that the ANC had accused his KwaZulu warriors of virtually the same crime. In the end I asked him once again: Would you meet Nelson Mandela if such a meeting could be brought about? His response was a most grateful yes. There was no coyness, no playing hard to get. Buthelezi was ready for dialogue.

MY LAST CONVERSATION with Nadine Gordimer administered, without doubt, the ultimate chagrin of my "diplomatic" shuttle. I was now armed at least with Buthelezi's consent and could not wait to convey this to her. She, like Nelson Mandela, had already warned me of the ANC's fervid democratic catechism— I encountered it so often, delivered like a creed of religious submission, that I would mentally recite it even as it was intoned by yet another ANC affiliate, including one or two of its writers. It went beyond liturgy, however. Indeed, it effected, and was acted upon with, such conformity, being virtually synonymous with "party discipline," that it could be counted upon to prevent Nelson Mandela from taking any step without the full approval of the Executive Committee. Nadine was therefore hesitant but agreed to lay "The Plan" before the ANC—Mandela and Buthelezi to Nigeria or wherever, secretly ferried thither in one of Babangida's presidential fleet.

Some days and several more postapartheid funerals later, I was off to Cairo to lay ambush for a heavyweight pair from within the ANC caucus, courtesy of information from my "reformed" Marxist acquaintance of the Lisbon exchange—or was it in fact Nadine? I am no longer certain. Perhaps the unexpected softening of the formerly doctrinaire revolutionary of the Lisbon encounter had imbued in me an inordinate optimism. No matter, I sought help from the embassy in Cairo, specifically requesting the young man who had rescued me from the near debacle of the All Africa Games. He had been posted away, but his replacement was only too eager to lend himself body and soul to the scheme. He succeeded in tracking down the elusive ANC voyagers, who, it appeared, were on a fund-raising mission. The young diplomat also sent a message home in case there was need for a rapid follow-up by Babangida or his foreign minister. I was not overanxious to meet the two travelers without an intermediary or at least some indication about their probable disposition. Nadine could help, and I was due to phone her anyway, since she had finally undertaken to lay the proposal—albeit without great enthusiasm—before the next meeting of the ANC Executive Committee. That meeting had now taken place.

It was indeed a most expectant one-man intervention force that made the call, joined by the embassy official, who had entered into the spirit of the chase. It was the briefest of my telephone exchanges with Nadine on the subject, but it had the effect—perhaps because of her own ambiguous position over the project—of transporting me vividly into the distant conference room where Nadine had introduced the initiative. I could almost swear that I saw each face seated around a table at the other end of the continent as the putative life expectancy of "The Plan" was summarily terminated. Nadine gave off a kind of throaty giggle; it was either a subconscious echo of the guffaws that had rent the discussion room or an embarrassed reaction of her own. Still, she eventually broke through her giggle to report, "The meeting broke up in a bout of derisory laughter."

I think a spasm of shock must have surged across my face because the diplomat sitting across the hotel room half rose from his chair, appearing more concerned with my well-being than with any message from a distant South Africa. He looked anxious as he asked me if I was all right. My reply was a revelation of my inner projections, even to me: "She's just informed me that they are laughing all the way to the cemetery."

Of course, those were not Nadine Gordimer's words. They were, however, the words I used also when I telephoned Oje Aboyade at home to signal the termination of my mission that very night. I asked him to be certain to transmit the message to Babangida just as I had phrased it and to let him know that I now considered the idea stillborn and was returning my meddlesome self to more rational pursuits. I was not born for the diplomatic world.

. . .

THE NO-DIALOGUE rhetoric continued for some months, escalating in intensity even as the sheer statistics of reprisals settled into a numbing spiral. Then one day, several select assassinations and indiscriminate massacres later, including the detonation of bombs at political gatherings, right on the heels of yet another fire-breathing ANC bulletin that promised to wipe out Inkatha and Inkatha's like response, news emerged that Nelson Mandela had quietly shunted aside his Executive Committee and traveled out on his own to meet Buthelezi.

Not, I am certain, that Mandela ever accommodated the latter designation within his rich humanism—but the avatar had transcended the "general."

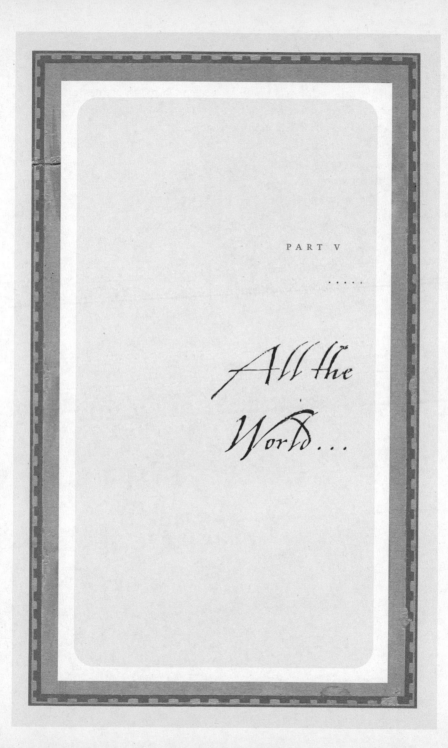

PART V

. . . . .

All the

World . . .

Tonight We Improvise

. . . . .

U SUALLY ONE SEES THEM IN STILL PHOTOS—IMAGES OF DYING CATTLE IN a land overtaken by drought, now landmarked by carcasses and skeletons, withered shrubs, and dry water holes. Occasionally, however, the video camera takes charge, lingers over a calf that is reduced to nothing but skin stretched over a cage of ribs and the final contractions of emaciated muscles. Flies settle and crawl over what remains of moisture on the prostrate beast, mostly around the eyes, ears, and nostrils. It makes a feeble attempt to lift itself, scuffing dirt with the sides of its hooves, then settles back on its side, immobile. Its enlarged eyes stare blankly into the lens. This disproportioned frame with extended ribs sinks slowly into immobility. At some point, you know the calf is doomed, its life slowly ebbing into the sands. The lens lifts toward the desiccated horizon, rises directly upward to reveal a cloud of swooping vultures, suspended, circling, blotting out the pitiless sun.

What I have tried to convey here—complete with circling vultures—is exactly what a director sees as he watches his play die slowly on the stage: the convulsions, the evident lack of nutrition, but above all the ebbing away of any animating spirit. And though the director-cowherd may turn away from the pathetic sight as often as he wants or flee the theater, the image remains branded on his retina and haunts him even in the bar where he has taken refuge. It hangs from the ceiling above the bed on which he has flung himself in despair. He knows the vultures are circling. On the review pages, the corpse is exhumed, mocked, and disemboweled and its tattered shrouds hung up as a warning to all other foolhardy adventurers. This, in fact, is almost a deed of mercy, a kind of public therapy that dissipates the intensity of the agony of the previous night. Nor is one speaking of the malicious or simply uninformed critic, the reveler in fascist power whose ex-wife is probably bleeding him to death through alimony and who must bleed someone else in revenge. No, when the playwright or director *knows* that a death has been enacted onstage, and not one that was called for by the script, he simply bleeds internally and goes into hiding.

A death is, of course, vastly different from a disaster, that unscripted incident that inflicts on the director no worse consequence than the loss of a handful of hair or a temporary homicidal or manic fit. Most directors know them firsthand, especially those first nights when everything appears to go wrong—lines are forgotten, the set collapses, a crucial technical effect is premature, or the lead actor has a seizure in midsentence. Such mishaps are gradually remedied, especially in a theater culture where the critic understands his or her trade from within, as part of the creative totality of the dramatic occupation, and does not confuse his role with that of a feudal executioner whose only function is one of instant decapitation.

It goes without saying that from the commencing decision to stage a play, irrespective of the process that brings it about, through the casting of actors to the end product, the director bears the ultimate responsibility—including even the choice of the play—for what appears on stage. He or she basks in the glow of a successful production and remains the architect of his or her own woes. However, I am certain the actual goings-on behind the scenes, which vary from the hilarious to the tragic, often prove more riveting than the actual public product, having driven many a director close to suicide or onto the psychiatrist's couch. Yet again, many unorthodox, unsung, and unacknowledged remedies have been known to rescue if not the theatrical event itself, at least the actors and company's spirit from collapse. Such efforts give the word "improvisation" a totally new meaning and may eventually lead to a new understanding of theater sociology. But first, to put that elastic theater routine in its place, a case against that very directorial equipment: improvisation.

Joan Littlewood and a Lumumba Fixation

In 1970—but perhaps the notion had been gestating long before then—the erratic genius Joan Littlewood got it into her head that only one man of the entire black race could take on the role of Patrice Lumumba, the martyred leader of the newly independent Republic of the Congo, in Conor Cruise O'Brien's *Les Anges Meurtriers*. That man was none other than Wole Soyinka, recently emerged from prison detention in Nigeria. Perhaps some kind of parallelism was working on her mind—the nation of Congo just emerging from Belgium's colonial detention, W.S. regaining his liberty from a military power? So obsessed was Joan with the idea that she refused to fill that part while I was still struggling to regain my passport, rendering even my appearance in Paris somewhat precarious. For Joan, that was only a minor problem. She continued to rehearse other scenes, confident that the spirit of Lumumba would eventually descend on the Nigerian government.

It did. I traveled to Paris after the other actors had been at work for more than three weeks, leaving me even less than that to master my role. The performance company was a mini–United Nations. There were French film actors, used to playing detectives and/or romantic leads—such as Jean-Pierre Aumont, with his record of pairing with quite a number of glamorous stars. Others were straightforward stage actors. The black Francophone actors—Senegalese, Congolese, Malians, et cetera—were a mixture of professionals and amateurs; the Congolese were musicians who had never stepped on anything but a concert platform. Naturally, the director press-ganged the musicians into acting roles. The list was rounded out with British and Irish actors; Joan liked to have around her a sprinkling of tried-and-tested products of the Joan Littlewood method, based on the principle of inspired lunacy and a blithe disregard of the playwright's text, stage instructions, intentions, even language. Such a radical proceeding had transformed and invigorated the British theater of the sixties and seventies, and Joan was now ready to destabilize French theatrical concepts with her unique style.

I was only a few days into rehearsals before I concluded that Joan Littlewood was mad, stark raving mad, and that the only person who deserved to be institutionalized before her was myself. She knew that I did not speak French, yet she had insisted on casting me in a play to be performed in *la langue française*. With nothing more than proficiency in reading the language, never having conversed in it, I had agreed to act in that medium. At least I had an excuse: I had emerged from prison detention not long before, so it could be claimed that my mind was still somewhat scrambled. What excuse did Joan have?

The French—as the world knows only too well—are extremely language-proud. They can forgive most things, including even watering down their wine, but they take strong exception to the murder of their language. The British complement in that company spoke with an accent that, even to my untutored hearing, was perhaps fractionally worse than mine. In addition, however, I had the terrible disadvantage of not being able to *hear* French at that stage, having never interacted with the Francophone world for any meaningful period. In short, I never could understand what the other actors were saying even after I had mastered my lines.

Now, regarding that little problem, learning one's lines, how did Joan Littlewood solve it? With a tape recorder, into which she had all Lumumba's lines recorded. And that tape recorder—with earphones when necessary—played into my ears every waking moment: eating, drinking, walking, defecating, right up to the moment of falling asleep and first thing on waking up. A French-speaking Lebanese, "Nadine," was attached to me as speech coach. This also helped, especially as we grew closer and closer and thus spent time in each other's company over and above the call of duty—an intense relationship that, but for my other marriage in Nigeria—national politics—would have resulted in elopement.

The lines were crammed and some intelligible delivery mastered. Instead of a correct French accent, however, the language-finicky audience would be treated to the experience of listening to their proud heritage passed through a Lebanese-Yoruba wringer. One problem still remained: how to ensure that Mr. Lumumba could understand what the others were saying in about ten different accents at any given moment. This was beyond even Joan Littlewood's genius, and it was left to me to find my own salvation.

The route to that salvation was, however, made nearly impassable by the methodology of the director herself, Joan, the compulsive improviser. She encouraged her performers to play around with both text and action onstage, especially during performance, more than content to have these altered from one show to the next. Well, improvisation is all very well when you can understand what the other person has just improvised. It's no good improvising "Have they dined?" when your bodyguard has just informed you that mercenaries are blasting their way into your bedroom.

Seizing a moment when the company was assembled onstage, I pointed out to them the marvelous example of the precision actor and French elocutionist Jean-Pierre Aumont, who played the U.N. Secretary-General Dag Hammarskjöld, shot down in his plane over the turbulent Congo. This actor was so precise, so coordinated, that you could time his physical gestures and vocal gradations in advance, calculate the precise distance his fingers would travel as he moved to slide the handkerchief out of his breast pocket, pause at a dramatic angle, then raise his hand to mop, ever so gingerly, the sweat beads on his forehead. John Wells—one of Joan's British imports—and I speculated that there were the exact same number of sweat drops on Aumont's forehead at

every performance. Certainly no one could fault the precision of his movements onstage, and his deployment of the French language manifested the
same daunting precision. His bloodless performance was, of course, a matter
of taste.

Improvise your heads away—I warned them all—when you are interacting
with one another, but not with me. You will get only the response I have
crammed with such difficulty. I won't pick up what you've just said, and if by
chance I do, I shall not attempt any French composition. Not only that, I know
how long you should take to deliver your speech. If you exceed the time limit, I
will come in, whether you're done or not.

John Wells, the satirical writer/actor, was the worst offender. He was the
original Esu* behind the scenes, a totally irrepressible agent of mischief and
with a horrible accent from which any music lover instinctively recoiled. That
did not faze him one bit, and he remained incorrigible till the end of the run.
Sometimes he would say, "You've ballsed up things pretty badly here, Mr. Lumumba, haven't you?" knowing very well that I would still follow with my response, "Yes, we're very proud of the start we've made." Fortunately, his accent
was mostly incomprehensible to French audiences.

Now, that was where Jean-Pierre Aumont was a godsend. His lines never
varied and were delivered to within a tenth of a second either way, night after
night and performance after performance. In return for the disdain with which
he regarded the International Conglomerate of Accents, however, the company spent most of the time sending up his undeniably robotic performance.
I was the only one without that consolation; I needed every ounce of concentration—onstage and offstage—in those terrible weeks that saw my politics of
African liberation overcome all rational judgment, making me the fellow subversive of a madcap director in the demolition of the French linguistic heritage.

YEARS LATER, PRESIDENT FRANÇOIS Mitterrand conferred on me the prestigious title of Chevalier de la Legion d'Honneur. The ceremony was conducted
by his ambassador in Nigeria. Some years after, the earlier-narrated conference of Nobelists hosted by Mitterrand took place, and I found myself at
the Elysée Palace, my spoken French vastly improved and a brief thank-you
speech, memorized, rippling off my tongue like an above-average *vin courant*. I
was taken aback by what appeared to be a set, inhospitable expression on his

---

* Yoruba god of mischief, the unpredictable factor.

face as he offered me a limp handshake. For a long time, I could not understand what I had done to deserve such a rebuff.

I have formulated several theories but have finally settled on this possibility: the honor had been awarded to someone whom Mitterrand only knew by name. The day of our encounter at the Elysée, however, there flashed through his mind the image of a Nigerian actor who had stood on a historic stage in the very heart of Paris and massacred his precious language.

No wonder he froze!

A Festival Improvised

Who could resist the promise of Siena? A theater festival right in the midst of Chianti country, and timed for the wine harvest of the year 1992? I gathered together the old hands of my dormant theater company, the Orisun Theatre, set aside all other work to complete a new play—*From Zia with Love*—and headed for the Italian vineyards. Alas, the festive context of the festival fell far short of the promise. Wine festival there was not. As we drove through vineyards from our billets to rehearsal spaces through picturesque Siena—verge to horizon draped in grapes ready for harvesting, the air heady with the fragrance of imprisoned juice—our imaginations were set ablaze with processions of gaily costumed maidens with full baskets of grapes drawn on ancient carts, mandolins and pipes in the hands of leather-kitted vignerons, kettledrums astride donkeys, a rain of wine-drenching onlookers and a bride of Bacchus crowned on the doorstep of city hall. Each day, we awaited notice of the festival, even some quaint rituals on the streets that would relieve the hours of hacking away at the unwieldy material of the dramatic text. No notice ever came, not even a drum signal.

We were lucky to make hay, nearly literally, while the sun shone. During that time of year, rain, we had been stoutly assured, was something unheard of—it was like Atlanta all over again, where snow had been unheard of for fifty years! And so the performances were mostly billed for the open air, even though some makeshift arrangements had been made for alternative venues in Siena in the absolutely unthinkable event that it rained. It *never* rained in summer, swore the people of Siena and the organizers—an article of faith to which a mostly reliable quality of the grape harvest had largely contributed. The festival venue comprised the sprawling, sloping grounds of an ancient castle framed so close against the sky that one felt that the sky was simply the roof of a performance dome. Acting spaces were dotted all over the open grounds, usually with a renovated lodge as dressing and storage rooms. Our production, like most others, was blocked and rehearsed all five weeks on the open-air stage.

The presiding deity would prove not to be Dionysus, the sunshine deity of the grapes. He kept away, probably sulking on some distant mountaintop about the cancellation of his festival, thus creating a vacuum that was instantly filled by the dark, brooding Sango, he of thunder, lightning, and torrential downpour.

Even before his full-blown manifestation, the omens were all around us. A third of the company took ill. Worse was to come riding in on Sango's wind. The god of lightning, rage, and thunder had also taken charge at home. A rain—of bullets—was beating the walls and streets of Lagos. The people had risen against a hike in the price of petroleum products, and the police had responded with fire. Now it was all anxiety for the company, uncertain how their families were affected. They wore their apprehension on their faces, and it played havoc with rehearsals.

They had been away from home for more than two weeks. Reports filtered through to us of mounting casualties. The actors spent most of their allowances on telephone bills, calling families and friends but mostly obtaining no coherent—or else contradictory—responses. Sometimes the line would break off in midsentence—the Italian telephone exchange was every bit as rudimentary as the Nigerian. There were rumors of a coup. Panic set in. Tunji Oyelana, the resourceful musician, was able to get through to his wife on an obliging line, his conversation crowded with messages from the company to their families, followed by depression at the thought that bad news was being kept from them.

Suddenly I had an inspiration, probably quickened by my own disquiet at being away from home at such a time. Certainly, my concentration suffered from time to time, however much I pretended not to be affected by the general mood.

I scheduled lengthier rehearsals for that week in order to increase, by one day, the next weekend break. The company was to spend that time resting and studying their lines. With an excursion into Rome also organized for the interested, the company was fully occupied one way or another when I took off for Nigeria, armed with letters and verbal messages from virtually every member for their families. I was entrusted with the task of bringing back truthful news of the situation.

Before late evening of my Friday-afternoon arrival on an Alitalia flight, I had accomplished my mission, spoken to members of the artistes' families, assessed the current state of the siege, and begun to prepare for my return on Saturday. Then I paused. What else could I do to boost the morale of the company? Foremost in my mind was how to relieve them of the tedium of the bland diet—to the average Nigerian taste—that the catering department was churning out. Personally, I was quite amenable to pasta, but for most of the actors, pasta was a diet for the sick or convalescing, and in any case, the portions were roundly damned as inadequate.

The first candidate for the relief package was obvious: the Nigerian farina, *gari*, prolonged deprivation of which has turned many a Nigerian to either crime or religion. To return without even a token quantity, merely symbolic, would have counted as an act of nonconcern or, worse, sadism. I was already resigned to the fact that this would have to be one of the exceptional flights where I could boast of checked-in luggage. Next, hot peppers, some dried fish, other seasoning items, some lightweight delicacies around which the starving Nigerians could improvise on the canteen cuisine.

Then I had yet another flash of inspiration! Or maybe it was simply a burst of madness. At the bottom of my freezer, a long, low-slung container of infinite capacity that preserved the rewards of my hunting forays, was a member of the civet cat family, the *eta*. For months it had awaited the right occasion for barbecuing, stuffing, smoking, and other forms of posthumous torture. It was unskinned, frozen rock-solid, and thus could be guaranteed to retain its edibility, even after thawing, for at least forty-eight hours. I hesitated. It seemed an improbable idea, but—was it really? I did not know the Italian laws regarding importation of live, cooked, or frozen game. It seemed unwise to contact the Italian Embassy for information in case it proved negative. In any case, I could always claim that it was a weekend and the embassy had been closed. Was it worth the risk?

I was already corrupted by my friend Femi Johnson, who would buy cheap, oilproof suitcases specially for the importation of yards of strung-together salami, boulders of Parmesan cheese, and even entire haunches of cured ham from Italy to cater to his special cravings. I bugged him relentlessly over this embarrassing habit but had no qualms about assisting him at demolition time. However, in Femi's case, he loaded himself with foreign matter on his way home, not outward, when penetrating foreign borders. How would the natives take to such a potential health hazard? Coming from Africa, of course, it had to be nothing less! The more I thought of it, the more appealing was the idea. The promised wine festival had failed to materialize; well, we would improvise! As a private bonus, I would be able to boast of beating my friend at his own game, albeit with the trafficking direction reversed. Most compelling, however, was the picture I conjured up of the faces of the troupe as I delivered letters from their families, assuring them that everyone was safe and the nation was not completely on fire. Then, pulling at the zipper, I would slowly unveil the offering.

The decision made, I dug out a respectable-looking bag comfortably capacious for my uncomplaining traveling companion and padded its interior with foam and newspapers. Just before heading for the airport, I inserted the *eta*, crouched in full rigor mortis, and sealed the bag. Saturday night, I was airborne for Rome, arriving on Sunday morning.

Then came the question: What would be my response if some overassiduous Customs officer chose to open that bag? That was soon resolved; he would be assailed by a factual but embroidered introduction to the ways of theater culture. A theater festival was taking place in Siena for which the frozen animal was an essential stage prop. This was an event that involved a ritual for which no stuffed or symbolic substitute could serve. I would create a grandfather of all fusses, threaten an international incident, demand to call the embassy, lie that I had checked the beast's admissibility with an official at the Italian Embassy, scream racism, invoke cosmic disasters—including a wretched wine harvest for all of Italy—if the ritually blessed and consecrated animal were not laid out on its appointed altar within the next twelve hours! In short, I was resolved not to leave Rome airport without that beast. If it came to that, I would even threaten to pull my company out of the festival. What would they do anyway? What could they do? What business was it of theirs, a frozen quadruped that was not after an immigration visa and would soon be cleansed and purified in ritual flames? It was clear, they would have to let the cadaver in.

There was a conference attached to the festival, and Bode Sowande, a playwright, lecturer, and director, had traveled from London for that purpose. We found ourselves clearing Immigration at the same time. Good or bad augury, it was time for some rapid improvisation. I said to him, "Listen, Bode, I am carrying *gari* and a few other items of consumption for the company. I don't know about the Italian Customs, but they might try to be awkward. If we are pulled aside for luggage inspection, let me do all the talking." Bode was more than willing. As if Customs were waiting specially for us, an official blocked our exit through the "Nothing to Declare" passage and waved us both to "Something to Declare."

Here we go, I sighed. Ogun, it is now your turn. You offered me this sacrificial beast on a previous outing; now it's your duty to ensure that it arrives at the destination where it will do the maximum good. Am I selfish, Ogun? No. Did I leave that beast in my private refrigerator awaiting consumption by me alone, maybe with Femi Johnson, who will surely raise hell when he learns that the *eta* is gone? No. Do I smuggle drugs? Arms? Certainly not. Sex slaves? Diamonds? Am I a trafficker in any contraband? If you agree that the answer to all the foregoing is "no," then regard this animal as your companion dog, preserved for offering. Blind those Customs officers to its presence or cover them in illusions like Pentheus at the hands of your sibling, Dionysus, whose festival we had expected to celebrate but who remains frustratingly elusive. Send these infidels dancing to ethereal music in honor of the tropical *eta*, miraculously transformed into the watchwolves of Romulus, guardians at the Roman gates.

I unbuckled Bode's bag, chatting loudly with him about the festival and lamenting what a disappointment it had been that the wine part of the festival had been canceled. I lauded Italian wine over and beyond its own claims and complained that the rehearsal facilities were inadequate, but that this disappointment was constantly tempered by the beauty of the Italian countryside and its unmatchable wines. If those officers understood that much English, they gave no sign. With a flourish, I opened Bode's two bags and let my hand hover absentmindedly over the zipper end of the criminal one. The chill of the frozen meat had penetrated to the outside of the bag, with a film of moisture covering the outer skin. If the Customs officer so much as laid a finger on the bag, even with the dismissive intent of pushing it aside, there was no way his curiosity would not be aroused. I tugged at the zipper. The officer had become bored. He looked over the bags and waved us on.

Once safely ensconced in a car, heading toward Siena, I revealed to Bode the nature of the bag's contents, nearly causing him to have a heart attack. In Siena, when the beast was unveiled, the delight on the faces of the company was, as I anticipated, an unquantifiable reward. Then, to cap it all, the Nigerian ambassador in Rome, Rekya Attah, having learned of the artistes' privations, arrived in her car with pots and deep bowls brimming with Nigerian food. By now, a rough fire had been built by the company in the field outside the Nigerian quarters, and the smell of singeing hair and burned skin soon attracted the other troupes. In twos and threes they emerged from their rooms, incredulous eyes confronted by a roasting *eta*, the size of a medium-sized sheep, at the edge of the rows of vines that dipped vertiginously from the artistes' row of houses.

What followed, three hours later, was a riot of a feast, with the *eta* as centerpiece. Music flowed, and a spontaneous festival began. That evening, there were no patrons in the festival cafeteria. The bus that came to take the actors for dinner was sent back empty, prompting even the organizers to jump in and return with it to investigate. Again, the bus returned empty; they opted to remain and partake of the festivities.

Pity that the opening night of the play was one of those events that recall the image of the dying calf. As the rain pelted down, one of the lead actors, Yomi, discharged from the hospital just in time for the performance, hobbled about on crutches, in deep pain from a sciatic nerve. Playing opposite him— there were just the pair of them onstage—the other actor (perhaps empathetically afflicted!) blanked out on his lines, totally and irremediably, leaving the stage entombed in one of those silences that all directors dread. To ensure that he could not extricate himself from the marshland of silence, a bunch of children burst onto the stage wing, led by an Italian mamma, a schoolteacher, who could not understand what the company was still doing onstage—the hall had been booked for her pupils' end-of-school concert, following *Zia,* and she had come to take possession. Struggling to find his place, the actor returned to a point that had been played more than forty minutes before. The Italian sound manager, totally lost, put on the next music cue anyway, judging that it was about time it came on.

We lost the play that night. Still, the spirit of the impromptu festival of *eta* appeared to take over and redeemed the remaining performances.

A Digression on the Purpose of "Accidents"

Few cultures are known to exist where the beginnings of drama have not been traced to the rituals of the society. It goes without saying, therefore, that the fortunes of a play may depend on a respect or disrespect for ritual observance, especially in those instances when Ritual comes knocking on the stage door, unbidden, and is either welcomed or denied entry. My 1981 production of *The Road* at the Goodman Theatre in Chicago proved to be, beyond a doubt, yet another of those instances of a clear correlation between a ritual/festival denied and the consequences for a production.

My assistant in that production, Malcolm, was uncharacteristically late for rehearsals one Sunday night. He had driven home for the weekend break, and as he was on his way back, racing to return in time for the Monday resumption of rehearsals, a deer ran onto the highway and attacked his motorcar, getting the worst of the encounter. Thereupon Malcolm proceeded to wait until the State Police arrived!

The story was so surreal that at first I thought he had been hallucinating. Are you sure you were struck by a deer? I persisted. No, the deer ran across the highway, he tried to quibble. I was having none of that. Did the deer collide with your car or not? He admitted the incident and even offered to show me the dent in his car.

Then I thought it all had to do with insurance. Was a police on-the-scene report essential to ensuring that his car was repaired on his policy? Apparently not. Then I proposed: Well, maybe the animal was not dead and he was awaiting an ambulance—the Euro-American world is filled with animal lovers of the decidedly lunatic fringe, and maybe it would be considered cruel if he put the animal in the trunk of his car, even for the purpose of taking it to the nearest veterinary clinic. That would still appear a ridiculous proceeding, but I was willing to make allowances. But no, the animal was quite dead, he assured me, dead as warm venison. So what was the problem?

It was the law, he explained. He was not permitted to take the game away. In the United States of America, when game decides to commit suicide by car, it is only the police who can remove it! Malcolm plummeted in my estimation, from that moment, to a level from which it took quite a while for him to recover. The law? What did the law want of a dead deer—to perform a postmortem? Was Malcolm a closet vegetarian? I projected myself onto those moments of involuntary deerslaughter and the tame surrender of legitimate kill. Scene: *Commuters rushing to and fro, minding their own business. Self-sacrificial deer jumps onto the road, hits oncoming car with violence (also damaging the vehicle!). Victim driver has been working on* The Road, *a play about the god Ogun, sacrifice, ritual, and a mystic quest, knows very well that the director would gladly relieve him of any burden of guilt—if any is felt—by organizing an after-rehearsal convention on the mythological symbolism of a stricken deer, even if it required motoring to some wasteland where a bonfire would attract little attention.* Malcolm, in short, had a ritual responsibility to have thrown that deer into the boot of his car and reported to the director of this production, who could not be bound by any impious American law under which policemen took charge of such carcasses, which then totally disappeared from sight.

To this day, no one has offered me a credible answer to the question: What happens to the mammals that are carted away by the State Police? Are they incinerated? Sold as dog food? Sent to veterinary teaching hospitals for dissection? Ha! And my assistant tamely hands over warm-blooded wild game to the police—it was most cowardly conduct, an act of betrayal and repudiation of every new knowledge I had imparted to the company. It was unacceptable conduct in a close collaborator. I refused to speak to him outside professional contact for days and viewed him with deep suspicion for at least a week afterward.

It would be my fate to be present at such deviant conduct in later years—once at Cornell University, with Skip Gates and a visiting collaborator from the days of the Orisun Theatre, Femi Euba. Skip was at the wheel of his car when we came upon a freshly slain deer, still warm to the touch, victim of a hit-and-run driver perhaps, no more than ten seconds ahead of our vehicle. Our duty to the world of rationality and ritual was to pick up that deer, repair to Skip's ample garden, and commence proceedings. I had no cooperation. On the contrary, Skip moved his car far from the carcass to ensure that I did not myself heave it into the car. I was becoming schooled in the peculiarity of Americans, so I contented myself with letting him know that he had inflicted a mortal wound on our friendship. The Chicago experience remained my introduction to the wastrel habit of American drivers after they have been victims of assault by rampaging game. A little more education, and such drivers would know that there was only one explanation for such "accidents"—they are a gift from Ogun and should be honored as such, atop a funeral pyre to the accompanying music of popping corks and roasting peppers.

It was that play, *The Road,* appropriately, that commenced the formulation of the image of the dying calf for any disasters I would later incur onstage. The contribution to that dismal experience by the lead actor was of such a nature and dimension that he became known as "the Black Hole," so resolutely did he suck the energies and vitality of the rest of the company into the antimatter of his stage presence. The play should have been retitled, for that production, *The Eclipse.* As for the director—hidden in a corner seat, having long abandoned the pointless exercise of note taking, I had only one wish left in the world: to sink into the theater vomitorium and be deposited directly into the underworld. Since that vanishing trick refused to oblige, I considered myself guilty of a double dereliction of duty by failing to step onto the stage in the middle of the ongoing performance to apologize to the audience for having abused their evening out, and would they please leave now and collect their entry fees at the box office—with a glass of champagne plus canapés, compliments of the establishment, and free theater seats for the rest of the season? And if anyone felt that this was not sufficient to assuage their assaulted dignity, they were invited to remain behind and witness an impeccable demonstration of a classic exit, to be performed by the director, in that terminal idiom known as *seppuku.*...

When that evening is contrasted with another in the same theater, the production of *Death and the King's Horsemen,* the difference is instructive. This was a production that was bedeviled by more than the usual problems, giving off the feeling, sometimes, that the entire project was under a severe psychic attack, threatening the very survival of the actors. Despite such malevolence, however, this production, in Chicago and at the John F. Kennedy Center for the Performing Arts in Washington, D.C.—not its post-Nobel revival at Lincoln Center for the Performing Arts, New York!—proved to be an aesthetic and critical success, a rare combination. It earned a *New York Times* accolade as one of the twelve best productions of that year.

In Chicago, however, where it made its American premiere, accidents of a physical nature threatened its very emergence on stage—accidents on the highways, within the city, and within the theater. Unlike with *The Road,* no divine signal in the form of a productive accident came our way, only debilitating ones, such as that of "Mrs. Pilkings," the wife of the district officer in that play, whose leg remained in a plaster cast till only a few days prior to performance, duplicating the cast-in-plaster-cast spectacle of Siena. No equivalent of Abraham's ram was spied entangled in the rigging, pointing us in the direction of what the gods demanded; instead, it was a stagehand who did his best to substitute. He landed barely one inch from the concrete flooring and the certainty of a shattered spine. Another day, giving directions from beside a plush curtain that covered an exit in the auditorium, I escaped, literally by sheer whiskers, the certain pulverization of my chin. I felt my goatee swept violently aside by an offensive weapon that had been inadvertently launched by one of the actors awaiting his entry—of course it had to be the actor who was also a fanatical bodybuilder! My beard was swept aside, and such was the gale force that followed in the wake of that truncheon that I finally understood the origin of the expression "a close shave." I was astonished to find my beard still intact. And then the illnesses—in so many ways, the seeds of serene Siena appeared to have been sown in the wilds of Chicago.

There was a clear demand by invisible forces for some rite of exorcism. The black actors were of the same mind, but the management, though fully in agreement that some kind of psychic remedy was called for, balked at the proposed format. The Chicago bylaws, I was made to understand, forbade the slaughtering of a ram within city limits. What of a cockerel? I inquired. It made no difference; the Chicago city fathers definitely frowned on the conversion of public buildings into private butcheries. The accidents continued. The management let it be known that its position had not changed but noted that it was not equipped to prevent any illegal act that was committed without its knowledge. It was thus left to the company to let the management know roughly between what hours the company might commit any purely conjectural illegal act.

After the theater had closed on the appointed night, which was to be during a week of the theatrical run of another play, the entire company, black and white, plus the technical director assembled under the stage, gathering around an outsize white cockerel, smuggled in by one of the actors. Kola nut was offered, libation—moonshine, for lack of palm wine in its distilled form, *ogogoro*—was poured. The bird was put out of its misery. I improvised a ritual, sprinkling blood in hidden corners beneath the stage and smearing some more on the spots of the major near accidents. The cockerel was then prepared in the apartment of one of the actors and consumed, each member of the cast eating a piece, however small.

Miraculously, the accidents ceased. Not one more actor so much as stubbed a toe in the darkened theater, tripped over wiring, or suffered from food poisoning, neither during the rest of the rehearsals nor through the lengthy run, not even when the production left the scene of the sacrificial cockerel and transferred to the Kennedy Center in Washington, D.C. If the spate of accidents had continued, I had my defense: substituting a cockerel for a ram and other forms of improvisation onstage are all very well for humans, but the deities reserve the right of a final, critical approval or rejection.

From Ghetto to Garrison

. . . . .

OF COURSE IT FEELS GRAND AND COMPARATIVELY STRESS-FREE TO WORK occasionally in theaters where everything is predictable—the stage mechanics work, actors are paid, there is a set division of labor, and so on—but I confess that such ventures leave me hankering for the more precarious existence that characterizes much of theater culture on the African continent. There, theater is not so much a noun as it is a verb; theater is where theater *happens*.

Unlike my first, semiprofessional theater company, the 1960 Masks, I created the Orisun Theatre principally as a political vehicle. Its first home, the Mbari Writers and Artists Club, Ibadan, was its nurturing home, and that environment became a formative factor in the distinct characteristics of the Orisun Theatre. Mbari was located at the base of the Dugbe market hub in the chaotic city of Ibadan, a crossroads of beggars and touts, pickpockets and gangsters, improvised motor parks, open urinals, lunatics, street vendors and itinerant preachers, beer parlors that were recruitment centers and haunts of freelance thugs high on marijuana, local gin, and the guarantee of protection from their political masters, no matter what mayhem they caused. Often it struck me that the daily street theater, to which most people remained oblivious, was far superior to anything that we could mount on the stage, but of course, while that demanded no entrance fee, payment could be exacted in rather unpleasant ways. Certainly the drama of the very environment contributed markedly to the development of the character of the Orisun artiste, an existence on the thin edge of survival, and the ability not just to identify with but to merge, chameleon-like, with the colors, sounds, and pulses of its habitués.

It was only just, therefore, that *The Beatification of Area Boy*, a play evolved from the Nigerian slums in Lagos and from the improvisational working method of Orisun—it actually began as a series of sketches—would prove, fortuitously, the vessel on which the Orisun impulse would travel, and along the same route that African slaves had taken to "the New World." It certainly provided me one of the most unforgettable—frustrating but infinitely rewarding—theatrical ventures I ever engaged in, and at a time when I desperately required some form of relief—its production took place during the high season of the anti-Abacha struggle.

First, however, *Beatification* made its—unexpectedly poignant—premiere at the West Yorkshire Playhouse in Leeds, England, under a British director, Jude Kelly. On the eve of its premiere came news of the hanging, by Sani Abacha, of the writer and environmental champion of the Ogoni, Ken Saro-wiwa, and his eight comrades. I was not present at the opening, but the news predictably cast a pall over the theater and created a quandary for the artistes—to cancel the event as a gesture of protest and respect or to dedicate the performance to their memory. They decided on the latter.

Six members from the Orisun workshop in Nigeria, the Sisi Clara Workshop, including three pioneers of that company, traveled to England to participate. I was involved in the production, unusually, as I prefer to leave a director of any of my plays to his or her own devices, but Jude Kelly was no less determined to block all my escape routes! As I lent a hand to her efforts, I returned wistfully again and again to that play's interrupted maturation in its own spawning ground and wondered whether the Yorkshire production would ever be seen by its intended audiences in Isale-Eko (Lagos), in Dugbe (Ibadan), the original Orisun home, or indeed in other Nigerian main cities—Kaduna, Enugu, Benin, Jos, or Port Harcourt. The production toured Europe, the United States (Brooklyn), and Australia, always to uplifting reviews and reception, but it remained, for me, just another successful production. Not even its transfer to the violent environment of Brooklyn came close as a substitute for Dugbe or Isale-Eko.

Then a Jamaican producer, Sheila Graham, ran across the play in a drama bookshop, read it, and said to herself—But this is Jamaica! This is Kingston, Jamaica, even if it did set out from Lagos! Sheila sought me out in Atlanta, where I was teaching at Emory University. A few months later, I was in Jamaica on a reconnoitering visit. I visited the various performing spaces, and, among the choices, never was a decision so well made in advance by the very social topography of a place!

As I confessed in my program notes, the easiest part of the production turned out to be the choice of a theater. Among all the contenders, including the far more modern Little Theatre, it was quite straightforwardly a case of— no contest! I settled for the Ward Theatre the moment I was driven through a pulsating community to confront this antique-looking structure from the Victorian Age. It was as if I had been transported to Broad Street or Yaba in Nigeria's Lagos! Groundnut sellers, cigarette hawkers, rickety stalls with the usual knickknacks were all on display; layabouts lolled on broken walls, tree stumps, and pavements in various stages of boredom and alert opportunism. Present and vacantly ambulatory was the regulation quota of an indulged street lunatic or two, probably high on ganja . . . summatively, an exterior of dust and noise and vitality but also—an efficient sound-insulated interior! It was a most unusual combination. Much as, confessedly, I feel at home in street theater, I also prefer major productions without unscripted "noises off." The environment of the Ward Theatre was unbelievably the identical environment of Glover Hall in Lagos, whose boards had often played host to Orisun Theatre and its parent company, the 1960 Masks.

The *process,* however, proved to be no such easy walkover! Never before has that eve-of-performance greeting "Break a leg!" held such resonance as during the entire preparation of *Beatification.* Over the project, more than a mere leg was broken—literally this time—for better or worse: social mythologies, insularity, professional attitudes, aptitude limitations, conventions, performance concepts, taboos, and so on, not to mention my own stoic ceiling and personal endurance record! The very violent context of "the Area Boy Project" in Kingston also provided a powerful antidote to the pessimism that daily threatened my existence from the stubborn tenacity of a dictator's hold on my own political space, the daily reports of new atrocities on the populace, accompanied by news of capitulation and collaboration by much of the political class.

Focusing on *youth, youth, youth!*—that all-too-familiar marginalized, disadvantaged, frustrated, exploited, underutilized, straining-at-the-leash-of-opportunity, but also often dangerously romanticized *youth*—proved most efficacious as a restorative agent. There was also Tunji Oyelana, my dogged collaborator, as a constant reminder of an unending mission. He was, after all, a founding member of Orisun. Now, as co–musical director of the production, he was a figure of continuity: thirty-plus years of collaboration, the product of a rather stubborn social-artistic impulse that had begun even before the nation's independence. All the same, when one embarks on a creative adventure in an environment that is paradoxically both familiar and estranged, it is always wiser to prepare for the roadblocks of the latter, girding oneself for a bare-foot journey into unknown territory.

It was a welcome break—the first and only sustained break—from work-ing to topple Abacha's regime and being hunted in turn by his goons. That is, I was insulated even from news about Nigeria. The long reach of the menace was, however, accorded due place, and I was assigned a police "minder" by the government for most of my stay in Jamaica. I felt reasonably safe, however; Ja-maica was itself such a violent place that I felt that Abacha's agents would have met their match locally before they came within a stone's throw of their quarry.

I found myself thrust into a bubbling, undirected ferment of uneven talent, a dubious mix of professionals, semiprofessionals, and rank amateurs, several of them unaccustomed to the discipline that is basic to the theater profession. It helped that Tunji Oyelana was also available to take some of the strain. Tunji, with his wispy goatee and avuncular manner, never set out directly to be accounted a political dissident, but his consistent and stubborn streak of conviction, even when strictly engaged in an artistic pursuit, would invariably result in his being marked down for negative attention by successive regimes.

After the West Yorkshire Playhouse production, he had been unable to re-turn to Nigeria, having been singled out for reprisals by the Abacha regime for his prominent role in that project. He had further compounded his pariah sta-tus by comments in interviews on the BBC and in a documentary that was made of the production and shown on Nigerian television. By now I had been formally declared a wanted man by the regime, and quite a few colleagues paid a heavy price even for association that had preceded the regime. As frequently happened, warnings from highly placed contacts reached us in time, and the other actors could take due precautions in their mode of reentry into the coun-try. Until the death of Sani Abacha, Tunji's home and office in Ibadan remained under constant surveillance.

It was not simply a play project intended solely for rehearsals, perfor-mances, and dispersal. The Kingston venture was approached by Sheila Gra-ham, from the very beginning, as one that would not merely rehabilitate the disadvantaged youths of Jamaica but transform the degraded inner-city envi-ronment. Would-be artistes were invited through advertisements and media promotion to apply for places in what was dubbed "the Area Boy Project." They underwent auditions and a final selection process—hundreds, apparently, ha applied! They also differed from Orisun in the quality of their backgrour much of which sometimes made the Nigerian sixties environments of Is

Eko or Dugbe seem like boarding schools in comparison. They were young—the youngest was ten, the "granddaddy" twenty-two, with a deep baritone operatic voice—but mostly they were all still in school, yet already adult and life-stressed in various ways.

"Mamma," for instance, a battle-scarred sixteen-year-old, was living alone and taking care of her younger sister. Her father had long since abandoned the family, and later her mother had died. She took in washing and did other odd jobs to survive and ensure that her sister went to school. "Clipper"—no one appeared to be without a nickname, and I wondered if this was another survival strategy, creating a deflective personality—was a boy cadet who was clearly enamored of the glamour and discipline of the military, while "Chicken," perhaps one of the handful without a notable background of trauma, attended rehearsals under the ambiguous shadow of her stepfather. His principles were against his stepdaughter appearing onstage, but he found all the attention paid to Chicken's evident talents irresistible.

"Molewa," by contrast, had a Rastafarian father, also remarried, who proudly appeared at rehearsals, seeking every opportunity to discuss world politics with me and to appear in photographs. "Sally," fourteen, had lost an eye in mysterious circumstances. The widely accepted story was that she had been battered by a drunken father, but she persisted in her tale of a mysterious bird that had flown in through the window of her home one day and—smack into her eye! She claimed that the seemingly blind eye was not truly blind but was her eye into another world with whose denizens she could commune. For this reason she would not agree to visit an eye specialist. "Aston" had lost his brother in a shoot-out; during rehearsals, his father would also die, victim of another shoot-out. And Tanya Thomas would lose her life at fourteen, a few weeks after the close of *Beatification*. She walked out of her home one normal morning and straight into a bullet from the crossfire of a gang war....

Jamaica *was* a space of violence. I knew that already. I had received my education on that island years before, during Carifesta, the Caribbean Festival of the Arts, when, ignorant of the turf wars that were being waged between the "garrisons," two colleagues—Kole Omotoso and Abiola Irele, both university lecturers—and I had come close to a messy end with a taxi driver on a lonely road. Now I was thrust amid the products of those hard beginnings, amid ouths who had been forbidden to cross the lines of close neighborhood. emy lines were clearly demarcated. Touching in their idealism and inno- e, plaintive yet messianic were the voices of our young recruits:

My dream is to see the world come together and live as one in peace and love and stop the killing.

I have learnt that you cannot categorize everyone as the same, each person has their own feelings, you need to know how to deal differently with each person.

If we don't pull the "turfs" together, Kingston is not going to survive.

I believe that we as young people can make a difference in the community.

Those were the voices of the garrison children, seeking liberation into a world of creativity and fulfillment, into which they also sought to liberate their community. At least half of them had emerged from broken homes. Most had known violence firsthand or indirectly, in one form or another. In the worst of the "war zones"—as they are actually described!—residents often slept beneath, not on, their beds, for fear of being killed before morning by stray bullets crashing through their thin walls at night. "Theater" was a strange concept to many. They had grown up learning to know their own turfs and accepting that it was dangerous to stray across certain streets or cross borderlines.

It was the politicians who created these garrisons. In order to guarantee and seal tight their political fiefdoms, they built schools in them, clinics and recreation centers of sorts, and created jobs—usually in construction--for their supporters and their dependents, some of whom doubled the job of foreman or supervisor with the more powerful position of being or serving the "dons" of the garrisons, controlling lives from infancy to death, which for many was sudden and violent. The marijuana trade sustained many; so did trafficking in harder drugs.

The garrisons, polarized in deadly destructiveness, went by exotic names: Tel Aviv, Barbican, Tivoli Gardens, Trenchtown, and the like. A full generation had been raised, gone to school, married, raised their own families, and sometimes died without stepping across the street that separated them from the next garrison. Even schooling was uneven, since sometimes the "wars" prevented pupils from emerging from their homes for long periods at a time. During our rehearsals, it was not unusual to receive frantic messages for help that had somehow been smuggled out from a youth—a stripling of upward of eighteen years—who had been locked up by his mother to prevent him from leaving home for fear of his getting killed. She would mount guard over the door and swear that he would leave home only over her dead body. Public transportation traversed these streets, moving through one garrison into the next, but you simply did not get down from the bus until you were safely in your own neighborhood.

I was pursued, I sometimes felt, by the violence from which I had sought to escape, if only for a while. I had an early taste of it one afternoon when I toured the garrisons to obtain a flavor of this Lagos live-alike, stopping in a bar from time to time for a beer and conversation. I was accompanied—a condition to which I was learning to adjust—by an assigned security officer in mufti, mostly to validate my presence in suspicious neighborhoods. Less than two hours after we left Trenchtown, a shoot-out occurred right outside the bar where we had sat. The female bartender, a buxom wit of immense vitality with whom we had passed an enjoyable half hour or so, caught a stray bullet and was killed. For some moments, I wondered, could Abacha's roving squads have successfully tracked me down, hit the right place, but mistimed their operation? But no, it was nothing more than the daily dose of local garrison violence.

That violence constantly intruded, but violence had become part of residents' lives. After each rehearsal, it was a quasi-military operation to ensure that these youthful enthusiasts got home safely, and there were times when the police came to rehearsals or radioed my minder to pass on a message: either we let the kids return home early on account of information of an impending gang war, or else the gang war would commence and we should keep the affected members with us for the night. Every constraint only made them more resolved to break free, and this theater activity was their personal and collective instrument.

It was thus the Orisun experience raised several levels, an intense, life-and-death Kingstonian strain. Brief, occasional theater sketches outside rehearsals for *Beatification* served as outlets for long-repressed experiences and emotions. Gradually, tentatively, they moved toward the creation of their own ensemble within the production company. Stringing together their sketches with songs, they designed their own very special show, all boundless energy and exuberance. For their first outing as an independent ensemble, they settled, poignantly, on the title *Border Connections*—most of them were crossing borders for the first time in their lives. Creative borders, obviously, but also violent, artificial borders that had been deliberately erected by the absentee political kingpins. Their obsessive theme was thus political manipulation, the exploitation and division of their communities. They decried the violence that ruled and ruined their lives and depicted the agonies of mothers constantly obliged to bury their children. The titles of the sketches reflected a touching crusading zeal: "Youth Oppressed," "Mi Son Dead," "Mi Hungry, Mi Angry," "Isn't There Another Way? Put Down de Gun!" They were apostles of change and hope.

It seemed a forlorn cry, doomed from its very utterance, but, incredibly, the "dons" who had heard of the show and watched it on television or on other neutral ground embraced it as a revelation. They negotiated "command performances" on their turfs, over which they proudly presided and played host. These were men who would end a twenty-year friendship in a burst of gunfire for no other cause than a suspicion that one had been "dissed"— disrespected—by a lifelong friend. Rape was a way of life for most. Beneath the bravado of the warlords, however, was an infinite war-weariness, for which the message of the youths offered prospects of eventual relief and a change in social sensibilities. The proof was not long in coming: the "dons" passed the word among rival gangs that it was time for a cessation of random violence! Was flirtatious eighteen-year-old Patrine being proved right? In her mission statement, the formal declaration that each participant made of his or her assessment of the Area Youth program, as it was renamed, she declared, "The youth have displayed the power to change and the will to conquer and eradicate violence from our society." The dons appeared to have subscribed to that. They sent out the word: *Bring out the guns, or bury them.*

Of course it was by no means over. The emergence of a band of evangelists does not transform any community overnight, not where there are those who feel threatened, who see their domination of society through the tactics of fractionalization being eroded by a youthful gospel of oneness. A performance of *Border Connections* on November 23, 2000, in one of the inner-city community centers, had to be canceled owing to what was publicly acknowledged as "war in the community," and the waste of young Tanya Thomas at the unfulfilled age of fourteen remained a harrowing reminder of the enormity of their task. However, the Area Youths operated on a different kind of battlefront, where the conquering band remained undeterred. "What we captured," proclaimed Theresa Whyte, one of the older members of the group, "was something we can't let go. We'll never let it go."

They did not. What started out as a movement of youthful idealism became the Area Youth Foundation, touring to worldwide acclaim. I receive the occasional postcard, e-mail, even newsletter.

BEATIFICATION WAS, BY no means, an easy exercise. Undertaken as a collaboration with Sheila Graham's quaintly named "The Company" by the University of the West Indies and Emory University, Atlanta, where I was teaching at the time, it was supposed to mark the beginning of a special relationship between the two universities. That sisterly bonding nearly foundered before it began. I was obliged to walk off the production once, agreeing to return only when the company had persuaded itself and its recruited members that it wanted a serious, professional production. The situation had become *impossible*! Before the show was finally over, from first casting to performance, I had rehearsed for *each* role, in a large cast, an average of two and a half actors—surely an unprecedented turnover rate in the history of most theater productions!

The Orisun experience may prepare a director for the unexpected, but it was not in the running for an entry in the *Guinness World Records* in directorial self-flagellation! I let loose on the assembled cast and production team and took off, laying out conditions for my return. We did not succeed in regrouping for another two and a half weeks. By the time I returned, however, the company had succeeded, among other creative insurmountables, in filling the role of one of the two principal characters in the play. The "professionals" also appeared to have finally imbibed the dedication of the younger, rawer elements in the troupe—*they* were the professionals, at least in commitment!

The lighting director, however, continued his existence in his accustomed, invisible, and unique time zone. I began to wonder if he was a phantom of The Company's creation, perhaps one of the famed West Indian zombies, from his capacity for sustained evaporation. He remained so despite the efforts of Rex Nettleford, the university rector, to trap him in the world of the living. Zombie or not, he barely escaped a truly terminal, irreversible death from a beckoning stage prop on the very day of the premiere! After disappearing throughout the crucial countdown days, Mr. Lighting Tech turned up only five hours before opening, blithely announcing that he had less than two hours to work under my direction, as he had yet another performance to light that same evening! Then, sticking to that time concession as if he had swallowed an alarm clock, he left the control booth, sauntered across the stage, and headed toward the exit, his tongue cheerfully tripping off the traditional theater greeting, "Break a leg." I succeeded in keeping my hands off the iron rod only by retorting "Break your neck!" but he was already halfway to his next engagement—no doubt in a rummery—and I doubt if he heard or cared.

Vinnie Murphy, from Emory Theater, had arrived that morning for the premiere with a university delegation. Like most directors who worked in conditions that approximated the norm, he was accustomed to technicals that took a steady, meticulous week. They found me in an empty theater, awaiting the levitation of the lighting director. I was still waiting there till late afternoon, occupying the time in brief spurts of activity with individual actors and other crew members. They helped me to preserve my outward calm.

The opening performance was thus, as in many such productions, a technical-cum-dress rehearsal. In addition, however, it was the first complete run-through of that play ever to take place—that is, its first uninterrupted performance in the correct order of scenes—thanks to the rotating absence of the principal actors. When Murphy returned to Atlanta, he took to regaling his students with the account of how he had actually witnessed a full-length production lit in an hour and forty-five minutes, but I doubt if any of them believed that it was anything but a ploy to work them like slaves in future Emory productions.

To watch the company leaping up and down onstage like a family of long-restrained, high-spirited monkeys the moment the curtain closed to sustained applause, *knowing*, with their newly honed theatrical sensibilities, that they had indeed brought off a singular, nearly impossible theatrical feat despite flawed moments here and there, savoring the vindication of unaccustomed days of discipline, self-privation, and creative exploration, engulfed by bodies as I emerged from backstage and they screamed the roof down, turning somersaults, breaking into spontaneous snatches from their *Border Connections*, was a most affecting moment. I rescued Chicken from her self-pitying corner—she had forgotten to make a costume change in one scene—and made her join the others. I told her, Consider this: but for the Lighting Zombie, you would have had a lighting cue. Soon she was feeling less suicidal.

They basked in the adulation of the families and friends who swarmed backstage, responded to the slightly more formal felicitations and suggestions of Rex Nettleford and his colleagues from Emory, Rudolph Byrd and Vinnie Murphy, then Sheila Graham and the city worthies. What they did not know was that—again on so many levels, since theater has no parallel in this territory of largesse (and denial!)—despite frequent bouts of despondency, theirs was easily the most valued single gift that I had received throughout the four dark years of the struggle against the tyranny of General Sani Abacha.

PART VI

Bernard Shaw Was Right!

How the News Came to Me

. . . . .

GEORGE BERNARD SHAW IS REPUTED TO HAVE SAID, "I FIND IT EASY TO FOR-give the man who invented a devilish instrument like dynamite, but how can one ever forgive the diabolical mind that invented the Nobel Prize in Literature?"

Yes, the Nobel was born of dynamite, but did that mean that it must transmit the shock waves of dynamite, and for so long afterward? It is not my business to account for how it came to take such a hold on the imagination of the world, to the extent that when I find myself in a number of countries, in Asia especially, the first question asked me is nearly always "What must we do to bring the Nobel Prize to this country?" It is a question that never ceases to astonish, even shock me—why should people worry their heads over a prize whose mode of selection they can in no way influence? Indeed, why should one *strain* for a prize? If it comes, fine; if it doesn't, what was one before the prize? Why should one notice the existence of a prize for anything?

Acknowledged competitions, I understand. At least one knows what the rules are. In my youth, I sent in my poems and short stories to the arts festivals in colonial Nigeria, won a bronze medal or two—it was always a bronze medal, for some reason—and was highly elated. My competitiveness was restricted to such adventures. It retained its keenness, perhaps, until I returned home from my studies in the United Kingdom and created my theater company. From then on I became increasingly indifferent to the very notion of competition, which can only mean that, somewhere deep down, I was persuaded that competitions in the world of creativity are meant for the young or the early adult, not for the mature, self-cognizant being. Contradicted though I am by the existence of numerous prizes of great prestige, much sought after and undoubtedly enhancements of one creative enterprise or another, I have experienced no urge to revise my visceral conviction.

The third-hardest part of the Nobel is to be found in the expectations of others—in the main. As a laureate, one is expected to be different from whatever one was before. So confident and self-fulfilling is that expectation that in some cases a difference is noticed—with marked approval or resentment—even by those who encounter a Nobelist for the first time! Others simply demand, even wordlessly, that one act differently, eat differently, talk differently, dress differently, walk differently, abandon former haunts, former preoccupations, former idiosyncrasies, and former likes and dislikes, and don, overnight, a totally fictitious persona that corresponds to their fantasies. Certain chores become too commonplace for the Nobelist, and the poor sod is faced—thank goodness!—with desertion if he fails to deliver on their expectations.

Second place, nearly in dead heat with the first, goes to the loss of the final shred of anonymity, especially hard for those who carry around with them a landmark of luxuriant moss that passes for a head of hair. This, however, can be ameliorated by a good stock of hats. Such disguises are not perfect, but at least they give one a running start. The prime place, however, belongs to one's overnight transformation—in the conception of most in one's own community—into the drinking buddy of Bill Gates.

There are compensations, however, and mine came right at the beginning. Not too many of the laureates, I am certain, could have relished coming into knowledge of their award the way it occurred in my case. Let me recall, first of all, the previous year, 1985, in which all kinds of speculators had been deservedly chastised for their premature celebrations, the Nigerian media most especially. It is a pity that no one can get a comprehensive copyright on one's own being, so that public speculations about any individual's prospects in any field become actionable infringement on one's privacy. How the rumors began, only the gods can tell, but there they were, and I at the distasteful center of it all. Confronted by confident predictions plastered all over the pages of the Nigerian newspapers, pursued by journalists in the weeks leading up to the announcement in October 1985, then pursued after the deflation of *their* prophetic presumptions, just to be asked what I felt, my answer oscillated among "Let that be a lesson to you all," "Serves you all right," "No comment," "Now can I get on with my writing?" and the like.

However, the media had learned its lesson, so in 1986 all was silent. Indeed, I did not even recall that the time of the Nobel was at hand as I took leave of Cornell University, where I was then teaching, boarded a plane, and headed for Paris to chair the executive meeting of the International Theatre Institute (ITI). I was to stay with my cousin Yemi Lijadu north of Paris, where he had an apartment. I arrived early in the morning. I hated those flights from the East Coast of America to Europe. They are what I call the overnight neither-nors— not long enough to permit a decent sleep and too long to prevent one from dozing off. My routine after such flights is to crawl into bed, close all the blinds, put on my eyeshade, and sleep for between two and three hours. As I was getting into Paris at an early hour, Yemi would normally have left the keys with a neighbor or in an agreed-upon hiding place and taken himself off to work.

This time, he was home. I found him in a state of barely suppressed excitement, his slight goatee bobbing up and down, his dark cheeks dancing with the well-being of French wines and lunches, not to mention the results of his own kitchen prowess. Before I could set down my bags, he had commenced his "dramatizer routine," one that had become second nature. If Yemi had exciting news to deliver, he would never do it straight--the more exciting, the greater the garnishing. This time he surpassed himself with so many peripherals, incidentals, and parentheses that I finally had to interrupt.

"Yemi, who is dead?"

"Dead? No! Oh no, just wait, I am trying to—"

"Yemi, what's the bad news?"

"Bad news? No, exciting news. But wait, of course you couldn't have heard..."

Finally, at some point, he ran out of delaying prefaces and side commentaries and came to the point. When he did, I sighed and shook my head. "You too! You mean you failed to learn from last year?"

He shook his head vigorously. "No, no, this time, it looks like it. Solidly. The press have been all over UNESCO."

"Yemi, I am tired. I need to sleep." And I went off to the bathroom. He followed.

"You have to start thinking what to tell them. How are you going to handle it? And there's a journalist from Stockholm who is coming here any moment."

I screamed, "You invited him here?"

That was the ultimate betrayal: Yemi, the normally protective Yemi, had allowed a journalist to invade my (his) sanctuary.

"I haven't had any rest myself since yesterday. You'll find out when you get to UNESCO."

I disappeared into the bedroom. I heard the phone ringing incessantly. I indignantly refused to take any calls and crawled into bed. Finally there was one I had to take—it was Anne-Marie, the secretary of ITI. She wanted to know when I was arriving at the meeting, because, she said, the press was going mad.

"Did you invite them?" I asked.

"No."

"Then ignore them."

"I can't do that. You're the only one who can send them away. We can't function here. They've taken over the entire frontage of rue Miollis. No one can do anything."

"Anne-Marie, I am going to sleep. And then I shall turn up for the meeting two hours late, as already agreed. Good night—or good morning, if you prefer."

"You'll have to go and face the press sooner or later," Yemi offered.

"Yemi, aren't you supposed to go to work?"

He shrugged. "All right, I'm off. But look, er . . . I promised that journalist. His newspaper sent him all the way from Stockholm, so it's a serious matter, you know. He explained to me—as soon as the decision is made, the committee starts tracking you all over the world. Please, when he comes, let him in."

"Yemi, I don't live on speculations. I came to Paris for the ITI meeting, and that's all I have on my mind."

The bell rang. "Aha, I think that's him."

"He's your guest. You do what you want with him."

I pushed deeper into the bed while his voice pursued me. "I made him promise he won't even attempt an interview. All his newspaper wants is for him to be with you when the news is made official. That's all."

Now, at this stage, surely something must have begun to give. I have gone over and over those moments, trying to discover when it was that my wall of disbelief and/or indifference began to crumble, the moment when I said to myself, Suppose it is true after all? I'm afraid I have never recovered that moment. I think the slamming of the door as Yemi let in the journalist could have been it; I cannot swear to it. I was sure of only one thing—I wanted, needed, my two-hour sleep before confronting the executive of the International Theatre Institute, where I presided over a group of genuine theater artists, researchers, and theater historians, as well as ideological apparatchiks from the Soviet bloc, for whom even administrative choices entered a party-line framework. The

Berlin Wall was not yet down. One required, ideally, a solid night's sleep before dancing on such a trampoline. Deprived of that, nothing should disturb a measly two-hour preparatory sleep, duly fortified by a double espresso. Through the sheets I heard Yemi say good-bye as he left for work, assuring me that he had extracted from the correspondent a promise that I was not to be disturbed, that he was prepared to wait, and that all he wanted was to be the first to see me after the news was formally announced.

I ignored him and pulled the blanket closer around my head, heard the door slam as Yemi left for work. About two minutes passed in the marvelous, soothing silence of his apartment, so high up that the demented traffic noise below arrived through bales of cotton fluff, and all the neighbors had gone to work. I sank effortlessly into the first stage of sleep. Any moment, and I would be wholly gone—when suddenly, there were voices in the apartment. Who else now? Who else had this sole journalist let into the apartment? Cameramen? I threw myself out of bed and marched into the living room. Well, there he was, and all alone, this Nordic figure humped over the television set and twiddling the buttons! I watched him for some time, and then he turned around and saw me.

"Oh, I am sorry if I disturbed you. You are, of course, Wole Soyinka."

I stared at him through bloodshot eyes. He continued, "Your cousin let me in. I was trying to tune into Bernard Pivot's culture program. That is where the announcement will be made."

At which point I surrendered all further thoughts of sleep. I shut the door and went into the bathroom to take a shower. It was better going to the ITI meeting than staying cooped up with this journalist.

I took my time, dressed, and got ready for UNESCO. I brewed some coffee and then, realizing I wasn't really being gracious to my cousin's guest, decided to offer him some. He accepted gratefully, and we both sat in the living room for what I expected would be only until we finished our coffee. Then I would leave him to his own devices. If he chose to follow me to UNESCO, that was his business. But he soon put paid to all that.

"Everybody is waiting for you at UNESCO," he said, as if he had read my thoughts.

"So I'm told. There must be a back way of getting in for my meeting."

He smiled. "I don't think you'll be having much of a meeting. I don't think there is much work going on at the UNESCO Annex right now. When I left, the excitement was really high."

I decided to take him on. "You know something? This nonsense happened last year also, only it happened at home, in Nigeria. The press there behaved exactly the same way as the reporters here appear to be doing. It came to nothing. I was just as far from taking them seriously then as I am now. I don't believe in speculations."

He shook his head. "Oh, I think this is more than mere speculation, Mr. Soyinka. My newspaper specially sent me to track you down and—"

"Oh yes, that's right. To do what, exactly? I warned my cousin that I am not giving any interviews."

"No, I don't want an interview. Although of course, if you do wish to say anything . . ."

"Nothing."

"That's fine, that's absolutely fine. All I need is that you allow me simply to be with you until the announcement is made. That's all. We're not asking too much."

I shrugged.

Then he saw the radio and dashed toward it. "I'd better put this on too. The radio may broadcast it before Pivot."

So the man began fiddling with the tuning knobs of the radio, seeking to lock in on the arts program. Then he would dash across the room again, tune the television set to another program, then return it to Bernard Pivot. Across the room again he dashed—always at a crouch—to try another radio channel. I saw his face becoming anxious, and quite frankly, I began to enjoy his discomfiture. There was I, a candidate for this much-envied prize, ensconced in a room with a journalist who was waiting on tenterhooks for the announcement, and all I was thinking was, Serves you right; this will teach you not to indulge in idle speculations. I think I must have a sadistic streak somewhere in me after all, because I really was enjoying the creases of anxiety that began to form on the man's face. He kept muttering to himself, "But it's eleven o'clock now, well, almost." A few minutes later: "But now it's actually past eleven. The announcement was to have been made at eleven." And he actually looked at, then shook his watch. He made the occasional check with me, as if I had agreed to be his fellow news monitor: "You didn't hear anything, did you? Do you think I missed it on the radio?"

The Norwegian, or Swede, was interrogating the radio when a man walked into Bernard Pivot's program and handed him a piece of paper. Pivot excused himself, adjusted his glasses, and read it, then faced the discussion panel while the camera focused on him. "Breaking news," as the Americans call it, and Pivot smoothed out his piece of paper and made his statement. The Swedish

Academy had announced the winner of the Nobel Prize in Literature for 1986, and the winner was—the writer from Nigeria . . . and he managed to garble my name. Across the room, the Nordic journalist continued his frantic struggle with radio static.

I suppose it is time to attend—as honestly as one can—to some personal dissection. The first admission I must make, and truthfully, is that I did not sense any quickening of my pulse. Did I know this writer? I was not sure. Was I asking, Did I hear right? No, I did not ask such a silly question. My French was sufficiently competent, the man had referred to the Nobel Prize in Literature, and he had coupled my name with it. So there it was. The trouble was that the announcement had been made in the most ordinary fashion, quite routinely, so it did not really tie in with all the excitement with which I had been confronted from the moment I had stepped into my cousin's apartment, beginning with his long rigmarole. Nor was it linked to the Scandinavian gentleman still fiddling with the radio controls and wearing a lengthening frown on his face.

I continued to sip my coffee and watched him return to his chair, from which he proceeded to give his undivided attention to the Bernard Pivot program. It ended some twenty minutes later, and now the man really looked defeated, totally baffled.

"But that's the end of the program," he announced piteously.

I nodded in agreement.

"But what happened? The official announcement should have been made. It was supposed to be on Pivot's program."

"Do you mean, the Nobel Prize in Literature?"

Irritated, he snapped, "Of course. At eleven o'clock."

I told him, matter-of-factly, "But it was announced."

He looked thunderstruck, and I saw immediately what was going on in his mind: he had been chasing the wrong quarry. But I wasn't being mischievous in prolonging his agony. I think that, in taking my time, I was also passing the news to myself. I did not feel I owed the intruder any special treatment, so there was no reason why we should not both learn of it at the same time, my absorption rate having been slowed down, probably, by the transatlantic flight.

"Well, well, what . . . ? Who? Tell me."

I shrugged, I think. "You were right. It was me."

Now he really was staring wide-eyed. "You? But when? What happened?"

"You were fiddling with the radio. Someone walked up to Pivot and handed him a piece of paper. He looked at it, and he made the announcement."

"It was you? Well? Well?" Now his voice was accusing. "But why didn't you call me? That's what I was waiting for."

I was not sure how to answer him, how to explain it, so I simply reminded him, "You didn't ask me to." I picked up the coffee cups and took them to the kitchen.

"But you are saying nothing," the man protested, following me. "What are your reactions? What do you feel?"

Did he expect me to fall down in a faint? Or burst into a Yoruba ululation? I did not understand the man's question. Just what did he want? What was the idea behind coming to trap me in my cousin's apartment—so he could report on my reactions? It seemed to me that the world—or his section of the world—was quite mad. Immediately, of course, the phone had to ring, and it was Anne-Marie on the line. "You have to come here at once. You simply have to come. Nobody can move or get past the press corps. This place is a madhouse."

"I did not invite them. Get whoever invited them to get rid of them."

"You're not being reasonable. Please try and be reasonable. They know already you're in Paris. There is no way they'll leave here unless you come."

"I am not coming," I insisted, and I meant it. Suddenly, all I wanted was the accustomed peace and quiet of my cousin's apartment, or something better. My next course of action, I felt, what I really wanted for myself, was to throw out the journalist and resume my interrupted sleep. I shook my head ruefully as I rinsed the coffee cups, realizing it was too late for that prospect, what with the lethal stuff I had just swallowed.

"Well," snapped Anne-Marie, "don't complain if they invade your hiding place."

I hadn't thought of that, but Yemi evidently had, because a few moments later, he was charging into the apartment, ready to drag me to UNESCO, with the aid of the French gendarmes if necessary. I decided to go quietly. I saw the face of the journalist, intently reading my own, looking for what, exactly, I still had no idea. He followed us to UNESCO and disappeared among the crowd.

As Yemi drove toward the frontage of No. 1, rue Miollis, I regretted my decision. I suddenly realized that there was an option available, one that I should have taken, and that was—to head in the opposite direction, toward Charles de Gaulle airport, and disappear from sight. But then I would have needed the cooperation of my cousin. For what struck me was that there were no more microphones, no more cameras, no more tripods, flashbulbs, or notepads left anywhere in the world. All had been miraculously and aggressively assembled at No. 1, rue Miollis. I was attacked—there is no other way of describing it—by a bristling, rearing, snarling pack of hunting hounds straining at the leash, blotting out the world of reality. For the first time, I understood how the metaphor "newshound" came about. I tried to duck back into the car, but Yemi, abandoning all cousinly responsibilities, had pulled away, leaving me at the mercy of the rampaging horde. Questions ripped through the air like tracer bullets. I mumbled inaudibly, mostly to myself, asking where I had thought I was heading when I first set pen to paper, then found that someone had managed to take charge and was imposing some kind of order, so that I could at last make sense of a few questions and provide some coherent but uninspiring answers. I was then dragged through the melee and hustled into the office where the ITI executive meeting had assembled. A bottle of champagne appeared miraculously, and now I was feeling safe among my ITI colleagues; never before had I appreciated what a lovable, harmonious family this was, until I had run the gauntlet of the press.

The press would not leave so soon, and we decided to adjourn an impossible meeting. Already I had made up my mind: I would have to escape from UNESCO, then flee Paris on the next available flight, whenever that was. I never wanted to see a news camera, flashbulb, or microphone again for as long as I lived. All I could think of was the 2.6 hectares of bushland that I had acquired and on which I had already laid the foundations of a modest cottage. The vista that opened up before my eyes was W.S. thrashing through the dense forest to that patch of absolute tranquillity, forsaking the world forever. I had not taken the full measure of what I had gotten myself into, but if it was anything like what confronted me at the UNESCO Annex, beginning with what should have been a routine arrival in my cousin's apartment, I wanted no part of it. "Abeokuta, here I come" was all I could think as I gulped down the champagne, looked around the conference room at the faces of my colleagues, and apologized silently for the abandonment that was coming to them, if only they knew it. I had made up my mind to retire from the world, simply—disappear!

T̸horns in the Crown

. . . . .

AND THEN CALAMITY STRUCK, AND FROM A TOTALLY UNEXPECTED DIREC-
tion. I arrived in Nigeria on October 14, to what came close to being a national
mood of euphoria, formally abetted by the wily IBB, who sent his minister of
culture, Tony Momoh, to spring an ambush as I arrived at the airport. Accompanied by carefully selected colleagues, among them J. P. Clark, Tony Momoh
brought with him a letter that conferred me with national honors. It was a carefully executed fait accompli, but one that was not especially difficult for me to
accommodate. By October 1986, Babangida had been in office for two years,
and at that time—a fact that many Nigerians find most convenient to forget—
could lay claim to the approval of much of the nation, in whose mind the terror
reign of Buhari and Idiagbon was still fresh.

That Nobel-induced festive mood came to an abrupt—and bloody—ending.
It had not lasted even a week when the nation was plunged into mourning, relieved only by a surge of outrage. An unprecedented event had taken place in
Nigeria: assassination by a letter bomb. The victim was an investigative journalist whose biting columns had disturbed the peace of many complacent
crooks in government.

Dele Giwa was breakfasting in his study with a London-based colleague,
Kayode Soyinka—no relation—when he opened a parcel that had just been delivered to him by a motorcycle courier. He took the full brunt of the explosion
on his lap. His guest was blown across the room, with permanent damage to
his eardrums. Nothing remained of Dele's thighs and legs but pulp.

Only a few weeks before, Dele Giwa, a copublisher and editor of *Newswatch*, Nigeria's earliest version of newsmagazines in the format of *Time* and
Newsweek, had been summoned by Babangida's head of national security,

Colonel Halilu Akilu, where he had undergone an encounter that had shaken him to his heels. He later confided in his solicitor, Gani Fawehinmi, that he feared for his life, and additionally he raised a public outcry. Dele Giwa claimed that Akilu had accused him of gunrunning, or of possessing knowledge of gunrunners and dissident groups who wanted to overthrow or destabilize Babangida's government. The charges were so preposterous that Dele Giwa had only one conjecture: this was a red herring, designed to prepare the ground for his already decided elimination.

A few days after his public outcry, Halilu Akilu telephoned to assure him that all was well, that the charges had been thoroughly investigated and there was nothing to worry about. To reassure him even further, Akilu informed Dele that President Babangida wished to speak to him to allay his fears. Later still, the security chief again telephoned Dele Giwa to ask him for directions to his house, informing him that Babangida wished to send him some documents. This was the background to the well-publicized remark that Dele Giwa made on receiving the package. As he proceeded to open it, he observed to his guest, Kayode Soyinka, "This must be from the president."

Immediately after, the murderous explosion.

I saw Dele Giwa on the very night of my arrival in Lagos. After the impromptu official reception at the airport, I fled to the home of my junior sister Yeside, in Suru-lere, a partially developed part of the suburb and thus reasonably quiet, where I had decided to spend the night. Fooled again! A handful of friends knew that I sometimes stayed with her and were lying in wait: Deji Akintilo, the budding entrepreneur; Yemi Ogunbiyi, an editor at *The Guardian;* Vera Ifudu, the broadcaster; Sunmi Smart-Cole, the photographer; and a handful of others. The determined celebrants were committed to making an evening, even a night of it. Vera Ifudu and Deji Akintilo lived only a few blocks from Yeside's, and, after a brief tussle, we moved to Ifudu's place.

It was about an hour before midnight when Dele arrived, casual but rumpled in a loose shirt and equally loose Bermuda shorts, looking like an American on vacation. In his hand was a bottle of his favorite XO cognac. He had already gone to bed when someone—Yemi Ogunbiyi, undoubtedly—had called and broken the news to him, informing him also that an impromptu party had commenced at Vera Ifudu's. Dele had promptly shaken himself out of bed, grabbed a bottle he had earmarked for some other event, and driven to join the group. He left, like most of the others, in the early hours of the morning, by which time I had long since retired.

Dawn found me on my way to Abeokuta, the only place from which I could mount effective defenses against any further encroachment. I needed time to sort out my thoughts, the enormity of the award having finally begun to percolate through to my mind. The media assault in Paris had merely impressed on me the monstrosity of the event; it was the palpable fervor with which my own nation had embraced the award that finally imbued it with exceptional value. I could not believe that even total strangers whom I had encountered as I left the airport, and since, had taken it so *personally*, that they saw in the award something that was individually and collectively theirs. It was not possible to underestimate the sense of triumph, of vindication, that rode on their responses— a disposition, if they could, to slaughter all the goats, cows, and chickens and milk all the palm trees within reach, in celebration. I realized now that I had to do some stock taking, and start studying how to cope with this avalanche of attention.

It was in Abeokuta that the news about Dele slammed into my mundane planning through the telephone. Given the background to the murder, one thought flashed instantly through my mind—the national award! I could not accept anything at the hands of the government. Not unless it could demonstrate, quite openly, that its hands were clean of the murder.

The following day, I called my friend Oje Aboyade, Babangida's righthand man. Your boss's hands are covered in blood, I told him. I cannot accept any honors from those hands. Neither will I accept any government representation at the Stockholm ceremony. The appointment agreed upon earlier with Aboyade over the telephone—to meet the dictator and discuss the modalities for a special ceremony for the national award—should be regarded as canceled.

Aboyade fell in with my position. We agreed to meet a few days later to discuss it, perhaps to agree on the wording of my letter of rejection, about which Oje was apprehensive—quite unnecessarily, in fact. Sending out a downright accusing or abrasive letter without any hard basis in fact, despite plausible deductions, was not an option.

First, a visit to the bereaved family, then prolonged discussions with his immediate associates, friends, and other journalists and a calm review of details of the events that preceded and surrounded the murder, and I felt ready to embark on my own plans for looking into the case. At the heart of those, as usual, was the Pyrates Confraternity, with its information network. We were, still are, *everywhere*—within the army, the police, Customs, the SSS, the media, and so on. Every member was a schoolmate of, married or related to, or professionally or otherwise connected with some listening source. I was not particularly close to the murdered man but, like many, had long admired his investigative verve and identified with his political attitudes, which were progressive and fearless.

Some, it was true, and in quite respectable quarters, considered his relationship with the government rather ambiguous—for no discernible reason. Some of his own close associates, even within *Newswatch,* were not long in beginning to rationalize his murder. One, and a close friend of his to boot, accused him of having been caught in a web of his own spinning, trapped in some power play in Babangida's court. There were even insinuations, including from his own colleagues in the media, that Dele had been silenced because he had uncovered some hard facts about drug dealing in high places and had been blackmailing the racketeers. Nigeria, alas, is the original rumor mill of the world, and the more untoward the event, the more creative and bizarre are the theories and concoctions that are bruited about as fact! Rumors, however, can provide useful leads, though not in the direction that the rumor purveyors intend, and this was where a loose network of information gatherers could best pursue the most disconnected clues. Nothing justified such a callous murder, nor the manner of his death, which could have equally eliminated any in his household: wife, children, relatives, visitors. At my urging, the Pyrates Confraternity posted a financial reward in the media—in hard currency—for any useful information.

Now I could concentrate on the president of the nation, who had been mentioned by the slain man as the supposed author of the deadly parcel. After hours of debate among Oje Aboyade, Yemi Ogunbiyi, and myself, we agreed that I would go ahead and keep the appointment as if nothing had happened to affect the agenda. It would then be my turn to spring an ambush—because Oje gave his word not to warn Babangida in advance that I now had negative thoughts about the national conferment. I would simply arrive with a formal letter, then set out my conditions for reinstating the honors.

"You can say what you like to him," Oje reiterated. "I'll back you up. The nation needs to get to the bottom of the crime, and if I find the situation untenable, I shall also hand in my resignation."

We met in IBB's office, the dictator all set to finalize the details of the participation of the Nigerian government in the Swedish event. Oje also came along, as did Yemi Ogunbiyi. No sooner were the courtesies over and we were seated in front of the vast presidential desk than he brought out a slim file from a drawer and carefully opened it, began to turn over some papers. It was Oje who stopped him.

"Mr. President, I think we've run into a snag. Maybe it would be better if you heard it directly from the horse's mouth."

Still unsuspecting, Babangida turned to me. "Oh, Professor, I am sure we can sort out whatever difficulties there are. Is the Stockholm date clashing with ours?"

I studied him very carefully, eyes glued to every gesture and motion of his hands and face. This was perhaps the most absurd test I have ever set myself: attempting to decide, within those first seconds, whether I was seated before an unconscionable killer or simply an innocent drawn into some fatal survival struggle that had been engineered by his subordinates. This was a soldier to whom killing was no stranger, a schemer who had had a hand in several coups d'état. I knew all about the rumors that surrounded him. Even his coup against Muhammadu Buhari has been strongly rumored to have been a preemptive coup for his own survival in the military, based on the assumption that Buhari was about to move against him and push him out of the army.

Among the rumors that were floating around the murder mystery was that the dead man had been investigating the mysterious death of one Gloria Okon, caught red-handed with hard drugs and said to be a "mule" of one of Ibrahim Babangida's close relatives. Had her death under arrest and hospitalization been "natural"? Was she dead at all? Had she been spirited abroad, another corpse interred, and a coroner's report fabricated? Dele Giwa was credited with having penetrated the seamy intrigues and then become ensnared within them—the Nigerian rumor mill is fecund, each story spun for a purpose that might divert attention away from, neutralize, or anticipate the rumors of others.

"Yes, Professor? Is there anything we can do from here to sort out the problem?"

I kept my eyes on him, my voice dispassionate (I hoped) as I said, "I'm afraid things have gone beyond any solution. Dele Giwa's death has put a stop to everything. I cannot see myself accepting these national honors. In fact, I don't think I can accept government participation in the Stockholm event. I would prefer that the government stayed out of it entirely."

A chill descended on the room, and a silence that held for ages. I only felt, not recognized, the presence of the other two. At that moment, it seemed that Babangida and I were the only beings in the soundproofed chamber. What I read in Babangida's face went beyond ceremonies and national honors. It was this: the dictator felt that he was about to be confronted with a new enemy where he had been led to believe that he might cultivate a potential ally. His initial expansive, amiable confidence had vanished. So be it, I thought to myself. I watched him slowly close the file, then slide it, almost imperceptibly, into the drawer. Then he asked, "Do you believe I, or the government, had a hand in Dele's death?"

"I have no idea. But I am amazed that up till now, your government has failed to set up a judicial inquiry into the bizarre murder."

Slowly, he slid shut the drawer, taking time to regain his composure. "Professor, I give you my word of honor," he began, very calmly, "I have never indulged in or encouraged any act of murder in my entire career. I am a soldier, and I've taken part in coups, but I do not plan murders. If I decided that Dele Giwa needed to be eliminated, I would put on my uniform, put a gun in my holster, drive up to his house, enter, and shoot him. But I would not for one moment engage in a sneak killing. I give you my word."

I scanned his face. Truthful? Or a suave, practiced actor? It was, we both knew, a decisive moment. Oje said nothing. Neither did Yemi. They left us alone, watchful.

"In that case," I said, finally, "do you agree to set up an independent judicial commission of inquiry? Transparently independent?"

"Of course," he said without hesitation. "In fact, it is something we're discussing right now. We've nearly finalized the composition, and I'll be giving them a time limit within which they must make a report. I want this matter cleared up as much as you, maybe even more. And we'll put someone in charge in whom the nation will have full confidence, I promise you that. Within the next month, the commission will begin sitting."

No, I did not thereby believe in Babangida's guilt or innocence. I suspended belief one way or the other. What I did believe was that a commission would sit, and in public. And I was confident that the offer of a reward from our side—hopefully augmented from other sources, his own journal, for instance—would loosen a tongue or two, however indirectly. It is never easy to keep secrets in Nigeria; it is just that secrets, when divulged, are tied up in many distractions. But hardly any crime has been committed in the nation whose perpetrators are not known to at least twenty other people. It was all a question of finding which one of them would speak under inducement, with guaranteed protection, or as a result of a falling-out among the conspirators. A judicial commission, sitting in public, would serve as our starting point.

. . .

THE INVESTITURE WAS a near disaster. I went to the wrong venue, itself a give-away about my enthusiasm and concentration on or attention to details. I had not studied the invitation card particularly well, and so when my brother stopped to see me the night before, I readily bought into his thinking that the venue would not be Lagos State House, as I thought, but Dodan Barracks, the seat of government. Lateness is a self-indulgent habit that I deplore, and I had positioned myself to take care of all traffic hazards and arrive at the venue at least fifteen minutes beforehand.

My consternation is best left to the imagination when, as I turned into the final avenue that led directly into the gates of Dodan Barracks, I encountered a motorcade belting out of the government seat with outriders and sirens blaring. It could only have been Babangida, but I checked with the driver anyway—had he seen and recognized the occupant of the protected vehicle? Well, he had not seen the face, but that was the usual security detail of Ibrahim Babangida. Even then, so thoroughly had I ingested the last information—my brother's choice of venue!—that it never crossed my mind that I could have been right all along. Otherwise, I would have ordered the driver to spin around and tail the convoy. I persuaded myself that maybe it was Augustus Aikhomu, Babangida's deputy, off to represent his boss at some other event, or a visiting dignitary being whisked to the airport. So we proceeded to the gate, where the expression on the face of the security official who recognized me told the entire story even before he opened his mouth—yes, that had indeed been the head of state speeding to Lagos State House to pin a medal on my chest.

We changed direction and pursued the convoy, breaking every traffic rule on the way. Of course the streets had been sealed off around the security perimeter of the State House. They were opened for the president's convoy to pass through and immediately closed off after him by trigger-ready soldiers and patrolling SSS agents with walkie-talkies and bulging armpits. All other vehicles were diverted to a different approach. I leaped out of the car and dashed up to the nearest soldier, whose face fell on seeing who it was. He found my gasped expla-nations superfluous and broke into a run. I jumped back into the car, and he led the way, screaming for the roadblocks to be moved—which was how I arrived only ten minutes late, having nonetheless broken the golden rule of protocol.

Thoroughly flustered as I was, I had time to notice, within the select crowd, even more desperately flustered faces. Among them was one that clearly scowled its displeasure, muttering something about how typical this was of W.S. It

THORNS IN THE CROWN / 321

had the predictable effect of ending my fluster abruptly, then getting me riled, angry, and aggressive. It was the wrong moment for a voice to be raised in protest at my unintended discourtesy, keeping a head of state waiting. I turned to snap back at that voice but was forcefully steered into the place of conferment. All I wanted at that moment was simply to turn around and tell them all to forget the ceremony.

When the ceremony was over, I learned that, as usual, some of the panic had been caused by the standard quota of *ab'obaku*,* who had voiced loud, indignant opinions that I had deliberately set up Babangida in order to humiliate him publicly, that I had never had the slightest intention of showing up or accepting the honors. This despite the fact that my brother Jamani patiently explained that he had himself discovered his error at the eleventh hour, that he had misled me, and that I was now busy finding my way to the State House!

No, there had never been any thought of my reneging on a clear understanding: the ceremony would go forward as planned, and the commission on Dele Giwa's death would be inaugurated. I intended to keep my side of the bargain and expected Babangida to keep his.

WEEKS PASSED. The national conferment had nearly been forgotten, yet no further word on the commission emerged from Dodan Barracks. I set up another meeting with Babangida, determined to obtain some answers. What stage had been reached? Why had the commission's composition not been announced and its terms of reference publicized? Why were no dates set yet for its commencement and its duration? Babangida again brought out his file, spread out his hands, and pleaded for a fair hearing.

"What was I supposed to do? You see it here"—he isolated a piece of paper and some news clippings—"your friend, your fellow activist, Gani Fawehinmi, has filed a criminal action in court, accusing two highly placed security agents of committing the murder—Halilu Akilu, my national security adviser, and Colonel Togun of military intelligence. Still, we went ahead with our publicized moves to set up the commission, and what does Gani do? He continues to breathe down our necks, threatens fire and brimstone in further court proceedings that would stop the commission from being sworn in and beginning its work. He claims that the matter is now sub judice in the criminal courts. Of course, it stopped us in our tracks. We have no choice but to let the criminal charges run their course."

---

* Literally, "one who dies with the king"; an unregistered power courtier.

. . .

GANI! BRILLIANT AND ERRATIC, a great humanist and compulsive loner, more than deserving of his Bruno Kreisky Award for Human Rights, yet nearly every colleague, collaborator, or beneficiary of Gani, virtually without exception, has gone through a phase of temporary derangement, wondering whether it would not be much better, for the sake of the very cause that Gani advocated, if he were to be heavily sedated, kidnapped, and hidden away, then revived and released only when the challenge had been resolved. Commissions of inquiry, even when cynically instituted, are productive exercises guaranteed to reveal much outside the official "terms of reference." In short, commissions provide the very opportunity to expose even what they attempt to conceal, thus throwing the issue back onto the court of public judgment and, sometimes, future reckoning. The one-judge commission set up to investigate the 1977 burning of Kalakuta Republic, the commune of the musician Fela Anikulapo Kuti, under Obasanjo's regime, cynical though its formal conclusions were, did succeed in removing all ambiguities in the public mind concerning the question of guilt. The role of Obasanjo's military regime was laid bare beyond all doubt, and the exercise gave birth to what became a public refrain for all suspected state crimes thereafter: "Unknown soldier."

Dele Giwa's murder predictably aroused public outrage at its most intense, a passion for truth and justice at all costs, and Gani had placed himself, as always, at the forefront. It was during this heated period that Gani encountered one of the accused, Colonel Togun, at the airport, and the defiant manner of that officer had produced the expected reaction in the volatile advocate: he not only openly accused the colonel and his superior, Halilu Akilu, of Giwa's murder, he also proceeded to seek the leave of the courts to file a private criminal suit against the two officers. Gani had set a trap for himself. His request was granted and he sued. Never averse to publicity, he also continued his campaign of open accusation in the media, naming names.

The accused's acquittal was predictable. Emboldened by the judgment, the two men sued their tormentor for defamation and won substantial damages. The immediate damage was more far-reaching, however: Babangida—willing or unwilling in the first place—could take shelter behind a threatened legal interdiction, and he did. All we had left was the assertion of his innocence and the hope of a leak from within the evident conspiracy at the very highest level of Babangida's security organization. The independent commission was stillborn. It was left to the rest of the nation to continue the search for the truth—with one hand tied behind the back and a leg amputated.

To Stockholm and Back

. . . . .

ONLY TWO YEARS BEFORE THE NOBEL, I HAD RECEIVED THE ENRICO MATtei Award for the Humanities, and the Enrico Mattei Foundation was basking in the satisfaction that it had recognized my work before the Nobel Academy did. Now, on the way to Stockholm, I received an invitation from the foundation to pass through Italy as a guest. I accepted with alacrity. I find Italy and Italians congenial in the main, and I was ready to leave Nigeria for a while, with its recent memory of the murder of a friend who had roused himself from his bed to celebrate my award.

Though I am basically irreligious—certainly in the sense of not being a worshiper at any shrine—the notion of sacrifice, or *saara*, the surrogate, is one that I share with most faiths, Christianity included. Certainly *saara* in the Yoruba traditional mode was routine even in the Christian household into which I was born. Childbirths, funerals, supplications to ward off danger whether from birthing or voyaging: from the pastor himself, the head of the Anglican church, all the way down to his catechist or lay readers, the bookseller, the organist, and the extended neighborhood of Christians, Muslims, and orisha devotees, hardly any household did not respond to such milestones or occasions with the *saara*, when food was cooked and taken around to neighbors and children were invited to the celebrant household to eat, drink, and play with the children of their hosts. To me, *saara* has always been instinct.

No, I was not in fact making *saara* for myself. I have, I like to think, a very personal, intuitive understanding with my protector demiurges. They take when they please. When I lose money or anything valuable, I tell myself that the insatiable demons have been at it again. I once lost—in 1962—my only manuscript of *The Strong Breed*, a play that dealt—interestingly—with the notion of sacrifice! Such a loss, for a writer yet pubescent in his career, was not easy to absorb. After the shock, I consoled myself by saying that the gods of creativity had really been out for their tithe. When, a year later, nearly to the day, I felt a sudden surge of total recollection, sat down, and tapped out the one-act play nonstop, I merely groused at the invisible light-fingered deity: What took you so long?

Sacrifice, preferably as a voluntary act, is part of communion. Once, every New Year, it was de rigueur that I sacrifice a ram for my family—or, to be specific, for my children. At least, it was them I thought about. *Saara* is simply a way of life. A powerful attachment to this function was thus responsible for my first act after I left for Rome, thinking of all I had done or left undone. Foremost on my mind was the large Nigerian contingent—taking up half a Boeing 707—that would be attending the ceremony. I sent a message to my sister Yeside to ensure that, before the plane took off, she would get hold of a hefty white or black ram, slaughter it, and distribute the meat to neighbors and family.

I also hold the view that there should be no beggars in society, that it is the responsibility of the state, the community, to look after its less fortunate, either create a means of livelihood for them or else house and feed them in some kind of commune, not leave them on the streets, dependent on the uncertain generosity of others. Mostly, I do not offer money to beggars. My visit to Italy—en route to Stockholm—proved to be one of those occasions when I contradicted myself yet again.

What happened was this: I found myself on the receiving end of further generosity from the Enrico Mattei Foundation, the ENI (AGIP) people. I was set up in a luxurious hotel where if I chanced to sneeze, the management came running. I was not allowed to pay for anything. I was provided with an escort who was extremely pleasant and charming but talked my head into a coma. She was entrusted with a budget for shopping—outfitting me for the cold of Stockholm. I picked a modish coat that looked as if it would withstand the promised day of the Apocalypse when Hell itself freezes over. It took me a whole half hour to decide on that coat—I who normally whisk in and out of a shop with two shirts, two undershirts, four underpants, and two pairs of trousers while the average shopper is still spinning in the revolving door. In the end I did not even buy the coat at the shop where I first saw it but only on encountering it again, after I had purchased a pair of fur-lined dress boots whose soles were guaranteed not to slip on ice. What else? The budget was not yet exhausted, so off we went again—didn't I need some handkerchiefs? Socks? A shaving set? Anything else I would like to do?

Well, it so happened that the restored Sistine Chapel was just being opened to the public, amid great controversy. Had it been aesthetically enhanced by the cleanup or banalized by the face-lift, in tonalities rendered garish and bereft of emotional appeal? The controversy had raged throughout the European artistic world. I remarked offhandedly that it would be interesting to view the frescoes I had last seen as a student. However, the queue that we drove past put paid to such thoughts. It wound itself endlessly around and around the Vatican walls, then disappeared into a sloping tunnel in a distant neighborhood. I shook my head.

The following morning, I received a call. An hour later, we were walking into the chapel through a side entrance where a curator's assistant was waiting for us. He made his apologies—the notice was short and he had earlier commitments—and left us alone. Thus began a private, exquisitely privileged viewing of the ceiling and other murals before the chapel was open to lesser mortals. If there is one aesthetic thrill over and above what is engendered in contemplating works of art, it is the internal dialogue with such works in a space of unabashed selfishness, a discovery that I made through attempts to address the strange phenomenon of millionaire collectors who pay fortunes for "hot" works of art that they cannot publicly display, share with others, or acknowledge openly as being a member of their extended family. To the questions "Why do they do it? What do they derive from it?" I came to the conclusion that the essence of art induces a certain communicant dimension that is best apprehended in a space of private solace, even when the object of contemplation is of criminal origin. It thus becomes easy to picture—and understand—these high-heist millionaires in their secret bunkers, contemplating their possessions with the morning espresso before going out into the philistine world of Mammon that, paradoxically, also provides the means to this very private, aesthetically charged space.

Not having the means to engage whatever local Mafia happened to be art-inclined in transporting the Sistine Chapel, or indeed any individual canvas or sculpture, from across the globe to Abeokuta, I luxuriated in the unanticipated viewing space of the Sistine Chapel, emptied of virtually all humanity. The only trouble was my charming escort, who would not stop talking, insisting on giving me a guided tour even though I continually reminded her that I had visited that chapel years before it was closed down for restoration. When she began to gush over what she referred to as the "contact point" of creation—the finger of God animating the prone figure of Adam or something along those lines I reached the end of my tether and was ready to explode. Fortunately for b of us, I recalled that this again was the donor deity at the game of exactions—operating through Esu, the mischievous one—taking his own share of my pleasure by inflicting such unnecessary agonies on me. It was hard though, very hard. I left the Sistine Chapel persuaded—what with my escort's Italo-American accent still rattling in my ears—that the Nobel had condemned me to a life where the savoring of unalloyed pleasure no longer existed. One way or another, I would always encounter a fly in the froth of my palm wine.

Considering the foregoing, I should seek no excuse for breaking my rules later that night. Ordering a sacrificial ram for the home front was one thing, but this other—what came next—was truly out of character. However, I appeared to have been receiving, receiving, receiving! And so, walking down the steps of the Piazza di Spagna, where Rome's beggars of every national origin congregate, suitably rid of my escort, I began to experience an unusual urge. I walked around for a while, stopped at a bar to prime myself, then left the piazza with my hands clutching fistfuls of lire but stuck firmly in my pockets. After some dithering, I turned around by a circuitous route and returned shame-facedly to another bar. I knew I needed to, was deeply impelled to, would have no peace unless I did, but was equally resolved not to submit to the unusual urge. Finally, I had had enough of my shilly-shallying. I selected a quiet Gypsy woman with an infant, one of the nonaggressive kind rather than the intrusive, even truculent breed. I am preternaturally immune to the other kind—those who thrust their stumps in your face in front of hotels or at traffic jams or bare their bodies to expose acid-eaten flesh that looks like some nightmare creation of Hammer Studios.

I emptied the lire into her hands and fled. Even so, my urge to make *saara* locally remained unassuaged. I took a few more turns around the piazza, dodging from time to time into the side streets, doused my—totally paranoid—sense of embarrassment with a shot of grappa in a bar, then surged out again. And suddenly there he was, the scruffy, bearded twentieth-century Michelangelo of indeterminate origin. I dashed across the road, transferred the other fistful of notes, the rest of my Enrico Mattei shopping budget, into his unbelieving hand, and vanished around the nearest street corner. Out of his sight, I waited a few moments, then walked back to peek around the wall. The incredulous, then rapturous expression on his face was worth the Nobel Prize a hundred times over. I was now free to proceed to the main business of the evening: seeking out a small, secluded, no-frills trattoria with an instantly recognizable ambiance of the single-minded "Eat" as in "Eatalian," far from the maddening world of tourists. I embarked on a very private celebration of my unexpected award, a simple ritual that I had imbibed from my friend Femi Johnson: I ordered a sumptuous dinner.

It was meant to be a solitary act of celebration, but in fact, I was not completely alone. I had never met any of the other Nobelists, but, going through the list of my designated classmates for that year, I had been struck most pleasantly by the name of the laureate in medicine who, to round off good auguries, was a native of the very country that was playing pre-Stockholm host to me; that name was Rita Levi-Montalcini. I ordered a bottle of Brunello di Montalcino!

STOCKHOLM. THE ELEGANT GRAND HOTEL, overlooking a canal, sleek yachts, cruise ships, and well-lit piers. My obligatory event—the acceptance speech before the academy—appeared to have gone well. The Nigerian contingent was enlivening the staid streets with colors, textures, and exotic sounds. In short, all was well with the world, and only one dread hung over my ease: Would I escape before the descent of snow?

It was the night before the award ceremony itself, virtually midnight. I had settled down to sleep and was awakened by the phone. The voice was extremely querulous.

"I wish to speak to Professor Soyinka."

"Who is this?"

"Who is this? It is a man looking for his wife everywhere. Tell Wole Soyinka to send down my wife."

"Excuse me, but who is this speaking?"

"Who? Why do you ask me who it is speaking? Who are *you*, in any case? I said I wanted to speak to Wole Soyinka. Isn't this his room?"

"I am Wole Soyinka, and this is my room. Now, who are you, and what do you want?"

"You're Wole Soyinka? You *are* Wole Soyinka? And you ask me what I want? I am telling you to send down my wife right now. Or bring her to the phone. I know she's in there with you."

The last mists of sleepiness were shredded from my eyes, leaving me not merely wide-awake but fully alert. And now the man began to unburden himself, lumbering back and forth in tones that were successively belligerent, maudlin, coarse, and deferential. "Why should you be having a party in there with other people's wives?"

"First of all, Mister Whoever-you-are, I am not having a party—"

"Don't lie to me. You are a famous man, and you shouldn't be lying. Do you think I can't hear noises in the background and music being played?"

"—secondly, I do not know your wife. And now I am going back to sleep."

And I put down the telephone, angry that the hotel staff had put a call through to my room when, as was my habit, I had instructed that all incoming calls should be blocked. The entire stay so far had been organized with impeccable efficiency, and I couldn't understand how there could have been such a serious slipup. I took the precaution of going to the doors and double-checking all the locks. It was a sumptuous, sprawling suite, with doors leading to the kitchenette, another door to the balcony. This bizarre awakening might spring further surprises.

Again the phone rang. I picked it up, and before I could even say a word, the same voice was ranting at me: "Mr. Soyinka, will you please tell your boys to give me back my wife."

My "boys!" Now, what was this new development in the mystery of the missing wife? I became rather intrigued. Numerous speculations flew through my mind. Who was this man? Could there have been a case of mistaken identity, or was it a thoroughgoing setup gone wrong?

By now it was well past one o'clock at night.

"So now it's my boys who took your wife? Listen, I'll give you one minute to make sense," I warned, "and then I shall call the police."

The words came tumbling out. "Call the police! Call Interpol if you like, and then you'll have to explain if you have been brought to Stockholm to abduct other people's wives. You all came to my nightclub. You danced with my wife, and then you took her to your hotel to continue partying. I want her back, and now you're pretending she's not there. You may think you're world famous, I don't care if the world thinks you're famous, that doesn't give you the right to go around breaking up my marriage. . . . Hey, talk to me, Mr. Famous! Answer me, will you? . . . Hello . . . hello. . . . are you there? If you think you can hang up on me . . ."

At last something rang a bell. Earlier that evening, some of the "boys" had indeed invited me to accompany them to a nightclub. They had been at the club the previous night and had been effusively welcomed by the lady proprietor. She had invited them to return the following night—indeed, to make her club their late-night haunt throughout their stay—but had also sent a special invitation to me to accompany them. She was a collector of sorts, and in addition to the nightclub, she ran an African arts gallery. Her husband was from one of the East African countries. The "boys" painted a glowing picture of the nightclub, decorated with African motifs, serving African snacks, and playing African music. I asked them to convey my regrets to the lady, however, having made the decision to avoid any potential incidents, to which even the most staid boozery is always prone. I began to picture what had happened: the "boys" must have gone there and left with the hostess to continue partying elsewhere.

As gently as I could, I tried to explain to him where he might find his wife—not at the Grand Hotel, where all the Nobelists were lodged, but at one of the other two hotels where the Nigerian contingent was staying. He repaid me with an earful.

"Oh, are you still there? Why do you continue to talk to me from upstairs? You're too big to come down and talk to me? I am standing here in this cold lobby while you're enjoying yourself in the warmth of your room. You can't do the polite thing and come down to talk to me, is that it?"

For the first time since that telephone intrusion, I had found something that interjected a light note into the proceedings. The thought of me going down to this enraged and basically incoherent stranger, already smarting from the loss of his wife's companionship, maybe with lurid thoughts in his head of a gang of randy Nigerians taking turns warming up her Swedish or whatever blood, was so idiotic that I laughed out aloud. That only sent him into a new bout of rage.

"You may laugh at me, sir. Because you're a big man and I am a nobody. But let me tell you, I have my rights. I am also a human being and won't be trampled on by you."

I cut short my merriment. "I am laughing at you because you dare take me for a moron. You actually expect me to leave the safety of my room to come and confront you, a total stranger in a strange hotel in the middle of the night? Now, listen, I am going to put down the phone, and if you dare call back again, I guarantee you'll sleep in a police cell tonight."

I put down the phone and dialed the operator. Our hosts had not even left it to us to take the initiative of instructing the operator about calls. Instead, we had been consulted about how we wanted calls and other forms of intrusion to be fielded. Any caller whose name was not on the list simply did not get through, and of course a "block" message was sacrosanct. So how...!

The operator explained that the man must have been calling from within the hotel, probably from the lobby, thus bypassing the switchboard. He could only do that if he had my room number, however, and how he had managed to obtain it was a mystery. So I asked the operator to connect me quickly to the hotel's security detail. "There's a lunatic in the hotel lobby," I informed him. "You'll find him at one of the house phones, still trying to dial my room." Moments later, the security officer phoned back. Yes, indeed, there had been a man, an African, at the phones, but he had left just a few moments before. The guard had looked outside, and he thought it was the same man he had seen getting into a car.

My official aide-de-camp from the Foreign Ministry was given the report the moment he arrived the following morning, and of course it became quite a moderate-sized scandal. The response of the Nigerian squad was to set up its own round-the-clock protection unit. During the day, they moved physically into the lobby of the Grand Hotel, and they would not depart until I was safely locked in my room. First thing in the morning, they were back.

The woman in question was interrogated. She admitted that she had in fact booked a room at the Grand Hotel before the arrival of the laureates so as to be able to hand me a present personally—a commissioned painting. So the husband was indeed right in some of his suspicions. Was it all an innocent jape? The lady had taken the trouble to book a room well in advance so as to have easy movement into and out of the hotel occupied by the laureates, never mind that she lived in the suburbs of Stockholm.

I received a note from her afterward. She was very upset that she was now obliged to move out, having earned herself a hostile interrogation by hotel security and some discreet checks by the police—all undeserved, she protested. I was bombarded by messages sent through every Nigerian she met. She even attended, quite legitimately, a party organized by our embassy; she was on the regular embassy guest list, it seemed, or at least had acquired a genuine invitation. However, by then, the "boys"—Olu Agunloye, Deji Akintilo, Yemi Ogunbiyi, and others—had formed a cordon sanitaire around me and would not let her get within spitting distance. Each time she attempted to move in my direction during the party, she was physically blocked. I was not aware of all this at the time, though I did notice some deft footwork, some strange concerted movements and signals going on around me.

Not that she gave up, so desperate was she to explain her side of the story and hand over the present. Her "husband" was not a husband as such but a business partner with whom she had once lived, but that affair was long over, even though they still maintained their business relations, including running the nightclub. She desperately wanted me to visit her gallery and wrote me a letter asking for a face-to-face meeting. I replied, thanking her for the present and her hospitality to my compatriots, sympathizing with her for her ordeal with her business partner and the police; I did not consider a meeting necessary, however, and regretted that it would not be possible.

Swiftly pushed to the forefront of my mind, from the moment the irate "husband" uttered his first accusation, was the scandal—also involving a woman—in which Martin Luther King, Jr., was very nearly embroiled in Oslo when he received the Nobel Peace Prize. The CIA was alleged to have engineered that incident.

THE NOBEL APPEARS to be a bug whose bite is craved, sometimes without any sense of discrimination or inhibition. The best-organized siege that was laid to my newly acquired sponsorship clout—as perceived by the outsider—was a whirlwind "courtship" by the wife of a former European minister who had established a quite impressive philanthropic foothold in East Africa, especially with children. Hers was a bold, direct, and quite impressive semiofficial campaign. At first, I did not know what she wanted.

I received a message that the lady had flown in by private plane the morning of the ceremony. She could be present in Stockholm only for the day, as the plane was taking her somewhere else for another engagement and she had to be back at her African station some time later. My recollections of this highpowered encounter are somewhat imprecise, as so many encounters took place at the same time. If she did indeed arrive that morning, an advance party must have preceded her, because, when I came down to the lobby, an impressive area had been devoted to literature by and about her. Coffee-table publications, expensively produced, jostled with brochures, photographic displays, citations, and a few artifacts from the regions where she had worked with children. There was a huge tome of a register for visitors to the mini-exhibition to sign, and it was not enough just to sign it. Visitors were also urged to write their impressions—in effect, testimonials to the humanitarian work being done by the lady.

The madam had an able assistant—a suave, lanky government official—whose duty appeared to be to prepare visitors in advance for the phenomenon they were about to encounter, enumerate her virtues, her selfless dedication to The Cause, and ensure—or perhaps this service was performed only for myself?—that they were not fooled by her reticent and inhibited nature. He owed it to her mission to place her achievements in perspective and lamented how the world had so far failed to appreciate them sufficiently, but was confident that I, as a discerning person, would see how this kind of work needed to be catapulted into world attention. She had met numerous African leaders; I would see the glowing testimonials they had written when we arrived at the exposition. As for her journeys by boat—her favorite mode of transportation, it seemed, and one that enabled her to penetrate the continent with tons and tons of supplies for undernourished and sick children—they were epics in themselves. First, the boats had to be cajoled from their owners or sponsors; than—I believe he explained—she sailed around the world obtaining supplies and medicines from governments, companies, and other donors. She next sailed around African ports, from which commenced yet other grueling journeys into the interior—using jeeps, camels, and any other form of transportation, breaking through into neglected areas where no one had trod before.

At some point we finally came upon the lady, waiting dutifully by her exposition. She piloted me through the eloquent photographic essays on the table: she fending off African heat in a safari outfit complete with pith helmet, with supplies in the boat, with one prime minister after another, then masses of photographs of her with African babies in her arms, crawling all over her, scrawny babies, plump babies—before and after—testimonies galore, and heavy photo publications—about Voyages I, II, and III, and now the preparations for IV. The "reticent" lady went over the ground already covered by her able spokesman, filled in gaps, presented me copies of these backbreaking tomes, then wondered how best to package the books for convenient transportation. No sooner was the thought spoken than she seized her wine-red Cartier briefcase, flung its contents on the table, then began to stuff it with books, photographs, brochures . . . and of course I was to keep this expensive designer briefcase, and, while I was at it, did I smoke? I was mumbling that I did smoke the odd cigar now and then when from nowhere an elegant Cartier lighter appeared, still in its case. And then there was a third item that was pressed into my hands, and of course I was not to worry—it would all be sent up to my room since she appreciated that I did not have much time and we should really go now and have that coffee together. It was kind of me to spare her that much time, but she just wanted to draw my attention to the children's books especially, the ones that contained the children's spontaneous songs to her, expressions of their childlike faith in her works, much more important than any tribute a head of state might pay or any state decoration she might receive. Mr. Soyinka, what you could do for this cause . . .

"Ah yes, madam, what would you like me to do?"

"I am preparing a new book, and how wonderful it would be if you could write the foreword, endorsing our efforts and—yes—wouldn't it be wonderful if you could compose a poem on this work for the children of Africa, and it would be a poem both in your own language and in English, and we would translate it into other languages? I think it is something those children would understand. Did I tell you that they call me the White African Mother? It's in one of those children's tributes. So if you wrote a poem..."

"I have to warn you, I do not find it that easy to simply sit down and scribble a poem to order. Not even the simplest-looking poem."

"Well, it needn't be a poem, Mr. Soyinka. It could be simply something from your own tribe. Are you Ibo? That would be Biafran, not so?"

"I am Yoruba."

"Aah, of course, Yoruba. I know about the Yoruba, very rich culture. So, some kind of children's Yoruba poem, which you would translate for us. Something that has to do with a mother's care for her children. The relation between mothers and their children is something that struck me so forcefully as I traveled all over the place. We are like that in my country, you know. So do you think you could do this for the cause? It would be like a kind of dedication to the work of the White African Mother...."

"White African Mother," I said. "You'd like a poem to the White African Mother?"

"Or some Yoruba saying that could be adapted, something to do with the mother. I am sure you still retain some songs, something from your own childhood."

I nodded with full comprehension. "Well, you'll have to give me some time to think about it. This hectic atmosphere does not exactly facilitate regressions into childhood, you realize."

She was fully understanding but abundantly prepared. "Actually, my aide and I were thinking about that, and we found what might be the solution. An original poem can come later if you feel like it, a traditional song or saying. But we brought along this poem, and it's already translated into English, ready to go into the new book. So what is needed is for you to translate it back into your own language, Yoruba, and then dedicate it to these children's White African Mother. Anything else you care to send later on, that will be more than kind, Mr. Soyinka. Do you think the translation is something you can do in the next few days? I have to be gone. My government was very kind to lend me a plane, but now it must take me back. But my assistant—there he is, you've met already—will be staying around with the exhibition. You can copy your translation directly into the large book I showed you, and then, with the dedication, it will appear in this new publication."

It would be easier dealing with the gentleman assistant, I decided. I stood up, feeling battered and bruised. I had actually dared to imagine that all she sought was the use of my newly augmented profile to promote her work on the continent, obtain more support from African governments especially, and call attention to the plight of the children. Well, maybe that was the ultimate goal. The enthronement of a White African Mother might just open up the sluice gates of the milk of human kindness. She kindly let me go to prepare for my morning's engagements, and I took my leave, unsure whether I should kiss her hand or give her a filial embrace. Her assistant dutifully followed with the spoils of the encounter, determined to see me to my room.

"Did she mention the other matter?" he asked.

"You have more than one project? Apart from the boat campaign?" I was most impressed. Being a White African Mother, I would have thought, was already a full-time job.

He rolled his eyes, shook his head in despair. "I say it all the time, she is a very reticent lady. Too reticent for her own good. She said nothing about the nomination?"

"Nomination? You mean as the White African Mother?"

"No, Mr. Soyinka, that is only to show how she is perceived in Africa. How she is loved and respected, like a mother. We feel that with that kind of acknowledgment, if you, Mr. Soyinka, can give support to the idea, she will definitely win the Nobel Peace Prize. I have to tell you, Mr. Soyinka, that the lady is too reticent, which is why the government gives her some staff to help her. She has been nominated before but did not win. We feel that, again next year, she has a hundred percent chance with your support. This is a work that is done in Africa, for Africans, for the African children, and you are now the African Voice. This is why we came to see you; we need your support for it to take place."

I gave myself a few seconds for the idea to sink in, then scrambled for a solution. "I'll tell you how we will proceed. Our ambassador here happens to be a woman, very cultured, very sophisticated, and most caring. I have known her for nearly twenty years. I shall speak to her. I assure you, she'll be most happy to take this on—I mean, continue where I leave off. Maybe you can leave a set of these publications with her?"

His eyes lit up. "Certainly. Certainly, Mr. Soyinka. We'll be delighted to do that."

It was a very happy man who deposited my "gifts" in a convenient spot in my room, bowed his gratitude, and took the good news back to the White African Mother. On my part, I cast my eyes in the direction of the gods of restitution in whatever corner of my suite they were chuckling and asked, "Is this a mere foretaste? Do you have more exactions riding on the Nobel?"

Three Lost Years

. . . . .

AFTER A FEW MONTHS OF RESISTANCE, I SURRENDERED. THERE WAS CLEARLY a price to be paid by Nobel Prize winners, most especially one from the African continent. No one had prepared me for it, but I soon found that I had embarked on the rites of restitution. I handed over 1987 to the implacable Swedish deity of dynamite and fulfilled my duties, swearing silently that the moment the next beauty queen was crowned had better be recognized as my hour of liberation. I had been stretched to the limit. My constituency was always wide—in the creative industry, in home politics and those of the continent, in issues of human rights —which, for me, includes the right to life, a commitment that led to my creation of a national Road Safety Corps and the unglamorous labor of hounding homicidal maniacs off the Nigerian highways and educating them the hard way.

This constituency had swollen beyond all rational projection. Still, I consoled myself, perhaps a year was not too heavy a price to pay. I found myself compelled to acknowledge that, in the Third World especially, my presence at a number of events appeared to induce so much plain, undisguised pleasure, generated such a sense of collective vindication for a variety of causes—and in the least expected places—that some of the satisfaction bounced back to me. I could even persuade myself, sometimes, that I had got the better part of the bargain. There is pleasure in giving pleasure—even as one feels that a portion of oneself is constantly shed in the effort, that one is being, literally, eaten piecemeal. No matter, one year, and that was it! The year 1987 proved indeed to be a dry year for creativity; I produced not even so much as an occasional poem that I can recall. I envisaged 1988 waiting in the wings, when the frustrated mind would slide back gradually into a creative normality.

I could not have been more mistaken; 1988 went the same way, only it was much, much worse. So did most of the following year, and then 1990 began to look like it was following the example of the others. It took a while for me to realize that my increasing unease went beyond the nonevent of *not* writing; that had never been a problem. I have never felt under a compulsion to write. If I felt noncreative, for months, for a year, I underwent no pressure, no sense of a dereliction of duty. There were always other things to do with one's time.

This time, however, I did not merely not write, I did not *wish* to write, did not wish to think creatively in any direction, to be involved in any creative project. I was indifferent to any artistic activities around me. Abroad, I rarely visited the theater. No concerts, no opera, no jazz clubs. My short list of books marked down for reading expanded beyond the normal growth rate—oh, I still browsed through the review pages of journals, I could somehow manage that, but it was more an accustomed drug on which my system had grown dependent, not an act of pleasure, curiosity, or enlightenment. I jotted down titles because I feared that the phase might pass suddenly, and I could not rely on my memory. Mostly, I simply did not care. I was overwhelmed by the futility of everything I had ever done or known in the realms of literature and the arts. Even during normal times, this was always a question I deplored, but if that intrusive brigade with the perennial "What are you working on now?" only knew what leaped to the tip of my tongue during this period, they would have recoiled at the furnace that raged within me and regretted their unintended temerity. They were not to know of course, but a huge void had settled into my life, usurping the habitat of a vital presence.

I remained in thrall to this absence, whose memory still haunts me, as it does so many others in varying degrees—from Ibadan and Lagos to London, Beirut, Cannes, Cairo, or Bergamo—a now-disembodied life force that pops up in the midst of festivities, not dampening the spirit but resurrecting bereavement, a throbbing amputation but mostly evoking the presence of an enlivening guest, bringing with his recollection a sense of wonder at the unimaginable plenitude that we had all shared in the sheer being of this individual.

WHY DID HIS FAMILY choose to abandon his body in an obscure German village called Wiesbaden? Was it envy? Hate? And why, when I finally brought him home, did they frustrate the anticipation of so many to bid him adieu, to pay simple tribute to him as friends, acquaintances, business partners, even business rivals who respected him for his remarkable enterprise and flair? Why? And then, unavoidably, my own nagging sense of guilt. Seven months of total rupture—had it been truly necessary? Really unavoidable?

I have tried to imagine my attendance at the Nobel Prize conferment without Femi, that instinctive embodiment of pleasure and celebration. It would have been such a hollow event. The Nobel was made for O. B. Johnson! He had to be there for the ceremony to have any meaning, for any rite of celebration to become a rounded experience, once one has incurred a life sentence for the crime of knowing OBJ for even one day. And so I felt profoundly grateful to the ancestors that they had intervened to ensure that I was not deprived of the attendance of one who was capable of *enjoying* and enlarging the occasion in ways I never could, right there in the flesh, absorbing the panoply of it, ingesting and exuding it through his own larger-than-life persona as a shared acquisition over which he exercised the major right of possession.

MI O R'IKU L'OJU E—no, I read no death in his eyes. Neither did any of his insurance colleagues in Cairo, where, according to reports, he performed his accustomed gastronomic feats and enlivened the gathering of brokers. We parted company in London, his plaints pursuing me into my taxi because I would not change my flight, return to Nigeria via Cairo, and share with him the excitement of his induction into the marvels of Egypt.

A week later, working in my study in Abeokuta, a car drew up. I recognized it from the window and went to open the door. It was Gboyega, Femi's personal chauffeur.

"I've been asked to come for you, sir."

"When did he return?"

"Just two days ago, sir."

"And he's been working nonstop in his office as usual, I bet."

I thought I detected a faint hesitation, but he said, "Y-yes, sir."

"Well, tell him me too, I'm still tied to my desk. When I've cleared it—maybe by the weekend—I'll see him."

His next words came out in a rush. "Please come, sir. It was Madam who sent me, not him. He's taken ill and been rushed to hospital. It is quite serious, sir."

"Femi? In hospital?"

"It happened in his office. They sent for Dr. Soyanwo. He ordered an ambulance, but it did not arrive in time, so a car took him to hospital."

I broke loose from the spell and dashed back into the house. An hour and a half later, I was by his bedside at Ibadan University Teaching Hospital. Femi had begun the fight for his life.

It was a stroke. Two seizures, it would seem. When the first had happened, Femi had thought he had merely had a fainting spell. He had come to, found himself on the floor, and somehow succeeded in pulling himself back to his desk. Then he had been stricken a second time. One of his secretaries had looked in and found him on the floor.

His wife, Folake, who now sat beside him, visibly distraught, had taken the call at home, but she was merely informed that her husband was feeling poorly and a doctor had been summoned. Next she learned that Femi had been taken to hospital. Her first thought was to send a driver to go and find "Prof," bring him over from wherever he was and whatever he was doing. Now she sat with her head bowed, wringing her hands. As soon as she saw me, she was convulsed afresh with sobs.

I sat by his bedside, looking at my friend, a drip in his arm and a tube up one nostril. His discomfort was nearly palpable; he tossed about and unconsciously tried to rip the tube from his body, so his other arm had been tied to the bed. Sometime later, Femi opened his eyes, rolled them toward me, and tried to speak. I gestured to him to be quiet—there would be time enough for that. He appeared to fall asleep again but mostly tossed around in a state of half consciousness. A doctor entered, an acquaintance. He patted me on the shoulders and tried to convey his sympathy. His examination over, I followed him outside, and we discussed Femi's condition.

Two to three hours later, I said to Folake, "You can go home now. Go and pack his things and send them over, then get some rest yourself while you can. There is nothing more you can do here." It took the doctors and me a long while to convince her to move.

FEMI'S CONDITION did not improve. The decision became unavoidable: he would have to be flown abroad for specialized treatment. Inevitably, and with a sense of belatedness, I remembered how Femi had tried to interest some doctors to start a home-based diagnostic hospital. It was an idea that had come from his annual checkup in the favorite health spot of the nation's politicians, top military, and other well-heeled members of society. Once Femi had found himself in a queue behind the then prime minister, Tafawa Balewa, ruler and ruled equalized by the bleached hospital smock that covered their otherwise naked bodies, by the urine and excrement samples and diagnostic cards that they carried as they moved from one room, cubicle, or window to the next. It was typical of Femi's creative mind to seek remedies at home: *If I must carry my own shit in my hand, why should I do it abroad rather than here?* He tried to interest a few doctors in the idea—my own brother, his namesake, among them. He asked them to prepare estimates and offered to put up the working capital. Whatever stage his efforts had reached at the time of his illness, they were clearly too late to help him. The premier teaching hospital in the nation lacked even the drugs required to stabilize his condition before he could be flown abroad.

And so—a familiar scenario for a teaching hospital—an all-out search! In all of Ibadan, the drugs could not be found. Throughout Lagos also—once the nation's capital and still its commercial center—this critical drug was equally unavailable! Finally news came that a pharmacy in a most unlikely city, Ilorin, had a small stock in store. A driver was dispatched. In anticipation, the air ambulance was alerted, perhaps even the same plane that had once flown his brother, Bolus, to Germany after a horrifying motor accident. It would take off from Germany as soon as the word was given, fully equipped for any emergency. The news grew graver by the day. A blood clot had been discovered in Femi's brain, and now we were looking at what, for us laymen, was going to be critical brain surgery. Suddenly, time was ranged against us. In the meanwhile, Femi tossed between full consciousness and partial incapacitation. He understood all that was going on around him, was lucid enough to mutter one of his favorite mantras from time to time: *"Iku lo m'eja kako."**

It was a familiar self-mocking lament for a moment of frustration, for any form of constraint—no different, for instance, from an inability to embark on or expand a business venture owing to a lack of an opening or capital. Only after the event, rewinding the reel of our last moments together in all their detail, did its prophetic pertinence strike me or anyone else. In any case, I was preoccupied with practical concerns: How quickly could I wind up my affairs, reschedule appointments, and so on and prepare to join Femi in Germany?

FEMI WAS BROUGHT out from the ambulance; his stretcher was laid on the tarmac for some fresh air, awaiting his transfer into the ambulance plane. The clearance papers for the plane's departure were being processed. I stood some distance away, to let him and his wife have a few moments alone before his departure—she had just been told that there would be no room for her in the

---

* "It was death that curled up the supple fish."

plane. My eyes swept over trees, horizon, tarmac, and parked planes, contemplated the slim craft that would bear Femi away, then came to rest on the stretcher. In obedience to some strange pull, I walked slowly back toward the couple. Femi must have heard my footsteps, because he tried to move his head and see behind him, but he only succeeded in rolling his eyes skyward, then tried to extend his scope of vision to embrace whatever it was that approached.

As I looked down on the stretcher, I received a jolt, rather like an electric shock, a crude intimation of finality. Nothing had prepared me for the plea for help that I encountered when my eyes looked into my friend's. His, glassy and mud brown, rolled upward to encounter mine, eloquent in their depth of bewilderment. *What is happening to me?* they pleaded. *Help me up out of this pit, just help me emerge from this darkness.* Femi's eyes appeared to dissolve and sink into a deep, endless tunnel, fathomless. I stood above these opaque windows and stared into their roiling recesses, encountering nothing but space, just space, infinite space into which I was violently pulled, so that I felt weightless. I came to and found that I had leaned over and encased his free hand in both of mine.

I withdrew slowly, chilled to the bone, acknowledging that he had withdrawn himself from the world, even as my hands left his. For I knew, in that moment, that I had left Femi at the very end of the tunnel, within that fathomless space, that the friend who lay on that stretcher would not return home in the form we knew—and cherished.

DESPITE THAT MOMENT, I was unprepared when the news came. I had permitted myself to banish the sad, eloquent glimpse that I had received of Femi's certain destination and restored him in my mind to his familiar surroundings. That dark presentiment, I decided, had been nothing but the product of my own fears. The doctors, the omniscient ones, had sent word back that we could banish all anxiety. From being extremely grave, there had been an upward swing in his condition, said the experts. I telephoned the hospital and received their reassurance—the pressure on his brain had eased, his condition had stabilized to such an extent that the surgeons were now prepared to operate on him. He was alert, could speak, and was fully aware of his surroundings and of the preparations for the operation. He had even shown signs of recovering his habit of self-deprecation. What stupid fears! It was in a buoyant mood that I prepared to ensure my arrival in Frankfurt in time for his operation or as soon as possible afterward, taking as much work as I could with me. Every moment I could spare would be spent with him during the period of his convalescence.

I was on my building site when the news came. The workers had left for home, and I had gone there to look at the progress they had made and, as always, marvel at my temerity in expanding the scope of the house I had planned originally—just a cottage with plenty of grounds. The Nobel Prize had, however, engendered grandiose ideas—a writers' annex, no less, to play host to three or four writers, artistes, or researchers for a few months every year. It was an ambitious concept, one that was still within my means at the time, but of course it played havoc with the original, quite modest architectural plans. Once modified, they dragged in their wake further modifications as the building progressed. Femi's words constantly rang in my ears in absent complaint: "I want to be involved in the project, you hear, make sure I am involved in it right from the beginning." The hell, I thought, you built that Golden Pillar, Broking House, from scratch, keeping me out. You'll see this only after it has been roofed and is ready for occupation!

It was typical of the irrationalities that sometimes marked our skirmishes. After all, the funds that had enabled me to make a start had come from Femi in the first place. On the advice of my bank manager, I had placed a substantial chunk of my Nobel Prize money in a fixed deposit for the first six months, where, if it conformed to habit, it was supposed to earn me some interest. I had not realized that after the expiration of the first six months this deposit would be automatically reinvested for the next six months, and so on and so on, unless I gave instructions to the contrary.

Blithely, a month or two after the first half year, I attempted to withdraw what was needed to shore up my grand project with gravel, clay blocks, cement, steel rods, and labor. Nothing doing, said the bank manager, your money will not be available till the end of the year. Femi, amazed as usual at my naiveté in money matters, immediately wrote a check for what was needed to break ground, purchase material, and rescue my building schedule.

Now I stood alone on a mound of gravel, surveying my domain wistfully, wondering how soon I might see it finally materialize into the edifice I could picture so clearly in my mind. Motunde, my young ward and grounds manager, drove up in my jeep. She had long since finished her own work and normally would have had no cause to return to the building site. I wondered what determined visitor had penetrated my rented home and sent her racing to warn me. Though she was young enough to be taken for my daughter, I would often wonder if our roles were not really reversed—she the patient, indulgent guardian and I a precocious but unpredictable ward. That was the way she had resolved to relate to me, to my frequent amusement.

I watched her take her time descending from the jeep, then walk slowly toward me. To her normal expression of ambiguous, often unsettling affection was now added the quiet but determined air of one who had come to take command of a crisis situation. This change in her bearing was familiar, and I simply waited for her to reveal the cause. When she came close, she stood still and looked at me wordlessly for some moments. Then, abruptly, she shook her head as if to rid it of some unbearable pressure and turned her gaze away, as if she wanted me to follow that gaze beyond the twilight gathering over the rim of the surrounding hills and see what I feared to know. I understood instantly. I think I let out a deep sigh, walked away from her, and stared into space.

She walked over to stand facing me, her large eyes bathing me in compassion. I asked her to leave, said that I wanted to be alone. She did not argue. I wandered off the building grounds, walking along the red laterite tracks that passed for roads. I did not feel bereaved or sad. I felt nothing but rage—rage at myself for permitting hope, even having seen what I had in the dark glassy tunnel of my friend's eyes. How could I have permitted myself to be so blinded by the pronouncements of mere doctors when I had glimpsed the truth and bidden him good-bye? For it was that moment on the tarmac that returned to rebuke me, the definitiveness of my gaze into the opaque tunnel and my encounter with the abyss of emptiness. If I had kept faith with that unambiguous intimation, I would by now have ceased grieving and could have turned my foreknowledge into a source of strength from which others, more needful, could draw solace.

INVOLVED OR NOT in the planning, designing, or laying of brick on brick, Femi was integrated into this house yet struggling to take shape. His laughter and interminable stories formed part of the foundation, echoed in advance of the raising of the walls. It was impossible not to see him striding from his bedroom—assigned to him right from the designing—to the dining room, groaning with fatigue as he took off his boots on a return from a hunt in my own locality, reminiscing on the highs and lows of the day, already looking forward to the next outing. It seemed incredible that there was nothing physical left of Femi to inhabit the grand undertaking, nothing but an elusive shadow that I vaguely grasped as an impossible absence.

It is only when a house has been lived in, when its walls have been pawed, its doorstep scraped by feet, and its humanity defined by the blend of human sweat, waste, and cooking that it may earn the right, through some accident of abandonment, to become a ghost house. Without having once leaked at the roof, however, without having squeaked at the doors, echoed with music, eaves-dropped on a domestic quarrel, or played voyeur at the rites of love, this mere statement of intent, crisscrossed only by foundation channels, pocked by excavated mounds of sand and stacked clay bricks—my home to be, my long-dreamed-of sanctuary—had suddenly become a ghost dwelling.

PART VII

Nation and Exile

$\mathcal{T}$he Road to Exile

. . . . .

I never feel I have arrived, though
I journey home. I took the road
That loses crest to questions. . . .

IBRAHIM BADAMASI BABANGIDA, THE GENIAL DICTATOR, HAD TAKEN THE nation for a long and twisted election ride that lasted nearly five years. From his first proclaimed date for handing over power to his ousting in 1993, when he "stepped aside," Babangida set up commissions for the "return to civilian rule" and took his time studying their reports. He decided on election dates, postponed them, banned and unbanned politicians at will, detained some and released them, set down rules and impossible conditions for the registration of parties, set the same rules aside, promulgated two ideologies—*a little to the left and a little to the right*—created two political parties that would supposedly reflect both, wrote the party constitutions, built two identical headquarters in the capital of each state of the federation, subsidized individual contenders simply to engender false hopes, changed the balloting system, the registration system, the primary system, and so on, then began all over again. Finally, in May 1993, bowing to pressure from the international community, the dictator permitted the elections to take place.

The voting was completed, with more than two-thirds of the results released into the public domain by the Electoral Commission and showing a clear indication that Bashorun Abiola was headed for a victory, when Babangida annulled the entire process. His response to the avalanche of cautionary articles, satirical cartoons, public rumblings, threats, reasoned advice even from within the military, and passionate denunciations that inundated private and public spaces and the media was to remain holed up in his fortress, silent. By now I had given up all hope of reformation of a fumbling yet manipulative mind. I resisted all appeals to resort to the telephone, call the dictator, and remonstrate with him. Indeed, I contributed only one published tract—"There Is Life After Power, IBB"—and that only after much persuasion from multiple directions, including within the military. Not for the first time, I felt that words had reached the limit of their effectiveness. In the adage of the Yoruba, the dog that is fated to lose its way in the bush will remain deaf to the hunter's whistle.

It was the final insult, a contemptuous thwarting of the popular will. There was a lull, a period of utter disbelief; then civic movements commenced plans for contesting such brazen arrogance. I had traveled to Europe to wind up overseas commitments in readiness for what promised to be a protracted struggle when, on June 26, 1993, the people took to the streets. A graduated strategy of protests and street demonstrations was swept aside by public impatience—or even, possibly, by the regime's agents provocateurs, the government's massive countermeasures being already primed for preemptive action. I had been part of the planning, so I really did not have much of a choice—I prepared to return to Nigeria. It turned out to be the kind of a journey that, in calmer moments after the event, I would come to regard as a mirror reflection of the nation's journey toward democracy—every bit as laborious, twisted, and unpredictable, an obstacle race devised and overseen by the wily manipulator to whom Nigerians had given the name "Maradona."

I was frankly annoyed that yet another crisis was devouring my life, making me shortchange other constituencies—principally the creative. Once again, a part of myself was being placed on hold, and it was clear that this was going to be a long hold. I wound up my affairs as fast as I could, then braced myself for yet another period of turmoil.

The main uprising was in Lagos. Lagos has always tended to be volatile, and, additionally, Lagos was the base of the dispossessed president, even though he was an indigene of Abeokuta. On the morning of June 27, I was at Charles de Gaulle airport, ready to board my plane. So were dozens of other passengers bound for Nigeria. Then came the announcement that all passengers dread—at least those who have anxious ones awaiting their arrival or business to attend to at the end of the flight, or who simply want to get home, shake the dust of alien lands off their feet, and sleep in long-abandoned beds. No, the flight was not postponed, delayed, or canceled. It simply was not going to touch down in Lagos. Owing to unrest in Nigeria, and in Lagos especially, the airline had been advised not to fly into Lagos. It would go only as far as

Cotonou. Dissatisfied, I spoke directly to a flight officer. The report that his airline had received was that rioters had taken over Lagos, traffic was halted everywhere, and the entire city was paralyzed. Fatalities had occurred in double digits. There was mention of a curfew.

There was an ominous incident at the French airport that morning, and perhaps it played a role in the airline's decision not to land in Lagos—unlike others flying from other European airports. At the beginning, it did look as if it were simply another false alarm—an absentminded passenger had left a shopping bag on a bench, and the area was cordoned off. The French SWAT machinery went into action, and eventually the package was blown up in a mild, controlled explosion. It was sufficiently near our departure gate for my curiosity to be aroused, so I spoke to one of the police officers who had been left behind to guard the debris. The bag, it turned out, had contained a small radio. After poking through it, the bomb squad had determined that the radio was packed with some timers, detonators, and other bomb-related materials, though it contained no real explosives. The owner of the bag could not be traced, but everything pointed to him or her as being one of the Lagos-bound passengers. It was not a comfortable prelude to returning home. I could not help surmising that the owner had panicked for some reason—perhaps at the sight of an approaching officer—and decided to abandon the compromising baggage. Was this linked in some way to the confrontation that was building up in the nation over the aborted elections?

Knowing the volatility of Lagosians especially, a delay of even a day or two might mean that it would become impossible to enter Lagos at all. It was not a pleasant prospect, having to wait out the protests in Europe. How would I explain it to others? How would I explain it even to myself, who, after all, bore the responsibility for traveling out just before the planned eruptions? The airline staff proposed that the next day's flight might be able to enter Lagos and offered to put the passengers up for the night. That was not only dangerously late for me, but there was no guarantee that the next flight would not undergo the same fate. There was only one solution—to fly into neighboring Cotonou with Air France, then travel overland to Lagos the following morning, by taxi if necessary. I had friends in Cotonou from whom I might be able to borrow a car and a driver. I would play it by ear. This was one instance when I definitely lacked prescience, but my passage into exile was about to begin—only I was journeying in the wrong direction.

Paulin Houtounji was minister of culture in the Republic of Benin at the time; he was a feisty academic philosopher with a small, compact frame, now tending toward a slightly comic rotundity, who never allowed his stammering impediment to prevent him from saying whatever he had in his head. On arrival, I decided, I would check in to a hotel, then contact him. Air France may have exaggerated the Lagos situation—other flights did land without any problem in Lagos, we found out later—but then, many passengers also found themselves compelled to pass the night at the airport and all of the following day, and the next, as the streets were impassable. Still, if I wanted any confirmation about the grimness of the situation in Lagos, Paulin soon settled that for me when I appeared in his office the following morning. He snorted his disbelief, struggled with his stammering for even longer than usual, then exploded.

Lagos? He declared to everyone within earshot that I was mad. He had no problem providing a car to take me to the border at Seme, but after that, I would be on my own. Both his car and driver, as well as his secretary, were at my disposal for as long as I needed them, but I would discover, he assured me, that Seme was as far as either could go, no matter how willing they were. No vehicles had been able to cross the border for the past thirty-six hours. Official diplomatic vehicles, commercial transport, whatever—everything was being turned back. Paulin insisted that his secretary accompany me in the hope that, along the way, she might talk some sense into me and bring me back in time for a reunion lunch in the sane environment of Cotonou.

I must confess here to an irrational presumption of my ability to penetrate any space, however hostile. It has to do, I suspect, with a deeply lodged rejection of restriction of my movements, be it on the authority of the state, of an individual or circumstance, or of some material impediment directed at me, personally or generally. Perhaps it is not so much irrational as it is nonrational; that is, I tend not to subject such challenges to the process of reasoning. If the space is obviously unbreachable, then, of course, it simply never occurs to me to want to go there. It poses no challenge whatsoever since it has placed itself beyond my human interest. Need also has something to do with it: Do I *need* to go from Apanla to Oponlo? I do? Good! I need, therefore I shall. Obstacles are supposed to disappear, simply because *oga** needs to go. It is one of the mysteries of my existence—looking back, that is, oh yes, only on looking back after the event, after several such instances. Only then does it strike me that I have conducted myself in a nonrational manner. At the time, however, the situation is outside the province of reasoning. *Have need, will travel.* End of doubts and beginning of motion.

---

*. Boss; master.

. . .

THE APPROACH TO the Nigeria-Cotonou border told the story at first glance. For miles we cruised past a long line of vehicles parked along the road right up to the border, unable or unwilling to cross. On the Benin side of the border, a few quickly conducted interviews with motorists painted an even bleaker picture.

I crossed over to the Nigerian side of the immigration post. There I met those who had earlier risked penetrating the Nigerian space beyond the safety of the border post. They returned within an hour of their venture either with damaged vehicles or with depleted pockets, having been forced to pay a toll for getting even as far as the first roadblock mounted by demonstrators. Checkmate? Well, at least I was now standing on Nigerian soil. I sent back Paulin's car, his secretary's voice ringing in my ears till the last moment, urging me to return with them and take up the lunch offer in the affable company of Paulin.

The taxi drivers on the Nigerian side were mostly strolling aimlessly around the border post, usually a beehive but now unnervingly emptied of any noticeable motion. They lolled in the tree shade or hung around the exits with their eyes strained in the direction of Lagos, determined perhaps to be the first to catch any bit of news emerging from there through some luckless traveler. I stood with my all-purpose bag in front of the Immigration office. Resting against a windowsill was an easily identifiable secret service agent—the notorious SSS—perhaps the one in charge of that sector. He recognized me, looked astonished, but was instantly alert. I told him that I needed to get into Lagos.

"Prof," he said, "I don't think it is wise to go into Lagos today. In fact, I don't think you'll be able to get in at all." He waved his hand in the direction of the idle groups of men and abandoned vehicles. "None of them will risk it. Some tried, and they've brought back sad stories."

"And you? What kind of stories have you got?"

"Stories? That's what I have just told you."

"Intelligence reports," I said bluntly.

He laughed. "*Haba,* Prof!"

We went among the taxi drivers, and the response was uniform—and firm. Even as we approached, a number of them scrambled up, waiting expectantly. I wasted no time in disappointing them.

"I am in no position to tell you anything," I said. "I've been away nearly a week, so you know more than I do. I flew in only last night from Paris, through Cotonou. That's because the captain refused to fly us into Lagos. Now, which of you is taking me into Lagos?"

Almost in concert, their gazes fell away, some to the ground, others to overhead wires or distant spaces above my head. Their feet scuffed the dust, and a few shoulders drooped. These were fervent admirers who, in different circumstances, would have fought one another for the delight of dropping me off wherever I chose. This was different. Finally one said, simply:

"*Oga* Wole, *eko o da o.*" *

Yes, I already accepted that Lagos had gone sour. And I understood that it was simple logic not to wish to venture into Lagos. The taxis were their sole livelihoods, and it made no sense to drive them into an inferno. And even risk their lives in the process. The only problem was that I needed to get into Lagos. Surely somebody had to understand that!

Another proposed that I wait another day, and then we would see how the situation developed. One came forward, pointed needlessly to his bandaged head with a bandaged hand. He proceeded to narrate the hot reception he had encountered, the bloodthirsty gang that pursued him even as he drove his car in reverse gear at full speed until he found a safe place to turn around. He nodded his head in the direction of his clutch of stranded passengers, seated in the shade some distance away.

"*Oga,* dose na my passengers. You fit go ask dem if you like. Dose rioters break my windshield even as I dey already reversing back. Na God save me self. Hn-hn. *Eko ti daru.*" †

"Babangida done spoil everything. *Afi ki e ba wa le lo!*" ‡

Heatedly I replied, "And how do you expect us to chase him out if you won't even take me into Lagos?"

One of them spoke decisively. "Prof, you won't be able to do much if you run into one of those gangs of wild ruffians and get killed."

SSS interjected at this point, "What are you talking about? Nobody is going to touch Prof, you all know that."

"Aah, you haven't seen these ones. *Won o m'oju.*§ Many of them are high on drugs. They'd have done their damage before they even recognize who it is."

"No, they won't touch Prof," someone else conceded.

I quickly pressed the advantage. "I tell you what—each time we approach a roadblock, I shall come out of the car so they'll see me clearly. I guarantee they'll let us through. If I fail, we'll simply turn back."

---

* "Master Wole, Lagos is not good."
† "Lagos is in chaos."
‡ "You have to chase him out for us."
§ "They recognize no one."

"Prof, there is something else you haven't thought of," offered yet another. "Let's say we get you into Lagos. How do *we* get back?"

They all looked up in anticipation—*Let's see how he deals with that.* I had no response, of course. I tried to lighten the atmosphere. "I could provide you with a laissez-passer. Special passport. We'll have it signed on the way in, by the leader of each roadblock." Only the SSS man joined me in a brief chuckle. The general mood remained somber; the silence was thick with fear.

"Come with me, Prof," said SSS abruptly.

He led the way to where a solitary driver had remained in his taxi, doors wide open and the seat flattened out as far as it would go, fast asleep. "Hey, wake up!" The driver sat up, rubbing his eyes. "I have a passenger for you," said SSS.

"Where to?" the man demanded.

"Where to? Where you dey take your taxi go? Lagos, of course."

The driver giggled and began to sink back into sleep. "*Oga*, I beg. Make you let man sleep." Just then his eyes caught sight of me, and he snapped fully awake. "Hey, na Prof! Prof, na you wanting to go Lagos?"

I nodded.

"The road is ba-a-ad. Very bad. This *oga* no tell you?"

"I know. But we'll get there, don't you worry. I'm in the car with you, don't forget."

Have need, will travel. As we approached that lone driver, I just *knew.* Right from the preliminaries, I had deposited my bag on the backseat of the vehicle—this was one fish that would not get away. The same arguments ensued. *Yes, maybe they know you, but the first rock that is hurled at the taxi won't know who you are. And even if we make it, how will I get back?* But by now I had thought up a solution to that one. Abeokuta was my ultimate destination, I told him, but if passage to Abeokuta proved truly impossible, I would remain in Lagos. He would stay at my place, no matter what, and leave only when the rioting was over. Someone else would drive me into Abeokuta. He thought deeply about this as I stood over him, vulnerably crouched in the space of the front seat, and mentally bullied him. It was not clear if the SSS man had some hold on him that he subtly exerted or if the man was anxious to rejoin his family, who, he told us, were all based in Ota, halfway between Lagos and Abeokuta. There was the factor also—I felt this instinctively as we made our way toward him—that he had unwittingly rendered himself susceptible by isolating himself from the others. This placed him outside the protection of the collective rationality. No matter why, he finally agreed, comic in his dolefulness, with an air of one who felt he was being led to a place of no return. And thus began the most night-marish journey of my existence—well, one of the most nightmarish.

THE ROADBLOCKS WERE made up of empty petroleum barrels, discarded tires and wheel hubs, vending kiosks, blocks of wood and tree trunks, huge stones ... anything at all that could form a barrier for any moving vehicle. The strategy for that day was "Stay home. No movement on the roads," its purpose being to shut down the cities in a national campaign of civil disobedience. This was where all semblance of uniformity ended. The methods of enforcing the strategy varied from roadblock to roadblock, as did the levels of interpretation.

The freelance hoodlums had taken over, or else they had been conceded place, through plain force majeure, by the authorized monitors of the stay-at-home campaign. At some roadblocks there was a going fee; you paid it and were allowed to pass—but that safe conduct lasted only until the next barrier. Sometimes the fee was a gallon or more of fuel siphoned from your car, and then you were permitted to proceed—until the next barrier. The rows of parked vehicles at various roadblocks, with disconsolate passengers taking shelter in the shade of trees, milling aimlessly about, told the stories of those who had managed to navigate a few roadblocks, only to meet their Waterloo at the next. Some vehicles had clearly run a gauntlet of missiles, cudgels, and even fists; others could have arrived directly from the film set of *Jurassic Park*—one could have sworn there were abnormal teeth marks in the bodywork. The stories had only slight variations: some drivers had been obstinate, tried to force their way through the vigilantes, or had attempted to point out—logically, they thought—that they had paid "tolls" at earlier roadblocks, and were they not part of the same army fighting for the same cause?

Hadn't I been here before? I seemed doomed to find myself in a replay, with even the violent faces taking on familiar features. It was 1965 all over again, after the rigging of the elections in the "wild, wild West." There we were, driving to Lagos in my friend Bola Ige's car, on the old Ikorodu road, heading for Lagos. The same crowds, the same passion or desperation, the same opportunism, all wrapped in violence, so often gratuitous. Between Sagamu and Lagos, a distance of some forty kilometers, we had encountered no fewer than three dozen roadblocks. Several were within clear view of one another, and the guardians of each barrier clearly saw a vehicle being "cleared" just a few yards away, yet the new set stopped the same vehicle and extorted what money they could before letting it through. The occasional dead body lay on the verge of the road, usually burned to death, some unfortunate political figure who had been recognized and whose crimes, in that mindless moment, were considered to merit instant justice. Faces are either passports or death warrants, depending on circumstances. Fortunately, ours were the former and constantly validated. Again and again we were let through to shouts of solidarity. Some ran ahead and cleared our passage.

Inevitably, however, there would be the totally unimpressionable stalwart who did not give a damn whether it was Bola Ige, Wole Soyinka, Jesus Christ, Mohammed, or even Obafemi Awolowo in person.... *Who cares who the hell it is? We are suffering.* The face becomes one extended snarl, its bloodshot eyes incinerate the air.... *Who cares? They're all the same. None of them knows what suffering is. If they want to pass here, they must pay something.* Others to the rescue: *Are you mad? Don't you know who these are?* But the leveler is unmoved; if anything, he becomes more truculent, interposes his body between the car and the barrier.... *To hell with all of them! They have to pay, otherwise no way!* And the sudden, brittle sound of a bottle smashing against the car and its neck miraculously in the hand of this implacable toll collector, its jagged end pushed virtually into Bola's face since his was the nearer, mere inches away. *You want I put this for your face? Put your hand for pocket and pull out money, my friend!* I am frightened for Bola, but inside? Mad, raging mad! But there is nothing to do except play for time, play for those extra seconds until the others can leap on him from behind, pin his arms behind him, and yank him away. The scene repeats itself, with variations. Mostly any such extortionist holdup is apologetic, even ingratiating.... Oga, *we never chop since morning, leave us something make we put for mouth.* We do not have to wonder what it must be like for other motorists, since we are sometimes obliged to go to their rescue, vouch for their political bona fides. Finally someone with overriding authority plonks himself down on the hood of the car and we drive steadily through until we have cleared all the barriers around Ikorodu. Our last sight of this sergeant major of the vigilantes is of him commandeering another vehicle going in the opposite direction to take him back to his post; that vehicle is the envy of other motorists.

THIRTY YEARS LATER, and here I am undergoing the identical rites of passage. As we approach each barrier, I poke out my head, and most of the time, this more than sufficient to clear the way. In between such blissful passages I spend my time trying to guess how soon we will come upon the drug-crazed tion with the burning eyes, one who will refuse to countenance any Before long, we encounter the barracks lawyer.... *You people gave the everyone should stay at home, now you're breaking your own rules.* I wonder how much more gleeful he would have been if he had known that I myself had initiated the stay-home strategy, selling it to the campaign as a variant on continuous street demonstrations, with their often numbing fatalities—a few days on the streets, the next few within doors. That way, the army and police would not know exactly what to expect from day to day. *Stock up on food and drink, close down the towns and cities, turn the streets into ghost spaces, and let Babangida rule over emptiness!*

I turn on my interlocutor in mock aggression: *And is this your home? I don't see your kitchen. Where is your shithouse?* He gives a half-ashamed smile while others laugh at his discomfiture. The barrier is lifted. But finally the inevitable occurs, and we encounter the no-exemptions type, albeit somewhat diffident and uncertain. At the very least, he insists, we must supply a bottle of petrol— the forces of resistance must be sustained by taxation of the rich, in cash or kind. Thin and wispy, he is probably still in school but has already established himself as the ideological guru of the barricade. I tell him to get lost and engage the obvious leaders in a discussion on the prospects of the resistance. Then, through the corner of my eye, I observe a suspicious movement. The sly revolutionary has only pretended to slink away; he is actually engaged in prying open the cover of the petrol tank and now, obviously well practiced at the task, has a rubber tube already snaking down into the tank. I dash out of the car and snatch the tube away, warning him that if he tries it again I will make him drink the petrol, then throw a lighted match down his throat.

Profiting from the 1965 experience, I take to picking up a guard at one barrier, dropping him at the next, and picking up a new one. One or two ask for money to get back to their station—never more than half a mile distant—but I remind them that taxis are not running. Then the impudent grin. *Oh,* oga, *you self, you know say na for take buy something for chop!* That's better, I grin back, just come clean with me and we'll get along. A handful of small-denomination naira changes hands—at least they did earn their pay. The backup plan remained the same: if we encountered a truly unbreachable roadblock, we would simply remain there until a more influential stalwart came along. It never did happen, but progress remained excruciatingly slow. I started out from Coto-u at about eight in the morning. Normally the journey into the heart of s would take two hours. Now it was already five hours later, and we had d only some fifty kilometers. I became increasingly anxious.

taxi driver was beginning to enjoy himself. Even the faint smallpox s jet-black, fleshy face appeared to glow with delight at our progress.

From a timorous beginning, his palms sweaty, his lips mumbling prayers, as we approached the early roadblocks, he had gradually convinced himself that I exercised absolute control over even the most dangerous ruffian or situation.... *Ah,* oga, *na you alone, for all of Nigeria, unless for say someone like Gani Fawehinmi or Doctor Beko, or say Femi Falana fit pass this road as we dey pass through today.* I watched him grow more and more confident, then bold and aggressive. The very back of his neck was quite expressive; if I were dissolving roadblocks as if by magic, then he too had become the ultimate miracle worker. He began to ignore our rule: *Slow down, wait for me to be recognized and let me do the talking. Above all, do not open your mouth.* Not anymore.

He took offense at having to slow down at all. *Whas the matter with you? You no get eyes? You no see who I dey carry for inside car?* He took umbrage at any delay in removing a tire rim or log of wood, at having to negotiate broken bottles. *You people, you no think how all this broken bottle fit begin cause tire puncture?* He became personally affronted by any query from the vigilantes. *Thas the way with our people, is the person trying to help common man that they no respect.* I became tired of rebuking him, simply resigned myself to undoing his braggadocio by popping out my head, getting down, and turning on the lubrication tap, gesturing that he be ignored. Underneath his bluster, however, was simple anxiety—he wanted to be out of the string of roadblocks and back in the calm security of his home.

Of all the taxi drivers, why had I landed this one? Well, the answer to that was straightforward enough, I reminded myself—he had been the only one stupid enough to take on the trip. When admonitions failed to work, I resorted to threats. If he had not so obviously been a pious, abstemious type, full of homilies and prayerful thanks to Jesus, I would have suspected him of sneaking a drink when I was not attentive. He was certainly high on something— was it some slow-fuse marijuana he had been smoking before I came upon him? Finally I grew weary and half threatened: *At the next roadblock I shall tell the vigilantes to detain you. I'll take over your taxi, and then you can pick it up tomorrow.* The bloodshot eyes in his round face looked as if he believed me. Anyway, it held him in check, but worse was to come—the bravado began to peel off. I watched it physically vaporize as we approached the outskirts of Lagos.

Fifty, maybe sixty kilometers in five hours? It finally got to me, and I became anxious. The tension in the air became palpable as we moved nearer to Lagos. The roadblocks became more frequent; so did the sight of damaged vehicles and, worst of all, corpses. At the sight of the first corpse, my driver simply disintegrated as a human being. We encountered abandoned roadblo and one could see that they had been violently dismantled, smashed through by forces that were clearly not of the popular resistance. Lurking around the peripheries of such posts were the temporarily destabilized vigilantes. They had changed tactics and become mobile forces, swooping out from hiding places to enforce the implacable "No movement" order, inflict what damage they could on the erring motorist, and then retreat before the forces of law and order came into sight. The frequency of corpses increased, but with a marked difference; these were not victims of immolation but of neat, clinical bullets. Danger was thick in the air, accompanied by an acrid sting in the nostrils; it penetrated through to and invested the taxi, and I finally understood what I had been watching. All that bravado? The man was undergoing a long-drawn-out attack of hysteria. It was a strange experience, watching a human being disintegrate before my very eyes, and so rapidly.

There is a turnoff, a few miles before the junction known as Mile 12, that offers a direct route to Ota, on the way to Abeokuta. I decided that it might be best for us to use that route. It would take us to yet another possible route into Lagos, a hardly used road and therefore certain to be less patrolled by the vigilantes. The driver was falling to pieces and no longer capable of thought. I offered to take over the driving several times, but the steering wheel had become a crutch. It was an object of familiarity; it offered the last crumbs of friendship and security that were left to him in a situation into which he had been tricked. I could read that accusation forming itself slowly on his face—tricked! Everything else had been taken from him. The steering wheel was his last hold on any personal reality, and he was not about to give it up. Suburbia turned gradually to greenery as we took the diversion through rural land, lined by cassava bushes and okra and vegetable farms.

The roadblocks diminished and, where encountered, were far less aggressive but no less dangerous. On those deserted stretches through mostly farmland, a car and its passengers could simply disappear forever. The personnel at these nonurban barriers were far less frenzied, less overtly menacing. They watched you approach with lazy, indifferent eyes, watched you approach the barrier with total unconcern, remained inhumanly still as they waited for you to make the first move. I leaned out of the car, spoke to them in Yoruba. These were mostly farmers and villagers. They moved slowly. I could read on their faces their difficulty in accepting that someone like "Prof" would be on such roads at that hour, but then, moments later, I would read again that they had decided that this was the most natural thing in the world. The lethargy would disappear, to be replaced by concern for my safety and an evident boost in their morale. The barrier would be pushed aside, warnings given about other barriers farther on: *Tell them you've just been through Agbara village and that you met Yekini.*

And then the skies opened and a deluge began. I tapped my driver on the shoulder and told him to cheer up. The rains would at least send the vigilantes seeking shelter, so we would have easier passage from then on. He was beyond consoling. We finally came to a decision point—the fork where one road led to Ota, then on to Abeokuta. The other led to Ipaja—and Lagos. At first he badly wanted to go to Ota, where he would rejoin his family the soonest. Ota suited me also, since this was closer to Abeokuta. Suddenly, however, he no longer wanted to go to Ota. The road was much too abandoned. He saw armed robbers everywhere—they would have taken over the deserted roads by now, he swore. They were not interested in any revolution; all they did was take advantage of the uprising and rob people of their vehicles. On that lonely stretch, he whimpered, we did not stand a chance—much better to take our chances where the Lagos people were out in force. *At least people there get sense,* oga. Yes, suddenly his earlier tormentors were the more rational.

And so we turned toward Lagos. Several more roadblocks, and we were on the main dual carriageway that links Lagos through Agege to Abeokuta. He knew some shortcuts, according to him, which meant, of course, that in a short while we were totally lost. This was a part of outer Lagos where I had never been, and this same driver, who had earlier boasted that all of this sector was his regular beat, became thoroughly befuddled. Moreover, the rain now took on an intensity like a third force intervening in the confrontation. Visibility approached zero. We arrived in a fairly well populated suburb and found that we had come upon a recent battleground. The streets were mostly deserted. A few stragglers moved cautiously from time to time, first peeking out from a door or window barely cracked open, then stepping out. We stopped one and asked for directions into Agege. He pointed, then warned, But you mustn't go that way. Soldiers? I asked. No, but it all came to the same thing. These were the Mobile Police, the "Kill-and-Go," also known as MOPO. They had just shot six people in the area. If you go past that side street, he said, you will see the bodies. They came in, shooting wildly. And they've just chased some of the demonstrato' in the direction of Agege, so I advise you not to go there. Was there anot' route? Oh yes, we could go back the way we had just come, then take the right at the roundabout....

At the roundabout, we came upon the remains of what had been the best-constructed barrier yet. The hulks of long-discarded vehicles, nothing left of them but skeletal frames and rust, lay across the approaches. Heavy wooden logs had been inserted between the eye sockets—once side windows—as reinforcements. It was possible to find a passage, but only by weaving through, slowly, sometimes with one set of wheels on the broken curb. We succeeded, and without getting down to move any obstacles aside, only to come to yet another barrier, this time more makeshift than before. This was where we heard the first shots, followed almost immediately by the sound of a heavy engine at full speed, and it was clear that the vehicle was heading our way. The driver hesitated, stalled the car right in the middle of the road. I screamed at him, "Hurry up, pull over, pull over!"—only to bite my tongue as I realized that I had only made him more nervous. Miraculously, he succeeded in restarting the engine and pulled onto the grass verge just as a Peugeot station wagon roared around the corner, virtually on two wheels and loaded with at least eight MOPO bristling with arms. In what was obviously a well-practiced maneuver, the two front doors were flung open at the same time with booted legs that held the doors stiff, turning the entire vehicle into a battering ram. The barrels went flying off the road as the motor vehicle crashed through. Two policemen from the rear seats then leaped out, guns at the ready, and raced around the barrier in an obvious attempt to find whoever had been manning it and cut them down. The vehicle roared off, leaving the two policemen behind, presumably to sweep the environment clean of any rebels. I guessed that the patrol car was engaged in dropping more of those killers at various stops at top speed and would return the same way to pick them up.

By now the rains had eased off, though the clouds were regrouping in readiness for a new discharge. We watched the MOPO maneuvers for a while, and then I asked the driver to pull back onto the road. Driver? No. I no longer had a driver. The creature that attempted to restart the taxi and operate the steering wheel was some kind of animated jelly whose lips moved and uttered some half-human gibberish. From time to time I could make out Yoruba words that suggested that he was thinking about his wife and children and the home that he had last seen nearly a week before. Gone was the last shred of that earlier ~avado that had sustained him as our passage continued its near-magical ~rse from Idi-iroko. But he had not yet touched the nadir of his collapse.

~directed him toward one of the policemen, who had clearly gotten weary ~sweeping operations and was now resting under a tree, presumably awaiting the return of the van. All I wanted to do was to ask for directions—we needed to get ourselves out of that embattled zone, and the policeman seemed to me the most obvious person to ask. We parked some distance away, so as not to make him jumpy, then I came down and approached him in the most nonthreatening manner I could muster. If I had had a white flag, I probably would have held it aloft, intoning "Peace, brother man, I come in peace."

His jaw dropped and his eyes opened wide as I approached. "Wait, wait, wait, am I seeing... Wait, is this not the Professor?..."

His eyes were bloodshot and he stank of alcohol, unquestionably a particularly lethal brand of *ogogoro*. When he stood up unsteadily to salute, he forgot that the gun was resting on his lap. It clattered down, but he ignored it.

I waved my hand around the deserted space. "You appear to have been having some trouble."

"But, Professor, you are here? In this place? Sir, this place is very dangerous."

"We drove in from Idi-iroko. As a matter of fact, we took this route to avoid the battle zones around Lagos—at least, so I thought—but they seem to be all over the place."

"Where you want to go, sir?"

I hesitated. "Well, right now, if I could get to Allen Avenue or as close by as possible.... My house is in that area."

"The ground is bad, *oga*. Too many killings today. The ground is very bad. What you see here is not the worst. My advice, sir, is, don't try to go into Lagos."

For a while I stood thoughtfully. The clouds had grown inky dark, and there were rumblings that appeared to warn that the earlier downpour would have been child's play by comparison. Only four in the afternoon, and it felt more like midnight. The more I reviewed the situation, the more distant appeared even my now-adjusted goal of reaching the heart of Lagos. I asked the policeman if there was any kind of hotel, motel, or lodging rooms in that area. He proceeded to describe one, so I waved to the driver to bring his car nearer so he could take the directions himself. I thus committed one of my many errors of that day. The Kill-and-Go did indeed begin by trying to give directions, but his words were slurred and his arms waved so imprecisely that neither my companion nor myself could tell in what direction he pointed—in any case, in backtracking to repeat his last direction, he contradicted everything he had said before. The sooner we extricated ourselves from him, I thought ...

thanked him, assuring him that we were now fully enlightened. I asked the driver to move on. The next moment, however, this drunk had opened the front door and was thrusting himself into the empty seat.

"No, no, there's no need to come with us. We can find the hotel perfectly from your instructions. Thank you so much."

But he was struggling to bring his body, then his gun, into the car. "*Oga,* this place is dangerous, very dangerous."

"I know. That's why we've decided to stay in a hotel for the night."

"Yes, and that's why I must accompany you. Sir, I can't let anything happen to you. How will the papers carry it, eh? That something happened to Professor Wole Soyinka in our juri... juri... jurisidintion? God forbid bad ting!"

"Nothing will happen, I promise you. We've managed so far from Seme. I assure you, we're quite capable on our own."

"Sir, you don't understand. I must make a report when I get back to the station. I have to tell my *oga* that I find Professor Soyinka on the road, trying to get to Lagos. And do you know what he will ask me? Sir, he will say, did you escort him? And when I tell him that I left you on the road, first he will give me a dirty slap! Sir, I swear to you, he will give me a dirty slap, then he will lock me in the guardroom."

"I'll give you a note if you like."

But he was no longer listening. His gun, which he had somehow persuaded to enter the car before him, was now wedged between him and the driver, who, by now, had no more willpower, no form of volition visible on his face or discernable in his limbs. And no wonder, since he was now staring, riveted, at the gun, whose slanted muzzle was pointing directly at his head. I leaned forward and pushed it away from him and toward the unwanted passenger, who gratefully assumed temporary control of his weapon.

"Thank you, sir. Ah, you don't understand, we all done see fire for eye today, and yesterday. But yesterday na child's play compare with today. As we break down one barricade, these people build it up again. Nothing anybody can do to them, they just won't give up. Too many people killed. So you see, sir, I just can't leave you like that, the streets are not safe and my *oga* will kill me if 'e hear say I abandon you. But I can bring you safe to the hotel, and I stay with you until things cool down...."

I felt my patience slipping away. Then I had an idea. "Where is your police station?"

"Not far from here. Is just around that corner."

"Good. We go there first. Then we go to the hotel."

His gin-glazed eyes took on a manic gleam, but it was all delight. "You mean...you want go first to our station?"

I nodded. He beamed as if he had won a lottery.

"You say, sir? I mean, you say you want come and greet our *oga*?" Beginning with an overwhelmed tremolo, his voice waxed ecstatic. "You mean, you will... oh my God, when I enter police station with you, sir, nobody will believe my luck. Nobody, sir! That is me get the luck to bring you to introduce you to the station...."

We got to the station, and I told the driver to stop at the gate. He protested immediately: "No, no, it's all right to go in. Go inside, driver."

I stopped the driver. "No. This is as far as we go. We'll drop you here. Listen, you're very kind, and I appreciate your concern. What you don't seem to understand is that your being in the car is the greatest danger to me. Do you think you can manage to understand that? All the people you've been fighting since yesterday, you think they want to see your uniform right now?"

He appeared to mull that over. I thought I detected a tiny light of comprehension in his eyes. Then he grew sad. "But, *oga*, we're all fighting for the same thing. Only we have no choice. We have to carry out orders. But, Prof, make I tell you, even as we discuss this matter in the barracks, everybody, all of us, we want these soldiers to go. I am an Abiola man myself, first and to last. The whole country know say he win this election, so why Babangida refuse to go?"

I patted him on the shoulder, pushed the snout of the gun away from my driver's face for the last time, and opened the door for him. "We shall win, don't you worry. And tell your *oga* it was I who refused your protection. Explain to him what I said, that anyone in uniform is a danger to me right now—he'll understand."

I watched him walk up the driveway toward the main block of the police complex, his uniform sticking to him from the soaking he had had, more a bedraggled chicken than a Kill-and-Go SWAT machine. Since he was also thoroughly soaked on the inside, my mind flew to an item on Chinese menus that I had never sampled but often wondered about—"Druncken Chicken," as it was spelled—and I used to wonder if the chicken were made drunk before being dispatched or alcoholized after the terminal event. Still, I hoped he would arrive in one piece, which seemed very much open to question, since he chose to drag his gun along the ground. The rain continued to pelt down, but this did not appear to bother him one bit. At that moment, he struck me as perhaps the unhappiest being in the universe.

. . .

A TEEMING CROWD of humanity is an awe-inspiring phenomenon. As an objective spectacle, that is all it is, a spectacle, but when you are within it, when you are one of the bits and pieces that make up the tumult, you become one with it, you share in the force that it represents and you endure a loss of identity, except as a compressed lump within the crowd. I confess that I have never *experienced* being fully melted into the pack, so I can only approximate. When I am caught in one, I cannot wait to find a way out of the swarming promiscuity. The safest crowds are those that are made up of a majority of individuals who know *why* they have coalesced into one, why they have chosen to jettison their individual identities to form a new substantive, a *mass.* One can talk to such a crowd. One can reason with it; one can even modify its purpose and direction. Above all, however, one can re-create such a crowd, transform the solidified mass of humanity and turn it, at its most violent, toward pacifism or, from its most pacific condition, make it heave, a mountain in convulsion. I had lots of tutelage in mob characteristics on that day of my foolhardy plunge into Lagos—not for the first time, but never in such heavy and sustained doses.

When we had found a hotel—in reality a suburban brothel and general-congregation bar for nightlifers and day drifters in shadowy rooms—I set down my bags and devoured a long beer. I discharged my long-suffering driver, paid him generously above the agreed fare. I offered him a room for the night, but he was under some kind of spell. Nothing would make him share my comparative safety—to him I spelled danger, deadly peril, and his instincts warned him that he could recover his damaged self only by extricating himself from my presence. Had he also come to *hate* me? I wondered.

The rain had stopped, but darkness was approaching as I set off for my Lagos home on the pillion of a motorcycle taxi, known as an *okada,* one form of transportation that could at least maneuver its way effectively through the obstacles that now sprouted up virtually every few yards. The stoppages and interrogatories by vigilantes did not diminish, but they were brief and apologetic. The motorcycle aroused less instinctive hostility than a motorcar, and the shock of recognition easily did the rest. If only I had known it at the time, it was a practice ride for a future escape through the forest that lay between Shaki and the border with Benin. Instead of lashing branches, however, this was a forest of arms and limbs that tugged at my body and threatened to unseat both the driver and me. At their stubborn insistence, I addressed a batch of my captors—before a few sentences, others poured out of crevices like soldier ants from hidden warrens. All sought a reassuring voice, craved some knowledgeable view of the future. I had nothing to offer but hope.

I appeared to have entered a war zone, the scene of recent battles, mostly one-sided. Corpses littered the streets, casualties with horrifying wounds, and patches of caked blood discolored the tar and sometimes the gray concrete divider on the motorway. Those smears often suggested that a wounded man had tried to climb the barrier, perhaps vainly seeking cover on the other side, failed, but left his trail on the winding slab of cement. I began to reassess my progress, finally giving up all hope of reaching Abeokuta. I adopted, purely by default, this improvised set of insurgents that multiplied by the hour. Too many groups had lost contact with their leaders and simply did not know what to do next—stay put, or disband and resume the protests the following day? Had the stay-home order been intended for two, three, or four days, or was it to last a full week? What would happen afterward? Was there a change of tactics that they knew nothing of? *Prof, what are we doing here? Why are we not training? Prof, I'm volunteering. Take me, take me with you, I know you have an army in the bush, just take me along.* Clutches here and there surrounded their radios, hoping to obtain some direction, some news of what was happening elsewhere. Darkness approached, and some groups began to prepare bonfires, resolved to spend the night at barricades. Students had commandeered station wagons and dump trucks. They wore white T-shirts marked with the Red Cross emblem and ferried bodies and the wounded to first-aid centers and hospitals. That day was one of the finest in the mottled career of university students, and I could only wish that the lessons of their conduct would inform their lives, collectively, forever.

I was warned against military and MOPO drive-past snipers, the hit-and-run specialists; it seemed that many casualties had been sustained that way, and on the motorbike I was a recognizable target. Eventually I was prevailed upon to transfer to another car with a volunteer driver wearing the Red Cross T-shirt and cap. It was not long before I ran into a new source of anxiety. At a recent killing ground that had been personally supervised by a military commander identified as Sani Abacha—he had arrived with a truckload of soldiers, the soldiers had poured out, and Abacha had given the order to open fire— a policeman stopped me and pulled me aside. The deaths that had taken place, he warned, were nothing compared to what would come at night, yes, that very night. He implored me to ensure that the demonstrators did not stay outdoors overnight. He had overheard an officer giving orders to another to mobilize soldiers for a night operation. They were to clear out any remaining barricades and take care of any sleeping protesters that were encountered.

I headed back to Ipaja, where I had earlier woven through barricades and backstreets on the motorbike. This time, we drove on the main road at snail speed. In no time at all, I was engulfed by a teeming humanity that stretched miles and miles on both sides of the Ipaja junction between Ota and Lagos. I was awed by this phenomenon. It felt as if hundreds of bodies were sitting on the car, on the hood, hanging from the windows, clearing a route that only drew more and more people until there was not a visible patch of that road, only heads and bodies, all threatening to crush the life out of the steel body of this misused vehicle. A man in a tracksuit, one of those who appeared not to be of the crowd yet exerted some confident authority, pushed his way forward. Through the window, I told him what I had heard and asked him if he could disperse the crowd with the fall of darkness. No, he said, you had better do it; in fact, I don't think they will let you through unless you address them.

With a joint effort, we succeeded in pushing the door against bodies to provide just sufficient space for me to emerge. Before I knew what was happening, arms had raised me onto the concrete divider, and next, I was standing on the roof of the car. The vehicle vanished, instantly swallowed by the human throng. If I had thought before that I had obtained an unforgettable sense of the massed impact of a crowd density, I now discovered that I had sensed nothing yet. The sight from my new vantage point reduced my sense of individuality to a mere speck. The world appeared to have been emptied into a skyline of heads and torsos pressed into immobility, yet seething with life.

Somehow, silence fell over the crowd. Then a roar and then silence, a roar again that rose and fell, and that vibrant silence that sucked the neigborhood into a tense expectancy. I shook my brain awake from stupefaction, succeeded in locating my voice. There was nothing to say except to commend their steadfastness, assure them of the certainty of victory. *But now you must disperse. Don't be fooled by pretenders. You know your leaders, they will reach you by radio. Do not stay out on the streets tonight. Go home and return in the morning, when you can see from which direction the enemy is coming in to strike. You've taken enough casualties. Don't let them slaughter you under cover of darkness. Go to your beds, but be back at your posts in the morning.*

LYING IN MY OWN BED late that night, my mind running through the reel of the day's events from the departure point at the Seme border, I found myself compulsively trying to occupy the skin of some luckless stray from the enemy camp who found himself entombed within the inhospitable pulse of such humanity.

By the Waters of Babylon

. . . . .

BETWEEN THE CONCLUSION OF THE JUNE 12, 1993, ELECTIONS, AND JUNE 26 of that year—three days before the date on which the military should have handed over power to the victorious candidate—the nation stood still. One felt that sense of congealment, of eerie immobility, nearly palpably, as if a hundred million people were massed in an outsize stadium, compelled to hold their breath. In only one section, raised like a press or adjudicators' box, did there appear to be a semblance of life. This was the law courts, where the noise and frenzy seemed resolved to make up for the loss of vitality elsewhere. There, case and countercase were filed between Babangida's surrogates on the one hand and the president-elect on the other. The former wanted to legitimize the obliteration of the results of a concluded contest, turning it into a nonevent, while the other fought the travesty of a reality in which millions had participated. The frenzy of litigation only warned how deceptive was the lethargy that had descended on the rest of the arena, filling it with an ominous expectancy.

During that month, the military regime launched one of its crudest, most cynical assaults on the already battered independence of the judiciary. It imported a rookie state magistrate from distant Edo state to hold court in the federal territory, Abuja, on a case that was clearly a federal matter. She was flown in by a presidential jet plane, sat at midnight, and found in favor of the regime—the elections, she declared, were illegal. The aggrieved parties took the hint and filed for redress in other state courts, of higher jurisdiction. Those judges ordered the regime to release the remaining results immediately and install the winner in power, one such judgment adding, "even if the heavens fall!" The heavens did not fall, but a self-outmaneuvered despot did.

I. B. Babangida had defied the courts and dug in, but his ousting was only a matter of time. Within a month after the elections, his formidable array of ar-mored cars, guns, bribes and wiles, tear gas, and batons notwithstanding, Ibrahim Babangida was forced out of office. There was nothing soldierly or dignified about his departure. The Yoruba—as always!—have a malodorous but apt expression for the manner in which colonial powers, forced to grant independence to their colonies, invariably made their exit: *Oyinbo su s'aga*— "Before leaving, the white man defecated on the throne." Even thus did Babangida make his bow. The dictator attempted to cushion his departure—or to pave the way for his anointed?—by appointing a civilian surrogate to rule the nation. That poisoned mantle fell on a Chief Ernest Shonekan, a gangling business executive, formerly of the British Unilever Company, with a history as obliging figurehead or point man for Babangida's creative transitional ploys. Shonekan's appearance as a recycled tool of despotic machinations was a re-newed affront to the nation. His official title, this time, was head of the Interim National Government, which quickly prompted a more popular sobriquet: "the King of ING."

That Babangida was casting about within the ethnic group and hometown of the nationally elected president, Bashorun M.K.O. Abiola, merely added in-sult to injury: Here, suck on this. Sure, I took your *gurudi*,* but here's *guguru*.† Much of the nation felt affronted by this patronizing gesture, but none more than the elected president's immediate constituency, the Yoruba West. As a fel-low Yoruba and partial townsman—the other part being Ijebu—of Abiola and Shonekan, I took the insult personally. Was this how low Babangida estimated the pride and sense of justice of that part of the nation to which I belonged? At great expense and human sacrifice, the entire nation, not just one section, had made a choice, and here was one individual usurping the will of a hundred million people, reducing a national voice to a gesture of sectarian appease-ment.

Came June 27, and the *gururu* was spat out and spat upon and the days of rage began. With the dictator's departure—he "stepped aside," in his own words—and the installation of the substitute, the direct violence of three days subsided into a campaign of attrition, shifting levels of civil disobedience. The already-tried strategy of citizens-stay-at-home was revived. Trade unions went on strike, citing one grievance or another, but underlying it all was the real

---

* A flat corn-and-coconut candy.
† Local popcorn.

cause, rejection of illegitimate power. The centers of commerce, Lagos most prominently, were turned into ghost towns. Shonekan became a prisoner, ostracized by his own people, isolated in his Aso Rock fortress but playing at being head of state. The real power lay with his chief of army staff, Sani Abacha, who watched him with amused contempt, awaiting the right moment to make his move.

The stalemate exacted its price, however. It took a strange toll on the fighting spirit of some of our noted civil rights leaders, as well as the supportive media—they grew impatient, even desperate. They began to utter the once unthinkable, calling on the army to step in, dethrone Shonekan, and install the truly elected man in the presidency. At the forefront of the choir was my unpredictable ally Gani Fawehinmi, who, with increasing stridency, abandoned the forensic for the mystical. Gani added and subtracted, analyzed and synthesized dates, signs, portents, and other arcane ingredients to arrive at a clairvoyant conclusion: destiny, he declared, had laid its hand on the head of the chief of staff for this solemn duty—to oust the civilian usurper and install the choice of the people. He identified the date by which the stars would align for the inevitable event. I was nonplussed. Hadn't the nation learned, from bitter experience, that you do not entrust a hyena with even the mere whiff of meat, however rotten?

I could not help thinking how little this differed in methodology from the invocational motions of the women of Abeokuta when the cup of power had been dashed from the lips of their own son. Their response was to resurrect an ancient rite of anathemization. They made the ritual *akara*, the fried bean cake, devoid of all condiments but impregnated with deep, ancient curses. They stripped to the waist and surged out in silent procession to place the *akara* at crossroads and other spots of ancestral significance. It was a fearful ritual, its potency stamped on the grim-faced procession.

If not provably felled by the women's necromancy, Babangida had at least fallen to the accompaniment of other civic chants of rejection. His surrogate, Ernest Shonekan, would in turn be swept away on the tide of cabalistic numerology invoked from the legal redoubt of my friend Gani—with some assistance, undoubtedly, from the inordinate ambitions of a little man called Sani Abacha.

On his part, Shonekan continued to twitch within other invisible webs spun by forces he little understood. It also appeared that Babangida, or perhaps simply his loyalists acting independently, became concerned at the tenacity of popular resistance. Prompted or not by the master schemer himself, these loyalists moved to seek ways of neutralizing the problematic load their boss had deposited on the seat of power as his parting gift.

First came a visit from a young ambassador to South Africa, Tunji Olagunju, who pretended that he was just passing by, learned that I was staying in Lagos with my usual host, Yemi Ogunbiyi, and stopped to pay his respects. It was transparent that he had been sent to discuss the political impasse—to test the ground, as it were. Olagunju proposed plans that would involve the abandonment of the presidential elections, perhaps leading to a repetition of the exercise, the setting up of a government of national unity, and so on. Abiola would be free to participate in both. I quickly let him know that the "abandonment" clause was a nonstarter. The nation had chosen, and that choice must be respected.

Olagunju's visit turned out to be preparatory for another, and at a higher level. The next caller was another Babangida affiliate, General Mohammed Gusau, national security adviser to the Babangida regime, now continuing his chief bodyguard role to the King of ING. He tried to break through the initial awkwardness of the meeting by a comment on what I knew already—that the filing cabinet in the State Security Service dedicated to the subject of Wole Soyinka was not a cabinet at all but an entire room, filled from floor to ceiling with surveillance reports, news clippings, photographs, tapes from tapped conversations, departmental assessments, and more—but: "Believe me, Prof, the summative view is that you act on principle, and everyone in the service has a great respect for you." I assured him that I also believed that "the service" acted on its principles, but what a pity its principles were constantly at variance with the people's. There was further mutual-assessment banter for a little while longer, and then, very strangely, came the question: *Why had I requested to see him?*

At first taken aback, I proceeded to correct him gently. Olagunju, I said, had asked me if it might help if some individuals, high up in government, intervened in the crisis, and would I agree to meet one or two of them? Yes, I did agree. I had, however, never met him, did not know who he was—so why should I have asked to see him? Gusau feigned surprise, but, that gambit over—whatever he hoped to gain by it remained a mystery—we got down to business: how to break the political deadlock.

I proposed an unannounced minisummit in next-door Republic of Benin including Ernest Shonekan, the usurper; Bashorun Abiola, the president-elect; his defeated opponent, Bashir Tofa; the chairmen of their political parties, and a few arbitrators cum moderators from either side. They would meet away from public pressure and work out a formula for the transfer of power. I insisted, however: *there must be absolutely no military participation.* The military was out, discredited, unwanted, and mistrusted. Elections had been held, and now the elected candidate must take over the reins of government. Agreement would be reached on a government of national unity—to restore trust and confidence—but Abiola must occupy the driving seat. Gusau demurred on the total exclusion of the military, setting out the advantages of their presence. I agreed in part but insisted: *strictly as observers.* They would not participate in the discussions or try to influence them in any way. Their role would be to listen, bear witness, and return to report to their constituency. Gusau accepted the amendment. We agreed that a resolution was urgent, indeed, that it must take place within the month. The nation was breaking down; it had become ungovernable and would remain so as long as Shonekan remained in power.

The following day found me at the embassy doorstep of our neighbor the Republic of Benin. The ambassador was away in Cotonou, the capital, which could not have worked better in our favor. A signal was sent to him by his deputy, so he could immediately begin consultations with his minister of foreign affairs, obtain the blessing of the Beninois president, and so on. Word came back as expected: the meeting was more than welcome, and all was prepared—a weekend dash across the border by all the principals, no publicity, no fanfare. If all went well, the nation would wake up the following Monday to learn that civil society had seized the initiative and resolved the crisis its own way. It all struck me as déjà vu, but this was easier territory than my earlier foray into peace brokering. I began to wonder if there wasn't a diplomatic career waiting for me whenever the dramatist's stream of inspiration ran dry.

Contacts with the principals were immediately initiated. Was Gusau sincere, or was the purpose of these visits merely to test, through me, how resolute the opposition remained and how mobilized? We never did find out. The termination of that undertaking came from Aso Rock: Shonekan, we were informed, was developing other ideas that would shortly be made public. Was he indeed? Were they his? Come to think of it, was the King of ING ever possessed of any idea beyond the delusion of power? Or did he simply take orders from his handlers, that is, Sani Abacha and his power-hungry hyenas? It was impossible to tell. Abiola and his advisers were more than prepared for the Benin summit when, suddenly, all was scuttled.

The bets on Chief Ernest Shonekan were now placed not on whether he would survive but on how brief his tenure would be. He was probably the only individual in all of Nigeria who did not know this. In November 1993, Sani Abacha decided that the comedy had run long enough and moved to bring down the curtain. Surrounded by his praetorian guards, he presented Shonekan with a letter of resignation and ordered him to sign it. Shonekan, we learned, actually made some kind of protest, which must have generated some barracks merriment among the putschists.

I was horrified at the jubilation even among the die-hard democratic combatants in the nation. The media, for once, lost its habitual watchfulness, and some proceeded to censor my articles, on the grounds that they were too strong. Abacha, many believed, actually meant well and would shortly fulfill their democratic expectations. Sani Abacha! Was this not the officer who had commanded the detachment that had opened fire on unarmed protesters in the Ipaja sector on June 28? Sani Abacha had single-handedly been responsible for some two hundred dead, shot in cold blood, within Lagos state alone! He had given orders for a severe crackdown nationwide, deploying specially selected troops to ensure that his orders were carried out. During the same public protestations, he once appeared on television, a puffed-up officer bristling with arrogance, to threaten the Lagos state governor with unilateral action if that politician failed to put down the unrest in his state. The elderly governor shrugged and told him that he might as well take over his state that very moment, since he lacked the means to effect any cessation of popular protest. Abacha did not take over the state, but he did his best to decimate its population. In any case, while the continent has known an exception or two—military caretakers who actually handed over power to civilians unfairly dispossessed of that power—you simply do not employ an alcoholic as a security guard in a distillery.

A pall had descended on the nation, but not many were yet willing to acknowledge that we were approaching Arthur Koestler's darkness at noon—not even Moshood Abiola, the president-elect, who agreed to deal with Sani Abacha on the face value of his protestations. With Yemi Ogunbiyi in tow, I called on my friend Ibrahim Alfa, the vice air marshal whom we had involved in the Benin scheme. We found him in like mood, sunk deep in dolefulness, cradling a glass of his favorite German Riesling.

"Sani came to see me the night before the coup," he admitted, "told me that he was taking over—to bring stability to the nation! I was horrified. I asked him why he would want to do such a thing, and he replied that the people wanted it. They felt he was the only one who could put an end to the anarchy.

'All right,' I told him finally, 'but be sure you don't stay longer than three months, just enough time to install the elected president.' Of course I said that only because he was going to take over anyway. Everything was already prepared. Inwardly, I shook like a leaf and began to think seriously of relocating. Abacha in charge of Nigeria? The man has the brain of a lizard."

IT PROVED IMPOSSIBLE not to feel and express outright contempt for the lizard's promulgation of his own unending program of transition to civilian rule. The process of self-entrenchment was blatant enough, but most depressing of all was its lack of originality—Abacha had decided that any scheme of deception employed by Babangida was worthy of emulation; simply multiply the brazenness of it twice or thrice over, and it would become palatable to the public. If it proved not to be, the obvious remedy was force-feeding, and with as much brutality as could be mustered.

At first, the new dictator permitted the civilian state governors and legislatures, elected under the interim arrangements of Babangida's gradualist ruses, to remain in office. Suddenly, with a Cromwellian flourish, he sent them packing: the political class had not learned its lesson, the legislators were not serious, corruption reigned unbridled, and so on. The public crowed approval: serves the bickering moneybags right! Emboldened, he began to toy with the captive populace. Inauguration of yet another constitution-writing body, one-third of which would be his own nominees. A new timetable for civilian restoration, then another. Arrests. Detentions. Constitutional Assembly sent on enforced vacation, returned sober and compliant. Mysterious assassinations, generally attributed to armed robbers. Abrupt retirements of the more professional soldiers. Deployment of suspect military units to the civil war front in Liberia. Flights of targeted individuals, including the dictator's earlier collaborators. Phantom plots against the regime—it took only a moment to make up an attempted coup d'état, then weave a net elastic enough to contain the entire population if necessary.

Now increasingly suspicious of the dictator's true intent, the press found itself under siege as it fought back. Under Ibrahim Babangida, his sadistic agents would simply wait until the daily or weekly print run had been completed, then swoop down on the editorial houses and cart off their irreplaceable haul. At a lecture at the University of Lagos, I challenged them: "Why do you let Babangida's police raid your offices, your printing presses, cart off copies of your journals without a fight? Have you never heard of underground publishing? Set up more than one editorial office, and divide up your pages among various presses. Use fronts. Scatter your editors, and let your journalists link up with them by telephone, fax, or carrier pigeon, if it comes to that!"

When, two or three years afterward, Abacha came into power, their guerrilla tactics appeared to have been readied and honed overnight. The garage behind my Abeokuta office on Lalubu Street was perhaps the earliest office of the samizdat. It was already being used for clandestine meetings by a youthful group working out plans for making Abeokuta a no-go area for Abacha's forces of occupation. There they prepared torrid pamphlets and organized their distribution. The journalists among them put their training to good use. I left the gates to my office compound open when I went home. They came at night and left by morning, leaving the garage clean of any evidence of their nocturnal presence or activities.

The ascendancy of raw, naked power was rapid. Abacha's police had graduated from merely seizing editions and setting fires to media houses; they now took to seizing journalists themselves, then taking their relatives—including wives and children—hostage, to force a wanted journalist or suspected dissident to turn himself in. A notorious episode, photographed by another journalist, showed an SSS agent pressing his pistol to the head of a six-year-old boy, screaming "Where is your father?" even as his mother was bundled into a waiting vehicle. Not long after occurred, albeit in a muted key, the curious incident around my son Tunlewa.

A botched kidnapping? Or just a clumsy attempt to identify and enter him, even at the age of four, into the surveillance album? Whatever their purpose, the agents were clearly handicapped by the fact that, as they skulked behind some flowering shrubs at his school in Ikeja, a Lagos suburb, they were uncertain which of the pupils was who. So they called out the name "Tunlewa" in the direction of a bunch of children going by. Their aim was to see which of the children would turn around. David, my nephew, who shared the same car pool, was already walking toward the car. He heard the name and turned around instinctively, wondering who was hailing his cousin, expecting to see him coming toward the car that would take them home. But strange men pointed urgently toward him, all friendly smiles: *Yes, you, you are young Soyinka, aren't you?* David shook his head, turned, and quickened his steps toward the safety of the car. Once home, he spoke to his mother about it, but guardedly, such was the impression of some impending danger that the incident had left on even his youthful senses.

That event took place against the background of more than a year's round-the-clock, hardly subtle surveillance on our rented bungalow in Ikeja, as well as my private office in Abeokuta, where I gave most of my press conferences, the offices of the Ogun state chapter of the national union of journalists being just around the corner and always eager for a political statement.

Curiously, the same journalists worried more about the safety of their contributor than about themselves, sometimes censoring something I had written for fear that it would prove the last straw for Abacha. It took weeks of angry pressure from me before *The News* finally published what was probably my defining prediction, an article written soon after the Abacha takeover and a year before my flight. There I warned that the new ruler was a killer, that "this man would gaol, torture, kidnap, maim and kill at will simply in order to remain in power." I knew him. I had studied him. I made it my business to follow the careers of a number of the military players on the Nigerian political field. Sani Abacha was a psychopath, certifiably so. Now head of state and commander of the most celebrated armed forces in West Africa, his security machinery translated into action his paranoid assessment of individuals opposed to his rule. Around my office, the attempt by Abacha's agents at invisibility was so laughable that a foreign visitor, a Swiss producer and cultural animator, Niggi Popp, could not contain himself. Long after I had opened the door to let him in, he remained on the doorstep, surveying the street. Then, in a loud, provocative tone, as if he wanted to make absolutely certain that he was overheard by the furtive presences, he demanded to know what I had done to deserve a horde of snoopers attempting to merge with the local color.

Of the constant visitors who came to check on my "state of health," the most wryly bewildered was perhaps Kunle Ajibade, one of the younger generation of investigative journalists. Kunle was a correspondent for *The News* in Abeokuta and one of the pioneers of the samizdat publication, toward which I had nudged his profession some years before. He would himself undergo the experience of a mock trial and incarceration—without ever losing his sense of the absurd. Kunle came almost ritualistically to my office, sat opposite my desk, and, with a mixture of amazement and expectancy on his face, demanded to know: "But, Prof, why haven't they come for you?"

"Why? Do you want them to?"

"No, but it doesn't make sense. By now they should have taken you in."

"Well, they haven't. So, what's your problem?"

"Well, I simply don't understand what you're still doing here," he persisted. "It's either you should be heading out of the country, or they should be pulling you in."

It was such a persistent puzzle for him that I teased him, insisting that he was hoping for a scoop, making sure that he was on the spot when Abacha's men did come for me. The opposite was true, of course, especially as Kunle sometimes took it on himself to censor the odd article or interview that I granted him, having resolved to protect me from myself! "But, Prof," he would protest in his high-pitched voice, "if we had published that article as you wrote it, we would have lost you to Abacha right away! And then where would I obtain my exclusive interviews?"

This much one must say for police surveillance: its helicopters certainly provided the nation some rich moments of comic relief, for which I insist on claiming credit. In the early months of 1995, unable to find their way to my house—the nearby villagers always misled uninvited visitors, sent them in all directions, and left them going around in circles—the police resorted to scouting the terrain from the air. Thereafter they buzzed over the house whenever they wanted some diversion or relaxation. Finally tired of their game, I summoned a press conference, issued a tongue-in-cheek warning, and sounded the war drums in the hyperbolic accents of a famous cri de coeur that had once been wrung out of one of Abacha's predecessors in office, Olusegun Obasanjo.

A retired general turned statesman at the time of his famous outburst and member of the Commonwealth's Eminent Persons Group set up to negotiate the end of apartheid, Obasanjo enjoyed the distinction of being the first African leader to breach the prison walls of Robben Island and actually meet Nelson Mandela. Deeply incensed by the intransigence of the Boers and frustrated by the slow progress of the liberation struggle, the general forgot his role as negotiator and let forth a most unusual rallying cry: "Where are our famed metaphysical powers? Is it not possible to call on our ancient spiritual forces to smash the apartheid system? Where is our juju force? Where is our much-vaunted *epe** potency?"

And so, in response to the aerial aggression against my domestic peace, I belted out an extended war chant modeled on the general's bellow of rage: "But for my humanity and the compassion that I feel for the innocent officers in that craft, I would have taken traditional measures against this noisome intruder. If the police boss, Comassie, doubts me, I dare him to return alone or with that cowardly torturer, Ismail Gwarzo. I shall teach them that there are powers beyond the white man's machine guns, rockets, and missiles. I shall stand outside

* Curses.

my house and recite some potent *ofo,* incantations from antiquity that will bring the craft spiraling down into my cassava fields!"

The journals made a feast of it! Playing along, they churned out caricatures of this Ijegba warrior with matted hair and beard, cowrie shells strung around my neck, a belligerent conch or horn in hand, pens and pencils vying with quills and amulets in my hair, one arm raised toward the intruder in the sky. More than a few were witty and hilarious. I framed my favorite and hung it behind my living room bar. In exile, my mind easily reverted to that cartoon when I learned that my house had been smashed up on the pretext of seeking the opposition radio, making me wonder if it was still hanging there, if it had caught the eye of one of the invaders with a sense of humor and ended up in his pocket, or if I would find it lying amid a heap of smashed furniture.

It all helped to ease a people's tension, dispersing the real aura of menace with ridicule. I did not fool myself, however. Even at that stage, it had become clear to me that the space for such mock heroics was rapidly contracting and that comic turns were becoming indistinguishable, literally, from gallows humor. Such moments became rarer and rarer. Civil society was knuckling under. There never is a shortage of willing collaborators within civil society, and the roll of recruits lengthened by the day. The prospect of a slave plantation, more than a hundred million at the last census, subject to the whim of one man, stared me in the face. It was time to revitalize public sensitivity to what was happening, where it was all headed, and incite its will toward self-recovery. Wearily, I acknowledged that it was time for some drastic initiative.

IN AUGUST 1994, surrounded and menaced by fully armed and kitted mobile police who pressed their faces against windows and a metal grille that surrounded the open assembly hall, I held a press conference at the Mayflower School, Sagamu, run by the late schoolmaster and social reformer Tai Solarin. There, with a detailed map, I outlined plans to expand an exercise we had undertaken during the sit-tight season of Ibrahim Babangida when we embarked on a walk from the Labor headquarters in Oju-elegba, on Lagos's outskirts, to Ikoyi. This time we would advance to the scope of Martin Luther King, Jr.'s march on Washington, D.C., and confront the lizard in its hole—mobilize the people and embark on a Million Man March on Abuja! We would converge from all four points of the compass, march on Abuja, and *invest* the seat of government until the tyrant was dislodged. We commenced plans in earnest.

A few weeks later, I was returning from a light hunt in the surroundings of my Abeokuta home one morning when I came upon three security agents. They had been waiting for me since very early in the morning, early enough to have found me if I had not gone into the bush. The "State Annexe"—the demure name for the offices of the State Security Service throughout the country—had just earned itself a rocket from Aso Rock, the seat of government. It appeared that the director's predecessor in office had earlier received a memo to pull me in and interrogate me about my public statements and activities. That luckless official had failed to track me down for weeks, when, lo and behold, I appeared on the front pages of the media yet again, not only spouting off but organizing a march that would converge on Aso Rock from all corners of the nation. A sizzling signal scorched the desk of his successor. The commander in chief demanded instant explanation: How could I be at once untraceable, yet conspicuously present in the national media, even to the extent of holding a press conference in that very town? The new director did not await a renewed warning. He dispatched three of his men with orders to stake out my house night and day and bring me in the moment I appeared.

They could not very well take me into their station carrying a firearm, albeit a simple shotgun, so they let me into my house. I deposited the armory and feathered victims, showered, and changed my clothes. I followed them by car to their office, which was in fact in the same neighborhood—albeit tucked away—as my personal office in Lalubu. As I was not sure if I were heading straight for detention, I scribbled a note and left it with my house help: *"If I am not back by a certain time . . ."* It had become routine, even second nature, to many, and my house help knew where to deliver the note.

I entered to strained smiles. The director brought out a bulging file and extracted and pushed toward me the memo from Aso Rock. His office had gone to incredible lengths to track me down—in Lagos, Ibadan, Abeokuta. . . . His voice was tinged with irrational rebuke: *But where were you, Prof?* I waited until he had rid himself of the umbrage from high up into which I had plunged his office by my elusiveness—of which I knew nothing! At the time, I had not begun any attempt at subterfuge. The trouble was that I was in perpetual motion, since we were mobilizing at all hours of the day and night. Methodically, he reviewed my recent activities, imploring me to understand that the government was not trying to curtail my freedom of expression or right to legitimate activities. Then he moved straight to the point: "Professor Soyinka, this million man march of yours, how do you propose to carry it out?"

"The details were spelled out at my press conference," I pointed out.

"Well, you realize, I'm new on this case. I've just been transferred from

Benin—you know, I was the one in charge of that armed robbery case, you know, the notorious Anini—that implicated one of our officers. I didn't really have much time left to follow much else of what was going on in the country."

I obliged, first pointing out that the stated theme, "One Step for Freedom," itself summarized the overall strategy. "Obviously, we are not going to march all the way to the capital, Abuja—if you take Lagos alone, we're speaking of over eight hundred kilometers to the capital. Maiduguri, in the far North, is at least seven hundred. The idea is to create a relay of marchers. Some will accompany the main column no more than a few steps and return to their homes. Others will merely walk from one end of a city to another. The main column will take off from wherever they are based and proceed along designated routes. Their places will be taken by others while they are transported in vehicles to the next stage—you may call it a massed exercise in leapfrogging. Of course, those who are capable of it are free to walk all the way. But the climax will be the convergence at the outskirts of Abuja, when we'll march en masse on Aso Rock."

The man had begun to shake his head. "Professor Soyinka, do you think you can achieve all this?"

"Why not? It's all being very carefully coordinated. Schools, mosques and churches, private clinics, market women, students, factory workers, and so on, they're all going to be involved. Several schools have already offered their premises as stops on the way. Give or take a day or two, we'll all be in Abuja in a week."

"But this is a massive undertaking!"

I agreed with him, pointing out, however, that the people were more than willing.

"Professor Soyinka, let me be candid with you: only one organization has the capability and the resources to mount a vast operation like the one you're telling me about, and that's the military. I want you to understand that this is the thinking in Aso Rock, and frankly, I agree with them."

"You couldn't be more wrong. And we're going to prove you all wrong."

"Oh, I don't think so, sir. I think that, surely, you will not be allowed to prove anything."

"Why? If the government thinks the march will fail, then what is it worrying about? All you have to do is watch us fall flat on our faces."

"Ah, but Prof, that's the point. The government thinks that you can succeed."

I expressed puzzlement. "You're contradicting yourself."

"No—you, you, sir, you, Professor Soyinka. The government is convinced that if there is anyone in the country who can pull it off, it's you."

I confessed to being flattered but assured him that there were thousands of others with even better organizational skills and resources: the trade unions, farmers and market women's organizations, student movements...

"But the international connections, Professor! Your 'shopping list'! All those items which you solicited at your press conference: camp beds, sleeping bags, first-aid kits, iron rations, banners, boots and backpacks, a hundred thousand balloons—even walkie-talkies! And of course you will need money. This kind of operation requires money. Taken together with all those costly items, it is certain that you are relying on outside sources."

"Both inside and outside," I conceded.

He pounced. "So you agree that foreign bodies are involved in this."

I demurred. "Well, I don't know that we can call them 'foreign bodies.' We have lots of Nigerians living outside who are just as determined to take the nation back to democracy."

He sighed and brought out another folder, much slimmer. His demeanor turned primly official. "Sir, it is now my duty to pass on to you, formally, the message from the government. If you don't mind, I must ask my immediate assistants to be present. I am required to read you this message in the presence of witnesses, after which I shall report back to Aso Rock."

He pressed the bell; two assistants entered and took their seats. It was clear that they had been awaiting the summons. He cleared his throat.

"I am about to pass on the message from Aso Rock," he said, and his colleagues nodded. " 'Professor Soyinka, the government has been disturbed by the announcement of your intention to march on Aso Rock with over a million people. While it is not the intention of this regime to clamp down on anybody's freedom of movement, the government is of the opinion that this may lead to a serious breach of peace. Your group may encounter other groups who disagree with you and may try to stop you. This would lead to a breakdown of law and order. It is therefore the firm intention of the government—in fact, the government considers it its duty—to prevent your march at all costs. This government will act in the best interest of national security.' "

The riot act had been read. He tucked the piece of paper back into its file, then extracted another and pushed it toward me. "And now, please, Mr. Soyinka, you have to write a statement."

I was baffled. "A statement?"

"Yes. Those are my instructions. From headquarters."

"A statement about what?"

"About everything that has taken place here. The ... er ... conversation I've had with you, the fact that I have read out this directive of government—everything, in fact, that has transpired here. I would strongly advise that you include a sentence stating that you have called off the march."

"Oh no, I cannot do that."

"Professor Soyinka, the government has decided that this march cannot take place."

"Sure, I understand the position of the government. You've made that abundantly clear."

"And the message says clearly that the government will do everything within its power to prevent your march."

"That's plain enough, but I have no authority to call off the march. I have to consult with others."

A pause. Clearly this was unexpected. Then: "How soon can we have a response?"

"As soon as possible."

The director sighed. "Professor, I wish you could find your way to calling off that march."

"I've told you, a decision cannot be made by me alone. In any case, what's the hurry? The march is still months away. We are only at the beginning of organizing."

"Well, I'm afraid you will have to put that also in your statement. You have to say something in reference to the government position that I have just read to you. Those are my instructions. Please ..." And he pushed the statement form to me again and offered me a pen.

I offered him a compromise. I was tired, I sighed, and in any case, I would rather type out a statement at home. I needed time to digest everything he had said, reflect on it, and provide a well-thought-out response.

"My officer can follow you home and bring it back?"

"What of tomorrow?"

"Tomorrow? I have to report back to headquarters."

"Maybe by tomorrow I will have succeeded in contacting some of my colleagues. You do want an early response, you said. So? Why don't we simply make it one statement instead of two or three? If I gave you an answer tomorrow and the others rejected it ..."

He pounced eagerly on this. "All right. Tomorrow morning, then. In the meantime, I shall send a message to reassure them at headquarters that we found you at last and that we've had an amicable meeting. But please sign here, on the government's letter, that you've seen this. That way I can send a signal right away that we've had a frank and amicable meeting."

"Yes, you may do that. It has been an amicable meeting." I signed the document.

I was amicably accompanied to my car. We agreed on noon the following day for collection of the "statement," to allow more time for contacts to be made. I returned home and typed out a brief statement acknowledging that we had had a frank but cordial meeting, that the message of the government had been conveyed to me, and that I would make a due response after consultations with my colleagues.

Noon the following day, and the assigned officer was at my house to collect the statement. He read it, chuckled, shook his head, and proceeded to place it in the folder he had brought with him. I asked him what he found so funny.

"Prof, there is nothing here to indicate that you're calling off the march."

"No. I've tried all morning and I still haven't reached any of my collaborators."

"Prof, there is no phone in this house. And you haven't left the house all day."

"How do you know? Do you know this neighborhood better than I?"

The smile never left his face even as he cast a casual look around him, ensuring that there was no one within earshot. "Prof, you don't know me. You saw me for the first time yesterday, but please believe what I am about to tell you and take my advice."

"Yes?"

"Don't go on that march."

"I've told your boss, it's not my decision alone."

"Don't go on that march, Prof. And leave the country. Please, sir, as soon as possible. And don't even tell anyone before you leave."

A few nights later, other pursuers would catch up with me, expressing agreement with the man from State Annexe—but the motivations could not be more different. Among them, the most passionate was the old man Pa Ajasin, a constant in the democratic struggle, now in his eighties, one of the recipients of the brutality of another dictator, General Buhari. He had sent more than a dozen emissaries to track me down, but it was Olu Agunloye who knew where to find me to deliver the same message, the same passionate plea: *Do not go on that march. Do not take anyone on any march. Abacha will mow them down in their thousands without losing a wink of sleep—remember June.*

. . .

FROM DANGER TO SAFETY, the river crossing had taken less than ten minutes. In real time, however, it had lasted days, weeks, even months. Half a dozen times at least, I had prepared to leave the country, only to draw back at the last moment. Hours before dawn, I pulled on my boots and sat on the doorstep, ready to take off as if on a routine hunt, knowing, however, that this step would end only when I had crossed the national border. The sun rose and I withdrew into the house, exchanged the shotgun for my laptop, and sat down to work. Within Abacha's camp, our sympathizers came close to despair. A fishing boat had been readied in Lagos, stood up, and summoned again, earning me the imprecations of its owner, Chief B.A., a normally cautious businessman, who threatened to personally hand me over to Abacha if I ever commandeered his craft again and failed to board it. A colleague accused me of seeking martyrdom. Others wavered, uncertain of the hazards—and outcome—of any choice. A handful felt that it might be a good thing for the cause—*if that madman made the mistake of arresting you!* Oh yes, they argued, then the world would have to ask what was the fate of lesser beings, and Abacha would learn just what it meant to fly that far in the face of international censure. Even in Oyo town, halfway to the border, my friend Francis Oladele, a pioneer of the Nigerian film industry, urged me to remain—Abacha would not dare, he insisted. Deep within the cells of my marrow, I already knew better. I tried to make light of the dilemma, justified another day's delay by going for a final hunt. We would read the entrails of any bird or mammal that fell, I proposed, then make a decision. No one laughed.

I dawdled, not because I underestimated the complex despot but because of a deep resentment that, at sixty years of age, I was again about to be dislodged from my home—and by a being I truly despised. I knew his record from the civil war; so did the army. Abacha had been a prime player on the killing fields of the Midwest region—men, women, even children—after the Biafran forces had been routed. The future Maximum Ruler did not discriminate. It was sufficient for him to be spurned by a woman or lose her to a rival for a killing to be guaranteed. Shehu Yar'Adua, then army chief of staff, had recommended his dismissal from the army; not that I knew this at the time, any more than I knew that—irony of ironies—the man who had overruled this recommendation was none other than General Olusegun Obasanjo, then commander in chief and head of state. Years later, Obasanjo would come within mere whiskers of death by firing squad under the machinations of this same psychopath, while Yar'Adua perished in prison, his arms tied behind him, as he was forcibly injected with poison. Not for a moment did I believe that the Nobel had conferred a charmed life on me. "He wouldn't dare touch you!" Not touch me? This man, I knew, would gladly flavor his *tuwo** with the *ngwam-gwam*[†] of my head. No, it was simply that often-fatal contradictory state of mind—I knew that it was time to leave but did not want to.

I had developed a lethargy whose primary cause I continued to refuse to admit to myself: that this exile could only be an embattled one from which there would be no retreat. That prospect made my return an uncertainty, and I had grown deeply attached to the tranquillity of my private environment. Despite frequent forays into the cauldron of the nation's politics—indeed, perhaps on account of those very eruptions—the quiet rhythm of my Abeokuta retreat had become essential to my desperate need for an inner equilibrium. It had nothing to do with a "creative environment"—it was an interweave of tactility, smells, the muted sounds and silences that compensated for the often-resented public impositions. I knew of nowhere else in the world where I would rather be, at any moment and for any stretch of time. At sixty, the thought of an indefinite separation from my Ajebo sanctuary was intolerable. My preference was to go underground and become truly "elusive"—but within reach of my cactus patch.

Objectively, however, I had no answer to the insistence of my embattled colleagues. We needed an opposition radio, and I was the one, they felt, who could bring it about. The wife of the imprisoned president-elect, the combative Kudirat Abiola, later to be felled by an assassin's bullets in a busy Lagos street, would wring her hands, lamenting whenever we met, "Prof, *radio ti a o ni yi, o nje wa n'ya.*"[†] I promised her that she would have her radio; this was one contribution I had decided that I must make, from the outset. In my hunting expeditions, miles from human habitation and even lost in forest fastness, I had frequently come upon incongruous sounds that could only have come from a radio. Following the direction of the sound, I would come upon cattle drovers with transistors, their only connection to the outside world.

There were, however, other pressures from every side, an unfair imposition, I sometimes felt, from a collective undertaking: only W.S. could mount a successful overseas campaign for the democratic front or mobilize resources if, as seemed increasingly likely, we had no choice but to engage in armed resistance.

---

* A corn mealie, popular in northern Nigeria.
† An eastern Nigerian delicacy made from the chopped-up head of a sheep or goat.
† "Prof, this radio that we lack, it is causing us much grief."

Much mythology surrounded these expectations. Still, I could not deny that I did possess some advantages that others lacked—nothing approaching the magical potency that they all imagined, but what did it matter anyway? It was one of the factors that went into reinforcing the nation's morale. Today, many still believe that I raised millions that sustained the democratic cause and that Charles de Gaulle's commandos during the French Resistance were mere Boy Scouts beside the warriors I had infiltrated through the Nigerian borders, awaiting only my signal for the final liberation of the nation!

The irony of my night ride through the Nigerian forests would remain lost on me until much later. That is, I did not even recollect at the time that, only a year and a half before, I had been forcing my way *into* Nigeria in a nearly equally outlandish manner, through a series of man-made obstacles that were no less determined than Nature's slip soil, gullies, boulders, and tree branches that sometimes threatened to decapitate my driver and me. Even a mild equivalence in the police role had not been lacking—a tense moment at embarkation, when I clearly identified a man as a border agent, but one who was cold sober and intense, and I wondered if I had not left my departure till too late after all. The precautions we took had been thorough enough—only a handful of people had been involved—so I had full confidence that our security had not been breached. The arrangements had been in place for months and only awaited my decision to activate them: false trails, improvised exits, the familiar hunting expeditions that were so well known to the SSS that its code name for me was "Antelope." As a matter of fact, I did find that rather troubling, if not downright unflattering. Was this all they thought of me? As game to be hunted down and eaten? Not that I was after anything glamorous, I did not aspire to any of the more lordly species—assuming that the SSS had been generous enough to have offered me a choice. After all, the name I had chosen for myself during the 1983 fight in Oyo state against an earlier fascism, that of the National Party of Nigeria, was the modest "Tracker." Still, I consoled myself that perhaps "Antelope" was a concession to my supposed elusiveness, or my passion for hunting. If I hoped, however, that my namesakes in the bush would learn that we were now bound together in this unsolicited naming rite and lose their suspicious attitude toward me during my incursions, I was mistaken. They continued to make our encounters as meager and as frustrating as possible.

For the urban denizens, I had loudly announced plans for rehearsals of *The Beatification of Area Boy,* to keep the SSS reassured of my continued presence in the country all through December. We tied down the obvious government spy squad around my office by having my car driven there with regularity even when I was nowhere near the office and maintained a semblance of normal activity through the usual stream of callers, some of whom had been given appointments that I never meant to keep—they would understand everything in due course! That ruse must have worked well enough, since the SSS detail along Lalubu Street continued to haunt my office dutifully for a full week after my escape, when I finally presented myself at the UNESCO headquarters in Paris for a press conference. Sani Abacha went berserk and dismissed the top echelon of the immigration officers at the Idi-iroko border, through which he naively presumed that I had made my escape.

Yet, at the departure point, an unmistakable agent had surfaced who pretended to be just one of the nocturnal crowd. While we waited for the canoe to arrive, he hung around, avidly scanning my features whenever he thought I was not looking, quickly taking his eyes off me when I turned my gaze on him. When a rough meal of watery beans and *gari** was prepared for my escorts and me, famished as I was, I took one look at it and my expression showed that I would prefer to fast until we reached the Benin side. This volunteer minder could not wait to offer to dash over to a not-too-distant goods shack where he could obtain some bread and tinned sardines, and even a bottle of stout. I told him, factually, that I did not drink stout but lied that I was not hungry. If he had insisted, I would have accompanied him, as I had also resolved not to let him out of my sight until we left.

The tensest moments came as we began to board the canoe, after the loading of goods was done. This helpful figure of indeterminate functions took out his flashlight and began—quite unnecessarily but acceptably—to beam it against the floor of the craft, guiding the feet of the passengers. When it came to my turn, however, he shot the beam straight into my face and kept it there. I pushed his hand away. Even with his eyes hidden by his flashlight, behind all his unctuous concern for my safety, I could see a pair of fevered eyes fastened on my face, attempting to recollect its features—or was it memorize them? I hoped it was the latter, but, prepared for the worst, my hand closed around the Glock pistol I still had strapped to my waist. After that grueling ride, which had brought me just one river's width from safety, I firmly decided I was not about to become an actor in any weepy movie of last-minute reversals, where the fugitive, with one foot virtually on the soil of freedom, is dragged back into captivity to the wailing of violins!

The sudden roar of the canoe's outboard motor drowned the sounds of any

---

* Farina made from cassava.

orchestra waiting in the wings, and the facial inspector leaped back onshore. It took no more than five minutes, and we crossed the innocent stream that demarcated the spaces of two nations. The "wharf" on the Benin side was a broad, flat slab of rock on which the reverse-track contraband was already waiting, laid out in neat rows. There were a few minutes to wait while the motorcycles, then the bales of merchandise, were off-loaded. I stood apart from the jostling bodies, staring across the stream, this moment of separation branding itself onto a template of infinite sadness.

For one who had sworn to himself that no tyrant would ever again chase him beyond the bounds of his nation, it was a moment of bitter defeat. Even when the choice is willingly made, exile sinks into one as a palpable space of bereavement. At that moment, I believe I died a little.

What I tasted in my mouth was worse than ashes; I distinctly felt the crunch of cold cinders between my teeth, and it set them on edge. The riverbank was spare of cover on the Benin side, so now that we had parted company from dense, overhanging foliage, the clouds also parted to bare the landing of all subterfuge in a wash of moonlight, as if to ensure that this place of leave-taking would be deeply etched on my mind—every detail of that moment, the stolid slab of rock basalt, the bales of smuggled goods, the practiced motions of the passengers as they emptied the canoe of jute bags, outsize cartons, cylindrical portmanteaux that I thought had disappeared with the advent of cheap, infinitely expandable plastic suitcases, "Ghana-must-go"* bags, sealed baskets, and tied-up bundles. With the casualness of practiced hands, the canoe operators piled rolls and boxes in improbable shapes across the carriers of the now off-loaded motorcycles or hauled them onto the heads of waiting porters. Already the canoe was spluttering toward the opposite bank, and the question that came to mind was—When again? In that moment of self-pity, the line that sprang to my mind came straight from childhood, when I had made a habit of appropriating to myself those lyrical lines that the Bible could offer. I tried to recollect—was this from the Song of Solomon or the Psalms of David? *By the waters of Babylon, we lay down and wept…*

… except that I did not feel in the least like weeping. A huge wave of rage swept through and engulfed me, voiding all other emotions. Would he triumph in the end, the tyrant who had brought this upon me? Just how much was required of any individual in his lifetime? Was my life now bound together with that of a killer, albeit in absolute power, in a struggle to the death? How

---

* The local name for an all-purpose jute bag, later notorious for underhand dealings.

long would it take before a savaged people woke up, recovered their sense of worth, and knocked him off his pedestal into a hole so deep that generations to come would seek his remains in vain? What role would I play in this, for how long, and at what cost? The rest of my life? Would I perish in the attempt? Mercifully, there was not much time for further self-pity. All too soon, it was time to climb back on the pillion and resume the journey, riding at a more humane pace through the Benin forest.

THE INSIDES OF my thighs ached. These were muscles that had never been subjected to an endurance test, and I marveled yet again how the body so easily takes for granted every strand of muscle or ligament that makes it function, forgetting that some simply never come up for use in years or even decades. Even if I had been a chronic jogger, it would never have occurred to me to prepare my inner thighs for a ten-hour journey on a motorcycle pillion. Three times I was compelled to ask my pilot to stop while I walked up and down, improvising exercises to regain circulation and loosen up the muscles as they were repeatedly assailed by severe cramps. They ached so badly that I began to fear that I might have done permanent damage to myself, some calamity such as uncontrollable muscle spasms in the future. For a hapless passenger, with nothing to do except stay glued to the seat of the motorcycle, the night passage was fertile ground for the direst imaginings. In addition to three stops, I was thankful when we came to streams that had to be forded or when we stopped to refuel the tank from the spare jerry cans with which we were amply supplied. I was even thankful for spills in sudden marshes or loose soil. As we rode deeper into the forest, my face was steadily lashed by branches. My driver would do his best to sound a warning as a branch loomed up around a corner and he ducked, but it was mostly pointless. I took vicious slashes, began to wonder if the branches were exacting vengeance for the nocturnal disturbance of the peace of the forest. I could hardly complain; my companion took far more whipping than I did.

Occasionally, we ran into night caravans of smugglers, strung out in a line, loads of every form of merchandise on their heads, but mostly of cloth and plastic vessels: plates, bowls, and other utensils, flasks. They had obviously come up from the Lagos factories and had a ready market in Benin and Togo, neither of which, I presumed, had any such factories. Using the clandestine routes meant that they could not only avoid payment of duties but also escape harassment by rapacious Customs officers, whose exactions could prove even more onerous than the legal Customs duties. From not too far off, muffled by dense vegetation, came the sound of a truck engine, retreating. I guessed that the driver had taken his passengers as far as he could on a barely motorable route, disgorged them, and was returning to the collection point for the next group. It struck me again and again as absurd, this separation of peoples into artificial nations, peoples who, despite their occasional wars, nevertheless regarded one another as one of a racial kind. Now they had to brave the forests and unpredictable border patrols in order to ply their time-ordered trade, gather at feasts of reunion, and celebrate their ancestral bonds.

I thought then of the people of Bobo-Dioulasso in Burkina Faso, to the northwest of Nigeria, of whose annual homecoming for the obsequies of the departed I had learned during my research days. That custom was only a focus for a much larger purpose, however. At this annual festival, all the people came together, both from the nation's metropolis and from beyond the borders of the nation that had once been known as Upper Volta, bringing news, retrieving relationships, and "burying" those who had died outside the community, but now with appropriate rites that involved weeks, even months, of preparation. I wondered if I would one day be brought home, even symbolically, to rest among my own people.

It was then, I now believe, as the motorcycle plunged southward into the Republic of Benin, placing a stamp on my exile, that I formulated the last wishes for my remains, which became an obsessive catechism: *If I should die outside my own borders, bury me in whatever alien land I expire in—as long as Sani Abacha still bestrides the nation at the time of my death!* The thought of Bobo-Dioulasso set off the fear, and I recoiled in horror at the prospect—that the gloating feet of such a ruler should trample over the same soil that held my remains. It would later become an all-consuming dread, perhaps the only visceral fear that I nurtured throughout my years of exile. I imparted strict instructions to my family: let no well-meaning relation even think of bringing my body home as long as that monstrosity holds sway over the portion of earth that I consider my own! Lost on me was the irony that, only seven years before, I had been incapable of one moment of tranquillity until I had brought home the remains of my friend Femi Johnson and reinterred him in the earth of Ibadan.

WE HAD SET out from Oyo just before daybreak in order to hole up at Iseyin until the motorcyclists joined us for a ride that would begin before the onset of darkness. It was a routine safety precaution, but in fact, I needed a final ramble in the woods, if only as a token farewell. Two birds fell, and I sent them back to

Francis with my escorts. Now I wished I had kept one—a small fire, a rushed barbecue, bliss. Instead, nothing had passed my lips since morning. I thought briefly of the streams we had forded and dismissed them—they were not the answer to my thirst. With the prolonged privation, my mood had hardened, my concerns had undergone a drastic change! Democracy, Sani Abacha, the SSS, and the rest of the impositions of the world faded into irrelevance. The moment the motorcycle wheels began to churn deeper into the Republic of Benin, with the bush track yielding to motorable though still untarred road, all my worldly and spiritual desires took on a marvelous simplicity, a reduction to the barest essentials that were projected onto two events and two events only. They shimmered behind eyelids that were caked with squashed moths and other winged life of the night, wracking me with anticipation.

One was a long, cold shower. Next, a long, cold beer. For both, at that moment, I was prepared to barter even my cactus patch. My throat was caked with dust; I felt I could taste pollen, bugs, and grime all the way down into the remotest coils of my intestines. The prospect of the materialization of those two events took on an agonizing intensity. After a ride of another two hours, the lights of human habitation replaced the swarms of fireflies that sometimes turned the bushes into fantasy groves, suggesting possible sources of inspiration for Fagunwa's *Ogboju Ode Ninu Igbo Irunmale.** I felt my tongue rattle in the dried gulch that passed for the cavern of my mouth and I swallowed hard in the agony of expectation. The sparse lines of electric poles meant only one thing: beer, and refrigerated! I began to look out for familiar signs that would indicate the watering holes of the inhabitants of that region of Benin.

The lamps on the tubular poles were virtually transformed into advertising beacons for that single commodity—a supremely chilled beer. I understood, for the first time, the essence of mirages, since, from time to time, I could swear that I saw a sweaty beer bottle thrust itself out of a billboard and reach toward me, cold to the touch, only to melt away again into the dark surroundings of the pool of illumination provided by the motorcycle lamp. Then, in a reversal of normal expectations, instead of the lighted road lamps becoming more frequent as we approached the first township, they stopped abruptly, even though the poles retained their precisely spaced levitations from the dark and their lamps, unlit, were visible in the moonlight. When we entered Tchaourou, the nearest border town to our point of incursion, only the moon provided any glimmering of light. Then I observed that there were no lights visible in the

---

* *The Fearless Hunter in the Forest of a Thousand Demons*—trans. W.S.

houses, not even the town center, which, to make matters worse, appeared completely deserted. It was not long past midnight, so what kind of town was this? Clearly not a rural habitation, yet the inhabitants appeared to have retired with the poultry.

It turned out that, most inopportunely, we had timed our arrival for the Oro* Festival of Tchaourou. No one was permitted in the streets, all lights were extinguished—not even a cigarette could be lit out of doors—and women in particular could not be seen. It also meant, of course, that the late-night bars were closed.

My guide could not have been more disconsolate as he returned from conversing with a cluster of men who sat on their porch, speaking in low voices. He soon grew cheerful, however, and assured me that the situation would be remedied somehow once we were safely within the compound of his "uncle." It also meant having to find his uncle's home with his lamp switched off. This was no simple task. Our destination proved to be a kind of way station for travelers of both night and day who had good reason to evade encounters with Customs officers and the police. The house was just outside the township itself and could be approached only by two-wheelers such as ours. Threading our way toward it between the warren of houses was no different, it struck me, from swerving around natural obstacles in the forest, except that here, they were recumbent goats and sheep, upturned cooking pots and pails, stacks of firewood, open hearths, pestles and mortars propped against walls in narrow passages, even water wells—all had to be carefully navigated. Fortunately, the moonlight was generous. We made it safely, my pilot stopping to speak to two or three of the locals and deliver messages.

When we arrived at the household of his "uncle," the welcome was spontaneous but also instinctively wary, marked by curiosity. Even in my disheveled condition I stood out conspicuously, an obvious stranger. Eyes followed me, but no questions were asked. Perhaps my pilot operated by telepathy, or the whispered conversations he had held earlier had involved couriers racing ahead through hidden passages, for, unknown to me, a miracle lay in wait. I had barely time to note that the "uncle" in whose home I had been billeted had his radio tuned to news from Nigeria when, courtesies over, he pointed to a seat, then waved toward a low table.

Standing in splendor on that table was that which I had spotted from the moment I entered the room but from which I had stolidly turned my gaze, fear-

* A masquerade of the male secret cult.

ful that a sudden visual assault might make it vanish. But—yes—it was indeed a bottle of beer, moist and cold to the touch, the loveliest object that fugitive humanity could ever hope to set eyes upon. In a moment, its existential mission was fulfilled. It sat depleted but transfigured in the effusiveness of my gratitude. Next came the other half of the unspoken covenant. A crude shed in the open yard, with only a token cover to shield its user from passing eyes—within it stood a bucket of water. I threw all inhibition to the winds, peeled off my clothes, and began to scrub the dust, grime, and squashed flies off my body. And my hair received a rare soapy cleansing; it had become a haven for every species of bug and moth that ever coursed the night paths of the tropical forest, my hat having flown off early on the ride. When I was hardly done, my ears picked up a long-forgotten sound that suddenly violated the calm of the night.

Oro Festival! It said it all. I could have been in Isara, my paternal village, within an identical warren of mud houses that are so familiar in a typical Yoruba town. Even the red baked earth, with its mild contortions and undulations, mimicked Isara. When the masquerade arrived, it went from house to house, decanting blessings and receiving tokens of the people's gratitude. I remained outside, beside the door, in the shadow cast by the roof of the house under that strong moon, watching this denizen of the spirit world flit from house to house, vanish within, and emerge a few moments later with his retinue. Around us, retreating and advancing, was the whine of the bullroarer. Seated on the ground, my legs stretched full length, I rested my strained back against the wall of my dwelling for the night, shirtless, basking in the night of Oro that the firmament appeared to honor with such a vast, luminous sky. Or perhaps it was the otherworldly Oro that chose to call human attention to the splendor of that night by ordering all terrestrial lights extinguished. Certainly—and how could it appear otherwise to a voyager who had just survived the hostility of the night forest?—it seemed to me that I had never known a night so deep, so eternal and serene. All rage was gone, all physical pain subsided. I chuckled to myself as I recalled that moment of panic, now remote and unreal, when I had thought that the busybody at the departure wharf had no other mission in life but to haul me back to Abacha's insatiable dungeons. My sense of peace was like a velvet cape that floated down to cover my seminudity. I could not stem a wave of nostalgia for what I had known, longing for what could be, lamenting how simple life really was: a cold shower, a cold beer, and then an ancestral presence that roamed the night to touch a people deep down, within that secretive space where their communal soul resides.

An Oro spirit mask whirled gradually in my direction. It was a most unnerving moment, because, a microsecond before, I had happened to look down to my right side, my eye caught by a twin spot that was boldly reflecting in the moonlight, glowing so brightly that I thought a pair of fireflies had settled on my skin. I saw what it was and was deeply embarrassed—had I broken the taboo? For they turned out to be the luminous bead of the Glock. I had retained this incongruous object next to my skin throughout the journey for self-defense. It had become such a part of my attire for so many months past that I had come to feel undressed without it. Thus, after my shower, even here, I had routinely restored it to its place, beneath my waistband. I snatched at it, yanked it out, and stuck it under my buttocks. I was in the shade of the roof, however, and no one appeared to have observed anything unusual. The masquerade procession moved to accept me into a community into whose bosom I had been thrust so unceremoniously. Oro spun around and around before me while I watched listlessly. One of his attendants offered me a kola nut over which Oro had whispered some incantation. It was all so familiar, albeit an infrequent manifestation. With only a variation here and there, this was a scene that tended to insinuate itself, unbidden, into telling moments of my existence. I took the kola nut and bit into it. Oro chanted what were clearly prayers in a low tone as one who communed with intimate forces. Silently, spontaneously, I muttered mine alongside his own. It was a deep, heartfelt, impossible craving: I prayed that the peace of this night, this pool of infinite solace, might endure forever.

DAWN ENDED THE magic of the night, ushering in a harsh pronouncement on my future existence. I stayed yet another night on the way to the Beninois capital, Cotonou, in Ouesse, in a hotel, to be alone and to ease myself body and soul into that future. I had need also to shop for mundane items: a pair of casual sandals and a shirt, but, most important, a new hat to hide my giveaway head of hair. Abacha's agents, we knew, had already infested Cotonou, thick as flies. I kept, as the expression goes, total "radio silence," even toward my family. My companions to the edge of the forest would have returned with news that my departure had been without any untoward event and that there had been no sign of pursuit.

Fifty hours after my departure from Abeokuta, I was in Cotonou, announcing myself at the reception booth of the French Embassy. The French ambassador in Lagos had sent word ahead—he was one of the few in on the secret, and indeed a willing contributor to one of my other optional escape plans. On my way to the embassy, I stopped at a café. As I fortified myself with an espresso, it struck me as a wryly defining moment of transition. Kola nut and coffee, both courted for their caffeine, yet culturally divergent in their essential natures—the ritual apprehension, cultural significance, and social symbolism of one, and the straightforward, consumerist absence of complication of the other. I needed no further reminder that the brief idyll of the night of Oro had indeed been a blissful culmination to the violence of exodus. The world of the espresso was worlds apart from that of the ritual kola nut of which I had so un-expectedly partaken. If I had any inclination to return to my cactus patch, it was now too late. I had submitted myself to an unalterable rite of leave-taking, and the prediction that lingered in my mouth was that of the kola nut, bitter and gritty.

Diplomatic Recruit

. . . . .

THERE WAS AN OLD ENEMY AWAITING ME IN EXILE. OFTEN, MY OUTSIDE ENgagements had been conditioned by his real or projected presence in the environment. Invitations to conferences, workshops, lectures, and so on were subjected to a selective process based on avoidance of this implacable foe as the first principle of well-being, or indeed survival. Alas, the first casualty of my new state of exile, I soon realized, was—volition. I had lost the right to choose my engagements. I was also precluded from taking refuge in hibernation like some of the most sensible mammals on Earth, as obligations forced me into that enemy territory again and again. After a few days' grace, Old Man Frost—to give him his nom de guerre—arrived in all his malevolent majesty to welcome me formally into exile, his "keen tooth"—thus certified by the non-tropical-blooded Bard himself—only a fraction less dreadworthy than Abacha's vampiric fangs. My talismanic adoption, since student days, of Shakespeare's "Blow, blow, thou winter wind . . . thy tooth is not so keen," hummed through tenderized nostrils, was sheer bluff, lacking in true defiant conviction, as invisible icicles scythed through successive layers of padding.

"Freeze, freeze, thou winter sky. . . ." My reinduction took place on my way to Harvard University in Cambridge, Massachusetts, after a short stay in Paris and London, weighing options. One winter blast sliced through my trousers as I stood outside Boston's airport, awaiting transportation. No one had informed me that my sentence of exile would be served in the Arctic wastes. How could I have forgotten that this climatic zone shared the same latitude as Cornell University, whose topography—so reminiscent of my own university at Ife— had actually succeeded in holding me down in the years between 1984 and

1987! That was a record three years in succession, but then I was still imbued with the masochistic recklessness of a borderline middle age. Even so, I had found more reasons to travel back to Nigeria than were warranted by necessity, and, in the end, offers of a tenured association had fallen on frozen ears.

Now, ten years later, one visitation of the northern wind from the Great Lakes activated my rights to limited choice. Ahead of the next winter, I bade adieu to my disconsolate academic host, Skip Gates, and fled southward to Emory University in Atlanta, much closer to the tropics. A surprise lay in wait: Old Man Frost had leapfrogged ahead of me, and I actually arrived during the infamous 1995 blizzard, Atlanta's first since the 1930s, I was told! I did not believe one word of that and felt like suing the university for deception over my working environment.

Still, the treachery was not repeated the following year, nor the next, and I settled in—a sarcastic expression if ever there was one—to be joined by my now intolerably menaced family, whose exit was also another cloak-and-dagger episode. Preparations were aided and abetted by the French ambassador in Lagos, Garrigue-Guyounaud, while my younger friends—Yemi Ogunbiyi, Olu Agunloye, and others—carried out the physical part of decoys, espionage, disinformation, and the eventual passage of the fugitives to safety. From friendly Cotonou, I monitored their progress, and we traveled back to Atlanta together via Paris, where the U.S. Embassy awaited them with the necessary papers. It was a huge weight taken off my mind. The surveillance over their residence in Ikeja had reached a pitch of intensity that signaled the likelihood of some imminent development of a sinister kind. Additionally, our man in Abuja, "Longa Throat," had urged their evacuation, and that had settled all further equivocation.

The U.S. Embassy in Paris also had a message for me—at least, one of its diplomats did. I was given a draft letter being prepared to protest the action of one Arpad Bosch, a highly placed official of the World Intellectual Property Organization (WIPO), an affiliate of the United Nations. This international civil servant had chosen to award WIPO's highest recognition, a medal for the defense of intellectual property, to one Sani Abacha for his championing of intellectual rights. Arpad had even traveled to Nigeria for the honor of decorating the dictator in person. Such an act was typical of the grotesque gestures that would surface from time to time on the part of the international community, and they never ceased to baffle me. Are you sure? I asked. It was true enough. Could it be, I suggested, that Abacha had undertaken to pursue foreign book royalties for Nigerian authors, mistaking them for oil royalties? The transit through Paris took a little longer than we had planned, but in the end the action was formally repudiated and the official forced to leave the organization.

This was symptomatic of my new role within the exiled opposition, and I took it in stride as an additional compensation for the stress I had undergone in extracting my family from danger. Similar battles were already being fought elsewhere as the foreign handlers of the Nigerian dictator sought to buy him respectability in the outside world, including attempts to name professorial chairs and fellowships after him at some American universities. The luckier of these institutions were those about which we had preknowledge; they could at least withdraw before the opposition publicly intervened and the scandal blew wide open. The others—two or three at least—were forced to make painful and embarrassing withdrawals, returning funds that they had already added to their coffers.

Hardly had my family begun to adjust to Atlanta when Winter's unconscious ally Sani Abacha won the fight to set up a consulate in Atlanta, now rated as the major bastion of opposition in his estimation—higher than New York and Washington—once it came to his ears that W.S. was hibernating there. Abacha's millions triumphed over the scruples of the City Council, and his killers were brought to rest right on my doorstep.

As I was obliged to travel extensively, my family was left vulnerable. This sinister addition to Atlanta's residents left me with no choice but to move them as far from Atlanta as I could—first to Rancho Cucamonga, then Upland, always on the other side of the American landmass, and—*southward*—in California. My peace of mind reasonably secured, I was free to extend myself as much as duty required. Only my head of department, his secretary, and the university president, William Chace, knew that I no longer lived in Atlanta. My activities were organized on an ad hoc basis, while I stayed at the Emory Conference Center Hotel. Student lectures, seminars, public interventions—including a memorable public dialogue with Archbishop Desmond Tutu—and other engagements took place en route to other parts of the world or the United States.

When Abacha declared me a wanted man in 1996 and placed me—with a number of others—on trial for treason, Chace, a most astute political being and former antisegregation activist, immediately read the implications and placed me under police protection. When the dictator's specially created smear brigade began its offensive through the publication of an obscenely libelous journal under the cynical name of *Conscience International*, circulated worldwide, with a special complimentary copy to Emory's president, he promptly raised the level of protection. The university police, usually in mufti, met and escorted me going through the airport and kept a watch on my safety, until I learned to "forget" to notify them of my movements. Not all the protestations of my head of department, the even more solicitous Rudolph Byrd, could persuade me to change my seemingly careless disposition. It was not that I underestimated the risks, but by then, we had an effective organization. I simply preferred the less obvious measures that our membership in Atlanta and environs—including a strong presence of Nigerian taxi drivers—willingly provided.

I HAD NOT left Nigeria by the hazardous route just to imbibe the air of foreign climes, and I soon set about gathering a number of exiles—students and workers—together to create the National Liberation Council of Nigeria (NALICON). There was already an opposition movement, the National Democratic Coalition (NADECO), in existence. It had been formed within Nigeria by a combination of former military officers and political veterans who had finally resolved to challenge Sani Abacha's dictatorship.

In late 1995, NADECO issued a number of ultimatums to Sani Abacha, the most crucial of which was a deadline by which to quit office. Abacha responded in a way that should have been predictable to those seasoned politicians and men of war: he came down heavily on them and scattered them to the four winds. Using brute force—arrests, firebombing, and bullets, as well as economic blackmail; forcing banks to call in their loans, pauperizing their businesses, and so on—he quickly brought some to their knees, while the more resolute fled into exile. They regrouped and resumed their activities outside. To the intense resentment of several of its members, I did not consider for one moment being part of NADECO but was more than ready to collaborate with it in every way. With the exception of two or three members, I was temperamentally ill suited to that company. One of their principal spokesmen had already compromised himself badly with Abacha, having canvassed for a business contract, and on terms that provided the dictator some of his earliest propaganda coups against the opposition—he had simply published the outrageous terms of the proposal.

It went beyond business compromises, however. The first "getting-to-know-you" meetings with NADECO made it clear that this was a ponderous organization, top-heavy and with competitive egos. Singly, its membership boasted experience and dedication; collectively, however, they tended to indulge in peripheral contests that consumed time and eroded their political credibility. There was a civil service approach to the making of tactical decisions for the overthrow of a tyranny. NADECO became an even more difficult working partner with the arrival of my favorite political maverick, Chief Tony Enahoro, who, paradoxically, thrived on endless meetings, copious minutes, points of order, standing orders, and the moving and seconding of motions, counter-motions, and amendments to motions. Worse still, his arrival appeared—without his intending it—to galvanize the already simmering rivalries within the movement, causing them to burst open. It was difficult to associate the combative chief with the same activist who had challenged Sani Abacha in the streets of Lagos and barely escaped with his life. I began to avoid meetings that should normally have enhanced our collective efforts, since they led nowhere and only ate up time and scant resources—flying across the Atlantic Ocean or the American landmass deserved some concrete justification in planning and results! Bickering was tearing that group apart, amid intrigues and the politics of ranking. Little did I know that NALICON, especially when it moved to ex-pand its membership, would come close to foundering on the same boulders of petty ambition.

Actual undertakings were a different matter, and there collaboration was not too difficult, especially on the diplomatic front. The case for the Nigerian people against a despotic regime had to be placed before the world, the inter-national community challenged to come to the aid of the people. This was one activity into which I was immediately co-opted, both through expectations and my own objective recognition of my "international profile," which placed me at an advantage. It did not take long, however, for a long-held suspicion to harden into an absolute certitude—if I were destined for a late-life change of career, it was not meant to be the diplomatic profession. Though I could turn myself into a yo-yo like the famous Middle East shuttle diplomat, I was still no Henry Kissinger. Still, willy-nilly, this became my primary field of assignment.

The average human composition—the range in which I group myself—has ensured that there is a limit to how many heads of state the body is built to encounter; how many ignorant—willfully or genuinely so—foreign affairs ministers it can educate, how many cause-famished pressure groups it can co-opt; under how much solidarity by human rights organizations it can bask; how many meetings of EU/UNESCO/UNO/OAU caucuses it can attend; into how many diplomatic gatherings it can be escorted like Dresden china or else gate-crash; how many "working" lunches, dinners, and so on, it can absorb; how many congressmen and -women and parliamentarians—feisty, outraged, or impotently sympathetic—it can lobby; how many bureaucracies it can infiltrate; how much mealy-mouthing it can stand; how many compromises it can withstand; how many promises are left for it to believe in; how many immigration officers it can mentally eviscerate; how much debt—both moral and material—it can accumulate; how many slanderous countercampaigns it can endure; how many safety measures it can tolerate; how many distractions it can overcome; how many betrayals it must anticipate.... Every day, it seemed as if I had reached the end of my tether, yet I dared not give up.

I accosted uncertain prospects, not even always within the targeted nations themselves but in their embassies, sometimes in a hotel suite where a head of state, a foreign or defense minister, or simply an influential politician was visiting and an ambush could be hastily organized, especially for leaders from the African continent. Great Britain after the ascendancy of the Labour Party, a willing Canada, a sometimes ambiguous France, a consistent European Union, and the United States—at least at the beginning—were the most sustained recipients of such diplomatic importunings, sometimes undertaken by our collaborator, NADECO, and sometimes jointly. But at least NADECO had two experienced hands in this field, perhaps even more: one had been a minister of foreign affairs, the other a career ambassador.

Always with a succession of tightened jaws, grimaces, silent imprecations, moments of deflation, elation, imprisoned laughter—well, one could always chuckle afterward, but at the time ... hardly a laughing matter.

The Germans were a mixed bag. The junior minister of home affairs, who had the attitude of an undertaker deprived of a corpse, had been unbearably curt. My visit was not even so much on behalf of our own struggle as in solidarity with our German chapter; NALICON had begun to sprout chapters in several countries. The chapter had joined forces with a group of Nigerians who had fled—or claimed to have fled—Abacha's persecution and had entered Germany illegally. They had sought sanctuary in a church, backed by its servants of God and their followers, but the earthly ministry was determined to evict and deport them. Our reception by this thin-faced undertaker hovered between diplomatic incivility and downright rudeness, the ultimate and unpardonable expression of which was—according to our German-domiciled Nigerian liaison—his failure to offer us coffee and biscuits! Knowing nothing of these protocols, I was still left with his vocal nuance and body language—and were they eloquent!

I responded by signaling an end to the meeting. I summoned my best Humphrey Bogart lopsided smile, got up with my "entourage" from our now clearly confrontational side of the table—the setting appeared to be always:

government on one side, delegation on the other, (missing) line of coffee/tea/ sparkling water and biscuits in the middle—and announced that there appeared to be no point in continuing with the session. My relief was unbounded on discovering that our Nigerian facilitator was even less of a diplomat than I; the missing coffee and biscuits, he insisted, demanded a stronger response, a total diplomatic rupture, maybe a challenge to a duel at dawn, sabers drawn on the banks of the Rhine.

Germany did make up for the boorish undertaker, however. The first opposition radio, Radio Freedom, enabled by the dissident general Alani Akinrinade, had been set up in early 1996 and was functioning inside Nigeria. Its range was limited, but it nettled the regime sufficiently for it to secure the expertise of the German Dornier company in the effort to track down the source of transmission. I flew to Germany. The foreign minister himself, Klaus Kinkel, was more than generous and affable when I again invaded the Rhineland—protocol of coffee/tea/biscuits being anything but lacking. Kinkel, whose grasp of profound issues was rather disparaged, we learned, by his compatriots, displayed an appreciable sense of humor when I reassured him that I had not come to deprive the German company of legitimate business. However, forget that biblical promise "Seek, and ye shall find," I urged. This is a time to *seek, but not to find.* Take Abacha's money and contribute a small percentage to our movement. The minister chuckled loud and long; he guaranteed the former but declared that it was beyond his ministerial powers to make a business enterprise part with hard-earned money. Still, through Kinkel's influence—or at least with a nod in that direction, I am persuaded—two of Germany's foremost foundations made contributions toward some of our logistical requirements, in addition to their own efforts at assisting some of our younger, imperiled writers.

Contradictions in the actions of some foreign governments remained baffling. An especially annoying instance was the plight of Cornelius Adebayo, a former governor of Kwara state in northwestern Nigeria. Having barely eluded a hit squad from Abacha, he headed for Ivory Coast, where he applied to enter Canada. But he found himself stuck for more than a year while both exile groups made strenuous representations, putting pressure on the Canadian government to allow him in, assuring its officials of Adebayo's bona fides. For an otherwise supportive government, this was a game of impenetrable ambiguity and cruelty that left a fugitive stranded in a place that was meant to be a temporary stop. It was incomprehensible, since the same Canadian government had shown itself so uncompromisingly hostile to the Abacha regime that it had been forced to close its embassy in Nigeria!

In many ways, the diplomatic field remained part of the battlefront, and once an eruption of that battle took place in a rather odd way. Long after the event, echoes of a day of—what else could have been responsible?—paranormal attack would assail my ears, a day when turbines of a hydroelectric power churned uncontrollably, pursued me from meeting to meeting with commissions of the European Parliament, vindicating my instinctive designation of water as an unruly tenant of the human intestines, especially its aerated version and when taken on an empty stomach! Never had a delegation's leader felt so mortified as a swallowed concertina or Scottish bagpipes insisted on participating in serious exchanges. All stomachs do rumble occasionally, but this was a marathon! In vain did I contract my stomach muscles, change seating positions, cough energetically, punch the offending guts surreptitiously under the table—all that provoked was a subversive will of its own, while my interlocutors did their best to pretend that a seismic event was not taking place right there, across the table. And it was not one of those one-off days when the work is done at one meeting, two, or three, all humanely spaced out. No, it had to be the day of the serial killer rounds, when one was ferried from room to room, from building to building, with little recovery time in between. Nothing, not even a quick lunch, could silence that windbag until after the last of the day's engagements. I was left to wonder if Abacha's long arm had finally caught up with me, since we knew that he engaged a round-the-clock squad of marabouts both to guarantee his survival and to pursue his enemies across the waters. No other explanation was possible, since the purpose was to undermine the talks—and this was evidently a stomach in demonic possession!

Even before the return of Abiola to the country, to be followed by his arrest, the United States had been a primary target of the opposition's diplomacy push. Less than a year into my exile and soon after the birth of NALICON, I requested the U.S. government to assist in dismantling the Korean-trained killer squad set up by Sani Abacha and placed under the command of the notorious Major Hamza al-Mustapha. Our contacts in Abuja—code-named "Longa Throat"—had supplied details of their secret location, a nondescript hotel in a crummy section of Abuja, their methods of operation, and a draft list of their targets. An overseas section was also being assembled; hence the resolve of the regime to establish consulates in Atlanta, where I was teaching, and also Houston, which had also been identified as a den of Nigerian dissidents. I passed the details on to Susan Rice, then at the Africa desk of the State Department, requesting assistance in dismantling or at least destabilizing the killers' operations. Not long after, the squad struck down Alfred Rewane, a close associate and backer of Abiola, right in his bedroom, shot him through a pillow placed over his head. They had gained entry into the protected home by using a fake delivery van that claimed to have come from Rewane's own factory. Kudirat, the combative wife of that ill-fated tycoon politician Abiola, had been another prominent victim, shot in a busy Lagos street. A number of other assassinations and disappearances have since been traced to this sinister force, including the failed attempt on the life of the proprietor of *The Guardian* newspapers, Alex Ibru. He survived but lost an eye and some fingers and remained badly traumatized for years.

Susan Rice, together with a fortyish, serious-faced colleague, Marc DeShaezer, had been part of a triumvirate with whom NALICON maintained direct contact in the White House. Occasionally, Anthony Lake, Clinton's national security adviser, would wander into his subordinate's office as well, as if by accident. A rather thoughtful, intellectual-looking type, Lake would listen intently to the discussion for some moments. Later, we met privately in his office. Rice and DeShaezer leaned significantly to the anti-Abacha cause, while the third, whose name my mind stubbornly refuses to retain, was insecure, pugnacious, and a miserable listener. I distrusted him on instinct, even before we had a sharp exchange. With no attempt to disguise his resentment, he groused that everyone expected the United States to pull their chestnuts out of the fire. I reminded him that most of the world's raging infernos had leaped from U.S. and European campfires. As the U.S. policy appeared to begin to shift toward accommodation of our enemy, I fantasized my invisible self slipping into his stuffy little office to catch him working on sneaky memos that advised against us, slipping them in the dead of night under the office door of his boss without the knowledge of his colleagues.

Rice exhibited a quiet intelligence and a deceptive guilelessness that could easily throw one off guard. Once, when we met her in her office after a spate of bombings began at home, she looked me in the eye and asked, without any preliminaries, if I were behind the campaign. The directness was unexpected, but I returned the look and told her no. The subject of violence having been broached, however, I asked her in turn—emphasizing that it was a purely hypothetical question—what the position of her government would be if the opposition found that it had no choice but to take up armed struggle. Not to plant bombs all over the place, but suppose we asked the government to open up some abandoned facilities in the United States for the training of volunteers— such mothballed facilities were scattered all over the American landscape— what would be the likely response? She appeared to mull that over for some moments, but in fact, the answer was already obvious on her face—after the Iran-*contra* affair, the United States was not overanxious to support any acts of insurgency, real or hypothetical. I imagined not, I replied, and there the matter ended.

It was, most ironically, South Africa that handed us our bitterest defeat. Civil society—the labor union, writers' groups, Chamber of Commerce, the individual institution known as Archbishop Desmond Tutu, and other public leaders—remained staunch, but the attitude of the government slid from lukewarm to the level, in one instance at least, of sabotage. This took place during efforts to weld all outside-based opposition groups into one. Toward that end, a congress was organized in Johannesburg in 1996, on the invitation of civil society. Kayode Fayemi and Olaokun Soyinka, my son, shuttled between London and South Africa, consulting with civic leaders, government officials, and representatives of the ruling party, the ANC. The go-ahead was given by the South African government. Passports were gathered and sent in a bunch to embassies in London and Washington for visas.

At the beginning, all went smoothly. Then, with no explanation other than that "instructions had been received," the London embassy not only stopped issuing further visas but became passionately attached to the passports when we moved to retrieve them. The timing was nearly fatal. Delegates had taken leaves of absence, wound up their affairs, and geared themselves up for the journey. Some had purchased their own cut-price tickets, nonrefundable. We could not change the dates. I turned to Norway for help, specifically to Jan Egeland, the secretary for foreign affairs, with whom I was already acquainted. The spontaneous response of the Norwegian government easily counted as one of the very high moments of our embattled existence. Visas were issued in record time, a number of flight tickets donated to the effort. Our friends in South Africa would not accept a shift of venue, however, refusing to accept a surrender of *their* democratic rights to the political whims of their government. It was a matter of principle, they said, and insisted that the conference be held as planned.

South African visas being already in the possession of half the delegates, there was only one solution: we ended up holding the conference simultaneously at two venues. I presided over the South African group in Johannesburg on the first day, while a colleague, Professor Ropo Sekoni, held the fort in Oslo. I then flew overnight to Norway and chaired the final session. A two-way flow of faxes and telephone lines united the two groups, making it possible to make joint decisions. When it was all over, I was left wondering whether it had all been a merely imagined event or one that had actually taken place. The minutes, resolutions, plan of action, and lists of participants, fortunately, testified that it had. Over and above mere records, however, was the testimony of the human body in silent protest—on the flight back to the United States, I remained without recollection of time passing, without any awareness of the plane taking off or landing.

I HAD HARDLY recovered from that exercise when, thanks to a meeting with the South African poet Breyten Breytenbach, a former prisoner of apartheid, we found an opening through which we could advance the newly unified organization from the beginnings made at the Johannesburg/Oslo meetings. The George Soros–sponsored Goree Institute in Dakar, of which Breyten was a board member, agreed to facilitate the second meeting of the umbrella group, now going by the name of the United Democratic Front of Nigeria (UDFN). That gathering took place over strong diplomatic representations by the Abacha regime. The Senegalese government replied that it did not make a habit of intervening in "cultural" meetings, which, to the best of its knowledge, this was meant to be, since it was sponsored by the Goree Institute.

It was a moment to be savored, the solidarity of the Senegalese government with the democratic cause and the coming together of twenty-seven organizations spread all over the globe, from Australia to Canada. Alas, the affliction I sought to escape in NADECO traveled with the luggage of a handful—a mere quartet, American-based—of the delegates. It served to increase my bewilderment at the craving for position and power in human disposition, one that seems especially absurd when an intervention in the fate of millions is initiated from the position of a weak challenger. It proved to be a near death at nativity; a movement that had been formed to liberate a nation from the very bane of power found itself enmeshed in a tawdry tussle for position.

I had declined any formal position within the new body. This, however, signaled a contest for what the ambitious quartet read as an opportunity for self-promotion into a vacuum and the complete takeover of the organization. The plot had been hatched well in advance. It began from the moment that the liaison officer for Boston discerned, with absolute certainty, that I would not run for office and would remain content with my functions as an informal ambassador to the movement. The irony of such jostling was totally lost on the conspirators. One was a self-hating Igbira, a minority tribe from the Nigerian hinterland, whose yearning to be mistaken for a Fulani aristocratic scion had resulted in his changing his name from Daniyan to Dan'Iyan. Partnering him was an ambitious youth from Swarthmore College, Jude Uzowanne. The third member was a labor unionist from Edo in southern Nigeria, Tunde Okorodudu, an activist in his own right who fell under the spell of the fourth member and center of intrigue, the liaison officer for the U.S. Boston chapter, Maureen Idehen, a pharmacist who had worked closely with me and was central to the coordination of activities for much of the United States. Together, this Gang of Four—the accolade was spontaneously bestowed—succeeded in serving a timely lesson on the power lust even among a yet inchoate formation that sought to curb power at its most virulent and malignant.

It was a low point in the career of the anti-Abacha movement, suddenly compelled to confront the banal distractions of trite intrigues and personal ambitions. Expelling the miscreants took its toll. The liaison officer, the Boston-based Maureen Idehen, made off with our scant funds, leaving behind a trail of bad checks. I should have been warned by the extralong talons, garishly decorated, that she affected in place of fingernails, but this highly efficient intriguer was the daughter of an old schoolfriend and classmate. His visits to his daughter in Boston had even served as an updating source for much of what was happening on the ground at home, and his support of the cause was quite vocal. As it turned out, he had also immersed himself in position grabbing on behalf of his daughter, even to the extent of poring through the minutes of the Dakar meeting and placing transatlantic calls to argue with my son—elected secretary-general of the UDFN—to assert the position of his daughter in the movement. To say that the entire episode constituted a personal embarrassment would be understating an experience of intense chagrin. I had the unpleasant duty of reminding the doting father that he was not a member of the movement and would he kindly keep sons and daughters outside an already draining undertaking.

Ironically, it was the "vengeance" of one of the subversives that raised the profile of the opposition in the mind of the Abacha regime, far above its own ambitions or capabilities. A "confession" appeared in a Northern-based newspaper run by the brother of the inspector general of police, Alhaji Ibrahim Commassie, contributed by Jude Uzowanne. In it the writer claimed that he had been involved in the recruitment and training of a secret army, that he was in fact chief of staff of this force under my military command. In the meantime, naturally, he had had second thoughts, was now opposed to violence, had voluntarily quit the organization for this reason, and was doing his patriotic duty by revealing these terrorist plans.

Of all the fabrications put out by Abacha's men about our activities, this was by no means the wildest. In any case, armed struggle, even from the start, was a subject that was openly introduced into discussions. This young man's claims, self-ingratiating concoctions though they were, did have one decidedly negative effect. They had, after all, emerged from one whose earlier membership could not be denied, albeit that he was now expelled and had turned into a born-again pacifist. He had come into the UDFN through an affiliating group and been assigned the role of mobilizing the youth wing of the movement. If young Uzowanne's claim had been true, it would have been his second conversion within a year. Revelations came tumbling in, confirming earlier rumors of his instability. He was confronted with a position paper he had sent to Sani Abacha, outlining how the dictator could turn himself into the Pinochet of Nigeria. His intellectual prowess, of which he had no modest estimation, was humbly offered to Abacha for the historic transformation. A small, ambitious Walter Mitty character, emotionally unstable, Uzowanne would indeed have been a most unusual choice for a military assignment, additionally being shortsighted, virtually blind, behind his inch-thick lenses and of such physical insubstantiality that the slightest wind from the heat of New York streets threatened to blow him right off the sidewalk and on to summary execution by the traffic.

Alas, some of our supportive foreign embassies in Nigeria did swallow this "revelation" without any qualification and reported to their governments, which began to distance themselves from the opposition movement. This would have been a minor nuisance, on balance, since we were also positively served in other ways by this egregious piece of fiction. Certainly it played havoc on Abacha's peace of mind; all reports indicated that it contributed to imbuing in him a holy terror at the very mention of W.S. or NALICON.

Such fears were further bolstered on a daily basis by a formidable weapon in our armory: Radio Kudirat, sponsored by Sweden and Norway, with some help also from the U.K.'s Westminster Foundation. I had made the acquisition of the radio, formerly named Radio Democrat, my obsessive priority from the moment I had stepped into exile and embarked on my diplomatic shuttle. Radio Freedom had played its part, but it had been limited in coverage, vulnerable, and intermittent. Much too soon, it had fallen silent altogether. With the powerful and secure transmitters of Radio Kudirat, however, the entire nation was covered. Almost everyone tuned in to its two-hour transmissions every evening, including soldiers in their barracks. Prisoners behind walls looked forward to this daily treat, huddled around transistor radios brought in by their wardens. No single event boosted the morale of the opposition as did reports of its corrosive effect on Abacha's equilibrium filtering back to us. The regime struck back in a number of ways, employing the same instrumentation of propaganda. One of its most sinister plots was to circulate rumors in the prison where the former head of state Olusegun Obasanjo was being held that a Wole Soyinka squad was on its way to storm the prison and rescue the inmates. In the confusion, of course, the former head of state would be gunned down.

GENERALLY, I PREFERRED working quietly and individually. Indeed, it would be an understatement to say that I am more than allergic to being a part— especially a leader—of a delegation. However, a scouting mission undertaken by Kayode Fayemi with his long-standing colleague, the ebullient, irrepressible Tajudeen Abdulraheen, a roving new-generation pan-Africanist, resulted in our most sustained, structured diplomatic offensive in Africa, with generous help from the Canadian government. The UDFN divided the continent in two, after identifying those governments that might be persuaded to pay attention to what was happening to us in Nigeria. Two delegations took off, not particularly bubbling with optimism, but at least we would leave no room for later excuses—*Why didn't they come to us? We would have helped.*

It proved a sound recommendation. A number of the government leaders we visited either feigned ignorance of or were genuinely uninformed about the degree of repression in Nigeria. If the latter were true, one could only wonder what their diplomatic representatives were doing to earn their salaries and privileges, what kind of reports even a mentally retarded but innately honest observer could possibly relay home except that the most populous nation in Africa was rapidly sinking into a state of power insanity that shamed a continent to whose aid nearly the entire world had rallied—however belatedly— when it was confronted by the humiliation of apartheid. If my remarks to the bosses of those diplomats resulted in only one of them being deprived of his sinecure, those mostly frustrating visits, undertaken as an unavoidable duty, would have been worth it.

The tour was not a total loss, however. There were at least two noteworthy encounters with African leaders, though drastically divergent in the impressions they made on me. One was with the Ugandan president, Yoweri Museveni, who, as it happened, occupied a very special position in relation to our struggle. None other than Moshood Abiola, the elected Nigerian president, still in prison, had funded Museveni's revolt against the tyrannical misrule of Milton Obote, the former Ugandan president, who had been dethroned by the homicidal buffoon Idi Amin Dada, restored by the idealistic Julius Nyerere of Tanzania, yet proceeded to surpass, it is arguably estimated, the atrocities unleashed on that nation by Idi Amin, the "Conqueror of the British Empire." I was on my best diplomatic behavior and resisted a strong impulse to remind Museveni that our fight was also that of his benefactor, especially when he took time off from our urgent concerns to pontificate about the "grammar-spewing intellectual elite" who should be held responsible for the woes of the African continent.

I had not known that this was a familiar Museveni line of peroration, or I would have spared myself the irritation. Still flushed with the victory of his guerrilla movement, he received our delegation late into the night. It was difficult to envisage him as a guerrilla fighter, since he proved to be a poor listener—a guerrilla in the bush must *listen,* common sense dictates, even to the language of the leaves! The Ugandan leader struck me as being more suited to his former profession as a schoolteacher, and an opinionated one at that, with an often embarrassing estimation of the profundity of some of his most commonplace notions or comments. Still, once we succeeded in dismounting him from his hobbyhorse, he proved quite positive. Abdulraheen, then resident in Uganda, ensured that our host and I ended up in an inner room, where we spoke with greater confidentiality. Contact continued for some time afterward, through a specially assigned minister. Nothing material emerged from this supportive direction, however, though we were able to ensure that Abacha's regime received no comfort from Uganda, especially within the Commonwealth. Proposed meetings with our contact minister each time he was due in Europe had a way of being called off at the last moment. Still, I had to accept the fact that Alice Lukwena's Lord Resistance Army was stretching the headmaster's attention to the limit in the northern part of the country.

A year or so after our meeting, while our struggle was still on, we did meet again, this time in Davos, Switzerland, at the World Economic Forum, where we shared a podium. I was still appreciative of the attention Museveni had paid us in Uganda and so was able to react indulgently when he resumed his patchy pronouncements on African history, half-baked theories of African social development, and whatever else, all delivered magisterially and with a bland indifference to the thematic assignment of the panel. Afterward, I ran into some of his aides and implored them: "Look, you people must really try and place your man under some kind of restraint, or one day soon he'll be taken to task on a public platform and ridiculed." They broke into laughter, and one replied, "Professor Soyinka, why are you complaining? You only had him for an hour and then you're gone; we undergo this every day. We can't escape him."

Impossible to imagine a greater contrast than Paul Kagame, then only the vice president of a nation that had undergone a near-unspeakable horror, the likes of which the African continent had never experienced in oral or recorded history. No visit that I undertook, either on my own or in delegation, could have been more poignant, yet more bracing, than that to Rwanda, where Kagame's liberation forces had routed the *genocidaires* and were pursuing them into neighboring countries but mostly into the Central African jungles. At the same time, a government of restoration was being positioned, confronted with the impossible task of suturing the mangled nerve endings of Rwanda's national being, restoring confidence in its corporate existence. Kagame, seven foot plus, every inch exuding intelligence and discipline, was a formidable force to encounter, and without any effort on his part to appear one. Even when he said "I am a fighting man," it was a statement that spoke of a disciplined vocation, delivered without a trace of bravado. It was a considered summation of a personal temperament that was also validated by the Rwandan circumstances. The same objective assessment informed his accounts of some of the horrors perpetrated by the Hutus on both Tutsis and Hutu objectors and his accusation of French complicity, and justified his decision to terminate French as an official language of the nation. It made his confidence credible when he stated that despite the seemingly terminal sentence on national unity, his mission of reunification was already predetermined.

With the same grounding in reality, Kagame went on to explain that it was necessary for him, the victorious Tutsi, to cede the top position of president to a member of the Hutu tribe while contenting himself with being the political second in command. A number of Hutus had also been victims or else had been coerced into collaborating with the murderers. It was essential for the purposes of rehabilitation that one of the majority Hutu be seen as occupying the top position. We had, however, built up an intimacy so quickly and effortlessly that he admitted—with a slight, apologetic smile that lit up his wafer-thin face, sculpted like a wedge of the *abata* kola nut—that yes, it was a temporary arrangement. When the fighting part was over, it was indeed likely that he would take over the political reins—but: "The arrangement suits me. I'm a fighting man. I love fighting."

One of the continent's extremely rare breed of leaders, I thought, and if there was a moment in our search when I felt that yes, we could confidently entrust our people into the hands of one man, it was there, in Rwanda. Indeed, recalling my brief student flirtation with soldiering, I could not help thinking how fortunate it was that Her Majesty's government had been unable to call on such a talent in its recruitment exercise. Kagame is a leader beside whom one would willingly march into battle and indeed relish the moment of confrontation with an overwhelmingly superior force.

The morning after our meeting was one that I awaited with dread, but it was a solemn obligation, not one that could be evaded. One should *see*, even if one had already imagined. We were driven around to two or more of the "museums" that had been created to document the killing rage of Rwanda, testaments yet again to the unfathomable propensity of man that leads him to butcher and mutilate his own kind. Among such memorials was the optimistically named Mandela's Park. There were others that were simply plain fields, with rows upon rows of white crosses. We visited a hut stacked high with skulls, hundreds and hundreds of skulls, some with bullet holes, others with the unmistakable gash of the machete, a curator calmly dusting the exhumed skulls and skeletons. The most poignant was a church into which the victims had fled, several deliberately lured with the promise of sanctuary, before the Hutu army, assisted by the vigilante killers—the *intehamwe*—was summoned. The bodies, now skeletons, were left exactly where they had fallen. These were the clothed skeletons, and the stories of their deaths were superfluous. The most enduring image of all was a baby's skull with a panga still embedded in it.

THESE WERE NOT, of course, victims of war but of organized butchery; nevertheless, the lessons remained sobering and apposite, reinforcing a constant openness on the part of our opposition groups to dialogue at every turn. Not that NALICON or UDFN ever made direct overtures to the Abacha regime—any such initiative, we knew, would only have provided material for hilarious propaganda. To every leader whom we did meet, however, we took pains to stress that same message—that the Nigerian crisis could still be resolved by dialogue— and we ensured that we did not turn our backs on any such opportunity.

Abacha's first reach toward us came early, toward the end of 1995, through Vice Air Marshal Ibrahim Alfa, my beanpole friend who had revealed the details of Abacha's visit to him on the eve of the 1993 coup. Alfa's message was direct: "Abacha wants to negotiate. He says, choose your time and place, send your representatives, and he'll send his." Ibrahim took back my answer: "First, free all your prisoners." For months I heard nothing further. Then came an apologetic message from Ibrahim, advising me to ignore any further invitations, not just from him but from any other direction. "The man is not serious," he said, "he has other plans, and I hate being used for a charade. He's only pandering to public opinion, wants to be able to claim that he's made overtures to the opposition." Ibrahim resigned his commission as go-between and ambassador extraordinare and returned the use of the jet plane assigned to him from Abacha's fleet.

There was a falling-out. Abacha had Ibrahim's bank—Alpha Bank—listed among "distressed banks" and imposed impossible conditions for its recertification. He attacked Ibrahim's other businesses and sought to pauperize him for his refusal to openly endorse the dictator's regime. They had a confrontation, during which Ibrahim protested, "Sani, why are you doing this to me? You know my bank is solvent." Abacha feigned surprise, swore that he had nothing to do with the harassments and would look into the mistake. Ibrahim read the signs, withdrew from his normal Lagos/Abuja beat, and retired to the safety of his village in the North. He died not long after. It was impossible to determine if his death had come naturally or been assisted.

The second and final overture, several months later, was the stuff of melodrama. It involved a famous "seer" who had warned the superstitious leader that his salvation lay in finding a common ground with the opposition, specifically with W.S., who, he warned, was protected by "a certain aura." Abacha must be credited with an evenhandedness in this respect: he dealt with both Muslim marabouts and Christian prophets, plus a sprinkling of indeterminate psychic consultants whose gory prescriptions had provided some of the content of my play *King Baabu*. So hush-hush was the operation with the "seer" that the religious leader was persuaded to host some kind of church convention. Abacha's secret service personnel then dressed up as reverend delegates and went into secret sessions with the "seer" to decide on the best approaches to the archdissident. They reported back to their boss, and the search then began for an emissary who could be trusted by the designated opposition leader. Someone remembered that my son-in-law, Tola Onijala, was a diplomat in the Foreign Service— and that was how Tola became the dictator's emissary to me in Washington.

He brought the same message as Ibrahim Alfa: a meeting at a venue of our own choosing and without preconditions. Again I made the obvious response: before I would even bring the proposal before the UDFN and NADECO, there had to be one precondition, and that was the release of all prisoners. Tola argued that my purpose was being defeated by such insistence. I warned him— in confidence—of Ibrahim Alfa's assessment of these overtures, an assessment that I fully shared. We had no time for cosmetic meetings that would then be presented to the world as serious attempts at resolution.

Tola held on to his conviction that Abacha's proposed meeting offered the best venue in which to present such demands. If we insisted on that precondition and the meeting was aborted, the nation—and the world—would blame the opposition, and the prisoners would remain Abacha's hostages. Finally I said, "All right, we'll make it a test. He's merely attempting to buy time to consolidate his rule, but take back the message that we've agreed to meet without preconditions. Our representatives will be ready whenever he is."

That was the last we ever heard of Abacha's accommodational intent. No one in the opposition lost a second's sleep or let down his or her guard in deference to Abacha's approaches. On his part, at some moment that was difficult to determine but was definitely after these overtures, Sani Abacha raised the stakes in his assault on all opposition. Officers whose loyalties were deemed suspect fell victim to attacks by "armed robbers," while others, like one luckless Customs officer, Omitola, a cousin of the fugitive general Alani Akinrinade, were disposed of in bomb explosions. After the death of Alani's cousin, his office was raided, and, naturally, bomb-making equipment was "discovered" in all its sophisticated glory. Originality was given scant consideration, since a check bearing Akinrinade's signature was also found within the car—just as a copy of Wole Soyinka's *The Man Died* had lain beside the body of the journalist Bagauda Kaltho in the bathroom of the Kaduna Hotel. It was a season of maximum saturation of every known elimination device, including, as would later be discovered, poisoning, which, in all likelihood, was the cause of a number of sudden, mysterious deaths, especially within the military.

No one was excessively surprised when, after what he must have deemed a decent interval, the no-nonsense, "incorruptible" General Buhari agreed to serve Sani Abacha, manning the so-called Petroleum Trust Fund with a free hand to dispense millions as he pleased. At home and abroad, the specter of assassination hovered over every mind. Plots were manu-factured to resolve the nightmare of resistance through the route of judicial lynching, and opposition figures were rounded up, cynically accused of responsibility for the assassination *of their own colleagues!*

As for the external opposition that continued to elude his roving assassins, Abacha unleashed a novel weapon—not original, but certainly unprecedented in its unprincipled inventiveness and its venomous intensity. He resorted to the weapon of slander.

A Digression on the Power of Slander
The spate of assassinations intensified, but assassinations were not only of one kind. Protecting ourselves against the obvious, we had overlooked the

other kind—that of character. Not that it mattered; that is one assault weapon against which no human individual or organization has ever invented an adequate response. The Sani Abacha propaganda unit went into action and commenced its toxic rampage with the launching of the most virulent publication in the history of propaganda, the cynically titled *Conscience International*.

My son Ilemakin was the first to alert me to the existence of the journal; he had seen it on sale in a London magazine store that specialized in off-mainstream and foreign journals. My picture decorated the cover, which of course was designed to attract the curiosity of Nigerian, and indeed African, readers. Within Nigeria itself, it was not on sale but was distributed free. Once, at a high-society wedding in Ibadan, a few dozen copies were unloaded on unsuspecting guests, who eagerly grabbed their copies and took them home, only to discover the putrid contents.

Each issue was devoted, nearly exclusively, to one prominent opposition figure at a time. I had the dubious honor of launching the series: Vol. 1, No. 1. At the very first glance, my mind leaped in the direction of the anti-Semitic product of the czarist era that was later absorbed into the armory of Nazi propaganda, *The Secret Protocols of the Learned Elders of Zion*. That feeling of empathy with an ancient, visceral violation did little to lift, in moments when I recollected its contents, the mottled cloud that would suddenly envelop my innermost space, even in the midst of the most energetic public activities. *The Protocols* had been directed at an entire race of millions; this was dedicated to a single individual, meant to be absorbed by just one human psyche without a dissipation in numbers.

The journal was produced under the direction of a Chief Abiola Ogundokun, an infamous politician who had served under Shehu Shagari, president of the nation between 1979 and 1983. Ogundokun's real claim to fame was that he had jumped bail in the United States after being charged with rape in a Baltimore hotel. He returned home a fugitive in disgrace—but not in the eyes of Shehu Shagari, who promptly made him a director of a government-owned chain of newspapers. Thereafter he was allocated one hatchet job after another, a series of dirty undertakings that even some of the notorious enforcers of his political party, the NPN, would not touch. Year after year, regime after regime, Ogundokun's career underwent the usual ups and downs until Abacha's talent scouts spotted him in a condition of abject penury. He was clothed, fed, set up in an office in Abuja, and generously supplied with funds. His assignment: to publish a journal of unprecedented grossness in the history of the Nigerian yellow press, as an offensive against all real and imagined threats to Abacha's regime.

Collaborating with Abacha's point man was the similarly qualified Major R.O.A. Salawu, who had been drummed out of a state organ that owed its existence to my initiative—the first Road Safety Corps in Nigeria, probably in all of the African continent. The Corps constituted my "citizen response" to the insensate slaughter on the Nigerian roads, especially between Ibadan and Ile-Ife, where I lectured, a veritable "slaughter slab" that devoured my colleagues and students and made a mockery of my efforts to fill the latter's brains with knowledge. Major Salawu, alas, proved to have been more preoccupied in the nonhumanitarian aspects of the undertaking and eventually found himself, at my insistence, charged in court with more than thirty counts of stealing, forgery, conspiracy, and so on. Then came the Abacha coup and the trial was stalled, and stalled, and eventually hiccupped to a stop. The thieving major was mysteriously reabsorbed into the same organization, which, being the brainchild of the now-exiled dissident, had become a nest of subversion in the dictator's mind. The Corps was undermined, its autonomy and public integrity badly compromised. It was only a matter of time before Salawu teamed up with his soul mate, Chief Abiola Ogundokun, in the service of the greatest reprobate of them all, General Sani Abacha.

In a lighter mood, I sometimes speak of the earth-shaking achievements of fellow Nobel laureates whose discoveries bestow palpable luster to the Nobel directory of recognition. Some have solved the riddle of DNA, others have transformed communication technology, yet others have found the cure for hitherto incurable diseases, and so on and on. None of them, however, except this writer, I boast, has ever waxed a musical record. (For all I know, this may be an unfounded claim, but it makes a good story!) That record, an LP, was titled *Unlimited Liability Company*. It was made in 1983, at the height of the profligate rule of the National Party of Nigeria. One solitary verse in the lyrics, in the vernacular pidgin English, was devoted to the U.S. escapade of Ogundokun:

> *Another Director is a Wanted Man*
> *He commit rape for Washington D.C.*
> *He run come home, you give 'am bigger post*
> *As Director of a chain of newspapers*

The randy chief had never forgotten nor forgiven.

The least putrid ingredient in this toxic broth—from which the rest can be imagined—was the invention of a daughter, then twenty-seven years old,

whom W.S. was supposed to have fathered on one of his students. So thorough was the propaganda work that a physical daughter was launched, albeit
furtively, on society. A most garrulous young lady, she visited members of my
family, circle of friends, and colleagues, an ex-governor or two, and others to
advertise her parentage. Obviously not so well coached, however, or perhaps
weaned on pulp novelettes, she volunteered a slight embellishment: she was
the daughter of a housemaid in my family employ, and knowledge of her true
paternity had come through a deathbed revelation by her mother. While we
battled Abacha from abroad, the young lady, named Yinka—to rhyme with
Soyinka, perhaps?—was welcomed among the well-to-do, ate free in restaurants, partied in discos and nightclubs, all expenses on the house, and generally lived off a land peopled mostly by Sani Abacha's opponents. Her claims did
not alarm me as much as the dangers posed by her infiltration of my family and
circle of colleagues. I took action as soon as I learned of this new "family member" and caused a letter to be circulated through her known haunts, though
this did little to stem her freeloading career.

It was not an original ploy. "Unacknowledged" children already long in the
tooth do have a habit of turning up after the death of a prominent figure; the
variant here was that the confectioners of the sob story did not even wait for
my passing away! Equally unoriginal, but of mind-numbing diabolism, was the
squalid catalogue of attributed crimes that were indeed based on actualities—
only they belonged, right down to the most sordid detail, to Major R.O.A.
Salawu, even as set out in the police charges against him.

Beneath my outward insouciance—this must be admitted—the contents
of that journal drilled a corrosive hole into the most secretive core of my being.
I had to improvise, go through processes of trial and error—from immersion
in overwhelming symphonic music that drowned out the voices in my head to
spells of meditation, those exercises that stood me in such good stead in prison
solitary—to counter the threatened erosion of my combative consciousness.
My outer shrug was a lie; we had work to do, and others needed the impervious
confidence of my leadership. For the sake of the opposition, as well as for my
family, I had to hide the suppurating wound that ate into my vital organs. Several nights I lay awake, wondering if any human psyche was really equipped
with an internal armor strong enough to protect the essence of his being
against a seepage of such venomous intensity.

Yes, those publications did succeed in depriving me of several nights of my
accustomed sleep and even ate into my waking preoccupations. My concentration would trail off occasionally in the midst of a discussion, as a phrase in a

tract of irredeemable vileness flashed across my mind. While I was reading a book, minutes would sweep by—five, ten, maybe fifteen, or more—and I would find myself still on the same page, unable to recall what lines I had read, what the book itself was that I held in my hand. Over and over again this would happen until I gave up after hours of zero absorption.

I was not unaccustomed to gossip, defamation, and slander. I doubt very much if any people in the world can match the conglomeration called Nigeria in the propensity of its inhabitants toward the game of character denigration; it is all part of a justly remarked-upon creative energy, unfortunately much of it of a negative, even self-destructive temper. This brand of the abuse of inventive energy has driven many valuable individuals away from any form of civic commitment or public service. In this publication, however, the most tenuous restraints had been jettisoned. A total stranger, a doppelgänger with an odious smirk, was being invented between the lurid pages, and I was swamped by this illicit being, this fake persona who dispensed spores of corruption guaranteed to percolate through the most protective layers of society.

Group therapy sessions, so favored in the United States, represent for me the ultimate in the abject abandonment of human dignity, self-respect, and the human will, a negation of that very private space within which, declares my temperament, the deepest wounds are healed. But then it must be understood that I have a deep contempt for much that goes under the name of psychiatric practice, especially in the United States. "I have an appointment with my therapist"—and off he/she goes for a weekly, twice-, thrice-weekly session with a shrink. Obviously these remarks do not apply to those genuinely in need, victims of diagnosed mental illnesses and disturbances. Among my acquaintances, alas, are several who make a fashionable pastime, or simply a very chic consumptive habit—like attending wine-tasting sessions—out of viable modes of treatment for psychiatric disorders. So how is it that I have caught myself wondering why no psychiatrist appears to have considered a particular area in which I have felt that I could do with some serious counseling myself, and of the group variety? For this is the stark truth: during that dark period, I sometimes felt that perhaps I could have done with a group session over this one experience: slander! Forget the dismissive shrug of the shoulders, the snarl of genuine contempt for the purveyors of degrading fantasies; something sticks to the soul and succeeds in dragging down the spirit, intermittently and sometimes for prolonged spells.

I understand why the word "smear" is such a preferred expression— yes, one feels smeared, dirtied, polluted. Feeling pure and uncontaminated within is all very well, but anyone who has ever accidentally stepped into dog excrement—a guaranteed event in some neighborhoods of New York—knows that you can scrape your shoes as much as you like against the pavement, step deliberately into puddles, and then rub the soles against tarmac, gravel, patches of grass, even mud; that peculiar, nauseous odor of *dog shit* simply never disappears—or, what really matters, you feel it never does! The smell hangs around you or—again this is what matters—you are convinced that it does. Even after you have finally reached home, taken your shoes off, and left them outside, the sense of a foul stench continues to dog you. And of course as you walk alongside or share public spaces with others, the question surfaces—can they *smell* you?

Slander is very much in that vein. Even among colleagues and acquaintances professing the usual trust and respect—well, they have heard, of course, but do they believe? When they say "Oh, no one believes a word of that," are they really thinking "Hmm, the dirty hypocrite, exposed at last"? Maybe, after all, a few sessions among those theragroupies would have helped. With this particular affliction, I believe, there is need for a forum where one can compare notes. No holding of hands in a circle, no group meditation, none of the "confessional" attitude, no passivity roles in the face of simulated assaults—no, none of that! Simply an orgy of music and poetry, lots of wine—very robust— the favorite food of each participant, video clips of libelers undergoing mild forms of social censure, such as being flayed alive, slowly roasted over an open fire, tarred and feathered, publicly castrated, or simply splayed over an anthill from dawn to dusk under an unblinking sun, while the more energetic among the victims are provided with air guns and darts, for target practice on the effigies and photographs of such vile social malcontents. Brushes, pots of paint, and broad canvases for some action painting should, of course, be provided for the more artistically minded.

Within the opposition, a few voices did propose a campaign of retaliation, targeting some of the more notorious props of the regime, such as Thomas Ikimi, the minister for foreign affairs, and Walter Ofonagoro, the minister of information. It was pointless going after the principal himself—no mind was equipped with the fiendish imagination that could invent crimes to beggar the reality of atrocities committed by the innermost core of the Abacha regime. I shot down the idea, however. The mental and practical energies that would be expended on such sterile activities were best reserved for psyching ourselves up for the irreversible moment when—or if—we actually committed to armed struggle. We never did reach that moment, but, as the Bard said, *The readiness is all!*

*R*equiem *for an Ecowarrior*

. . . . .

THE CALLS UPON THAT STATE OF READINESS WERE NOT SLOW IN COMING, but none equaled the brutal clamor of the event of November 10, 1995, an event that addressed the world in the most lacerating accent yet, even by the savage register of General Sani Abacha's rule. The event was primarily designed for the Nigerian populace—it warned, very simply, that a new force had come into being, a force that admitted no constraints or scruples, was contemptuous of world opinion, and would remain deaf to the counsel of the most revered. This event was therefore timed to make the maximum impact on global aware- ness, to serve notice to political watchers, Amnesty International, Human Rights Watch, and other busybodies that the threshold for the impunity of power had been lowered below their meddlesome projections. The United Na- tions felt sufficiently exercised to send a commission of inquiry after the event; its members were treated with derision by Abacha's government, most directly and publicly by the minister for foreign affairs, Chief Thomas Ikimi, who pro- ceeded to lecture them on the limits of their mission. For most of us in the opposition—certainly for me—the state murder of Ken Saro-wiwa and his eight companions signaled the futility, indeed the death, of dialogue.

The trial of the Ogoni Nine, right from the beginning, was a proceeding that would be farcical but for its lethal implications. The defense lawyers, led by Gani Fawehinmi, had been openly taunted, subjected to indignities—on orders—harassed, and even roughed up as they arrived for each day's hearing. Stricken by remorse, one state witness had confessed on videotape that he and others had been offered lavish inducements to perjure themselves and were coached on what evidence to give—especially against Ken Saro-wiwa. The hanging judge Justice Ibrahim Auta dismissed this damning rebuttal of the state's case as irrelevant. Frustrated and unwilling to continue to be counted as part of a deadly charade, the defense lawyers withdrew—albeit controversially—leaving the accused to conduct their own defense. A travesty of justice could now proceed, unimpeded by and indifferent to the presence of international observers, a number of whom were, in their turn, barred from future proceedings. Every form of protest or intervention merely served to feed the arrogance of power. The spectacle played out its tragicomic script right on to the designated end.

The verdict—guilty—was fully expected. Very few individuals, however, believed that the sentence—death by hanging—would ever be carried out. I was not among the optimists. Power had mounted the head of the dictator; it needed its periodic nourishment in blood.

KEN HAD SOUGHT me out years before in Abeokuta, perhaps in 1989, to seek support for his Ogoni Bill of Rights—the inception of a structured struggle by the people of a devastated, oil-soaked land. The Ogoni remain one of those minority people in the delta region in the South with a distinct history, language, and culture. Oil prospecting and extraction had doomed their land and impoverished their people, but conferred—and still confer!—on the rest of the nation, especially the military and its business conduits, limitless wealth from the proceeds of the very agent of their misery. The bill was a manifesto for Ogoni social, cultural, and economic justice. Seeking my voice on behalf of that cause, Ken came accompanied by a small delegation that included his son, Ken Junior. Intense, committed, and organized, they were demanding reparations for past abuse, neglect, and state robbery, as well as a degree of political autonomy.

I needed no persuasion. How many times had I flown over the Niger Delta—the main oil-prospecting part of the nation—and seen the landscape dotted with flues that burned night and day, several of them for decades? Even before Ken's visit, I had contributed to a special feature in *The Guardian* (Nigerian) on the destruction of Ogoni land by the oil companies, the degradation of ancient farmlands, the pollution of fishing ponds, and the poisoning of the very air. Saro-wiwa's struggle was thus joined to mine within that most fundamental condition of social being that I summarize quite simply as *justice*.

In the process of that struggle and its factional degeneration, four Ogoni chiefs had been murdered, denounced as collaborators with the military government and the oil companies. These were brutal, horrendous killings, totally indefensible. To the extent that the murders had been committed by Ogoni youth militants, members of MOSOP—the Movement for the Salvation of the Ogoni Peoples—who owed loyalty to Ken Saro-wiwa, their leader, who had failed to condemn the murders in the most rigorous language, Ken could be assailed with a measure of *moral* responsibility. But to accuse him of complicity, direct or indirect, was an act of cynical opportunism. To try him and his companions in a special "tribunal," a military contrivance albeit with a civilian judge as its figurehead chairman, then convict them on the "evidence" placed before the nation, was an act by minds totally devoid of all conscience, perhaps steeped in a diabolism that required human sacrifice. Finally, to proceed to hang those victims, even before they had exhausted all avenues of appeal open to them within the provisions of the decree that established the "judicial process," was a step that no sensible person ever thought possible—from the Ogoni infant in his village to the sage Nelson Mandela. Mandela arrived at the Auckland airport beaming with confidence and dismissing the anxious questions of journalists with a jovial wave of the hand. Had Abacha not personally assured him, in a telephone exchange, that he would not execute those men? After the deed, Mandela would give vent to his outrage in these unforgettable words: "General Sani Abacha is sitting on a volcano and I am going to make sure that it blows up under him."

I was due in Japan, but not for a number of days. I left early and detoured to Auckland where the Commonwealth heads of state were gathering for their biannual summit, and it was clear that they alone, at that stage, still commanded the weight of voices that might save nine innocent men from the gallows. My message to them was insistent, desperate, and even strident: "Only strong threats will save these lives, strong threats backed by unmistakable indications that such threats will be enforced if the sentence is carried out!" Occasionally I encountered a member of the governmental delegations who listened and thought hard and deep, as if resolved to influence attitudes within his delegation or the routine caucuses. I would then walk back onto Auckland's sunlit streets, desperately plucking courage from such meager signs.

Today, even after the tragic denouement, I am mildly surprised to find that it is not anger or bitterness I feel as my mind traverses the few years since then—only sadness, tinged of course with renewed pain, as I recall the responses of those leaders. In the main, very few of these heads of state of the Commonwealth—former colonies of Great Britain, from Canada through Asia and Africa to Australia—despite their varied experiences of humanity, had ever encountered, except in history books, the likes of Sani Abacha. Maybe even now they still believe that Hitler, Stalin, Pol Pot, and others were all mutants, perhaps created by undetected spores that spilled out of some secret Chernobyl, or by the singular gas seepage from our neighboring Cameroon's Lake Nyos that killed, in the 1980s, hundreds of sleeping victims between night and dawn. These leaders conveniently forgot the lesson of Idi Amin Dada within their own club of nations. The majority of their foreign ministers, ambassadors, advisers, political analysts, and so forth were versed in bloodless briefings, attuned to cynical lobbies, cocktail and diplomatic reception circuits where the formal attire is camouflage for both viper and dove, and the garb of atrocities is shed at the door with a crested visiting card. The rest, like the rulers they served, were potential clones of the Abacha breed and simply wondered what the fuss was all about.

I *knew* Sani Abacha—no, not personally, though we had met twice. It was simply his type that I knew intimately, a species that I had studied closely, lectured and written about. I did not share the confidence of the others, but I was hopeful—at least at the start. And it was just as well. We were all doomed to be eviscerated by an invisible blade wielded by a psychopath from a place called Abuja. My only saving grace was that I had already felt its thrust, long before the noose tightened around Kenule's neck.

Even now, I still relive those moments of intense isolation that leave you truly "spaced out"—as in spinning in outer space—an alien among supportive, courteous mortals, a feeling that clings to you, knowing that, among the teeming population of that island, you are one of the mere handful of creatures—no more than two or three, one of whom was Ken's son—who know with absolute certainty that a mass murder is about to be committed, yet you are powerless to stop it or persuade anyone to believe you. My final moment of certitude came from a chance crossing of paths.

On the streets of Auckland, where I exorcised my restlessness and frustration with incessant walking between appointments, a car drew up with young Ken, the son of the condemned man, and some workers from the Body Shop and other NGOs who were looking after him. Ken leaped out, holding a cyclostyled statement from Shell, the oil company. If ever there was a scripted form of Pontius Pilate washing his hands before handing Christ over to his executioners, this would be its very corporate equivalent! If anything untoward happened to the Ogoni Nine, the statement declared, others were to blame—the agitators whose aggressive tactics only hardened the mood of the military regime and undid all the careful work of silent diplomacy being undertaken by their company, and well-meaning others.

Yes, *we* were to blame, not Shell! Not the oil-exploration companies. Not the military regime, its corporate allies, its kangaroo courts, but us! I handed back this tract of self-exoneration, company unctuousness, and—it seemed clear to me—accessory knowledge. In my distraction, I thought I had spoken aloud, and flagellated myself long afterward for an outburst that lacked consideration for the son's presence. But he assured me much later that I had the sequence of events all wrong. For what I thought I had blurted out without thinking was "He's dead. They've decided to hang them. This statement—Shell knows of the decision already." Even today, however, the words still ring in my head as I thought I had heard them, clear as the tolling of a funeral bell.

Walking myself into a state of total exhaustion from a sweaty pace around the humid streets of Auckland, mostly along the harbor, I began to feel somewhat dizzy. Recognizing why—I had had only my usual morning espresso that day—I entered a restaurant off the beaten track, where I attempted to stuff my insides but again mostly drank. Then, instead of returning to my hotel, I went to the improvised office of the Body Shop. It was abandoned; the volunteers were between hotels, waylaying and canvassing whatever delegates they could. I knew why I remained there in that abandoned office—it was to await the news. I did not wish to be found, did not wish to be invited to join in canvassing one more statesman or delegate. I returned to my hotel room only when it was late and news of the confirmation of sentence by Abacha's military ruling council had been formally announced.

Now I had only one thought: to get out of New Zealand! I had an engagement in Japan—a gathering of Nobel laureates—but we were not expected for two more days. That was just too bad. I sent a message but did not really care whether or not I was met, or if I upset the protocols that appear to be encoded in the national genes of the Japanese. I had only one goal in mind—to escape the island that would shortly host a wake for complacent heads of state, their political advisers, and their pundits. They would fashion statements of indignation and perform other accustomed rites of assaulted dignity. That would be their problem; it was no longer mine. The statement from Shell may not have been a death warrant, but it was so clearly a death certificate that I no longer thought of Ken as being in the world of the living, and I had no wish to encounter politicians and statesmen after the event. Above all, I most certainly did not wish to speak to the press. "So what is your view on these executions, Mr. Soyinka?" Finally, I did not wish to witness the agony of a son when the now-inevitable hole in his life yawned before him. All of this sent me looking for the next plane out of Auckland heading in the direction of Tokyo, where I knew I would have a clear two days alone before I was again obliged to face the world.

I only obtained relief from this irrational dread of being pursued when the plane was airborne and out of New Zealand airspace. After arriving in Tokyo, ensconced in a temporary suite by my polite hosts, I awaited the expected.

IT CAME IN THE MORNING, in the form of a young journalist, ushered into my suite by a geisha-attired woman who had been specially assigned to look after me, sitting just outside my room at all times—I later discovered—as if my hosts from the *shimbun,* the publishing house, feared that I might go into a depression, do some kind of harm to myself. Ken Saro-wiwa and his eight companions, the young man said, had been hanged at Port Harcourt prison, shortly after their appeal was rejected by the Supreme Military Council of Sani Abacha.

Never were hosts more gentle, more sensitive, self-retiring yet solicitous. The editor of the newspaper house, the sponsor of the conference, called on me. His brief stay was virtually soundless. In the most delicate manner, he indicated that the contents of the envelope that he was leaving on the table were for me to use in any way I wanted, that it was a gift of sympathy from his fellow executives who wished to ensure that I lacked nothing, yet were conscious of my likely preference to be alone. If I wished to look around the city, however, I only needed to inform the lady by the door and she would get in touch with his office. Even the choice of the young journalist who broke the news could not have been more deft. He looked more like a medical intern with a practiced bedside manner, tried to hide his astonishment (and relief) that I took the news so well. How was he to know that I had prepared myself, that I had left Auckland wondering only how soon the killing would be carried out? He tiptoed his way out, saying that he knew I would wish to be alone. Not that he forgot his calling—he left his card on the table by the door. If at any time I wished to make a statement, he would remain on call.

Being prepared for the worst is always one thing; confronting its stark actualization is another. There is a point at which the mind threatens to fold up, succumbing to its own destructive power of evocation. How does one erase the image of a friend and comrade suspended in the immense loneliness of a prison yard? This was worse than mere depletion. My human landscape appeared to me irremediably desecrated.

The laureates, when we finally gathered, were founts of humanity. Mikhail

Gorbachev, architect of glasnost and perestroika, whom I was meeting for the first time, seemed awkward in his anxiety to offer solace. Mostly, he shook his head in bewilderment. "How could such a thing happen?" he repeated over and over. Was it really possible? Could a regime act with such brutality? And then, businesslike: "What should other governments, individuals, and organizations do?" About this he was specific—boycotts, sanctions, expulsion from world organizations—anything but platitudes! Gorbachev's horror was palpable. He was the first to sign the document of condemnation and call to action that I prepared and proposed to my colleagues as a collective reaction. All the laureates signed it, joined by our Japanese counterparts from various disciplines. This was one of the many posthumous resonances for Ken and his cause, but it was I who benefited from the therapy of having it vociferously adopted at the plenary gathering.

How ironic it seemed. Here was a product of the Soviet Union, which was once defined by—and still is sometimes inconceivable without—a Stalinist mentality. A product, perhaps even a sometime participant, in the operations of that most brutal era, the era of mock trials, banishments to arid wastelands, torture, forced psychiatric "medications," executions that saw the end of so many artists, writers, thinkers, workers, and peasants—yet here he was, actually shaking his head in disbelief at the crime of a dictator in some distant land called Nigeria. Gorbachev, with the unusual signature patch of a red birthmark on his forehead, hamming it up with the Japanese, donning and strutting around in the "peace jacket"—or was it "love jacket"?—that was presented to each of us. And his ebullient wife, Raisa, basking in the approbation of a world that had faced down a totalitarian monstrosity whose internal collapse owed so much to the resolve and planning of her husband and his fellow conspirators. I spent most of my stay observing Gorbachev, a once-powerful lord of a wide swathe of the globe, for all the world at peace with himself, oblivious, to all appearances, or maybe simply reconciled, to the ironic fate of "the prophet that has no honor in his own land." For by then, Mikhail Gorbachev's own people had turned on him. He was now fair game for every woe that had befallen the once-all-powerful nation, most especially its economic collapse. Greatly reduced in public reckoning, I thought, had become the great gift of liberty. The euphoria of freedom had all but evaporated within the Soviet Union.

The absurdities—albeit deadly—of ideological somersaults in the play of nations, the cruelties and absurdities of individual fates, all joined forces with personal self-revelations of that timely company—solemn, comic, self-mocking, an intercultural potpourri of experiences and futuristic schemes—to act as gradual restoratives to a battered psyche, contest its debilitation by ghosts of a horrific bereavement. I turned my mind to practical duties. The most efficacious antidote for grief— which I learned from the death of my friend Femi Johnson—comes in a practical conscription of the mind, its redirection toward some practical task, however distanced, but related. In Femi's case it had been quite simply the single-minded task of bringing his body home. I pursued his exhumation, accompanied him home from Frankfurt, and reinterred him in the cemetery of the Chapel of the Resurrection at the University of Ibadan. For Ken, not even knowledge of his remains was permitted; it was all classified, held close to the triumphalist chests of a predatory class, the military rulers. But his cause remained intact, one that, I quietly swore, we would someday bring to fruition.

Ken Saro-wiwa's death also served as a well-earned rebuke to my fatalism in exile. At least I enjoyed the freedom to go in search of a resting place, in case Abacha did succeed in fulfilling his plans for me. Saro-wiwa's relatives were not even permitted access to his body. Some reports claim that it took four attempts to hang him, others said it took more. What is undisputed is that the initial attempts failed, that he was taken down from the scaffold while his companions were executed, so that he witnessed it all and then took his turn.

I was left with the sense of a compulsive burden of debt to Ken, his companions, and their cause. Not even my long poem, written nearly a year after his death, "Calling Josef Brodsky for Ken Saro-wiwa," which I failed twice, at Emory University and in Purcell Hall in London, to read to the end in public, overcome by emotion, seemed to discharge that burden. Indeed, both the title and subterfuge—fastening on Josef Brodsky, the Russian dissident poet, as a courier between Ken and me—was self-revealing....

> *I play*
> *The simple messenger, dared thus far*
> *To link two kindred souls from worlds apart*
> *In passage to the other world*

I had tried and failed to write to, for, in memory of, in homage to, in posthumous dialogue with Ken after his death, yet I needed to, needed to purge my psyche of yet another failure, one that, unlike the death of Moshood Abiola, had involved a desperate effort from the moment that I knew, with absolute certainty, that Abacha was resolved on Saro-wiwa's death. Dirging his end through another combative soul was the formula that finally worked.

The dismal proceedings of Kenule's murder in a Port Harcourt prison were videotaped on orders of the dictator, who held viewing sessions afterward with some of his officers, not all of whom knew in advance to what macabre feast they had been summoned. A witness has since revealed that one of the dictator's young aides fainted during a viewing. Abacha turned around and laughed. "Look at him," he mocked, "and he calls himself a soldier."

I am persuaded that I have always known that human aberrations such as Sani Abacha exist; I have learned to identify them since childhood, although, of course, mostly by intuition at that age. It is sufficient, a modest life mission, to ensure that such monsters do not enjoy the last laugh, do not rob individual beings of the fundamental right to a dignified life and a dignified exit, afflicting one's living thoughts with echoes of the brutal laughter of power over the courageous, farewell words of a fighter or the tread of triumphal boots that desecrate the peace of that rightful bequest from the cradle—the cactus patch.

"Lord, receive my soul," Kenule Saro-wiwa shouted as he stepped on the scaffold, "but the struggle continues."

Within such a commitment, I believe, is captured the essential teaching of that paradox, the Yoruba god of the restless road and creative solitude, the call of the lyric and the battle cry: Ogun.

$\mathcal{A}$rms and the Man

. . . . .

Now we come to the question: would we have resorted to armed struggle to rid the nation of the dictatorship of Sani Abacha? How does one come to terms with issues of pacifism and violence, make peace with their moral questions? Did we actually begin preparations for armed struggle?

The question of willingness to take up arms against a cruel despot was not one with which I found myself suddenly confronted. I had once resolved it in a minor mode during the Western Nigerian uprising of 1964–65, which had necessitated the takeover of the broadcasting station in Ibadan. Several within the opposition movement, however, found themselves faced with what, for me, was familiar though not fully settled territory. I have pondered numerous times the many faces of violence, its limpet attachment—it would seem—to the very genes of humanity. I could not deny its existence in some accommodating space within mine. I felt no special urge to pry it off and exclude it absolutely from the means of retrieval of a people's violated dignity, a community that defined my own existence as a human being. A monster had reduced us, collectively, to a plantation of slaves, and the word "liberation" could not be restricted to being a mere rhetorical device.

I was burdened with a special responsibility beyond mere leadership. Not many within the movement could claim to have been thrust, as I was, with an uncanny predilection, into situations that straddled the divide between peace and violence, compelling a constant review of the imperatives of both, each circumstance a unique instruction on its own. I had not escaped even the Irish "troubles." During my stint as a fellow in Churchill College, Cambridge, in 1970, I was invited to lecture in Belfast at the very height of the violence. Our lodgings were situated on a street whose entry points were heavily sandbagged positions—in what had once been a normal, cozy neighborhood. I arrived at night, thus missing out on the sight of the fortifications. I woke up early the following morning—a Sunday—and sauntered out in all lordliness, little dreaming that eyes were watching me from behind curtains, taking note, passing on news of an intruder through the local bush telegraph. The streets were eerily empty, a sensation that eventually percolated through to me, even though I felt no particular alarm. I had, however, set up a panic among my hosts: a black face in the streets of Ireland, at that time in 1970, meant only one thing—a serving soldier in the British forces and thus fair game for the IRA. Search parties were immediately sent out, and later, we were formally informed that an IRA cell had been alerted.

A year or so later, I would find myself setting up a meeting between the Irish Provos and the "Regulars." Only one and a third names have stuck to my memory from that experience: Seamus Towney and, the one-third, Macsomething. One side wanted a return to the violent days; the other was for a political solution. The two factions had just begun to tear each other apart, and an effort was being initiated, before the conflict became irreversible, to come to a resolution. During the run of Les Anges Meurtriers in Paris, Joan Littlewood, in whose Blackheath home I would sometimes meet not only the literary but the violent compatriots of the playwright Brendan Behan, asked me one day if I could find a safe house for the two factions in Paris. They had agreed to meet in secrecy and resolve their differences.

Through Nadia, the secretary to my Lumumba in Conor Cruise O'Brien's play, I secured an apartment just off Boulevard St.-Michel, owned by the daughter of the proprietor of one of the huge brasseries in that arrondissement, Titi C. It was all appropriately cloak-and-dagger. The Irish belligerents slipped away from under the nervous eyes of British agents, traveled on a cross-Channel ferry. The address had been sent to them in Ireland. On landing, they were informed in which letter box—that of an untenanted apartment—the key was hidden. Their meeting lasted nearly all night. By morning, they had boarded the ferry, headed for the Irish seas.

As I complained to Mary Robinson, then the Irish prime minister, when we met in Davos, Switzerland, two decades later, the intrusion of W.S. into Irish contemporary history had sunk into the Irish seas without a ripple. I had looked forward to the outcome as others might the result of a World Cup final, and to the private celebration of my unsung triumph—together with Nadia and Titi C.—in the cause of peace. Fortunately I had no active consciousness, at the time, of the existence of a Nobel Peace Prize, or I would have felt very badly done by when, not long after, the peace effort succumbed to the superior lure of bombs and guns. Unable to fire a public salvo at those fratricidal letdowns, I moped around for some days afterward and boycotted Irish literature and music for some weeks longer. Fortunately, I never had taken to Irish whisky.

To concede genuine revulsion at the phenomenon of violence does not, however, contradict an acceptance of its sometime necessity—and even justice. There are those who *relish* violence; there is no other word for it. They are juiced up at the prospect of its eruption, and some even consciously seek it out. Others merely reconcile themselves to violence but, having done so, direct it in as practical, minimalist, and humane a way as is compatible with the objectives, propelling it toward that moment when one may look back with relief at the jettisoning of such a phase that violates one's loftiest ideals, celebrate its termination, and hope—*Never again?*

I have recognized and accepted my membership in this latter group since I became conscious of injustice and the tendency to domination as ingrained aspects of the conduct of society and individuals. I have always found it abnormal that violence should be offered as a normal commodity of exchange between individuals or that nations should conduct their diplomacy through the pulverization of one another's cities and the decimation of their populations. To gauge the greatness of nations—as my earliest history texts would have it—by their capacity and cunning for destruction and award the title of "Great" to successful warmongers in a confused context with nation building and social enhancement has always struck me—well, as far back as I can recollect—as a perversion of human values. To respond to terror with violence or attempt to defeat violence with its own instrumentality is, however, unblameworthy. I admire the saints—the Gandhis, the Martin Luther Kings, the Dalai Lamas, the Aung San Suu Kyis, the Gautamas, and all—but I cannot aspire to companionship with them.

Many were the encounters I had with loving apologists of rabid power during the Abacha era, those who tried their best not to know of the violence that was meted out daily to their fellow citizens, often right before their eyes. The more daring made efforts to reassure me that the dictator was a muchmisunderstood man who cared very deeply about the potholes in the roads— *Prof, I am not saying he's perfect, but you should see how he's been rehabilitating the roads*—or else lauded his commitment to sanitizing the banking system— *Those mushroom banks, Prof, he's really putting an end to their activities*—and so on and so on and so on! Such encounters, often in airports or hotel lobbies during exile, never failed to call to mind one occasion in which I was physically caught up in the web of absurdity that is sometimes spun by violence. A common enough occurrence in domestic settings, this was acted out in the public arena. I have thought often of my interlocutors, the Abacha apologists while he lived, as actors in that street scene—they on the receiving end, our dictator as the natty young man who doled out that violence in the full confidence that he had a submissive partner, and a tolerant environment. That scene remains my favored morality tale, both as a moment of self-revelation—in addition to its cautionary lesson—and of my contempt for a tendency toward "reasoned" submissiveness or its partner, the psychologically induced, a probable masochistic streak.

AN EVENING—YES, I admit it—of egregious folly! New York, Upper Manhattan, 1970s. I was returning from some function or other in the company of my host, Joseph Okpaku, a trained engineer turned publisher, literary critic, and business adventurer from Benin, then domiciled in the United States. Joe was driving. A taxi overtook us, then swung sharply to the curb, screeching to a stop just a few yards from one of those apartment buildings with an awning and sidewalk carpet running from street to door, presided over by a stolid doorman in uniform, fully braided, at least an ex-boxer or -wrestler—in short, well able to take care of himself and any disturber of the peace. Before the taxi had rolled to a complete stop, the curbside door flew open and a woman leaped out, screaming at the top of her lungs and running—obviously—toward the protective presence of the doorman. After her leaped a man, who caught up with her in a couple of strides and pinned her against the wall. The taxi drove alongside the pair—perhaps, we thought, he still had his fare to collect. Joe had also pulled up, and together we watched.

"Get back in the car!" the man screamed at her. "No, no!" she screamed back. "Leave me alone! Help!"

The next sound we heard was the crunch of her head against the wall as the man took her face in his hands and *bang, bang, bang* against the wall. Over and over again went that head against that wall, as if the neck would snap. The man would stop briefly, step back, point, and order the woman once again to get back in the taxi. We watched in anticipation—that is, anticipation of help from the doorman. Nothing. He simply watched, stolidly.

The man grabbed her again, ready to resume his pounding, but the woman broke loose and fled screaming along the sidewalk, the man in pursuit. The taxi crawled alongside and we crawled behind it, still expecting the doorman to intervene. When her companion caught up with her again and resumed the same process, with such increased violence that I felt I could feel those bangs reverberate against the wall of my stomach, some unseen force must have lifted me out of the car and catapulted me forward, because the next thing I knew, I was standing over the man. I could only assume that I had knocked him down—from behind!

Well now, what next? Having knocked him down, what was I supposed to do? Had I gotten myself into a fight? Was Joe calling the police? Would the doorman at last act as a decent citizen and come to my aid? I dared not take my eyes off the fallen bully, dared not turn my back on him. I had no thought of doing anything to incapacitate him before he turned his fury on me, and I certainly could not leave him lying there while I regained the sanity and protection of Joe's vehicle. In short, I felt stuck, and I now began to feel stupid in the bargain. Not for long, however, since matters were taken out of my hands by a staccato of blows on my shoulders from behind. Reinforcements? From within the taxi? But no, the ownership of those tiny fists was soon established when I heard that earlier screaming voice now whining, "Don't you dare hurt him. I love him! I love him!"

My jaws began to lose their tautness. I felt my mouth distinctly slacken, opening slowly in silent questioning of my hearing. Now thoroughly scared, I hoped that the footsteps that I heard running up were Joe's, which indeed they were. The tattooing persisted, accompanied by increasing protestations of love. I dared not turn around, dared not take my eyes off the prostrate figure. I simply wished that the wind would whisk me away from that spot and deposit me in my Isara village, where human beings still conduct themselves with some measure of normality.

Recovering some volition, I bent over the man, all red lights flashing as my mind resumed functioning in the mode of extreme caution. There were passersby, quickening their pace as they skirted our group, and I believe that it was at that moment that I first became conscious that the surrounding humanity, including the three central figures—assailant, victim, and doorman spectator—were white. Solid pink-white upper-class Manhattanites. That is, I finally came down from the clouds of righteous and impulsive fellow feeling, landed plumb in the heart of habitual violence, the U.S.Alien land. Strange people! Until that moment, I had seen only three human beings, devoid of racial identity, one of whose head was about to be reduced to squashed melon. So I bent down, apologetic. My sole concern was now, very simply, self-preservation, and the instant question on my mind was—was Lover Boy carrying a knife? Or, worse yet, a gun?

I helped him up, tenderly, cooing contritely, my arms hooked under his armpits. Each hand took turns to dust him down so that he remained constantly half pinioned in a helpful manner. I felt no weapons. All the time, I uttered purring, conciliatory noises.

"My mistake, sir. You're not hurt, are you? Obvious misunderstanding. We were far away, misjudged the situation, you understand? Very, very clumsy of me . . ."

Lover Boy—straight from a tailor's fitting session, it seemed—ignored me, adjusted and smoothed down his jacket, and ordered his consort, "Get in the taxi!"

"That's it!" I eagerly concurred, ushering them both toward the taxi. Once they were inside, the door slammed against them, I took a giant step backward. "Take her home, please, and sir, beat her shitless. I mean, beat her to a shitty pulp."

The words sounded somewhat familiar, and I recalled that I had used similar lines in *The Trial of Brother Jero*. It only made me wax more creative. I retreated even farther, ever backward, keeping my eye on the taxi, whose occupants had fallen silent. Joe was now closer to me, and I grew more confident. "That's right, sir, please love each other to death, but I implore you, first beat the living shit out of the lady. She needs it, she deserves it, and you'll be fulfilling both a lover's and a civic duty."

As we passed the doorman, he now appeared to have woken up, ready to advertise his role as a concerned citizen and spectator. I could not believe my ears at his fatuous inquiry: "What happened there? What did he say to her?"

At which point, I did not care that he still struck me as a cross between Mike Power, the Nigerian wrestler, and Sonny Liston at the height of his reign of demolition. I stopped, fixed him with a glare full of naked Ijegba hatred, then ejected onto him a brief, semicoherent, but pithy summary of my assessment of him, his race, and his sick society. There was so much violence stored up in me that I think I secretly wished he would take a swing at me and connect, if only to remind me forcefully that there are societies where the norm is to remain uninvolved, even if murder is being committed right under one's foreign nose.

Thank goodness, my compatriots who refused to "get in the taxi" far outnumbered those who were not only content to go for the ride but narrated to the outside world the idyllic vistas through which their purring limousine was being driven, and its utopian destination. The majority of Nigerians were being forced, not even into taxis but into Black Marias, straight from domestic haven or workplace and, sometimes, directly into hearses. Their screams for help did not come from them alone or reverberate against our gut linings as exiles but rose from within ourselves. The only question that was left to us was: What form should such self-help take? If we were compelled to embrace violence, we had to analyze the conditions of violence and mediate its unpredictable nature with a controlling, discriminating philosophy of violence.

ONE EVOLVES SPECIFIC rules of engagement simply from habit, even if only as a theoretical framework from within which one can endure, morally, a violent world. Combatants in war know the nature of the terrain into which they are thrust, an unambiguous arena of violence. However, even within the conceded space of violence, codes of restraint must exist. For instance, I have always considered the taking of innocents as hostages a despicable form of struggle, a pathetic mimicry of the renegade state that takes its entire people hostage. I always took my leave, thankfully and painlessly, of rhetoricians of sweeping, nondiscriminating violence, especially during those heady days of Marxist and Troskyite arrogation, now supplanted by a jihadist competitiveness of all religious colors. "There are no innocents." Thus are the slaughter and kidnapping of innocents justified in the name of a Higher Cause—secular or religious. The right word is "megalomania," a presumptuousness of a divine right of the random appropriation of lives. It has always struck me as merely blasphemous, no matter how just one may find the fundamental causes to which such catechisms attach themselves.

In the solitude of moral conscience, there is a genuine dilemma when one is confronted by the specter of actually generating violence. Such a dilemma is a natural product of reflection. It is a recollection of one's humanity, bringing to the forefront of one's thoughts the invisible future, the potential transformation—for the better—of the social entity that must pay the price of bloodshed and social disruption. When it is glaring that power has gone rabid in society and the reality of daily existence is that of ongoing terror, cruelty, and repression, there is really little room for hand-wringing or agonizing. The choice is made, and then the mind is set free to address the management of such an unwanted commodity, to set limits on its deployment in the cause of redress and restitution. The schooling of the individual participant is crucial: a keen and constant assessment of the ultimate goal and an awareness of the danger that such a goal can be corrupted by divergences from a code of conduct that must be set beforehand and subscribed to collectively.

After the first Persian Gulf War and the release of prisoners, I was riveted by a program of interviews with some of the former prisoners of war. A pair of infiltrators from the anti-Saddam coalition force, two Britishers from the Special Unit—those adepts of derring-do who precede an invasion and establish tactical vectors in the empty dunes behind enemy lines—had been surprised by a mere child of some six or seven years. He had wandered far from his home and stumbled on their hideout. For several moments, the invaders had stood staring at the seeming apparition, moments during which they could have shot, knifed, or smothered him.

Said the Special Unit man, "My training was really to have killed him, but I couldn't do it." The child was allowed to run off. He reported the presence of the intruders to his parents, who alerted their local army unit. The capture of the intruders and their imprisonment followed swiftly. I have often compared that moment to the "there are no innocents" combatants of Ireland, both the Ulster Defence Association psychopaths and their soul mates within the Irish Republican Army who think nothing of tossing a bomb into a pub or blowing up a crowded shopping mall. Nor do I find any enlightenment in suicide bombers, never mind the sobering thought that some do it out of total, terminal conviction, their entire consciousness consumed by the indignity of what to them is an existential negation—that is, life is not living when lived as such but may be validated, indeed purified, when sacrificed in avenging its indignity: "I die, therefore, I am"; or, better still, "I die, and thus—become." Yet others immolate themselves in this manner out of the expectation of a reward: the guarantee of resurrection in the eternity of a sybaritic paradise. They believe in this recompense, and that is the true inducement to their surrender to self-immolation.

The accidental casualty that is inflicted on innocents in the course of a conflict—I detest the expression "collateral damage" when applied to human lives—occupies a different level of responsibility and censure, to be judged on the efforts made by participants in the conflict to avoid such violations of innocence or neutrality. But that disingenuous mantra "Violence is violence" requires repudiation as an abdication of all moral responsibility, an attempt to justify any level of criminality under the untenable, indeed obnoxious, argument that when the consequences are the same, the causes acquire a moral equivalence. The glorification of random violence in particular leaves no room for moral ambiguity, that conditioning of the mind that declares all of humanity culpable and deserving of random punishment for being whole while others are mutilated or satiated while others are starving, for sleeping soundly while others are insomniacs—indeed, for being alive while others are dead!

. . .

ONE MORE INSTRUCTIVE encounter, this time with the thrill seeker, the vicarious collaborator in indiscriminate violence. Traveling between London and the United States in the summer of 1971, I found myself an object of attention by a young, eager face from Egypt, a member of a group on its way to attend some kind of youth event sponsored by the United Nations. I was working at my portable typewriter, and he could not resist coming over to ask me if I was a writer. I confessed to the crime. Where was I from? Nigeria, I said. He was clearly dying to engage me in conversation, perhaps because there were just the two black faces in the plane, those of my female companion and me. The youthful interloper—he could not have been more than nineteen—plunged straight into the politics of colonialism but did not really take too long to ask the question on his mind: How did we, in Nigeria, view the Palestinian problem?

"With support for the displaced Palestinians," I responded. "They deserve their own homeland."

We discussed the plight of the refugees, the ambiguous role of the United Nations, and the likelihood (or unlikelihood) of peace in the Middle East in our lifetime. He was then unaware that the Nigerian government—and most African nations—had broken off relations with Israel after the Six-Day War with Egypt: Israel had been warned not to advance into any portion of the African continent but had ignored the warning. So the Organization of African Unity had exhorted all its members to break off relations, and several had. When I revealed that Nigeria had indeed been one of the first to do so, it was all he could do to refrain from throwing his arms around me. Our love feast underwent a sudden hiccup, however, when, with a confident, even gloating smile on his face, he asked, "Ah, my friend, so what do you think of the blow struck by the liberation movement against Switzerland?"

I thought I was sure what he meant, but I asked anyway, "A blow against Switzerland? When was this?"

"But you must have heard. The plane—*boom!*"

I studied him with some keenness, put my work aside, and said carefully, "If you have any friends in the PLO, I suggest you tell them that that kind of outrage is certain to lose them the support they enjoy right now among most African governments—and peoples."

He stopped dead. My companion, an African American, gave a wry smile, as if to say, Well, end of in-flight romance.

"And you?" asked this young man of righteous intensity. "What do you think?"

"Sickening," I said.

Slowly, he sank down on his knees beside me, the intent would-be tutor of a backward child. "But you see, the Swiss government had been supporting the Zionist cause. And Swiss business—they pour millions and millions into Jewish business, and that money is used in turn to suppress the Palestinian movement."

"I don't know about your facts," I told him, still in the same comradely mode. "You probably have information that I do not, but even if that were true, does it justify the murder of innocents?"

His face was wreathed in that understanding smile— the patient, dedicated teacher accommodating a retarded pupil. "Ah, my Nigerian friend, you have to understand that the Swiss government is guilty of the deaths of many innocent Palestinians at the hands of the Israelis. This was a plane owned by the Swiss government. The profits find their way sooner or later into the hands of the enemies of the Palestinians."

I decided to change tack. "For how long have the North Vietnamese engaged first the French and then the Americans in a bloody war of liberation?"

He looked puzzled. I spoke as gently as I could. "Well, at least two decades taken together, wouldn't you say?" He nodded agreement.

"Well, then," I continued with self-conscious gentleness, "would you claim that their cause is any less just than others? Than the Palestinians', for instance? For nearly twenty years they've fought superior forces armed with the most sophisticated weaponry, defeated one, and brought the other to a virtual standstill. Explain to me why they haven't chosen to go around blowing innocent people out of the air. Do you think they are mentally retarded? Trapped in antiquated notions?" The effort to keep my voice even was becoming frayed. "Do you think it possible there may be some valid principles—even pragmatic reasoning—behind such restraint? Some careful political calculations? Well, tell me, whose choice strikes you as being more politically rational and/or morally superior to the other? Which one do you find arrogant and insulting?"

At the time, inquiries had not uncovered the source and details of the Swissair attack, only that the plane had exploded in the skies, the work of an altimeter bomb. Yet to come was the revelation of the callousness with which the perpetrators had set out to gain the affection of two females, invited them home on holiday, and then made excuses that they had been prevented from traveling at the last moment; they would join their women later. An engagement had been concluded with one; a marriage was to follow shortly afterward. What was more natural than that the bride-to-be should agree to take her fiancé's suitcase with her? In short, in addition to the total strangers aboard, there were two beings with whom they had broken bread and drunk wine, whom they had fondled, and to whom they had made love—then sent to their deaths, making them the instruments of their own annihilation. The cynical details were yet to be uncovered, but one could still approach the outrage clinically, devoid even of that personalized dimension. My liberation warrior continued to stare at me with an expression that I could not immediately decipher, and I decided to restrict our scope of discussion to overall strategic choices, even within the brutal parameters of armed struggle.

"Any liberation war," I pressed on, "involves more than mutual destruction. It is also a war of opinion, a contest for support, for solidarity. In other words, all action should be guided by considerations of a long-term advantage. So when one side acts with a brutal contempt for innocent lives, it alienates potential support. Doesn't that stand to reason?"

"But first we have to defend ourselves," he insisted. "And we defend ourselves by attacking the profit machine of our enemies or all who support our enemies."

"Wait a minute," I said. "You don't believe that travelers will start avoiding Swissair, do you?"

He shrugged. "At least it may make them think twice. Certainly the profits of Swissair will be cut, and that will affect their policies."

I smiled at him. "Permanently? That is, even if at all?"

"At least Switzerland will experience some commercial insecurity. A blow has been struck at the Swiss industrial machine."

The homicidal thrill of the vicarious killer—Oh yes, I have been here before, I said to myself, heard it all too often. In a moment, he would begin to drool openly. It was time to encourage the young man to return to his seat so I could resume my work.

"Oh, undoubtedly," I reassured him. "The blow was heard all around the world. However, with your permission, I intend to retain my moral outrage. That was a thrill killing, nothing to do with a liberation war. It is even impious—you assume the power of life and death over *all* of humanity. I find that arrogant. Offensive. I come from a culture that despises such tactics. It's an assault on my humanity."

And that was when I received what I still consider a prime candidate for the most profound insult of my life. It grates, it rankles, to this very day, whenever

I recall it. This youth, at least a decade below my age, this weasely, pampered, pimply, unripe specimen of humanity who had earlier bubbled with the effervescence of an anticipated week or fortnight vacation at a youth jamboree, courtesy of the United Nations, in the very heartland of "Zionist apologists and supporters," arranged his face into a sweet, understanding smile, appropriating to himself a power of absolution that normally resides in the voice of one who has witnessed much, suffered much, but understood and transcended it all. Looking up at me from his bent knees, he let me know, in effect, that I had his full sympathy, that the only mission that he now had left in the world was to comfort and exonerate me from the implications of utterances that, presumably, would have been a capital crime from the lips of other mortals.

"Ah, but I understand," he said. "You are a writer, a poet."

I was terribly conscious of the mischievous smile on the face of my female companion. We had been together long enough since my release from prison for her to grasp what my fingers itched to do at that moment. My strangulated voice, stressed beyond the endurance limits of the metal skin of a contraption that did not permit such responses, one that was also headed for a destination where such impulses, if given rein, would have to be sternly answered on landing, miraculously succeeded in forcing from me a response in a nonmanic mode.

"Perhaps I should let you know this," I said—and my calmness of voice was deserving of a medal for composure under enemy fire—"I have just emerged from prison detention in my own country." It gained his attention, but this only knotted up my insides even more violently. "I am sorry I have to bring it up, I don't like talking about it, especially to a total stranger, but you should know that I did not earn that prison spell from being a poet. We recently concluded a civil war; I was imprisoned on account of my role in that war. Wait"—I saw his face undergoing yet another instant plastic surgery; I was about to be insulted with comradely sympathy—"that was not my first brush with the law. The first time, I was on trial for armed robbery."

I do not recall any further exchanges after that, since I returned immediately to my typewriter. He did say something, but it was lost on me. Indeed I do not recall when or how he left and returned to his seat, only that he could not have prolonged his stay, since he was still intact when I saw him seated among his companions an hour or so later on my way to the bathroom, and there was no sense of any bruising on my knuckles. I had decided to ignore him altogether, but the sight of this commander of life and death, this fount of understanding of the lofty, idealistic, but pitiably innocent world of the poet, a youth seated among his friends, all of them so full of life, so fired up with anticipated thrills and new experiences in the despised but accommodating United States, proved unbearable. My imagination projected youths like him and his companions in that ill-fated plane or another like it, with a doomsday parcel tucked in one of their rucksacks. I stopped and looked at him, at his companions, then back at him. He returned the look with some fear and uncertainty. I confess that I rather enjoyed that look.

"By the way, I knew no one on that plane," I said to him, "but I easily could have. Maybe a friend, a relation, or even a comrade from our own very modest struggle, not so earth-shaking as yours. If I had ... well, just be careful where you're going—I mean, to whom you say such things. Some of us—poets—are not exactly poets. We live sometimes—beyond the word."

MY ETHICAL CODE on violence evolved through numerous such encounters, but not only from them. I am, after all, an assiduous student of history and a product of a world still in thrall to the mandates of violence. I did not really sit down to ask questions of my temperament but listened to its responses to nonpacific situations, both real-life and as articulated by others. As the century began to close upon the struggle against Abacha, so did our choices contract.

It was indeed approaching a time to prepare, having clarified in our minds what we would and would not do, how to preserve our humanity even in the midst of violence. There were zones of potential help that we meticulously avoided. For instance, contacts were made on behalf of the movement with some warlords in Liberia; we turned down the idea. And once I received a personal invitation from a rebel leader in Sierra Leone who felt that we should make common cause. It was not until much later, indeed after my return home, that I came to uncover how the contact had ever come to be made.

In the ranks of that rebel leader was a former journalist and radio broadcaster. We had done programs together on the BBC; indeed, he had interviewed me more than once on Nigerian arts and politics. The timing of this reaching out to us was, in fact, well judged. The Nigerian army under Sani Abacha was considered an army of occupation by quite a sizable section within Sierra Leone, thus this rebel leader was persuaded that he was involved in a genuine war of liberation. We were equally resolved to unseat a dictator in Nigeria; that made us natural allies—thus went his reasoning. He would confront the Nigerian war machine on Sierra Leonean soil while we eroded its base within Nigeria.

His calculations did not lack affirmation within the military itself. By

1996, many Nigerian soldiers, even units, had begun to fraternize with rebel forces. They saw no reason why they should be in Sierra Leone, fighting for democracy, while that commodity was denied them and their families at home, and under the most brutal conditions. And there was massive discontent and suspicion among the officers and men. Some Southern officers had become convinced that Abacha was using the war in Liberia and Sierra Leone either to keep them from intervening at home or to decimate their ranks, while simultaneously installing his own regional minions in cushy political positions at home, turning the war into a money-spinning industry over their body count. I once encountered a former U.S. ambassador to Nigeria, Thomas Pickering, in Washington, D.C. In the course of reviewing his tour of duty in Nigeria, he revealed how Sani Abacha, while chief of staff, had brought him an invoice for the hiring of transport planes for ECOMOG troops, a cost that the U.S. government had promised to underwrite. One look at the figures, and the ambassador had screamed. More calmly, he had reminded Abacha that the United States had a lot of experience in airlifting troops all over the world. Abacha, he said, had quietly withdrawn the invoice, and he never brought it back; he had simply added two zeros to the figures.

Disillusionment was therefore at its highest, and morale at its lowest, especially after the costly 1996 attempt by the Nigerian Army to reinstall President Ahmad Tejan Kabbah in office in Sierra Leone. That effort had resulted in the rebel forces marching on the capital, Freetown, penetrating close to the very heart of the city, and nearly routing the Nigerian forces. The Nigerian soldiers, in the main, simply did not want to fight. There was an instance, one of many, when a commander actually arranged for his unit to be "captured" by a rebel force. After some weeks of fraternizing, they arranged similarly to be released—"as a gesture of goodwill" by their captors. The charade was so transparent that the commander was later court-martialed and, I was informed, shot. The rebel commander was therefore not so illogical in thinking that we could have something in common with his cause. And at that stage, the war in Sierra Leone had not truly degenerated into a state of mindless atrocities in which a generation of young recruits, sometimes as young as six or seven, were turned into drug-crazed killers, agents of defilement and torture. The frenzy of amputations, thrill killings, rapes, and arson had not begun. Scattered incidents, yes, but they had not attained the status of a competitive policy of near-indiscriminate dehumanization. We decided to keep our distance, but it would be false to say that the offer was not objectively considered.

We did seek help elsewhere—in Ethiopia, Eritrea, South Africa, Rwanda,

Uganda, Burkina Faso—and not necessarily from their governments. The responses were, as expected, varied. Some assisted with logistics, others with mobility, some were generous with sweet words, yet others lent us expertise. Burkina Faso was especially liberal with travel documents, and the president, Blaise Compaoré, was spontaneous and sympathetic. His ambassador in France kept in constant touch, letting me know when his leader was likely to pass through Paris, in case I wished to arrange a further meeting. However, the war scenario in the West African subregion, in which Compaoré was clearly playing a controversial role, made us somewhat chary. We withdrew further and further from someone who was clearly disposed to be a keen ally, whose nation harbored a large Nigerian population and was strategically positioned in relation to Nigeria. Through General David Mark, another dissident general who had escaped Abacha's net quite early in the game, we learned that our abandonment of that resource had not stopped Abacha's intelligence service from reporting that I had a trained army of infiltrators already positioned in that country.

We prepared shopping lists, followed leads that took us to both dubious and idealistic corners. We allied with the rump of the ill-fated Ogboru-Orkar warriors who had tried and failed to topple the regime of Ibrahim Babangida. (Most were war-weary.) A Vietnam veteran who had once been a business associate of the imprisoned president Moshood Abiola, a voluble, boastful, and ultimately unproductive ally, appeared to have a recurrent boatload of arms anchored somewhere on the high seas, ready for delivery but requiring a down payment that our combined lifetime resources must have found hilarious. In the end, all that we gained from him was the privilege of being used! He smuggled himself into a photo opportunity during my encounter with President Clinton, set up for a university commencement. He then took the photographs into a bankruptcy court hearing as proof that he had used his resources to back a democratic struggle—headed, of course, by none other than the Nobel laureate in the photograph. He presented a folder of news clippings of my denunciations of the regime and its human rights abuses. Clinton's presence was proof that he had the tacit approval of the U.S. government; thus his "contributions" should be declared tax-deductible.

If only we had a fraction of his business adroitness! Still, we did set up a financial unit, tried out the most arcane routes for generating funds. Our allied financial wizards prepared plates for liberation bonds in readiness for D-Day. Others set up small ventures specifically for the cause—one, Bola Tinubu, who had escaped from Abacha's dragnet through a hospital window and would later become the elected governor of Lagos state, set up a trade in rice with Taiwan! Lacking even the most rudimentary sense of trade, I stuck to my own narrow groove for generating funds: I accepted lecture engagements anywhere, anytime, for virtually any fee or none at all. Propagating the cause was itself an essential resource on which we could draw.

Numerous factors continued to push us beyond the line of mere readiness. Indeed, less than a year before Abacha's death, we found ourselves, within NALICON, compelled to reassess the state of the struggle. It was not difficult to confront the truth: that the route that the democratic movement had traveled so far—albeit creatively and sometimes courageously—was close to a dead end. Every moment saw Abacha consolidating himself deeper in power and terror. More and more opposition voices were being silenced while the political figures were falling like ninepins under the spell of power. If you cannot beat them, they shrugged, join them. There was no question about it, the so-called masses were losing hope.

Thus, for us on the outside, it was time to reexamine our level of commitment.

A new impetus was needed. One by one, the opposition movements at home were being emasculated. The pioneering group the Campaign for Democracy was barely functioning. Most of the internal leaders—Dr. Beko Ransome-Kuti, Femi Falana, Shehu Sani, and others—were either in jail without charge, sentenced in kangaroo tribunals, awaiting trial on treason charges, or otherwise incapacitated. Gani Fawehinmi, the civil rights lawyer, continued to shuttle into and out of jail, perpetually harassed, his chambers shot up occasionally as a warning, his night watch leaving a blood trail that dragged over a paved courtyard and a gate, for all the world like a film sequence, as he tried to clamber to safety. That Gani had won the Bruno Kreisky Award for Human Rights only appeared to incense Abacha all the more, making him an even more desirable target for persecution and, indeed, elimination. Our NADECO partners within the country, constantly exposed, lived under the sudden visitation of the assassins' bullets. In plain daylight, at a petrol station at a busy intersection of Lagos, the elderly but vigorous Abraham Adesanya, a former senator, unbelievably escaped death as his car was drilled through and through by the submachine guns of Abacha's killer squad. The combative wife of the imprisoned president, Kudirat Abiola, was not so lucky. She was waylaid in full traffic flow in the morning rush hour, stopped, and shot through the head. Not until after Sani Abacha's death and the dismantling of his murder organization would it be discovered that one of her closest confidants and political advisers had been an agent of Sani Abacha and had indeed provided details of her movements on that day to the assassins.

Sani Abacha appeared to have it all his own way, even as the nation hoped, futilely, that he would soon overreach himself—at least, through his overassiduous servitors. His confidence and impunity further bloated by capitulations and defections from the ranks of well-known political figures, Sani Abacha moved to announce, yet again, new plans for a return to civilian rule, but this time with a difference. A new electoral body was set up, armed with that now-routine Nigerian democratic variant: the power to approve the formation of new parties. Five such consortiums were eventually approved, three of them being instantly recognizable as the personal property of Sani Abacha. Even before their formal registration, all three had announced the name of their flag bearer for the presidency—none other than the incumbent, General Sani Abacha. The "independence" of a fourth, funded and owned single-handedly by Abacha's former minister of petroleum, Dr. Don Etiebet, was short-lived. Its existence degenerated into farce when its founder, owner, and presidential candidate emerged from several days' seclusion in his home to renounce his presidential ambitions and defect, with all appropriate apologies, to one of Sani Abacha's parties. That seclusion, it turned out, had been a spell of house arrest, broken only by visits from Abacha's man of all purpose, officially his security adviser—the sinister Major Hamza al-Mustapha.

This left only one party. It put up a determined fight, led by Alhaji M. D. Yusuf, a former head of the secret service of an unusually liberal cast of mind, and of Fulani extraction. The nation did not hold its breath while it awaited the outcome. Even so, all bets were wrong. What most people had imagined was that this last party would be allowed free play in order to give the elections a semblance of choice. After all, the electoral machine was firmly under Abacha's control, and any results could be announced even before the completion of voting. Abacha's handlers were taking no chances, however. At a meeting held in Kaduna to select and anoint that party's own presidential candidate, Abacha's storm troopers, headed by the same Major al-Mustapha, made an unscheduled appearance with a "goodwill message" from the head of state. The authentic leaders of the party walked out of their own meeting in protest against the intrusion. The rump that remained behind had no difficulty in concluding the meeting with a formal adoption of Sani Abacha as the presidential candidate. Thereafter, all five parties became known—in the coinage of my late friend Bola Ige—as the five fingers of one leprous hand.

After which it was the turn of traditional rulers—the obas, obis, emirs, chiefs, and other titled heads. One after another, they visited Aso Rock to endorse their new king—a coy heir apparent to his own crown—who continued to deny that he had any ambitions to transform himself into a civilian president but said he would submit, albeit reluctantly, to the wishes of the people. The "people" soon made their wishes known, most vociferously, through the antics of a flamboyant impresario with an eye on the main chance. The young man appeared from nowhere, launched an amorphous body with the rousing title of YEAA—Youths Earnestly Ask for Abacha—and proceeded to launch what he billed as a Million Man March on Aso Rock. My aborted 1994 march on Abuja to demand the exit of Abacha from Aso Rock had been cynically turned on its head; this time, the march was to plead with the dictator to remain in power as a civilian head of state! Armed with a bottomless campaign chest from a treasury that was flung wide open to any such ventures, this upstart, Kalu—who also swore that he would commit suicide if Abacha failed to heed their plea—organized a musical extravaganza in Abuja, at which political office seekers—men and women, former military officers, ex- and aspiring governors, and a sprinkling of traditional rulers—gyrated to rousing rhythms from prodigally remunerated musical groups. It was an awe-inspiring performance, one that plumbed the very abyss of self-degradation, a veritable wallowing in sycophantic sludge that, it would appear, some peoples accumulate in their passage toward self-definition and national becoming.

For the musicians, the repercussions were instant. As they returned to their hometowns, their erstwhile fans were waiting, but not with the welcome banners to which they were accustomed. Many went into hiding, issued statements that claimed that they had been duped into performing. In some cases, this was true. The campaign for self-succession took place during the buildup period to the global soccer madness known as the World Cup, and some bands had been taken in by the tale that this was a fund-raising event for the Green Eagles, as the Nigerian national team was known. Most knew the truth but could not resist the mouthwatering inducements. The response of the erstwhile fans, among others, was one cheering note, but a challenge also—it was a crop whose harvesting could not be long delayed, or it would shrivel in the heat of a tyrant's desperation. There were other responses that were no less encouraging, all indicative of a mood that needed to be reinforced and structured before it dissipated from battle weariness.

Abacha's campaign moved with increasing boldness and impudence. It was now the turn of the most palpable bastions of resistance, the physical, peopled arena, to be subdued. A well-known Abacha crony of Yoruba stock, a commodity supplier for the operations of ECOMOG—the West African peacekeeping forces—in Liberia and Sierra Leone during Abacha's tenure as the Nigerian Army chief of staff, suddenly appeared as point man for his benefactor. This was another "Triple A," Alhaji Alao Arisekola, a long-standing shadow player in Ibadan politics. He proceeded to organize a public rally at the Ibadan Liberty Sports Stadium at which his now-adopted political protégé, Sani Abacha, would be presented as presidential candidate to the Ibadan people.

A reedy, normally self-retiring specimen more given to sneaky, behind-the-scenes activities and intrigues than overt confrontations, the Yoruba Triple A astonishingly discovered a hidden promotional verve in his psyche and became a public promoter of the Abacha regime. Indeed, the obsession of this trader, possessed of the messianic destiny of Abacha, was matched only by his contempt for his own people, the Yoruba, who, by contrast, had mostly held his protégé, Abacha, in deep abhorrence since the imprisonment of Moshood Abiola, the elected president of the Nigerian nation.

The Alhaji's performances on radio and television on the single-minded mission of imposing Sani Abacha on the Nigerian people were quite complex. They went beyond gratitude to a business benefactor and revealed astonishing depths of self-loathing. Once, on television, he chastised his fellow Yoruba in the most scabrous language, denigrating whatever qualities he held responsible for their hatred of domination:

"The Yoruba people are too clever for their own good. Because they are educated, they think they know everything and so never recognize where their true interests lie. That makes them act stupidly. If the Yoruba had any sense in their heads, they would have long realized that it is not the portion of the Yoruba race to rule this nation. God has given the Northerners that mandate. The sensible position, therefore, would be to adopt Sani Abacha as a divinely chosen leader and cooperate with him. That way, their interests would be well protected."

The Northern scion and original propagator of the divine right to rule, Alhaji Maitama Sule, a former Nigerian representative to the United Nations, could not have preached it with greater conviction.

Now it was time to present the divinely anointed to the Yoruba, and Ibadan, his hometown, was Triple A's logical launching pad. The entire forces of the police and army were placed at the business mogul's disposal. A moderate rent-a-crowd had already taken up positions within and around the stadium with YEAA caps, T-shirts, and a few flags. Motorcades and delegations trickled into the stadium, the demeanor of the latter for all the world like that of chain gangs being led to roadside labor. The governor's motorcade would invade the stadium at any moment. Triple A himself arrived in his distinctive armor-plated Mercedes stretch limousine with police escorts and screeching sirens—and promptly ran into an ambush. Unknown to him, a fair portion of the rent-a-crowd were infiltrators from the camp of Comrade Ola Oni, a Marxist agitator from time immemorial, who, with a handful of resisters, had plotted all night in a small lecture room at the University of Ibadan campus. They had moved at an amazing pace through the warrens of Ibadan to mobilize the populace and set them up at strategic positions. Triple A take Ibadan for Abacha? Never! they swore.

There were running battles. Lives were lost, prisoners taken, but the Alhaji's forces were routed. He took refuge in an outside broadcasting van of the television station, sat upon for his own safety by policemen as the opposition combed the nooks and corners of Liberty Stadium, searching for him. Triple A then emerged after dark with a handful of his reconstituted bodyguards and moved to exact revenge for his public humiliation by combing the hospitals one by one, looking for the wounded. At Oluyoro Hospital, he and his men dragged out the wounded—anyone who looked as if he had been in a fracas and was not one of his followers—and shot them in cold blood, shot the doctor who was operating on them, routed the remaining medical attendants, and left other patients without aid.

THE SWOLLEN FACE of Olisa Agbakoba, with one eye closed and blackened—an image that was splayed all over the Nigerian media—told the entire story of a similar contest in Lagos. Olisa, an Igbo living in Lagos, was a human rights lawyer who had immediately responded to Kalu's YEAA by threatening a Two Million Man counterrally of his own within Lagos. He recharged the flagging mood of the opposition and the people responded, coming out in defiance of the cynical orders of the police—the peacekeepers who continued to ban all public gatherings, pronounced them illegal, but were always at the protective service of the YEAAs and AAAs and allied groups.

Although, like that of Comrade Ola Oni, Agbakoba's defiant public rally was to ensure that Abacha did not claim the city of Lagos as conquered territory, it was also partly a response to the wavering that had become apparent in the attitude of some foreign governments, which had begun sliding toward a policy of accommodation. Their diplomatic representatives were telling us bluntly, both outside and within the country, "The opposition appears to have

faded away. There is no real action on the ground." It was an outrageous sentiment. No real action? It was not the opposition that placed its own people in
prison dungeons and subjected them to torture. Those victims had not voluntarily submitted themselves to their jailers but had been arrested for *doing
something*! And their innocent relatives and dependents were being held hostage, even children—but *there is no real action*! The sad truth was that most of
these governments were eager to return to business as usual. Abacha looked
more and more impregnable every day, and they feared that their business
interests were being jeopardized through the principled policy of denying a
tyrant their recognition.

In the same breath, however, the same governments repudiated any notion
of armed resistance! The few bombs that went off—attributed at the time
to the opposition—were vigorously condemned by these governments. One
government—again our friends the Canadians—demanded from me an unambiguous pledge to refrain from violent tactics. I refused. The nation was
being subjected to a sustained regimen of state violence, yet here we were,
hamstrung in every way, being asked for a pledge to eschew violence. It struck
me as absurd, as it did Chief Tony Enahoro, the chairman of NADECO
Abroad. Indignantly he refused to make any such pledge. We both realized
that this would cost us much financial assistance from both the Canadian and
other governments, but it was not a pledge that we could make honorably.

It was an ironic situation since, even at that stage, we continued to explore
strategies for avoidance of a dreaded resolution in an unpredictable armed
struggle.

Not surprisingly, the basic handicap of the opposition groups remained—
funds. Not even funds for what those governments imagined—explosives,
arms, and ammunition—but funds for basic engagement in the most peaceful
activities, such as public demonstrations, just enough to print posters and
leaflets and pay for transportation, fuel, first aid, and medical bills. Both
NADECO and UDFN received urgent appeals from Olisa Agbakoba, who had
grasped the full foreign implications of Abacha's expanding campaigns for
"popular approval" and recognized the need to thwart or counter them. His
desperate appeal to us on the outside for his Lagos campaign was one of the
lowest moments for me personally, since I understood the critical nature of his
undertaking. The public face of resistance had to be bolstered, or else other
governments would join Bill Clinton in what—in our view—surely ranked
as the most execrable pronouncement of his career. Asked, as he stopped in

Senegal on his 1998 African tour, what would be his reaction toward Aba-cha's now-apparent bid for self-succession, the leader of the world's most popu-lous democratic nation replied, in obvious reference to the fifteen-year-old self-transformation of Flight Lieutenant Jerry Rawlings of Ghana into a civil-ian president, Well, it is not unknown where a military dictator has taken that route, shed the military uniform for the civilian, and thereby saved his country from the edge of chaos. As long as he is able to win the people's mandate!

Words to that effect, of such devastating potential for numerous other na-tions in Nigeria's shoes, made Susan Rice, by then Clinton's undersecretary of state for Africa, throw herself into damage control. She issued an immediate disclaimer, insisting that her president's words had been taken out of context or distorted, assured the world that America's policy toward unelected rulers remained the same, and so on. Too late. The damage had been done, and it was extensive. Abacha no longer needed to await the steamrolled affirmation of the people's will. The words had hardly rolled off Bill Clinton's tongue than Abacha shed all further coyness and declared himself a presidential can-didate. The appeal for material help from the home front attained a truly fran-tic intensity.

Was armed struggle still avoidable?

By now the opposition groups were financially drained. It was a pitiable sum that we succeeded in transmitting to Olisa Agbakoba from NALICON—a thousand dollars! Sadder still, it was the only contribution, as we later dis-covered, that Olisa received from outside. YEAA's Kalu spent that much at one sitting in a bar with his cronies. Nonetheless, with even more meager con-tributions from other sources from within, but mostly relying on volunteer work, Olisa and his colleagues succeeded in flooding the streets of Lagos with demonstrators, breaking up and regrouping under the weight of police at-tacks. Banners were raised and leaflets distributed, and a jubilant media boosted a remarkably courageous outing, against all conceivable odds, that was equaled only by that of Ola Oni's doughty warriors of Ibadan.

Both Abacha's ploys and the responses by the internal opposition—tenacious but weakened by increasing casualties—indicated only one course of action: a new "front" to keep the momentum of the struggle alive and keep the evil day of armed struggle at bay for as long as possible. It did not have to be anything dramatic; all that mattered was that the war be taken to the Abacha regime, on Nigerian soil, relying on the people themselves to provide a net-work of protection for identified but elusive organizers. Psychological warfare appeared to be a prerequisite: panicking and eroding the confidence of an oppressive regime and, at the same time, boosting the morale of the active opposition and the prostrate populace.

I could not deny the logic of this step any longer, nor evade the fact that I was the obvious choice to spearhead the new initiative. After all, there had been so many sightings of W.S. by Abacha's agents, leading to police and troop movements on a massive scale, high alerts at airports, ostentatious surveillance of known W.S. haunts and hosts, inflicting unpleasant experiences on a handful of travelers who happened to bear the slightest resemblance to the fugitive—at least in the eyes of overzealous security agents of a paranoid ruler. We were aware that these sightings, nearly all of which were mythical, were a constant source of strength to the opposition. Indeed, we would later discover that some of these sightings had been deliberate inventions, not by Abacha's security agents and propagandists but by opposition plants who had fed them to the agents! It was time to flesh out this apparition and earth it within Nigeria. The move would resuscitate a flagging resolve and structure the sporadic acts of defiance into a sustained campaign of civil disobedience—more accurately, a resumption of the civil disobedience campaign of June 1993, when the elections had been annulled, and the follow-up of November, when a spirited effort had been made to remove Ernest Shonekan, the parting gift of the ousted dictator Ibrahim Babangida. The ground needed to be softened up, made accommodating, if the ultimate weapon of resistance—armed struggle—could not be avoided.

At the third full meeting of the new opposition group, the UDFN, in Pittsburgh in March 1998, I announced that our gathering would be the last outside Nigerian soil and that the next meeting would be in Abuja, the nation's capital. The elation and raucous applause were expected, but only a handful of attendees were aware that this was the formal announcement of a new phase in the struggle, not simply a morale booster. Sola Adeyeye, our bearded secretary-general with the bearing of a bantam cock, now a member of the House of Representatives, was one of the few. Taken into confidence, he promptly swore that I would not reenter Nigeria without him. I felt guilty that I could not inform my deputy, Julius Ihonvbere, then program officer at the Ford Foundation, or other key members such as Kayode Fayemi, the fusslessly methodical organizer who had made a detailed study of military mentality. I feared that they would strenuously object and probably summon a meeting of the Governing Council of the UDFN to overrule the decision. It would not have changed my mind; I had completed my own analysis of our situation and was in no mood for arguments to which I had no intention of contributing.

My family, safely ensconced in California, had to be treated on an individual basis. The most troubling decision concerned my wife, Folake. Her reaction was predictable, and it was no time for emotional entreaties. I briefed my two sons, Olaokun and Ilemakin, both operating from England. I thought the elder, Olaokun, a medical doctor, would be ruled by a pragmatic approach and accept the supportive but crucial role that I was entrusting to him—from the outside. He shocked me by his adamant response: if I were going in, so was he—and as advance guard! His brother, Ilemakin, made matters even worse by declaring that he would not be left behind. Over my dead body, I decided, even as I agreed to include them in the infiltration team; they would learn soon enough that they had been ditched when I made my first broadcast from within Nigeria!

Only three non-Nigerians either had knowledge of or were involved in the planning of my return. One was a German quasi-diplomat who worked for a foundation—he agreed to organize a noisy cultural event as decoy on the day of our entry into Nigeria. That was a brief alliance with a most unsettling termination, for the man would back off shortly after, denying even the generous sum he had contributed unsolicited, as well as his offer to take up all further travel expenses. So fervent was his dissociation that I anxiously called up my young companion on that visit, Kayode Fayemi, seeking assurance that I had not suffered a brain fever in Hanover, where the meeting had taken place. The crucial exchange had been necessarily private, but, fortunately, on emerging from the man's office, I had transferred the donated sum, all in hard currency, to Kayode. Now I sought to know if it had been phantom currency notes that I shoved into his hands, evaporating perhaps as soon as we had left Germany! Kayode's reassurance saved me from a fear of stress-induced delusions.

Of more durable material was the second ally, whose name it does no harm to mention. This was Gerry Feil, a long-standing collaborator in a medley of projects—artistic and political—and in myriad ways since my earliest brush with renegade regimes. Gerry's cluttered studio in the Village in downtown New York was virtually surrendered to me for use whenever and for no matter what. It was the venue for meetings that required the highest security, for leaving and retrieving messages, or simply for getting some sleep. It was just as well for us that an FBI operative's recommendations for "taking care of Mr. Gerry Feil," wrongly suspected of aiding the revolutionary Weathermen in the sixties, had not been implemented. As revealed in a book* by another operative, now retired, Gerry was to have been locked in a car, suspended on the edge of a cliff, and "made to sweat until the bastard reveals all he knows." Gerry, alas for him, had had the misfortune some years earlier of leaving his car in the custody of a filmmaker who was making a documentary about the Weathermen.

The FBI agent has since been exposed for the lunatic he was, but I would have stayed miles away from Gerry had I known at the time how dangerous a revolutionary he had been regarded in some FBI circles! Not that this would have prevented me from making use of the professional makeup skills of his colleagues in the film industry. These practical aids were essential not only for a successful reentry, but for the ability to move openly yet remain undetected.

My voice would be a problem when introduced in zones infiltrated by the police, but not one that a semi-trained actor keeping a low profile could fail to overcome, even without voice-distorting gadgets. This problem did not arise for the formal broadcasts, however, and I had prepared the speech that would be transmitted over Radio Kudirat the moment our small team set foot again on Nigerian soil. After that, any UDFN statements would issue first from within the nation's boundaries and only then be rebroadcast by Radio Kudirat from its Scandinavian base. Thanks to Reporters sans Frontières, we still laid claim to an idle, mobile FM radio transmitter, stored in the basement of an apartment building in the very heart of Paris—the shortwave Radio Kudirat had rendered it temporarily redundant by successfully covering the entire space of the Nigerian nation on its own.

The third non-Nigerian was our man in Paris—still an international civil servant for UNESCO, Nigerian but of French nationality—whom I asked to prepare to take possession of the transmitter and travel with it to Cotonou in the Republic of Benin. From there it would travel to Lagos, a repeat exercise of the first incursion of any opposition radio onto Nigerian airwaves in 1996: Radio Freedom, a venture that had been made possible by the dissident general Alani Akinrinade. Early in 1996, the first mobile transmitters had been secretly tested in the Republic of Benin, dismantled, smuggled piecemeal into Nigeria by women traders and other volunteers, then reassembled within the country. Among such volunteers were the mild-looking Dapo Olorunyomi, a journalist; Kayode Fayemi, who from writing doctorals on military domination had become an agent for its reversal; and the self-effacing "Lemi." Like Olorun-

---

* M. Wesley Swearingen, *FBI Secrets: An Agent's Expose* (Boston: South End Press, 1995).

yomi, Lemi had once enjoyed Abacha's hospitality and lived to tell the tale. My private nickname for Lemi was "the Gecko"—he had a natural gift for blending into walls, which perhaps had helped him to survive and secure his eventual "ransom" from Abacha's dungeons. The impact of Radio Freedom on the Nigerian populace, the first time that the monopoly of state broadcasting had ever been breached, had been nothing short of galvanizing. The transmission could only cover a few square miles at a time, but its mobility made it appear far more extensive in its coverage. A search for that transmitter had also provided the pretext for the military invasion of my Abeokuta home, the real purpose of course being to destroy whatever could be destroyed. The new radio, our gift from Reporters sans Frontières and more powerful than Radio Freedom, would follow the same route and operate in the same way, only this time its broadcasts would be picked up and rebroadcast all over the country by Radio Kudirat.

At the lagoon village of Ganvie in Cotonou, in the neighboring Republic of Benin, a canoe with an outboard motor and two escorts were placed on standby, ready to take me into Nigerian waters. They were provided by a Nigerian businessman who, despite his careful cultivation of a low profile, enjoyed seemingly unlimited reaches into the ranks of the Beninois police and Customs commands. This entrepreneur had already assigned us isolated, mostly disused warehouses in which we were free to store whatever we wished. If our incursion into Nigerian territory had its desired effect, a psychological front would be effectively established and the nation might be spared a war of insurrection. If not, the people would be primed for resistance.

$\mathcal{A}$ Final Mission

. . . . .

I HAD ONE MORE "DIPLOMATIC OFFENSIVE" TO EXECUTE BEFORE DEPARTURE, and that was to go to Israel, a country I had never before visited. Among the preliminaries for venturing into the lion's den in that year, 1998, one that NALICON had designated the Year of Liberation, was the fullest possible penetration and, we hoped, disruption of Sani Abacha's security apparatus. He had inherited it from his predecessor, Ibrahim Babangida, and it was run largely by the Israelis. Even before my flight from Nigeria, a notorious, irrepressible multiple agent of successive governments, Godwin Daboh, had once offered to draw me into a plot to topple Sani Abacha. Among his—largely improbable— boasts was that he had a direct connection with the Israeli-run security operations as well as intimate links to the Israeli government. If we could come to an agreement about the composition of the civilian succession, he would simply contact the Israeli government, which would then authorize its nationals to do whatever was necessary. The army, he assured me, was ready to move and install the winner of the 1993 presidential elections in Aso Rock.

Daboh was most specific, even down to technical details. One switch, he said, controlled the entire security gadgetry of Aso Rock—communication, lights, signals, and so forth. Without it, Abacha would be stripped naked, suddenly bereft of protection. Daboh claimed to know the Israeli engineering firm that had set up the entire circuit. He swore that he had the blueprints in his possession, or at least that he had access to them at any time of his choosing. If I had tarried long enough, I have no doubt that he would have claimed that he had the remote control button right in his pocket and might even have offered to demonstrate a fraction of its efficacy!

It was an embarrassment to have Godwin Daboh screaming all this at me virtually at the top of his voice in the courtyard premises of the Lagos Magistrate Court, where I had gone to institute a civil suit against Abacha's usurpation of power. That was a purely symbolic gesture; we knew in advance which way the judge, a well-known AGIP (Any Government in Power), would make his ruling. Daboh was nothing if not consistent: "Stop wasting time on a case with a predictable judicial outcome. Let's get to work on something practical." Hurriedly, to shut him up, I agreed to a fictitious rendezvous and fled!

The Israeli security connection was real, however, and it was one of the first targets of the opposition groups, once we moved into exile. NADECO had already taken the initiative and written to the Israeli government to protest the technical support still provided to a brutal dictator in the area of security. Questions were raised in the Knesset, and NADECO received a letter of assurance that all Israelis had been told to withdraw from any activities that implicated a direct or indirect collaboration with the Abacha regime. My visit was a follow-up. It was no longer sufficient for the Israelis to have withdrawn; we now required active support from the government, especially in its intelligence section.

This had to be the last such engagement! Each moment carried the same thought: I was freeing myself of the mind-numbing itinerant diplomacy, leaving the field to the NADECO stalwarts, to whom this was meat and drink, but also, on our side, to NALICON, to Kayode Fayemi, whom I had watched navigating those shoals with increasing self-assurance.

The chauffeur arrived. I attended a Knesset meeting, then met with individual members of that house, including the female representative who had introduced the original motion that barred any further collaboration with the Abacha regime. They all gave reassurances of strict compliance by Israeli citizens with the directives. Brief meetings with small committees, representatives of the various coalitions that made up the government, the opposition, a politician or two who had been in Nigeria and wanted a few minutes just to ask about old friends ...

Then followed a quiet lunch with Shimon Peres and an abrupt change of mood. The secluded restaurant, clearly not open to the public, aided the transition, more like a private, discreet clubhouse where members of the government might take visitors for confidential exchanges, and my host hinted as much, though he added that he enjoyed dining there by himself, since it was one place where he knew his thoughts would not be interrupted. Peres was no longer prime minister. His party was in opposition, but Israeli politics were such that he still wielded a great amount of influence in government. Shimon

Peres—we had interacted before on a few occasions—always struck me as one of that rare species: a politician of principle, even in the heated combat zone that his nation had become. We engaged the Palestinian issue only toward the end; I had not traveled to Israel for a conference on Middle East politics, but of course, how could that eye of a global storm be completely avoided? When I began to outline the developments in the Nigerian predicament, he nodded in familiarity with the subject. Israel, he responded, was committed to democracy, and he gave me his solemn assurance that even though he was no longer in government, he could and would ensure that his nation did not overtly or covertly act in any way that would give joy to the Abacha regime.

I continued more cautiously as I went on to explain that my visit was exploratory and I would be followed shortly by a team that would be led by someone by the name of Alani Akinrinade, formerly a general in the Nigerian Army. I wrote down the name for him. How soon could they visit, and could he facilitate their visas? As soon as they wish, he said, just give me a few days' notice. He would also make a call to the relevant consulate. I provided indications of the new thinking of the opposition—that we had to begin operating from within, preparing for any eventuality. I watched his reaction as I stressed that we were not thinking yet of armed conflict but could no longer rule out any measure, that the situation was deteriorating so rapidly that we expected more than mere neutrality or diplomatic niceties from the Israeli government. What we needed above all was help to penetrate Abacha's security network— we could do, for a start, with some sophisticated technological gadgets.

Shimon Peres listened, expressed himself as one who was already working on a problem and could be relied upon not to take refuge in evasion. The afternoon passed quietly. We spoke like old friends, an older man whose life had encompassed much, the other, younger but infected with his presence, so that he began to feel prematurely aged deep inside. Peres introduced the Palestinian situation, as if to draw parallels—not of politics but of the frustrations of conflict—running lightly over the numerous and abortive attempts at peace. His voice, a deep rumble as if emerging from deep caverns of thought, was a mixture of quiet resolve, tinged with some regret that logical policies, in his reckoning, had failed to result in his vision, conceding a barely disguised anxiety for the future. Only during this part of our exchange did his measured rhythm change character, revealing a deep anger at and contempt for his predecessor, Benjamin Netanyahu, whose imported brand of Zionism he found depressingly barren. Regardless of my view of Israeli policies toward Palestinians, being with Peres simply as a human being and a leader of people made me marvel all over again how it ever came about that the Abachas of the world could actually dare aspire to any rank of leadership, even of a pack of hyenas. I felt quite contented. Even if we obtained nothing from the resources within Peres's scope of influence, his wistful gaze left me feeling that this was a friend who shared similar ideals and who wished with all his heart that the world were different from the one we both inhabited.

It was one of those balmy afternoons when a glow settles over one, inexplicably, although in this case I could attribute it to the serene atmosphere of our meeting place, the fussless attention of the waiters, the calm exchanges, and the quiet attentiveness displayed by a host toward the concerns that had brought me thousands of miles around the globe. In addition, I was already feeling the sense of satisfaction that comes with knowing that I was shutting down one particular line of duty and freeing myself for the next. It struck me as a fitting end to shuttling around to foreign lands, attempting to assess what others might or might not give, urging on the former and adjusting to the latter, mentally casting about, even within an encounter, for where one might turn next in the rounds of exploration. I had never really felt cut out for this role, and it was an added bonus to be about to end it on an altruistic, though powerless, note—altruistic, because I was concluding an unwanted career in a land upon which I truly wished I could bestow something in turn: a just resolution of its own travails. Perhaps my visit to the Holocaust Museum that morning also had something to do with this feeling. The measured, modulated voice that read out the list of victims in that somber yet riveting space still echoed in my head, albeit muted, even sepulchral, coursing around the retentive skull.

THERE WAS SOME TIME before my final engagement—an informal one, just a reception, in the home of Professor Yacov Zvi of the University of Jerusalem, whose invitation to lecture had served as cover for my visit. It was a long-standing invitation, one that I had warned him I might wish to take up with only a few days' notice. I decided on some sightseeing. My chauffeur, every bit of whom reeked of Mossad, the Israeli secret service, took me to Old Jerusalem.

At the foot of Temple Mount, known also as the Noble Sanctuary, I excused my minder, since I prefer to explore new places by myself, without a guide or running commentary, even without a map or guidebook. I descended into the crypts, the grottoes, the temples and mosques, the reliquaries, and the mythologies of the spirit. It was not difficult to decipher the architectural rivalries inscribed on walls, the altered passages, sealed-up niches and alcoves, sealed-up archways and altars as one faith supplanted another, temple turned to church to mosque to church and then to temple or mosque again, each attempting to eradicate the manifest presences of the last but with the signatures of each faith still visible, if only vestigially, sometimes cohabiting the same space as if in an optimistic testament to the potential accommodativeness of the human spirit. There was no doubt about it: a communion of sheer spirit, elevated above theology, sect, or creed pervaded every niche, perfumed the air with the rich distillation of numinous presences. My path crossed those of other tourists. They were not many and would be more truthfully described as pilgrims, since their faces, even bodies, radiated the awareness of being in a place of history, hallowed by the passage of prophets and seers. It was approaching dusk when I emerged and stood looking down over the plains.

The next moment, I was hailed by name, by voices whose accents were distinctly familiar. They turned out to be from a busload of Ghanaian soldiers, a detachment from the U.N. peacekeeping force in Lebanon who had motored to Jerusalem to visit the holy sites. I waved to them. Encountering them so far from home within this foreign space, bound on a mission of peace, immediately moved me in a strange way, as if it were some kind of message from the distant coast of a continent where my cactus patch was eternally lodged and from within which my obsessive mission acquired its enigmatic endorsement. Within the mandates of peace and strife, this encounter struck me, quite inexplicably, as a gracious, indeed benign, portent.

The bus was already pulling out when some of them recognized my head of hair—always the giveaway!—and excitedly stopped the driver. I was mobbed. They insisted on taking souvenir pictures and obtaining autographs. One of them was reading an anthology of African writing. He proudly opened a well-thumbed page—he had been reading the section of my poems! That was unusual. Most of the time when I catch one of our own reading any work of mine, it's *The Lion and the Jewel* or *The Trial of Brother Jero*. Most frequently, however, they are reading Chinua Achebe's *Things Fall Apart*! It was one of those rare times that I was devoid of any sense of resented duty in that sometimes exasperating labor of signing autographs and posing for photographs; I signed most willingly and gratified the insatiable cameras. Finally they departed, and with the dwindling of the bus to a speck in the distance came a sudden silence that enveloped the dusk, as if that busload of peaceful warriors had been the last intrusive object, of either noise or motion, into a contemplation of timelessness. I resumed my gaze outward, but with a marked difference in response.

Not even the passage of a shy straggle of youthful visitors, wordless and reverential, disturbed the silence that had descended. One moment, I watched them pause at the Mount of Olives and stand still for several moments; then, as noiselessly as they had appeared, they were gone, seemingly swallowed up by the earth as they vanished down stone steps that led into the chambers, grottoes, and galleries of the mount. With their passage, it seemed as if, finally, the last human presence in the world had been sucked into the underworld. I slipped gradually into a consciousness that merged totally with my surroundings, the arid slopes that swept into an endless horizon from the splayed feet of Temple Mount, slipped into one of my inexplicable flotation experiences, those moments when a part of one's self appears to separate from the body and moves to inhabit a pure realm of sensations that have drifted in from all sides, emanating from nowhere, never defining themselves for what they are, what they portend, why they have chosen to assail that detached portion of the self within a neutral, elusive territory. Perhaps the self becomes more receptive in those moments when one has truly shed the encumbrances of options and submits only to a straightforward choice of action, or none at all. Certainly, the only identified thought that my mind had retained for the past hours had been—going home. The rest was up to others, and I felt supremely light-hearted and light-headed, readied only toward one direction, one uncomplicated goal, regaining my own terrain and moving anonymously on familiar earth—an end to the frenzy of "ambassadorial" hustling, leaving only the task of infiltrating, settling in, watching and waiting, preparing. I felt supremely at peace.

It crept over me gradually, the strange, yet familiar and always mystifying experience. I found myself entranced by a dusk that would remain memorable in its surreality, elusive to the grasp, impossible to apprehend. There is a most eloquent spirituality about that much-fought-over land—I, an adherent of none of the three principal faiths that inhabit it, testify to this.

I remained with a vast silence at the confluence of embattled slopes, bathed, however, in a protective calm, a now-placid crossroads of multiple civilizations and faiths. Sunset had descended. My gaze swept over centuries of history—strife, trade, and spirituality. It brought with it a slow wave of melancholy, settling imperceptibly on the pores of the skin. Then I felt I could sense the seepage of incense, spices, and unguents from ancient times, a sensation unprecedented on any foreign soil that had ever attempted to entice me into a shedding of my discrete sense of being. Unresisting, I submitted to the experience, hovered above eons of time, surrounded by a sough of winds in a dusk of absolute stillness.

Restored to my immediate surroundings, I wondered, Why? Why was this generous mat of peace so deeply soaked in hate? For I felt nothing but a protective cloak that opened into an endless vista to dissolve rocks, groves, and monuments, lifting from an air of peace from that patch of earth, one that, in those ineradicable moments, percolated through the soles of my feet, affirming the essence of that earth as the spiritual navel of the world. And I felt a gift had been passed to me. It was without definition, but it was, clearly, a much-sought-after bequest. It left me uplifted, endowed with infinite certitude of a resolution of all things. I felt, somehow, that the future was resolved and its truth transmitted to me—not revealed, since I had no idea what it was, only that I was already a secret confidant of the end of discord. And I knew it had to do with the nature of the mission that had brought me to this place. Temple Mount to some, Noble Sanctuary to others—I left the space subdued yet buoyant, curiously at peace with myself. I was no longer seeking; I had found. I had not known that condition of equanimity, of interior accommodation with the outer world, in many years, certainly not since my departure from home. There was no expectation of anything. But I felt no more anxiety, only a quiet trust in that moment, a serenity that transcended questions and uncertainties, as a pilgrim might feel who finds the mundane substance of his quest subsumed in a vision of eternity.

Outside the borders of my own land, this kind of intimation was rare. I once experienced a kindred sensation on a visit to the rockhills of Idanre, in Ondo, the western part of Nigeria, and a more contrasting landscape would be difficult to imagine—a rockhill that I elsewhere described as "a god-suffused grazing of primal giants and mastodons, petrified through some strange history, suckled by mists and clouds"! Yet there also, something similar had occurred, a silent intrusion of presences that would be conjured—or, more accurately, would levitate and dissolve—into a walk in the dead of night through the woods of a yet-virgin part of Molete, just outside Ibadan, more than two hundred miles from that originating experience and all of two years later. That took place in 1965, and it gave birth to the long poem *Idanre*. And occasionally I would undergo spells of quiescent self-dissolution in the moist, densely wooded grove of Osun, the goddess that presides over the city of Oshogbo, an hour's drive from Ibadan. But never before in a strange land, not entwined in a few moments of twilight communion with whatever deity or more presided over this land of such austere beauty, sibilant with ancestral whispers, so remote from the rancorous sermonizing of its intemperate clerics of separation and hate. It would take a year before I would revisit that scene in the lines:

Pondering war, I trod the sandal-paved stones
Senses lulled in light incense, brushed by hems
Of robes from distant sages, pilgrims of all faiths.
And the dark hour beckoned to me in hope.
From that seared land that I had sworn
I would not leave with empty hands, came a gift....

I went straight from Temple Mount to the reception in the home of my host, and there a persistent journalist finally trapped and interviewed me on the usual themes, of which the immediate politics of Nigeria were prominent. He was actually a pleasant young man, who impressed me with his unusually intimate knowledge of our situation, and I was content to speak to him quite extensively. On his way home, he turned on his car radio as usual and—could not believe the news that was emerging! He immediately spun around and raced to catch me before I left the reception, ran up the stairs, and attempted to drag me into another room where there was a television set. I resisted a little, mumbling protests about the improbability of the news he was repeating so excitedly. He turned on the box.

It seemed unreal, but I knew it was true. Sani Abacha, the cause of all my incessant peregrinations all over the world, had quit the scene, terminally. The journalist wanted my immediate reaction, had raced back at breakneck speed to obtain a scoop, hardly believing his luck. To him and a handful of the guests who had followed us into the television room, I shut off the exulting—no, not exulting, not euphoric, not even vindicated but simply accepting, grateful, and fulfilled—part of me and said, repressing a smile, "Have they carried out a postmortem? Has the man been cut in little pieces? Taken out his brain? Understand this—Sani Abacha has a feudal mentality. He may have faked his death simply to see who is mourning and who is dancing. Come back when the doctors have chopped him up to determine the cause of death."

But it was true. Deep within me, I knew that this time it was no wish-fulfilling rumor, of which there had been no shortage in the past.

It was as if an opaque glass had been shattered and I was confronted with the reality that lay hidden behind it, straining to be released. The element of doubt was not altogether absent, but it was more a distrust in the rapidity with which the intimations that had assailed me on the Noble Sanctuary were now clarified. The sudden opening of long-sought possibilities was the certain part; a lingering mistrust remained within my inner reality. Nonetheless, time was fractured; suddenly everything was in the past!

. . .

WAS I TRULY about to be relieved of four years of body-and-soul-sapping itinerancy? Years of disappointments, of reversals and the ambitions of little monstrosities lurking in corners of the abruptly vacated citadel of terror kept one in check, preached hard caution. Still, one could not but savor this prospect—the end to a clandestine existence, of planning, scheming, organizing, bullying, cajoling heads of state, defense ministers, dissident caucuses within Abacha-contented governments, sessions with military strategists and veterans of guerrilla struggle, retired or still active, sometimes actual combatants on furlough—East, West, Africa, South Africa . . . but now, a rescue? Suddenly, the shearing away of a crushing, life-altering burden?

Forty matured years distanced from the first reprieve of this nature—my volunteer flirtation with the Hungarian uprising—mentally dressed again for an outing that had been canceled at the eleventh hour, I wondered what my collaborators were feeling at that very moment. As profoundly relieved as I was, I hoped, but perhaps some of them would also be caught in that ambiguous zone of deflation that appears to surround such moments. All I experienced, once I had gained the peace and quiet of my hotel room, was an overwhelming urge to be home at that hour, undetected, maybe even wearing the grotesque disguise that would have been perfected by Gerry Feil's colleagues but grinning to myself underneath it, to stroll through my cactus patch, let the mood of the people percolate to me while it still flowed jubilantly, indifferent to tomorrow's uncertainties, and be part of their sense of vindication.

I longed to see especially those from whom it had been necessary—for their own health—to steer a clear path, those with whom I was known to have a close relationship. No attempt to make contact, no telephone calls, only the occasional verbal message through accidental meetings with mutual acquaintances at airports or in a hotel lobby: "Tell so-and-so we are alive and keeping safe." And often the careful, anxious messages from within: "Please keep your head down; we are all praying for you." The world of friendship and closeness had been split in two: there were those who were directly involved, at some level or another, in the single-minded mission of ousting a tyrant, accepting all attendant risks, and those who were at one with the cause but could not be seen to be involved, however remotely. For the former, one lived by the rules of comradeship and a respect for their chosen level of participation and risk taking. For the latter, one emptied all emotional storage tanks and hoped that maybe, someday, you would meet again.

Most burdensome of all, you also took the anguish of a nation with you everywhere, as familiar as your toilet kit, poring over reports, moving from high-level, highly publicized meetings to clandestine encounters, worrying about the insiders with a purely clinical, practical concern. Who are the latest arrivals in jail? How can you penetrate the walls to reach them, to let them know they are not forgotten? Who is left outside the walls, and how tightly is their existence now circumscribed? How can you get support to them? To their families? Is Radio Kudirat, the opposition voice that was making Sani Abacha frantic, reaching everyone? Often enough? Effectively enough? And sometimes, warnings from our listening posts, even from deep within Abacha's security system—those warnings were more safely delivered to us on the outside than to those inside; it removed the danger of a direct linkage and exposed such supportive sources to lesser risk. We then became the roundabout conduit to those who remained on the ground: *It's time for you to move—move out—now!!!* Or else: *Change your routine—drastically.* Or: *Vanish under, dig deep underground, and remain there.*

Move! Move some more and then—move again! And again and again! The sheer physicality of so many years had usurped the norm, overwhelming the rightful claims of spaces of serenity, creativity, the elusive space of resolution, even of contrary things. Was this about to end, and so suddenly? It was difficult to surrender to such an enticing, desperately craved prospect, one that translated simply as—*going home.* Not a sentimental homecoming but simply *going where one should never have left.*

WHEN MY CHAUFFEUR came to take me to the airport for departure, he, like the young journalist, was unable to contain his excitement. He rushed at me, and the words came tumbling out in a cascade.

"It's him! It's him! I know him!"

"Know whom?"

"Your new head of state, General Abdulsalami. At first, when I heard the name, I wasn't sure. But his picture was on the television screen this morning."

Well, should I have been surprised? What was more natural than that Mossad should know every one of our top military brass, and indeed lower-ranking officers? What, among other reasons, had brought me to Israel?

"Did you meet him in Nigeria?" I asked.

"No, here, in Israel! Every year. Some of his colleagues too. But he has a bad back and came for treatment. Every year I took him to the private clinic. Same clinic. Very nice person. He would stay maybe two or three weeks. Unfailingly.

While he received treatment, I would take his wife shopping. They were a very nice couple."

I did not need to pump him for information about the new face in Aso Rock. All the way to the airport, he spoke incessantly. "I can't believe it. I simply cannot believe it. Here am I driving you, and all these years I have been driving the general, and he turns out to be your new head of state."

"Well, you never know who you get to meet, especially in this profession of yours."

He blinked, did a double take—my imagination?—but certainly took another look at me through the rearview mirror.

"Oh, yes, running this car-hire service, one gets to meet so many people. The government likes to use our firm for important visitors." He drove thoughtfully for a while, then shook his head yet again. "Still, it's a miracle. Maybe you will also become the next head of state?"

I had to smile at that and comforted him with a pat on the shoulder. "Miracles were never intended to stretch that far."

PART VIII

Homecoming

An Interim Welcome—Official

. . . . .

PERHAPS, AFTER ALL, I AM A SECRET JUNKIE FOR A MEASURE OF THE UN-predictable, for a slight tinge of risk. Even a closet masochist? I am reluctant, indeed embarrassed, to admit to a vague discontent over my prospective return, but it is there, even palpable. Something is about to end, and I already experience a feeling akin to amputation. I know that at sixty-five, I should be grateful to glimpse the end of a nomadic imposition and the precariousness of certain forms of contestations, but there is this old man still nursing a twinge of deprivation, rather than overt, wine-cork-popping gratitude.

It seemed unreal, but all that was over. I could actually contemplate, then discuss with others, the ideal moment for our return, yet I found myself compelled to acknowledge a sneaky sense of disappointment scuffing the hairs on the old man's skin, one who was already several years a pensioner (albeit without a pension), already old enough to profit from the subsidized fares on California's railways and some airlines for a "senior citizen" status—another irritating coinage of the pseudolanguage of American "political correctness"—just what is wrong with the tried-and-tested "elder," "elderly," and so forth? Still, what a weird feeling it was to exercise that gerontocratic privilege for the first time on a San Bernardino Metroliner! Mentally I poured a libation for my admission to the new age-grade—a call, surely, to cease from further strife.

My momentous age-grade induction, ignored by all the world except the automatic ticket machine, preceded the moment of liberation by a clear two years. Perhaps, whenever I made the voyage home, I thought, I should be made to submit to a painful age-grade ritual since, on looking inward, I continually caught my elderly alter ego furtively drawing a dry tongue over his own teeth of discontent at a moment when I should have been salivating with satisfaction, savoring my own portion of a collective vindication, the true essence of the approaching homecoming.

Then the messages began to pour in—or, more accurately, the same message from multiple directions: the successor, General Abubakar Abdulsalami, himself former army chief of staff to the monster I had dubbed "Triple D"— Diminutive Demented Dictator—wanted us to meet. Was this a replay of the never-never Abacharian dialogue? I consulted with both NALICON and key members of NADECO. The feeling was unanimous: I should go and listen to what he had to say.

AS IF IN A beggarly compensation for the now-expunged thrill of a sneak return, we prepared for our meeting with Abdulsalami the way we had operated for nearly four years—only this time, our cautionary moves were not to thwart any danger to ourselves but to avoid contamination by the new political hangers-on. Nothing that we had inquired into remotely suggested that Abdulsalami was planning an Abacha-style act of treachery on American soil— on the contrary, this general appeared to have read the national (and international) mood right. He accepted that he was permitted just the one mission: to return the nation to apparent civilian rule and make a graceful exit. How thoroughgoing would be the transfer, how faithfully distanced from a mere surface change of baton, became the primary concern of the organized opposition.

As soon as he took over after Sani Abacha, Abdulsalami blithely announced that all exiles were free to return home. We found this extremely hilarious. There we were, subjects of "wanted" posters all over the country offering rewards for our capture—the posters had mostly been torn down or defaced, as a matter of fact—but the reality was that charges of treason, a capital crime, still hung over our heads. Abacha's men were still on the loose. Any policeman or soldier could arrest us on sight or shoot us "for resisting arrest." In what kind of a world, we asked, was this former associate of Abacha living? Did he understand how deeply the Abacha machinery had burrowed into the normal safeguards against arbitrariness? Had we survived Abacha's roving death squads all over Europe and America only to walk into a trap at home?

Cautiously, however, we had to admit the possibility that the new man might be serious. He had the treason charges against us formally withdrawn and their cancellation widely publicized. Even more remarkable was the fact that as soon as he began to plan his first overseas trip a few weeks after taking office, he was already instructing ambassadors to the nations on his itinerary to track me down and arrange a meeting. The democratic movement decided that we had nothing to lose. And so we met at the Palace Hotel in New York City. We set down unambiguous terms for meeting—this was strictly political business, not a courtesy visit. Next, to avoid that latter coloring and ensure that we did not find ourselves trapped among the usual train of appendages who had trailed him from Nigeria to Europe, where their ranks had been swelled at every stop, and who were now virtually swarming around him in New York, we insisted that the meeting should be set for a time when he had rid himself of his train. Most emphatically, I did not wish to run into the man who had become known as the King of ING—Ernest Shonekan, former head of the Interim National Government.

When the elections of June 1993 were abruptly annulled by Ibrahim Babangida, the nation became too hot for even that survivalist to juggle in his nimble hands. Violent demonstrations—especially in the West, where the winner, Moshood Abiola, came from—compelled him to "step aside," but not so far aside as to disinterestedly do the right thing, which was to hand over power to the elected president. He prepared a cushion—the Interim National Government—to break his fall, then named a pliant fall guy to head a nation of a hundred million restless souls. Babangida often deluded himself in presuming to understand the psychology of Nigeria's peoples. In nominating Shonekan to the position of head of state, he assumed that the Yoruba would be content with the swap—one Yoruba, any Yoruba, as long as it was one Yoruba for another! This crude gesture of appeasement only incensed the Yoruba. On the one hand, there was a president elected by the entire nation; on the other, a puppet nominated by a disgraced dictator who was bent on clinging to the last shreds of authority. Shonekan became a pariah among his own people.

Ninety days after his illegal occupation of Aso Rock, he was unceremoniously tossed out by Abacha, but even one hour in office would have sufficed for the company servant. It was still something to place on his résumé. To this today, this Egba king is probably the sole mind in our shared hometown, Abeokuta, that harbors the notion that he was ever a functional chief executive of the Nigerian nation.

It is one thing for a dog to cringe under the lash of a sadistic master; it stretches the pathology of cravenness to watch the whipped creature follow the same master around, licking his hand, whimpering for scraps, jumping to "fetch it" when a training stick is tossed, then racing to ingratiate itself with that master's replacement in competition with a hundred attendant curs in a roving kennel. After serving Sani Abacha in various menial roles, the presence of Ernest Shonekan in Abdulsalami's entourage even before the new dictator was a month at the head of affairs was a truly unsavory sight. We singled him out as one individual whom we absolutely did not wish to encounter during our meeting. It went beyond the one individual objection, however. We had to take measures to ensure that our visit was perceived for what it was—not a courtesy visit but a formal encounter with the new man at the helm of power, without any encumbrances.

And so we went into a relaxed version of the kind of security routine to which we had become accustomed when Abacha's agents were roaming the world at will. In getting to the rendezvous, for once, the restraining kennel insultingly known as a New York taxi came in handy in more ways than one; within it, one was truly invisible from the outside. Cooped in the constricted space with one's nose against the armored divider between driver and passenger, the fare is rendered incognito since the knees are drawn up to the face and the body sunk into the most uncomfortable seats ever designed for public transportation. It was a measure of my newfound liberation that I proceeded to vent, with my colleagues as captive audience but in full agreement, my long-pent-up aggression against this New York model of the taxi, also proliferating throughout the nation. No other word for it, those vehicles are rude, downright rude! That a driver deserves his protection from armed, usually drug-crazed urban bandits is one thing; that a modern nation, famed for space-age designs, one that had known the humane and commodious Checker cabs, could fail to design taxis that are considerate and respectful, yet protective of the driver, had always struck me as typical of an attitude of contempt for fare-paying humanity, as well as an indictment of the supineness of passengers from all over the world or a testimony to their forbearance. What, I now proposed, would prevent a one-day universal boycott by tourists as well as natives against such insolent conveyances? Or a blockade of the streets against them through civic action... It made a pleasant change to be able to launch a vitriolic outburst against a long-resented necessity that could not answer back. With a sense of relief, I knew I was already recovering my taste for earthshaking issues!

We had decided, as a base, on an Italian bar cum restaurant opposite the hotel, where we kept a lengthy watch on the premises to see who went in and came out. Sola Adeyeye, the mercurial secretary-general of the umbrella organization the UDFN, had taken on the task of inspecting the locality and securing our vantage point. I would wait in the bar until he and the third member of the team, our vice chairman, Julius Ihonvbere, were absolutely certain that all unwanted visitors had disappeared. Only then was I to enter the hotel and join the others. Wearing one of my lighter disguises, I shot out of the taxi trap—though "clambered" would be a more accurate word for the contortions needed to exit that mobile pit!—dived into the bar, and ensconced myself in the left corner by a window from which I could view the street without being seen. Adeyeye went into the hotel to negotiate my movements with Dr. Ibrahim Gambari, the ambassador to the United Nations who was in charge of Abdulsalami's visit; it was he who had finally tracked me down and arranged the encounter. So anxious was Gambari to ensure that "you do not suddenly decide on one of your vanishing acts" that he came over to the bar to assure me that all was clear and would I now follow him so as to avoid the wastage of even one minute? I asked, Where is Sola? Sola came charging through a moment later to insist that I stay put. The hotel lobby was still filled with all the unwanted and undesirable, he said. Julius followed shortly and confirmed it. I was quite contented with my position; the bar appeared to be sufficiently stocked for a prolonged siege.

Eventually Gambari prevailed on us to transfer into the hotel. The environment was not yet fully sanitized, but he proposed—quite reasonably—that we wait in his own room. That way, he could take us up to Abdulsalami's suite at a moment's notice, once the last visitor had departed. How he must have regretted his quite practical proposal—but that would come later. For now, the regret was all ours—we could not have chosen a worse moment. An elevator was just disgorging the last set of stragglers as we stepped into the lobby, and we were obliged to run the gauntlet. Several handshakes, hugs, and backslaps later with the not-so-leprous among them—even so, it seemed an eternity—we fled into the sanctuary of Gambari's room, where a few ladies, wives of some of the accompanying officials, also appeared to have found a haven. Among them was Gambari's wife, whom, to my now recurrent chagrin—considering that she had hosted me to sumptuous meals in calmer days, as she reminded me—I did not recognize! Gambari left us to our devices while he went up and down on his protocol duties.

On the coffee table were some publications. A picture on one cover stood out conspicuously—the photograph of the deceased dictator. Mentally, I retitled him "Quadruple D"—Diminutive, Demented, now Deceased Dictator. But why was it so conspicuously displayed? Worse was to be revealed. On the cover of this lavishly produced volume of selected speeches was the note "With a Foreward [yes, Foreward] by General Abdulsalami, Head of State"!

It was an inauspicious beginning. What message was this meant to convey? That the new military regime wished to enshrine the legacy of Sani Aba-cha? I browsed rapidly through Abdulsalami's introduction, then passed the book to Julius. He flashed through it, sighed, and passed it to Sola, who took one look at the cover and instantly exploded. His reaction was most telling of our individual states of mind, since it was not much different—I later reflected—from my earlier tirade against the insolence of New York taxis.

"Look at this! This is a book printed at great expense to be distributed to the whole world, and those illiterate officials can't even spell."

His outburst took us by surprise. "What? Spell what? What has spelling to do with it?"

"Didn't you notice? Don't you see how they've spelled 'Foreword'?"

I hadn't noticed, but now I did. I sighed. "Is the spelling something to bother about?"

"It's a disgrace. Look, this is supposed to be our window on the world. Everything that comes out of an embassy represents the image of the nation. It should be meticulously prepared, every dash and dot!"

Between Julius and me, we succeeded in bringing the discussion back into focus. "Two things strike me as sinister," I observed. "You can tell that this collection was in preparation while Abacha was alive. No doubt it was part of the campaign to turn him into a world statesman—remember, Nigeria has been trying to win a seat on the Security Council. The publication was clearly not ready by the time Abacha died, but did they pulp the copies or hide them away in some warehouse? No, they actually held off on the final production until they could co-opt the new head of state into writing a foreword."

"I bet Abdulsalami did not write that foreword himself," Julius observed.

"I bet he didn't even bother to read it," I agreed and proceeded to share the picture I had formed of what was clearly a typical con operation.

"Some bureaucrat—special adviser or whatever—goes to the new boss and says, 'Sir, we need some kind of continuity. It would look good in the eyes of the world if you paid a tribute to your predecessor. Here is a prepared text, sir. We are close to grabbing a seat on the Security Council, and this publication will clinch it. Once you've done your part in this—just this foreword, sir—you can put Abacha's regime behind you and carry on with your own program, et cetera, et cetera.' That's one possible scenario."

Both Julius and Sola nodded agreement.

"The second is—a million dollars or two have been voted and cornered by someone for this publication and a number of other Abacha sanitization projects. With Abacha dead, the lucky ministry in charge—Information or Foreign

Affairs, very likely the latter—knows that there is no point in going ahead with it. But are they about to give up that loot? No way. In all likelihood they've pocketed the bulk of it. So they rush through the publication, get Abdulsalami to endorse it. They print maybe two hundred copies, just enough to decorate the reading desks of a few of our embassies all over the world and send to foreign embassies in Nigeria. They tag several zeroes onto the end of the number they're supposed to have printed and distributed—all in the name of campaigning for a seat on the Security Council. And that's it! Who's going to bother about that particular budgetary item once Abacha is gone? It has fallen in the crack between two regimes."

Julius nodded. "Could be a combination of both scenarios."

"But the least they could do is spell 'Foreword' correctly!"

There was nothing I could do to suppress Sola's spelling bee in the bonnet. Unconsciously, we had all transferred to a vastly reduced territory of rights and wrongs, competence and improprieties, all nonlethal, on which the built-up passions of the past years were being gradually expended—from insolent taxis to spelling mistakes!

During welcoming pleasantries, that is, as each side keenly summed up the other, I was tempted to transmit to our host greetings from his regular Israeli chauffeur and watch his reaction. Then I decided against it. Who could tell if we would have to renew opposition against this new man and what form it might take? Instead, as soon as we were settled into our seats, I offered him the publication.

"What signal is this publication supposed to send? Is it an endorsement of the Abacha regime? Is it a message, a warning to the nation that this regime intends to walk in Abacha's steps, or what?"

Abdulsalami looked baffled, turned the booklet over in his hands, and turned to his ambassador for clarification. Gambari spluttered and launched a most curious counterattack: "But, Prof, what does this mean? You mean you were rifling through my private papers?"

All three of us responded almost at the same moment. "Private papers? A publication on your coffee table, displayed with other magazines? What are you talking about! Was this not meant for distribution?"

A sweaty Gambari then went into some long-winded explanation. He had received the publications from the ministry, he said, but they had been prepared a long time before and been designed—our guess had been right—to promote Nigeria's campaign for a seat on the Security Council. Obviously they couldn't be discarded, Gambari claimed; a lot of money had gone into the publication, and so, to make it current, the head of state had been invited to provide a foreword....

Bang on cue came our secretary-general's explosion: "And these people couldn't even spell 'Foreword' correctly!"

"Sola, could you ... ?"

The new head of state appeared intrigued, insisted that Sola should have his say—"No, no, I think it's an important observation. I really want to hear about this."

Our S-G needed no further prompting. Sola Adeyeye, a smallish, disproportionately dynamic scientist whose movements sometimes suggest to me what a tree sprite must be like if it existed in real life, is propelled by an inner force that feeds on the nearest anomaly in the way that life or humanity expresses itself, with a blithe unconcern for its immediate context. Then his eyes distend, his arms stiffen into lightning rods as he irradiates the object of attention with instant passion! I often suspect that it has to do with his occupation, that of a biologist, where the minutest specimen must be subjected to an expository procedure that more or less renders all items equal under the microscope. He launched into a tirade on the general sloppiness of our embassies abroad, pummeled the bureaucracy, excoriated the level of decay in public service that could possibly result in the disgraceful misspelling of such an important word. Abdulsalami clearly felt—or had decided that he should be seen to be—seriously concerned with this distraction. Inwardly, I fumed, wishing I could leave the two of them alone to thrash out the finer points of spelling, diplomacy, Nigerian image abroad, and so on while I awaited their conclusions in the Italian bar across the street. Julius struck the posture of the urbane international executive that he was—an intellectual who happened to be working for a foreign foundation at the time but who had not hesitated to throw himself into a political fray that now approached some form of conclusion—or respite. I looked to my deputy—he was nearer—to kick Sola surreptitiously on the ankle, but he seemed to be totally oblivious or indifferent to my impatience. It seemed ages, but finally we did get back to substantive issues. Our guess was right, however: Abdulsalami had not seen the finished product. Now he wanted to know everything about the publication.

It was a relief when Sola Adeyeye's background as a preacher, rather than a grammarian, took over some moments later—he was a Baptist who sometimes took to the pulpit in his church. Without a break in rhythm, he now launched a fiery and robust sermon directly at Abdulsalami—whatever god the soldier believed in, thundered our secretary-general, that god stood over him at this crucial moment of Nigerian history. Such a god would call him to strict accounting if he failed to toe the path of rectitude! A short span of time had been allotted to him, Abdulsalami, to rescue the nation from the morass into which it had been plunged by Abacha's regime. Adeyeye's eyes bored into the startled general, his beard stiffly pointed like a painting of one of the Old Testament prophets. "If you believe in any god, sir, if you believe that Allah is waiting for all of us on the Day of Judgment, you will ensure that you do not fail the nation at this critical moment." Abdulsalami's face appeared to weather the onslaught like that of a trained soldier who finds himself unexpectedly under fire, nodding from time to time in subdued agreement.

Julius followed, albeit in a different mode. Methodically, he outlined the position of the joint opposition movements over the period of transition. From his briefcase, he extracted copies of the memorandum from the conference of both internal and external groups that had been rapidly organized after Sani Abacha's death by the Centre for Development and Democracy, headed by Kayode Fayemi, one of the few structures that had emerged from and survived the democratic struggle. That meeting had been marked by a vastly different atmosphere from earlier encounters—for the first time, participants had not been obliged to sneak out through secret routes and return the same way, every step fearful and anonymity rigorously maintained. Now all was in the open, and while apprehensions remained about the intentions of the new regime, it was impossible not to be infected by the euphoria that clearly had enveloped the gathering.

Julius handed over the document. Its conclusion could be summarized in two central demands and read as the defining statement of the opposition: a transitional government of national unity to take over from the military and, simultaneously, the summoning of a sovereign national conference to debate and decide the future of the nation—its structure if it must continue as a federation, and its constitution.

Abdulsalami listened carefully, but it would appear that he had far more modest pursuits on his mind. "When are you coming home?"

We responded that certain conditions still needed to be fulfilled, and we enumerated them. Abdulsalami took notes, promised to look into them. He played the role not only of a good listener but of one who enjoyed listening to others talk—or maybe simply enjoyed letting others provide some earnest-sounding noises as background to his private thoughts and already decided intentions. I had the impression that nothing in the world could ruffle this man. We had spent nearly an hour together already. All had been said that we had come to say, and the encounter was now over, at least from our side. Each had sized up the other beneath the courteous exchanges. The general had kept his part of the bargain; he had received us alone, except for his ambassador and someone who appeared to be his secretary. He appeared to have no secret agenda, nothing outside his main commitment to supervise the transition to a new government and embark on whatever retirement plans he had worked out for himself. He did not divulge any hint of what path he and his military colleagues would take to achieve that goal, nor was there any glimmering on his placid face of his reaction to our proposals for taking the nation back to democratic rule. In the little that he said, he *appeared* convincing, but we had not come this far to take any politician or "militrician" at face value. Sola Adeyeye summed up our response to him in the same preacher accents, his keen-edged trowel of a beard aimed, it seemed, at Abdulsalami's heart: "You will be judged by your actions, not by your declarations."

Abdulsalami did not seem anxious to bring the meeting to a close. It was evidently his last engagement of the day, and I suspect that he was fascinated by the small group. I wondered if his thoughts strayed to the publication of our Walter Mitty, Jude Uzowanne; as the top soldier, he must have been compelled to address contingency plans in case of the genuineness of the alleged guerrilla threat. Whatever the rest of the military thought about our effectiveness, all sources—from visiting ambassadors to domestic servants—testified, both during and after Abacha's reign, that the dictator believed that we commanded the forces of hell, all of which had joined hands with hitherto unheard-of monsters from outer space to destroy him! Abacha's exceptional interview, perhaps the only one with a foreign newspaper (*The Washington Post*) was marked by an obsessive devotion to his favorite monster—"That Wole Soyinka, he is supposed to be a poet, to be writing poetry, but what he does is throw bombs all over the place, is that the function of a poet?"—all rattled off in his reedy voice. As Sani Abacha's chief of staff, Abdulsalami must occasionally have been witness to Abacha's famed paroxysms that had the opposition—and W.S. especially—as their trigger.

There were thus moments during our meeting when I felt that this soldier was sizing us up, wondering if this trio represented the forces that he must contend with if he succumbed to the temptation to cling to power. A quizzical look would pass over his face, and then he would seem to engage in a keener inspection of the team than was warranted by the subject under discussion. He had one of those faces that did not readily smile, simply because it was so relaxed that the entire head constituted itself into one simple, understated smile. It broke its mold only when we came to the subject of victims—both military and civilian—who had been framed by Sani Abacha and were still held in jail, a full month after Abdulsalami had taken office.

Why, I demanded, had General Olusegun Obasanjo been released from prison but not Generals Diya and Adisa, Colonel Gwadabe, and others? Abdulsalami replied that their cases were being closely studied. That was clearly evasive, and I insisted that the continued denial of their freedom was illogical, an unwarranted endorsement of the process that had landed them in prison in the first place.

General Oladipo Diya, Abacha's former second in command, whom Abdulsalami had replaced, was widely believed to have been framed, just like Olusegun Obasanjo. However, the conduct of some of these soldiers during trial had been far less than soldierly. The nation had been treated to video clips of the whimpering generals, secretly filmed by al-Mustapha, Abacha's chief security officer. Confronted with evidence of their alleged complicity in the coup attempt, a number of them had fallen on their knees, sobbing and pleading for forgiveness. In one scene, Abacha contemptuously handed his former chief of staff his handkerchief and gestured that he should wipe away his tears.

"Look, General," I protested, "there is no justifiable reason for their continued detention. What I propose is this: set them free immediately and reabsorb them into the army. Then you can legitimately court-martial them for cowardice under fire, and then—shoot them if you like. I won't complain."

Abdulsalami nearly fell off his chair as, for the first time, his placid mask cracked and he doubled over with laughter.

I had a personal matter that I had left to the last. "I think I should serve you notice," I warned, "I am going to sue your government."

"What for, Prof?"

"For gross defamation. I am going to sue your government, and your ambassadors are going to be summoned as witnesses."

Gambari was visibly startled, and I wondered if he already guessed that I was referring to the lurid invention of Abacha's propaganda machinery, the glossy product of the fugitive rapist Abiola Ogundokun: *Conscience International.*

"This packaged bundle of obscenities," I continued, "was sent to key Nigerian embassies throughout the world, several of which in turn distributed them to institutions, human rights organizations, and even the international media. The president of my university was sent a copy"—and here I turned to Gambari—"directly from the Information Department of our United Nations mission, with a complimentary slip signed by one E. Agbehir."

Again, Abdulsalami turned wordlessly to Gambari. The ambassador sighed, probably relieved that at least this publication had not been encountered by our delegation as a companion piece to the eulogy of Abacha as world statesman.

"All I know, sir," he stammered, "was that this box of magazines was sitting in the office of Agbehir, the information officer. I saw it one day when I entered the office, and I was attracted by the Prof's photo on the cover. So I took a copy and opened it. Almost immediately I realized what was inside. I dropped it, I remember saying, 'Uh-uh, I don't want any part of this. I don't want anything to do with this.' Later on, I found that the information officer had already sent me my own copy. I don't think I've even read it to this day. It must be sitting somewhere in my office."

"I am going to sue the government," I repeated quietly. "That's my first duty whenever I return to Nigeria. I'm serving you notice so that you don't complain that, after all, we had an amicable meeting, and so on. It's nothing personal, but I have to take you to court."

The man smiled his broadest yet, spread out his surprisingly soft hands, and said, "Prof, everybody is suing me. Obasanjo himself has threatened to sue for wrongful imprisonment. What am I supposed to do? So many people are going to sue this government. I am not saying you're not justified, but where are we going to get the money to pay all these damages?"

"Well, that's for you to worry about. I'm suing. It's a duty imposed on me. Anyway, that's the one item I have on my personal agenda—I needed to get it off my chest. We really should leave you now, I'm sure you have other people to see."

The photographer was summoned for the inevitable photographs. "But when are you coming home?" As we were set up, positioned, and repositioned for the satisfaction of the photographer, Abdulsalami continued to insist. "Next week? Next month? Everybody wants you back, you know. What am I to tell them when I return home?"

"Soon, soon," I kept responding. "Soon. I can't simply pull up roots and return just like that, you know. I have acquired quite a few responsibilities here."

"Well, at least a visit. Come home for a week or so, you can manage that. I'll give you my phone numbers. If you'd just let us know when you're coming..."

"I will. That's a promise."

In the vestibule, an official rushed in. "Your Excellency, I wonder if the Prof can delay a few moments. Madam is just coming in, and I'm sure the Prof would like to meet her."

"Where's she?"

"They're coming up in the elevator. They should be here in a moment."

"Ah, please wait, Prof. My wife won't forgive me if she knew you were here and I didn't hold you long enough for both of you to meet."

Mrs. Abdulsalami came in a short while later, accompanied by four women. It was a remarkable change. In the heyday of the "two Ms"—Mariam Babangida and Maryam Abacha—there would have been no less than a caravan of women, at least two dozen, if not thirty to forty, overdressed, overpainted, simpering satellites. Abdulsalami's wife was dressed very simply and, I soon discovered, had spent nearly the entire day observing the proceedings of the Supreme Court, herself being a judge. I spoke to her briefly, and could not help observing that she was somewhat ill at ease with me—not conspicuously, but she did seem a little short on spontaneity. I wondered which of my many reputations she had swallowed that had created that air of discomfort or if my entire surmise had been misplaced. Perhaps it was nothing but a cultivated judicial mien.

Later I was informed by a childhood friend of Abdulsalami that during the Abacha period, she had been very critical of the language of contempt that I employed toward Sani Abacha. She was in agreement with the content but belonged to that school of thought, quite prevalent among a substantial portion of our educated elite, that holds that a head of state was still a head of state, no matter what else he might be. This meant that he was entitled to the fullest respect from the nation's citizens. No matter what he did, you simply did not refer to him as "a murderous imbecile," "cretin," and other standard epithets that I found objectively descriptive of the man. Approval for the role I was playing in the struggle, yes. But it was wrong to be so abusive. A head of state was still "His Excellency."

As further knowledge was obtained of Abacha's plots to get rid of all probable or imaginary obstacles in his bid for self-perpetuation, it emerged that Abdulsalami had himself been next for the jump. During interrogation, which routinely involved torture, some of the accused coup plotters had been offered the chance to shorten their agony and even purchase their freedom or survival by implicating Abdulsalami in one of the phantom plots against the Abacha regime. This attempt had commenced, it turned out, right from the interrogations that had preceded the trials and convictions of General Diya and others.

A Colonel Lawan Gwadabe in particular, once one of Abacha's most trusted collaborators, had undergone horrendous torture in the effort to make him implicate his boss. He had been hung upside down, flogged, and had buckets of excrement poured over him.

Unfortunately for that colonel, he was, like his master, a devoted client of marabouts, one of whom sealed Gwadabe's fate by divining that he would one day become Nigeria's head of state. The prophecy reached Abacha's ears, and he promptly took preventive action. Perhaps the marabout also predicted a like elevation for Abdulsalami; those marabouts loved to please! Speculations were pointless with Sani Abacha, however. For whatever reasons in the murky recesses of what passed for his mind—and with steady prodding from his hatchet man, al-Mustapha—Abacha had begun the process of removing Abdulsalami from office and trying him for treason, with predictable results. Gwadabe was to have been the prime witness, but that loyal soldier, notoriously of Abacha's cast of mind in many other ways, refused to break. I wondered if, after learning that truth, Mrs. Abdulsalami would still be of the opinion that Abacha's anointed number one enemy had been too extreme in his choice of language.

THE PAST BEGAN to recede in the mind, ceased to influence daily habits and instincts or govern practical choices. Finally, I accepted my papers of release from the custody of fear and sent prudence on indefinite sabbatical. I could begin to act on the spur of the moment, plonk myself down at a table on the open pavement of a café or restaurant, walk the streets and enter recreation spaces with greater spontaneity, constrained only by my craving for anonymity. It was in this new mood that, headed for London, I accepted an offer of two tickets to Wimbledon from a Nigerian tennis coach, Jacob Akindele, who had been one of my volunteer marshals in the heyday of the Road Safety Corps. Jacob had a more impressive distinction, however—he could boast of having coached John McEnroe in his rookie days! In my mood of liberation, I prepared to venture into Wimbledon's hallowed precincts, my first such visit in more than forty years.

Not that I have ever been one for blood sports, least of all lawn tennis, whose genteel setting—most especially in England's Wimbledon—I have always considered a contradiction, the game itself being no more than a sublimation of the blood instinct that has stuck with such tenacity to every rung in the ladder of human evolution. Boxing is another matter entirely. It does not pretend to be anything else, and thus, I have never been averse to watching the occasional round of a boxing match, almost exclusively on television.

It was only natural that my mind should travel back to my last visit to Wimbledon as a fresh graduate, in the company of Barbara, my first wife, perhaps even then pregnant with Olaokun, my first son. Everything fell into place—this time Olaokun was bound to be in London, and I had two tickets. He also, I thought, must be feeling the pangs of withdrawal, having thrown himself into the fray body and soul, serving as secretary to the UDFN and neglecting the small computer publication business that had developed from his medical publication enterprise until it had gone bankrupt in the service of democracy. He had been compelled to return to his first profession, as a part-time doctor on call. I pictured him wondering what to do with himself now that he was deprived of preparations for preceding me into Abacha's lair, tried to gauge what his reaction would be when I informed him that I had never had the slightest intention of gratifying his wish! I called him up—did he wish to come with the old man? He was more than ready.

A summery day, the kind that Wimbledon aficionados pray for and sometimes get. Whatever was going on in Olaokun's mind, I did not know, and I wondered if his mother had ever told him that we used to take the bus and walk to Wimbledon during my stint at the Royal Court Theatre in 1958–59, when we lived in Maida Vale, Willesdon, and Putney, the last being nearest to Wimbledon. What went through the old man's mind, however, was the sheer air of freedom. I was walking among crowds without sprouting eyes all around my head, without being accompanied by a volunteer bodyguard or two, inconspicuous but close by. All I dreaded was to be recognized by anyone— *Just make them leave me alone,* I pleaded with the unseen gods.

Those deities are, however, practiced in turning a deaf ear. As we walked past the gates and began to drift through the crowd, the familiar sound shot through the air: "Prof! Prof! Professor Soyinka!"

I always know when I cannot bluff my way, pretending to be someone else. This was no voice of uncertainty, and, whoever it was, we were going to be ensconced within that place for the next few hours, when she would have lots of time to scrutinize me closely if I tried the gambit of self-denial. It is always an embarrassment when a "senior citizen" finds himself caught in a bald lie, especially by a mere juvenile.

I turned. She was petite and light-complexioned, and could easily have passed for an Indian. Yet it was not she who really caught my interest but her companion. Darker and of a somewhat more substantial build, she remained rooted by the entrance gate while the one who had called out ran forward excitedly. Not one probing step did she take in our direction. Her face read horror, unrelieved horror, her body—total petrification. She shrank progressively into her distant self, staring at the scene with wide-eyed apprehension.

The girl came up to me, her excitement bubbling over. "Yes, I knew it was you. I recognized you in spite of the hat." She continued breathlessly, "I've read your books, I admire them a lot."

"Thank you. And you? What's your name? Are you studying here?"

"Zainab, and I'm reading law."

I nodded, gestured toward Olaokun. "This is my son, Olaokun."

They shook hands. The congealed companion appeared to have thawed sufficiently to drag closer to our group on heavy limbs but remained several strides away. Her expression distinctly said, "Zainab is mad. She's stark raving mad. What's going to happen now?"

"When do you finish schooling?" I inquired.

"Oh, I've finished. I've qualified, but now I'm serving my attachment."

"Congratulations. So you're on holiday? You enjoy tennis?"

"I love it. But I'm not on vacation. I live in London."

I gave my self-deprecatory gesture. "I'm afraid I'm not very fond of tennis, but I wanted to see if I could recover my former taste for it, especially with the Williams sisters playing. When it comes to sports, I'm a racist. Are you also heading for Centre Court?"

"No," she sighed. And she mentioned the names of the players she had come to see.

"Well, I hope you enjoy your match." I made one more effort to include her shrinking companion in the exchange, nodded briefly toward her. And then, intrigued by this retiring girl, I decided on a little more time with both, wondering if there was a history that could be dredged up from my lamentable memory. Keeping my eyes not on the forward one called Zainab but on this other, I asked, "You did not tell me the rest of your name. Zainab what?"

The girl leaned forward, raised herself onto her toes, whispered in my ear "Abacha," and quickly drew back, still smiling, to watch my reaction.

I have, I have been told, a most expressive face, but I do wear, I have also been told, a companion mask that comes down even faster and hides the expression. This time, neither alternative was on call—there was certainly no need for the mask. I was neither startled nor alarmed; I took it all in stride. Neither internally nor by any outward gesture did I sense any instinct toward recoil. It's difficult to explain, but it seemed to me that the most natural encounter in the world had just taken place; it fitted into the pattern of so much that had happened over the past five years. Yes, within that mannered, manicured setting, to be accosted by and come face-to-face with the daughter of the man who had done his utmost to terminate my existence, and on a day when I was relishing my release from her father's custody—it all fit in. If I had any emotion at all, it was delight. After dropping her "bombshell" she had moved quickly back to watch my reaction, and I could see she was a little disappointed. She saw me smiling, and it was not faked. I admire chutzpah.

I nodded. "Ah, of course. So you're not coming back soon?"

She nodded, somewhat wistfully. I had, of course, recalled her being named in investigations into accounts that were suspected to hold her father's stolen billions. The Abdulsalami regime had set their recovery as a priority agenda—at least from all appearances—for his one year in office.

"You think you will sort out your problems with the regime?" I asked.

"Yes," she said, "we are talking with them."

I looked at the other girl, still immobilized and dumbfounded. I shook Zainab's hand once more, nodded to both. "Good luck. We must go and find our seats."

She flashed a smile at us, and we parted.

The games began. It was as I expected. At the end of the first set, I turned to my son and announced that I was leaving but that he should feel free to remain and watch the game to the end. We would arrange a rendezvous.

"You're not enjoying the game?" he asked.

"Not really. It's the atmosphere. Stilted. I may still come back for the last game, but I have something more interesting I would rather be doing."

"All right, I'll come with you."

We went out, giving our tickets to a couple among the loitering hopefuls. They could not believe our refusal to take their money. Only after we were out in the open air did I reveal my objective to my puzzled son. "I didn't feel right," I said. "I think maybe I was too abrupt. Let's find them. I want to buy that girl a drink."

"Who? The Abacha girl?"

"I may have left her thinking I hated her, just because I detested her father. We should have offered to buy them a drink. There was still time."

Olaokun nodded agreement. We set out to look for them in the other courts, in the pavilions, the bars, everywhere. No luck.

I felt strangely sad. My day of outing would have been perfect if I had been able to offer a drink to the pert, daring girl and her petrified companion, with words that could be something like "Here's to your generation. Try to wean yourself from the past."

THE KING IS DEAD; long live the king! Or, more accurately: the usurper's dead; long live the heir presumptive?

Moscow Road, London, housed an apartment—20 Alexander Court— whose ready hospitality I had scrupulously denied myself during the usurper years. It belonged to a young friend, Deji Akintilo. A businessman in the oil sector, he would have qualified for Abacha's instant reprisals if that dictator's "international observers" had reported any signs of him fraternizing with the enemy. The air of liberation had also touched this den of potential subversion, and it became the trysting ground for a high-level contact, with its owner act- ing as intermediary for yet another emissary from Nigeria armed with a confi- dential message.

I was setting out for Europe, so I agreed to meet the mystery man in the London apartment. He turned out to be one of the young generation of quietly aggressive entrepreneurs, a former medical doctor who had turned to business. Dr. Tunde Soleye's not-so-open background was that of a close confidant of General Abdulsalami, with whom he had grown up in Kwara state.

The doctor came straight to the point. His mission was on behalf of a pow- erful political consortium which was in the process of deciding the future of the nation. The transition program was a reality, Soleye assured me, and this group needed to make an immediate decision. They wanted Wole Soyinka to run for president.

I was not taken aback. It was not the first of such offers of the crown, among which, on the scale of ego vitamin, my favorite remained that of Gen- eral Joseph Garba, once the commander of the national brigade of guards that had toppled General Yakubu Gowon in 1975, and then foreign minister in the ensuing regime. On retirement from the army, he became a "mature student" of the Harvard School of Law, from which he graduated, later venturing into politics. In 1995 he decided to run for the presidency under Sani Abacha's own transition charade. To this end, he revisited Harvard, where I was then teach- ing, booking himself into a hotel for two nights to acquaint me with his ambi- tion, discuss his chances, and outline his vision, only to undermine it all by declaring: "There is only one person in Nigeria for whom I am prepared to sink my own ambition and that's you. You should run. My real preference—I'll be sincere with you—is to have you run." And he proceeded, with some passion, to set out the reasons for his conviction.

I reminded him that there had been an election. Someone had won that election and that person was in prison. Joe's view was that the nation had to move beyond that election. We remained divided on that, but I sincerely wished him luck. Joe Garba and I had become very good friends. He was an honorable man and I truly wished that the political field were not polluted by the immorality of Abiola's predicament. Joe would have made a very good president.

Now, once again, the crown was up for grabs, and a "powerful consortium" had gone head hunting, settling on mine. I could read the reasoning behind it. The dispossessed and now dead president-elect was a Yoruba, from my own part of the nation, indeed from the same town as I, Abeokuta. A section of the nation had been wronged, and some pragmatic politicians thought it expedient to make amends—or at least appear to do so. It was a replay of the "King of ING" scenario, albeit under a democratic "legitimation."

With Akintilo offering vigorous support, Soleye urged, "You should take it. They want you, and, any way you look at it, you are entitled to it. You've paid your dues. It will cost you nothing, and the nation needs you."

My immediate objection was that I would not make a unifying president. An influential caucus in the North—a feudal elite whom I had never spared, and who in turn had indoctrinated their constituency with the convenient notion that I hated the North in its entirety—viewed me with great suspicion. To make the ideal president, I would first have to dismantle that lie, and that, I knew, would require making undeserved concessions.

The doctor shook his head—those misconceptions had vanished with the five-year taste of Abacha. The consortium, he assured me, included powerful figures from that very part of the nation; it was a pity, but he could not mention names.

So I sought refuge in my lack of resources. I could not fund myself even for a local government election. What little money I had left from the Nobel, even bolstered by intensive lecture rounds, had gone into the struggle. Dr. Soleye smiled indulgently. "That is the least of your worries. Your campaign budget is guaranteed. You will not spend a penny of your own money."

Over dinner and late into the night, the exchanges continued, but it was mostly a one-sided affair. I could not subscribe to Abdulsalami's rushed transition program, I reminded both, any more than I believed that I was temperamentally suited to managing a nation such as Nigeria. If the proposal had been to act as a short-term interim president in keeping with the opposition's manifesto, there would have been a viable basis for consideration. Possibly. This nomination, however, smelled distinctly of manipulation by the very forces I had often publicly castigated. I had no inclination for the rigors, the ordeal of a campaign, yet it was clear that the election would be "won" for me anyway. One could read the blueprint of authority that would emerge: a head of state with built-in obligations to undemocratic forces. A hostage.

"The position is yours," Dr. Soleye repeatedly urged. "Take it. It has to be now. This chance will never come your way again."

Wearying of the pressure, I conceded one or two days to think it over, but that was only to end the long night. I had just won my liberty and could not contemplate its abandonment so soon, and in such a questionable manner. The transition from plain Mr. Citizen to heir presumptive simply stalled, even at the thought of it. I deeply craved a personal space, and it beckoned from the surroundings of my cactus patch. A disappointed Soleye took back my message, leaving behind the even more disconsolate proprietor of 20 Alexander Court.

Where the Earth Says Welcome!

. . . . .

Business-class seat, courtesy of Lufthansa, which had donated the ticket for my return: my journey is pampered, not one that requires slipping in through one secret route or another to supervise plans for a war of attrition. The air of unreality continues to taunt, pervades the soothing interior of the plane as the events and plans of the past five years course through my mind, wreathed in a whiff of discontent. It was an impossible hope, that months of planning would end so tamely, on a routine passenger flight, treated like some privileged species by both the staff and other passengers! I had schooled myself differently, existed within a totally contrasting reality. The word was—deflation! While not seeking to be a victim, I had been primed to return to claim quite simply—if need be—my cactus patch. Everything about this palpable present, therefore, feels as contrived as the sudden, sordid death of the dictator Sani Abacha in the arms of Asian prostitutes flown into Abuja for one of his periodic orgies. For five years, the existence of this man had dominated my own; it was still difficult to believe that he would vacate that position of power with barely a whimper. The prospect of a peaceful resolution of the Nigerian crisis through the mediation of a successor, the choice of dialogue over confrontation, probably with violence, was a luxury we had begun to deny ourselves.

That which I had thought of as being unnaturally absent—emotion—still does not return as I actually step down from the plane into the airport. Clinically I observe a difference in the Murtala Muhammed Airport from my last recollection. This new airport appears—disciplined. Restrained. It is immediately apparent that security is tight. The last time I arrived in Lagos airport with such advance preparations had been on the occasion of receiving honors for the Nobel Prize, whose announcement had caught me in Paris. Protocol this time is just as efficient but less rambunctious. The airport commandant leads the way. Only a few voices punctuate the unnaturally empty passages: "Welcome! Welcome back! Prof, you are most welcome! Welcome back to Nigeria, sir!" As I watch the starched back of the commandant, I wonder on whose side he was during the struggle to remove his erstwhile boss. Certainly he would have shot me outright had he succeeded in laying his hands on me during those years when his boss held sway over the nation.

Our plane has arrived early. It overflew Lomé, a scheduled stop, for one reason or another—it would return there afterward—so we have landed an hour and a half before the scheduled time. The protocol officer is full of apologies; I will have to wait in the VIP lounge for a while. He has a list of the NADECO stalwarts who have been given passes—"Pa" Abraham Adesanya, Arthur Nwankwo, Bola Tinubu, Ayo Adebanjo, and a host of others—and most have yet to show up. But Arthur Nwankwo is already there, he informs me—Arthur Nwankwo, one of the foolhardy ones who snuck out of the country to attend a meeting of the allied democratic resistance in London. Olu Agunloye—my covictim in the libelous assault of *Conscience International*—has wangled his way in somehow. Yet even those who have passed through the security zone are disappointed. They had planned to join the formal welcoming group right up at the door of the aircraft, but we have arrived impossibly early.

A grin breaks through my face as I recall a flight from Paris to Cotonou, quite early into the fight against Abacha. Already Cotonou was heavily infiltrated by Nigerian undercover agents, but we had our own people there too, and they knew every one of Abacha's spies. Both sides kept watch on each other and sometimes even fraternized. Early in the game, I would walk up to a group—usually of two or three—in the lobby of a hotel, cheerfully identify them to themselves, and buy them drinks. Going to Cotonou, just a stone's throw from Lagos, was risky but not as foolhardy as it might sound—at least, not then. Ghana, much farther away, was more dangerous. Its leader, Flight Lieutenant Jerry Rawlings, was well known as an Abacha ally and was even on his payroll, as would later be revealed by Abacha's chief security adviser, Ismail Gwarzo. We had a dependable base in Benin. I openly addressed Nigerian groups in the capital, Cotonou, and in the ancient harbor town of Porto-Novo, a visit that was sponsored by Professor Albert Tedjevore, my elder collaborator in more than a few African causes. At one stage, the Abacha regime had threatened Matthias Kerekou, the Beninois head of state, with serious consequences for harboring "enemies of Nigeria." Himself a former, but now reformed, dictator, he refused to be intimidated, though he did pay a "brotherly visit" to Abuja to reassure the paranoid ruler. After his visit, we received a message of reassurance but one that urged us to please conduct our activities with greater discretion. The loss was Abacha's agents'; we could no longer buy them drinks.

That roundabout flight into Cotonou had made a transit stop at Ouagadougou, Burkina Faso. I stood in the doorway, at the top of the stairs, as the plane was refueled. The pilot also came out to stretch his legs.

I turned to him and asked, "Suppose, for any reason, we are unable to land in Cotonou—due to weather conditions or whatever—what would be your alternative airport?" Without any hesitation, he replied, "Lomé, in Togo." "Well," I continued, "suppose the weather was also bad in Lomé, or there was a coup and the airport was closed. Which would be the next choice?" "Abidjan" was the response. "What of Lagos?" I asked. "No," he replied, and shook his head very firmly, "we don't go to Lagos. For one thing, we couldn't even be guaranteed aviation fuel." So I thanked him and then added, "Please, if for any reason you find yourself compelled to head for Lagos, just find me a parachute and open the door so I can jump out." The hostesses, standing by, laughed aloud but the pilot did not. He nodded quite seriously and said, "I understand. Don't worry. We won't land you in Lagos."

Looking at the back of the commandant, who turned around from time to time to grin his welcome at me, I wondered what role he would have enjoyed playing during the Abacha period if my plane had taxied down Lagos tarmac on an unscheduled stop. It was a permanent nightmare that all our dissident exiles underwent, and one of our NADECO associates, a minister under a former regime, had actually undergone that undesired experience. Security officers had boarded the plane—this had become a routine security measure—and looked over all the passengers to search for fugitives. It seemed that they did recognize him but pretended not to. Yet another fugitive within our own organization, UDFN, had found himself trapped in a plane that had been similarly diverted to Lagos. He had succeeded in overcoming his initial paralysis when he realized that he was about to descend into the lion's jaws, signaled to a hostess, and confided his plight to her. The captain loaned him his jacket and cap and kept him in the cockpit until the plane took off again.

The emptiness of the airport is most striking—at four-thirty in the afternoon, it is abnormal. Later I would learn that even essential workers had been cleared from the arrival section of the airport, all in the name of security!

Do they plan to keep this up for every arrival? I enter the VIP lounge to encounters with beaming faces, emotional embraces, and crisp military salutes. Later, I observe that the protocol officer is hovering around uncertainly, so finally I ask him what he wants. He whispers nearly inaudibly, "Your passport, sir." But I have no passport, I inform him. The commandant has overheard the exchange and bellows, "Are you asking for his passport? Take yourself out of here!" But the tone is lighthearted. Again, I would later discover that orders had been given that if any Immigration officer so much as dared to ask me for any papers, he was to lose his job on the spot; obviously the protocol officer was not aware of this. I have my U.N. laissez-passer on me, and I also have a courtesy diplomatic passport from a friendly African government, but my position over this is straightforward: it was the Nigerian government that seized my national passport, and I have no intention of using any other passport to enter my own country.

THE CAT-AND-MOUSE GAMES that had resulted in the seizure of my passport had taken place at this very airport, on the Nigerian side of the Immigration post. The first round ended with the seizure of my national passport, on my way to attend a meeting at UNESCO. The second time, I was headed for the inaugural meeting of the International Parliament of Writers in Paris. Neither setback was unexpected; indeed, I routinely told my Lagos hosts, the Ogunbiyi couple, to keep my dinner waiting just in case.

I had become an adept in the rites of travel restriction and its manifold forms—one anticipates but one never really becomes inured to its destabilizing impact. Movement is the palpable essence of freedom. That seems obvious enough, since restraint is its negation, but it needs to be stated and restated. Freedom expresses itself in many ways, but its real essence is movement— that is, the right to exercise the choice to move or not to move. Even thought, which is so marvelously secured from the encroachment of chains and walls— thought, as we learned in school, is made possible only through the motion of electrical charges in the brain.

The first time it happened to me, it was some time in 1965, at the time of the Western Region insurrection. I was stunned. It seemed that the world itself suddenly stood still, so that I experienced a distinct vertigo. "You are telling me I cannot travel? That I cannot leave the country?" And the unbelievably matter-of-fact but quaintly official response: *That's right, sir. We have instructions that you are not to be allowed to proceed out of the country.* The bloodless, expressionless face behind the desk, calmly tucking your passport into a drawer! And sometimes the elaborate deception, a charade with a foregone conclusion: *Will you step this way, sir?* Which way? What for? *Just follow me, please.* And so into an office, where a higher-up is waiting. *Is that all your luggage?* No, I've checked a suitcase. *In that case, could you go with the officer and bring it here?* And so these strange hands invade your luggage, piece by piece, item by item, pore through your papers, turn the suitcase upside down, looking for heaven knows what else—sometimes for long enough to ensure that you miss your flight. Or else simply keep you waiting, speaking into the telephone to some unseen powers beyond, glancing at you from time to time, fingering the passport like a strange, lethal disease, to-ing and fro-ing, then at the end: *Sorry, sir, you are not allowed to travel.* And so you learn, bit by bit. You learn never to check any luggage, and you either send whatever papers you need ahead of you or find a friendly passenger to take them for you, because it is papers that enthrall them most of all. They want to understand what is in the papers, why even a scrap of paper should be part of your luggage, what it says, what it hides, what subversive magic it performs. So you ensure that you have no papers with you but your passport. And above all, no address book. How do they cope these days, I wonder, with the world of computers and near-impregnable passwords?

The last bout had been tense, very tense. When my national passport was seized at the earlier attempt to travel to Paris for a meeting at UNESCO, Federico Mayor, the director general, had been outraged and had immediately ordered that a UNESCO passport be sent to me. Within days, his Lagos office had contacted me and handed me the new passport. Armed with the UNESCO document, I resumed my attempt to breach the Immigration barrier. We knew the results beforehand; the only question that remained was—would they stop at merely preventing my travel, or would I end up at an unwanted destination? Within the informal circle of our inchoate democratic movement, the debate was tense. At the time, we had not yet arrived at the option of exile, only at a choice of remaining above- or underground. One assertive view was that it was better not to tempt fate at all by going to the airport, that it was best to take the plunge once for all and disappear from sight.

Things came to a head when I began to organize the Million Man March on Abuja in May 1994. The State Security Service invited me for an interview and gave me a clear message from Aso Rock: Abandon the march, or you will be held responsible for the consequences. But it was also from within the same SSS that the warning came to me: Keep away from the airports!

It might be difficult to understand—sometimes it does puzzle even me a little—but I was obliged to engage in that final proof at the airport, nevertheless. Brinksmanship, perhaps, but quite within rational limits, since we knew enough to be fairly certain that a clear decision had not been made over my fate. Moreover, the political capital to be made from the failure of the Abacha government to respect a U.N. passport was not something that we could lightly discard. Within the Abacha camp, the situation was fluid. Various options were being considered about how to silence me. The minister of foreign affairs, the unctuous Thomas Ikimi, one of Nigeria's breed of Uriah Heeps, had proposed that I be given an "enhanced" Aung San Suu Kyi treatment—confined to my house, allowed access to visitors, and so on, and then, after a decent interval, whisked off to a distant prison. Others proffered even more drastic, immediate ideas. Still, it was in the early days, when international opinion counted for something with Abacha and his advisers; they were not yet so firmly entrenched that they could afford to alienate that community altogether.

The moment I arrived at the airport, with virtually no luggage, and presented my passport at Immigration, I knew that I was not going to leave the country. The pit of my stomach also informed me, very clearly, that I had taken a nearly unpardonable risk in coming to the airport at all. After a while, you simply know. It is inexplicable. A man is seated at the desk. He takes your passport. He is the Immigration officer. Standing over him is a man in mufti, a superfluous presence in that booth, except of course that he is there to scrutinize passengers, even those whose names have not shown up in the computer that is located, and slyly consulted, beneath the desk. The Immigration officers and the SSS agents are clearly not on the best of terms. The latter are usually arrogant, filled with an inordinate sense of power. They consider not just Immigration officers but all other officials—and passengers, including visitors—inferior beings. Yet—thank goodness—there are exceptions to be found among them!

It is only natural that a bond should exist among "inferior" beings, a silent but palpable hostility toward overweening superbeings. It has to be this current of sympathy that transmits itself to the potential victim, and the greater the danger, the stronger the current. It is not so much that they speak directly to you, it is a language in their body, eloquent, effortlessly communicated to others with whom they share the bond of this imposed "inferior" status. Since they know what is happening or what is about to happen, they emit a silent wave of despair or anguish, a deep resentment, and a sense of impotence. It flashes past you, and your antenna picks it up—I think that is all there is to it. And so, when you arrive at the Immigration counter and hand over your passport, there is a way in which the officer does *not* look at you that is beyond verbal expression. You sigh inwardly—Uh-oh, here we go again! Then follows the immediate question: Where, in the course of this night, shall it all end?

The SSS agent, of course, stands there as if indifferent to your presence. He is just passing the time of day, has no interest whatever in the immigration process. He does not care that the Immigration officer and you are engaged in a defining moment: *Sorry, Mr. Soyinka, I'm afraid you cannot travel.* Oh, really? And why not? *I have no idea, sir, but you cannot travel.* In that case, can I have my passport back? The SSS man is obviously bored by this uninteresting exchange, he knows it all beforehand and he knows how it will end, so he steps backward, maybe to see something more worthy of his attention at the Customs or security check, which is just behind the line of Immigration booths, or else to pick his nose more comfortably. As for you, you have to make a clear statement, so you insist on having the passport back, but the response is just as clear as it is expected: *I have instructions to detain your passport.* Detain my passport? Do you see what passport that is? That is a United Nations passport. It is not the property of the Nigerian government, so you have no right to it! *I'm sorry, sir, I have instructions to detain it.* Of course I demand it back once more, just for the record: I don't think you understand—that passport is property of the United Nations, not of the Nigerian government. I want it back! *Well, sir, all I can do is give you the address where you can go and claim it.* When? *Tomorrow morning, if you like!* In that case, I want a receipt for it! *I'm just preparing it, sir. The address is on the receipt—that's where you go to reclaim the passport. I suggest you telephone in advance to make an appointment—this is the telephone number.*

Work at the other booths has slowed virtually to a stop. The officers are still flicking through the pages of passports, looking over immigration forms and stamping them, but their minds are elsewhere, their minds are within this one booth, and their motions have become heavy with apprehension. It weighs on the air and percolates through to you. The SSS man has become less and less interested in what is going on, his covert eyes having taken in what is on the form to ensure that no secret information is being passed from one lesser being to another. Now he is merely sightseeing, taking the air, and refuses to have his equanimity disturbed by any unseemly row. Yet even if he had retained his earlier attentive position, virtually looking over the shoulder of the Immigration officer, he would have missed the tense whisper that issued from the closed lips of the latter: *Please, Mr. Soyinka, go now. Please go. Leave the airport.*

That Immigration officer does not look up, not even with the sparest of glances. He busies himself pushing my passport into an envelope, then into a drawer, pulling up a file or whatever. And then once more: *Go now, please!*

Hardly the time to compliment him on his impressive ventriloquial skill. I permit myself a departing tirade against fascism, the abuse of my human rights, the commencing rape of the nation, and so on, and so on. "You can tell Abacha I said that he thinks he owns this country, but he does not. And we'll reclaim it even if he fills all the airports with his goons and his mimic Gestapo...." Noises of support and sympathy reach me from the other travelers as I snatch my carry-on and move toward the exit with a set face. Anyone would think I was about to commence a one-man march right there and then go and yank Abacha off his seat! I rage past incoming travelers—*Prof, what happened? Have they stopped you again?* But I only increase my pace, snarling invectives as my eyes search for my escorts, whom I had warned not to leave the departure hall until the plane was actually airborne and friendly ground staff had assured them, as prearranged, that I was actually inside the plane.

AND NOW I AM BACK to these same stressful grounds, five years later, within the same airport, the circumstances much closer to those in 1986, when a reception committee awaited me after the announcement of the Nobel Prize for that year. But I feel far less harried than on that occasion, when I had not expected an exultant intervention of the Nigerian government—and a military dictatorship at that—in a foreign award, thinking, very foolishly in hindsight, that I was returning home to a haven of peace, away from the European journalists, who appeared bent on rending me limb by limb. The contrasting sense of peace on this occasion is further augmented by the flushed figure of the army commandant, who has just reentered the VIP lounge, sweating, hot, and bothered.

"Professor, the crowd is becoming impossible to control!"

I find this puzzling. The airport had seemed quite empty to me. Arthur Nwankwo interjects, "There is quite a crowd outside. We could enter only because we had passes."

I ask him, "When are the others coming?"

"Any moment now," Arthur replies. "The plane arrived early...."

"I know, I know!" the commandant wails. "It overflew Lomé. But what do I do about the crowd?"

I make a proposal: "Do you think I should go and show my face?"

"I don't know, I don't know. If anything goes wrong... I'm worried. But they say we must wait for the rest of the delegation before escorting you out."

Before we can assess the situation any further, a breathless inspector of police—or some officer of such ranking—rushes in and informs the commandant that the situation is getting out of hand. The crowd is threatening to break through the security cordon.

"You see what I mean? Oh God, I just want this night to be over so I can go home to my family and sleep." And he rushes out with the inspector.

Ten minutes later he is back, and this time his immaculately pressed uniform is rumpled, his cap askew, and his swagger stick flailing wildly.

"Professor, we have to do something about the situation. They think we're holding you here against your will, and they're threatening to break down the barriers and force their way in. The security forces are going to be overwhelmed any moment."

"In that case..."

"There is one man in particular. Most uncooperative. I warned him I would arrest him, and he dared me to go ahead. He wanted to come in and I said no, he had no permit. We have strict instructions that only those with passes can come in. We are in charge of your safety, and we can't afford to take any chances."

"Who is the man?"

"I don't know him. The man sounds quite educated, so I was very disappointed. I expected someone like him to understand the situation but he's the worst, the very worst of them. Very bad-tempered. They all call him 'Doctor' ..."

"Doctor?" That wouldn't be Agunloye, who was already inside. "Is the man short, tall, thin, fat, or what?"

"Stocky. Dark complexion. He's throwing his weight all over the place, inciting the crowd."

I laugh. "I think I know who that is. My advice is, let him in."

"But the crowd will just follow him in."

"No, you let just him through. Announce that he's coming in to see things for himself. Once he comes in and sees I'm all right, he will go back and calm down the others."

The commandant only looks more confused and uncertain. "I don't know, Professor...."

Suddenly it becomes clear that he simply does not wish to face the crowd another second without me, so I get up. "Let's go. It's too bad about the rest of the welcoming delegation, but I'd better go and show my face."

The relief on the commandant's face confirms my suspicion. "Thank you, Professor, thank you. I think that's the best thing to do right now. Let's go, sir."

We have barely reached the hall containing the duty-free shops when we encounter "Dr. Troublemaker" himself in golfing shorts, a "Welcome Home" T-shirt, and a "Welcome Kongi" cap, accompanied by some half-dozen others, all of whom were sensibly let in by the next in command after the harried departure of the commandant. They had been mandated to go and investigate what was happening and report back to the crowd. The commandant points a shaking swagger stick at Yemi Ogunbiyi.

"That's the man! He's got in! You see what I mean? He has forced his way in!"

"Look at this *yeye* man," Ogunbiyi retorted. "You've been creating unnecessary tension for the crowd."

The rest is lost as the cause of all the commotion is himself smothered in hugs. The next moment both the troublemaker and the commandant are engaged in friendly insults as we double-quick march our way through the corridors. I am escorted through the departure, not the arrival, section, so we march through the line of security and scanning equipment and approach the Immigration kiosks, where the officer warned me off five years before with his ventriloquist performance. A blur of salutes, beaming faces, and shy "Welcomes" from passing airport staff, very restrained, as if yet under watchful eyes. Still I feel no particular excitement. Now we are right at the infamous line at which so many Nigerians lose their passports, vanish into interrogation rooms, and from there are rendered invisible for long spells. Officers leap to attention, salute follows salute. It is all a very correct welcome, nearly emotionless, as if they are adhering to some strict textbook of protocols. But I *know* them. These are longtime conspirators in furtive transmissions, and I know what is really going on inside their minds, so, after passing through, I stop, turn around slowly, and, summoning a deadpan face, I demand, "Which of you last seized my passport?"

A moment of double-take, and the tension is dissolved. Now their laughter roars out loud, their uniforms vanish, and their stiffened bodies explode in a gamut of emotions. In turn, I distinctly feel myself thawing—not much, but definitely responding to the human warmth.

Outside, twilight has descended. The vast departure hall is virtually empty. It strikes me yet again as strange—there were no passengers milling around on the departure side of Immigration, in the lounges, or around the duty-free shops, and now, none at the entrance to Immigration—and this at about six in the evening. I find it extraordinary that the airport should be so free of teeming humanity at this hour. To complete the unusual feeling of a deserted hub, hardly any of the varied uniforms of airline staff are visible—none since the occasional stragglers we met on our way from the VIP lounge.

And then something makes me turn around, and—there they all are, choking the long balcony that runs above the departure hall where they must have been herded, just to empty the floor. Whose idea of security was this, in heaven's name! I wave, and that is when the gods of vocal decibels turn loose. The pent-up torrents of "Welcome" cascade in my direction, and at that very moment a wave of humanity, from the opposite side, comes crashing through the shut gates of the main entrance, and then it becomes a matter of struggling to keep my feet on the ground or be crushed. The Pyrates—that fraternity of unending controversy—are on hand and form a protective phalanx to clear a path to the waiting vehicles. Their tactics are not working quite as well as they might and threaten to create further tension. Bola Ige, friend and political ally since student days, has joined up, and together we succeed in shouting instructions over the crowd noise. The Pyrates change tactics, and we move more easily through the crowd, but the arms that reach out for a handshake, a grab, even a touch are like a forest of bamboos, slashing and whipping. A fear that my arm might be torn out of its socket—*Haven't I been here before?*—is soon submerged under the greater fear that some of the crowd might get knocked down and be trampled upon. The scene seems primed for inevitable disaster, and it is now only a question of what form of injuries many would sustain. Then again I find myself compelled to direct my concerns to myself—it has become obvious that it is this very idiot, fast losing his balance while worrying over others, who would prove the likeliest casualty. The loss of balance changes to a sensation of being choked, and I hear the police officer shouting in a panic, "They're going to kill him! They're going to kill him!"

I realize that the "him" is none other than me. I had earlier felt a hand on my throat, desperately clutching at my windpipe and attempting to choke me. It has happened twice already and I peeled off the hand, not even thinking that it was the same hand, but those of different people trying to save themselves from falling or being crushed. But I had felt the choke hold, so when I feel the hand again, I grasp it and turn to look for its owner. The next moment the hand is torn from mine and I catch a faint glimpse of its owner being borne halfway down—no, not deliberately, simply from the sheer weight of the crowd. The gray "French" suit looks familiar—I last saw it in the VIP lounge, but the chaos is so overwhelming that I cannot recall who was wearing it. Suddenly a voice rises in song, strongly, taming the din:

> *Kaabo o, ku abo*
> *Kaabo o, ku abo*
> *Omo a b'ile soro, omo a b'ile soro*
> *K'ilke y'anu, ka a bo* *

And something gets through to me at last. It is a song I last heard in my paternal hometown, Isara, the song with which I was received at the entrance to the town and led in procession to the oba's palace, where the *oba* and his chiefs and priests had laid out a triumphal gathering for the returning "son of the soil." At that unforgettable welcome by the town, even the highest of the chieftaincy hierarchy had been caught unprepared for a unique moment, very rare in occurrence. This was when the potent *egungun,* the most numinous and dreaded of the ancestral guardian spirits of the town, emerged. As it whirled around, it made a sudden leap toward the table of honor and, in one swirling movement, enveloped me in its garments so that I vanished completely from the sight of mortals. For what seemed an eternity, I was shrouded, sucked into the dark abode of ancestors. One moment I was watching, a spectator like the rest, and suddenly I was no one, drained of all palpability, transported from plain daylight into the immensity of an eclipse, from within which the voice of the *egungun* rose in spells and incantations, invoking blessings from the living, the dead, and the unborn. This face, whose features I could not discern in the total darkness of the charged tent, chewed on a kola nut and squirted its grainy juice into my face, unhitched a gourd from within the recesses of its linings, sloshed the contents into its mouth and spat it onto my face, then unleashed a stream of invocations that seemed to emerge from the very bowels of the earth. Then the voluminous tent was lifted and the *egungun* rose to its height and raced out of this charged circle, headed toward its sanctuary, acknowledging no one else, not even the oba, his handlers in hot pursuit, clearing the way to ensure that he did not touch any other being until he had completely melted from human sight. It was a sudden, breathless emanation, and it left the gathering paralyzed with awe.

This song, now filtered through the enveloping twilight, was one that I

---

* "Welcome, welcome / You who speak and the earth / Opens its mouth in wonder / Welcome."

would permanently associate with my reception, living, into the bosom of the ancestors. Its accent differed in the mundane setting of an airport, but it swept me back to that day when, without being an initiate, with no warning and no self-preparation, I partook of communion with the deepest mysteries of earth, and the munificence of the ancestors.

> *Omo a b'ile soro, omo a b'ile soro*
> *K'ilke y'anu, ka a bo…*

Oh yes, finally, at this homecoming, I feel deeply stirred, but the tangle of arms and bodies brings me back to the present, struggling not to be dragged down and probably inducted—literally this time—into the realm of the departed as we battle our way to the waiting vehicles. Finding some hidden energy from nowhere, I succeed in forcing a stop even as I am borne onward, my feet now barely touching the ground. I find my voice and take back some control of the situation.

A despairing appeal for order: "Listen, please! All of you, listen to me! I want nobody to get hurt. No one must get hurt today, not at this homecoming. So please, stand aside, and let us move toward the car."

Someone loudly demands that I should address them.

I belt out a few sentences above the din, and somehow, we make it to the line of cars. In front of the jeep, I see the wearer of the gray French suit being resuscitated. It is Arthur Nwankwo, it was he whose hand had been at my throat, clutching for support as he was overcome by waves of dizziness. Finally, he had collapsed and fainted, fortunately being rescued before he was trampled upon by the crowd. I am hustled into Olu Agunloye's jeep, but still the crowd will not let go. There are hands banging on the windows and clinging to fenders, bodies splayed on the hood. Again, the feeling of déjà vu, recollecting the nightmare drive from Idi-iroko to Ipaja during the demonstrations to terminate Babangida's rule. The police are frustrated. I open my window, thinking to shake a hand or two—a kind of symbolic good-bye for now. A great mistake, and I curse myself for failing to learn from the earlier grabs at my arm. This time, I come really close to dispensing with a ligament or socket—I am not sure which, but something definitely feels as if it has given. Then the arm is somehow extricated and the vehicle takes off. I sink back into the obscurity of the jeep with relief.

No, there is no question about it this time—at long last, my viscera yield and concede: *I am back in the place I never should have left.*

Acknowledgments

FIRST ACKNOWLEDGMENT GOES TO MY RELAY OF EDITORS, ANN GODOFF, Ileene Smith, and Will Murphy. To this heroic triad, I extend, additionally, one hand in sympathy, and the other as a sign of exoneration for any flaws in this tract, since I am quite certain that these are the result of my own decisions.

For data checks, I am deeply indebted to Kunle Ajibade, Tunde Awosanmi, Laolu Akande, Etienne Galle, my French translator, and Bankole Olayebi, my Nigerian editor. They have had to compensate for the diary I have never kept and for a kaleidoscopic mental gadget that sometimes pretends to the function of memory, not to mention the loss of useful documentation, the result of raids on my home during the Nigerian season of dictatorship insanity or simply of a peripatetic existence.

My gratitude to the W.E.B. Du Bois Institute, Harvard University, and the International Institute of Modern Letters, University of Nevada, for conditions of attachment that enabled me to devote some time—in between global crisscrossings—to another biographical undertaking, one which, in my more rational moments, I had sworn I would not extend beyond "the age of innocence," as delimited in *Aké: The Years of Childhood.*

Lastly, it would be churlish not to acknowledge the industry of those assiduous scribblers whose monographs, conference papers, and so forth, on the life of this subject finally goaded me into abandoning a rational decision: not to pursue the task of recollection and reflection beyond the age of innocence—calculated at roughly eleven and a bit. While, unlike those authoritative voices, I still hesitate to claim definitive knowledge of the subject, I can at least flaunt the advantage of having lived with him all his life, without even a day off, which is far longer than has any other being on the literary planet.

WOLE SOYINKA is a writer of global stature,
the first African ever to receive the Nobel Prize
in Literature. Soyinka was imprisoned in
Nigeria for his opposition to dictatorship. He
is the author of *Aké: The Years of Childhood* and
Climate of Fear, based on the prestigious Reith
Lectures he delivered on the BBC. He now
divides his time among Southern California,
the United Kingdom, and his homeland.